SAXON® MATH

Course 1

Stephen Hake

Solutions Manual

SAXON®

HOUGHTON MIFFLIN HARCOURT
Supplemental Publishers

www.SaxonPublishers.com
800-531-5015

Printed in the U.S.A.

ISBN 978-1-591-41817-7

13 2266 14

4500465669 A B C D E F G

Solutions Manual

Answers

Solutions

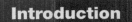

The *Saxon Math Course 1 Solutions Manual* contains answers and solutions that support daily instruction and cumulative assessment in the *Saxon Math Course 1* program.

Daily Power Up

Answers for Power Up facts, Mental Math, and Problem Solving are found in this manual, beginning on page 1. Answers for the optional Power Up facts begin on page 10.

Answers for Power Up facts, Mental Math, and Problem Solving are also located on the corresponding page of the *Saxon Math Course 1 Teacher's Manual.* In addition, the *Teacher's Manual* includes a step-by-step script with a complete solution for every daily Problem Solving exercise. The scripts are found on the interleaf "Power-Up Discussion" page that precedes each lesson.

Daily Lessons and Investigations

Complete solutions for the *Saxon Math Course 1 Student Edition* lessons—Practice Set, Written Practice, and Early Finishers—are located in this manual, beginning on page 82. Answers for these problems are also found on the corresponding *Teacher's Manual* pages and on the *Saxon Math Course 1 Answer Key CD.*

Answers and solutions for the Investigation exercises are located in the same resources—this manual, the *Teacher's Manual*, and the *Saxon Math Course 1 Answer Key CD.* Answers for those Lesson and Investigation Activity Masters that are utilized as worksheets are found in this manual, on page 37.

Course Assessments

Answers and solutions for the Baseline Test, Power-Up Tests, Cumulative Tests, Benchmark Tests, and the End-of-Course Exam are located in this manual. Complete solutions for the Performance Tasks and Performance Activities are also located in this volume, beginning on page 393. Answers for the Placement Test can be found on page 9 of the *Saxon Math Course 1 Course Assessments* book.

Reteaching

Answers for the *Saxon Math Course 1 Reteaching Masters* are located in this manual, beginning on page 38.

Answer Key CD

Answers to Power Up Mental Math and Problem Solving, Practice Sets, Written Practice, Early Finishers, and Investigation exercises are located on the *Saxon Math Course 1 Answer Key CD.* This resource provides pdf files of the pages in the *Saxon Math Course 1 Student Edition.* Answers are placed adjacent to each problem. These pages are identical to the reduced student pages located in the *Teacher's Manual.*

Adaptations for Saxon Math

If you are using *Adaptations for Saxon Math Course 1,* the answers for Targeted Practice, Fraction Activities, Facts Practice, and the Quick Tests are located in Volume 2 of the *Adaptations* binder.

Power Up A

Facts Add.

4 + 6 10	9 + 9 18	3 + 4 7	5 + 5 10	7 + 8 15	2 + 3 5	7 + 0 7	5 + 9 14	2 + 6 8	3 + 9 12
3 + 5 8	2 + 2 4	6 + 7 13	8 + 8 16	2 + 9 11	5 + 7 12	4 + 9 13	6 + 6 12	3 + 8 11	7 + 7 14
4 + 4 8	7 + 9 16	5 + 8 13	2 + 7 9	0 + 0 0	6 + 8 14	3 + 7 10	2 + 4 6	7 + 1 8	4 + 8 12
5 + 6 11	4 + 7 11	2 + 5 7	3 + 6 9	8 + 9 17	2 + 8 10	10 + 10 20	4 + 5 9	6 + 9 15	3 + 3 6

Power Up B

Facts Add.

7 + 7 14	2 + 4 6	6 + 8 14	4 + 3 7	5 + 5 10	3 + 2 5	7 + 6 13	9 + 4 13	10 + 10 20	7 + 3 10
4 + 4 8	5 + 8 13	2 + 2 4	8 + 7 15	3 + 9 12	6 + 6 12	3 + 5 8	9 + 1 10	4 + 7 11	8 + 9 17
2 + 8 10	5 + 6 11	0 + 0 0	8 + 4 12	6 + 3 9	9 + 6 15	4 + 5 9	9 + 7 16	2 + 6 8	9 + 9 18
3 + 8 11	9 + 5 14	9 + 2 11	8 + 8 16	5 + 2 7	3 + 3 6	7 + 5 12	8 + 0 8	7 + 2 9	6 + 4 10

Power Up C

Facts Subtract.

8 − 5 3	10 − 4 6	12 − 6 6	6 − 3 3	8 − 4 4	14 − 7 7	20 − 10 10	11 − 5 6	7 − 4 3	13 − 6 7
7 − 2 5	15 − 8 7	9 − 7 2	17 − 9 8	10 − 5 5	8 − 1 7	16 − 7 9	6 − 0 6	12 − 3 9	9 − 5 4
13 − 5 8	11 − 7 4	14 − 8 6	10 − 7 3	5 − 3 2	15 − 6 9	6 − 4 2	10 − 8 2	18 − 9 9	15 − 7 8
12 − 4 8	11 − 2 9	16 − 8 8	9 − 9 0	13 − 4 9	11 − 8 3	9 − 6 3	14 − 9 5	8 − 6 2	12 − 5 7

Power Up D

Facts Multiply.

7 × 7 49	4 × 6 24	8 × 1 8	2 × 2 4	0 × 5 0	6 × 3 18	8 × 9 72	5 × 8 40	6 × 2 12	10 × 10 100
9 × 4 36	2 × 5 10	9 × 6 54	7 × 3 21	5 × 5 25	7 × 2 14	6 × 8 48	3 × 5 15	9 × 9 81	5 × 4 20
3 × 4 12	6 × 5 30	8 × 2 16	4 × 4 16	6 × 7 42	8 × 8 64	2 × 3 6	7 × 4 28	5 × 9 45	3 × 8 24
3 × 9 27	7 × 8 56	2 × 4 8	5 × 7 35	3 × 3 9	9 × 7 63	4 × 8 32	0 × 0 0	9 × 2 18	6 × 6 36

Power Up E

Facts Multiply.

8 × 8 64	3 × 9 27	6 × 7 42	5 × 2 10	0 × 0 0	3 × 8 24	4 × 6 24	5 × 8 40	2 × 9 18	9 × 9 81
6 × 1 6	2 × 6 12	3 × 3 9	4 × 5 20	5 × 5 25	8 × 6 48	4 × 2 8	7 × 7 49	7 × 4 28	5 × 3 15
6 × 9 54	8 × 4 32	5 × 9 45	4 × 3 12	7 × 8 56	2 × 2 4	6 × 5 30	2 × 7 14	8 × 9 72	3 × 6 18
4 × 4 16	5 × 7 35	3 × 2 6	7 × 9 63	6 × 6 36	3 × 7 21	2 × 8 16	0 × 7 0	9 × 4 36	10 × 10 100

Power Up F

Facts Divide.

7 $7\overline{)49}$	3 $9\overline{)27}$	5 $5\overline{)25}$	3 $4\overline{)12}$	6 $6\overline{)36}$	3 $7\overline{)21}$	10 $10\overline{)100}$	2 $5\overline{)10}$	0 $4\overline{)0}$	4 $4\overline{)16}$
9 $8\overline{)72}$	7 $4\overline{)28}$	7 $2\overline{)14}$	5 $7\overline{)35}$	8 $5\overline{)40}$	4 $2\overline{)8}$	1 $8\overline{)8}$	3 $3\overline{)9}$	3 $8\overline{)24}$	6 $4\overline{)24}$
9 $6\overline{)54}$	6 $3\overline{)18}$	7 $8\overline{)56}$	2 $3\overline{)6}$	6 $8\overline{)48}$	4 $5\overline{)20}$	8 $2\overline{)16}$	9 $7\overline{)63}$	2 $6\overline{)12}$	6 $1\overline{)6}$
8 $4\overline{)32}$	5 $9\overline{)45}$	9 $2\overline{)18}$	8 $8\overline{)64}$	5 $6\overline{)30}$	3 $5\overline{)15}$	7 $6\overline{)42}$	8 $3\overline{)24}$	9 $9\overline{)81}$	9 $4\overline{)36}$

Answers

Power Up G

Facts Reduce each fraction to lowest terms.

$\frac{2}{8} = \frac{1}{4}$	$\frac{4}{6} = \frac{2}{3}$	$\frac{6}{10} = \frac{3}{5}$	$\frac{2}{4} = \frac{1}{2}$	$\frac{5}{100} = \frac{1}{20}$	$\frac{9}{12} = \frac{3}{4}$
$\frac{4}{10} = \frac{2}{5}$	$\frac{4}{12} = \frac{1}{3}$	$\frac{2}{10} = \frac{1}{5}$	$\frac{3}{6} = \frac{1}{2}$	$\frac{25}{100} = \frac{1}{4}$	$\frac{3}{12} = \frac{1}{4}$
$\frac{4}{16} = \frac{1}{4}$	$\frac{3}{9} = \frac{1}{3}$	$\frac{6}{9} = \frac{2}{3}$	$\frac{4}{8} = \frac{1}{2}$	$\frac{2}{12} = \frac{1}{6}$	$\frac{6}{12} = \frac{1}{2}$
$\frac{8}{16} = \frac{1}{2}$	$\frac{2}{6} = \frac{1}{3}$	$\frac{8}{12} = \frac{2}{3}$	$\frac{6}{8} = \frac{3}{4}$	$\frac{5}{10} = \frac{1}{2}$	$\frac{75}{100} = \frac{3}{4}$

Power Up H

Facts Multiply or divide as indicated.

$\begin{array}{r}4\\ \times 9\\ \hline 36\end{array}$	$\begin{array}{r}4\\ 4\overline{)16}\end{array}$	$\begin{array}{r}6\\ \times 8\\ \hline 48\end{array}$	$\begin{array}{r}4\\ 3\overline{)12}\end{array}$	$\begin{array}{r}5\\ \times 7\\ \hline 35\end{array}$	$\begin{array}{r}8\\ 4\overline{)32}\end{array}$	$\begin{array}{r}3\\ \times 9\\ \hline 27\end{array}$	$\begin{array}{r}9\\ 9\overline{)81}\end{array}$	$\begin{array}{r}6\\ \times 2\\ \hline 12\end{array}$	$\begin{array}{r}8\\ 8\overline{)64}\end{array}$
$\begin{array}{r}9\\ \times 7\\ \hline 63\end{array}$	$\begin{array}{r}5\\ 8\overline{)40}\end{array}$	$\begin{array}{r}2\\ \times 4\\ \hline 8\end{array}$	$\begin{array}{r}7\\ 6\overline{)42}\end{array}$	$\begin{array}{r}5\\ \times 5\\ \hline 25\end{array}$	$\begin{array}{r}2\\ 7\overline{)14}\end{array}$	$\begin{array}{r}7\\ \times 7\\ \hline 49\end{array}$	$\begin{array}{r}1\\ 8\overline{)8}\end{array}$	$\begin{array}{r}3\\ \times 3\\ \hline 9\end{array}$	$\begin{array}{r}0\\ 6\overline{)0}\end{array}$
$\begin{array}{r}7\\ \times 3\\ \hline 21\end{array}$	$\begin{array}{r}5\\ 2\overline{)10}\end{array}$	$\begin{array}{r}10\\ \times 10\\ \hline 100\end{array}$	$\begin{array}{r}8\\ 3\overline{)24}\end{array}$	$\begin{array}{r}4\\ \times 5\\ \hline 20\end{array}$	$\begin{array}{r}6\\ 9\overline{)54}\end{array}$	$\begin{array}{r}9\\ \times 1\\ \hline 9\end{array}$	$\begin{array}{r}2\\ 3\overline{)6}\end{array}$	$\begin{array}{r}7\\ \times 4\\ \hline 28\end{array}$	$\begin{array}{r}8\\ 7\overline{)56}\end{array}$
$\begin{array}{r}6\\ \times 6\\ \hline 36\end{array}$	$\begin{array}{r}9\\ 2\overline{)18}\end{array}$	$\begin{array}{r}3\\ \times 5\\ \hline 15\end{array}$	$\begin{array}{r}6\\ 5\overline{)30}\end{array}$	$\begin{array}{r}2\\ \times 2\\ \hline 4\end{array}$	$\begin{array}{r}3\\ 6\overline{)18}\end{array}$	$\begin{array}{r}9\\ \times 5\\ \hline 45\end{array}$	$\begin{array}{r}4\\ 6\overline{)24}\end{array}$	$\begin{array}{r}2\\ \times 8\\ \hline 16\end{array}$	$\begin{array}{r}8\\ 9\overline{)72}\end{array}$

Power Up I

Facts Write each improper fraction as a mixed number. Reduce fractions.

$\frac{5}{4} = 1\frac{1}{4}$	$\frac{6}{4} = 1\frac{1}{2}$	$\frac{15}{10} = 1\frac{1}{2}$	$\frac{8}{3} = 2\frac{2}{3}$	$\frac{15}{12} = 1\frac{1}{4}$
$\frac{12}{8} = 1\frac{1}{2}$	$\frac{10}{8} = 1\frac{1}{4}$	$\frac{3}{2} = 1\frac{1}{2}$	$\frac{15}{6} = 2\frac{1}{2}$	$\frac{10}{4} = 2\frac{1}{2}$
$\frac{8}{6} = 1\frac{1}{3}$	$\frac{25}{10} = 2\frac{1}{2}$	$\frac{9}{6} = 1\frac{1}{2}$	$\frac{10}{6} = 1\frac{2}{3}$	$\frac{15}{8} = 1\frac{7}{8}$
$\frac{12}{10} = 1\frac{1}{5}$	$\frac{10}{3} = 3\frac{1}{3}$	$\frac{18}{12} = 1\frac{1}{2}$	$\frac{5}{2} = 2\frac{1}{2}$	$\frac{4}{3} = 1\frac{1}{3}$

Power Up J

Facts Write each mixed number as an improper fraction.

$2\frac{1}{2} = \frac{5}{2}$	$2\frac{2}{5} = \frac{12}{5}$	$1\frac{3}{4} = \frac{7}{4}$	$2\frac{3}{4} = \frac{11}{4}$	$2\frac{1}{8} = \frac{17}{8}$
$1\frac{2}{3} = \frac{5}{3}$	$3\frac{1}{2} = \frac{7}{2}$	$1\frac{5}{6} = \frac{11}{6}$	$2\frac{1}{4} = \frac{9}{4}$	$1\frac{1}{8} = \frac{9}{8}$
$5\frac{1}{2} = \frac{11}{2}$	$1\frac{3}{8} = \frac{11}{8}$	$5\frac{1}{3} = \frac{16}{3}$	$3\frac{1}{4} = \frac{13}{4}$	$4\frac{1}{2} = \frac{9}{2}$
$1\frac{7}{8} = \frac{15}{8}$	$2\frac{2}{3} = \frac{8}{3}$	$1\frac{5}{8} = \frac{13}{8}$	$3\frac{3}{4} = \frac{15}{4}$	$7\frac{1}{2} = \frac{15}{2}$

Answers

Power Up K

Facts

Complete each equivalent measure.		Write a unit for each reference.
1. 1 cm = 10 mm	13. 10 cm = 100 mm	**Metric Units:**
2. 1 m = 1000 mm	14. 2 m = 200 cm	25. The thickness of a dime: millimeter
3. 1 m = 100 cm	15. 5 km = 5000 m	26. The width of a little finger: centimeter
4. 1 km = 1000 m	16. 2.5 cm = 25 mm	
5. 1 in. = 2.54 cm	17. 1.5 m = 150 cm	27. The length of one big step: meter
6. 1 mi ≈ 1610 m	18. 7.5 km = 7500 m	
		U.S. Customary Units:
7. 1 ft = 12 in.	19. $\frac{1}{2}$ ft = 6 in.	28. The width of two fingers: inch
8. 1 yd = 36 in.	20. 2 ft = 24 in.	
9. 1 yd = 3 ft	21. 3 ft = 36 in.	29. The length of a man's shoe: foot
10. 1 mi = 5280 ft	22. 2 yd = 6 ft	
11. 1 m ≈ 39 in.	23. 10 yd = 30 ft	30. The length of one big step: yard
12. 1 km ≈ 0.62 mi	24. 100 yd = 300 ft	

Power Up L

Facts

Write the abbreviation.	Complete each equivalence.	Complete each conversion.
Metric Units:	Metric Units:	14. 2 liters = 2000 milliliters
1. liter L	7. 1 liter = 1000 milliliters	15. 2 liters ≈ 2 quarts
2. milliliter mL	U.S. Customary Units:	16. 3.78 liters = 3780 milliliters
U.S. Customary Units:	8. 1 cup = 8 ounces	17. 0.5 liter = 500 milliliters
3. ounces oz	9. 1 pint = 16 ounces	18. $\frac{1}{2}$ gallon = 2 quarts
4. pint pt	10. 1 pint = 2 cups	19. 2 gallons = 8 quarts
5. quart qt	11. 1 quart = 2 pints	20. 2 half gallons = 1 gallon
6. gallon gal	12. 1 gallon = 4 quarts	21. 8 cups = 2 quarts
	Between Systems:	22–23. A two-liter bottle is a little more than 2 quarts or $\frac{1}{2}$ gallon.
	13. 1 liter ≈ 1 quart	

Power Up M

Facts Write each percent as a reduced fraction and decimal number.

Percent	Fraction	Decimal	Percent	Fraction	Decimal
5%	$\frac{1}{20}$	0.05	10%	$\frac{1}{10}$	0.1
20%	$\frac{1}{5}$	0.2	30%	$\frac{3}{10}$	0.3
25%	$\frac{1}{4}$	0.25	50%	$\frac{1}{2}$	0.5
1%	$\frac{1}{100}$	0.01	$12\frac{1}{2}$%	$\frac{1}{8}$	0.125
90%	$\frac{9}{10}$	0.9	$33\frac{1}{3}$%	$\frac{1}{3}$	Rounds to 0.333
75%	$\frac{3}{4}$	0.75	$66\frac{2}{3}$%	$\frac{2}{3}$	Rounds to 0.667

Power Up N

Facts Complete each equivalence.

1. Draw a segment about 1 cm long. 1 cm
2. Draw a segment about 1 inch long. 1 inch
3. One inch is how many centimeters? 2.54
4. Which is longer, 1 km or 1 mi? 1 mi
5. Which is longer, 1 km or $\frac{1}{2}$ mi? 1 km
6. How many ounces are in a pound? 16
7. How many pounds are in a ton? 2000
8. A dollar bill has a mass of about one gram.
9. A pair of shoes has a mass of about one kilogram.
10. On Earth a kilogram mass weighs about 2.2 pounds.
11. A metric ton is 1000 kilograms.
12. On Earth a metric ton weighs about 2200 pounds.
13. The Earth rotates on its axis once in a day.
14. The Earth revolves around the Sun once in a year.

15. Water boils 212 °F
16. 100 °C
17. Normal body temerature 98.6 °F
18. 37 °C
19. Cool room temperature 68 °F
20. 20 °C
21. Water freezes 32 °F
22. 0 °C

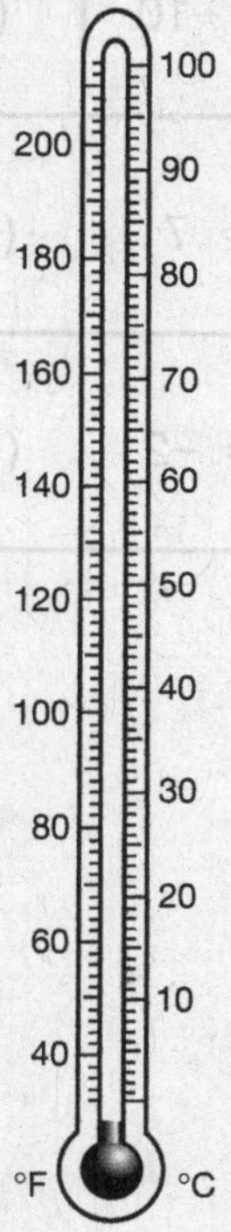

Power Up O

Facts Simplify.

(+3) + (−4) = −1	(−2) + (+2) = 0	(−3) + (+4) = 1	(−3) + (−4) = −7
(−5) + (+2) = −3	(+5) + (−2) = 3	(−5) + (+5) = 0	(−5) + (−2) = −7
(−6) + (−2) = −8	(+6) + (−2) = 4	(+6) + (−6) = 0	(−6) + (+2) = −4
(−2) + (+8) = 6	(−2) + (−8) = −10	(+2) + (−8) = −6	(+2) + (+8) = 10

Power Up P

Facts Simplify.

(−3) − (+3) = −6	(+10) − (−10) = 20	(−3) − (−3) = 0	(−3) + (−3) = −6
(−4) − (+6) = −10	(−7) − (−1) = −6	(+4) + (−6) = −2	(+10) + (−8) = 2
(+5) − (−2) = 7	(−2) − (+5) = −7	(−2) + (+5) = 3	(+5) + (−2) = 3
(−10) − (−8) = −2	(+7) + (+1) = 8	(−5) − (−2) = −3	(−7) + (+3) = −4

Power Up Q

Facts Simplify.

$(-3)(-6) = 18$	$\frac{-8}{-4} = 2$	$(-2)(+5) = -10$	$\frac{+5}{-5} = -1$
$(-6)(+4) = -24$	$\frac{-15}{5} = -3$	$(-2)(-8) = 16$	$\frac{-10}{-5} = 2$
$(+3)(-6) = -18$	$\frac{+15}{-3} = -5$	$(-5)(+2) = -10$	$\frac{+20}{+5} = 4$
$(-3)(6) = -18$	$\frac{-4}{-4} = 1$	$(+4)(+6) = 24$	$\frac{12}{-4} = 3$

Add.

7 + 2 9	9 + 4 13	2 + 8 10	6 + 5 11	4 + 4 8	3 + 9 12	8 + 4 12	5 + 7 12
9 + 7 16	4 + 7 11	7 + 5 12	5 + 4 9	3 + 4 7	6 + 8 14	2 + 5 7	8 + 8 16
6 + 3 9	2 + 9 11	7 + 8 15	8 + 3 11	5 + 9 14	3 + 6 9	9 + 9 18	4 + 9 13
5 + 8 13	9 + 5 14	4 + 5 9	8 + 6 14	2 + 3 5	6 + 6 12	5 + 2 7	7 + 3 10
3 + 8 11	8 + 9 17	2 + 2 4	7 + 6 13	5 + 5 10	6 + 9 15	3 + 7 10	9 + 8 17
4 + 2 6	3 + 3 6	6 + 4 10	4 + 8 12	9 + 3 12	2 + 4 6	8 + 5 13	7 + 9 16
7 + 4 11	2 + 6 8	5 + 3 8	9 + 6 15	4 + 3 7	6 + 7 13	3 + 2 5	8 + 7 15
5 + 6 11	8 + 2 10	3 + 5 8	6 + 2 8	7 + 7 14	4 + 6 10	9 + 2 11	2 + 7 9

Subtract.

7 − 0 7	10 − 8 2	6 − 3 3	14 − 5 9	3 − 1 2	8 − 6 2	4 − 4 0	11 − 8 3
5 − 3 2	7 − 5 2	2 − 1 1	6 − 6 0	8 − 4 4	2 − 2 0	13 − 6 7	15 − 8 7
7 − 2 5	14 − 7 7	8 − 1 7	11 − 6 5	3 − 3 0	16 − 7 9	5 − 2 3	12 − 4 8
10 − 9 1	6 − 2 4	13 − 9 4	4 − 0 4	10 − 5 5	5 − 1 4	10 − 3 7	12 − 6 6
13 − 8 5	7 − 4 3	10 − 7 3	0 − 0 0	12 − 8 4	5 − 5 0	4 − 3 1	8 − 7 1
17 − 8 9	6 − 0 6	10 − 6 4	4 − 1 3	9 − 5 4	9 − 0 9	5 − 4 1	12 − 5 7
16 − 9 7	7 − 1 6	18 − 9 9	11 − 3 8	13 − 7 6	8 − 2 6	11 − 5 6	5 − 0 5
12 − 3 9	16 − 8 8	9 − 1 8	15 − 6 9	11 − 4 7	13 − 5 8	1 − 0 1	8 − 5 3

Multiply.

6 × 8 48	5 × 7 35	3 × 3 9	6 × 2 12	4 × 7 28	9 × 3 27	8 × 5 40	2 × 4 8
7 × 2 14	4 × 5 20	8 × 2 16	8 × 6 48	2 × 9 18	5 × 6 30	9 × 7 63	4 × 9 36
8 × 9 72	7 × 9 63	2 × 6 12	3 × 8 24	7 × 8 56	9 × 6 54	3 × 2 6	6 × 7 42
5 × 2 10	3 × 7 21	8 × 7 56	6 × 3 18	2 × 2 4	7 × 7 49	9 × 8 72	4 × 3 12
7 × 6 42	8 × 8 64	4 × 8 32	3 × 5 15	8 × 3 24	9 × 5 45	2 × 7 14	5 × 8 40
6 × 6 36	2 × 3 6	4 × 4 16	5 × 3 15	9 × 9 81	3 × 9 27	8 × 4 32	7 × 3 21
4 × 6 24	7 × 5 35	3 × 6 18	6 × 9 54	5 × 4 20	9 × 4 36	2 × 5 10	6 × 4 24
5 × 9 45	3 × 4 12	6 × 5 30	2 × 8 16	7 × 4 28	4 × 2 8	5 × 5 25	9 × 2 18

Divide.

$\begin{array}{r}5\\4\overline{)20}\end{array}$	$\begin{array}{r}7\\9\overline{)63}\end{array}$	$\begin{array}{r}4\\1\overline{)4}\end{array}$	$\begin{array}{r}2\\7\overline{)14}\end{array}$	$\begin{array}{r}1\\3\overline{)3}\end{array}$	$\begin{array}{r}3\\8\overline{)24}\end{array}$	$\begin{array}{r}0\\5\overline{)0}\end{array}$	$\begin{array}{r}4\\6\overline{)24}\end{array}$
$\begin{array}{r}4\\4\overline{)32}\end{array}$	$\begin{array}{r}7\\8\overline{)56}\end{array}$	$\begin{array}{r}0\\1\overline{)0}\end{array}$	$\begin{array}{r}2\\6\overline{)12}\end{array}$	$\begin{array}{r}6\\3\overline{)18}\end{array}$	$\begin{array}{r}8\\9\overline{)72}\end{array}$	$\begin{array}{r}3\\5\overline{)15}\end{array}$	$\begin{array}{r}4\\2\overline{)8}\end{array}$
$\begin{array}{r}1\\5\overline{)5}\end{array}$	$\begin{array}{r}8\\8\overline{)64}\end{array}$	$\begin{array}{r}0\\3\overline{)0}\end{array}$	$\begin{array}{r}7\\4\overline{)28}\end{array}$	$\begin{array}{r}7\\7\overline{)49}\end{array}$	$\begin{array}{r}2\\2\overline{)4}\end{array}$	$\begin{array}{r}9\\9\overline{)81}\end{array}$	$\begin{array}{r}4\\3\overline{)12}\end{array}$
$\begin{array}{r}9\\2\overline{)18}\end{array}$	$\begin{array}{r}1\\6\overline{)6}\end{array}$	$\begin{array}{r}5\\3\overline{)15}\end{array}$	$\begin{array}{r}5\\8\overline{)40}\end{array}$	$\begin{array}{r}0\\2\overline{)0}\end{array}$	$\begin{array}{r}4\\5\overline{)20}\end{array}$	$\begin{array}{r}3\\9\overline{)27}\end{array}$	$\begin{array}{r}8\\1\overline{)8}\end{array}$
$\begin{array}{r}6\\2\overline{)12}\end{array}$	$\begin{array}{r}9\\5\overline{)45}\end{array}$	$\begin{array}{r}7\\1\overline{)7}\end{array}$	$\begin{array}{r}2\\4\overline{)8}\end{array}$	$\begin{array}{r}0\\7\overline{)0}\end{array}$	$\begin{array}{r}2\\8\overline{)16}\end{array}$	$\begin{array}{r}8\\3\overline{)24}\end{array}$	$\begin{array}{r}5\\9\overline{)45}\end{array}$
$\begin{array}{r}3\\7\overline{)21}\end{array}$	$\begin{array}{r}5\\2\overline{)10}\end{array}$	$\begin{array}{r}7\\6\overline{)42}\end{array}$	$\begin{array}{r}3\\1\overline{)3}\end{array}$	$\begin{array}{r}6\\4\overline{)24}\end{array}$	$\begin{array}{r}2\\3\overline{)6}\end{array}$	$\begin{array}{r}6\\9\overline{)54}\end{array}$	$\begin{array}{r}3\\6\overline{)18}\end{array}$
$\begin{array}{r}4\\8\overline{)32}\end{array}$	$\begin{array}{r}1\\1\overline{)1}\end{array}$	$\begin{array}{r}4\\9\overline{)36}\end{array}$	$\begin{array}{r}9\\3\overline{)27}\end{array}$	$\begin{array}{r}7\\2\overline{)14}\end{array}$	$\begin{array}{r}5\\5\overline{)25}\end{array}$	$\begin{array}{r}8\\6\overline{)48}\end{array}$	$\begin{array}{r}0\\8\overline{)0}\end{array}$
$\begin{array}{r}0\\6\overline{)0}\end{array}$	$\begin{array}{r}2\\5\overline{)10}\end{array}$	$\begin{array}{r}1\\9\overline{)9}\end{array}$	$\begin{array}{r}3\\2\overline{)6}\end{array}$	$\begin{array}{r}9\\7\overline{)63}\end{array}$	$\begin{array}{r}4\\4\overline{)16}\end{array}$	$\begin{array}{r}6\\8\overline{)48}\end{array}$	$\begin{array}{r}2\\1\overline{)2}\end{array}$

Answers

Mental Math

Lesson 1

a. 60
b. 600
c. 120
d. 1200
e. 90
f. 900
g. 12 in.
h. 10 mm

Lesson 2

a. 540
b. 260
c. 270
d. 770
e. 480
f. 480
g. 24 in.
h. 20 mm

Lesson 3

a. 7000
b. 2600
c. 3020
d. 920
e. 4500
f. 4370
g. 36 in.
h. 30 mm

Lesson 4

a. 2920
b. 8420
c. 7740
d. 2850
e. 1490
f. 9050
g. 3 ft
h. 100 cm

Lesson 5

a. 760
b. 870
c. 7200
d. 790
e. 5800
f. 640
g. 7 days
h. 24 hours

Lesson 6

a. 2900
b. 8400
c. 770
d. 9740
e. 1560
f. 2980
g. 60 seconds
h. 60 minutes

Lesson 7

a. 500

b. 1000

c. 350

d. 2200

e. 400

f. 500

g. 52 weeks

h. 365 days

Lesson 8

a. 2800

b. 786

c. 8920

d. 920

e. 2400

f. 360

g. 6 ft

h. 200 cm

Lesson 9

a. 168

b. 89

c. 7720

d. 810

e. 360

f. 165

g. 20 in.

h. 366 days

Lesson 10

a. 68

b. 870

c. 279

d. 50

e. 250

f. 3200

g. 9 ft

h. 300 cm

Lesson 11

a. 120

b. 1200

c. $5.75

d. 691

e. 4100

f. $3.50

g. 10 cm

h. 2

Lesson 12

a. 240

b. 2400

c. $17.50

d. 475

e. 2500

f. $7.50

g. 36 in.

h. 0

Answers

Lesson 13

a. 1500

b. 15,000

c. $9.25

d. 3830

e. 4000

f. $15.00

g. 1000 mm

h. 10 years

Lesson 14

a. 3200

b. 18,000

c. $15.00

d. 590

e. 250

f. $2.50

g. 100 years

h. 11

Lesson 15

a. 28,000

b. 2400

c. $25.00

d. 92

e. 6100

f. $17.50

g. 10 decades

h. 0

Lesson 16

a. 96

b. 92

c. 170

d. 84

e. 750

f. 7500

g. 2 yds

h. 1

Lesson 17

a. 170

b. 256

c. 192

d. 73

e. 1900

f. $2.50

g. 2000 mm

h. 5

Lesson 18

a. 92

b. 128

c. 126

d. 72

e. 90 ft

f. 14 days

g. 48 hours

h. 1

Lesson 19

- **a.** 192
- **b.** 138
- **c.** 138
- **d.** 83
- **e.** 83
- **f.** $7.50
- **g.** 20 decades
- **h.** 10

Lesson 20

- **a.** 138
- **b.** 192
- **c.** 1840
- **d.** 92
- **e.** 92
- **f.** $25.00
- **g.** 120 minutes
- **h.** 12

Lesson 21

- **a.** 168
- **b.** 228
- **c.** 83
- **d.** 487
- **e.** $3.50
- **f.** 12
- **g.** 12 months
- **h.** 4

Lesson 22

- **a.** 216
- **b.** 168
- **c.** 65
- **d.** 317
- **e.** $6.50
- **f.** 24
- **g.** 3 yds
- **h.** 25

Lesson 23

- **a.** 310
- **b.** 180
- **c.** 96
- **d.** 1550
- **e.** $4.50
- **f.** 42
- **g.** 3000 mm
- **h.** 2

Lesson 24

- **a.** 144
- **b.** 300
- **c.** 86
- **d.** 1250
- **e.** $5.50
- **f.** 34
- **g.** 4 yds
- **h.** 5

Lesson 25

a. 258
b. 225
c. 86
d. 2500
e. $3.75
f. 15
g. one centimeter
h. 4

Lesson 26

a. 238
b. 224
c. 93
d. 600
e. $3.25
f. 16
g. 25
h. 2

Lesson 27

a. 364
b. 198
c. 82
d. 306
e. $2.75
f. 43
g. 4 ft
h. 10

Lesson 28

a. 336
b. 255
c. 85
d. 1250
e. $1.75
f. 18
g. one foot
h. 5

Lesson 29

a. 301
b. 256
c. 92
d. 375
e. $2.75
f. 35
g. equal
h. 50

Lesson 30

a. 288
b. 210
c. 94
d. 535
e. $7.25
f. 36
g. 98
h. 49

Lesson 31

a. 100
b. 222
c. 57
d. $8.75
e. 21
f. 60
g. 60 seconds
h. 8

Lesson 32

a. 300
b. 1580
c. 73
d. $6.50
e. 120
f. 6
g. 16 square feet
h. 10

Lesson 33

a. 500
b. 203
c. 84
d. $7.25
e. 240
f. 12
g. 18 square inches
h. 7

Lesson 34

a. 900
b. 1130
c. 63
d. $9.50
e. 500
f. 15
g. equal (or neither)
h. 12

Lesson 35

a. 1300
b. 344
c. 76
d. $15.00
e. 120
f. 360
g. 10 cm
h. 4

Lesson 36

a. 1700
b. 2875
c. 47
d. $12.50
e. 160
f. 48
g. 52 weeks
h. 8

Answers

Lesson 37

a. 2100

b. 387

c. 47

d. $20.00

e. 260

f. 250

g. 30 in.

h. 1

Lesson 38

a. 2500

b. 750

c. 37

d. $3.75

e. 75

f. $4.00

g. 56 cm

h. 8

Lesson 39

a. 2900

b. 270

c. 38

d. $9.50

e. 175

f. 25

g. 83

h. $\frac{1}{2}$

Lesson 40

a. 3300

b. 2250

c. 35

d. $6.75

e. 480

f. 48

g. 3 hours

h. 7

Lesson 41

a. 1000

b. 675

c. 55

d. $5.25

e. 350

f. 60

g. 5 ft

h. 12

Lesson 42

a. 500

b. 875

c. 75

d. $9.25

e. 500

f. 58

g. 100 mm

h. 3

Lesson 43

a. 900

b. 520

c. 65

d. $25

e. 600

f. $7.00

g. 6

h. 6

Lesson 44

a. 1300

b. 461

c. 85

d. $11.25

e. 700

f. $0.15

g. 8

h. 7

Lesson 45

a. 1700

b. 875

c. 95

d. $10.75

e. 750

f. $4.00

g. 81 square cm

h. 7

Lesson 46

a. 2100

b. 447

c. 55

d. $8.25

e. 475

f. 20

g. 6 mm

h. 7

Lesson 47

a. 3700

b. 261

c. 37

d. $7.75

e. $6.25

f. $2.50

g. 15

h. 1

Lesson 48

a. 200

b. 580

c. 81

d. $5.25

e. $7.50

f. $0.25

g. The radius is half of the diameter.

h. 9

Lesson 49

a. 1000

b. 340

c. 39

d. $1.75

e. $15.00

f. 40

g. 18.84 cm

h. 5

Lesson 50

a. 1800

b. 315

c. 85

d. $2.44

e. $12.50

f. 500

g. 112

h. 1

Lesson 51

a. 1000

b. 272

c. 35

d. $5.63

e. $75.00

f. $1.00

g. 1 day 12 hours

h. 20

Lesson 52

a. 1000

b. 218

c. 349

d. $22.50

e. $2\frac{1}{2}$

f. 800

g. 5 in.

h. 25

Lesson 53

a. 1800

b. 290

c. 151

d. $12.50

e. 5

f. 40

g. 31.4 ft

h. 11

Lesson 54

a. 1500

b. 336

c. 474

d. $13.75

e. $4\frac{1}{2}$

f. 900

g. *Answers will vary.*

h. 100

Lesson 55

a. 2600

b. 379

c. 276

d. $7.50

e. 7

f. 30

g. 1 yd 2 ft

h. 4

Lesson 56

a. 2000

b. 112

c. 199

d. $8.25

e. $7\frac{1}{2}$

f. 1200

g. 1000 cm

h. 8

Lesson 57

a. 3400

b. 715

c. 101

d. $6.25

e. 9

f. 20

g. a century

h. 1

Lesson 58

a. 150

b. 165

c. 449

d. $20.00

e. $12\frac{1}{2}$

f. 1000

g. 13

h. 5

Lesson 59

a. 300

b. 629

c. 51

d. $7.25

e. $3.00

f. 20

g. 48

h. 15

Lesson 60

a. 1500

b. 179

c. 949

d. $11.25

e. $2.50

f. 2000

g. 2, 3, 5, 7

h. 25

Answers

Lesson 61

a. 3000

b. 533

c. 551

d. $5.75

e. 25

f. 30

g. $\frac{1}{6}$

h. 100

Lesson 62

a. 200

b. 1675

c. 252

d. $11.00

e. $12.00

f. $2.50

g. 4 minutes

h. 2

Lesson 63

a. 700

b. 370

c. 252

d. $6.00

e. 15

f. $0.25

g. 72 in.

h. 0

Lesson 64

a. 1200

b. 4950

c. 238

d. $15.00

e. $5.00

f. $7.50

g. 2 m

h. 8

Lesson 65

a. 300

b. 536

c. 195

d. $17.50

e. $1.50

f. $0.75

g. 11, 13, 17, and 19

h. 1

Lesson 66

a. 800

b. 475

c. 184

d. $3.50

e. $20.00

f. $3.00

g. a decade

h. 1

Lesson 67

a. 1300

b. 291

c. 144

d. $8.50

e. $2.50

f. $0.30

g. 3 yd

h. $2\frac{1}{2}$

Lesson 68

a. 400

b. 1775

c. 294

d. $6.25

e. $12.00

f. $12.00

g. 1 m

h. −1

Lesson 69

a. 900

b. 480

c. 264

d. $4.25

e. $3.50

f. $1.20

g. equal

h. 1

Lesson 70

a. 1400

b. 575

c. 162

d. $6.25

e. $30.00

f. $25.00

g. 6 cm

h. 0

Lesson 71

a. 2400

b. 268

c. 344

d. $1.25

e. $4.50

f. $2.50

g. 5 in.

h. 1

Lesson 72

a. 375

b. 325

c. $2.97

d. $10.01

e. $2.20

f. $25.00

g. 46

h. 15

Answers

Lesson 73

a. 448
b. 325
c. $3.96
d. $4.98
e. $7.00
f. $0.35
g. 30
h. 21

Lesson 74

a. 690
b. 700
c. $4.95
d. $3.02
e. $0.60
f. $12.50
g. 101
h. 11

Lesson 75

a. 3024
b. 375
c. $5.97
d. $4.49
e. $3.20
f. $1.25
g. 27
h. 1

Lesson 76

a. 832
b. 535
c. $7.96
d. $5.01
e. $0.90
f. $95.00
g. 24
h. 5

Lesson 77

a. 1555
b. 315
c. $9.95
d. $9.49
e. $1.60
f. 0.065
g. 148
h. 10

Lesson 78

a. 1300
b. 1775
c. $8.97
d. $17.01
e. $0.80
f. 175
g. 386
h. 25

Lesson 79

a. 1842

b. 580

c. $11.96

d. $8.74

e. $48.00

f. 12.5

g. 1000 liters

h. 8

Lesson 80

a. 1260

b. 550

c. $14.95

d. $2.01

e. $1.20

f. 0.375

g. 4 qt

h. 0

Lesson 81

a. 2177

b. 750

c. $39.96

d. $12.49

e. $11.00

f. 7.5

g. 2000 mL

h. 9

Lesson 82

a. $\frac{1}{2}$

b. 134

c. $4.98

d. $2.50

e. 25

f. 20

g. 8 oz

h. 3

Lesson 83

a. $\frac{1}{3}$

b. 875

c. $11.97

d. 7

e. 0.025

f. 680

g. 4000 mL

h. 3

Lesson 84

a. $\frac{2}{3}$

b. 844

c. $8.98

d. $2.50

e. 750

f. 24

g. 16 oz

h. 2

Answers

Lesson 85

a. 36
b. 375
c. $15.96
d. $2.50
e. 0.75
f. 700
g. 3 L
h. 30

Lesson 86

a. 3600
b. 680
c. $13.98
d. $0.50
e. 8
f. 3
g. 2 cups
h. 11

Lesson 87

a. 4900
b. 625
c. $24.95
d. $1.70
e. 0.625
f. 900
g. 2
h. 10

Lesson 88

a. 6400
b. 570
c. $3.96
d. $0.50
e. 15
f. 3
g. 5000 mL
h. 11

Lesson 89

a. 8100
b. 595
c. $47.94
d. $54.00
e. 0.875
f. 720
g. 45 cubic inches
h. 3

Lesson 90

a. 10
b. 746
c. $4.96
d. $8.00
e. 37.5
f. 4
g. 64 cubic centimeters
h. 2

Lesson 91

a. 35

b. 125

c. $34.95

d. $250.00

e. 0.125

f. 840

g. 2 pints

h. 7

Lesson 92

a. 1500

b. 536

c. 12

d. $5.25

e. 125

f. 20

g. 15

h. 3

Lesson 93

a. 2400

b. 184

c. 6

d. $8.46

e. 0.012

f. 750

g. 25

h. 1

Lesson 94

a. 3500

b. 722

c. 40

d. $3.64

e. 2

f. 32

g. 54

h. 21

Lesson 95

a. 4800

b. 287

c. 20

d. $8.27

e. 0.175

f. 1650

g. 70

h. 3

Lesson 96

a. 6300

b. 614

c. 30

d. $4.11

e. 1.5

f. 25

g. 4 pints

h. 9

Lesson 97

a. 1000

b. 267

c. 15

d. $15.57

e. 0.001

f. 1500

g. 1 liter

h. 3

Lesson 98

a. 2000

b. 743

c. 24

d. $1.28

e. 1250

f. 9

g. 4 cups

h. 2

Lesson 99

a. 3000

b. 291

c. 12

d. $17.74

e. 0.375

f. 450

g. equal

h. 11

Lesson 100

a. 4000

b. 930

c. 50

d. $18.11

e. 80

f. 30

g. 4 pints

h. 15

Lesson 101

a. 6000

b. 370

c. 25

d. $24.29

e. 0.0375

f. 1000

g. 1 liter

h. 10

Lesson 102

a. 12,000

b. 612

c. 20

d. $52.50

e. 6

f. 750

g. 8 pints

h. 50

Lesson 103

a. 3000

b. 293

c. 10

d. $9.64

e. 0.875

f. 25

g. 10,000 mL

h. 90

Lesson 105

a. 8000

b. 417

c. 100

d. $20.19

e. 0.075

f. 22

g. 8 quarts

h. 11

Lesson 106

a. 24,000

b. 779

c. 50

d. $0.55

e. 120

f. 720

g. 2000 mL

h. 5

Lesson 107

a. 10,000

b. 226

c. 20

d. $22.88

e. 0.06

f. 6

g. 8 pints

h. 6

Lesson 108

a. 4900

b. 146

c. $5

d. $17.22

e. 0.75

f. 20

g. 3000 mL

h. 7

Lesson 109

a. 12,000

b. 937

c. $2

d. $3.13

e. 50

f. 21,000

g. 4 cups

h. 3

Answers

Lesson 110

a. 8100

b. 476

c. $25

d. $11.60

e. 0.08

f. 7

g. 12.56 yd

h. 20

Lesson 111

a. 16

b. 245

c. $24

d. $1.41

e. 50

f. 4

g. 240 cubic feet

h. 25

Lesson 112

a. 18

b. 288

c. $12

d. $7.47

e. 0.05

f. 15,000

g. 3 in.

h. 7

Lesson 113

a. 12

b. 152

c. $50

d. $90.50

e. 0.012

f. 4

g. 31.4 mm

h. 0

Lesson 114

a. 28

b. 2880

c. $50

d. $5.64

e. 125

f. 36,000

g. Find the length, width, and height to find the volume.

h. 10

Lesson 115

a. 12

b. 4563

c. $0.25

d. $0.41

e. 0.005

f. 8

g. $\frac{1}{2}$

h. -1

Lesson 116

a. 6

b. 2240

c. $1.25

d. $9.47

e. 37.5

f. 20,000

g. 84; 69

h. 7

Lesson 117

a. 14

b. 2280

c. $20

d. 25%

e. 24

f. 42,000

g. 34; 86

h. 9

Lesson 118

a. 18

b. 10

c. $8

d. 25%

e. 6

f. 90,000

g. 899; 562

h. 8

Lesson 119

a. 9

b. 42

c. $35

d. 50%

e. 56

f. 200

g. 89; 55

h. 10

Lesson 120

a. 18

b. $48

c. 12

d. 100%

e. 320

f. 6000

g. mode: 908; range: 746

h. 1

Answers

Problem Solving

Lesson 1 25, 36, 49

Lesson 2 18

Lesson 3 14 dots

Lesson 4 A, C, D and E are inside the curve; B and F are outside the curve

Lesson 5 $\boxed{76} + 9 = \boxed{85}$ and $\boxed{58} + 9 = \boxed{67}$

Lesson 6 *From top to bottom:* 140 books, 130 books, 100 books, 80 books, and 50 books

Lesson 7 The pully is not in equilibrium; The right side will be heavier.

Lesson 8 246, 264, 426, 462, 624, and 642

Lesson 9 *Answers will vary depending on students' positions.*

Lesson 10 *Answers will vary. See student work.*

Lesson 11 *See Teacher's Manual for table of answers.*

Lesson 12 55

Lesson 13 8 dots

Lesson 14 8 seconds; 24 seconds; 40 seconds

Lesson 15

$$\begin{array}{r} 417 \\ -\ 396 \\ \hline 21 \end{array}$$

Lesson 16 17, 20, 21

Lesson 17 7 pans of lasagna

Lesson 18 *Four possible combinations are:* 3 quarters, 1 dime, 3 nickels; 2 quarters, 5 dimes; 1 half-dollar, 1 quarter, 5 nickels; *or* 1 half-dollar, 4 dimes, 2 nickels

Lesson 19 31 different rectangles

Lesson 20

Lesson 21 20

Lesson 22 Truston should give Melina 4 tickets and Sergio 2 tickets.

Lesson 23 4 bracelets

Lesson 24 north; 10 steps away from the big tree

Lesson 25

$$\begin{array}{r} 819 \\ -\ 452 \\ \hline 367 \end{array}$$

Lesson 26 83

Lesson 27 108

Lesson 28 7 stamps; 64 stamps; 9 stamps

Lesson 29 $\frac{1}{4}$

Lesson 30 *See* Power-Up Discussion *for explanation.*

Lesson 31 4 nickels and 3 dimes

Lesson 32 7, 11, 13

Lesson 33 1, 2, and 4 dots; 14 dots

Lesson 34 A

Lesson 35

$$\begin{array}{r} 108 \\ \times\ \ \ 9 \\ \hline 972 \end{array}$$

Lesson 36 8 bicycles; 16 wagons

Lesson 37 $\frac{1}{2}$ goat; $1\frac{1}{2}$ piglets; 3 ducks

Lesson 38 ACR, ARC, CAR, CRA, RAC, RCA

Lesson 39 27 cubes

Lesson 40 *Sample:* $2 \times 2 + 2 - \frac{2}{2}$

Lesson 41 Singles court: perimeter = 210 ft; area = 2016 sq. ft; Doubles court: width = 36 ft; perimeter = 228 ft; area = 2808 sq. ft

Lesson 42 Second: 2 ft; Third: 1 ft; Fourth: $\frac{1}{2}$ ft; Fifth: $\frac{1}{4}$ ft

Lesson 43 3 colors; paint opposite faces the same color

Lesson 44 C 

Lesson 45

$$\begin{array}{r} 999 \\ +\ \ 9 \\ \hline 1008 \end{array}$$

Lesson 46

$$\begin{array}{r} 99 \\ 9\overline{)891} \\ \underline{81} \\ 81 \\ \underline{81} \\ 0 \end{array}$$

Lesson 47 No; *See* Power-Up Discussion *for explanation.*

Lesson 48 12 sack lunches

Lesson 49 The distances are equal.

Lesson 50 1 cup

Lesson 51 28 dominoes

Lesson 52 2 ways

Lesson 53 16 different numbers

Lesson 54 0 m (The paths are equal distance.)

Lesson 55

$$\begin{array}{r} 146 \\ 6\overline{)876} \\ \underline{6} \\ 27 \\ \underline{24} \\ 36 \\ \underline{36} \\ 0 \end{array}$$

Lesson 56 

Lesson 57 1200 eggs

Lesson 58 15 combinations

Lesson 59 744,000,000 miles

Lesson 60 3 painted faces: 8 blocks;
2 painted faces: 12 blocks;
1 painted face: 6 blocks;
no painted faces: 1 block

Lesson 61 1024 mm; a table

Lesson 62 390 ft

Lesson 63 *Diagram* A

Lesson 64 history: blue folder; math: green folder; science: red folder

Lesson 65

$$\begin{array}{r} 238 \\ \times\ \ \ 7 \\ \hline 1666 \end{array}$$

Lesson 66 25 cm

Lesson 67

$$\begin{array}{r} 142{,}857 \\ \times\ \ \ \ \ \ \ \ 7 \\ \hline 999{,}999 \end{array}$$

Lesson 68 2 socks

Lesson 69 72 in.^2 or $\frac{1}{2}$ ft^2

Lesson 70 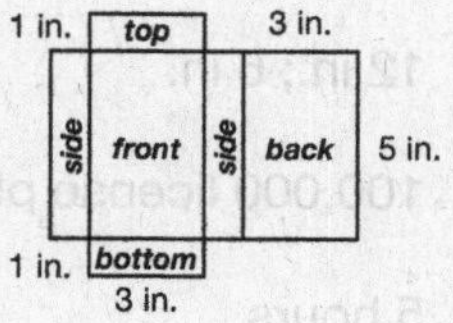

Lesson 71 91 blocks; 81 blocks

Lesson 72 36

Lesson 73 6 ways

Lesson 74 The tablecloth should be shifted 2 in. to the right and 2 in. back; 50 in.-by-92 in.

Lesson 75 97,531

Lesson 76 Sarang: 31 seconds; Gemmie: 29 seconds; Joyce: 27 seconds; Karla: 25 seconds

Lesson 77 57 pages

Lesson 78 192 seconds (or 3 minutes, 12 seconds)

Lesson 79 12 combinations

Lesson 80 10,000 phone numbers

Lesson 81 dime; penny

Answers

Lesson 82 1

Lesson 83 >; >; *see script for context.*

Lesson 84 To start, turn both timers over at the same time. When the three-minute timer runs out, a game turn begins. At that point there is one minute left in the 4-minute timer. When the 4-minute timer runs out, immediately turn it over. When it runs out again, play stops.

Lesson 85
$$\begin{array}{r} 136 \\ \times \quad 7 \\ \hline 952 \end{array}$$

Lesson 86 30

Lesson 87 21

Lesson 88 1, 3, 3, 3, 3, 7; *or* 1, 1, 1, 3, 7, 7

Lesson 89 12 in.; 6 in.

Lesson 90 100,000 license plates

Lesson 91 5 hours

Lesson 92 98

Lesson 93 $\frac{7}{10}, \frac{3}{10}, \frac{3}{10}, \frac{2}{3}$

Lesson 94 $\frac{5}{12}, \frac{1}{2}, \frac{7}{12}, \frac{2}{3}$

Lesson 95 Yes

Lesson 96

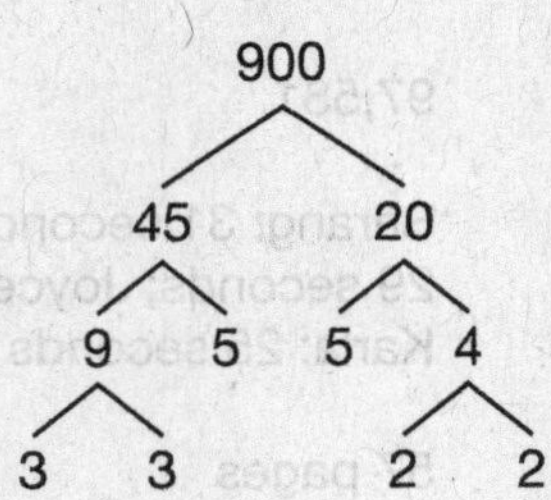

Lesson 97 80; 90

Lesson 98 10 handshakes

Lesson 99 9 sheets

Lesson 100 10 different triangles

Lesson 101 6

Lesson 102 1234 × 56 ≠ 69,106; *or* The product is incorrect. *See* Power-Up Discussion *for explanation.*

Lesson 103

Lesson 104 Saturday

Lesson 105 $\frac{\boxed{3}}{4} + \frac{\boxed{1}}{6} = \frac{11}{12}$ and $\frac{\boxed{1}}{4} + \frac{\boxed{4}}{6} = \frac{11}{12}$

Lesson 106 *Check student diagrams;* 15 = 9 + 4 + 1 + 1; 18 = 9 + 9; 20 = 16 + 4

Lesson 107 $1.30

Lesson 108 15 handshakes

Lesson 109 6,760,000 license plates

Lesson 110
$$\begin{array}{r} 91 \\ 11\overline{)1001} \\ \underline{99} \\ 11 \\ \underline{11} \\ 0 \end{array}$$

Lesson 111 4 students

Lesson 112 60 cards

Lesson 113 10 triangles

Lesson 114 25 grams; $4x + 25 = x + 100$

Lesson 115 10 = 7 + 3, *or* 10 = 5 + 5
15 = 11 + 2 + 2, *or* 15 = 7 + 5 + 3, *or* 15 = 5 + 5 + 5
20 = 17 + 3, *or* 20 = 13 + 7

Lesson 116 125 gram; $3x + 250 = x + 500$

Lesson 117 *See student work;* 30, 60 and 90

Lesson 118 90 minutes

Lesson 119 Grandfather's method: 50 miles; Grandmother's method: 48 miles; Grandfather

Lesson 120 The treasure is on the island furthest to the east.

Lesson Activity Master 3

~~1~~	(2)	(3)	~~4~~	(5)	~~6~~	(7)	~~8~~	~~9~~	~~10~~
(11)	~~12~~	(13)	~~14~~	~~15~~	~~16~~	(17)	~~18~~	(19)	~~20~~
~~21~~	~~22~~	(23)	~~24~~	~~25~~	~~26~~	~~27~~	~~28~~	(29)	~~30~~
(31)	~~32~~	~~33~~	~~34~~	~~35~~	~~36~~	(37)	~~38~~	~~39~~	~~40~~
(41)	~~42~~	(43)	~~44~~	~~45~~	~~46~~	(47)	~~48~~	~~49~~	~~50~~
~~51~~	~~52~~	(53)	~~54~~	~~55~~	~~56~~	~~57~~	~~58~~	(59)	~~60~~
(61)	~~62~~	~~63~~	~~64~~	~~65~~	~~66~~	(67)	~~68~~	~~69~~	~~70~~
(71)	~~72~~	(73)	~~74~~	~~75~~	~~76~~	~~77~~	~~78~~	(79)	~~80~~
~~81~~	~~82~~	(83)	~~84~~	~~85~~	~~86~~	~~87~~	~~88~~	(89)	~~90~~
~~91~~	~~92~~	~~93~~	~~94~~	~~95~~	~~96~~	(97)	~~98~~	~~99~~	~~100~~

Investigation Activity Master 10

1. 45°
2. 90°
3. 30°
4. 150°
5. 135°
6. 165°
7. 60°
8. 165°
9. 90°
10. 180°
11. 105°
12. 150°

Investigation Activity Master 17

Section A

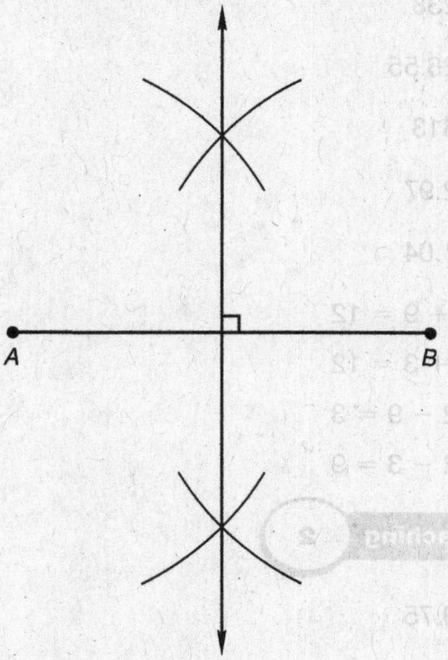

Section B

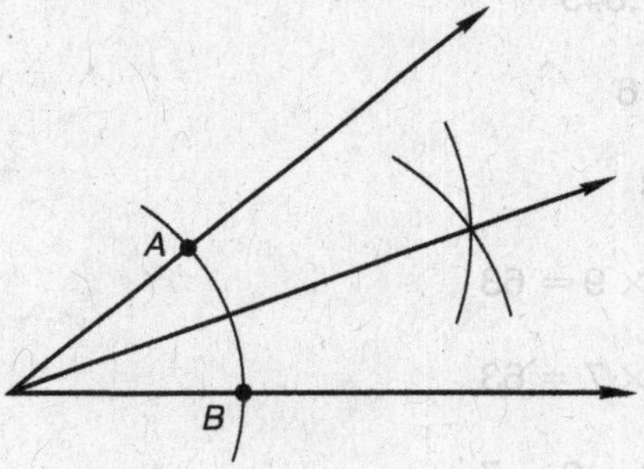

Answers

Reteaching 1

1. 4238
2. $28.55
3. 3313
4. $2.97
5. $1.04
6. 3 + 9 = 12
   9 + 3 = 12
   12 − 9 = 3
   12 − 3 = 9

Reteaching 2

1. $9.75
2. 2,044
3. 11,845
4. 416
5. 23
6. 7 × 9 = 63
   9 × 7 = 63
   63 ÷ 9 = 7
   63 ÷ 7 = 9

Reteaching 3

1. 18
2. 27
3. 34
4. 12
5. 35
6. 36
7. 27
8. 41
9. 90
10. 13
11. 25
12. 785

Reteaching 4

1. 8
2. 13
3. 32
4. 24
5. 96
6. 375
7. 7
8. 16
9. 9

Reteaching 5

1. 8
2. 32
3. 8
4. 8
5. 36
6. 10

Reteaching 6

1. 15
2. $\frac{3}{5}$
3. 10
4. 5
5. $2.75
6. $\frac{3}{10}$

Reteaching 7

1. line, segment, ray
2. C
3. $3\frac{1}{2}$ inches
4. 22 mm

Reteaching 8

1. 8 cm
2. 60 mm
3. 20 inches
4. 4 inches

Reteaching 9

1. \$0.24, \$2.40, \$24
2. $<$
3. $=$
4. $>$
5. $<$

Reteaching 10

1. 48
2. 35
3. 40
4. A. 329
5. 16, 19, 22
6. 16°F

Reteaching Inv. 1

1. 11–15
2. 0–5
3. 6
4. 15

Reteaching 11

1. 55 steps
2. 253 pages
3. 48 tomatoes
4. 74 miles

Reteaching 12

1. five million
2. hundred thousands
3. 3
4. 23,402,000
5. 26,880
6. 5

Reteaching 13

1. 73 students
2. 222 years
3. 45 years
4. 365 pages

Reteaching 14

1. –2
2. –4
3. 5°
4. 13°

Reteaching 15

1. 25 bags
2. \$7.80

3. 15 rolls

4. 234 cards

Reteaching 16

1. 48,000
2. 5400
3. 800
4. 9000
5. 200
6. 5000 km

Reteaching 17

1. $1\frac{5}{8}$
2. $3\frac{3}{4}$ inches
3. $4\frac{3}{16}$ inches
4. $5\frac{3}{8}$ inches

Reteaching 18

1. 6
2. 36
3. 125
4. quiz 3
5. 20

Reteaching 19

1. 1, 3, 5, 15
2. 1, 2, 3, 6, 9, 18
3. 1, 3, 7, 21
4. C. 4
5. B. 17

Reteaching 20

1. 6
2. 3
3. 9
4. 12
5. 5

Reteaching Inv. 2

1. $\frac{3}{5}$
2. $\frac{5}{8}$
3. 50%
4. $>$
5. $<$
6. D. 80%

Reteaching 21

1. A. 2612
2. B. 1395
3. A. 3456
4. C. 7938

Reteaching 22

1. 6 eggs
2. 10
3. 27
4. 20
5. 16 answers
6. 750 tickets

Reteaching 23

1. $\frac{15}{16}$
2. $\frac{2}{3}$
3. $\frac{12}{13}$
4. $\frac{3}{2}$
5. $\frac{3}{1}$

Reteaching 24

1. $\frac{4}{5}$
2. 1
3. $\frac{5}{6}$
4. $\frac{5}{8}$
5. 0
6. $\frac{7}{9}$

Reteaching 25

1. $3\frac{2}{3}$
2. $6\frac{1}{4}$ inches
3. $1\frac{1}{5}$
4. 4, 8, 12, 16, 20, 24
5. 10, 20, 30, 40, 50

Reteaching 26

1. $\frac{3}{4}$
2. $\frac{2}{3}$
3. $\frac{3}{5}$
4. $6\frac{1}{6}$
5. $3\frac{1}{2}$
6. 7
7. $3\frac{1}{4}$

Reteaching 27

1. A. radius
2. 11 inches
3. A. segment *AB*
4. $\frac{1}{2}$
5. 36 cm

Reteaching 28

1. $\angle B$ (or $\angle ABC$ or $\angle CBA$)
2. acute angle
3. $\angle FGH$, $\angle HGF$, $\angle G$
4. right angle

Reteaching 29

1. $\frac{3}{10}$
2. $\frac{4}{3} = 1\frac{1}{3}$
3. $1\frac{1}{3}$
4. $\frac{1}{3}$
5. $\frac{9}{10}$
6. $\frac{4}{3}$

Reteaching 30

1. 20
2. 14
3. 18

Answers

4. $\frac{7}{3}$

5. $\frac{5}{3}$

6. $\frac{5}{4}$

Reteaching Inv. 3

1. ∠*RQN* or ∠*NQR*, ∠*RQS* or ∠*SQR*

2. 135°

3. ∠*MQN* or ∠*NQM*

4. ∠*MQS* or ∠*SQM*, ∠*SQN* or ∠*NQS*

Reteaching 31

1. 80 square tiles

2. 35 square-inch tiles

3. 224 sq. ft

4. 176 square centimeters

5. 9 square inches

Reteaching 32

1. 406

2. 7300

3. 3 hr 30 min

4. 2 hr 12 min

Reteaching 33

1. $\frac{2}{5}$

2. $\frac{3}{5}$

3. $\frac{3}{4}$

4. $\frac{3}{25}$

5. $\frac{1}{5}$

6. $\frac{1}{2}$

Reteaching 34

1. 3

2. 9

3. 2.14

4. 6

5. 2

6. 9

Reteaching 35

1. $\frac{28}{100} = \frac{7}{25}$

2. 0.07

3. 0.056

4. 0.19

5. 7.3

6. four and twenty-one hundredths

Reteaching 36

1. $1\frac{3}{4}$

2. $3\frac{5}{8}$

3. $4\frac{7}{10}$

4. $1\frac{1}{3}$

5. $3\frac{2}{5}$

6. $4\frac{1}{6}$

Reteaching 37

1. 1.5
2. 0.12
3. 3.84
4. 3.16
5. 6.97
6. 1.1

Reteaching 38

1. 1.32
2. 9.83
3. 40.3
4. 3.48
5. 14
6. $7\frac{2}{3}$

Reteaching 39

1. 0.070 = 0.07
2. 1.44
3. 0.0312
4. 0.048
5. 0.0552

Reteaching 40

1. 1.47
2. 1.21
3. 5.68
4. 4.7
5. 2.69
6. 5.37

Reteaching Inv. 4

1. qualitative
2. quantitative
3. closed-option survey
4. seventh graders

Reteaching 41

1. $\frac{3}{5}$; 0.6
2. 20 questions
3. \$10
4. \$ 0.76
5. \$24.33
6. \$4.76

Reteaching 42

1. 12
2. 6
3. 32
4. 35
5. $\frac{2}{2}$
6. $\frac{3}{8}$

Reteaching 43

1. 2.44
2. 0.42
3. $\frac{5}{7}$
4. $3\frac{5}{8}$
5. 5.2
6. $\frac{7}{4}$

Answers

Reteaching 44

1. 3.04
2. 0.091
3. >
4. <
5. >

Reteaching 45

1. 0.36
2. 0.045
3. 0.27
4. 0.31
5. 0.054
6. 0.975

Reteaching 46

1. 650
2. 875.6
3. 357.9
4. 240
5. 8.1
6. 60

Reteaching 47

1. 31.4 inches
2. 628 mm
3. 31.4 cm
4. about 126 inches
5. 18.84 cm

Reteaching 48

1. $2\frac{5}{7}$
2. $3\frac{2}{3}$
3. $2\frac{3}{4}$
4. $1\frac{4}{5}$
5. $4\frac{6}{8}$

Reteaching 49

1. 0.036
2. 105
3. 1.3
4. 5.1
5. 2.5

Reteaching 50

1. 2.4
2. 0.3
3. 6.8
4. 4.5

Reteaching Inv. 5

1. 85
2. 88

3.

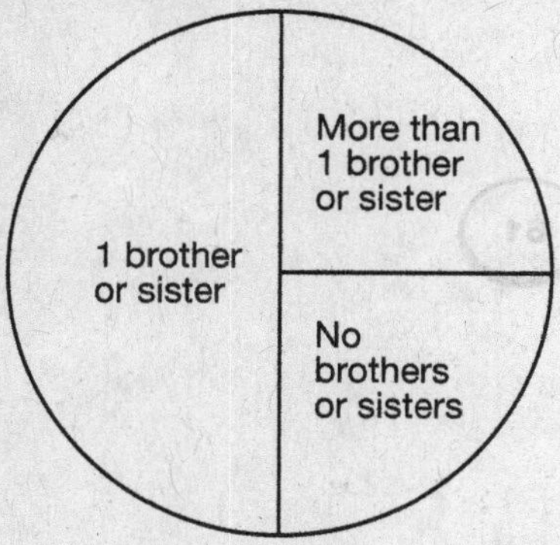

4. only one brother or sister

Reteaching 51

1. 2.4
2. 0.5
3. 3.69
4. 0.94
5. $1.49
6. $0.67

Reteaching 52

1. 9.54
2. 0.38
3. 0.715
4. 0.036
5. 0.0225
6. 0.879

Reteaching 53

1. Fill them with zeros.
2. $1\frac{1}{4}$
3. $1\frac{1}{3}$
4. $1\frac{1}{5}$
5. $1\frac{1}{3}$

Reteaching 54

1. 3
2. $\frac{1}{8}$
3. $\frac{5}{8}$
4. $\frac{1}{3}$

Reteaching 55

1. $\frac{5}{6}$
2. $\frac{3}{4}$
3. $\frac{1}{8}$
4. $1\frac{1}{8}$
5. $\frac{1}{4}$

Reteaching 56

1. $\frac{9}{20}$
2. $1\frac{3}{10}$
3. $\frac{1}{6}$
4. $\frac{5}{12}$
5. $<$
6. $=$

Reteaching 57

1. $\frac{8}{9}$
2. $1\frac{1}{12}$
3. $1\frac{3}{10}$

4. $\frac{1}{6}$

5. $\frac{3}{8}$

6. $\frac{5}{12}$

Reteaching 58

1. $\frac{1}{2}$

2. $\frac{1}{6}$

3. 20%

4. 50%

Reteaching 59

1. $4\frac{5}{6}$

2. $11\frac{1}{8}$

3. $7\frac{1}{9}$

4. $4\frac{1}{12}$

5. $5\frac{7}{8}$

6. $5\frac{1}{2}$

Reteaching 60

1. 5

2. a square

3. 36 inches

4. 12 mm

5. 96 cm

Reteaching Inv. 6

1. 6

2. 5

3. 6

4. 27

Reteaching 61

1. $1\frac{2}{3}$

2. $1\frac{5}{8}$

3. $1\frac{5}{12}$

4. $7\frac{7}{8}$

5. $8\frac{1}{8}$

6. $7\frac{1}{3}$

Reteaching 62

1. $\frac{8}{3}$

2. $\frac{15}{4}$

3. $\frac{15}{8}$

4. $\frac{29}{6}$

5. $\frac{5}{6}$

6. $1\frac{3}{8}$

Reteaching 63

1. $13\frac{1}{8}$

2. $1\frac{1}{3}$

3. $2\frac{1}{10}$

4. $2\frac{3}{8}$

5. $3\frac{2}{3}$

6. $1\frac{5}{8}$

Reteaching 64

1. C
2. A
3. B
4. D. trapezoid
5. false

Reteaching 65

1. 2 · 2 · 7
2. 3 · 3 · 5
3. 2 · 2 · 2 · 2 · 2
4. 2 · 3 · 3 · 3

Reteaching 66

1. $1\frac{2}{3}$
2. $1\frac{2}{3}$
3. $6\frac{2}{3}$
4. 8
5. $4\frac{3}{8}$
6. $3\frac{3}{8}$

Reteaching 67

1. $\frac{4}{9}$
2. $\frac{5}{9}$
3. $\frac{5}{8}$
4. $\frac{7}{11}$
5. $\frac{7}{10}$
6. $\frac{6}{7}$

Reteaching 68

1. $\frac{4}{9}$
2. $1\frac{4}{5}$
3. 2
4. $2\frac{1}{3}$
5. $1\frac{9}{14}$
6. $\frac{2}{3}$

Reteaching 69

1. 4 cm
2. 60°
3. 110°
4. *Possible answer:* ∠*RSQ* and ∠*QST*
5. *Possible answer:* ∠*RSQ* and ∠*RSU*

Reteaching 70

1. $2\frac{1}{2}$
2. $6\frac{2}{3}$
3. 6
4. 3
5. $3\frac{2}{3}$
6. 11

Reteaching Inv. 7

1. B
2. (−1, 3)

3. 16 units

4. 15 sq. units

5. (1, 1)

6. (2, −1)

Reteaching 71

1. 24 sq. cm

2. 52 cm

3. 156 sq. cm

4. 100°

5. 80°

Reteaching 72

1. Write the fractions with common denominators.

2. Simplify the answer by reducing or converting improper fractions.

3. $\frac{1}{6}$

4. $\frac{1}{3}$

5. $\frac{1}{7}$

6. $\frac{3}{16}$

Reteaching 73

1. $2^2 \cdot 3^2$

2. $2^3 \cdot 5^2$

3. $\frac{53}{100}$

4. $8\frac{1}{2}$

5. $\frac{2}{5}$

6. $1\frac{1}{4}$

Reteaching 74

1. 0.6

2. 0.375

3. 5.75

4. 6.5

5. 2.75

6. 4.8

Reteaching 75

1. 30%

2. 40%

3. 6%

4. 92%

5. 85%

6. 80%

Reteaching 76

1. $<$

2. $=$

3. $>$

4. $<$

5. $>$

6. $<$

Reteaching 77

1. 9 eggs

2. 120 flowers

3. 8 runners

4. 20 students

Reteaching 78

1. $\frac{1}{2}$
2. 4 cups
3. 2 quarts
4. 16 cups

Reteaching 79

1. 10 cm^2
2. 70 cm^2
3. 15 cm^2
4. 4 sq. cm
5. 27 sq. mm

Reteaching 80

1. 40 red flowers
2. 6 girls
3. 12 vans
4. 24 pieces of white chalk

Reteaching Inv. 8

1.

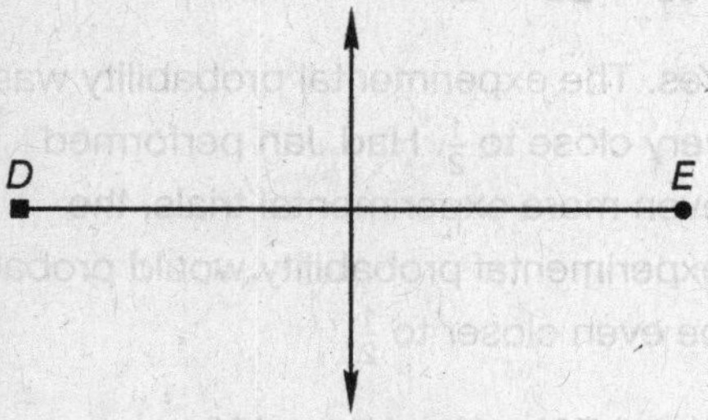

2.

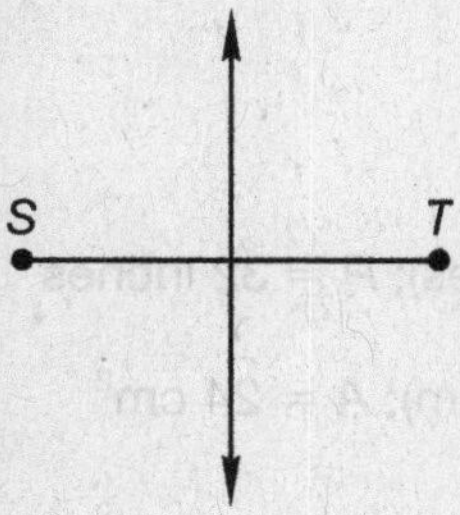

3.

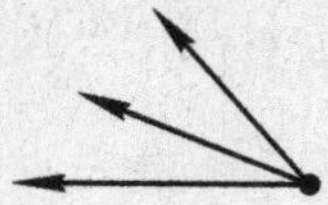

4.

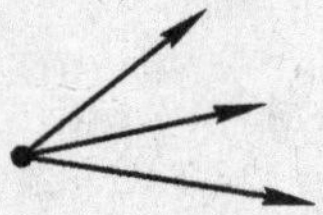

Reteaching 81

1. 32 inches
2. 14 inches
3. 54 inches
4. 18 ft^2
5. 5 cm
6. $50\frac{mi}{hr}$

Reteaching 82

1. 264 $in.^3$
2. 144 cm^3
3. 125 $in.^3$
4. 16 sugar cubes
5. 72 $in.^3$

Reteaching 83

1. B. $\frac{16}{20}$
2. $\frac{3}{7} = \frac{9}{21}$
3. $\frac{9}{5} = \frac{18}{10}$
4. $\frac{6}{5} = \frac{30}{25}$

Reteaching 84

1. 29
2. 16
3. 13

Answers

4. 7

5. 30

6. 9

Reteaching 85

1. 16
2. 35
3. 27
4. 20
5. 28
6. 6

Reteaching 86

1. 78.5 cm^2
2. 50.24 cm^2
3. 12.56 cm^2
4. 153.86 $in.^2$
5. 452.16 $in.^2$

Reteaching 87

1. 0.14
2. $1\frac{3}{4}$
3. $4\frac{1}{2}$
4. 4
5. 0.19
6. 6

Reteaching 88

1. 6 girls
2. 8 boys
3. 6 B's
4. 24

Reteaching 89

1. B. 3 and 4
2. C. 5 and 6
3. 50
4. 60
5. 80
6. 14

Reteaching 90

1. 360°
2. 45°
3. south
4. west

Reteaching Inv. 9

1. 1a. $\frac{4}{10}$ 1b. $\frac{5}{10}$

   1c. 10%

2. 1a. $\frac{52}{100} = \frac{13}{25} \approx \frac{1}{2}$

   2b. Yes. The experimental probability was very close to $\frac{1}{2}$. Had Jan performed even more experimental trials, the experimental probability would probably be even closer to $\frac{1}{2}$.

3 3a. About 7% 3b. About 408

Reteaching 91

1. $P = 4s$; $P = (4)(8 \text{ inches})$; $P = 32 \text{ inches}$
2. $A = lw$; $A = (4 \text{ cm})(6 \text{ cm})$; $A = 24 \text{ cm}^2$

3. $P = 2b + 2s$; $P = 2(3 \text{ inches}) + 2(5 \text{ inches})$; $P = 16$ inches

4. $A = \frac{1}{2}bh$; $A = \frac{1}{2}(5 \text{ cm})(8 \text{ cm})$; $A = 20 \text{ cm}^2$

Reteaching 92

1. 8
2. $1\frac{7}{9}$
3. 6
4. 2
5. 59
6. 3500

Reteaching 93

1. A. acute triangle
2. 36 inches
3. 9 inches
4. an acute triangle
5. true

Reteaching 94

1. 40%
2. $14\frac{2}{7}\%$
3. $37\frac{1}{2}\%$
4. 92%
5. 40.6%

Reteaching 95

1. 56 dollars
2. 315 cents
3. 600 miles
4. 270 students
5. 390 cm per second

Reteaching 96

1. 15, 18
2. 16, 21
3. 16, 20
4. 40, 50

Reteaching 97

1. 110°
2. ∠8
3. 70°
4. ∠4
5. line h
6. ∠5

Reteaching 98

1. 50°
2. 40°
3. 60°
4. 360°

Reteaching 99

1. 0.8, 80%
2. $\frac{3}{50}$, 0.06
3. $1\frac{7}{10}$, 170%

Reteaching 100

1. −9
2. 3

Answers

3. −4

4. −12

5. 14°F

6. 8°C

Reteaching Inv. 10

1. $\frac{1}{10}$

2. $\frac{1}{36}$

3. $\frac{1}{45}$

4. $\frac{3}{14}$

Reteaching 101

1. 9 boys

2. 16 girls

3. $\frac{4}{3}$

4. $\frac{3}{5}$

5. $\frac{2}{3}$

Reteaching 102

1. 6000 lb

2. 3000 g

3. 32 oz

4. 8 oz

5. 500 grams

6. 1000 lb

Reteaching 103

1. 34 m

2. 46 m

3. 28 in.

4. 18 cm

Reteaching 104

1. Minus 2 equals a negative 2.

2. Minus a positive 2 equals a negative 2.

3. Plus a negative 2 equals a negative 2.

4. The negative of a positive 2 equals a negative 2.

5. −8

6. +4 or 4

7. −6

8. +6 or 6

9. +12 or 12

10. 0

Reteaching 105

1. 20 students

2. 25 students

3. 20 questions

4. 24 questions

5. 2 team members

Reteaching 106

1. 7

2. 8

3. 6

4. 2

5. 3

6. 9

Reteaching 107

1. 31 m^2
2. 144 cm^2
3. 24 mm^2
4. 21 $in.^2$

Reteaching 108

1. translation
2. rotation or reflection
3. rotation or reflection
4. translation and reflection

Reteaching 109

1. 15 in.
2. *A* and *C*
3. $\angle K$
4. 36 mm^2

Reteaching 110

1. 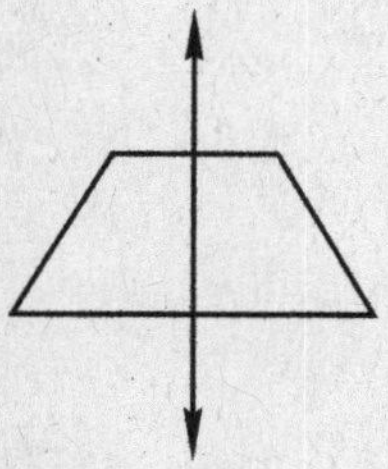

2. 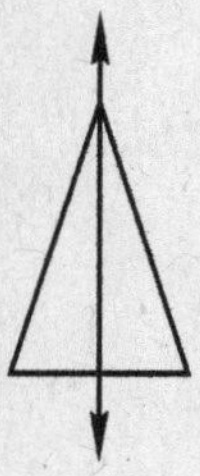

3. 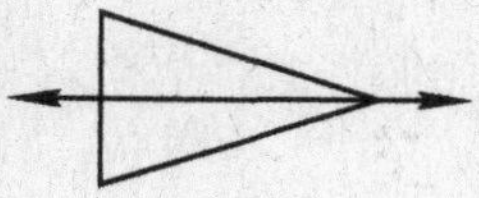

4. 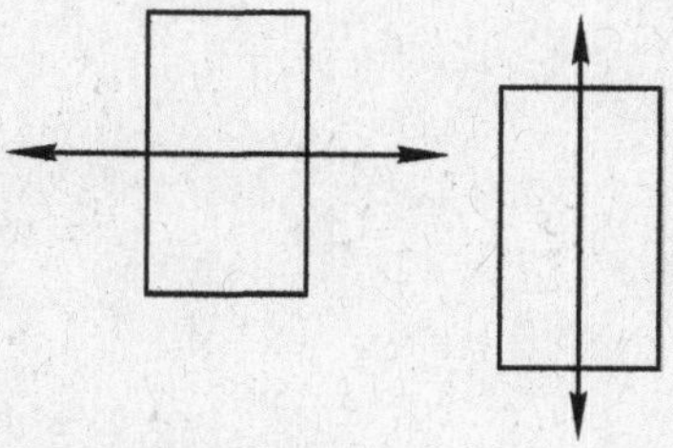

Reteaching Inv. 11

1. 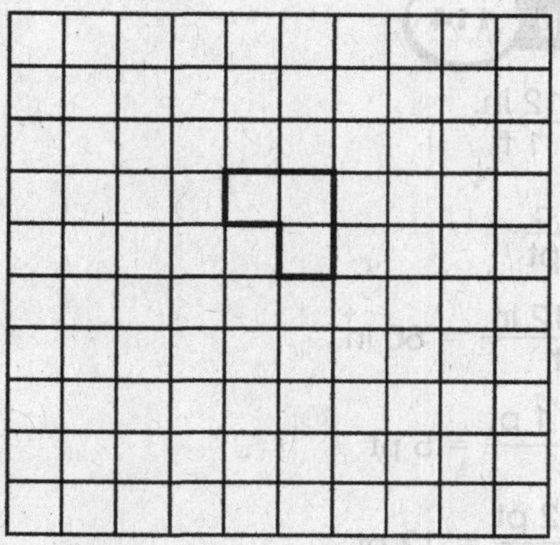

Reteaching 111

1. 24, 24, 24, 25
2. 2 tickets
3. 4 cars
4. 25, 25, 26

Reteaching 112

1. 24
2. −48
3. −35
4. −3
5. −7
6. +5

Answers

Reteaching 113

1. 3,500,000
2. 1,500,000
3. 2700
4. 1 ft 6 in.
5. 5 ft 8 in.
6. 6 min 30 sec

Reteaching 114

1. $\frac{1 \text{ ft}}{12 \text{ in.}}; \frac{12 \text{ in.}}{1 \text{ ft}}$
2. $\frac{1 \text{ pt}}{2 \text{ c}}; \frac{2 \text{ c}}{1 \text{ pt}}$
3. $\frac{5 \text{ ft} \times 12 \text{ in.}}{1 \text{ ft}} = 60 \text{ in.}$
4. $\frac{10 \text{ c} \times 1 \text{ pt}}{2 \text{ c}} = 5 \text{ pt}$
5. $\frac{6 \text{ qt} \times 2 \text{ pt}}{1 \text{ qt}} = 12 \text{ pt}$
6. $\frac{12 \text{ qt} \times 1 \text{ gal}}{4 \text{ qt}} = 3 \text{ gal}$

Reteaching 115

1. $\frac{1}{12}$
2. $\frac{1}{24}$
3. $\frac{1}{14}$
4. $\frac{1}{3}$
5. $\frac{8}{15}$
6. $\frac{11}{15}$

Reteaching 116

1. $224.00
2. $327.00
3. $500.00
4. $640.00

Reteaching 117

1. 25 students
2. 16 players
3. 27 people
4. 32 students
5. 10
6. 40

Reteaching 118

1. about 28 sq. units
2. about 33 sq. units
3. about 29 sq. units
4. about 35 sq. units

Reteaching 119

1. 500
2. 750
3. 125
4. 75
5. 200
6. 300

Reteaching 120

1. 63 cm^3
2. 201 cm^3
3. 785 cm^3
4. 1696 cm^3

5. 4710 cm^3

6. 226 cm^3

Reteaching Inv. 12

1. $SA = 726 \text{ cm}^2$; $V = 1331 \text{ cm}^3$

2. $V = 35 \text{ m}^3$

3. $SA = 260 \text{ mm}^2$

4. $V = 96 \text{ yd}^3$

Answers

Baseline Test

1. C. 43
2. B. 9.67
3. D. 22.25
4. A. 45,600
5. D. 36¢
6. B. 6
7. A. $2\frac{1}{2}$
8. C. 6
9. B. $1\frac{1}{2}$
10. C. $\frac{2}{3}$
11. D. 6
12. A. 2,500,000
13. C. 20 mm
14. B. 1 meter
15. D. 0.2
16. D. 144
17. C. 10
18. A. 10.3
19. B. 280,000
20. A. 0.01, 0.1, 1.0
21. C. $\frac{3}{9}$
22. D. 45 miles
23. B. 23 students
24. A. 80
25. B. $\frac{1}{2}$
26. C. $6.36
27. A. 128 ounces
28. B. $13.75
29. D. $\frac{4}{5}$
30. A. 300 miles
31. D. 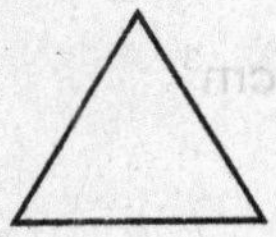
32. C. 
33. B. 70 mm
34. B. 20 inches
35. C. 96 sq. in.
36. A. $\frac{2}{5}$
37. C. 6
38. D. 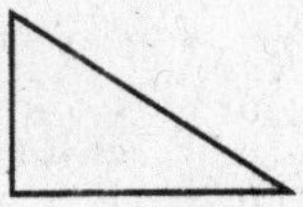
39. A. 
40. C. 9 sq. ft
41. B. $-2 < -1$
42. A. 27
43. D. 3
44. D. 5
45. C. $(6 \times 3) + (6 \times 4)$
46. C. 12
47. A. $\frac{1}{2} \times \frac{1}{2} < \frac{1}{2} + \frac{1}{2}$
48. B. 8
49. C. -3
50. D. Point *D*

Power-Up Test

1. Wes

2. $2\frac{1}{2}$ minutes

3. 3 dimes and 4 nickels

4. 56 seats

5. 1 and 6

6. 6 possible routes

7. 24 glubs $= \frac{1}{2}$ dort

8. 5, 7, 9

9. *Answers will vary; check student work* (8 possible solutions).

10. $$\begin{array}{r} \underline{8}37\underline{2} \\ -\,2\underline{4}65 \\ \hline 59\underline{0}7 \end{array}$$

11. 75

12. Celia (oldest)
Marcos (youngest)

13. 4 possible combinations

14. 9 yd × 3 yd, 7 yd × 5 yd

15. 6 pieces

16. $ 20

17. 6 handshakes

18. 50 daisies

19. 10 cm^2

20. 11 bounces

21. $300

22. two games: DD or LL
three games: DLL or LDD
four games: DLDD or LDLL
five games: DLDLD, DLDLL, LDLDD, or LDLDD

23. Yes; *Answers will vary.*

Answers

Cumulative Test 1A

1. 6 + 12 = 18 12 + 6 = 18
   18 − 12 = 6 18 − 6 = 12
2. 15 × 5 = 75 5 × 15 = 75
   75 ÷ 5 = 15 75 ÷ 15 = 5
3. 5268
4. $2.15
5. $7.00
6. 40 quarters
7. 8 groups
8. 35 pencils
9. $16.45
10. 168
11. 3444
12. 27,024
13. 27,336
14. 1202
15. 125
16. 15
17. 12
18. 53
19. 742
20. 17

Cumulative Test 1B

1. 5 + 11 = 16 11 + 5 = 16
   16 − 11 = 5 16 − 5 = 11
2. 4 × 16 = 64 16 × 4 = 64
   64 ÷ 4 = 16 64 ÷ 16 = 4
3. $12.23
4. $6.51
5. $3.48
6. 15 nickels
7. 12 players
8. 31 days
9. 7402
10. 1460
11. 3839
12. 9200
13. 12,240
14. 1036
15. 144
16. 21
17. 4
18. 47
19. 1638
20. 18

Cumulative Test 2A

1. $2.76
2. $9.50
3. 5693
4. 2969
5. 1692
6. 28
7. $8.77
8. 18
9. 506

10. 63

11. 34

12. $\frac{3}{8}$

13. 40

14. $2\frac{3}{4}$ in.

15. miles

16. 60 mm

17. 18

18. C. 4321

19. $4\overline{)20}$ $20 \div 4$ $\frac{20}{4}$

20. $10 + 20 = 30$ $20 + 10 = 30$
$30 - 20 = 10$ $30 - 10 = 20$

Cumulative Test 2B

1. $5.63

2. 3 pencils

3. 2112

4. 417

5. 1224

6. 602

7. $18.84

8. 3

9. 32

10. 35

11. 51

12. $\frac{3}{10}$

13. 18

14. 27 mm

15. inches

16. 40 mm

17. 32

18. C. 7654

19. $8\overline{)16}$ $16 \div 8$ $\frac{16}{8}$

20. $11 + 22 = 33$ $22 + 11 = 33$
$33 - 22 = 11$ $33 - 11 = 22$

Cumulative Test 3A

1. 20 rolls

2. 561 years

3. ten thousands

4. ten million

5. 3

6. 431,720

7. 165 steps

8. 12°F

9. $\frac{2}{5}$

10. $<$

11. 42,650

12. 3216

13. $10.00

14. 506

15. 25

16. 8

17. 592

18. 7

19. 80 mm

20. $8 \times 15 = 120$ $15 \times 8 = 120$
$120 \div 8 = 15$ $120 \div 15 = 8$

Answers

Cumulative Test 3B

1. 13 players per team
2. 156 years
3. thousands
4. four billion
5. 11
6. 20
7. 176 steps
8. 2°F
9. $\frac{1}{8}$
10. >
11. $9.23
12. 4648
13. $3.50
14. 402
15. $4.17
16. 12
17. 1904
18. 6
19. 6 cm
20. $8 + 15 = 23$ $\quad$ $15 + 8 = 23$
    $23 - 8 = 15$ $\quad$ $23 - 15 = 8$

Cumulative Test 4A

1. 2
2. 3
3. 216 pages
4. 9°
5. 65
6. 29
7. 38,000
8. 2500
9. 41
10. 8
11. 61
12. 1, 2, 3, 6, 9, 18
13. $9.75
14. 6
15. Friday
16. 5 answers
17. $1.75
18. 60 mm
19. 75
20. $2\frac{1}{2}$ in.

Cumulative Test 4B

1. 5
2. 5
3. 117 pages
4. 18°
5. 118
6. 26
7. 4400
8. 9000
9. 72
10. 8
11. 50
12. 1, 3, 7, 21

13. $7.80

14. 8

15. 22 points

16. 2 points

17. $3.75

18. 32 mm

19. 81

20. $1\frac{1}{2}$ in.

Cumulative Test 5A

1. 170

2. $\frac{13}{15}$

3. 17,105,000

4. 2700

5. B. 1632

6. $2\frac{2}{5}$

7. 60

8. 12

9. 6

10. $\frac{7}{12}$

11. 36 miles

12. 8

13. $\frac{5}{6}$

14. $\frac{7}{12}$

15. $\frac{2}{5}$

16. 1

17. 50%

18. $\frac{3}{8}$

19. $2.75

20. $>$

Cumulative Test 5B

1. 300

2. $\frac{13}{16}$

3. 21,286,000

4. 3900

5. C. 3624

6. $5\frac{1}{3}$

7. 4610

8. 7

9. 5

10. $\frac{4}{15}$

11. 240 miles

12. 18

13. $\frac{2}{3}$

14. $\frac{3}{8}$

15. $\frac{5}{8}$

16. 1

17. 25%

18. $\frac{7}{12}$

19. $3.75

20. $<$

Cumulative Test 6A

1. $6\frac{3}{4}$ inches

2. $\frac{7}{8}$

3. 1400

4. 63

5. 74

6. 1, 2, 4, 5, 10, 20

7. 8

8. B. diameter

9. 9 pencils

10. 0

11. $\frac{2}{3}$

12. $\frac{3}{8}$

13. $1\frac{2}{3}$

14. $6\frac{1}{3}$

15. $\frac{3}{4}$

16. 12

17. 9 in.

18. $\frac{3}{2}$

19. 40, 48, 56

20. ∠*C* or ∠*ACB* or ∠*BCA*

Cumulative Test 6B

1. $7\frac{1}{4}$ inches

2. $\frac{2}{3}$

3. 2000

4. 24

5. 123

6. 1, 3, 11, 33

7. 9

8. C. circumference

9. 15 books

10. $\frac{2}{5}$

11. $\frac{3}{4}$

12. $\frac{2}{15}$

13. $1\frac{1}{2}$

14. $8\frac{2}{5}$

15. $\frac{2}{3}$

16. 24

17. 15 cm

18. $\frac{4}{3}$

19. 49

20. ∠*B* or ∠*ABC* or ∠*CBA*

Cumulative Test 7A

1. 1800

2. $\frac{3}{2}$

3. 32 in.

4. 120 square tiles

5. 3

6. 0.012

7. 506

8. 12 in.

9. $\frac{47}{100}$

10. $<$

11. 0.35

12. $1\frac{2}{5}$

13. $\frac{2}{5}$

14. 30

15. 27

16. $\frac{1}{2}$

17. 110

18. $1\frac{1}{3}$

19. $\frac{4}{5}$

20. 32 answers

Cumulative Test 7B

1. 5300
2. $\frac{6}{5}$
3. 40 cm
4. 150 square tiles
5. 8
6. 1.5
7. 5070
8. 14 in.
9. $\frac{7}{10}$
10. >
11. 0.03
12. $1\frac{2}{7}$
13. $\frac{3}{5}$
14. 575
15. 30
16. $\frac{2}{3}$
17. 550
18. $2\frac{2}{3}$
19. $\frac{3}{5}$
20. 30 answers

Cumulative Test 8A

1. $\angle BDC$ or $\angle CDB$
2. 5
3. $\frac{4}{5}$
4. 9000
5. 19
6. 81 pages
7. 4
8. $\frac{3}{5}$
9. $4\frac{1}{3}$
10. $\frac{3}{8}$
11. $\frac{1}{4}$
12. 1 hour 53 minutes
13. 24
14. 100 square-inch tiles
15. 3
16. 10.05
17. 1.5
18. 5.54
19. 0.09
20. 0.045

Cumulative Test 8B

1. $\angle ADB$ or $\angle BDA$
2. 2
3. $\frac{3}{4}$
4. 13,000
5. 29
6. 83 pages
7. 7
8. $\frac{2}{5}$
9. 5
10. $3\frac{2}{3}$
11. $\frac{1}{3}$
12. 6 hours 15 minutes
13. 6

14. 48 square-inch tiles
15. 4
16. 3.12
17. 1.2
18. 10.56
19. 0.04
20. 0.048

Cumulative Test 9A

1. 45
2. $1\frac{1}{3}$
3. 9 in.
4. 180 sq. ft
5. 10.12
6. $20
7. 18
8. C. 70%
9. 4
10. $\frac{7}{100} = 0.07$
11. 4
12. $5\frac{1}{3}$
13. $\frac{1}{3}$
14. 15.13
15. 1.73
16. 0.0884
17. $1\frac{1}{3}$
18. 8
19. 0.175
20. C. $\overline{SR}$

Cumulative Test 9B

1. 60
2. $1\frac{1}{2}$
3. 25 cm
4. 132 sq. ft
5. 12.05
6. $15
7. 16
8. A. 30%
9. 7
10. $\frac{9}{100} = 0.09$
11. 24
12. $3\frac{3}{5}$
13. $\frac{1}{4}$
14. 13.68
15. 1.66
16. 0.0276
17. 7
18. 6
19. 0.375
20. D. $\overline{SQ}$

Cumulative Test 10A

1. 0.58
2. 3
3. $1.28
4. 8000
5. 2005
6. 96

7. $\frac{3}{4}$

8. 20

9. $\frac{5}{8}$

10. 12

11. 10,000 sq. cm

12. 31.40 in. or 31.4 in.

13. 10.2

14. 0.77

15. 10.12

16. 0.024

17. 0.041

18. 1.5

19. $4\frac{3}{5}$

20. 1250

Cumulative Test 10B

1. $\frac{7}{9}$

2. 7

3. $1.12

4. 1000

5. 209

6. 46

7. $\frac{2}{3}$

8. 36

9. $\frac{7}{8}$

10. 8

11. 1161 sq. mm

12. 31.40 ft or 31.4 ft

13. 21.05

14. 0.99

15. 17.07

16. 0.0156

17. 0.076

18. 4.1

19. $2\frac{2}{3}$

20. 350

Cumulative Test 11A

1. 25.12 cm

2. 0.0375

3. 88 mm

4. 480 sq. mm

5. $\frac{6}{5}$

6. 15 dimes

7. 2.3

8. =

9. 80.08

10. 2.9

11. $5\frac{1}{3}$

12. $1\frac{2}{3}$

13. $\frac{1}{6}$

14. $\frac{2}{3}$

15. 0.0375

16. 0.0375

17. 10

18. $\frac{7}{8}$

19. $\frac{6}{7}$

20. 3.7

Answers

Cumulative Test 11B

1. 18.84 cm
2. 0.00972
3. 70 mm
4. 300 sq. mm
5. $\frac{4}{3}$
6. 10 pennies
7. 2.9
8. >
9. 20.2
10. 6.73
11. 6
12. $3\frac{3}{5}$
13. $\frac{3}{10}$
14. $\frac{4}{5}$
15. 0.0045
16. 0.075
17. 5
18. $\frac{5}{8}$
19. $\frac{3}{10}$
20. 0.8

Cumulative Test 12A

1. $\frac{1}{3}$
2. 48 in.
3. 96 sq. cm
4. 3
5. 7.73
6. 0.71
7. 0.081
8. 94 inches
9. D. 9
10. $\frac{1}{2}$
11. $2\frac{2}{3}$
12. 0.05
13. 30
14. 123.4
15. $1\frac{1}{10}$
16. $\frac{11}{20}$
17. >
18. $6\frac{1}{6}$
19. $5\frac{1}{2}$
20. $0.66

Cumulative Test 12B

1. $\frac{1}{2}$
2. 42 in.
3. 108 sq. cm
4. 8
5. 18.76
6. 2.25
7. 0.084
8. 157 inches
9. C. 4
10. $\frac{2}{3}$
11. $\frac{3}{8}$

12. 0.24

13. 40

14. 1.234

15. $1\frac{1}{12}$

16. $\frac{7}{15}$

17. $<$

18. $7\frac{1}{4}$

19. $5\frac{2}{3}$

20. $0.76

Cumulative Test 13A

1. 4 sq. ft

2. $\frac{4}{4}$

3. $\frac{1}{3}$

4. $\frac{1}{2}$

5. D. 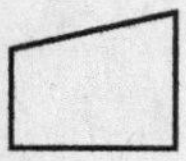

6. $2 \cdot 2 \cdot 2 \cdot 5$

7. $<$

8. $13.99

9. $5.94

10. 20.01

11. 2.66

12. 0.0486

13. 0.028

14. 15

15. $2\frac{1}{3}$

16. $3\frac{1}{2}$

17. $1\frac{5}{8}$

18. $3\frac{1}{3}$

19. 8 vertices

20. $\frac{5}{8}$

Cumulative Test 13B

1. 16 sq. in.

2. $\frac{3}{3}$

3. $\frac{2}{3}$

4. $\frac{1}{2}$

5. D. 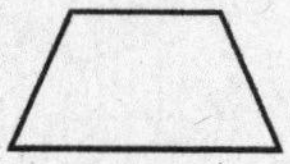

6. $2 \cdot 5 \cdot 5$

7. $>$

8. $15.89

9. $9.90

10. 33.67

11. 2.91

12. 0.21

13. 0.0375

14. 25

15. $3\frac{1}{2}$

16. $8\frac{1}{3}$

17. 1

18. $3\frac{1}{4}$

19. 12 edges

20. $\frac{2}{3}$

Answers

Cumulative Test 14A

1. 9
2. 121 sq. cm
3. 8.75
4. 0.0144
5. 55
6. 0.075
7. C. 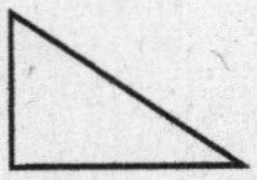
8. >
9. $26.45
10. 450
11. 15
12. $\frac{7}{10}$
13. $7\frac{1}{8}$
14. 8
15. 72 mm
16. $\frac{2 \cdot 2 \cdot 2 \cdot 3}{2 \cdot 3 \cdot 5} = \frac{4}{5}$
17. $3\frac{3}{4}$
18. $\frac{7}{8}$
19. C. 
20. $\frac{1}{4}$

Cumulative Test 14B

1. 4
2. 144 sq. mm
3. 0.7
4. 0.0156
5. 45
6. 0.035
7. C. 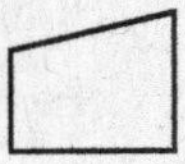
8. <
9. $20.49
10. 0.045
11. 7.5
12. $1\frac{5}{8}$
13. 14
14. 27
15. 6 cm
16. $\frac{2 \cdot 2 \cdot 2 \cdot 3}{2 \cdot 2 \cdot 3 \cdot 5} = \frac{2}{5}$
17. $2\frac{1}{3}$
18. $\frac{3}{5}$
19. B. 
20. $\frac{1}{3}$

Cumulative Test 15A

1. 24 sq. cm
2. $2.72
3. >
4. Point D
5. (3, −2)
6. B. pentagon
7. $\frac{3 \cdot 3 \cdot 5}{2 \cdot 3 \cdot 3 \cdot 3} = \frac{5}{6}$
8. 0.25
9. $0.12 = \frac{3}{25}$
10. 24

11. 1.82
12. 0.36
13. 12.5
14. 0.145
15. $1\frac{11}{12}$
16. $10\frac{1}{10}$
17. $2\frac{3}{8}$
18. 4
19. 3
20. 4.3

Cumulative Test 15B

1. 72 sq. cm
2. $3.63
3. $<$
4. point H
5. (2, −3)
6. 8 sides
7. $\frac{2 \cdot 3 \cdot 3 \cdot 3}{3 \cdot 3 \cdot 3 \cdot 3} = \frac{2}{3}$
8. 0.8
9. $0.15 = \frac{3}{20}$
10. 24
11. 2.95
12. 0.09
13. 8
14. 0.125
15. $1\frac{5}{8}$
16. $11\frac{1}{3}$
17. $3\frac{11}{12}$
18. 12
19. 3
20. 10.8

Cumulative Test 16A

1. $\frac{1}{4}$
2. 84%
3. 24 sq. cm
4. 10 units
5. 6 sq. units
6. $>$
7. 8 months
8. false
9. $\frac{3}{5}$, 18 girls
10. 10
11. 16.02
12. 0.35
13. 0.036
14. $\frac{1}{2}$
15. $7\frac{1}{4}$
16. $\frac{1}{2}$
17. 3
18. 36
19. $1\frac{1}{5}$
20. 0.57

Answers

Cumulative Test 16B

1. 2 quarts
2. 86%
3. 6 sq. cm
4. 12 units
5. 9 sq. units
6. <
7. 10 muffins
8. true
9. $\frac{2}{5}$, 24 minutes
10. 10
11. 23.17
12. 0.68
13. 0.052
14. $\frac{1}{2}$
15. $8\frac{1}{8}$
16. $3\frac{5}{8}$
17. 3
18. 28
19. $\frac{6}{7}$
20. 5.5

Cumulative Test 17A

1. $\frac{4}{5} = 0.80 = 0.8$
2. 48 cm^2
3. 60%
4. 314 cm
5. 44 mm
6. 90 sq. mm
7. 50°
8. $\frac{3}{2}$
9. (−1, 2)
10. 1500 tickets
11. 26 in.
12. 22
13. 360 $in.^3$
14. 15
15. 8.9
16. 0.15
17. $5\frac{3}{8}$
18. $1\frac{3}{4}$
19. $4\frac{1}{2}$
20. $1\frac{1}{3}$

Cumulative Test 17B

1. $\frac{3}{5} = 0.60 = 0.6$
2. 48 cm^2
3. 80%
4. 628 cm
5. 36 cm
6. 60 sq. cm
7. 50°
8. $\frac{4}{3}$
9. (−2, 3)
10. 16 questions
11. 30 in.
12. 2

13. 200 in.^{3}

14. 15

15. 1.78

16. 1.14

17. $3\frac{1}{4}$

18. $2\frac{3}{4}$

19. 8

20. $\frac{3}{4}$

Cumulative Test 18A

1. 50 seeds

2. 8 girls

3. 24 cm

4. 24 sq. cm

5. 1.79

6. 0.081

7. 0.045

8. 30

9. C. 4 and 5

10. $1\frac{1}{3}$

11. $\frac{5}{6}$

12. 6

13. 4

14. $1\frac{4}{5}$

15. 62.8 cm

16. 314 cm^2

17. $\frac{3}{4} = 0.75$

18. 300 cm^3

19. 6 faces

20. (−2, −2), (8, −2), or (2, 6)

Cumulative Test 18B

1. 40 seeds

2. 18 boys

3. 12 cm

4. 6 sq. cm

5. 1.7

6. 0.086

7. 0.075

8. 50

9. C. 5 and 6

10. $1\frac{1}{2}$

11. $\frac{3}{4}$

12. 2

13. 3

14. $1\frac{3}{5}$

15. 62.8 in.

16. 314 in.^{2}

17. $\frac{13}{20} = 0.65$

18. 1000 cm^3

19. 12 edges

20. (1, 0), (−5, 0), or (5, 6)

Cumulative Test 19A

1. 0.5

2. 90

3. 25%

4. 8 edges

5. 54 sq. cm

6. C. right triangle

7. 26

8. $2\frac{1}{4}$

9. 15

10. 12

11. 12

12. 35

13. 4.43

14. 8

15. $14\frac{1}{6}$

16. $\frac{7}{12}$

17. $\frac{3}{5}$

18. $33\frac{1}{3}\%$

19. 3.75; 5.25

20. 20 units

Cumulative Test 19B

1. 0.5

2. 19

3. 40%

4. 5 faces

5. 30 sq. cm

6. D. right triangle

7. 7

8. $6\frac{1}{4}$

9. 12

10. 24

11. 30

12. 36

13. 6.83

14. 6

15. $10\frac{1}{8}$

16. $\frac{11}{12}$

17. $1\frac{1}{3}$

18. $66\frac{2}{3}\%$

19. 3.75; 6.25

20. 18 units

Cumulative Test 20A

1. 16 finches

2. $\frac{1}{36}$

3. a. $\frac{3}{5}$ b. 60%

4. a. $\frac{1}{20}$ b. 0.05

5. 12 students

6. 180 sq. mm

7. 56 mm

8. 80°

9. 360°

10. 30

11. −8

12. 2

13. 60 cm^3

14. 4

15. 11

16. 1.75

17. 15

18. 1.4

19. 18°F

20. 113.04 in.^{2}

Cumulative Test 20B

1. 9 geese
2. $\frac{1}{36}$
3. a. $\frac{2}{5}$ b. 40%
4. a. $\frac{1}{25}$ b. 0.04
5. 10 students
6. 48 sq. cm
7. 32 cm
8. 105°
9. 360°
10. 20
11. −7
12. 4
13. 27 cm^3
14. 2
15. 5
16. 10.75
17. 12
18. 2.3
19. 13°F
20. 200.96 in.^{2}

Cumulative Test 21A

1. $0.16
2. 50 people
3. (1, −2)
4. 61
5. 24 sugar cubes
6. 24 cm
7. 62.8 cm
8. 4000 pounds
9. 15
10. 15 boys
11. a. 1.6 b. 160%
12. a. $\frac{9}{10}$ b. 90%
13. a. $\frac{1}{10}$ b. 0.1
14. 3.05
15. −1
16. 10
17. $10\frac{5}{12}$
18. 10
19. $1\frac{1}{2}$
20. 24 sq. cm

Cumulative Test 21B

1. $0.81
2. 30 students
3. (2, 3)
4. 133
5. 27 sugar cubes

Answers

6. 34 cm

7. 314 cm^2

8. 1000 pounds

9. 18

10. 12 boys

11. a. 2.2 b. 220%

12. a. $\frac{7}{10}$ b. 70%

13. a. $\frac{1}{20}$ b. 0.05

14. 5.45

15. 0

16. 0.0024

17. $3\frac{5}{12}$

18. 15

19. $1\frac{1}{3}$

20. 30 sq. cm

Cumulative Test 22A

1. 40°

2.

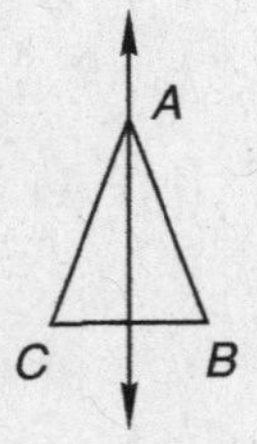

3. $2\frac{2}{3}$

4. $5\frac{1}{3}$

5. 4.125

6. −2, 0.2, $\frac{1}{2}$

7. 12 sq. units

8. −13

9. $\frac{1}{15}$

10. 13

11. a. 1.2 b. 120%

12. a. $\frac{3}{10}$ b. 30%

13. a. $\frac{7}{20}$ b. 0.35

14. 80 cu. in.

15. 314 $in.^2$

16. 7 to 9 or $\frac{7}{9}$

17. 8

18. 11

19. 36 m

20. 50 sq. m

Cumulative Test 22B

1. 30°

2.

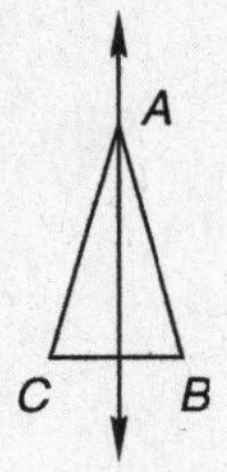

3. $1\frac{5}{6}$

4. 3

5. 4.625

6. −3, 0.35, $\frac{3}{4}$

7. 12 sq. units

8. −12

9. $\frac{2}{9}$

10. 7

11. a. 1.25 b. 125%

12. a. $\frac{7}{10}$ b. 70%

13. **a.** $\frac{3}{20}$ **b.** 0.15

14. 96 blocks

15. 100.48 in.

16. 9 to 7 or $\frac{9}{7}$

17. 12

18. 9

19. 50 m

20. 118 sq. m

Cumulative Test 23A

1. 27, 27, 28, 28

2. 1,500,000

3. 3^4

4. $\overset{2}{\cancel{8}}\ \cancel{qt} \times \frac{1\text{ gal}}{\underset{1}{\cancel{4}}\ \cancel{qt}} = 2\text{ gal}$

5. H

6. $\frac{1}{5}$

7. 45 cm

8. 15 ft

9. 31.4 in.

10. 42 m

11. 80 sq. m

12. **a.** 0.75 **b.** 75%

13. **a.** $\frac{1}{50}$ **b.** 2%

14. **a.** $1\frac{1}{5}$ **b.** 1.2

15. 5.025

16. 3

17. 28

18. −8

19. 40 sq. cm

20. $25.00

Cumulative Test 23B

1. 28, 28, 29

2. 1,500,000,000

3. 2^6

4. $8\ \cancel{qt} \times \frac{2\text{ pt}}{1\ \cancel{qt}} = 16\text{ pt}$

5. S

6. $\frac{1}{5}$

7. 12 in.

8. 25 sq. cm

9. 62.8 in.

10. 32 cm

11. 48 sq. cm

12. **a.** 0.25 **b.** 25%

13. **a.** $\frac{1}{25}$ **b.** 4%

14. **a.** $1\frac{1}{2}$ **b.** 1.5

15. 9.73

16. 30

17. 36

18. −6

19. 48 sq. mm

20. $30.00

Benchmark Test 1

1. D. 7 inches
2. C. $\frac{3}{4}$
3. A. $\frac{120}{30}$
4. D. 7
5. C. between 38 yd and 42 yd
6. C. 10
7. B. 6
8. D. diameter
9. D. 10
10. B. $\frac{4}{7}$
11. C. $\frac{7}{8}$
12. D. $\frac{3}{8}$
13. C. $1\frac{1}{3}$
14. D. 6
15. C. $\frac{3}{4}$
16. C. 18
17. C. 16 cm
18. C. $\frac{4}{3}$
19. D. 64
20. C. obtuse
21. C. 80
22. B. 25%
23. D. $\frac{7}{12}$
24. B. $\frac{2}{5}$
25. D. Jasmine

Benchmark Test 2

1. D. $\frac{2}{3}$
2. C. 36 inches
3. D. 96 cm^2
4. C. 5
5. A. 5.96
6. C. 0.76
7. D. 0.064
8. C. 5 ft
9. B. 9
10. A. $\frac{2}{1}$
11. B. $2\frac{1}{4}$
12. C. 0.24 pounds
13. B. 20
14. C. 37.8 liters
15. C. $1\frac{3}{10}$
16. D. $\frac{1}{15}$
17. D. $\frac{1}{6}, \frac{1}{2}, \frac{2}{3}$
18. B. $6\frac{1}{4}$
19. C. $4\frac{2}{3}$
20. C. 74¢
21. B. 100 by 4
22. C. 9
23. B. $\frac{3}{4}$
24. B. $\frac{1}{4}(60 - 48)$
25. A. $\frac{7}{16}$

Benchmark Test 3

1. A. 200

2. D. 16

3. B. 36 cm

4. B. 54 cm^2

5. A. 0.92 m

6. C. 0.075

7. B. 0.05

8. C. 40

9. D. 6 and 7

10. C. $1\frac{1}{5}$

11. B. $1\frac{3}{4}$

12. D. 15 ft^2

13. A. 3

14. B. 2.4

15. C. 31.4 cm

16. B. 78.5 cm^2

17. B. $\frac{3}{4}$

18. D. 360 $in.^3$

19. B. 12 edges

20. D. $(-1, -2)$

21. A. 6:23 p.m.

22. C. $-2, 0.3, \frac{1}{2}, 1$

23. B. $2^2 \cdot 3^2 \cdot 5^2$

24. B. 20%

25. D. 11

Answers

End-of-Course Exam

1. C. $304\frac{2}{5}$
2. D. 19.25
3. A. 1.55
4. A. 0.63
5. B. 5.2
6. B. $4\frac{1}{2}$
7. C. $1\frac{9}{10}$
8. C. $2\frac{2}{3}$
9. A. $1\frac{3}{5}$
10. C. $\frac{5}{7}$
11. B. 4
12. A. 2,500,000
13. C. 1200 mm
14. B. 2 m
15. D. 0.04
16. B. 10^7
17. C. 14 and 15
18. E. None correct
19. D. 26
20. C. 0.3, 33%, $\frac{1}{3}$
21. C. 18
22. D. 30
23. D. 31
24. B. 9
25. C. $\frac{1}{2}$
26. B. \$3.12
27. C. 13¢/oz
28. C. \$27.00
29. B. 84%
30. D. 1000 miles
31. B.

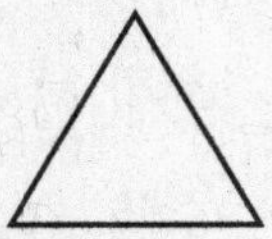

32. A. 52°
33. D. 70 cm
34. B. 62.8 in.
35. B. 54 m^2
36. A. 50 ft^2
37. A. 80 cm^3
38. C.

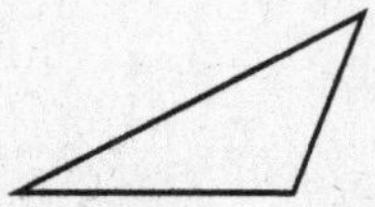

39. D. $\overline{TS}$
40. A. 5
41. B. −7
42. D. 144
43. C. 36
44. A. $2^3 \cdot 3$
45. D. $6 \cdot 20 + 6 \cdot 5$
46. B. 12
47. A. $\sqrt{9} < 2^2$
48. B. 100
49. D. 13
50. A. (−2, −3)

Baseline Test

1. $$\begin{array}{r} 43 \\ 22\overline{)946} \\ \underline{88} \\ 66 \\ \underline{66} \\ 0 \end{array}$$

C. 43

2. $$\begin{array}{r} \overset{1}{6}.50 \\ 2.47 \\ \underline{+\ 0.70} \\ 9.67 \end{array}$$

B. 9.67

3. $$\begin{array}{r} 23.45 \\ \underline{-\ 1.20} \\ 22.25 \end{array}$$

D. 22.25

4. $$\begin{array}{r} 608 \\ \underline{\times\ 75} \\ 3040 \\ \underline{4256\ } \\ 45{,}600 \end{array}$$

A. 45,600

5. $$\begin{array}{r} \$0.36 \\ 20\overline{)\$7.20} \\ \underline{6\ 0} \\ 1\ 20 \\ \underline{1\ 20} \\ 0 \end{array}$$

D. 36¢

6. $$\begin{array}{r} 3\frac{2}{3} \\ \underline{+\ 2\frac{1}{3}} \\ 5\frac{3}{3} \end{array} = 6$$

B. 6

7. $$\begin{array}{r} 4\frac{3}{4} \\ \underline{-\ 2\frac{1}{4}} \\ 2\frac{2}{4} \end{array} = 2\frac{1}{2}$$

A. $2\frac{1}{2}$

8. $\frac{3}{5} \times 10 = \frac{3}{5} \times \frac{10}{1} = \frac{30}{5} = 6$

C. 6

9. $\frac{3}{4} \div \frac{1}{2} = \frac{3}{4} \cdot \frac{2}{1} = \frac{6}{4} = \frac{3}{2} = 1\frac{1}{2}$

B. $1\frac{1}{2}$

10. $\frac{8}{12} = \frac{8 \div 4}{12 \div 4} = \frac{2}{3}$

C. $\frac{2}{3}$

11. **D. 6**

12. **A. 2,500,000**

13. $2\ \cancel{\text{cm}} \cdot \frac{10\text{ mm}}{1\ \cancel{\text{cm}}} = 20\text{ mm}$

C. 20 mm

14. **B. 1 meter**

15. **D. 0.2**

16. $12^2 = 12 \cdot 12 = 144$

D. 144

17. $\sqrt{100} = \sqrt{10 \cdot 10} = 10$

C. 10

18. **A. 10.3**

19. $692 \approx 700$
$412 \approx 400$
$700 \cdot 400 = 280{,}000$

B. 280,000

20. $0.01 < 0.1 < 1.0$

A. 0.01, 0.1, 1.0

21. $\frac{1}{3} \cdot \frac{3}{3} = \frac{3}{9}$

C. $\frac{3}{9}$

22.

Ratio	Actual Count
15 miles	N
1 hour	3 hours

$$\frac{15}{1} = \frac{N}{3}$$
N = 45 miles

D. 45 miles

23. $$\frac{22 + 22 + 25}{3} = \frac{69}{3} = 23$$

B. 23 students

24. 80 occurs most often, so it is the mode.

A. 80

25. **B.** $\frac{1}{2}$

26.
$$\begin{array}{r} \overset{1\,1}{\$5.87} \\ +\ \$0.49 \\ \hline \$6.36 \end{array}$$

C. $6.36

27.

Ratio	Actual Count
1 pound	8 pounds
16 ounces	N

$$\frac{1}{16} = \frac{8}{N}$$
N = 128

A. 128 ounces

28.
$$\begin{array}{r} \$13.75 \\ 2\overline{)\$27.50} \\ \underline{2} \\ 07 \\ \underline{6} \\ 15 \\ \underline{14} \\ 10 \\ \underline{10} \\ 0 \end{array}$$

B. $13.75

29. $$\frac{16}{20} \div \frac{4}{4} = \frac{4}{5}$$

D. $\frac{4}{5}$

30.

Ratio	Actual Count
60 miles	N
1 hour	5 hours

$$\frac{60}{1} = \frac{N}{5}$$
N = 300

A. 300 miles

31. **D.**

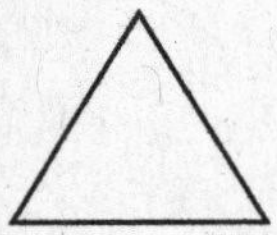

32. **C.**

33. perimeter = 20 mm + 15 mm + 20 mm + 15 mm
= 70 mm

B. 70 mm

34. Radius = Diameter ÷ 2
= 40 in. ÷ 2
= 20 in.

B. 20 inches

35. Area = 12 in. × 8 in. = 96 in.^{2}

C. 96 sq. in.

36. **A.** $\frac{2}{5}$

37. **C. 6**

38. **D.**

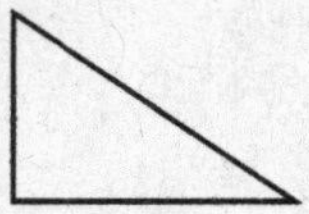

39. **A.**

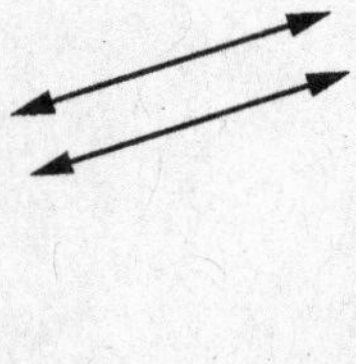

40. Area = 3 ft × 3 ft = 9 ft^2

C. 9 sq. ft

41. B. −2 < − 1

42.

$$\begin{array}{r} 15 \\ +\ 12 \\ \hline 27 \end{array}$$

A. 27

43. $5\frac{2}{3} - \left(4 - 1\frac{1}{3}\right) = 5\frac{2}{3} - 2\frac{2}{3} = 3$

D. 3

44. D. 5

45. 6 × 12 = 72
(6 × 10) + (6 × 2) = 60 + 12 = 72
(6 × 6) + (6 × 6) = 36 + 36 = 72
(6 × 3) + (6 × 4) = 18 + 24 = 42
(3 × 12) + (3 × 12) = 36 + 36 = 72

C. (6 × 3) + (6 × 4)

46. 36 ÷ 3 = 12

C. 12

47. A. $\frac{1}{2} \times \frac{1}{2} < \frac{1}{2} + \frac{1}{2}$

48. $x = \frac{12}{2} = 6$

$2 + x = 2 + 6 = 8$

B. 8

49. C. −3

50. D. Point *D*

Solutions

Practice Set 1

a.
$$\begin{array}{r} {}^{1\,1\,1} \\ 3675 \\ 426 \\ +\ 1357 \\ \hline \mathbf{5458} \end{array}$$

b.
$$\begin{array}{r} \$6.25 \\ \$_{1}8.23 \\ +\ \$12.00 \\ \hline \mathbf{\$26.48} \end{array}$$

c.
$$\begin{array}{r} {}^{6}\ \ \\ 5\,3\,\cancel{7}\,{}^{1}4 \\ -\ \ 1\,6\,8 \\ \hline \mathbf{5\,2\,0\,6} \end{array}$$

d.
$$\begin{array}{r} {}^{4\ \ \ 9}\ \ \\ \$\cancel{5}.\,\cancel{0}{}^{1}0 \\ -\ \$1.\,3\,5 \\ \hline \mathbf{\$3.\,6\,5} \end{array}$$

e.
$$\begin{array}{r} 6 \\ +\ 8 \\ \hline \mathbf{14} \end{array} \qquad \begin{array}{r} 8 \\ +\ 6 \\ \hline \mathbf{14} \end{array} \qquad \begin{array}{r} 14 \\ -\ \ 6 \\ \hline \mathbf{8} \end{array} \qquad \begin{array}{r} 14 \\ -\ \ 8 \\ \hline \mathbf{6} \end{array}$$

f. **25 − 15 = 10**
10 + 15 = 25
15 + 10 = 25

Written Practice 1

1.
$$\begin{array}{r} 25 \\ +\ 40 \\ \hline \mathbf{65} \end{array}$$

2.
$$\begin{array}{r} {}^{1\,2}\ \\ 137 \\ 89 \\ +\ \ \ 9 \\ \hline \mathbf{235} \end{array}$$ **people**

3.
$$\begin{array}{r} {}^{2}\ \ \ \ \ \\ \cancel{3}{}^{1}8\,7 \\ -\ \ \ 9\,3 \\ \hline \mathbf{2\,9\,4} \end{array}$$

4.
$$\begin{array}{r} {}^{4\ \ \ 9}\ \ \\ \$\cancel{5}.\,\cancel{0}{}^{1}0 \\ -\ \$3.\,7\,5 \\ \hline \mathbf{\$1.\,2\,5} \end{array}$$

5.
$$\begin{array}{r} \$5.22 \\ +\ \$4.15 \\ \hline \mathbf{\$9.37} \end{array}$$
I added the two amounts because I was combining what Tatiana earned with what she already had.

6.
$$\begin{array}{r} {}^{1}\ \ \ \ \\ \$1.25 \\ \$0.70 \\ +\ \$0.60 \\ \hline \mathbf{\$2.55} \end{array}$$

7.
$$\begin{array}{r} {}^{1}\ \\ 63 \\ 47 \\ +\ 50 \\ \hline \mathbf{160} \end{array}$$

8.
$$\begin{array}{r} {}^{1\,1}\ \\ 632 \\ 57 \\ +\ 198 \\ \hline \mathbf{887} \end{array}$$

9.
$$\begin{array}{r} {}^{2}\ \\ 78 \\ {}_{1}\ \ 9 \\ +\ 987 \\ \hline \mathbf{1074} \end{array}$$

10.
$$\begin{array}{r} {}^{1\,1}\ \\ 432 \\ {}_{1}579 \\ +\ 3604 \\ \hline \mathbf{4615} \end{array}$$

11.
$$\begin{array}{r} {}^{2\ \ 13}\ \ \\ \cancel{3}\,\cancel{4}\,{}^{1}5 \\ -\ \ \ 6\,7 \\ \hline \mathbf{2\,7\,8} \end{array}$$

12.
$$\begin{array}{r} 678 \\ -\ 416 \\ \hline \mathbf{262} \end{array}$$

13.
$$\begin{array}{r} {}^{6\ \ 15}\ \ \\ 3\,\cancel{7}\,\cancel{6}\,{}^{1}4 \\ -\ \ \ \ 9\,6 \\ \hline \mathbf{3\,6\,6\,8} \end{array}$$

14.
$$\begin{array}{r} {}^{2\,1}\ \\ {}_{1}875 \\ 1086 \\ +\ \ 980 \\ \hline \mathbf{2941} \end{array}$$

15.
$$\begin{array}{r} {}^{2}_{1}10 \\ 156 \\ 8 \\ +\ 27 \\ \hline \mathbf{201} \end{array}$$

16.
$$\begin{array}{r} \$\overset{2}{\not3}.{}^{1}4\,7 \\ -\ \$0.\,9\,2 \\ \hline \mathbf{\$2.\,5\,5} \end{array}$$

17.
$$\begin{array}{r} \$2\,\overset{3}{\not4}.{}^{1}1\,5 \\ -\ \$1.\,4\,5 \\ \hline \mathbf{\$2\,2.\,7\,0} \end{array}$$

18.
$$\begin{array}{r} \overset{1\,1}{\$0.75} \\ +\ \$0.75 \\ \hline \mathbf{\$1.50} \end{array}$$

19.
$$\begin{array}{r} \overset{1}{\$0.12} \\ \$0.46 \\ +\ \$0.50 \\ \hline \mathbf{\$1.08} \end{array}$$

20. **Sum**

21. **Difference**

22.
$$\begin{array}{r} 5 \\ +\ 6 \\ \hline 11 \end{array} \quad \begin{array}{r} 6 \\ +\ 5 \\ \hline 11 \end{array} \quad \begin{array}{r} 11 \\ -\ 6 \\ \hline 5 \end{array} \quad \begin{array}{r} 11 \\ -\ 5 \\ \hline 6 \end{array}$$

23. **16 + 27 = 43**
43 − 16 = 27
43 − 27 = 16

24. **50 − 29 = 21**
29 + 21 = 50
21 + 29 = 50

25. **One way to check is to add the answer (difference) to the amount subtracted. The total should equal the starting amount.**

Practice Set 2

a.
$$\begin{array}{r} \overset{1}{37¢} \\ \times\ 20 \\ \hline \mathbf{740¢}\text{ or }\mathbf{\$7.40} \end{array}$$

b.
$$\begin{array}{r} 37 \\ \times\ \ 0 \\ \hline \mathbf{0} \end{array}$$

c.
$$\begin{array}{r} 407 \\ \times\ 37 \\ \hline 2\,849 \\ 12\,210 \\ \hline \mathbf{15{,}059} \end{array}$$

d.
$$\begin{array}{r} \mathbf{\$1.68} \\ 5\overline{)\$8.40} \\ 5 \\ \hline 3\,4 \\ 3\,0 \\ \hline 40 \\ 40 \\ \hline 0 \end{array}$$

e.
$$\begin{array}{r} \mathbf{16\ R\,8} \\ 12\overline{)200} \\ 12 \\ \hline 80 \\ 72 \\ \hline 8 \end{array}$$

f.
$$\begin{array}{r} \mathbf{78} \\ 3\overline{)234} \\ 21 \\ \hline 24 \\ 24 \\ \hline 0 \end{array}$$

g. **5; 12; 3**

h. **8 × 9 = 72**
9 × 8 = 72
72 ÷ 9 = 8
72 ÷ 8 = 9

Written Practice 2

1.
$$\begin{array}{r} 11 \\ \times\ \ 7 \\ \hline \mathbf{77} \end{array}$$

2.
$$\begin{array}{r} \overset{8}{\not9}{}^{1}7 \\ -\ 7\,9 \\ \hline \mathbf{1\,8} \end{array}$$

3.
```
    1
   170
 + 130
 -----
   300
```

4.
```
     9
  4)36
    36
    --
     0
```

5.
```
   21
   386
    98
   1
 + 1734
 ------
   2218
```

6.
```
    4  9
   $5̸. 0̸¹0
 − $2. 2 5
 ---------
   $2. 7 5
```

7.
```
    6 9
   $7̸ 0̸.¹0 0
 − $4 7. 5 0
 -----------
   $2 2. 5 0
```

8.
```
     75¢
   × 12
   ----
    150
    750
   ----
   900¢  or  $9.00
```
Possible answer: I multiplied 75¢ × 12. The answer was more than one dollar, so I wrote the answer with a dollar sign and decimal point.

9.
```
    2 ¹0
    3̸ 1̸¹2
 −    8 6
 --------
    2 2 6
```

10.
```
    11
   4106
 + 1398
 ------
   5504
```

11.
```
    3 9 9
    4̸ 0̸ 0̸¹0
 −  1 3 5 7
 ----------
    2 6 4 3
```

12.
```
    0  9  9
   $1̸ 0̸. 0̸¹0
 −     $2. 8 3
 ------------
       $7. 1 7
```

13.
```
    405
  ×   8
  -----
   3240
```

14.
```
    25
  × 25
  ----
   125
   500
  ----
   625
```

15.
```
      48
   6)288
     24
     --
      48
      48
      --
       0
```

16.
```
       15
   15)225
      15
      --
       75
       75
       --
        0
```

17.
```
   $1.25
  ×    8
  ------
  $10.00
```

18.
```
     400
  ×   50
  ------
  20,000
```

19.
```
      125
   8)1000
     8
     --
     20
     16
     --
      40
      40
      --
       0
```

20.
```
        $2.25
   20)$45.00
       40
       --
        5 0
        4 0
        ---
        1 00
        1 00
        ----
           0
```

21. $6 \times 8 = 48$
$8 \times 6 = 48$
$48 \div 6 = 8$
$48 \div 8 = 6$

22. $36 \div 9 = 4$
$4 \times 9 = 36$
$9 \times 4 = 36$

23. $24 + 12 = 36$
$36 - 24 = 12$
$36 - 12 = 24$

24. **a.** $\begin{array}{r} 9 \\ +\ 6 \\ \hline \mathbf{15} \end{array}$ **b.** $\begin{array}{r} 9 \\ -\ 6 \\ \hline \mathbf{3} \end{array}$

25. $\text{divisor}\overline{)\text{dividend}}$ with **quotient** above

26. $\begin{array}{r} 39¢ \\ \times\ 6 \\ \hline 234¢ \end{array}$ **or $2.34**

27. $\begin{array}{r} 365 \\ \times\ 0 \\ \hline \mathbf{0} \end{array}$

28. $\begin{array}{r} \mathbf{0} \\ 50\overline{)0} \end{array}$

29. $\begin{array}{r} \mathbf{1} \\ 365\overline{)365} \\ 365 \\ \hline 0 \end{array}$

30. **One way to check is to multiply the divisor by the quotient. The answer should equal the dividend.**

Early Finishers Solutions

$(2 \times 100) + (8 \times 20) + (5 \times 5) + (20 \times 1)$
$+ (80 \times 0.25) + (25 \times 0.10)$
$+ (95 \times 0.01)$
$200 + 160 + 25 + 20 + 20 + 2.50 + 0.95$
$= \$428.45$

Practice Set 3

a. $\begin{array}{r} 45 \\ -\ 12 \\ \hline 33 \end{array}$ check: $\begin{array}{r} 33 \\ +\ 12 \\ \hline 45 \end{array}$

$\boldsymbol{A = 33}$

b. $\begin{array}{r} \overset{5}{\cancel{6}}{}^{1}0 \\ -\ 3\,2 \\ \hline 2\,8 \end{array}$ check: $\begin{array}{r} \overset{1}{3}2 \\ +\ 28 \\ \hline 60 \end{array}$

$\boldsymbol{B = 28}$

c. $\begin{array}{r} 15 \\ +\ 24 \\ \hline 39 \end{array}$ check: $\begin{array}{r} 39 \\ -\ 15 \\ \hline 24 \end{array}$

$\boldsymbol{C = 39}$

d. $\begin{array}{r} \overset{2}{\cancel{3}}{}^{1}8 \\ -\ 2\,9 \\ \hline 9 \end{array}$ check: $\begin{array}{r} \overset{2}{\cancel{3}}{}^{1}8 \\ -\ \ 9 \\ \hline 2\,9 \end{array}$

$\boldsymbol{D = 9}$

e. $\begin{array}{r} \overset{4}{\cancel{5}}{}^{1}2 \\ -\ 2\,4 \\ \hline 2\,8 \end{array}$ check: $\begin{array}{r} \overset{1}{2}8 \\ +\ 24 \\ \hline 52 \end{array}$

$\boldsymbol{e = 28}$

f. $\begin{array}{r} \overset{6}{\cancel{7}}{}^{1}0 \\ -\ 2\,9 \\ \hline 4\,1 \end{array}$ check: $\begin{array}{r} \overset{1}{2}9 \\ +\ 41 \\ \hline 70 \end{array}$

$\boldsymbol{f = 41}$

g. $\begin{array}{r} \overset{1}{6}7 \\ +\ 43 \\ \hline 110 \end{array}$ check: $\begin{array}{r} \overset{0}{\cancel{1}}\,\overset{0}{\cancel{1}}{}^{1}0 \\ -\ \ 6\,7 \\ \hline 4\,3 \end{array}$

$\boldsymbol{g = 110}$

h. $\begin{array}{r} \overset{7}{\cancel{8}}{}^{1}0 \\ -\ 3\,6 \\ \hline 4\,4 \end{array}$ check: $\begin{array}{r} \overset{7}{\cancel{8}}{}^{1}0 \\ -\ 4\,4 \\ \hline 3\,6 \end{array}$

$\boldsymbol{h = 44}$

i. $\underbrace{36 + 14 + 8} + n = 75$
$58 + n = 75$
$75 - 58 = 17$
$\boldsymbol{n = 17}$
check: $36 + 14 + 17 + 8 = 75$

Solutions

Written Practice 3

1.
$$\begin{array}{r} 25 \\ \times\ 12 \\ \hline 50 \\ 250 \\ \hline \mathbf{300} \end{array}$$

2.
$$\begin{array}{r} 25 \\ +\ 12 \\ \hline \mathbf{37} \end{array}$$

3.
$$\begin{array}{r} 25 \\ -\ 12 \\ \hline \mathbf{13} \end{array}$$

4.
$$\begin{array}{r} 75 \\ \times\ 31 \\ \hline 75 \\ 2250 \\ \hline \mathbf{2325} \end{array}$$
2325 cans

5.
$$\begin{array}{r} \$7.85 \\ \times\ \ 12 \\ \hline 1570 \\ 7850 \\ \hline \mathbf{\$94.20} \end{array}$$

6.
$$\begin{array}{r} \overset{0}{\not1}\,\overset{9}{\not0}\,{}^{1}2 \\ -\ \ 6\ 3 \\ \hline \mathbf{3\ 9} \end{array}$$
3 9 points

Possible answer: I subtracted 63, the number of points in the first half of the game, from 102, the total.

7.
$$\begin{array}{r} \$3.68 \\ \times\ \ \ 9 \\ \hline \mathbf{\$33.12} \end{array}$$

8.
$$\begin{array}{r} 407 \\ \times\ \ 80 \\ \hline \mathbf{32{,}560} \end{array}$$

9.
$$\begin{array}{r} 28¢ \\ \times\ 14 \\ \hline 112 \\ 280 \\ \hline \mathbf{392¢} \end{array}$$
392¢ or **$3.92**

10.
$$\begin{array}{r} 370 \\ \times\ \ 140 \\ \hline 14800 \\ 3700 \\ \hline \mathbf{51{,}800} \end{array}$$

11.
$$\begin{array}{r} 100 \\ \times\ \ 100 \\ \hline \mathbf{10{,}000} \end{array}$$

12.
$$\begin{array}{r} \mathbf{12} \\ 12\overline{)144} \\ 12 \\ \hline 24 \\ 24 \\ \hline 0 \end{array}$$

13.
$$\begin{array}{r} 12 \\ \times\ \ 5 \\ \hline \mathbf{60} \end{array}$$

14.
$$\begin{array}{r} {}^{2\,2\,1} \\ 3627 \\ 598 \\ +\ 4881 \\ \hline \mathbf{9106} \end{array}$$

15.
$$\begin{array}{r} \overset{4}{\not5}\,\overset{9}{\not0}\,\overset{10}{\not1}\,{}^{1}0 \\ -\ 1\ 3\ 7\ 6 \\ \hline \mathbf{3\ 6\ 3\ 4} \end{array}$$

16.
$$\begin{array}{r} \$\overset{0}{\not1}\,\overset{9}{\not0}.\,\overset{9}{\not0}\,{}^{1}0 \\ -\ \ \$0.\ 2\ 6 \\ \hline \mathbf{\$9.\ 7\ 4} \end{array}$$

17.
$$\begin{array}{r} 48 \\ -\ 16 \\ \hline 32 \end{array}$$
***A* = 32**

18.
$$\begin{array}{r} \overset{4}{\not5}\,{}^{1}2 \\ -\ 2\ 3 \\ \hline 2\ 9 \end{array}$$
***B* = 29**

19.
$$\begin{array}{r} 31 \\ +\ 17 \\ \hline 48 \end{array}$$
***C* = 48**

20. $\begin{array}{r} \overset{3}{\not{4}}{}^{1}2 \\ -\ 2\,5 \\ \hline 1\,7 \end{array}$

D = 17

21. $75 - 38 = 37$

x = 37

22. $38 + 75 = 113$

x = 113

23. $75 - 38 = 37$

y = 37

24. $\underbrace{6 + 8 + 5} + w = 32$

$19 + w = 32$

check: $32 - 19 = 13$

w = 13

25. **48 + 24 = 72**
72 − 24 = 48
72 − 48 = 24

26. **15 × 6 = 90**
90 ÷ 6 = 15
90 ÷ 15 = 6

27. $\begin{array}{r} \mathbf{10} \\ 20\overline{)200} \\ \underline{20} \\ 00 \\ \underline{00} \\ 0 \end{array}$

28. $\begin{array}{r} \mathbf{15} \\ \times\ \ \mathbf{8} \\ \hline \mathbf{120} \end{array}$

29. $\begin{array}{r} \mathbf{1} \\ 144\overline{)144} \\ \underline{144} \\ 0 \end{array}$

30. **To find a missing addend, subtract the known addend(s) from the sum.**

Early Finishers Solutions

a. $\begin{array}{r} 500 \\ 30\overline{)15000} \end{array}$; Petrov's family purchases 500 gallons of gasoline each year.

b. 500 gallons × \$2.89 per gallon = \$1445.00

Practice Set 4

a. $\begin{array}{r} 1\,3 \\ 7\overline{)9^{2}1} \end{array}$ check: $\begin{array}{r} 13 \\ \times\ \ 7 \\ \hline 91 \end{array}$

A = 13

b. $\begin{array}{r} 2\,2 \\ 20\overline{)44^{4}0} \end{array}$ check: $\begin{array}{r} 22 \\ \times\ 20 \\ \hline 00 \\ 440 \\ \hline 440 \end{array}$

B = 22

c. $\begin{array}{r} 15 \\ \times\ \ 7 \\ \hline 105 \end{array}$ check: $\begin{array}{r} 1\,5 \\ 7\overline{)10^{3}5} \end{array}$

C = 105

d. $\begin{array}{r} 1\,8 \\ 8\overline{)14^{6}4} \end{array}$ check: $\begin{array}{r} 8 \\ 18\overline{)144} \end{array}$

D = 18

e. $\begin{array}{r} 1\,2 \\ 7\overline{)8^{1}4} \end{array}$ check: $\begin{array}{r} 12 \\ \times\ \ 7 \\ \hline 84 \end{array}$

w = 12

f. $\begin{array}{r} 1\,4 \\ 8\overline{)11^{3}2} \end{array}$ check: $\begin{array}{r} 14 \\ \times\ \ 8 \\ \hline 112 \end{array}$

m = 14

g. $\begin{array}{r} 1\,2 \\ 30\overline{)36^{6}0} \end{array}$ check: $\begin{array}{r} 3\,0 \\ 12\overline{)36^{0}0} \end{array}$

x = 12

h. $\begin{array}{r} 60 \\ \times\ \ 5 \\ \hline 300 \end{array}$ check: $\begin{array}{r} 6\,0 \\ 5\overline{)30^{0}0} \end{array}$

n = 300

i. See student work.

Solutions

Written Practice 4

1. **4 carrot sticks**

$$
\begin{array}{r}
15\overline{)60} \\
\underline{60} \\
0
\end{array}
$$

2. **25 pennies**

$$
\begin{array}{r}
4\overline{)100} \\
\underline{8} \\
20 \\
\underline{20} \\
0
\end{array}
$$

Possible answer: I divided 100 pennies by 4 to make 4 equal groups of pennies.

3. **20 stacks**

$$
\begin{array}{r}
5\overline{)100} \\
\underline{10} \\
00 \\
\underline{00} \\
0
\end{array}
$$

4. **21 teams**

$$
\begin{array}{r}
14\overline{)294} \\
\underline{28} \\
14 \\
\underline{14} \\
0
\end{array}
$$

5.

$$
\begin{array}{r}
2\,\overset{7}{\not 8}\,{}^{1}0 \\
-\ 1\,5\,6 \\
\hline
1\,2\,4
\end{array}
\ \textbf{pages}
$$

6.

$$
\begin{array}{r}
\$0.75 \\
\times\ \ \ 42 \\
\hline
150 \\
\underline{3000} \\
\mathbf{\$31.50}
\end{array}
$$

7.

$$
\begin{array}{r}
12 \\
5\overline{)60} \\
\underline{5} \\
10 \\
\underline{10} \\
0
\end{array}
\qquad \text{check:} \qquad
\begin{array}{r}
\overset{1}{1}2 \\
\times\ \ 5 \\
\hline
60
\end{array}
$$

***J* = 12**

8.

$$
\begin{array}{r}
\overset{6}{\not 7}\,{}^{1}2 \\
-\ 2\,7 \\
\hline
4\,5
\end{array}
\qquad \text{check:} \qquad
\begin{array}{r}
\overset{1}{2}7 \\
+\ 45 \\
\hline
72
\end{array}
$$

***K* = 45**

9.

$$
\begin{array}{r}
37 \\
-\ 36 \\
\hline
1
\end{array}
\qquad \text{check:} \qquad
\begin{array}{r}
1 \\
+\ 36 \\
\hline
37
\end{array}
$$

***L* = 1**

10.

$$
\begin{array}{r}
\overset{5}{\not 6}\,{}^{1}4 \\
-\ 4\,6 \\
\hline
1\,8
\end{array}
\qquad \text{check:} \qquad
\begin{array}{r}
\overset{5}{\not 6}\,{}^{1}4 \\
-\ 1\,8 \\
\hline
4\,6
\end{array}
$$

***M* = 18**

11.

$$
\begin{array}{r}
\overset{1}{4}8 \\
+\ 84 \\
\hline
132
\end{array}
\qquad \text{check:} \qquad
\begin{array}{r}
\overset{0}{\not 1}\,\overset{12}{\not 3}\,{}^{1}2 \\
-\ \ \ 4\,8 \\
\hline
8\,4
\end{array}
$$

***n* = 132**

12.

$$
\begin{array}{r}
13 \\
7\overline{)91} \\
\underline{7} \\
21 \\
\underline{21} \\
0
\end{array}
\qquad \text{check:} \qquad
\begin{array}{r}
13 \\
\times\ \ 7 \\
\hline
91
\end{array}
$$

***p* = 13**

13.

$$
\begin{array}{r}
7 \\
\times\ 0 \\
\hline
0
\end{array}
\qquad \text{check:} \qquad
\begin{array}{r}
0 \\
7\overline{)0} \\
\underline{0} \\
0
\end{array}
$$

***q* = 0**

14.

$$
\begin{array}{r}
24 \\
6\overline{)144} \\
\underline{12} \\
24 \\
\underline{24} \\
0
\end{array}
\qquad \text{check:} \qquad
\begin{array}{r}
6 \\
24\overline{)144} \\
\underline{144} \\
0
\end{array}
$$

***r* = 24**

15.

$$
\begin{array}{r}
\mathbf{\$2.06} \\
6\overline{)\$12.36} \\
\underline{12} \\
0\,3 \\
\underline{0\,0} \\
36 \\
\underline{36} \\
0
\end{array}
$$

16.

$$
\begin{array}{r}
\mathbf{720} \\
8\overline{)5760} \\
\underline{56} \\
16 \\
\underline{16} \\
00 \\
\underline{00} \\
0
\end{array}
$$

17.
$$\begin{array}{r} \textbf{29 R 4} \\ 18\overline{)526} \\ \underline{36} \\ 166 \\ \underline{162} \\ 4 \end{array}$$

18.
$$\begin{array}{r} ^{2\,1} \\ 563 \\ 563 \\ 563 \\ \underline{+\ 563} \\ \mathbf{2252} \end{array}$$

19.
$$\begin{array}{r} \$3.75 \\ \underline{\times\quad 16} \\ 2250 \\ \underline{3750} \\ \mathbf{\$60.00} \end{array}$$

20.
$$\begin{array}{r} ^{1\ 1} \\ \$3.00 \\ \$2.86 \\ \underline{+\ \$0.98} \\ \mathbf{\$6.84} \end{array}$$

21.
$$\begin{array}{r} ^{0\ 9\ \ 9} \\ \$\not{1}\not{0}.\not{0}{}^{1}0 \\ \underline{-\quad \$6.\,4\,3} \\ \mathbf{\$3.\,5\,7} \end{array}$$

22.
$$\begin{array}{r} 12 \\ 3\overline{)n} \end{array} \qquad \begin{array}{r} 12 \\ \underline{\times\ \ 3} \\ \mathbf{36} \end{array}$$

The dividend is 36.

23. $5 \times m = 100$
$$\begin{array}{r} \mathbf{20} \\ 5\overline{)100} \\ \underline{10} \\ 00 \\ \underline{00} \\ 0 \end{array}$$

The other factor is 20.

24. $17 - 8 = 9$
$\mathbf{9 + 8 = 17}$
$\mathbf{8 + 9 = 17}$

25. $\mathbf{72 \div 9 = 8}$
$\mathbf{8 \times 9 = 72}$
$\mathbf{9 \times 8 = 72}$

26. $w + \underbrace{6 + 8 + 10} = 40$
$w + 24 = 40$
$40 - 24 = \mathbf{16}$
$\mathbf{w = 16}$

27.
$$\begin{array}{r} ^{2} \\ 23¢ \\ \underline{\times\ \ 7} \\ \mathbf{161¢} \end{array}$$
161¢ or **\$1.61**

28.
$$\begin{array}{r} 1 \\ 25\overline{)25} \\ \underline{25} \\ 0 \end{array}$$
$m = \mathbf{1}$

29.
$$\begin{array}{r} 0 \\ 15\overline{)0} \\ \underline{0} \\ 0 \end{array}$$
$n = \mathbf{0}$

30. **To find an unknown factor, divide the product by the known factor.**

Practice Set 5

a. $\underbrace{16 - 3} + 4$
$13 + 4$
$\mathbf{17}$

b. $16 - \underbrace{(3 + 4)}$
$16 - 7$
$\mathbf{9}$

c. $24 \div \underbrace{(4 \times 3)}$
$24 \div 12$
$\mathbf{2}$

d. $\underbrace{24 \div 4} \times 3$
6×3
$\mathbf{18}$

e. $\underbrace{24 \div 6} \div 2$
$4 \div 2$
$\mathbf{2}$

f. $24 \div \underbrace{(6 \div 2)}$
$24 \div 3$
8

g. $\dfrac{6 + 9}{3} = \dfrac{15}{3} = \mathbf{5}$ **(6 + 9) ÷ 3**

h. $\dfrac{12 + 8}{12 - 8} = \dfrac{20}{4} = \mathbf{5}$

i. **(6 + 9) ÷ 3**

Written Practice 5

1.
```
  $1.25        $5̸.0̸¹0   (4, 9)
+ $0.60      − $1. 8 5
  $1.85        $3. 1 5
```

2.
```
   ¹
   82
    8
 + 12
 102 kilograms
```

3.
```
  0 ¹0
  1̸ 1̸¹0
−   2 5
    8 5
```

4.
```
   25¢
 × 12
   50
  250
 300¢ or $3.00
```

5.
```
  4 ¹0
  5̸ 1̸¹6
−  1 4 9
   3 6 7
```

6. **To find the average number of pages she needs to read each day, divide 235 pages by 5.**

7. $5 + \underbrace{(3 \times 4)}$
$5 + 12$
17

8. $\underbrace{(5 + 3)} \times 4$
8×4
32

9. $800 - \underbrace{(450 - 125)}$
$800 - 325$
475

10. $600 \div \underbrace{(20 \div 5)}$
$600 \div 4$
150

11. $\underbrace{800 - 450} - 125$
$350 - 125$
225

12. $\underbrace{600 \div 20} \div 5$
$30 \div 5$
6

13. $144 \div \underbrace{(8 \times 6)}$
$144 \div 48$
3

14. $\underbrace{144 \div 8} \times 6$
18×6
108

15. $\$5 - \underbrace{(\$1.25 + \$0.60)}$
$\$5 - \$1.85$
$3.15

16.
7 × 9 = 63
9 × 7 = 63
63 ÷ 7 = 9
63 ÷ 9 = 7

17.
```
     24
 12)288
    24
     48
     48
      0
```


18. $\begin{array}{r} \textbf{\$0.40} \\ 25\overline{)\$10.00} \\ \underline{10\ 0} \\ 00 \\ \underline{00} \\ 0 \end{array}$

19. $\begin{array}{r} 378 \\ \times\ \ 64 \\ \hline 1512 \\ 2268\ \\ \hline \textbf{24,192} \end{array}$

20. $\begin{array}{r} 506 \\ \times\ 370 \\ \hline 35420 \\ 15180\ \\ \hline \textbf{187,220} \end{array}$

21. $\begin{array}{r} \$\overset{0}{\not1}\,\overset{9}{\not0}.\,\overset{10}{\not1}\,{}^{1}0 \\ -\ \ \$9.\,8\,9 \\ \hline \textbf{\$0.\,2\,1} \end{array}$

22. $\begin{array}{r} 63 \\ +\ 36 \\ \hline 99 \end{array}$ check: $\begin{array}{r} 99 \\ -\ 63 \\ \hline 36 \end{array}$

***n* = 99**

23. $\begin{array}{r} \overset{5}{\not6}\,{}^{1}3 \\ -\ 3\ 6 \\ \hline 2\ 7 \end{array}$ check: $\begin{array}{r} \overset{5}{\not6}\,{}^{1}3 \\ -\ 2\ 7 \\ \hline 3\ 6 \end{array}$

***p* = 27**

24. $\begin{array}{r} \overset{3}{\not4}\,\overset{12}{\not3}\,{}^{1}2 \\ -\ \ \ 5\ 6 \\ \hline 3\ 7\ 6 \end{array}$ check: $\begin{array}{r} \overset{1\,1}{376} \\ +\ \ 56 \\ \hline 432 \end{array}$

***m* = 376**

25. $\begin{array}{r} 60 \\ 8\overline{)480} \\ \underline{48} \\ 00 \\ \underline{00} \\ 0 \end{array}$ check: $\begin{array}{r} 60 \\ \times\ \ 8 \\ \hline 480 \end{array}$

***w* = 60**

26. $\underbrace{5 + 12 + 27} + y = 50$

$44 + y = 50$

$50 - 44 = 6$

$\boldsymbol{y = 6}$

check: $\begin{array}{r} {}_{2}5 \\ 12 \\ 27 \\ +\ \ 6 \\ \hline 50 \end{array}$

27. $\begin{array}{r} 9 \\ 4\overline{)36} \\ \underline{36} \\ 0 \end{array}$ check: $\begin{array}{r} 4 \\ 9\overline{)36} \\ \underline{36} \\ 0 \end{array}$

***a* = 9**

28. $\begin{array}{r} 8 \\ \times\ 4 \\ \hline 32 \end{array}$ check: $\begin{array}{r} 8 \\ 4\overline{)32} \\ \underline{32} \\ 0 \end{array}$

***x* = 32**

29. **7 + 11 = 18**
11 + 7 = 18
18 − 11 = 7
18 − 7 = 11

30. $\underbrace{3 \cdot 4} \cdot 5$

$12 \cdot 5$

60

Early Finishers Solutions

3 rooms × 2 gallons per room = 6 gallons;

$\begin{array}{r} \$45 \\ 6\overline{)\$270} \end{array}$; each gallon costs $45.

Practice Set 6

a. **Three fourths; $\frac{3}{4}$**

b. **Two fifths; $\frac{2}{5}$**

c. **Three eighths; $\frac{3}{8}$**

Solutions

d.

$$\begin{array}{r} \mathbf{36} \\ 2\overline{)72} \\ \underline{6} \\ 12 \\ \underline{12} \\ 0 \end{array}$$

$\frac{1}{2}$ of 72 is **36**

e.

$$\begin{array}{r} \mathbf{500} \\ 2\overline{)1000} \\ \underline{10} \\ 00 \\ \underline{00} \\ 00 \\ \underline{00} \\ 0 \end{array}$$

$\frac{1}{2}$ of 1000 is **500**

f.

$$\begin{array}{r} \mathbf{60} \\ 3\overline{)180} \\ \underline{18} \\ 00 \\ \underline{00} \\ 0 \end{array}$$

$\frac{1}{3}$ of 180 is **60**

g.

$$\begin{array}{r} \mathbf{\$1.20} \\ 3\overline{)\$3.60} \\ \underline{3} \\ 0\,6 \\ \underline{0\,6} \\ 00 \\ \underline{00} \\ 0 \end{array}$$

$\frac{1}{3}$ of \$3.60 is **\$1.20**

One third of \$3.60 is \$1.20 because \$1.20 + \$1.20 + \$1.20 = \$3.60

h.

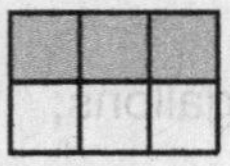

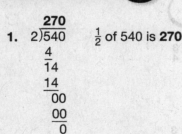

Written Practice 6

1.

$$\begin{array}{r} \mathbf{270} \\ 2\overline{)540} \\ \underline{4} \\ 14 \\ \underline{14} \\ 00 \\ \underline{00} \\ 0 \end{array}$$

$\frac{1}{2}$ of 540 is **270**

2.

$$\begin{array}{r} \mathbf{180} \\ 3\overline{)540} \\ \underline{3} \\ 24 \\ \underline{24} \\ 00 \\ \underline{00} \\ 0 \end{array}$$

$\frac{1}{3}$ of 540 is **180**

3.

$$\begin{array}{r} {}^{2\,2} \\ 346 \text{ miles} \\ 417 \text{ miles} \\ 289 \text{ miles} \\ \underline{+\ 360 \text{ miles}} \\ \mathbf{1412 \text{ miles}} \end{array}$$

4.

$$\begin{array}{r} \$\overset{1}{\not 2}\ \overset{9}{\not 0}.\ \overset{9}{\not 0}{}^{1}0 \\ \underline{-\ \$1\ 2.\ 0\ 8} \\ \mathbf{\$7.\ 9\ 2} \end{array}$$

5.

$$\begin{array}{r} \overset{1}{5}2 \\ \underline{\times\ \ 7} \\ \mathbf{364 \text{ days}} \end{array}$$

6.

$$\begin{array}{r} \mathbf{50 \text{ bills}} \\ \$20\overline{)\$1000} \\ \underline{100} \\ 00 \\ \underline{00} \\ 0 \end{array}$$

7. **Five sixths; $\frac{5}{6}$**

8.

$$\begin{array}{r} {}^{1\,1} \\ 3604 \\ 5186 \\ \underline{+\ 7145} \\ \mathbf{15{,}935} \end{array}$$

9.

$$\begin{array}{r} \$\overset{2}{\not 3}\ \overset{9}{\not 0}.\ \overset{9}{\not 0}{}^{1}1 \\ \underline{-\ \$1\ 5.\ 7\ 6} \\ \mathbf{\$1\ 4.\ 2\ 5} \end{array}$$

10.

$$\begin{array}{r} 376 \\ \underline{\times\ 87} \\ 2632 \\ \underline{30080} \\ \mathbf{32{,}712} \end{array}$$

11.
$$\begin{array}{r} 470 \\ \times\ 203 \\ \hline 1410 \\ 0000 \\ 94000 \\ \hline \mathbf{95{,}410} \end{array}$$

12.
$$\begin{array}{r} \overset{1\ 9\ \ 9}{\$\not{2}\ \not{0}.\ \not{0}^{1}0} \\ -\ \$1\,1.\,9\,8 \\ \hline \mathbf{\$8.\ 0\ 2} \end{array}$$

13. $596 - (400 - 129)$

$596 - 271$

325

14. $32 \div (8 \times 4)$

$32 \div 32$

1

15.
$$\begin{array}{r} \mathbf{502} \\ 8\overline{)4016} \\ 40 \\ \hline 01 \\ 00 \\ \hline 16 \\ 16 \\ \hline 0 \end{array}$$

16.
$$\begin{array}{r} \mathbf{400\ R\ 9} \\ 15\overline{)6009} \\ 60 \\ \hline 00 \\ 00 \\ \hline 09 \\ 00 \\ \hline 9 \end{array}$$

17.
$$\begin{array}{r} \mathbf{250} \\ 36\overline{)9000} \\ 72 \\ \hline 180 \\ 180 \\ \hline 00 \\ 00 \\ \hline 0 \end{array}$$

18.
$$\begin{array}{r} 60 \\ 8\overline{)480} \\ 48 \\ \hline 00 \\ 00 \\ \hline 0 \end{array}$$

check:
$$\begin{array}{r} 60 \\ \times\ 8 \\ \hline 480 \end{array}$$

$\boldsymbol{w = 60}$

19.
$$\begin{array}{r} 64 \\ +\ 46 \\ \hline 110 \end{array}$$

check:
$$\begin{array}{r} \overset{0\ \ ^{1}0}{\not{1}\ \not{1}\ ^{1}0} \\ -\ \ 6\ 4 \\ \hline 4\ 6 \end{array}$$

$\boldsymbol{x = 110}$

20.
$$\begin{array}{r} 7 \\ 7\overline{)49} \\ 49 \\ \hline 0 \end{array}$$

check:
$$\begin{array}{r} 7 \\ 7\overline{)49} \\ 49 \\ \hline 0 \end{array}$$

$\boldsymbol{N = 7}$

21.
$$\begin{array}{r} \overset{3}{15} \\ \times\ \ 7 \\ \hline 105 \end{array}$$

check:
$$\begin{array}{r} 15 \\ 7\overline{)105} \\ 7 \\ \hline 35 \\ 35 \\ \hline 0 \end{array}$$

$\boldsymbol{M = 105}$

22.
$$\begin{array}{r} \overset{5\ ^{1}4}{\not{6}\ \not{5}\ ^{1}3} \\ -\ 3\ 6\ 5 \\ \hline 2\ 8\ 8 \end{array}$$

check:
$$\begin{array}{r} \overset{1\,1}{365} \\ +\ 288 \\ \hline 653 \end{array}$$

$\boldsymbol{P = 288}$

23. $36¢ + 25¢ + m = 99¢$

$61¢ + m = 99¢$

$99¢ - 61¢ = 38¢$

$\boldsymbol{m = 38¢}$

check:
$$\begin{array}{r} \overset{1}{36¢} \\ 25¢ \\ +\ 38¢ \\ \hline 99¢ \end{array}$$

24. $\boldsymbol{\frac{1}{4}}$

25.

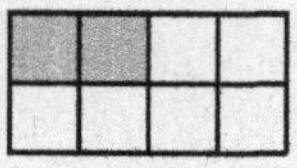

26.
$$\begin{array}{r} \$6.35 \\ \times\quad 12 \\ \hline 1270 \\ 6350 \\ \hline \mathbf{\$76.20} \end{array}$$

27.
2 + 4 = 6
4 + 2 = 6
6 − 4 = 2
6 − 2 = 4

28.
2 × 4 = 8
4 × 2 = 8
8 ÷ 2 = 4
8 ÷ 4 = 2

29.

```
   38
×  10
  380
```

30. **See student work. Sample answer: How much money is $\frac{1}{2}$ of $3.60?**

```
  $1.80
2)$3.60
  2
  1 6
  1 6
    00
    00
     0
```

$\frac{1}{2}$ of $3.60 is **$1.80**

Practice Set 7

a. **$1\frac{3}{4}$ in.**

b. **25 mm**

c. **2 in.; 5 cm**

d. **Ray**

e. **Line**

f. **Segment**

g. **A. Inches**

h. **C. Kilometers**

Written Practice 7

1.

```
   $0.25
×    100
  $25.00
```

2.

```
  ²
  3̸¹6 5 days
−   9 1 days
  2 7 4 days
```

3.

```
   ¹
   596
+  612
  1208 miles
```

```
     ⁸
  1 8 9̸¹0
− 1 2 0 8
    6 8 2 miles
```

4.

```
  117
2)234
  2
  03
   2
   14
   14
    0
```

5.

```
   $0.78
3)$2.34
   2 1
     24
     24
      0
```

6. **Three eighths; $\frac{3}{8}$**

7.

```
   2 1 1
    3654
    2893
+   5614
  12,161
```

8.

```
    ³ ¹⁰ ⁹
  $4̸ 1̸. 0̸¹1
− $1 5. 7 6
  $2 5. 2 5
```

9.

```
    28¢
×   74
   112
  1960
  2072¢  or  $20.72
```

10.

```
    906
×    47
   6342
  36240
  42,582
```

11.

```
  833 R 2
6)5000
  48
   20
   18
    20
    18
     2
```

12.

```
    50
16)800
   80
    00
    00
     0
```

13.
$$\begin{array}{r} \textbf{52 R 54} \\ 60\overline{)3174} \\ \underline{300} \\ 174 \\ \underline{120} \\ 54 \end{array}$$

14. $\underbrace{3 + 6 + 5 + 4} + w = 30$
$18 + w = 30$
$30 - 18 = 12$
$w = \mathbf{12}$

15. $\underbrace{300 - 30} + 3$
$270 + 3$
273

16. $300 - \underbrace{(30 + 3)}$
$300 - 33$
267

17.
$$\begin{array}{r} \$4.32 \\ \times \quad 20 \\ \hline \mathbf{\$86.40} \end{array}$$

18.
$$\begin{array}{r} 48¢ \\ \times \ 24 \\ \hline 192 \\ 960 \\ \hline \end{array}$$
1152¢ or **$11.52**

19.
$$\begin{array}{r} \mathbf{\$0.35} \\ 25\overline{)\$8.75} \\ \underline{7\,5} \\ 1\,25 \\ \underline{1\,25} \\ 0 \end{array}$$

20.
$$\begin{array}{r} 7 \\ \times \ 6 \\ \hline 42 \end{array}$$
$W = \mathbf{42}$

check:
$$\begin{array}{r} 7 \\ 6\overline{)42} \\ \underline{42} \\ 0 \end{array}$$

21.
$$\begin{array}{r} 16 \\ 6\overline{)96} \\ \underline{6} \\ 36 \\ \underline{36} \\ 0 \end{array}$$
$n = \mathbf{16}$

check:
$$\begin{array}{r} \overset{3}{1}6 \\ \times \ \ 6 \\ \hline 96 \end{array}$$

22.
$$\begin{array}{r} \overset{1}{\cancel{2}}\,\overset{0}{\cancel{1}}{}^{1}3 \\ - \quad 5\,8 \\ \hline \mathbf{1\,5\,5} \end{array}$$
$r = \mathbf{155}$

check:
$$\begin{array}{r} \overset{1}{1}\overset{1}{5}5 \\ + \ \ 58 \\ \hline 213 \end{array}$$

23. **60 − 36 = 24**
36 + 24 = 60
24 + 36 = 60

24. $\mathbf{1\frac{1}{2}}$ **in.**

25. **3 cm; 30 mm**

26. **9 × 10 = 90**
10 × 9 = 90
90 ÷ 9 = 10
90 ÷ 10 = 9

27. **To find a missing dividend, multiply the quotient by the divisor.**

28.
$$\begin{array}{r} \overset{1}{1}2 \\ + \ \ 8 \\ \hline 20 \end{array}$$
$w = \mathbf{20}$

check:
$$\begin{array}{r} \overset{1}{\cancel{2}}{}^{1}0 \\ - \ 1\,2 \\ \hline 8 \end{array}$$

29.
$$\begin{array}{r} \overset{0}{\cancel{1}}{}^{1}2 \\ - \quad 8 \\ \hline 4 \end{array}$$
$x = \mathbf{4}$

check:
$$\begin{array}{r} \overset{0}{\cancel{1}}{}^{1}2 \\ - \quad 4 \\ \hline 8 \end{array}$$

30. (a) **1000 millimeters**
(b) **B. The length of a hallway**

Early Finishers Solutions

a. $\frac{1}{5} \cdot 40$ players = 8 players

b. 8 × $45 = $360

Practice Set 8

a. 12 mm + 12 mm + 12 mm + 12 mm
= **48 mm**

b. 15 mm + 20 mm + 15 mm + 20 mm
= **70 mm**

c. 10 mm + 15 mm + 10 mm + 20 mm
= **55 mm**

d. 2 cm + 2 cm + 2 cm = **6 cm**

e. 1 cm + 1 cm + 1 cm + 1 cm + 1 cm
= **5 cm**

f. **15 cm**
4)60 cm
4
20
20
0

g. **Drawings will vary; check students' work.**

h. **B. Feet**

Written Practice 8

1.
  25
× 18
200
250
450 chairs

2.
0 ¹6 ¹4
~~1~~ ~~7~~ ~~5~~ ¹0
− 7 6 5
9 8 5 fewer cans

I subtracted 765 from 1750.

3. **28 teams**
5)140
10
40
40
0

4. 20 mm + 15 mm + 25 mm = **60 mm**

5. **$3.27**
2)$6.54
6
0 5
4
14
14
0

6. **218**
3)654
6
05
3
24
24
0

7. $\mathbf{\frac{3}{10}}$

8. **$2.25**
4)$9.00
8
1 0
8
20
20
0

9. **37 R 3**
10)373
30
73
70
3

10. **125**
12)1500
12
30
24
60
60
0

11. **20 R 20**
39)800
78
20
00
20

12. $400 \div 20 \div 4$
$20 \div 4$
5

13. $400 \div (20 \div 4)$
$400 \div 5$
80

14. $20 \times 12 = 240$
$12 \times 20 = 240$
$240 \div 20 = 12$
$240 \div 12 = 20$

15. $80 + 60 = 140$
$140 - 80 = 60$
$140 - 60 = 80$

16. 12 in. + 12 in. + 12 in. + 12 in. = **48 in.**

17. a. $6 + 4 = 10$ **b.** $6 \times 4 = 24$

18. $\$5.00 - \$1.48 = \$3.52$ (regrouped: $\overset{4}{\cancel{5}}.\overset{9}{\cancel{0}}{}^{1}0$)
M = **$3.52**

19. $\underbrace{10 \times 20}_{200} \times 30$
200×30
6000

20. $825 \div 8$ = **103 R 1**
8
02
0
25
24
1

21. $63 + 36 = 99$ check: $99 - 63 = 36$
w = **99**

22. $\underbrace{150 + 165}_{315} + a = 397$
$315 + a = 397$
$397 - 315 = 82$
***a* = 82**
check: $150 + 165 + 82 = 397$

23. $120 \div 12 = 10$
12
00
00
0
check: $12 \times 10 = 120$
w = **10**

24. $24 \times 8 = $ **192**

25. a. About 3 centimeters

b. 28 millimeters

26. Check to see if student's line is $2\frac{3}{4}$ in. long.

27. $\overset{1}{2}7 + 18 = 45$
***w* = 45**

28. $\overset{1}{\cancel{2}}{}^{1}7 - 18 = 9$
***x* = 9**

29. $\overset{2}{3}5 \times 4 = $ **140**

30. One way to calculate the perimeter of a rectangle is to add the lengths of the four sides.

Practice Set 9

a. 12¢, $1.20, $12

b. $\underbrace{16 - 8 - 2}_{6}$ (<) $\underbrace{16 - (8 - 2)}_{10}$

c. $\underbrace{8 \div 4 \times 2}_{4}$ (>) $\underbrace{8 \div (4 \times 2)}_{1}$

d. $\underbrace{2 \times 3}_{6}$ (>) $\underbrace{2 + 3}_{5}$

e. $\underbrace{1 \times 1 \times 1}_{1}$ (<) $\underbrace{1 + 1 + 1}_{3}$

f. $\frac{1}{2} > \frac{1}{4}$

g. 10 inches < 1 foot

Solutions

Written Practice 9

1. 18 books
$$\begin{array}{r} 18 \\ 8\overline{)144} \\ \underline{8} \\ 64 \\ \underline{64} \\ 0 \end{array}$$

2.
$$\begin{array}{r} 1\overset{5}{\not6}{}^{1}03 \\ -\ 1492 \\ \hline 111 \text{ years} \end{array}$$

3.
$$\begin{array}{r} 4 \text{ R1} \\ 2\overline{)9} \\ \underline{8} \\ 1 \end{array}$$
5 trips

4. **length = 2 cm**
width = 1 cm
perimeter = 2 cm + 2 cm + 1 cm + 1 cm
= 6 cm

5.
$$\begin{array}{r} \$2.90 \\ 2\overline{)\$5.80} \\ \underline{4} \\ 1\,8 \\ \underline{1\,8} \\ 00 \\ \underline{00} \\ 0 \end{array}$$

6.
$$\begin{array}{r} \$0.25 \\ 4\overline{)\$1.00} \\ \underline{0} \\ 1\,0 \\ \underline{8} \\ 20 \\ \underline{20} \\ 0 \end{array}$$
$0.25 ⟶ **25¢**

7. **One fourth; $\frac{1}{4}$**

8. **a.** 5012 ⓒ< 5120
b. 1 mm < 1 cm

9. **0, $\frac{1}{2}$, 1**

10. $\underbrace{100 - 50 - 25}_{25}$ ⓒ< $\underbrace{100 - (50 - 25)}_{75}$

11.
$$\begin{array}{r} {}^{2\,1} \\ {}_{1}478 \\ 3692 \\ +\ \ 45 \\ \hline \mathbf{4215} \end{array}$$

12.
$$\begin{array}{r} \$\overset{4}{\not5}\,\overset{9}{\not0}.\,\overset{9}{\not0}{}^{1}0 \\ -\ \$3\,1.\,7\,6 \\ \hline \mathbf{\$1\,8.\,2\,4} \end{array}$$

13.
$$\begin{array}{r} \$4.20 \\ \times\ \ 60 \\ \hline \mathbf{\$252.00} \end{array}$$

14.
$$\begin{array}{r} 78 \\ \times\ 36 \\ \hline 468 \\ 2340 \\ \hline \mathbf{2808} \end{array}$$

15.
$$\begin{array}{r} \mathbf{803} \\ 9\overline{)7227} \\ \underline{72} \\ 02 \\ \underline{00} \\ 27 \\ \underline{27} \\ 0 \end{array}$$

16.
$$\begin{array}{r} \mathbf{304} \\ 25\overline{)7600} \\ \underline{75} \\ 10 \\ \underline{00} \\ 100 \\ \underline{100} \\ 0 \end{array}$$

17.
$$\begin{array}{r} \mathbf{400\ R\ 14} \\ 20\overline{)8014} \\ \underline{80} \\ 01 \\ \underline{00} \\ 14 \\ \underline{00} \\ 14 \end{array}$$

18. $$\begin{array}{r} \mathbf{71\ R\ 36} \\ 100\overline{)7136} \\ \underline{700} \\ 136 \\ \underline{100} \\ 36 \end{array}$$

19. $$\begin{array}{r} \mathbf{1} \\ 736\overline{)736} \\ \underline{736} \\ 0 \end{array}$$

20. $$\begin{array}{r} \overset{2}{\not 3}\,\overset{9}{\not 0}\,{}^{1}0 \\ -\ 1\,6\,5 \\ \hline 1\,3\,5 \end{array}$$ check: $$\begin{array}{r} {}^{1\,1}\ \ \\ 165 \\ +\ 135 \\ \hline 300 \end{array}$$
$\boldsymbol{a = 135}$

21. $$\begin{array}{r} {}^{1}\ \ \\ 68 \\ +\ 86 \\ \hline 154 \end{array}$$ check: $$\begin{array}{r} \overset{0}{\not 1}\,\overset{14}{\not 5}\,{}^{1}4 \\ -\ \ 6\,8 \\ \hline 8\,6 \end{array}$$
$\boldsymbol{b = 154}$

22. $$\begin{array}{r} 16 \\ 9\overline{)144} \\ \underline{9} \\ 54 \\ \underline{54} \\ 0 \end{array}$$ check: $$\begin{array}{r} {}^{5}\ \\ 16 \\ \times\ \ 9 \\ \hline 144 \end{array}$$
$\boldsymbol{c = 16}$

23. $$\begin{array}{r} {}^{3}\ \\ 15 \\ \times\ \ 7 \\ \hline 105 \end{array}$$ check: $$\begin{array}{r} 7 \\ 15\overline{)105} \\ \underline{105} \\ 0 \end{array}$$
$\boldsymbol{d = 105}$

24. See student work.
5 cm

25. **C.** $\longrightarrow$

26. $\boldsymbol{\frac{1}{2} > \frac{1}{3}}$

27.
$$\begin{aligned} \mathbf{9 \times 11 = 99} \\ \mathbf{11 \times 9 = 99} \\ \mathbf{99 \div 11 = 9} \\ \mathbf{99 \div 9 = 11} \end{aligned}$$

28. $\underbrace{25 + 0}_{25} \ \textcircled{>}\ \underbrace{25 \times 0}_{0}$

29.
$$\begin{aligned} 100 &= \underbrace{20 + 30 + 40} + x \\ 100 &= 90 + x \\ 100 - 90 &= x \\ \mathbf{x} &= \mathbf{10} \end{aligned}$$

30. **Since 5012 is less than 5120, point the small end of the symbol to the smaller number, 5012.**

Practice Set 10

a. **. . . , <u>54</u>, <u>63</u>, <u>72</u>, . . . Addition sequence. Add 9 to the value of a term to find the next term.**

b. **. . . , <u>16</u>, <u>32</u>, <u>64</u>, . . . Multiplication sequence. Multiply the value of a term by 2 to find the next term.**

c. **Odd**

d. **72°F; 22°C**

Written Practice 10

1. **Add 8 to the value of a term to find the next term. . . . , <u>40</u>, <u>48</u>, <u>56</u>, . . .**

2. $$\begin{array}{r} 1776 \\ -\ 1620 \\ \hline \mathbf{156\ years} \end{array}$$

3. **The number 1492 is even because the last digit, 2, is even.**

4. **154 pounds**

5. $$\begin{array}{r} \mathbf{10\ mm} \\ 4\overline{)40} \\ \underline{4} \\ 00 \\ \underline{00} \\ 0 \end{array}$$

6. **$3.25**
2)$6.50
6
05
04
10
10
0

7. $\underbrace{4 \times 3 + 2}_{14}$ $<$ $\underbrace{4 \times (3 + 2)}_{20}$

8. **Three fourths; $\frac{3}{4}$**

9. **a.** 100
× 100
10,000

b. 100
\+ 100
200

10. 365
× 100
36,500

11. 146
× 240
5840
29200
35,040

12. 78¢
× 48
624
3120
3744¢ or **$37.44**

13. 907
× 36
5442
27210
32,652

14. **426**
10)4260
40
26
20
60
60
0

15. **213**
20)4260
40
26
20
60
60
0

16. **284**
15)4260
30
126
120
60
60
0

17. 28,347
− 9,637
18,710

18. $11.49
− $8.00
$3.49
***w* = $3.49**

19. $10.00
− $0.75
$9.25

20. $0.56
× 60
$33.60

21. **$1.55**
4)$6.20
4
22
20
20
20
0

22. $\underbrace{56 + 28 + 37}_{121} + n = 200$
$121 + n = 200$
$200 - 121 = 79$
$\boldsymbol{n = 79}$
check: $56 + 28 + 37 + 79 = 200$

23. $\begin{array}{r} \overset{1}{6}7 \\ +\ 49 \\ \hline 116 \end{array}$ check: $\begin{array}{r} \overset{0}{\cancel{1}}\overset{10}{\cancel{1}}\overset{1}{}6 \\ -\ 6\ 7 \\ \hline 4\ 9 \end{array}$

a **= 116**

24. $\begin{array}{r} \overset{5}{\cancel{6}}\overset{1}{}7 \\ -\ 4\ 9 \\ \hline 1\ 8 \end{array}$ check: $\begin{array}{r} \overset{5}{\cancel{6}}\overset{1}{}7 \\ -\ 1\ 8 \\ \hline 4\ 9 \end{array}$

b **= 18**

25. $\begin{array}{r} 15 \\ 8\overline{)120} \\ 8 \\ \hline 40 \\ 40 \\ \hline 0 \end{array}$ check: $\begin{array}{r} \overset{4}{1}5 \\ \times\ \ 8 \\ \hline 120 \end{array}$

c **= 15**

26. $\begin{array}{r} \overset{3}{2}4 \\ \times\ \ 8 \\ \hline 192 \end{array}$ check: $\begin{array}{r} 24 \\ 8\overline{)192} \\ 16 \\ \hline 32 \\ 32 \\ \hline 0 \end{array}$

d **= 192**

27. $5\overline{)20}$; $20 \div 5$; $\frac{20}{5}$

28. $\begin{array}{r} 12 \\ 3\overline{)36} \\ 3 \\ \hline 06 \\ 6 \\ \hline 0 \end{array}$

29. **346 + 463 = 809**
463 + 346 = 809
809 − 463 = 346
809 − 346 = 463

30. **32°F**

Investigation 1

1. **No. In the frequency table, the number of students who scored 20 is combined with the number who scored 19.**

2. **Each interval is 2 scores wide. One reason he might have arranged the scores in these intervals is to group the scores by A's, B's, C's, and D's.**

3. 𝍸 𝍸 II

4. **Answers will vary. See student work. Sample answer:**

Frequency Table

Birth Month	Tally	Frequency
Jan–Mar	𝍸 IIII	9
Apr–Jun	𝍸 II	7
Jul–Sep	𝍸	5
Oct–Dec	𝍸 IIII	9

5. **13–14**

6. **19–20**

7. **15–16**

8.

Frequency Table

Number Correct	Tally	Frequency
90–99	IIII	4
80–89	𝍸 II	7
70–79	IIII	4
60–69	III	3
50–59	II	2

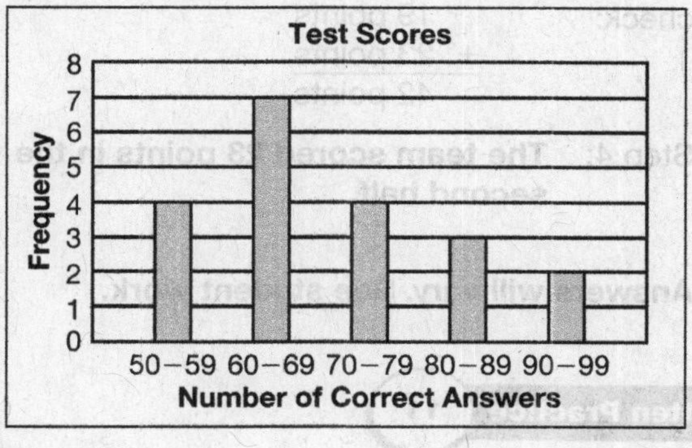

9. **Softball**

10. **D. Cannot be determined from information provided**

11. **Suggestion: Consider only girls' responses: consider only boys' responses. Discuss.**

12. **Consider eliminating some choices while adding others. Discuss.**

Extensions

a. **Answers will vary. See student work.**

b. **Answers will vary. See student work.**

Solutions

Practice Set 11

a. Step 1: Subtraction pattern

Step 2: $B - A = R$

314 pages − 129 pages = remaining pages

Step 3: **314 − 129 = R**

$$\begin{array}{r} \overset{2}{\cancel{3}}\overset{10}{\cancel{1}}{}^{1}4 \text{ pages} \\ -\ 1\ 2\ 9 \text{ pages} \\ \hline 1\ 8\ 5 \text{ pages} \end{array}$$

check:

$$\begin{array}{r} \overset{1\,1}{185} \text{ pages} \\ +\ 129 \text{ pages} \\ \hline 314 \text{ pages} \end{array}$$

Step 4: **Tim has 185 pages to read**

b. Step 1: Addition pattern

Step 2: $S + M = T$

19 points + M points = 42 points

Step 3: **19 + *M* = 42**

$$\begin{array}{r} \overset{3}{\cancel{4}}{}^{1}2 \text{ points} \\ -\ 1\ 9 \text{ points} \\ \hline 2\ 3 \text{ points} \end{array}$$

check:

$$\begin{array}{r} \overset{1}{1}9 \text{ points} \\ +\ 23 \text{ points} \\ \hline 42 \text{ points} \end{array}$$

Step 4: **The team scored 23 points in the second half.**

c. Answers will vary. See student work.

Written Practice 11

1. 8 + *l* = 21

$$\begin{array}{r} \overset{1}{\cancel{2}}{}^{1}1 \\ -\ \ 8 \\ \hline 1\ 3 \text{ laps} \end{array}$$

2. (a) $\begin{array}{r} 8 \\ \times\ 4 \\ \hline \mathbf{32} \end{array}$ (b) $\begin{array}{r} 8 \\ +\ 4 \\ \hline \mathbf{12} \end{array}$

3. $\underbrace{(6 \times 4)}_{24} \div \underbrace{(8 - 5)}_{3}$

$24 \div 3$

8

4. $20.00 − *m* = $7.75

$$\begin{array}{r} \$\ \overset{1}{\cancel{2}}\overset{9}{\cancel{0}}.\overset{9}{\cancel{0}}{}^{1}0 \\ -\ \ \ \ 7.\ 7\ 5 \\ \hline \mathbf{\$\ 1\ 2.\ 2\ 5} \end{array}$$

5. 8 + *g* = 74

$$\begin{array}{r} \overset{6}{\cancel{7}}\overset{14}{\cancel{4}} \\ -\ \ 8 \\ \hline \mathbf{6\ 6 \text{ pounds}} \end{array}$$

6.

$$\begin{array}{r} \$\overset{1}{0}.65 \\ +\ \$0.40 \\ \hline \mathbf{\$1.05} \end{array}$$

7.

$$\begin{array}{r} \overset{0}{\cancel{1}}\overset{14}{\cancel{5}}{}^{1}5 \\ -\ \ 8\ 7 \\ \hline 6\ 8 \end{array}$$

w = 68

check:

$$\begin{array}{r} \overset{1}{8}7 \\ +\ 68 \\ \hline 155 \end{array}$$

8.

$$\begin{array}{r} \overset{0}{\cancel{1}}\overset{9}{\cancel{0}}\overset{9}{\cancel{0}}{}^{1}0 \\ -\ \ 3\ 8\ 6 \\ \hline 6\ 1\ 4 \end{array}$$

x = 614

check:

$$\begin{array}{r} \overset{0}{\cancel{1}}\overset{9}{\cancel{0}}\overset{9}{\cancel{0}}{}^{1}0 \\ -\ \ 6\ 1\ 4 \\ \hline 3\ 8\ 6 \end{array}$$

9.

$$\begin{array}{r} 1000 \\ +\ \ 386 \\ \hline 1386 \end{array}$$

y = 1386

check:

$$\begin{array}{r} 1386 \\ -\ 1000 \\ \hline 386 \end{array}$$

10. $\underbrace{42 + 596} + m = 700$

$638 + m = 700$

$700 - 638 = 62$

m = 62

check: $42 + 596 + 62 = 700$

11. $\underbrace{1000 - (100 - 10)}_{910}$ ⓢ> $\underbrace{1000 - 100 - 10}_{890}$

12.

$$\begin{array}{r} \mathbf{125} \\ 8\overline{)1000} \\ \underline{8} \\ 20 \\ \underline{16} \\ 40 \\ \underline{40} \\ 0 \end{array}$$

13. $\begin{array}{r} \mathbf{98}\ \mathbf{R\,7} \\ 10\overline{)987} \\ \underline{90} \\ 87 \\ \underline{80} \\ 7 \end{array}$

14. $\begin{array}{r} 35 \\ \times\ 12 \\ \hline 70 \\ \underline{350} \\ \mathbf{420} \end{array}$

15. $\begin{array}{r} 600 \\ \times\ 300 \\ \hline \mathbf{180{,}000} \end{array}$

16. $\begin{array}{r} 1 \\ 365\overline{)365} \\ \underline{365} \\ 0 \end{array}$

$\mathbf{w = 1}$

17. Add 4 to the value of a term to find the next term.
2, 6, 10, <u>14</u>, <u>18</u>, <u>22</u>, . . .

18. $\underbrace{2 \times 3} \times 4 \times 5$
$\underbrace{6 \times 4} \times 5$
24×5
120

19. $\begin{array}{r} \mathbf{180} \\ 2\overline{)360} \\ \underline{2} \\ 16 \\ \underline{16} \\ 00 \\ \underline{00} \\ 0 \end{array}$

20. $\begin{array}{r} \mathbf{90} \\ 4\overline{)360} \\ \underline{36} \\ 00 \\ \underline{00} \\ 0 \end{array}$

21. $\begin{array}{r} {}^{2\,4} \\ 125 \\ \times\ \ 8 \\ \hline \mathbf{1000} \end{array}$

22. **$2\frac{1}{4}$ in.**

23. $\mathbf{\frac{5}{8}}$

24. 9 mm + 9 mm + 9 mm + 9 mm = **36 mm**

25. 1 + 3 + 5 + 7 + 9 = **25**

26. **$6\overline{)30}$, 30 ÷ 6, $\frac{30}{6}$**

27. $\begin{array}{r} \overset{2}{\cancel{3}}\,{}^{1}0 \\ -\ 1\ 7 \\ \hline \end{array}$ **1 3 boys** $\mathbf{\frac{13}{30}}$

28. **0°C**

29.
6 × 4 = 24
4 × 6 = 24
24 ÷ 4 = 6
24 ÷ 6 = 4

30. **Answers will vary. See student work. Sample answer: Before he went to work, Pham had $24.50. He earned some money putting up a fence at work. Then Pham had $37.00. How much money did Pham earn putting up the fence?**

Practice Set 12

a. **3**

b. **Ten billions**

c. **Twenty-one million, three hundred fifty thousand, six hundred eight**

d. **4,520,000,000**

e. $\frac{(6 \times 4)}{(6 - 4)} = \frac{24}{2} = \mathbf{12}$

Solutions

Written Practice 12

1. $\underbrace{(1 \times 2 \times 3)}_{6} - \underbrace{(1 + 2 + 3)}_{6}$
   $6 - 6$
   0

2. **93,000,000 miles**

3. **167 + *k* = 342**
   $$\begin{array}{r} \overset{2}{\cancel{3}}\,\overset{13}{\cancel{4}}\,{}^{1}2 \\ -\ 1\,6\,7 \\ \hline 1\,7\,5 \end{array}$$
   175 pancakes

4. **59 + *l* = 102**
   $$\begin{array}{r} \overset{0}{\cancel{1}}\,\overset{9}{\cancel{0}}\,{}^{1}2 \\ -\ \ 5\,9 \\ \hline 4\,3 \end{array}$$
   43 points

5. 10 mm + 10 mm + 18 mm + 18 mm
   = **56 mm**

6. $$\begin{array}{r} 10 \\ 6\overline{)60} \\ \underline{6} \\ 00 \\ \underline{00} \\ 0 \end{array}$$
   ***m* = 10**

7. a. $$\begin{array}{r} \mathbf{50} \\ 2\overline{)100} \\ \underline{10} \\ 00 \\ \underline{00} \\ 0 \end{array}$$
   b. $$\begin{array}{r} \mathbf{25} \\ 4\overline{)100} \\ \underline{8} \\ 20 \\ \underline{20} \\ 0 \end{array}$$

8. $\underbrace{300 \times 1}_{300}$ ⊜ $\underbrace{300 \div 1}_{300}$

9. $(3 \times 3) - (3 + 3)$
   $9 - 6$
   3

10. Multiply the value of the previous term by 2 to find the next term.
    2, 4, 8, <u>16</u>, <u>32</u>, <u>64</u>, . . .

11. $\underbrace{1 + 456}_{} + m = 480$
    $457 + m = 480$
    $480 - 457 = 23$
    $\boldsymbol{m = 23}$

12. $$\begin{array}{r} \overset{0}{\cancel{1}}\,{}^{1}0\,\overset{0}{\cancel{1}}\,{}^{1}0 \\ -\ \ 1\,0\,1 \\ \hline 9\,0\,9 \end{array}$$
    ***n* = 909**

13. $$\begin{array}{r} \mathbf{123\ R\ 4} \\ 10\overline{)1234} \\ \underline{10} \\ 23 \\ \underline{20} \\ 34 \\ \underline{30} \\ 4 \end{array}$$

14. $$\begin{array}{r} \mathbf{102\ R\ 10} \\ 12\overline{)1234} \\ \underline{12} \\ 03 \\ \underline{00} \\ 34 \\ \underline{24} \\ 10 \end{array}$$

15. 2 + 4 + 6 + 8 + 10 = **30**

16. **32 mm**

17. **2**

18. **Millions**

19. **6**

20. 1 × 10 × 100 × 1000 = **1,000,000**

21. $$\begin{array}{r} \overset{2\ 1}{\$3.75} \\ \times\ \ \ \ 3 \\ \hline \mathbf{\$11.25} \end{array}$$

22. $$\begin{array}{r} 0 \\ 22\overline{)0} \\ \underline{0} \\ 0 \end{array}$$
    ***y* = 0**

23. $\underbrace{100 + 200 + 300 + 400}_{} + w = 2000$

$$1000 + w = 2000$$
$$2000 - 1000 = 1000$$
$$\mathbf{w = 1000}$$

24.
$$\begin{array}{r} 24 \\ \times\ 26 \\ \hline 144 \\ 480 \\ \hline \mathbf{624} \end{array}$$

25.
$$\begin{array}{r} 25 \\ 25\overline{)625} \\ 50 \\ \hline 125 \\ 125 \\ \hline 0 \end{array}$$
$\mathbf{m = 25}$

26.
$$\begin{array}{r} 8 \\ \times\ 4 \\ \hline \mathbf{32} \end{array}$$

27. $\mathbf{3\overline{)27},\ 27 \div 3,\ \frac{27}{3}}$

28.
$$\begin{array}{r} 10 \\ -\ 7 \\ \hline 3 \end{array} \qquad \mathbf{\frac{3}{10}}$$
If 7 of the 10 marbles are red, then 3 of the 10 are not red.

29. 4,000,000,000,000

30. Answers will vary. See student work. Sample answer: What is the difference between the product of 2 and 5 and the sum of 2 and 5?

$(2 \times 5) - (2 + 5)$

$10 \quad - \quad 7$

$\mathbf{3}$

Practice Set 13

a. Step 1: Subtraction pattern

Step 2: $C - W = D$

Step 3: **26,290 − 18,962 = D**

$$\begin{array}{r} \overset{1}{\not 2}\,\overset{15}{\not 6},\overset{1}{}2\,\overset{8}{\not 9}\overset{1}{}0 \\ -\ 1\ 8,9\ 6\ 2 \\ \hline 7,3\ 2\ 8 \end{array}$$ people

Step 4: **7,328 people.**

b. Step 1: Subtraction pattern

Step 2: $L - E = D$

Step 3: **1215 − 1066 = D**

$$\begin{array}{r} 1\,\overset{1}{\not 2}\,\overset{10}{\not 1}\overset{1}{}5 \\ -\ 1\ 0\ 6\ 6 \\ \hline 1\ 4\ 9 \end{array}$$ years

Step 4: **149 years.**

Written Practice 13

1. $(8 \times 5) - (8 + 5)$

$40 \quad - \quad 13$

$\mathbf{27}$

2. 250,000 miles

3. Five hundred twenty-one billion

4. 5,200,000

5.
$$\begin{array}{r} 20 \\ \times\ \ 3 \\ \hline \mathbf{60} \end{array}$$ **years old**

A score is 20 so threescore is three 20s, which is 60.

6. 1000 − 487 = T

$$\begin{array}{r} \overset{0}{\not 1}\,\overset{9}{\not 0}\,\overset{9}{\not 0}\overset{1}{}0 \\ -\ \ 4\ 8\ 7 \\ \hline \mathbf{5\ 1\ 3} \end{array}$$ **tickets**

7. 692 − 405 = d

$$\begin{array}{r} \not 6\,\overset{8}{\not 9}\overset{1}{}2 \\ -\ 4\ 0\ 5 \\ \hline \mathbf{2\ 8\ 7} \end{array}$$ **miles**

8. 300; 99 and 101 are both one away from 100, so I added 100 three times. 100 + 100 + 100 = 300.

9. $\underbrace{9 \times 10}_{} \times 11$

90×11

$\mathbf{990}$

990; 9 × 10 = 90, 90 × 11 is like 9 × 11 = 99, so 90 × 11 = 990.

10. 4

11. **Billions**

12. 18 mm + 18 mm + 18 mm = **54 mm**

13.
$$\begin{array}{r} \textbf{54 R 32} \\ 100\overline{)5432} \\ \underline{500} \\ 432 \\ \underline{400} \\ 32 \end{array}$$

14.
$$\begin{array}{r} \textbf{2,000} \\ 30\overline{)60,000} \\ \underline{60} \\ 0\,0 \\ \underline{0\,0} \\ 00 \\ \underline{00} \\ 00 \\ \underline{00} \\ 0 \end{array}$$

15.
$$\begin{array}{r} \textbf{142 R 6} \\ 7\overline{)1000} \\ \underline{7} \\ 30 \\ \underline{28} \\ 20 \\ \underline{14} \\ 6 \end{array}$$

16.
$$\begin{array}{r} \textbf{\$1.52} \\ 3\overline{)\$4.56} \\ \underline{3} \\ 1\,5 \\ \underline{1\,5} \\ 06 \\ \underline{6} \\ 0 \end{array}$$

17. 3 + 2 + 1 + 0 (>) 3 × 2 × 1 × 0
6 **0**

18. **7**

19.
$$\begin{array}{r} \textbf{2640} \\ 2\overline{)5280} \\ \underline{4} \\ 12 \\ \underline{12} \\ 08 \\ \underline{08} \\ 00 \\ \underline{00} \\ 0 \end{array}$$

20.
$$\begin{array}{r} 1 \\ 365\overline{)365} \\ \underline{365} \\ 0 \end{array}$$

w = **1**

21. $\underbrace{(5 + 6 + 7)}$ ÷ 3
18 ÷ 3
6

22. **$1\frac{3}{4}$ in.**

23. **To find the perimeter of a square, either add the lengths of the four sides or multiply the length of one side by four.**

24.
$$\begin{array}{r} {}^{1\,3} \\ 125 \\ \times\quad 6 \\ \hline \textbf{750} \end{array}$$

25. **212°F**

26. **$7\overline{)21}$, 21 ÷ 7, $\frac{21}{7}$**

27.
$$\begin{array}{r} 102 \\ 8\overline{)816} \\ \underline{8} \\ 01 \\ \underline{0} \\ 16 \\ \underline{16} \\ 0 \end{array}$$

check:
$$\begin{array}{r} 102 \\ \times\quad 8 \\ \hline 816 \end{array}$$

a = **102**

28. $\begin{array}{r} 12 \\ \times\ 4 \\ \hline 48 \end{array}$ check: $\begin{array}{r} 12 \\ 4\overline{)48} \\ 4 \\ \hline 08 \\ 8 \\ \hline 0 \end{array}$

$b = 48$

29. $\begin{array}{r} 3 \\ 4\overline{)12} \\ 12 \\ \hline 0 \end{array}$ check: $\begin{array}{r} 4 \\ 3\overline{)12} \\ 12 \\ \hline 0 \end{array}$

$c = 3$

30. $\begin{array}{r} 61 \\ +\ 16 \\ \hline 77 \end{array}$ check: $\begin{array}{r} 77 \\ -\ 16 \\ \hline 61 \end{array}$

$d = 77$

Practice Set 14

a. −8 ⓪ −6 → −8 (<) −6

b. Negative eight

c. −3

d. −3, −1, 0, 2

e.

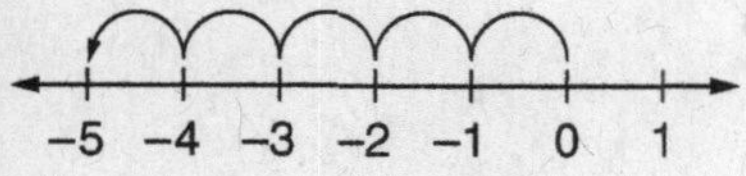

−5

f.

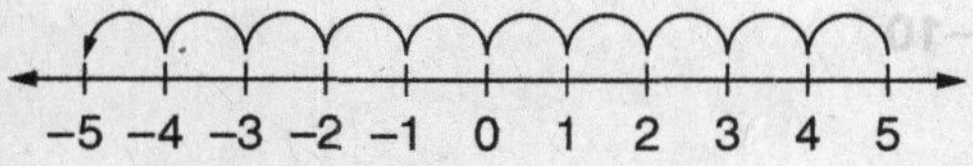

−5

g.

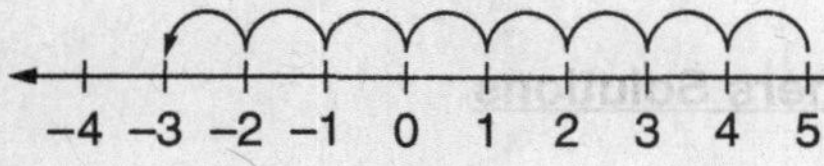

−3

h.

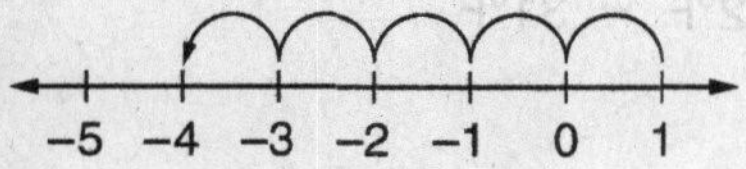

−4

i. True

j. −12°F

k. −186 ft

l. $\begin{array}{r} \$\,1\,8.\,\overset{4}{\not 5}\,{}^{1}0 \\ -\ \$\,1\,6.\,2\,5 \\ \hline 2.\,2\,5 \end{array}$; **−$2.25**

Written Practice 14

1. $\dfrac{(15 + 12)}{(15 - 12)} = \dfrac{27}{3} = \mathbf{9}$

2. Billions

3. 186,000 miles per second

4. −1

5. −3, −2, 0, 1, 5

6.

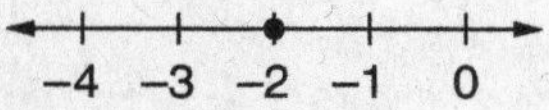

−2

7. 140 − 72 = *a*

$\begin{array}{r} \overset{0}{\not 1}\,\overset{13}{\not 4}\,{}^{1}0 \\ -\ \ 7\,2 \\ \hline 6\,8 \end{array}$ **students**

8. 1 + 2 + 3 + 4 (<) 1 × 2 × 3 × 4
10 **24**

9. 25 mm + 15 mm + 20 mm = **60 mm**

10. Divide the previous term by 2 to find the next term.
16, 8, 4, <u>2</u>, <u>1</u>, . . .

11. 500 − 365 = *d*

$\begin{array}{r} \overset{4}{\not 5}\,\overset{9}{\not 0}\,{}^{1}0 \\ -\ 3\,6\,5 \\ \hline 1\,3\,5 \end{array}$

d = **135**

12.

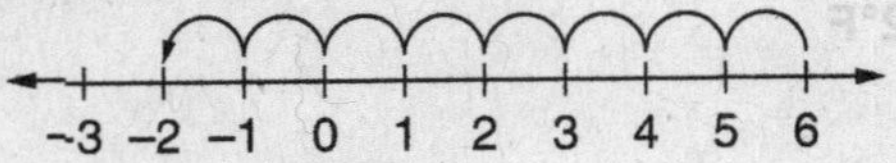

−2

13.

$$\begin{array}{r} \mathbf{10\ R\ 20} \\ 100\overline{)1020} \\ \underline{100} \\ 20 \\ \underline{00} \\ 20 \end{array}$$

14.

$$\begin{array}{r} \mathbf{3{,}015} \\ 12\overline{)36{,}180} \\ \underline{36} \\ 0\,1 \\ \underline{0\,0} \\ 18 \\ \underline{12} \\ 60 \\ \underline{60} \\ 0 \end{array}$$

15.

$$\begin{array}{r} \mathbf{31\ R\ 6} \\ 18\overline{)564} \\ \underline{54} \\ 24 \\ \underline{18} \\ 6 \end{array}$$

16.

$$\begin{array}{r} {}^{1\,2} \\ 1234 \\ 567 \\ \underline{+\quad 89} \\ \mathbf{1890} \end{array}$$

17.

$$\begin{array}{r} 310 \\ \underline{+\ 186} \\ 496 \end{array}$$

***n* = 496**

18.

$$\begin{array}{r} 11 \\ \underline{\times\ 10} \\ 110 \end{array} \qquad \begin{array}{r} 110 \\ \underline{\times\ 12} \\ 220 \\ \underline{1100} \\ \mathbf{1320} \end{array}$$

19.

$$\begin{array}{r} \$\overset{2}{\cancel{3}}.\overset{9}{\cancel{0}}{}^{1}5 \\ \underline{-\ \$2.\,9\,8} \\ \$0.\,0\,7 \end{array}$$

***m* = $0.07**

20. 4 cm; 40 mm

21.

$$\begin{array}{r} 100 \\ \underline{\times\quad 100} \\ 10{,}000 \end{array} \qquad \begin{array}{r} 10{,}000 \\ \underline{\times\quad\quad 100} \\ \mathbf{1{,}000{,}000} \end{array}$$

22. 5

23. To find the length of the object in millimeters, multiply its length in centimeters by 10.

24.

19 × 21 = 399
21 × 19 = 399
399 ÷ 19 = 21
399 ÷ 21 = 19

25. $\underbrace{12 \div 6}_{} \times 2 \ \textcircled{>}\ 12 \div \underbrace{(6 \times 2)}_{}$

$2 \times 2 \qquad\qquad 12 \div 12$

$4 \qquad\qquad\qquad 1$

26. $6\overline{)60}$**, 60 ÷ 6,** $\dfrac{60}{6}$

27. 6,400,000,000 people

28.

$$\begin{array}{r} \mathbf{4\ eggs} \\ 3\overline{)12} \\ \underline{12} \\ 0 \end{array}$$

29. −10

30. −1, 0, $\mathbf{\frac{1}{2}}$**, 1**

Early Finishers Solutions

a. 42°F + 33°F − 12°F = 63°F

b. 63°F − 32°F = 31°F

Practice Set 15

a. Step 1: Equal groups

Step 2: $n \times g = t$

Step 3: $n \times 25¢ = 450¢$

```
       18 cups
25¢)450¢
     25
     200
     200
       0
```

Step 4: **18 cups.**

b. Step 1: Equal groups

Step 2: $n \times g = t$

Step 3: $18 \times 12 = t$

```
   18
×  12
   36
  180
  216 parking spaces
```

Step 4: **216 parking spaces.**

Written Practice 15

1. **Answers will vary. See student work. Sample answer: In the auditorium there were 15 rows of chairs with 20 chairs in each row. How many chairs were there in the auditorium?**

2. **212° − 32° = *d***

```
  ¹
  2̸¹1 2
−   3 2
  1 8 0°F
```

The answer is reasonable because 180° + 32° = 212°.

3. **16 · 320 = *t***

```
  320
×  16
 1920
 3200
 5120 little O's
```

4. **31 − 3 = *d***

```
 ²
 3̸¹1
−  3
 2 8 days
```

5. 3 − 1 ⓪> 1 − 3
   2   −2

6. 2 − 5 = −3
   Negative three

7.
```
     7
  $ 2 8̸.¹0 0
− $ 2 5. 5 0
       2. 5 0; −$2.50
```

8. Subtract 2 from a term to get the next term.
   6, 4, 2, 0, −2, −4, −6, . . .

9. **−6°F; negative six degrees Fahrenheit or six degrees below zero Fahrenheit.**

10.
```
    0 9
  $ 1̸ 0̸.¹0 0
−   $ 0 . 1 0
    $ 9 . 9 0
```

11.
```
   $1.75
2)$3.50
   2
   1 5
   1 4
     10
     10
      0
```

12. **600**

13.
```
     ₂9
    ₁87
    654
+  3210
   3960
```

14.
```
    574
×    76
   3444
  40180
 43,624
```

15.
```
   480
9)4320
  36
   72
   72
    00
    00
     0
```

16.
```
     13 R 25
36)493
   36
   133
   108
    25
```

17.
```
        4
300)1200        check:    300
    1200                4)1200
       0                  12
                           00
                            0
                           00
                            0
                            0
```
$w = 4$

18.
```
   1
63)63           check:   63
   63                   × 1
    0                    63
```
$w = 1$

19.
```
  76            check:     1
×  1                   76)76
  76                      76
                           0
```
$m = 76$

20.
```
    0 9 9                     1 1
  $ 1 0 0 10     check:      $935
−      $ 6 5               + $65
   $ 9 3 5                 $1000
```
$w = \$935$

21. $\underbrace{3 + 12 + 27} + n = 50$

$42 + n = 50$

$50 - 42 = 8$

$n = 8$

check:

$3 + 12 + 27 + 8 = 50$

22. 30 mm

23. $\underbrace{(8 + 9 + 16)} \div 3$

$33 \div 3$

11

24. **Thousands**

25. **2**

26. $19 + 21 = 40$

$21 + 19 = 40$

$40 - 19 = 21$

$40 - 21 = 19$

27. **−3, −1, 0, 2**

28. $\frac{8}{17}$

29.
```
   3
   75¢
×   7
  525¢  or  $5.25
```

30. **0**

Early Finishers Solutions

a. 1933 − 1882 = 51 years old

b. 1945 − 1933 = 12 years in office

Practice Set 16

a. 60

b. 60

c. 50

d. 300

e. 400

f. 400

g. 4000

h. **8000**

i. **7000**

j.
$$\begin{array}{r} 400 \\ +\ 200 \\ \hline \mathbf{600} \end{array}$$

k.
$$\begin{array}{r} 700 \\ -\ 600 \\ \hline \mathbf{100} \end{array}$$

l.
$$\begin{array}{r} 30 \\ \times\ \ 30 \\ \hline \mathbf{900} \end{array}$$

m.
$$\begin{array}{r} \mathbf{20} \\ 30\overline{)600} \\ 60 \\ \hline 00 \\ 00 \\ \hline 0 \end{array}$$

n.
$$\begin{array}{r} 5000 \\ -\ 4000 \\ \hline \mathbf{1000} \end{array}$$ **fewer people**

o.
$$\begin{array}{r} 7000 \\ -\ 5000 \\ \hline 2000 \end{array} \qquad \begin{array}{r} 7000 \\ +\ 2000 \\ \hline \mathbf{9000} \end{array}$$ **people**

Written Practice 16

1. $\underbrace{(20 \times 5)}_{100} - \underbrace{(20 + 5)}_{25}$

100 − 25

75

2. **1803 − 1584 = *d***

$$\begin{array}{r} 1\,\overset{7}{\cancel{8}}\,\overset{9}{\cancel{0}}\,{}^{1}3 \\ -\ 1\,5\,8\,4 \\ \hline \mathbf{2\,1\,9} \end{array}$$ **years**

3. **5 · *g* = 140**

$$\begin{array}{r} \mathbf{28} \\ 5\overline{)140} \\ 10 \\ \hline 40 \\ 40 \\ \hline 0 \end{array}$$ **cards**

The answer is reasonable because 5 × 28 = 140.

4. **3**

5. **One hundred twenty-one million, sixty-eight thousand, seven hundred fifteen votes.**

6.
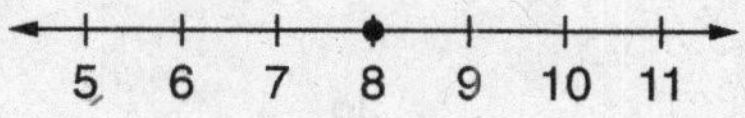

8

7. **57,000**

8. **600**

9.
$$\begin{array}{r} 300 \\ \times\ \ \ 400 \\ \hline \mathbf{120{,}000} \end{array}$$

10.
$$\begin{array}{r} {}^{1}\overset{1}{4}5 \\ 5643 \\ +\ \ 287 \\ \hline \mathbf{5975} \end{array}$$

11.
$$\begin{array}{r} \overset{3}{\cancel{4}}\,\overset{9}{\cancel{0}},{}^{1}3\,\overset{0}{\cancel{1}}{}^{1}2 \\ -\ 1\,4,\,9\,0\,8 \\ \hline \mathbf{2\,5,\,4\,0\,4} \end{array}$$

12.
$$\begin{array}{r} \mathbf{609} \\ 12\overline{)7308} \\ 72 \\ \hline 10 \\ 00 \\ \hline 108 \\ 108 \\ \hline 0 \end{array}$$

13.
$$\begin{array}{r} \mathbf{53\ R\ 67} \\ 100\overline{)5367} \\ 500 \\ \hline 367 \\ 300 \\ \hline 67 \end{array}$$

14. $\underbrace{(5 + 11)}_{16} \div 2$

16 ÷ 2

8

15. $2\overline{)\$5.00}$ = **$2.50**
4
10
10
00
00
0

16. $4\overline{)\$5.00}$ = **$1.25**
4
10
8
20
20
0

17. $0.25
× 10
$2.50

18. 325(324 − 323)
325(1)
325

19. 1 + (2 + 3) ⊜ (1 + 2) + 3
1 + 5 3 + 3
6 6

20. **It felt colder at 3 p.m. The wind chill at 3 p.m. was −10°F, and the wind chill at 11 p.m. was −3°F. It felt colder at 3 p.m. because −10 < −3.**

21. 60 · 72 = t
72
× 60
4320 times

22. 90 ft + 90 ft + 90 ft + 90 ft = **360 ft**

23. 80
− 30
50 more pounds Kg

24. 30
60
+ 80
170 pounds Kg

25. 60
× 7
~~420 pounds~~ Kg

26. **Answers will vary. See student work. Sample answer: How many more pounds of peanuts does the mother elephant eat each day than the baby elephant?**

27. $6\overline{)66}$ = 11 check: 11 × 6 = 66
6
06
6
0
***w* = 11**

28. 60 + 37 = 97 check: 97 − 60 = 37
***m* = 97**

29. $\overset{5}{\cancel{6}}{}^{1}0$ − 37 = 23 check: $\overset{5}{\cancel{6}}{}^{1}0$ − 23 = 37
***n* = 23**

30.
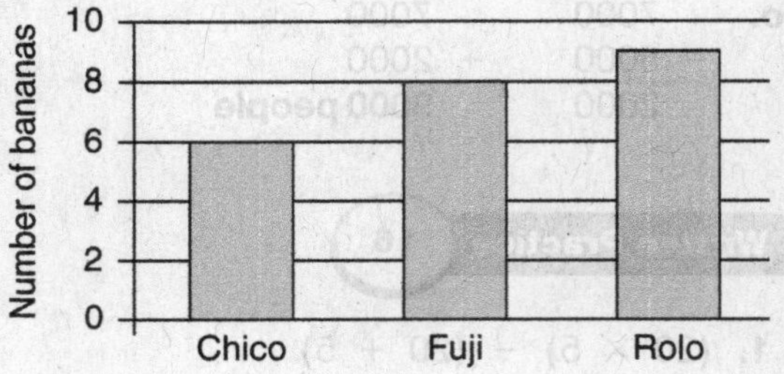

Practice Set 17

a. $\frac{9}{16}, \frac{5}{8}, \frac{11}{16}, \frac{3}{4}, \frac{13}{16}, \frac{7}{8}, \frac{15}{16}, 1, 1\frac{1}{16}, 1\frac{1}{8}, 1\frac{3}{16}, 1\frac{1}{4}, 1\frac{5}{16}, 1\frac{3}{8}, 1\frac{7}{16}, 1\frac{1}{2}$

b. $-2\frac{1}{2}$

c. $3\frac{1}{2}$

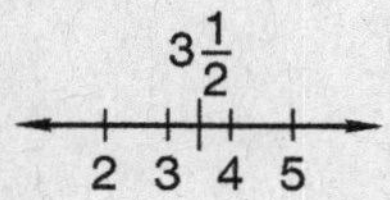

d. $1\frac{5}{6}$

e. $\frac{13}{16}$ in.

f. $2\frac{4}{16}$ or $2\frac{1}{4}$ in.

g. $3\frac{3}{16}$ in.

Written Practice 17

1.
$$\begin{array}{r} \overset{1}{1}2{,}500 \\ +\ 10{,}610 \\ \hline 23{,}110 \end{array}$$

2. 1969 − 1903 = *d*
$$\begin{array}{r} 1969 \\ -\ 1903 \\ \hline 66 \text{ years} \end{array}$$

3. 12 · 6 = *t*
$$\begin{array}{r} \overset{1}{1}2 \\ \times\ \ 6 \\ \hline 72 \text{ yards} \end{array}$$

4. 24 · 1000 = *t*
$$\begin{array}{r} 24 \\ \times\ 1000 \\ \hline \$\,24{,}000 \end{array}$$

5.
$$\begin{array}{r} 5000 \\ +\ 2000 \\ \hline 7000 \end{array}$$

6.
$$\begin{array}{r} 160 \\ 3\overline{)480} \\ \underline{3} \\ 18 \\ \underline{18} \\ 00 \\ \underline{00} \\ 0 \end{array}$$

7. $\frac{6 - 6}{3} = \frac{0}{3} = 0$

8. $b + a = c$
$c - a = b$
$c - b = a$

9. $\frac{2}{3}$

10. A square has four sides of equal length. So to find the perimeter, we add (10 cm + 10 cm + 10 cm + 10 cm), or we multiply (4 × 10 cm).

11. $3\frac{3}{16}$ in.

12.
$$\begin{array}{r} \$\overset{2}{\cancel{3}}.\overset{9}{\cancel{0}}{}^{1}0 \\ -\ \$1.75 \\ \hline \$1.25 \end{array}$$
y = $1.25

check:
$$\begin{array}{r} \$\overset{2}{\cancel{3}}.\overset{9}{\cancel{0}}{}^{1}0 \\ -\ \$1.25 \\ \hline \$1.75 \end{array}$$

13.
$$\begin{array}{r} 20 \\ +\ 30 \\ \hline 50 \end{array}$$
m = 50

check:
$$\begin{array}{r} 50 \\ -\ 20 \\ \hline 30 \end{array}$$

14.
$$\begin{array}{r} 0 \\ 12\overline{)0} \\ \underline{0} \\ 0 \end{array}$$
n = 0

check:
$$\begin{array}{r} 12 \\ \times\ \ 0 \\ \hline 0 \end{array}$$

15. 16 + 14 = 14 + *w*
30 = 14 + *w*

$$\begin{array}{r} \overset{2}{\cancel{3}}{}^{1}0 \\ -\ 14 \\ \hline 16 \end{array}$$
w = 16

check:
$$\begin{array}{r} \overset{1}{1}4 \\ +\ 16 \\ \hline 30 \end{array}$$

16. $19 \times 21 < 20 \times 20$
399 400

17. $100 - \underbrace{(50 - 25)}$
$100 - 25$
75

18. $5280 \div 44 = \mathbf{120}$
44)5280
44
88
88
00
00
0

19.
365
4 576
+ 50,287
55,228

20. Add 5 to a term to find the next term.
5, 10, 15, 20, 25, . . .

21. 9

22. 100)250,000 = **2 500**
200
50 0
50 0
0 0
0 0
00
00
00
0
0

23.
$3.75
× 10
$37.50

24. $\frac{1}{2}$ from carbohydrates, $\frac{1}{2}$ not from carbohydrates
3)26 = 13
26
0
about 13 grams

25. $1 + 3 + 5 + 7 + 9 + 11 = \mathbf{36}$

26. One way to find $\frac{1}{4}$ of 52 is to divide 52 by 4.

27. a. 25¢)100¢ = **4 quarters**
100
0

b. 25¢)300¢ = **12 quarters**
25
5
50
0

28. $\mathbf{\frac{3}{8}}$ **-inch mark**

29. $\mathbf{4\frac{1}{6}}$

30. 2)16 = 8
16
0
8 sixteenths of an inch

Early Finishers Solutions

Use an estimate: 800 sq. ft ÷ 2 = 400 sq. ft. Since one gallon of paint will cover about one-half the walls Manny plans to paint, he should buy one more gallon of paint.

Practice Set 18

a.
26 books
36 books
+ 43 books
105 books

3)105 = **35 books**
9
15

b. $96 + 44 + 68 + 100 = 308$
$308 \div 4 = \mathbf{77}$

c. $\frac{28 + 82}{2} = \frac{110}{2} = \mathbf{55}$

d. $\frac{86 + 102}{2} = \frac{188}{2} = \mathbf{94}$

e. $3 + 6 + 9 + 12 + 15 = 45$
$45 \div 5 = \mathbf{9}$

f. **12 in.**

g. **Between her thirteenth and her fourteenth birthdays**

h. **No**

Written Practice 18

1.
```
   1 1
   2068
 + 3940
   6008 peanuts
```
Addition pattern

2. $(11 + 12) + x = 32$
$23 + x = 32$
$32 - 23 = 9$
$\mathbf{x = 9}$ **teeth**
Addition pattern

3.
```
    53¢
  × 12
   1 06
   5 30
  $6.36
```
Multiplication pattern

4.
```
   5000
 − 2000
   3000
```

5. $9 + 7 + 8 = 24$
$24 \div 3 = \mathbf{8}$

6. $\frac{59 + 81}{2} = \frac{140}{2} = \mathbf{70}$

7.
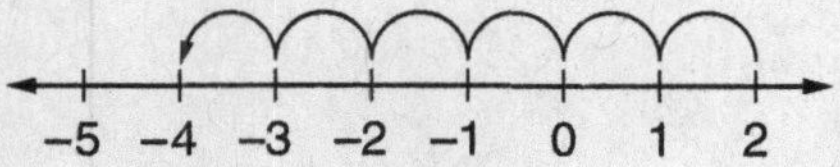

−4

8.
```
   $0.35
 ×   100
  $35.00
```

9.
```
      1,001
 10)10,010
    10
     0 0
     0 0
      01
      00
       10
       10
        0
```

10.
```
      2010 R 10
 17)34180
    34
     01
     00
      18
      17
       10
       00
       10
```

11.
```
     1 1
    $3.64
   $94.28
 +  $0.87
   $98.79
```

12.
```
   3 10  12 16
   4 1,  3 7 15
 −  1 3, 5 7 6
    2 7, 7 9 9
```

13.
```
    125
  ×  16
    750
   1250
   2000
```

14.
$4 \cdot 3 \cdot 2 \cdot 1 \cdot 0$
$12 \cdot 2 \cdot 1 \cdot 0$
$24 \cdot 1 \cdot 0$
$24 \cdot 0$
0

15.
```
    1
    84
 +  48
   132
```
$w = \mathbf{132}$

check:
```
  0 12
  1 3 2
 −  8 4
    4 8
```


16.
```
    39
6)234
  18
   54
   54
    0
```
$n = 39$

check:
```
     6
39)234
   234
     0
```

17. $(1 + 2) \times 3 = (1 \times 2) + m$

$3 \times 3 = 2 + m$

$9 = 2 + m$

$9 - 2 = 7$

$m = 7$

check:

$(1 + 2) \times 3 = (1 \times 2) + 7$

$3 \times 3 = 2 + 7$

$9 = 9$

18.

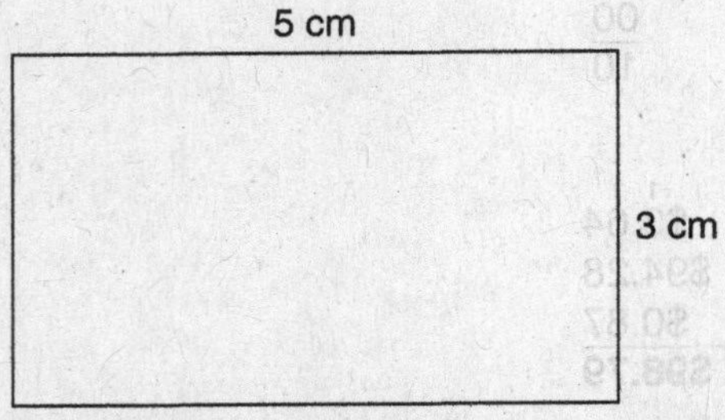

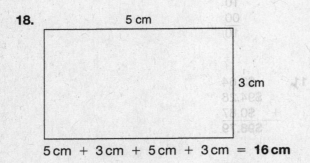

5 cm + 3 cm + 5 cm + 3 cm = **16 cm**

19. 2 + 4 + 6 + 8 + 10 + 12 = **42**

20. Multiply the value of a term by 2 to find the next term; 8

21. $500 \times 1 \ (=) \ 500 \div 1$

500 500

22.
```
   555
2)1110
  10
   11
   10
    10
    10
     0
```

23. Millions

24.
```
  ¹
  2¹00
-   80
  120 heartbeats per minute
```
1 2 0 heartbeats per minute

25.
```
   200
×   10
```
2000 times

26. Answers will vary. See student work. Sample answer: Walking increases a resting person's heart rate by about how many heartbeats per minute?
```
  ⁰
  1¹40
-   80
```
6 0 heartbeats per minute

27.
```
   ¹
   24 students
   27 students
+  33 students
   84 students
```
28 students
```
3)84
  6
  24
  24
   0
```

The average should be a central number between the least and greatest numbers being averaged. Since 28 is between 24 and 33, the answer is reasonable.

28. a.
10 dimes
```
.10)$1.00
     1 0
      00
      00
       0
```

b.
30 dimes
```
.10)$3.00
     3 0
      00
      00
       0
```

29.

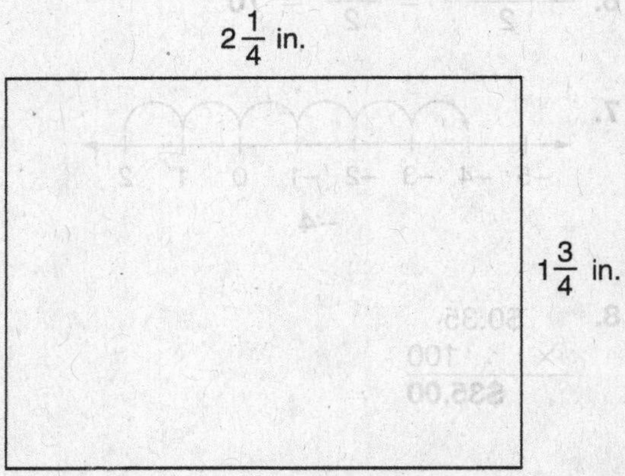

30. Combining, equal groups

Early Finishers Solutions

a. 1603 − 1518 = 85 cubic feet

b. 85 × \$0.67 = \$56.95

Practice Set 19

a. 1, 2, 7, 14

$$\begin{array}{r} 14 \\ 1\overline{)14} \\ \underline{1} \\ 04 \\ \underline{4} \\ 0 \end{array} \quad \begin{array}{r} 7 \\ 2\overline{)14} \\ \underline{14} \\ 0 \end{array} \quad \begin{array}{r} 2 \\ 7\overline{)14} \\ \underline{14} \\ 0 \end{array} \quad \begin{array}{r} 1 \\ 14\overline{)14} \\ \underline{14} \\ 0 \end{array}$$

b. 1, 3, 5, 15

$$\begin{array}{r} 15 \\ 1\overline{)15} \\ \underline{1} \\ 05 \\ \underline{5} \\ 0 \end{array} \quad \begin{array}{r} 5 \\ 3\overline{)15} \\ \underline{15} \\ 0 \end{array} \quad \begin{array}{r} 3 \\ 5\overline{)15} \\ \underline{15} \\ 0 \end{array} \quad \begin{array}{r} 1 \\ 15\overline{)15} \\ \underline{15} \\ 0 \end{array}$$

c. 1, 2, 4, 8, 16

$$\begin{array}{r} 16 \\ 1\overline{)16} \\ \underline{1} \\ 06 \\ \underline{6} \\ 0 \end{array} \quad \begin{array}{r} 8 \\ 2\overline{)16} \\ \underline{16} \\ 0 \end{array} \quad \begin{array}{r} 4 \\ 4\overline{)16} \\ \underline{16} \\ 0 \end{array} \quad \begin{array}{r} 2 \\ 8\overline{)16} \\ \underline{16} \\ 0 \end{array} \quad \begin{array}{r} 1 \\ 16\overline{)16} \\ \underline{16} \\ 0 \end{array}$$

d. 1, 17

$$\begin{array}{r} 17 \\ 1\overline{)17} \\ \underline{1} \\ 07 \\ \underline{7} \\ 0 \end{array} \quad \begin{array}{r} 1 \\ 17\overline{)17} \\ \underline{17} \\ 0 \end{array}$$

e. 23 is prime; 21 is divisible by 3 and 7, 25 is divisible by 5.

f. 31 is prime; 32 is even, 33 is divisible by 3 and 11.

g. 43 is prime; 44 is even, 45 is divisible by 3, 5, 9, and 15.

h. 42

i. 51

j. 33

k. $2 \cdot 2 \cdot 2 \cdot 2 = 16$

l. $2 \cdot 3 \cdot 3 = 18$

Written Practice 19

1.
$$\begin{array}{r} \mathbf{42} \\ 6\overline{)252} \\ \underline{24} \\ 12 \\ \underline{12} \\ 0 \end{array}$$

2.
$$\begin{array}{r} 1\,\overset{7}{\cancel{8}}\,\overset{15}{\cancel{6}}\,{}^{1}\cancel{3} \\ -\quad 8\ 7 \\ \hline 1\ 7\ 7\ 6 \end{array}$$
Fourscore and seven is 87, and 87 years before 1863 is 1776.

3. 69° − (−46°) = 69° + 46° = **115 degrees**

4. $7 \cdot g = 203$
$$\begin{array}{r} \mathbf{29\ turnips} \\ 7\overline{)203} \\ \underline{14} \\ 63 \\ \underline{63} \\ 0 \end{array}$$

5. 1 + 2 + 4 + 9 = 16
$$\begin{array}{r} \mathbf{4} \\ 4\overline{)16} \\ \underline{16} \\ 0 \end{array}$$

6. 36

7.
$$\begin{array}{r} \overset{3}{2}5\text{ mm} \\ \times\quad 6 \\ \hline \mathbf{150\text{ mm}} \end{array}$$

8. 30 mm

Solutions

9. 1, 2, 4, 5, 10, 20

$1\overline{)20}$ = 20; 2; 00; 00; 0
$2\overline{)20}$ = 10; 2; 00; 00; 0
$4\overline{)20}$ = 5; 20; 0
$5\overline{)20}$ = 4; 20; 0
$10\overline{)20}$ = 2; 20; 0
$20\overline{)20}$ = 1; 20; 0

10. 4

1, 3, 5, 15

$1\overline{)15}$ = 15; 1; 05; 5; 0
$3\overline{)15}$ = 5; 15; 0
$5\overline{)15}$ = 3; 15; 0
$15\overline{)15}$ = 1; 15; 0

11. C. 29

12. $100\overline{)250,000}$ = **2 500**
200
50 0
50 0
00
00
00
00
0

13. $60\overline{)1234}$ = **20 R 34**
120
34
00
34

14. $\frac{6 + 18 + 9}{3} = \frac{33}{3} =$ **11**

15.
$3.45
× 10
$34.50

16. $\$\,10.00 - \$\,1.93 = \$\,8.07$ (regrouped: 0 9 ^{9} ^{1}0)
check: $\$\,10.00 - \$\,8.07 = \$\,1.93$

w = **$8.07**

17. $4 \times 3 = 12$ check: $3\overline{)12}$ = 4; 12; 0

w = **12**

18.
$ba = c$
$c \div a = b$
$c \div b = a$

19. $-2, 0, \frac{1}{2}, 1, 3$

20. 123 ÷ 1 (>) 123 − 1
123 122

21. 9

22. 123,000,000

23. $2\overline{)\$11.00}$ = **$5.50**
10
1 0
1 0
00
00
0

24. $4\overline{)48}$ = **12 inches**
4
08
8
0

25. (51 + 49) · (51 − 49)
100 · 2
200

26. A. 2

27. 2 · 2 · 5 = 20

28. 12 + 12 + 6 = 30
$3\overline{)30}$ = **10 dictionaries**
3
00
00
0

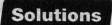

29.

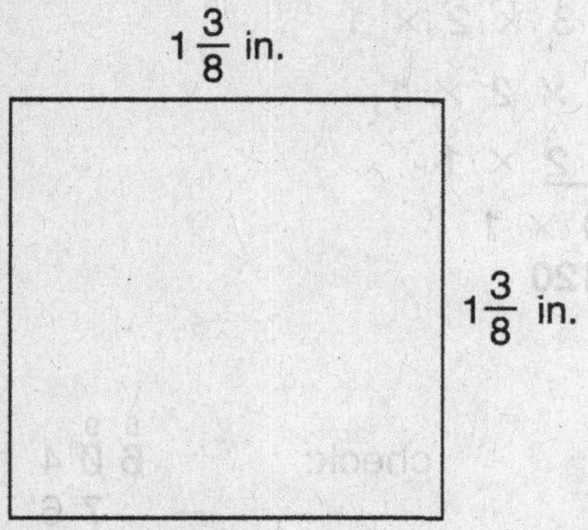

30. If the number is even, it is divisible by 2. All even numbers are divisible by 2. Odd numbers are not divisible by 2.

<u>**Early Finishers Solutions**</u>

a. $\frac{32 + 49 + 21 + 59 + 37 + 44 + 52}{7}$
$= 42$; 42 CDs

b. $47 - 42 = 5$; Yolanda's friends averaged 5 fewer than the reported average.

Practice Set 20

a. The factors of 10 are 1, 2, 5, 10
The factors of 15 are 1, 3, 5, 15
GCF is **5**

b. The factors of 18 are 1, 2, 3, 6, 9, 18
The factors of 27 are 1, 3, 9, 27
GCF is **9**

c. The factors of 18 are 1, 2, 3, 6, 9, 18
The factors of 24 are 1, 2, 3, 4, 6, 8, 12, 24
GCF is **6**

d. The factors of 12 are 1, 2, 3, 4, 6, 12
The factors of 18 are 1, 2, 3, 6, 9, 18
The factors of 24 are 1, 2, 3, 4, 6, 8, 12, 24
GCF is **6**

e. The factors of 15 are 1, 3, 5, 15
The factors of 25 are 1, 5, 25
GCF is **5**

f. The factors of 20 are 1, 2, 4, 5, 10, 20
The factors of 30 are 1, 2, 3, 5, 6, 10, 15, 30
The factors of 40 are 1, 2, 4, 5, 8, 10, 20, 40
GCF is **10**

g. The factors of 12 are 1, 2, 3, 4, 6, 12
The factors of 15 are 1, 3, 5, 15
GCF is **3**

h. The factors of 20 are 1, 2, 4, 5, 10, 20
The factors of 40 are 1, 2, 4, 5, 8, 10, 20, 40
The factors of 60 are 1, 2, 3, 4, 5, 6, 10, 12, 15, 20, 30, 60
GCF is **20**

i. **Answers will vary, but should show a list of numbers that are all multiples of 7 and have no greater common factor. Sample answer: 7, 14, 21.**

Written Practice 20

1. $(12 \times 8) - (12 + 8)$
$96 - 20$
76

2. **1,429,000,000 km**

3. **9**

4. **400**

5.

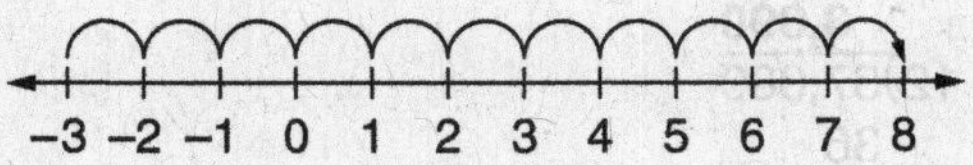

11°C

6. $31 + 52 + 40 = 123$

41 points per game

$$\begin{array}{r} 41 \\ 3\overline{)123} \\ \underline{12} \\ 03 \\ \underline{3} \\ 0 \end{array}$$

7. The factors of 12 are 1, 2, 3, 4, 6, 12
The factors of 20 are 1, 2, 4, 5, 10, 20
GCF is **4**

8. The factors of 9 are 1, 3, 9
The factors of 15 are 1, 3, 5, 15
The factors of 21 are 1, 3, 7, 21
GCF is **3**

9.
$$\begin{array}{r} \mathbf{\$0.81} \\ 4\overline{)\$3.24} \\ \underline{3\,2} \\ 04 \\ \underline{4} \\ 0 \end{array}$$

10.
$$\begin{array}{r} \mathbf{543\ R\ 2} \\ 10\overline{)5432} \\ \underline{50} \\ 43 \\ \underline{40} \\ 32 \\ \underline{30} \\ 2 \end{array}$$

11. $\frac{28 + 42}{14} = \frac{70}{14} = \mathbf{5}$

12.
$$\begin{array}{r} {}^{1\,1\ \ 1} \\ 56{,}042 \\ +\ 49{,}985 \\ \hline \mathbf{106{,}027} \end{array}$$

13.
$$\begin{array}{r} \mathbf{3{,}090} \\ 12\overline{)37{,}080} \\ \underline{36}\phantom{{,}080} \\ 1\,0 \\ \underline{0\,0} \\ 1\,08 \\ \underline{1\,08} \\ 00 \\ \underline{00} \\ 0 \end{array}$$

14.
$$\begin{array}{r} \$6.47 \\ \times\quad 10 \\ \hline \mathbf{\$64.70} \end{array}$$

15. $5 \times 4 \times 3 \times 2 \times 1$
$20 \times 3 \times 2 \times 1$
$60 \times 2 \times 1$
120×1
120

16.
$$\begin{array}{r} {}^{1\,1} \\ 528 \\ +\ \ 76 \\ \hline 604 \end{array} \qquad \text{check: } \begin{array}{r} {}^{5\ 9} \\ \not{6}\,\not{0}\,{}^{1}4 \\ -\ \ 7\ 6 \\ \hline 5\ 2\ 8 \end{array}$$
***w* = 604**

17.
$$\begin{array}{r} {}^{0\ \ 13\ \ 9} \\ \not{1}\,\not{4},\not{0}\,{}^{1}0\ 9 \\ -\quad 9\ 6\ 7\ 0 \\ \hline 4\ 3\ 3\ 9 \end{array} \qquad \text{check: } \begin{array}{r} {}^{0\ \ 13\ \ 9} \\ \not{1}\,\not{4},\not{0}\,{}^{1}0\ 9 \\ -\quad 4\ 3\ 3\ 9 \\ \hline 9\ 6\ 7\ 0 \end{array}$$
***w* = 4339**

18.
$$\begin{array}{r} 15 \\ 6\overline{)90} \\ \underline{6} \\ 30 \\ \underline{30} \\ 0 \end{array} \qquad \text{check: } \begin{array}{r} {}^{3} \\ 15 \\ \times\ \ 6 \\ \hline 90 \end{array}$$
***w* = 15**

19.
$$\begin{array}{r} {}^{1\,1} \\ 365 \\ +\ 365 \\ \hline 730 \end{array} \qquad \text{check: } \begin{array}{r} {}^{6\ 12} \\ \not{7}\,\not{3}\,{}^{1}0 \\ -\ 3\ 6\ 5 \\ \hline 3\ 6\ 5 \end{array}$$
***q* = 730**

20.
$$\begin{array}{r} 365 \\ -\ 365 \\ \hline 0 \end{array} \qquad \text{check: } \begin{array}{r} 365 \\ -\ \ \ 0 \\ \hline 365 \end{array}$$
***p* = 0**

21. **4**

22. $\underset{49}{50 - 1}$ ⓒ< $\underset{50}{49 + 1}$

23. 1, 3, 5, 7, 9, 11, 13, 15, 17, 19
19

24. **Since the four sides of a square have equal lengths, we divide the perimeter, 100 cm, by 4 to find the length of each side.**

25. **Student estimates may vary; $2\frac{4}{16}$ or $2\frac{1}{4}$ inches**

26. **a.** **8 bits**

b.
$$\begin{array}{r} 8 \\ \times\ 3 \\ \hline \textbf{24 bits} \end{array}$$

27. 12 + 24 + 36 + 48 = 120

$$\begin{array}{r} \textbf{30 golf balls} \\ 4\overline{)120} \\ \underline{12} \\ 00 \\ \underline{0} \\ 0 \end{array}$$

28. **A. 5**

29. **1, 2, 3, 4, 6, 8, 12, 24**

I found all the whole numbers that multiply to make 24.

$1\overline{)24}$ = 24, $2\overline{)24}$ = 12, $3\overline{)24}$ = 8, $4\overline{)24}$ = 6, $6\overline{)24}$ = 4, $8\overline{)24}$ = 3

$12\overline{)24}$ = 2, $24\overline{)24}$ = 1

30.
$$\begin{array}{r} \overset{0}{\cancel{1}},\overset{9}{\cancel{0}}\,{}^{1}00{,}000{,}000{,}000 \\ -\ 10{,}000{,}000{,}000 \\ \hline \textbf{990,000,000,000} \end{array}$$

Early Finishers Solutions

a. There are 15 prime numbers from 1 to 52 (2, 3, 5, 7, 11, 13, 17, 19, 23, 29, 31, 37, 41, 43, 47). There are also 36 composite numbers.
Week 1: $1
Prime number weeks: $3 × 15 = $45
Composite number weeks: $5 × 36 = $180
$1 + $45 + $180 = $226
Tino's total for the year will be $226

b. Tino will receive $1, plus $5 × 15, plus $3 × 36. $1 + $75 + $108 = $184. Tino would make less.

Investigation 2

1. **50%**

2. $\frac{1}{4}$

3. $\frac{1}{8}$

4. **75%**

5. **50%**

6. **50%**

7.

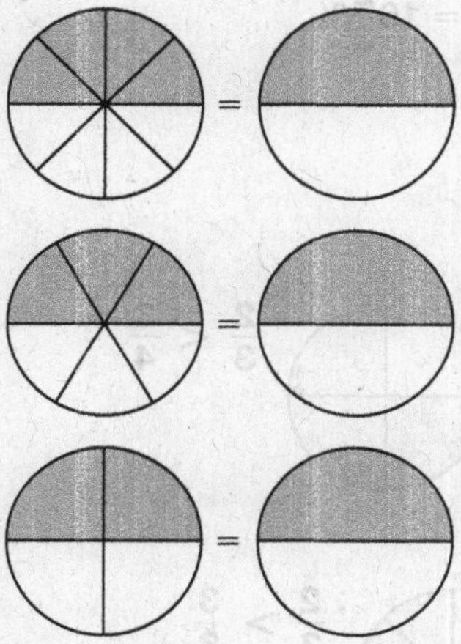

8. $\frac{1}{4}$

9. **3**

10. $\frac{1}{3}$

11. **2**

12. $\frac{3}{8} + \frac{2}{8} = \frac{5}{8}$

13. $1 - \frac{1}{6} = \frac{6}{6} - \frac{1}{6} = \frac{5}{6}$

14. $1 - \frac{1}{3} = \frac{3}{3} - \frac{1}{3} = \mathbf{\frac{2}{3}}$

15. $1 - \frac{1}{4} = \frac{4}{4} - \frac{1}{4} = \mathbf{\frac{3}{4}}$

16. $1 - \frac{3}{8} = \frac{8}{8} - \frac{3}{8} = \mathbf{\frac{5}{8}}$

17. $3\overline{)100}$ quotient 33 $= \mathbf{33\frac{1}{3}\%}$
$\underline{9}$
10
$\underline{9}$
1

18. $6\overline{)100}$ quotient 16 $= 16\frac{4}{6} = \mathbf{16\frac{2}{3}\%}$
$\underline{6}$
40
$\underline{36}$
4

19. 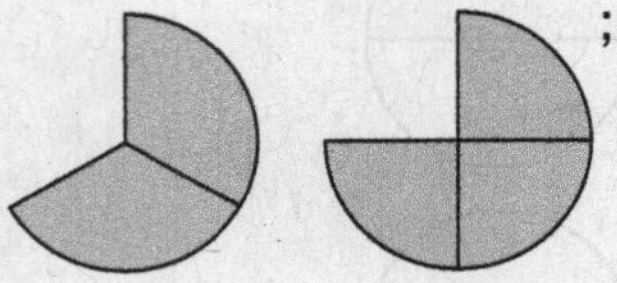 ; $\mathbf{\frac{2}{3} < \frac{3}{4}}$

20. 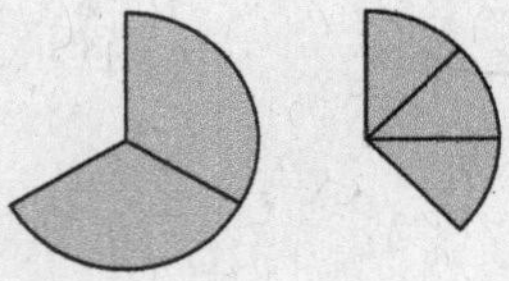 ; $\mathbf{\frac{2}{3} > \frac{3}{8}}$

21. 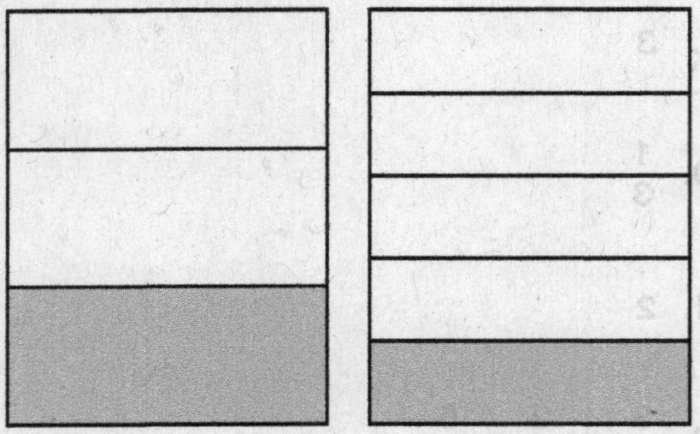

$\mathbf{\frac{1}{3}}$

22. **One possibility:**

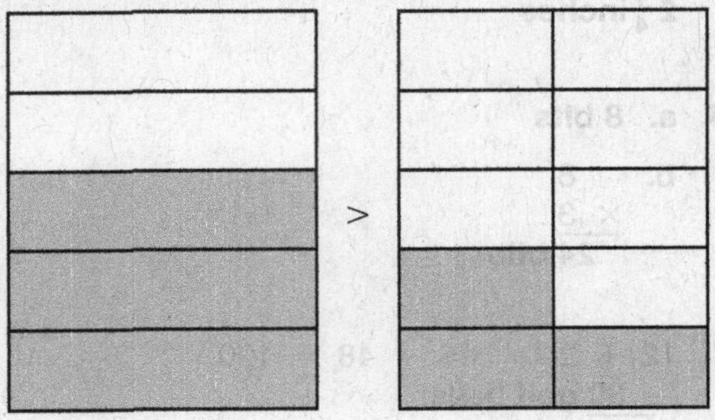

23.

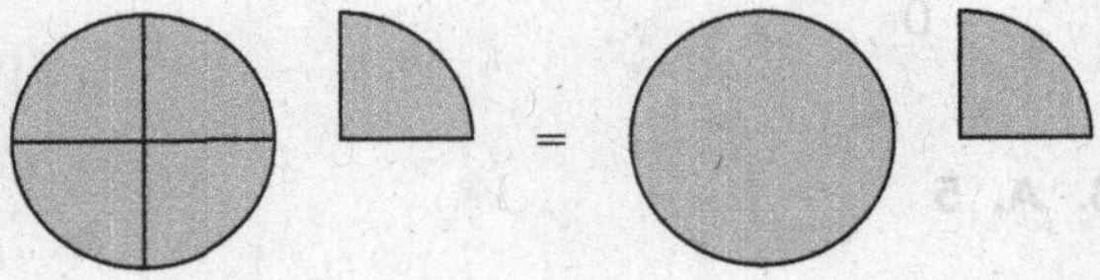

24. $\mathbf{1\frac{3}{4}}$

25. $\mathbf{1\frac{1}{2}}$

26. **6**

27. **6; Possible answer: We put our fraction pieces together and made two circles using six $\frac{1}{3}$s. Or: Three $\frac{1}{3}$s make one circle, so two circles use twice as many, 2 × 3 = 6.**

28. $\mathbf{1\frac{1}{3}}$

29. $\mathbf{1\frac{5}{6}}$

30. $\mathbf{\frac{6}{12}, \frac{3}{12}, \frac{4}{12}, \frac{2}{12}}$

Practice Set 21

a. 123; No, the last digit is not even.
234; Yes, the last digit is even.
345; No, the last digit is not even.

b. $1 + 2 + 3 + 4 = 10$
1234; No, the sum of the digits is not divisible by 3.
$2 + 3 + 4 + 5 = 14$
2345; No, the sum of the digits is not divisible by 3.
$3 + 4 + 5 + 6 = 18$
3456; Yes, the sum of the digits is divisible by 3.

c. **2, 3, 5, 10**

d. **2, 3**

Written Practice 21

1. $\underbrace{(8 + 5)}_{13} \times \underbrace{(8 - 5)}_{3}$
13×3
39

2. **1959 − 1787 = *d***
$$\begin{array}{r} 1\overset{8}{\cancel{9}}{}^{1}5\,9 \\ -\ 1\,7\,8\,7 \\ \hline 1\,7\,2 \end{array}$$
1 7 2 years

3. **16 · *w* = 240**
15 bowling balls
$$\begin{array}{r} 15 \\ 16\overline{)240} \\ \underline{16} \\ 80 \\ \underline{80} \\ 0 \end{array}$$

4. $\frac{3}{4}$

5. $\frac{17}{30}$

6. $\frac{3}{100}$

7.
$$\begin{array}{r} \$1.17 \\ 2\overline{)\$2.34} \\ \underline{2} \\ 0\,3 \\ \underline{2} \\ 14 \\ \underline{14} \\ 0 \end{array}$$

8. **Millions**

9. **256; Multiply the value of a term by 4 to find the next term.**

10. $\underbrace{64 \times 1}_{64}$ (<) $\underbrace{64 + 1}_{65}$

11. $3 + 6 + 5 = 14$
365; No, the sum of the digits is not divisible by 9.
$1 + 1 + 7 + 9 = 18$
1179; Yes, the sum of digits is divisible by 9.
$1 + 5 + 5 + 6 = 17$
1556; No, the sum of the digits is not divisible by 9.

12.
$$\begin{array}{r} 400 \\ 200 \\ +\ 200 \\ \hline \mathbf{800} \end{array}$$

13. The factors of 12 are 1, 2, 3, 4, 6, 12
The factors of 16 are 1, 2, 4, 8, 16
GCF is **4**

14.
$$\begin{array}{r} \mathbf{40\ R\ 30} \\ 100\overline{)4030} \\ \underline{400} \\ 30 \\ \underline{00} \\ 30 \end{array}$$

15.
```
     2,035
24)48,840
   48
    0 8
    0 0
      84
      72
      120
      120
        0
```

16.
```
   113
6)678
  6
  07
   6
   18
   18
    0
```

17.
```
   $4.75
×     10
  $47.50
```
$47.50

18.
```
  $10.00        check:   $10.00
− $0.87                − $9.13
  $9.13                  $0.87
```
***w* = $9.13**

19. $463 + 27 + m = 500$

$490 + m = 500$

$500 - 490 = 10$

***m* = 10**

check: $463 + 27 + 10 = 500$

20. **−2, 0, $\frac{1}{4}$, $\frac{1}{2}$, 1**

21.
```
   12        17
   16     3)51
 + 23       3
   51       21
            21
             0
```
17

22. **1, 2, 4, 7, 14, 28**

23. **2, 5, and 10**

24. **See student work.**

10 cm

25. $(12 \times 12) - (11 \times 13)$

$144 - 143$

1

26. **4 and 8**

27. 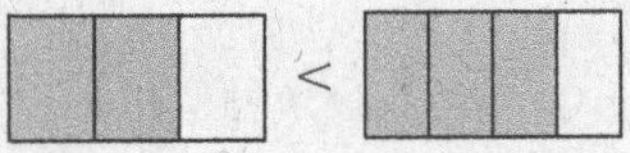

28. a. **8 bits**

b. **4 bits**

29. The factors of 20 are ①, ②, 4, ⑤, ⑩, 20.
The factor of 30 are ①, ②, 3, ⑤, 6, ⑩, 15, 30.
1, 2, 5, 10

30. Draw a circle ○. Through the center of the circle, draw a plus sign ⊕. Then draw a times sign through the center of the circle ⊛.

Early Finishers Solutions

22 − (15 − 10) = 17

Practice Set 22

a.

12 musicians

3 musicians
3 musicians
3 musicians
3 musicians

$\frac{3}{4}$ could play piano (first three boxes)

$\frac{1}{4}$ could not play piano (last box)

9 musicians

b.

$$3\overline{)\$4.50} = \$1.50$$

3
1 5
1 5
00
00
0

$4.50

$1.50
$1.50
$1.50

$\frac{2}{3}$ of $4.50 (first two boxes)

$\frac{1}{3}$ of $4.50 (last box)

$$\$1.50 \times 2 = \mathbf{\$3.00}$$

c.

$$5\overline{)60} = 12$$

5
10
10
0

60

12
12
12
12
12

$\frac{4}{5}$ of 60 (first four boxes)

$\frac{1}{5}$ of 60 (last box)

$$12 \times 4 = \mathbf{48}$$

d.

$$10\overline{)80} = 8$$

80
0

80

8
8
8
8
8
8
8
8
8
8

$\frac{3}{10}$ of 80 (first three boxes)

$\frac{7}{10}$ of 80 (last seven boxes)

$$8 \times 3 = \mathbf{24}$$

e.

$$6\overline{)24} = 4$$

24
0

24

4
4
4
4
4
4

$\frac{5}{6}$ of 24 (first five boxes)

$\frac{1}{6}$ of 24 (last box)

$$4 \times 5 = \mathbf{20}$$

f.

$$10\overline{)100} = 10$$

10
00
00
0

100%

10%
10%
10%
10%
10%
10%
10%
10%
10%
10%

$\frac{9}{10}$ of 100% (first nine boxes)

$\frac{1}{10}$ of 100% (last box)

$$10 \times 9 = \mathbf{90\%}$$

Written Practice 22

1. $(15 \times 12) - (15 + 12)$

$180 - 27$

153

2. $\mathbf{\frac{13}{50}}$

3.

$$1760 \times 26$$

10560
35200
45,760 yards

$$45{,}760 + 385 = \mathbf{46{,}145 \text{ yards}}$$

4.

12 apples

4 apples
4 apples
4 apples

$\frac{2}{3}$ were eaten (first two boxes)

$\frac{1}{3}$ were not eaten (last box)

8 apples

5.

16

4
4
4
4

$\frac{3}{4}$ of 16 (first three boxes)

$\frac{1}{4}$ of 16 (last box)

12

6.
$$\begin{array}{r} \$0.35 \\ 10\overline{)\$3.50} \\ \underline{3\ 0} \\ 50 \\ \underline{50} \\ 0 \end{array}$$

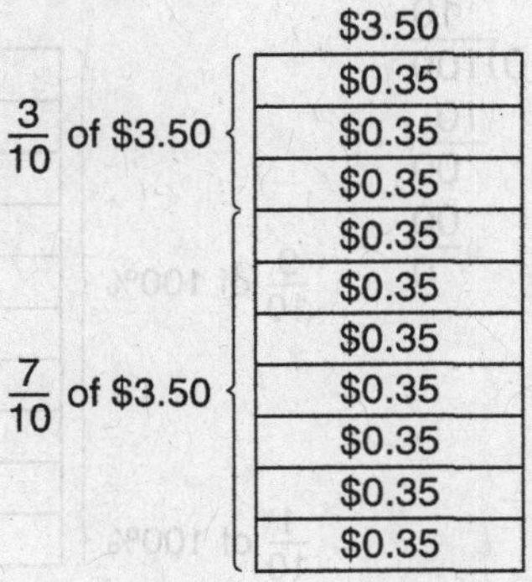

$$\begin{array}{r} \$0.35 \\ \times \quad 3 \\ \hline \mathbf{\$1.05} \end{array}$$

7.

700 ft

8.
$$\begin{array}{r} \overset{1}{1}5 \\ +\ \ 8 \\ \hline 23 \end{array} \qquad \text{check: } \begin{array}{r} \overset{1}{2}{}^{1}3 \\ -\ 1\ 5 \\ \hline 8 \end{array}$$

***w* = 23**

9.
$$\begin{array}{r} 345 \\ \times\ 15 \\ \hline 1725 \\ \underline{3450} \\ 5175 \end{array} \qquad \text{check: } \begin{array}{r} 345 \\ 15\overline{)5175} \\ \underline{45} \\ 67 \\ \underline{60} \\ 75 \\ \underline{75} \\ 0 \end{array}$$

***w* = 5175**

10.
$$\begin{array}{r} \$\overset{1}{0}.\overset{2}{3}6 \\ \$4.78 \\ +\ \$34.09 \\ \hline \mathbf{\$39.23} \end{array}$$

11.
$$\begin{array}{r} \mathbf{\$4.15} \\ 3\overline{)\$12.45} \\ \underline{12} \\ 0\,4 \\ \underline{3} \\ 15 \\ \underline{15} \\ 0 \end{array}$$

12.
$$\begin{array}{r} \mathbf{28\ R\ 20} \\ 35\overline{)1000} \\ \underline{70} \\ 300 \\ \underline{280} \\ 20 \end{array}$$

13. $\dfrac{7 + 9 + 14}{3} = \dfrac{30}{3} = \mathbf{10}$

14. **$45.00; First multiply 4 × $1.25 to get $5.00. Then multiply 9 × $5.00.**

15. **2**

16. Factors of 12
1, 2, 3, 4, 6, 12
Factors of 15
1, 3, 5, 15
GCF is **3**

17. **1, 2, 3, 5, 6, 10, 15, 30**

18. 2; Yes, the last digit is 0.
3; No, the sum of the digits is not divisible by 3.
5; Yes, the last digit is 0.
9; No, the sum of the digits is not divisible by 9.
10; Yes, the last digit is 0.
2, 5, 10

19.
$$\begin{array}{r} 20 \\ 5\overline{)100} \\ \underline{10} \\ 00 \\ \underline{00} \\ 0 \end{array}$$

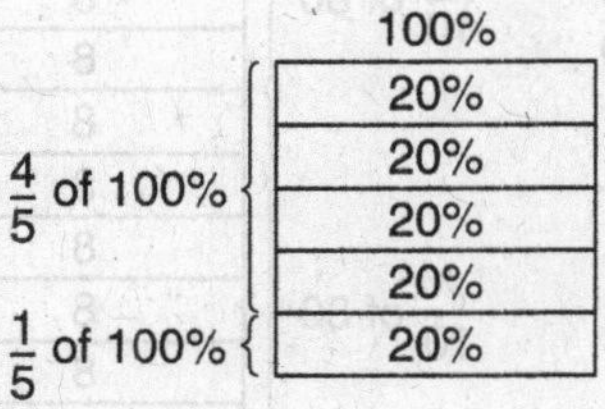

$$\begin{array}{r} 20\% \\ \times\quad 4 \\ \hline \mathbf{80\%} \end{array}$$

20. $\dfrac{1}{3}$ ⓧ $\dfrac{1}{2}$ → $\dfrac{1}{3} < \dfrac{1}{2}$

21. **C. 39**

22. $(3 + 3) - (3 \times 3)$
$6 - 9$
$\mathbf{-3}$

23. $\begin{array}{r} \overset{1}{4}3 \\ +\ 27 \\ \hline 70 \end{array}$ $\quad \begin{array}{r} 35 \\ 2\overline{)70} \\ 6 \\ \hline 10 \\ 10 \\ \hline 0 \end{array}$

24. 15 cm + 10 cm + 15 cm + 10 cm
= **50 cm**

25. $2\frac{1}{4}$ **in.**

26.

Corn bread

Wheat bread

A slice of wheat bread

27.

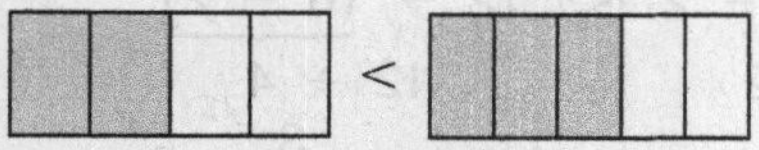

$\frac{2}{4}$ ⓒ< $\frac{3}{5}$

28. 1 year = 12 months

$\frac{1}{4}$ of a year { 3 months

$\frac{3}{4}$ of a year { 3 months, 3 months, 3 months

3 months

29. a. **8 bits**

b. **2 bits**

30. $c - t = p$
$p + t = c$
$t + p = c$

Practice Set 23

a. $\frac{\text{number of dogs}}{\text{number of cats}} = \frac{\mathbf{12}}{\mathbf{19}}$

b. $\frac{\text{number of girls}}{\text{number of boys}} = \frac{\mathbf{13}}{\mathbf{17}}$

$\begin{array}{r} \overset{2}{\cancel{3}}{}^{1}0 \\ -\ 1\ 7 \\ \hline 1\ 3 \end{array}$ girls

c. $\frac{\text{number of trucks}}{\text{number of cars}} = \frac{\mathbf{2}}{\mathbf{7}}$

d. $\text{time} = \frac{\text{distance}}{\text{rate}} = \frac{400 \text{ miles}}{50 \text{ mph}} =$ **8 hours**

e. $\frac{\$2.48}{4 \text{ qt}} =$ **\$0.62 per quart**

Written Practice 23

1. $\begin{array}{r} 30 \text{ cm} \\ \times\ 10 \text{ mm} \\ \hline \mathbf{300 \text{ mm}} \end{array}$

2. 30 problems

$\frac{2}{3}$ are finished { 10 problems, 10 problems

$\frac{1}{3}$ are not finished { 10 problems

20 problems

3. **About 100 yards**

4. $\text{mileage} = \frac{\text{distance}}{\text{fuel used}} = \frac{245 \text{ miles}}{7 \text{ gallons}}$
= **35 miles per gallon**

5. 25

$\frac{3}{5}$ of 25 { 5, 5, 5

$\frac{2}{5}$ of 25 { 5, 5

15

6.
```
      $3.60
10)$36.00
   30
    6 0
    6 0
      00
      00
       0
```

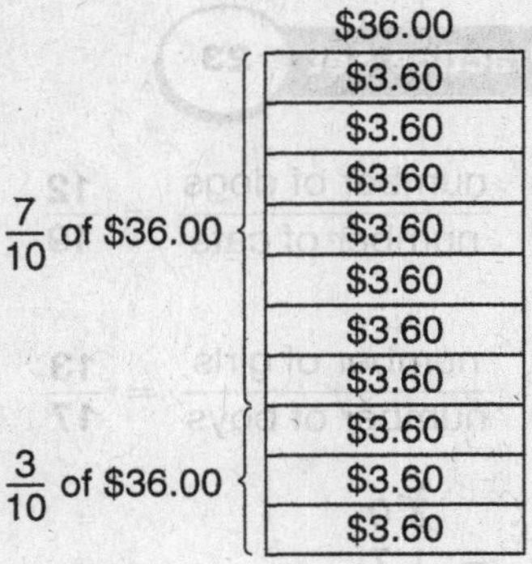


```
   $3.60
×      7
  $25.20
```

7. $\frac{7}{8}$

8. $1\frac{1}{8}$

9. **25%**

10.
```
   $3.75
×     16
   22 50
   37 50
  $60.00
```

11.
```
    $0.15
25)$3.75
    2 5
    1 25
    1 25
       0
```

12. **Millions**

13. **One way to find $\frac{2}{3}$ of a number is to first divide the number by 3; then multiply that answer by 2.**

14.
```
             1 00
$0.35)$35.00
        35
         0 0
         0 0
           00
           00
            0
```
check
```
   $0.35
×    100
  $35.00
```

$n = 100$

15.
```
   0 9 ¹1
  $1̸ 0̸. 2̸¹0
– $3. 4 6
  $6. 7 4
```
check:
```
   0 9 ¹1
  $1̸ 0̸. 2̸¹0
– $6. 7 4
  $3. 4 6
```
$m = \$6.74$

16. $\frac{3}{4}$ (<) 1

17.

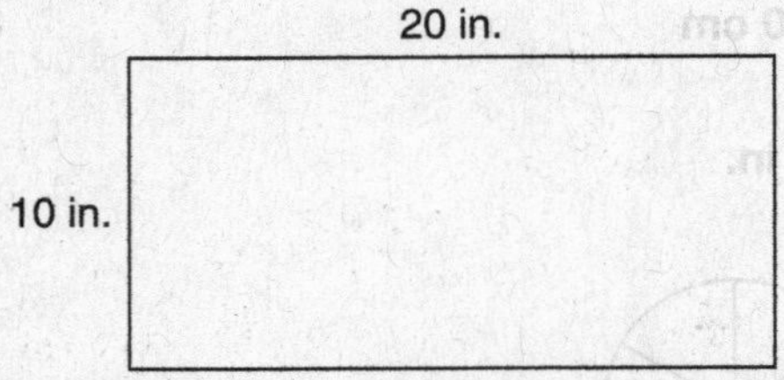

20 in. + 20 in. + 10 in. + 10 in. = **60 in.**

18. 2, 4, 8, 16, 32, 64 ....
64
To find a number, multiply the number before it by 2.

19. **Fahrenheit; Snow indicates a temperature at or below the freezing temperature of water, and 14° is below freezing on the Fahrenheit scale but far above freezing on the Celsius scale.**

20. $\underbrace{12 \div 6}_{2} - 2$ (<) $12 \div \underbrace{(6 - 2)}_{4}$

$2 - 2 = 0$ $12 \div 4 = 3$

21. Factors of 24
1, 2, 3, 4, 6, 8, 12, 24
Factors of 32
1, 2, 4, 8, 16, 32
GCF is **8**

22. 1 + 3 + 5 + 7 + 9 + 11 + 13 = **49**

23. a. **4**
b. **2**

24. $12\frac{1}{2}$**%**

25. $\frac{4}{8}$

26. $\frac{\text{competed in free style}}{\text{did not compete in free style}} = \frac{5}{11}$

```
  16
–  5
  11 did not compete
```

27. 23, 29

28. B.

29. 252; No, last digit is not a 5 or 0.
525; No, last digit is not even.
250; Yes, last digit is 0 and even.
C. 250

30. $\frac{\text{win}}{\text{loss}} = \mathbf{\frac{5}{9}}$

Early Finishers Solutions

$\frac{5}{6} \cdot 30$ students $=$ 25 students; 3×125 veggie sticks $=$ 375 veggie sticks

$375 \div 25 = 15$; Each student will eat 15 veggie sticks.

Practice Set 24

a. $\frac{3}{8} + \frac{4}{8} = \mathbf{\frac{7}{8}}$

b. $\frac{3}{4} + \frac{1}{4} = \frac{4}{4} = \mathbf{1}$

c. $\frac{1}{8} + \frac{1}{8} + \frac{1}{8} = \mathbf{\frac{3}{8}}$

d. $\frac{4}{8} - \frac{1}{8} = \mathbf{\frac{3}{8}}$

e. $\frac{3}{4} - \frac{2}{4} = \mathbf{\frac{1}{4}}$

f. $\frac{1}{4} - \frac{1}{4} = \frac{0}{4} = \mathbf{0}$

g. **Four eighths minus one eighth equals three eighths.**

Written Practice 24

1. $\$6.00 \times 5 = \$30.00$; $\$30.00 + \$5.00 = \mathbf{\$35.00}$

Multiplication pattern (equal groups); Addition pattern (combining)

2.

1 dozen eggs	
$\frac{3}{4}$ used	3 eggs
	3 eggs
	3 eggs
$\frac{1}{4}$ not used	3 eggs

9 eggs

3. $1760 \div 8 = 220$

$$\begin{array}{r} 220 \\ 8\overline{)1760} \\ \underline{16} \\ 16 \\ \underline{16} \\ 00 \\ \underline{0} \\ 0 \end{array}$$

220 yards; To find $\frac{1}{8}$ of 1760, I divided by 8.

4. $\frac{1}{4} + \frac{2}{4} = \mathbf{\frac{3}{4}}$

5. $\frac{7}{8} - \frac{4}{8} = \mathbf{\frac{3}{8}}$

6. $\frac{1}{2} + \frac{1}{2} = \frac{2}{2} = \mathbf{1}$

7. $\frac{1}{2} - \frac{1}{2} = \frac{0}{2} = \mathbf{0}$

8.

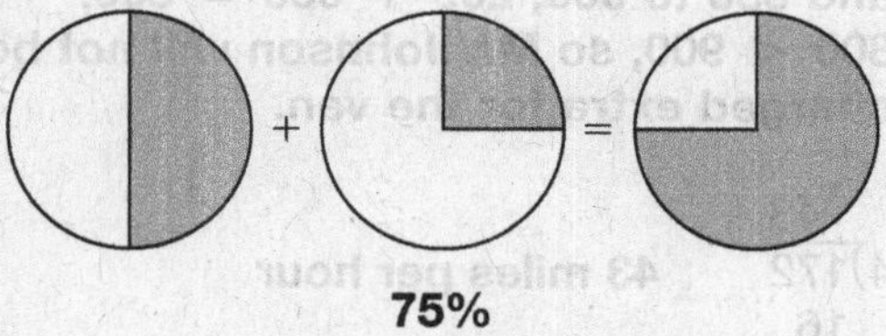

75%

Word problem: Answers will vary. See student work. Sample answer: $\frac{7}{8}$ of my family came to my party in two cars. If $\frac{4}{8}$ came in one car, what fraction came in the other car?

9. $\frac{\text{fiction books}}{\text{nonfiction books}} = \mathbf{\frac{41}{23}}$

10. **Add 123 and 321 and divide by 2.**

11. 25 feet $\times$ 4 = **100 feet**

12. **A. 21**

13.

$$9\overline{)1000} \quad \text{111 R 1}$$

$$\begin{array}{r} 9 \\ \hline 10 \\ 9 \\ \hline 10 \\ 9 \\ \hline 1 \end{array}$$

14.

$$32\overline{)22{,}422} \quad \text{700 R 22}$$

$$\begin{array}{r} 22\ 4 \\ \hline 02 \\ 00 \\ \hline 22 \\ 00 \\ \hline 22 \end{array}$$

15.

$$100\overline{)\$350.00} \quad \$3.50$$

$$\begin{array}{r} 300 \\ \hline 50\ 0 \\ 50\ 0 \\ \hline 00 \\ 00 \\ \hline 0 \end{array}$$

16. $\dfrac{1}{2} \bigcirc\!\!\!> \dfrac{1}{4}$

17. No; an estimate; I rounded 172 to 200 and 636 to 600; 200 + 600 = 800; 800 < 900, so Mr. Johnson will not be charged extra for the van.

18.

$$4\overline{)172} \quad \text{43 miles per hour}$$

$$\begin{array}{r} 43 \\ \hline 16 \\ \hline 12 \\ 12 \\ \hline 0 \end{array}$$

19. 44°F

20. 33,000,000

21. Factors of 21
1, 3, 7, 21
Factors of 28
1, 2, 4, 7, 14, 28
GCF is **7**

22. 123; No, the sum is not divisible by 9.
234; Yes, the sum is divisible by 9.
345; No the sum is not divisible by 9.
B. 234

23. $\dfrac{4}{4}$

24.

$$\begin{array}{r} 8 \\ \times\ 20 \\ \hline 160 \end{array} \qquad \text{check:} \qquad 8\overline{)160} \quad 20$$

$$\begin{array}{r} 16 \\ \hline 00 \\ 00 \\ \hline 0 \end{array}$$

$w = \textbf{160}$

25.

$$7\overline{)84} \quad 12 \qquad \text{check:} \qquad \begin{array}{r} 12 \\ \times\ 7 \\ \hline 84 \end{array}$$

$$\begin{array}{r} 7 \\ \hline 14 \\ 14 \\ \hline 0 \end{array}$$

$x = \textbf{12}$

26.

$$\begin{array}{r} 4\,\overset{7}{\cancel{8}}1 \\ -\ 3\ 7\ 6 \\ \hline 1\ 0\ 5 \end{array} \qquad \text{check:} \qquad \begin{array}{r} \overset{1}{3}76 \\ +\ 105 \\ \hline 481 \end{array}$$

$w = \textbf{105}$

27.

$$\begin{array}{r} \overset{1}{2}86 \\ +\ 592 \\ \hline 878 \end{array} \qquad \text{check:} \qquad \begin{array}{r} \overset{7}{\cancel{8}}\overset{1}{7}8 \\ -\ 2\ 8\ 6 \\ \hline 5\ 9\ 2 \end{array}$$

$m = \textbf{878}$

28. Madison

29.

$$\begin{array}{r} 14000 \\ -\ 10000 \\ \hline 4000 \end{array} \quad \textbf{About 4000 more people}$$

30.

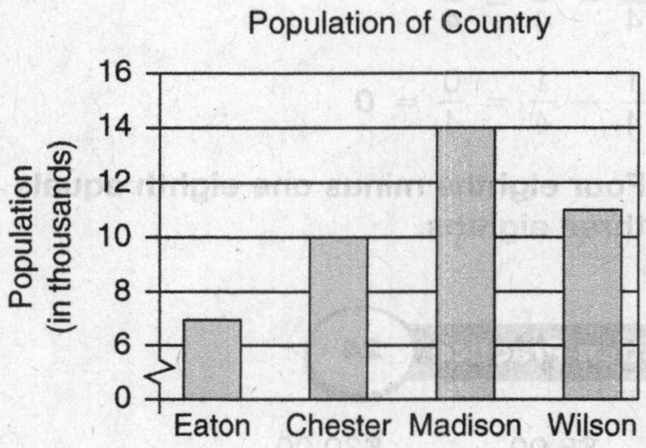

Population of Country

Early Finishers Solutions

a. $\dfrac{7}{8} \cdot 112$ members $= 98$ members

b. $11\overline{)98.00}$ $\dfrac{8.90}{}$ They will need 9 vans.

Practice Set 25

a. $\mathbf{3\frac{4}{8}}$ or $\mathbf{3\frac{1}{2}}$ **in.**

$$8\overline{)28}$$
$$\underline{24}$$
$$4$$

b. $\mathbf{14\frac{2}{7}\%}$

$$7\overline{)100}$$
$$\underline{7}$$
$$30$$
$$\underline{28}$$
$$2$$

c. $\mathbf{46\frac{7}{10}}$

$$10\overline{)467}$$
$$\underline{40}$$
$$67$$
$$\underline{60}$$
$$7$$

d.
12 × 1 = **12**
12 × 2 = **24**
12 × 3 = **36**
12 × 4 = **48**

e.
8 × 1 = **8**
8 × 2 = **16**
8 × 3 = **24**
8 × 4 = **32**
8 × 5 = **40**
8 × 6 = **48**

f.
8 × 3 = 24
12 × 2 = 24
24

g. $\mathbf{5\frac{5}{6}}$

$$6\overline{)35}$$
$$\underline{30}$$
$$5$$

h. $\mathbf{4\frac{9}{10}}$

$$10\overline{)49}$$
$$\underline{40}$$
$$9$$

i. $\mathbf{5\frac{5}{12}}$

$$12\overline{)65}$$
$$\underline{60}$$
$$5$$

Written Practice 25

1. $\left(\frac{1}{2} + \frac{1}{2}\right) - \left(\frac{1}{3} + \frac{1}{3}\right)$

$$\frac{2}{2} - \frac{2}{3}$$
$$1 - \frac{2}{3}$$
$$\frac{3}{3} - \frac{2}{3}$$
$$\mathbf{\frac{1}{3}}$$

2. **Carlos can find the average distance of the three punts by adding 35 yards, 30 yards, and 37 yards and then dividing the sum by 3.**

3. **149,600,000 kilometers**

4. $\frac{3}{8}$ in. + $\frac{1}{8}$ in. + $\frac{3}{8}$ in. + $\frac{1}{8}$ in. = $\frac{8}{8}$ in. or **1 in.**

5. **4 · *p* = 30**
$\mathbf{7\frac{2}{4}}$ or $\mathbf{7\frac{1}{2}}$ **inches**

$$4\overline{)30}$$
$$\underline{28}$$
$$2$$

6. $\frac{3}{3} - \frac{2}{3} = \mathbf{\frac{1}{3}}$

7. $\frac{1}{2}$ of 12 ⓖ $\frac{1}{3}$ of 12

$2\overline{)12}$ = 6; 12; 0 $\qquad$ $3\overline{)12}$ = 4; 12; 0

8.

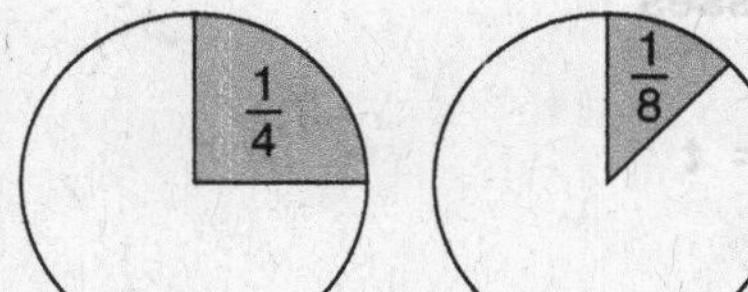

$\frac{1}{2}$ of $\frac{1}{2}$ $\qquad$ $\frac{1}{2}$ of $\frac{1}{4}$

$$\mathbf{\frac{1}{8}}$$

9. $9\overline{)100\%}$ = $\mathbf{11\frac{1}{9}\%}$

9
10
9
1

10. (a) **6**

(b) **3**

11. $\mathbf{\frac{1}{3}}$

12. $7\overline{)365}$ = $\mathbf{52\frac{1}{7}}$

35
15
14
1

13. $\frac{2}{3} + \frac{2}{3} + \frac{2}{3} = \frac{6}{3} = \mathbf{2}$

14. $\frac{6}{6} - \frac{5}{6} = \mathbf{\frac{1}{6}}$

15. $\underbrace{30 \times 40} \div 60$

$1200 \div 60$

20

16. $\frac{5}{12} - \frac{5}{12} = \frac{0}{12} = \mathbf{0}$

17. $\frac{\text{win}}{\text{loss}} = \mathbf{\frac{7}{13}}$

$\overset{1}{2}{}^{1}0$
$-\ \ 7$
1 3 losses

18. **10 · 25 = *t***

$0.25
× 10
$2.50

19. Factors of 24
1, 2, 3, 4, 6, 8, 12, 24
Factors of 30
1, 2, 3, 5, 6, 10, 15, 30
GCF is **6**

20. $100\overline{)100}$ = **1**

100
0

21. $\frac{8}{8} - \frac{5}{8} = \frac{3}{8}$

$m = \mathbf{\frac{3}{8}}$

check: $\frac{5}{8} + \frac{3}{8} = \frac{8}{8} = 1$

22. $12\overline{)144}$ = 12

12
24
24
0

check: $12\overline{)144}$ = 12

12
24
24
0

n = **12**

23.
3000
6000
+ 5000
14,000

24. $3\overline{)60}$ = **20**

6
00
00
0

60 students

$\frac{2}{3}$ liked peaches { 20 students / 20 students

$\frac{1}{3}$ did not like peaches { 20 students

40 students

25. **About 2 inches;**
$1\frac{14}{16}$ or $1\frac{7}{8}$ inches

26. **One possibility: Jan could draw segments from the center of the circle to the places where 12, 4, and 8 would be on a clock face.**

27. $4\overline{)15}$ = $\mathbf{3\frac{3}{4}}$

12
3

28. 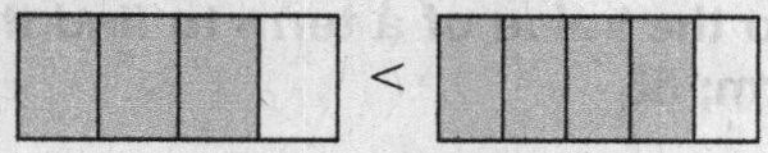

$\frac{3}{4} \bigcirc\!\!\!\!< \frac{4}{5}$

29. $25 \times 1 = \mathbf{25}$
$25 \times 2 = \mathbf{50}$
$25 \times 3 = \mathbf{75}$
$25 \times 4 = \mathbf{100}$

30. 910; No, sum is not divisible by 9.
8910; Yes, sum is divisible by 9 and last digit is 0.
78,910; No, sum is not divisible by 9.
B. 8910

The sum of the digits is 18 which is divisible by 9, so the number is divisible by 9, and the last digit is zero so the number is divisible by 10.

Practice Set 26

a. $\mathbf{\frac{1}{4}}$

b. $\mathbf{\frac{3}{4}}$

c.
$$\begin{array}{r} 12\frac{1}{2}\% \\ +\ 12\frac{1}{2}\% \\ \hline 24\frac{2}{2} \end{array}$$
$\frac{2}{2} = 1$
$24 + 1 = \mathbf{25\%}$

d.
$$\begin{array}{r} 16\frac{2}{3}\% \\ +\ 66\frac{2}{3}\% \\ \hline 82\frac{4}{3} \end{array}$$
$\frac{4}{3} = 1\frac{1}{3}$
$82 + 1\frac{1}{3} = \mathbf{83\frac{1}{3}\%}$

e.
$$\begin{array}{r} 3\frac{3}{4} \\ +\ 2\frac{3}{4} \\ \hline 5\frac{6}{4} \end{array}$$
$\frac{6}{4} = 1\frac{2}{4} = 1\frac{1}{2}$
$5 + 1\frac{1}{2} = \mathbf{6\frac{1}{2}}$

f.
$$\begin{array}{r} 1\frac{1}{8} \\ +\ 2\frac{7}{8} \\ \hline 3\frac{8}{8} \end{array}$$
$\frac{8}{8} = 1$
$3 + 1 = \mathbf{4}$

g.
$$\begin{array}{r} 3 \\ +\ 2\frac{2}{3} \\ \hline \mathbf{5\frac{2}{3}} \end{array}$$

h.
$$\begin{array}{r} \frac{3}{4} \\ +\ 4 \\ \hline \mathbf{4\frac{3}{4}} \end{array}$$

i. One and one eighth plus two and seven eighths equals four.

Written Practice 26

1.
$$\begin{array}{r} 3\frac{3}{4}\text{ mi} \\ +\ 3\frac{3}{4}\text{ mi} \\ \hline 6\frac{6}{4}\text{ mi} \end{array}$$
$\frac{6}{4} = 1\frac{2}{4} = 1\frac{1}{2}$
$6 + 1\frac{1}{2} = \mathbf{7\frac{1}{2}}$ **miles**

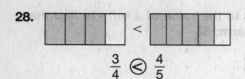

2.
$$\begin{array}{r} \mathbf{3}\text{ years old} \\ 12\overline{)36} \\ \underline{36} \\ 0 \end{array}$$

Solutions

3. 1 dozen = 12
$\frac{1}{2}$ dozen = 6
12 + 12 + 6 = **30 balloons**

Yes, there are 30 balloons and 30 children so there are enough balloons for each child to have one.

4. 1 m = 100 cm
1 km = 1000 m
$$\begin{array}{r} 1000 \\ \times \quad 100 \\ \hline \textbf{100,000 centimeters} \end{array}$$

5. $\frac{2}{3}$ in. + $\frac{2}{3}$ in. + $\frac{2}{3}$ in. = $\frac{6}{3}$ in. = $\frac{2}{1}$ in.
= **2 in.**

6. $\frac{1}{2} + \frac{1}{2} \; \textcircled{>} \; \frac{1}{2} \times \frac{1}{2}$
$\frac{2}{2}$ $\qquad \frac{1}{4}$
1

7. $$\begin{array}{r} 5\frac{7}{8} \\ + \quad 7\frac{5}{8} \\ \hline 12\frac{12}{8} \end{array}$$
$\frac{12}{8} = \frac{3}{2} = 1\frac{1}{2}$
$12 + 1\frac{1}{2} = \mathbf{13\frac{1}{2}}$

8. $$\begin{array}{r} 12\frac{1}{2}\% \\ 12\frac{1}{2}\% \\ + \quad 12\frac{1}{2}\% \\ \hline 36\frac{3}{2}\% \end{array}$$
$\frac{3}{2} = 1\frac{1}{2}$
$36 + 1\frac{1}{2} = \mathbf{37\frac{1}{2}\%}$

9. $\mathbf{\frac{12}{12}}$

10. Factors of 15
1, 3, 5, 15
Factors of 25
1, 5, 25
GCF is **5**

11. **Add 8 to the value of a term to find the next term; 56**

12. $$\begin{array}{r} \mathbf{2\frac{4}{5}} \\ 5\overline{)14} \\ \underline{10} \\ 4 \end{array}$$

13. $\frac{2}{5} + \frac{4}{5} = \frac{6}{5} = \mathbf{1\frac{1}{5}}$

14. $1 - \frac{2}{3}$ $\qquad$ check: $\frac{2}{3} + \frac{1}{3} = \frac{3}{3} = 1$
$\frac{3}{3} - \frac{2}{3} = \frac{1}{3}$
$n = \mathbf{\frac{1}{3}}$

15. Factors of 12
1, 2, 3, 4, 6, 12
Factors of 18
1, 2, 3, 6, 9, 18
GCF is **6**

16. $1 - \frac{3}{4}$
$\frac{4}{4} - \frac{3}{4} = \mathbf{\frac{1}{4}}$

17. $$\begin{array}{r} 3\frac{3}{4} \\ + \; 3 \\ \hline \mathbf{6\frac{3}{4}} \end{array}$$

18. $2\frac{1}{2} - 2\frac{1}{2} = \mathbf{0}$

19. 4671; No, the last digit is not even.
3858; Yes; the last digit is even and the sum of the digits is divisible by 3.
6494; No, the sum of the digits is not divisible by 3.
B. 3858

20. **31, 37**

21. $$\begin{array}{r} 5000 \\ - \; 4000 \\ \hline \mathbf{1000} \end{array}$$

22. $\mathbf{\frac{3}{4}}$

23. $\begin{array}{r} \$2.39 \\ \times \quad 4 \\ \hline \mathbf{\$9.56} \end{array}$

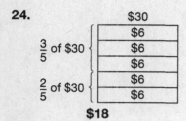

24.

	$30
$\frac{3}{5}$ of $30	$6
	$6
	$6
$\frac{2}{5}$ of $30	$6
	$6

$18

25. a. 25 millimeters

b. 1 inch

26. −1, 0, $\frac{1}{2}$, 1

27. $\begin{array}{r} 55 \text{ inches} \\ -\ 25 \text{ inches} \\ \hline \end{array}$

About 30 inches

28. $\begin{array}{r} \overset{1}{2}5 \text{ in.} \\ 55 \text{ in.} \\ +\ 40 \text{ in.} \\ \hline 120 \text{ in.} \end{array}$ $\begin{array}{r} \mathbf{40 \text{ inches}} \\ 3\overline{)120} \\ \underline{12} \\ 00 \\ \underline{00} \\ 0 \end{array}$

29. $\begin{array}{r} \overset{3}{\cancel{4}}{}^{1}0 \text{ inches} \\ -\ 2\ 5 \text{ inches} \\ \hline \end{array}$

About 1 5 inches

30. Answers will vary. See student work. Sample answer: What was the approximate total rainfall during the first three years?

$\begin{array}{r} \overset{1}{2}5 \text{ in.} \\ 55 \text{ in.} \\ +\ 40 \text{ in.} \\ \hline \end{array}$

About 120 inches

Practice Set 27

a. Diameter

b. Circumference

c. Radius

d. $\begin{array}{r} \mathbf{5 \text{ in.}} \\ 2\overline{)10} \\ \underline{10} \\ 0 \end{array}$ **The radius is half the diameter because two radii in opposite directions form a diameter.**

Written Practice 27

1. $\underbrace{(55 + 45)}_{100} \times \underbrace{(55 - 45)}_{10}$

100 × 10

1000

2.

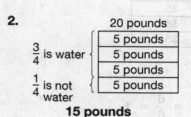

	20 pounds
$\frac{3}{4}$ is water	5 pounds
	5 pounds
	5 pounds
$\frac{1}{4}$ is not water	5 pounds

15 pounds

3. 306 − 249 = *d*

or

306 − *d* = 249

$\begin{array}{r} \overset{2}{\cancel{3}}\ \overset{9}{\cancel{0}}{}^{1}6 \\ -\ 2\ 4\ 9 \\ \hline \mathbf{5\ 7} \end{array}$ **students went outside**

4. $\begin{array}{r} \mathbf{2\frac{1}{2} \text{ in.}} \\ 2\overline{)5} \\ \underline{4} \\ 1 \end{array}$ **The diameter is twice the radius of a circle.**

5. 122; No, the sum is not divisible by 3.
123; No, the last digit is not even.
132; Yes, the sum is divisible by 3 and the last digit is even.
C. 132

6. 1,230,000

7. 10*p* = $12.90

$\begin{array}{r} \mathbf{\$\,1.29} \\ 10\overline{)\$12.90} \\ \underline{10} \\ 29 \\ \underline{20} \\ 90 \\ \underline{90} \\ 0 \end{array}$

$1.29 per pound

8. **24**

9.

65

$\frac{3}{5}$ of 65	13
	13
	13
$\frac{2}{5}$ of 65	13
	13

39

10.

$15

$\frac{2}{3}$ of $15	$5
	$5
$\frac{1}{3}$ of $15	$5

$10

11. $\frac{1}{6} + \frac{2}{6} + \frac{3}{6} = \frac{6}{6} = \mathbf{1}$

12. $\frac{7}{8} - \frac{3}{8} = \frac{4}{8} = \mathbf{\frac{1}{2}}$

13. $\frac{6}{6} - \frac{5}{6} = \mathbf{\frac{1}{6}}$

14. $\frac{2}{8} + \frac{5}{8} = \mathbf{\frac{7}{8}}$

15. (a) **8**

(b) **4**

16. $\mathbf{\frac{2}{3}}$

17. $\mathbf{\frac{1}{8}}$

18. $\mathbf{\frac{1}{2}}$

19. $52\overline{)2100}$ = **40 R 20**

$$\begin{array}{r} 208 \\ \hline 20 \\ 00 \\ \hline 20 \end{array}$$

20. $4\overline{)36}$ = **9 inches**

$$\begin{array}{r} 36 \\ \hline 0 \end{array}$$

21. $6\overline{)7}$ = $\mathbf{1\frac{1}{6}}$

$$\begin{array}{r} 6 \\ \hline 1 \end{array}$$

22. $18\overline{)432}$ = **24**

$$\begin{array}{r} 36 \\ \hline 72 \\ 72 \\ \hline 0 \end{array}$$

23. $\underbrace{(55 + 45)}_{100} \div \underbrace{(55 - 45)}_{10}$

10

24. 502; No, the last digit is not 0.
205; No, the last digit is not 0.
250; Yes, the last digit is 0.
C. 250

25. **One method is to add the digits of the number. If the sum of the digits is divisible by 9, the number is also divisible by 9.**

26. **2**

27. **Circumference**

28. $\mathbf{\frac{4}{5}}$ **There are four even numbers (2, 4, 6, 8) and five odd numbers (1, 3, 5, 7, 9), so the ratio of even to odd is 4 to 5.**

29.

$$\begin{array}{r} 37\frac{1}{2}\% \\ -\ 12\frac{1}{2}\% \\ \hline 25\frac{0}{2}\% \end{array}$$

25%

30.
$$\begin{array}{r} 33\frac{1}{3}\% \\ +\ 16\frac{2}{3}\% \\ \hline 49\frac{3}{3}\% \end{array}$$
$\frac{3}{3} = 1$

$49 + 1 =$ **50%**

Early Finishers Solutions

$2\frac{1}{4} + \frac{3}{4} + 1\frac{3}{4} = 3 + 1\frac{3}{4} = 4\frac{3}{4}$; $4\frac{3}{4}$ cups

Practice Set 28

a. **Observe students.**

b. **Obtuse**

c. **Right**

d. **Acute**

e. 

Obtuse angle

f. 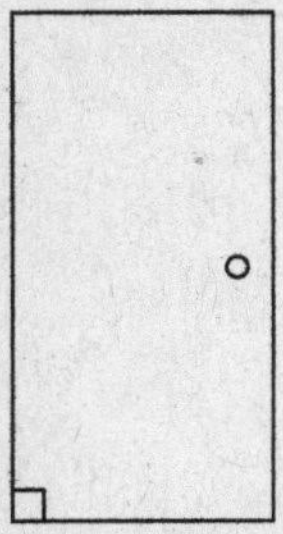

Right angle

g. $\angle 1$ and $\angle 3$

h. 

i. 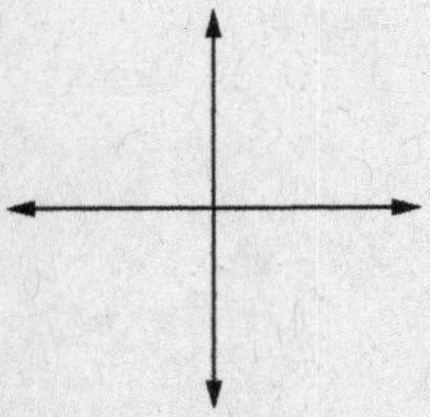

j. $\angle F$ (or $\angle HFG$ or $\angle GFH$)

k. $\angle G$ (or $\angle FGH$ or $\angle HGF$)

Written Practice 28

1. $\frac{1}{3} + \frac{2}{3} + \frac{3}{3} = \frac{6}{3} =$ **2**

2. **8 million people; Answers will vary. See student work. Sample answer: I found $\frac{1}{5}$ of 20 million by dividing 20 by 5 and got 4 million. Then to find $\frac{2}{5}$ I multiplied 4 million by 2 and got 8 million.**

3. $32g = 768$

24 peanuts
$$\begin{array}{r} 24 \\ 32\overline{)768} \\ 64 \\ \hline 128 \\ 128 \\ \hline 0 \end{array}$$

4. **(current year) − 1776 = *d***

5.
$$\begin{array}{r} 7\frac{2}{3} \\ 3\overline{)23} \\ 21 \\ \hline 2 \end{array}$$

6.
$$\begin{array}{r} 1\frac{2}{3} \\ +\ 1\frac{2}{3} \\ \hline 2\frac{4}{3} \end{array}$$
$\frac{4}{3} = 1\frac{1}{3}$

$2 + 1\frac{1}{3} =$ $\mathbf{3\frac{1}{3}}$

7.
$$\begin{array}{r} 3 \\ +\ 4\frac{2}{3} \\ \hline \mathbf{7\frac{2}{3}} \end{array}$$

8.
$$\begin{array}{r} 3\frac{5}{6} \\ -\ 1\frac{4}{6} \\ \hline 2\frac{1}{6} \end{array}$$

9. $\frac{1}{2}$

10.

	$24.00
$\frac{2}{3}$ of $24.00	$8.00
	$8.00
$\frac{1}{3}$ of $24.00	$8.00

$16.00

11. a.
$$\begin{array}{r} 10\% \\ 10\overline{)100\%} \\ \underline{10} \\ 00 \\ \underline{00} \\ 0 \end{array}$$

$$\begin{array}{r} 10\% \\ \times\quad 3 \\ \hline \mathbf{30\%} \end{array}$$

12. $\frac{1}{4}$

13.
$$\begin{array}{r} 26 \\ \times\ 11 \\ \hline 26 \\ 260 \\ \hline \end{array}$$
286 miles

14. $1 - \frac{1}{4}$

$\frac{4}{4} - \frac{1}{4} = \frac{3}{4}$

$m = \mathbf{\frac{3}{4}}$

check: $\frac{1}{4} + \frac{3}{4} = \frac{4}{4} = 1$

15.
$$\begin{array}{r} \overset{3}{\not4}\,\overset{11}{\not2}\,{}^{1}3 \\ -\ 2\ 9\ 7 \\ \hline 1\ 2\ 6 \end{array}$$
$w = \mathbf{126}$

check:
$$\begin{array}{r} \overset{3}{\not4}\,\overset{11}{\not2}\,{}^{1}3 \\ -\ 1\ 2\ 6 \\ \hline 2\ 9\ 7 \end{array}$$

16. a. $\angle PSQ$ or $\angle QSP$

b. $\angle QSR$ or $\angle RSQ$

17.
$$\begin{array}{r} 22 \\ 20 \\ 23 \\ +\ 23 \\ \hline 88 \end{array} \qquad \begin{array}{r} \mathbf{22}\text{ correct answers} \\ 4\overline{)88} \\ \underline{8} \\ 08 \\ \underline{8} \\ 0 \end{array}$$

18.
$$\begin{array}{r} \mathbf{12}\text{ inches} \\ 3\overline{)36} \\ \underline{3} \\ 06 \\ \underline{6} \\ 0 \end{array}$$

19. Factors of 24
1, 2, 3, 4, 6, 8, 12, 24
Factors of 36
1, 2, 3, 4, 6, 9, 12, 18, 36
Factors of 60
1, 2, 3, 4, 5, 6, 10, 12, 15, 20, 30, 60
GCF is **12**

20.
$$\begin{array}{r} \overset{0}{\not1}\,\overset{9}{\not0},{}^{1}0\,\overset{0}{\not1}\,{}^{1}0 \\ -\quad 9\ 9\ 0\ 9 \\ \hline \mathbf{1\ 0\ 1} \end{array}$$

21. $\underbrace{(100 \times 100)}_{10{,}000} - \underbrace{(100 \times 99)}_{9900}$

100

22.

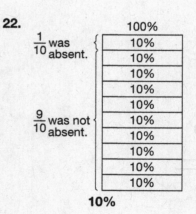

	100%
$\frac{1}{10}$ was absent.	10%
$\frac{9}{10}$ was not absent.	10%
	10%
	10%
	10%
	10%
	10%
	10%
	10%
	10%

10%

23.
$$\begin{array}{r} 509\frac{7}{10} \\ 10\overline{)5097} \\ \underline{50} \\ 09 \\ \underline{0} \\ 97 \\ \underline{90} \\ 7 \end{array}$$

24.

24 eggs

$\frac{3}{4}$ of 24	6 eggs
	6 eggs
	6 eggs
$\frac{1}{4}$ of 24	6 eggs

18 eggs

25. a. $\mathbf{3\frac{3}{16}}$ **inches**

b. 8 centimeters

26.
$6 \times 1 = 6 \quad 8 \times 1 = 8$
$6 \times 2 = 12 \quad 8 \times 2 = 16$
$6 \times 3 = 18 \quad 8 \times 3 = 24$
$6 \times 4 = 24 \quad 8 \times 4 = 32$
$6 \times 5 = 30 \quad 8 \times 5 = 40$
6, 12, 18, (24), 30
8, 16, (24), 32, 40

27. $\mathbf{\frac{1}{6}}$

28.
$$\begin{array}{r} 13 \\ -\ \ 7 \\ \hline 6 \end{array}$$ white stripes

$$\frac{\text{red stripes}}{\text{white stripes}} = \mathbf{\frac{7}{6}}$$

29. $\mathbf{3 \cdot 3 \cdot 3 = 27}$

30. 234; Yes, sum of digits is divisible by 9.
345; No, sum of digits is not divisible by 9.
567; Yes, sum of digits is divisible by 9.
B. 345

Practice Set 29

a. $\frac{1}{2} \times \frac{4}{5} = \frac{4}{10}$

$\frac{4 \div 2}{10 \div 2} = \mathbf{\frac{2}{5}}$

b. $\frac{1}{4} \times \frac{2}{3} = \frac{2}{12}$

$\frac{2 \div 2}{12 \div 2} = \mathbf{\frac{1}{6}}$

c. $\frac{2}{3} \times \frac{3}{4} = \frac{6}{12}$

$\frac{6 \div 6}{12 \div 6} = \mathbf{\frac{1}{2}}$

d. $\frac{5}{6} \times \frac{6}{5} = \frac{30}{30}$

$$\begin{array}{r} \mathbf{1} \\ 30\overline{)30} \\ \underline{30} \\ 0 \end{array}$$

e. $\frac{5}{1} \times \frac{2}{3} = \frac{10}{3}$

$$\begin{array}{r} \mathbf{3\frac{1}{3}} \\ 3\overline{)10} \\ \underline{9} \\ 1 \end{array}$$

f. $\frac{2}{1} \times \frac{4}{3} = \frac{8}{3}$

$$\begin{array}{r} \mathbf{2\frac{2}{3}} \\ 3\overline{)8} \\ \underline{6} \\ 2 \end{array}$$

g. $\frac{9 \div 3}{12 \div 3} = \mathbf{\frac{3}{4}}$

h. $\frac{6 \div 2}{10 \div 2} = \mathbf{\frac{3}{5}}$

i. $\frac{18 \div 6}{24 \div 6} = \mathbf{\frac{3}{4}}$

j.
$$\begin{array}{r} 30 \\ -\ 20 \\ \hline 10 \end{array}$$ boys

$$\frac{\text{number of boys}}{\text{number of girls}} = \frac{10}{20} = \mathbf{\frac{1}{2}}$$

Solutions

Written Practice 29

1.
$$\begin{array}{r} 2000 \\ \times \quad 8 \\ \hline \end{array}$$
16,000 pounds

2.
$$\begin{array}{r} 16 \\ \times\ 16 \\ \hline 96 \\ 160 \\ \hline \end{array}$$
256 dried beans

3.
$$\left(\frac{1}{2}+\frac{1}{2}\right)-\left(\frac{1}{2}\times\frac{1}{2}\right)$$
$$\frac{2}{2}-\frac{1}{4}$$
$$1-\frac{1}{4}$$
$$\frac{4}{4}-\frac{1}{4}$$
$$\mathbf{\frac{3}{4}}$$

4. $\frac{\text{win}}{\text{loss}} = \frac{6}{8} = \mathbf{\frac{3}{4}}$

5. $\frac{16 \div 8}{24 \div 8} = \mathbf{\frac{2}{3}}$

6. $\frac{1}{8} + \frac{3}{8} = \frac{4}{8}$
$\frac{4 \div 4}{8 \div 4} = \mathbf{\frac{1}{2}}$

7. $\frac{1}{2} \times \frac{2}{3} = \frac{2}{6}$
$\frac{2 \div 2}{6 \div 2} = \mathbf{\frac{1}{3}}$

8. $\frac{7}{12} - \frac{3}{12} = \frac{4}{12}$
$\frac{4 \div 4}{12 \div 4} = \mathbf{\frac{1}{3}}$

9.
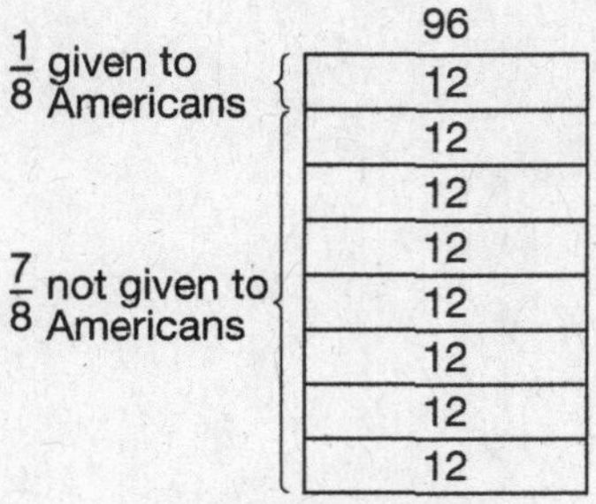

12 prizes

10. **. . . , 13, 16, 19, . . . Add 3 to a term to find the next term.**

11.
$$\begin{array}{r} 12 \\ -\ 5 \\ \hline 7 \end{array}$$
$\mathbf{\frac{7}{12}}$

12.
$$\begin{array}{r} \$3.60 \\ \times \quad 100 \\ \hline \end{array}$$
$360.00

13.
$$\begin{array}{r} \mathbf{500} \\ 100\overline{)50,000} \\ 50\,0 \\ \hline 00 \\ 00 \\ \hline 00 \\ 00 \\ \hline 0 \end{array}$$

14.
$$\begin{array}{r} 4\frac{2}{4} = \mathbf{4\frac{1}{2}} \\ 4\overline{)18} \\ 16 \\ \hline 2 \end{array}$$

15.
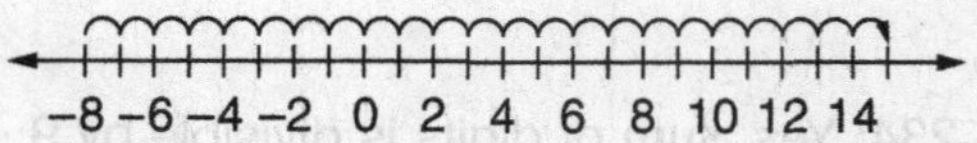

23°F

16. $m + \underbrace{496 + 2684}_{} = 3217$
$m + 3180 = 3217$

$$\begin{array}{r} 3\,2\,1\,7 \\ -\ 3\,1\,8\,0 \\ \hline 3\,7 \end{array}$$

m = **37**

check:
$$\begin{array}{r} 37 \\ 496 \\ +\ 2684 \\ \hline 3217 \end{array}$$

17.
$$\begin{array}{r} 1000 \\ -\ 857 \\ \hline 143 \end{array} \qquad \text{check: } \begin{array}{r} 1000 \\ -\ 143 \\ \hline 857 \end{array}$$
***n* = 143**

18.
$$\begin{array}{r} 20 \\ 24\overline{)480} \\ 48 \\ \hline 00 \\ 00 \\ \hline 0 \end{array} \qquad \text{check: } \begin{array}{r} 24 \\ \times\ 20 \\ \hline 480 \end{array}$$
***x* = 20**

19. $\underbrace{7 \cdot 11} \cdot 13$
$77 \cdot 13$
1001

20. **To estimate 4963 ÷ 39, first round 4963 to 5000 and round 39 to 40. Then divide 5000 by 40.**

21. $\frac{2}{3} \times \frac{3}{2}$ ⊜ 1
$\frac{6}{6} = 1$

22. 10 mm + 10 mm = 20 mm
60 mm − 20 mm = 40 mm
40 mm ÷ 2 = **20 mm**

23.
$$\begin{array}{r} 12 \\ -\ 40 \\ \hline \mathbf{-\ 28} \end{array}$$

24. $\left(\frac{1}{2} \times \frac{1}{2}\right) - \frac{1}{4}$
$\frac{1}{4} - \frac{1}{4}$
0

25. **a.** **∠*A*** and **∠*C***
b. **∠*B*** and **∠*D***

26. $\frac{2}{3} \times \frac{3}{5} = \frac{6}{15}$
$\frac{6 \div 3}{15 \div 3} = \mathbf{\frac{2}{5}}$

27. $\frac{3}{4} \times \frac{4}{3} = \frac{12}{12}$
$\frac{12 \div 12}{12 \div 12} = \mathbf{1}$

28.
$$\begin{array}{r} 12 \\ 2\overline{)24} \\ 2 \\ \hline 04 \\ 4 \\ \hline 0 \end{array} \qquad \frac{\text{radius}}{\text{diameter}} = \frac{12}{24} = \mathbf{\frac{1}{2}}$$

29.

Acute angle

30.
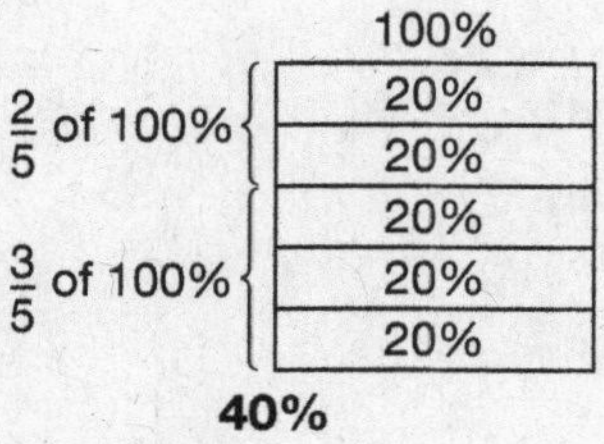

Sample answer: A whole circle is 100%, so $\frac{1}{5}$ of a circle is 20% and $\frac{2}{5}$ is 40%.

<u>Early Finishers Solutions</u>

$14 \cdot \frac{2}{7} = 4$ guards

$14 \cdot \frac{1}{2} = 7$ forwards

14 − (7 + 4) = 3 centers

Practice Set 30

a. Multiples of 6: 6, 12, 18, ㉔, 30, 36, . . .
Multiples of 8: 8, 16, ㉔, 32, 40, 48, . . .
LCM is **24**

b. Multiples of 3: 3, 6, 9, 12, ⑮, 18, 21, . . .
Multiples of 5: 5, 10, ⑮, 20, 25, 30, . . .
LCM is **15**

c. Multiples of 5: 5, (10), 15, 20, 25, . . .
Multiples of 10: (10), 20, 30, 40, 50, . . .
LCM is **10**

d. $\frac{\mathbf{1}}{\mathbf{6}}$

e. $\frac{\mathbf{3}}{\mathbf{2}}$

f. $\frac{\mathbf{5}}{\mathbf{8}}$

g. $\frac{\mathbf{3}}{\mathbf{1}}$

h. $\frac{3}{8} \times \frac{\mathbf{8}}{\mathbf{3}} = 1$

i. $4 \times \frac{\mathbf{1}}{\mathbf{4}} = 1$

j. $\frac{\mathbf{6}}{\mathbf{1}} \times \frac{1}{6} = 1$

k. $\frac{\mathbf{8}}{\mathbf{7}} \times \frac{7}{8} = 1$

l. $\frac{\mathbf{5}}{\mathbf{2}}$

m. $\frac{\mathbf{12}}{\mathbf{5}}$

Written Practice 30

1. 3, 6, 9, (12)
4, 8, (12)
$12 - 12 = \mathbf{0}$

2. 117 pounds

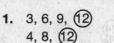

$\frac{2}{3}$ is water. { 39 pounds | 39 pounds }
$\frac{1}{3}$ is not water. { 39 pounds }

about 78 pounds

3. $$\begin{array}{r} 8 \\ 15\overline{)120} \\ \underline{120} \\ 0 \end{array}$$

$42 \cdot 8 = p$

$$\begin{array}{r} \overset{1}{4}2 \\ \times \quad 8 \\ \hline \end{array}$$
336 pieces of popcorn

4. $12 \times 1 = \mathbf{12}$
$12 \times 2 = \mathbf{24}$
$12 \times 3 = \mathbf{36}$
$12 \times 4 = \mathbf{48}$

5. Multiples of 4: 4, 8, (12), 16, 20, 24, 28, . . .
Multiples of 6: 6, (12), 18, 24, 30, 36, . . .
LCM is **12**

6. $$\begin{array}{r} \overset{5}{\cancel{6}}\,{}^{1}0 \\ -\;1\;2 \\ \hline 4\;8 \end{array}$$ $\frac{\text{commercial time}}{\text{noncommercial time}} = \frac{\mathbf{12}}{\mathbf{48}} = \frac{\mathbf{1}}{\mathbf{4}}$

$\frac{12 \div 12}{48 \div 12} = \frac{1}{4}$

Sample answer: An hour is 60 minutes, so if 12 minutes were commercials, then 48 minutes were not commercials.

7. $\frac{2}{5} + \frac{2}{5} + \frac{2}{5} = \frac{6}{5} = \mathbf{1\frac{1}{5}}$

8. $\frac{10}{10} - \frac{1}{10} = \frac{\mathbf{9}}{\mathbf{10}}$

9. $\frac{11}{12} - \frac{1}{12} = \frac{10}{12}$
$\frac{10 \div 2}{12 \div 2} = \frac{\mathbf{5}}{\mathbf{6}}$

10. $\frac{3}{4} \times \frac{4}{3} = \frac{12}{12}$
$\frac{12 \div 12}{12 \div 12} = \frac{1}{1} = \mathbf{1}$

11. $\frac{5}{1} \times \frac{3}{4} = \frac{15}{4}$

$4\overline{)15}$ = $3\frac{3}{4}$

12

3

12. $\frac{5}{2} \times \frac{5}{3} = \frac{25}{6}$

$6\overline{)25}$ = $4\frac{1}{6}$

24

1

13. Factors of 24: 1, 2, 3, 4, 6, 8, 12, 24

8

14.

$3.00

$24.00

\+ $6.50

$33.50

15.

$5.00

− $1.50

$3.50

16.

600

× 400

240,000

17. $\angle C$

18. $\frac{2}{3} \times \frac{2}{3}$ ⓐ $\frac{2}{3} \times 1$, where ⓐ is a circled $<$

$\frac{4}{9}$ $\quad \frac{2}{3} \times \frac{3}{3} = \frac{6}{9}$

19. $100\overline{)500,000}$ = **5,000**

500

00

00

00

00

00

00

0

20. $35\overline{)8540}$ = **244**

70

154

140

140

140

0

21. $7\overline{)100\%}$ = **$14\frac{2}{7}\%$**

7

30

28

2

22. $\frac{4 \div 4}{12 \div 4} = \frac{\mathbf{1}}{\mathbf{3}}$

23.

375

632

\+ 571

1578

$3\overline{)1578}$ = **526**

15

07

6

18

18

0

24. $6\overline{)36}$ = **6 inches**

36

0

25. **1**

26. $\frac{\mathbf{5}}{\mathbf{2}}$

27. $\frac{\mathbf{8}}{\mathbf{3}}$

28. $\frac{\mathbf{1}}{\mathbf{2}}$

29. $10\overline{)45}$ = $4\frac{5}{10}$ = **$4\frac{1}{2}$**

40

5

30. $\frac{3}{4} \times \frac{4}{1} = \frac{12}{4} = \frac{3}{1} =$ **3 inches**

Solutions

Early Finishers Solutions

a. 90 sandwiches; To find the number of sandwiches they should make, find the least common multiple of 10 and 18. Since 90 is the LCM that is greater than 80, they should make 90 sandwiches to have no left over slices.

b. $90 \div 10 = 9$ packages of bread
$90 \div 18 = 5$ packages of cheese

Investigation 3

1. 15°, acute

2. 45°, acute

3. 90°, right

4. 142°, obtuse

5. 38°, acute

6. 135°, obtuse

7.

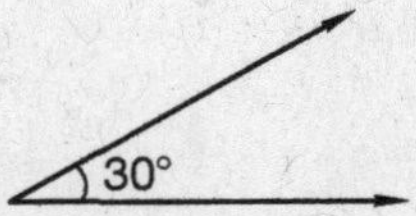

8.

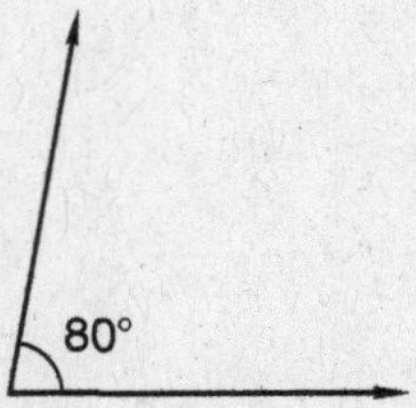

9.

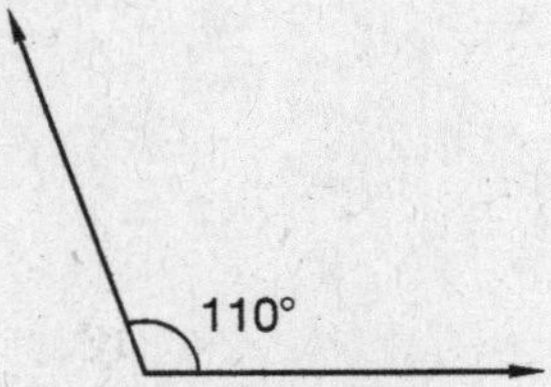

10.

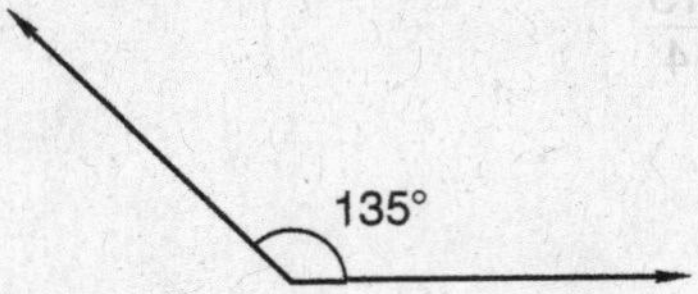

11.

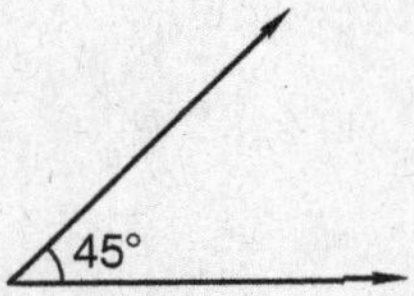

12.

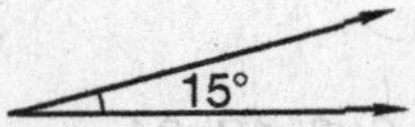

13. See student work.

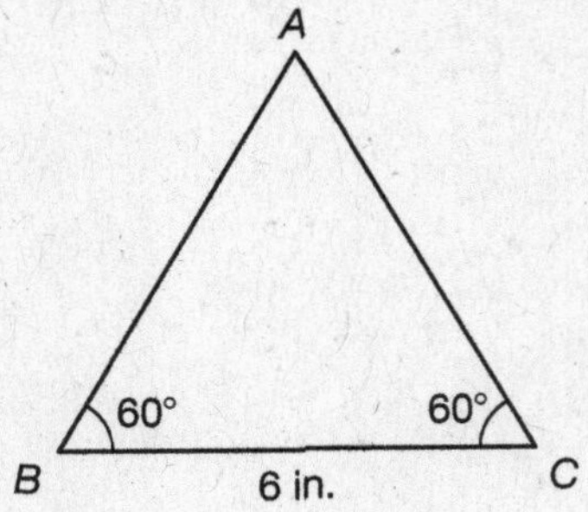

14. ***AB* = 6 in.; *AC* = 6 in.**

15. m $\angle A$ = **60°**

16. See student work.

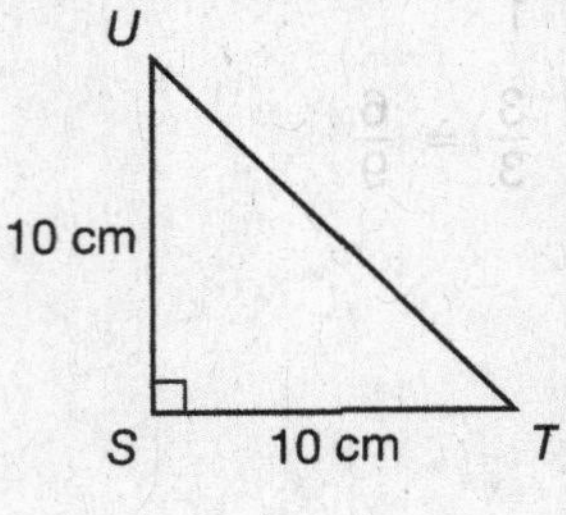

17. m $\angle T$ = **45°**; m $\angle U$ = **45°**

18. *TU* = **14 cm**

Practice Set 31

a. 6 square units in a row
$\times$ 4 rows
24 square units

b. 7 square units in a row
$\times$ 7 rows
49 square units

c. 8 m $\times$ 5 m = **40 sq. meters**

d. 12 m $\times$ 12 m = **144 sq. meters**

e. 5 $\times$ 5 = 25
5 inches

f. 5 in. $\times$ 4 = **20 inches**

g. 40 ft $\times$ 20 ft = **800 square feet**

h. **B. Square feet**

Written Practice 31

1. 4, 8, (12)
3, 6, 9, (12)

$$\begin{array}{r} 1 \\ 12\overline{)12} \\ 12 \\ \hline 0 \end{array}$$

2. **580,000,000 miles**

3. $$\begin{array}{r} 3\frac{1}{3} \\ 3\overline{)10} \\ 9 \\ \hline 1 \end{array}$$

4. 4 square stickers in a row
$\times$ 2 rows
8 square stickers

5. 10 tiles in a row
$\times$ 10 rows
100 tiles

6. 12 in. $\times$ 8 in. = **96 square inches**

7. 7 $\times$ 7 = **49**

Possible answers: 1. Add the next odd number (+3, +5, +7, +9, etc.)
2. To find the next term, multiply the number of the term by itself (1×1, 2×2, 3×3, 4×4, etc.)

8.

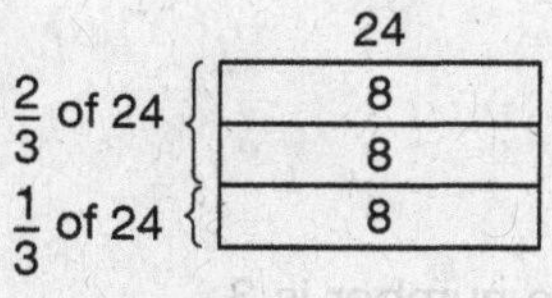

16

9. $$\begin{array}{r} \overset{3}{\cancel{4}}{}^{1}2 \\ -\ 2\,4 \\ \hline 1\,8 \end{array}$$
f = **18**

check: $$\begin{array}{r} \overset{1}{2}4 \\ +\ 18 \\ \hline 42 \end{array}$$

10. $\frac{1}{8} + \frac{1}{8} = \frac{2}{8} = \mathbf{\frac{1}{4}}$

11. $\frac{5}{6} - \frac{1}{6} = \frac{4}{6} = \mathbf{\frac{2}{3}}$

12. $\frac{2}{3} \cdot \frac{1}{2} = \frac{2}{6} = \mathbf{\frac{1}{3}}$

13. $\frac{2}{3} \times \frac{5}{1} = \frac{10}{3}$

$$\begin{array}{r} \mathbf{3\frac{1}{3}} \\ 3\overline{)10} \\ 9 \\ \hline 1 \end{array}$$

14. $$\begin{array}{r} 400 \\ \times\ \ 500 \\ \hline \mathbf{200{,}000} \end{array}$$

15. $$\begin{array}{r} \mathbf{\$2.00} \\ 10\overline{)\$20.00} \\ 20 \\ \hline 0\,0 \\ 0\,0 \\ \hline 00 \\ 00 \\ \hline 0 \end{array}$$

Solutions

16.
$$\begin{array}{r} 63 \\ \times\ 47¢ \\ \hline 441 \\ 2520 \\ \hline \end{array}$$
2961¢ or **$29.61**

17.
$$\begin{array}{r} \mathbf{210\ R\ 3} \\ 22\overline{)4623} \\ \underline{44} \\ 22 \\ \underline{22} \\ 03 \\ \underline{00} \\ 3 \end{array}$$

18. Smallest odd prime number is 3

$\mathbf{\frac{1}{3}}$

19. One third equals $33\frac{1}{3}\%$

$$\begin{array}{r} 33\frac{1}{3}\% \\ +\ 33\frac{1}{3}\% \\ \hline \mathbf{66\frac{2}{3}\%} \end{array}$$

20.
$$\begin{array}{r} 100 \\ -\ \ 90 \\ \hline 10 \end{array} \qquad \begin{array}{r} \overset{0}{\cancel{1}}\overset{9}{\cancel{0}}{}^{1}0 \\ -\ \ 8\ 9 \\ \hline 1\ 1 \end{array} \qquad \begin{array}{r} 111 \\ -\ 100 \\ \hline 11 \end{array} \qquad \begin{array}{r} 109 \\ -\ 100 \\ \hline 9 \end{array}$$

D. 109

21. 3,670,000,000 miles

22.
$$\begin{array}{r} 7 \text{ inches} \\ 2\overline{)14}\phantom{\text{ inches}} \\ \underline{14}\phantom{\text{ inches}} \\ 0\phantom{\text{ inches}} \end{array}$$

$$\frac{\text{radius}}{\text{diameter}} = \frac{7\text{ in.}}{14\text{ in.}} = \mathbf{\frac{1}{2}}$$

23. $\frac{3}{9} = \mathbf{\frac{1}{3}}$

24. $\mathbf{2\frac{5}{8}}$ **in.**

25. $\frac{3}{10} \times \frac{3}{10} = \mathbf{\frac{9}{100}}$

26. $\mathbf{\frac{4}{3}}$

27. $\mathbf{\frac{8}{8}}$

28.

24 students

$\frac{5}{6}$ scored 80% or higher	4 students
	4 students
	4 students
	4 students
	4 students
$\frac{1}{6}$ did not score 80% or higher	4 students

20 students

29. **a.** **∠*PMQ*** or **∠*QMP***

b. **∠*RMQ*** or **∠*QMR***

30. If the room is rectangular, first measure the length of the room and the width of the room. Then multiply the length by the width to calculate the floor area of the room.

Practice Set 32

a. **(2 × 100,000) + (7 × 10,000)**

b. **(1 × 1000) + (7 × 100) + (6 × 10)**

c. **(8 × 1000) + (5 × 10)**

d. 6000 + 400 = **6400**

e. 700 + 5 = **705**

f.
$$\begin{array}{r} \overset{10\ :\ 65}{\cancel{11}:\cancel{05}}\text{ a.m.} \\ -\ \ 7:15\text{ a.m.} \\ \hline 3:50\phantom{\text{ a.m.}} \end{array}$$

3 hr 50 min; Possible answer: If I add 3 hours to the starting time I get 10:15 a.m. Then if I add 50 minutes I get 11:05 a.m., which is the finish time.

g.
$$\begin{array}{r} 11:50\text{ p.m.} \\ +\ \ 3:30\phantom{\text{ p.m.}} \\ \hline 14:80\phantom{\text{ p.m.}} \\ 15:20\phantom{\text{ p.m.}} \\ \mathbf{3:20\text{ a.m.}} \end{array}$$

h.
$$\begin{array}{r} \overset{9\ \ \ 60}{\cancel{10}:\cancel{00}}\text{ p.m.} \\ -\ \ 4:30\phantom{\text{ p.m.}} \\ \hline \mathbf{5:30\text{ p.m.}} \end{array}$$

Written Practice 32

1. $\underbrace{(24 + 7)}_{31} \times \underbrace{(18 - 6)}_{12}$

   31×12

   372

2. $1836 - 1786 = d$

$$\begin{array}{r} 1\,\overset{7}{\cancel{8}}\,{}^{1}3\,6 \\ -\;1\,7\,8\,6 \\ \hline \textbf{5 0 years} \end{array}$$

3. **$0.14 per ounce**

$$\begin{array}{r} 16\overline{)\$2.24} \\ 16 \\ \hline 64 \\ 64 \\ \hline 0 \end{array}$$

4.

$$\begin{array}{r} 6{:}50 \text{ a.m.} \\ +\;3{:}30 \\ \hline 9{:}80 \end{array}$$

10:20 a.m.

5.

$$\begin{array}{r} 2 \\ 20\overline{)40} \\ 40 \\ \hline 0 \end{array} \qquad \begin{array}{r} 5 \\ 20\overline{)100} \\ 100 \\ \hline 0 \end{array}$$

$\mathbf{\frac{2}{5}}$

6.

$$\begin{array}{r} 90 \text{ ft} \\ \times\; 90 \text{ ft} \\ \hline \textbf{8100 square feet} \end{array}$$

7.

$$\begin{array}{r} 90 \text{ ft} \\ \times\quad 4 \\ \hline \textbf{360 ft} \end{array}$$

8. 1, 3, 5, 7, 9, 11, 13, 15

   This is a sequence of positive odd numbers. Add 2 to the value of a term to find the next term. 15

9. **(7 × 1000) + (5 × 100)**

10.

$$\begin{array}{r} \overset{0}{\cancel{1}}\,\overset{9}{\cancel{0}}\,{}^{1}0\,0 \\ -\quad 9\,9\,0 \\ \hline 1\,0 \end{array} \qquad \begin{array}{r} \overset{0}{\cancel{1}}\,\overset{9}{\cancel{0}}\,\overset{9}{\cancel{0}}\,{}^{1}0 \\ -\quad 9\,0\,9 \\ \hline 9\,1 \end{array} \qquad \begin{array}{r} 1009 \\ -\;1000 \\ \hline 9 \end{array} \qquad \begin{array}{r} 1090 \\ -\;1000 \\ \hline 90 \end{array}$$

C. 1009

11.

$$\begin{array}{r} \overset{1}{\$623} \\ \$494 \\ +\;\$380 \\ \hline \$1497 \end{array} \qquad \begin{array}{r} \mathbf{\$499} \\ 3\overline{)\$1497} \\ 12 \\ \hline 29 \\ 27 \\ \hline 27 \\ 27 \\ \hline 0 \end{array}$$

12.

$$\begin{array}{r} \$0.05 \\ \times\quad 100 \\ \hline \mathbf{\$5.00} \end{array}$$

13. $\mathbf{\frac{5}{2}}$

14.

$24	
$\frac{3}{4}$ of $24	$6
	$6
	$6
$\frac{1}{4}$ of $24	$6

$18

15. $\frac{3}{5} + \frac{3}{5} = \frac{6}{5} = \mathbf{1\frac{1}{5}}$

16. $\frac{3}{4} - \frac{1}{4} = \frac{2}{4} = \mathbf{\frac{1}{2}}$

17. $\frac{3}{4} \times \frac{1}{3} = \frac{3}{12} = \mathbf{\frac{1}{4}}$

18. $\frac{3}{10} \times \frac{7}{10} = \mathbf{\frac{21}{100}}$

19. $1\frac{2}{3} - 1\frac{1}{3} = \mathbf{\frac{1}{3}}$

20. One fourth of a circle is 25%.

$$\begin{array}{r} 25\% \\ \times\quad 3 \\ \hline \mathbf{75\%} \end{array}$$

21.

$$\begin{array}{r} 53 \\ +\;12 \\ \hline 65 \end{array} \qquad \text{check:} \qquad \begin{array}{r} 65 \\ -\;53 \\ \hline 12 \end{array}$$

$w = \mathbf{65}$

22.

$$\begin{array}{r} 30 \\ 8\overline{)240} \\ 24 \\ \hline 00 \\ 00 \\ \hline 0 \end{array} \qquad \begin{array}{r} 30 \\ \times\quad 8 \\ \hline 240 \end{array}$$

$q = \mathbf{30}$

23. $\begin{array}{r} 36 \\ -\ 15 \\ \hline 21 \end{array}$ girls

$$\frac{\text{boys}}{\text{girls}} = \frac{15}{21} = \mathbf{\frac{5}{7}}$$

24. Multiples of 4
4, 8, (12), 16, 20, 24
Multiples of 6
6, (12), 18, 24, 30
LCM is **12**

25.

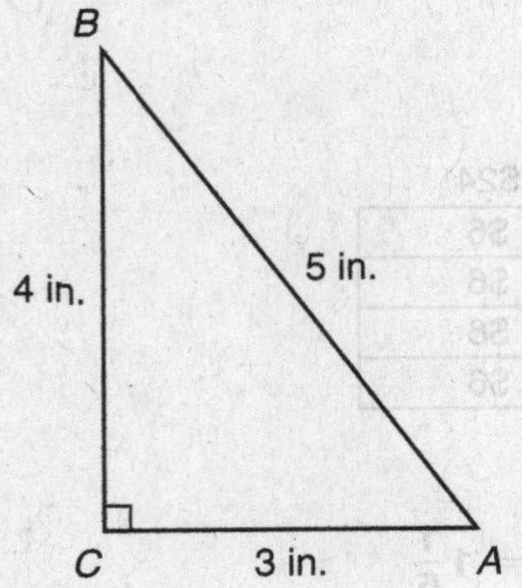

26. $\frac{24}{30} = \mathbf{\frac{4}{5}}$

27. $\begin{array}{r} \overset{10\,:\,75}{\cancel{11}:\cancel{15}} \text{ a.m.} \\ -\ \ 6:45 \text{ a.m.} \\ \hline 4:30 \end{array}$

4 hr 30 min

28. $\underbrace{(3 \times 100) + (5 \times 1)}_{305} \;\text{\textcircled{<}}\; 350$

29. $\mathbf{\frac{3}{10}}$

30. **To find the cost per ounce, divide the price of the box of cereal by the weight of the cereal in ounces.**

Practice Set 33

a. $\frac{80}{100}$

$$\frac{80 \div 20}{100 \div 20} = \mathbf{\frac{4}{5}}$$

b. $\frac{5}{100}$

$$\frac{5 \div 5}{100 \div 5} = \mathbf{\frac{1}{20}}$$

c. $\frac{25}{100}$

$$\frac{25 \div 25}{100 \div 25} = \mathbf{\frac{1}{4}}$$

d. $\frac{24}{100}$

$$\frac{24 \div 4}{100 \div 4} = \mathbf{\frac{6}{25}}$$

e. $\mathbf{\frac{23}{100}}$

f. $\frac{10}{100}$

$$\frac{10 \div 10}{100 \div 10} = \mathbf{\frac{1}{10}}$$

g. $\frac{20}{100}$

$$\frac{20 \div 20}{100 \div 20} = \mathbf{\frac{1}{5}}$$

h. $\frac{2}{100}$

$$\frac{2 \div 2}{100 \div 2} = \mathbf{\frac{1}{50}}$$

i. $\frac{75}{100}$

$$\frac{75 \div 25}{100 \div 25} = \mathbf{\frac{3}{4}}$$

j. **Possible answer: Write 40% as $\frac{40}{100}$ and then reduce by dividing 40 and 100 by 20 to get $\frac{2}{5}$.**

Written Practice 33

1. $\underbrace{(10 \times 15)}_{150} \div \underbrace{(10 + 15)}_{25}$

$$150 \div 25$$

6

2. **6690 − 3792 = *d***

```
   5 15 18
   6 6 9 10
 − 3 7 9 2
   2 8 9 8 kilometers
```

3. **14,000,000,000 years**

4. **(3 × 1000) + (4 × 10)**

5. 600 + 2 = **602**

6. $\mathbf{\frac{10}{10}; \frac{100}{100}}$

7. $\mathbf{\frac{3}{5}}$

8. 12 in. + 8 in. + 12 in. + 8 in. = **40 in.**

9.
```
   12 tiles in a row
 ×  8 rows
   96 square tiles
```

10. 56; No, the sum of the digits is not divisible by 3.
75; No, the last digit is not even.
83; No, the last digit is not even and the sum of the digits is not divisible by 3.
48; Yes, the last digit is even and the sum of the digits is divisible by 3.
D. 48

11.
```
   5000
 − 2000
   3000
```

12.
```
   $4.30
 ×   100
 $430.00
```

13.
```
        $16.08
 25)$402.00
     25
     152
     150
       2 0
       0 0
       2 00
       2 00
          0
```

14. $\frac{3}{5} \times \frac{20}{1} = \frac{60}{5} = \frac{12}{1} = \mathbf{12}$

```
   12
 5)60
   5
   10
   10
    0
```

15. $\frac{4}{5} + \frac{4}{5} = \frac{8}{5} = \mathbf{1\frac{3}{5}}$

```
   1 3/5
 5)8
   5
   3
```

16. $\frac{5}{8} - \frac{1}{8} = \frac{4}{8}$

$\frac{4 \div 4}{8 \div 4} = \mathbf{\frac{1}{2}}$

17. $\frac{5}{2} \times \frac{3}{2} = \frac{15}{4} = \mathbf{3\frac{3}{4}}$

```
   3 3/4
 4)15
   12
    3
```

18. $\frac{3}{10} \times \frac{3}{100} = \mathbf{\frac{9}{1000}}$

19. 2, 4, 6, 8, 10, 12, 14, 16, 18, 20
This is a sequence of positive even numbers. Add 2 to the value of a term to find the next term. 20

20.
```
   24        check:    47
 + 23                − 24
   47                  23
```
Q = **47**

21. $\frac{2}{1}$ or 2 check: $\frac{1}{2} \times \frac{2}{1} = \frac{2}{2} = 1$

w = **2**

22. **3 · 5**

23. **About 2 meters**

24. $\frac{5}{30}$

$\frac{5 \div 5}{30 \div 5} = \frac{1}{6}$; **Possible answer: Five over 30 reduces to $\frac{1}{6}$, and $\frac{1}{6}$ of 30 is 5.**

25. $1\frac{7}{10}$

26. a. $\frac{70}{100}$

$\frac{70 \div 10}{100 \div 10} = \frac{7}{10}$

b. $\frac{30}{100}$

$\frac{30 \div 10}{100 \div 10} = \frac{3}{10}$

27.

20 answers

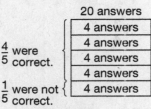

$\frac{4}{5}$ were correct.	4 answers
	4 answers
	4 answers
	4 answers
$\frac{1}{5}$ were not correct.	4 answers

16 answers

28. If the numerator is more than half of the denominator, the fraction is greater than $\frac{1}{2}$. If the numerator is less than half of the denominator, the fraction is less than $\frac{1}{2}$.

29.

$$\begin{array}{r} 8{:}45 \text{ p.m.} \\ +\ 6{:}30 \\ \hline 14{:}75 \\ = 15{:}15 \end{array} \qquad \begin{array}{r} 15{:}15 \\ -\ 12{:}00 \\ \hline \textbf{3:15 a.m.} \end{array}$$

30. $\frac{1}{16}, \frac{1}{8}, \frac{1}{4}, \frac{1}{2}$

Early Finishers Solutions

a. Area $= lw$

$\cong$ (31 m) (70 m)

$\cong$ 2170 m^2

b. Perimeter $= 2l + 2w$

$\cong (2 \times 31 \text{ m}) + (2 \times 70 \text{ m})$

$\cong$ 202 m

Practice Set 34

a. **Thousandths**

b. **4**

c. **2**

d. **Ones**

e. **Cent**

f. **Mill**

Written Practice 34

1.

24 members

$\frac{3}{8}$ were tenors.	3 members
	3 members
	3 members
$\frac{5}{8}$ were not tenors.	3 members
	3 members
	3 members
	3 members
	3 members

9 tenors

2.

$$\begin{array}{r} 8 \text{ ounces} \\ \times\ 3 \\ \hline \textbf{24 ounces} \end{array}$$

3.

$$\begin{array}{r} \overset{1}{8}{:}47 \text{ a.m.} \\ +\ 1{:}15 \\ \hline 9{:}62 \\ \textbf{10:02 a.m.} \end{array}$$

4. a. $\frac{60}{100}$

$\frac{60 \div 20}{100 \div 20} = \frac{3}{5}$

b. $\frac{40}{100}$

$\frac{40 \div 20}{100 \div 20} = \frac{2}{5}$

5. $\frac{100}{100}$ (=) $\frac{10}{10}$

6. $600 + 5 = $ **605**

7. **6**

8. a. $4\overline{)24}$ inches = **6 inches**

$$\begin{array}{r} 24 \\ \hline 0 \end{array}$$

b. 6 in. × 6 in. = **36 square inches**

9.

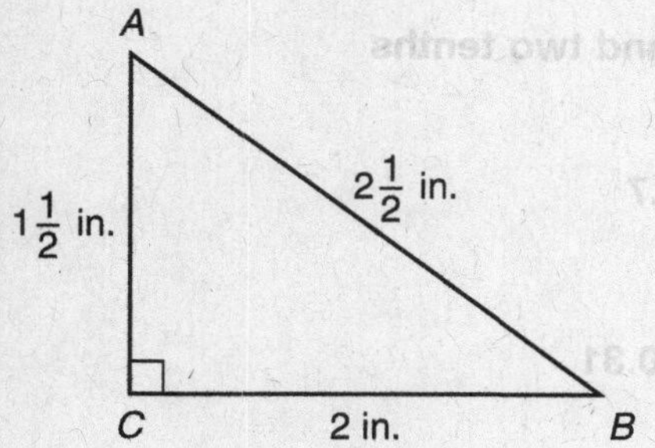

10. Multiples of 6
6,12,18, (24), 30
Multiples of 8
8,16, (24), 32,40
LCM is **24**

11. $10\overline{)\$5.60}$ = **$0.56**

$$\begin{array}{r} 5\,0 \\ \hline 60 \\ 60 \\ \hline 0 \end{array}$$

12. $\frac{9}{10} \cdot \frac{9}{10} = \mathbf{\frac{81}{100}}$

13. $30\overline{)900}$ = **30**

$$\begin{array}{r} 90 \\ \hline 00 \\ 00 \\ \hline 0 \end{array}$$

14. **36,800**

15. $6\overline{)144}$ = 24

$$\begin{array}{r} 12 \\ \hline 24 \\ 24 \\ \hline 0 \end{array}$$

check:

$$\begin{array}{r} 24 \\ \times\ \ 6 \\ \hline 144 \end{array}$$

$d = $ **24**

16.

$$\begin{array}{r} 144 \\ \times\ \ \ 6 \\ \hline 864 \end{array}$$

$d = $ **864**

check: $6\overline{)864}$ = 144

$$\begin{array}{r} 6 \\ \hline 26 \\ 24 \\ \hline 24 \\ 24 \\ \hline 0 \end{array}$$

17. $\frac{5}{2} + \frac{5}{2} \ (=)\ \frac{2}{1} \times \frac{5}{2}$

$\frac{10}{2} = 5 \qquad \frac{10}{2} = 5$

18. $\frac{3}{8} + \frac{3}{8} = \frac{6}{8}$

$\frac{6 \div 2}{8 \div 2} = \mathbf{\frac{3}{4}}$

19. $\frac{11}{12} - \frac{1}{12} = \frac{10}{12}$

$\frac{10 \div 2}{12 \div 2} = \mathbf{\frac{5}{6}}$

20. $\frac{5}{4} \times \frac{3}{2} = \frac{15}{8}$

$8\overline{)15}$ = $\mathbf{1\frac{7}{8}}$

$$\begin{array}{r} 8 \\ \hline 7 \end{array}$$

21. $\frac{6}{30}$

$\frac{6 \div 6}{30 \div 6} = \mathbf{\frac{1}{5}}$

22. **88 · $7.50 = *t***

$$\begin{array}{r} \$7.50 \\ \times\ \ \ \ 88 \\ \hline 6000 \\ 60000 \\ \hline \mathbf{\$660.00} \end{array}$$

Possible answer: At $10 each, 88 tickets would be $880. At $5 each, 88 tickets would be half as much, $440. Since $7.50 is halfway between $10 and $5, the total should be halfway between $880 and $440, which it is.

23. −6

24. $(80 \div 40) - (8 \div 4)$
$2 - 2$
0

25. 8

26.

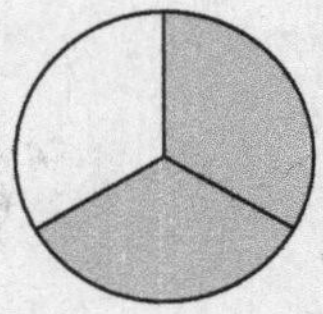

27. $12\overline{)5225}$ = $435\frac{5}{12}$
```
   435 5/12
12)5225
   48
    42
    36
     65
     60
      5
```

28.
```
   1
  12 ounces        10 ounces
  11 ounces      3)30 ounces
+  7 ounces        3
  30               00
                   00
                    0
```
10 ounces

29. $tr = d$
$d \div t = r$
$d \div r = t$

30.
```
   15           15
 5)75        10)150
   5            10
   25            50
   25            50
    0             0
```

Practice Set 35

a. $\frac{1}{10}$

b. $\frac{31}{100}$

c. $\frac{321}{1000}$

d. 0.3

e. 0.17

f. 0.123

g. Five hundredths

h. Fifteen thousandths

i. One and two tenths

j. $\frac{7}{10}$; 0.7

k. $\frac{31}{100}$; 0.31

l. $\frac{731}{1000}$; 0.731

m. 5.6

n. 11.12

o. 0.125

Written Practice 35

1. $\frac{3}{4} \times \frac{3}{5} = \frac{9}{20}$

2. 360 seeds

	360 seeds
$\frac{3}{4}$ sprouted	90 seeds
	90 seeds
	90 seeds
$\frac{1}{4}$ did not sprout	90 seeds

270 carrot seeds

3.
```
    1
   11:45 a.m.        14:00
 +  2:15           − 12:00
   13:60             2:00 p.m.
 = 14:00
```
2:00 p.m.

4. a. $\frac{23}{100}$

b. 0.23

5. **Ten and one hundredth**

6. **10.5**

7. a. $\frac{25}{100}$
$\frac{25 \div 25}{100 \div 25} = \mathbf{\frac{1}{4}}$

b. $\frac{75}{100}$
$\frac{75 \div 25}{100 \div 25} = \mathbf{\frac{3}{4}}$

8. $5000 + 600 + 40 = \mathbf{5640}$

9. **3**

10.
$$\begin{array}{r} 20 \text{ mm} \\ \times\ 10 \text{ mm} \\ \hline \mathbf{200 \text{ sq. mm}} \end{array}$$

11. $20 \text{ mm} + 10 \text{ mm} + 20 \text{ mm} + 10 \text{ mm}$
$= \mathbf{60 \text{ mm}}$

12.
$$\begin{array}{r} 100 \text{ centimeters} \\ \times\ 10 \phantom{\text{ centimeters}} \\ \hline \mathbf{1000 \text{ centimeters}} \end{array}$$

13. **−1, 0, 0.001, 0.01, 0.1, 1.0**

14. **About 1 meter**

15. $\frac{3}{5} + \frac{2}{5} = \frac{5}{5}$
$\frac{5 \div 5}{5 \div 5} = \frac{1}{1} = \mathbf{1}$

16. $\frac{5}{8} - \frac{5}{8} = \frac{0}{8} = \mathbf{0}$

17. $\frac{2}{3} \times \frac{3}{4} = \frac{6}{12}$
$\frac{6 \div 6}{12 \div 6} = \mathbf{\frac{1}{2}}$

18. a. $\mathbf{\frac{5}{2}}$

b. $\frac{5}{2} \times \frac{2}{1} = \mathbf{\frac{10}{2}} = \mathbf{5}$

19.
$$\begin{array}{r} 3\frac{2}{6} = \mathbf{3\frac{1}{3}} \\ 6\overline{)20} \\ 18 \\ \hline 2 \end{array}$$

20.
$$\begin{array}{r} 16\frac{4}{6}\% = \mathbf{16\frac{2}{3}\%} \\ 6\overline{)100\%} \\ 6 \\ \hline 40 \\ 36 \\ \hline 4 \end{array}$$

21. $3\frac{4}{4} - 1\frac{1}{4} = \mathbf{2\frac{3}{4}}$

22. $5 \ \textcircled{=} \ 4\frac{4}{4}$
5

23. $\mathbf{16\frac{2}{3}\%}$

24. $3 \times 18 \div 6 \ \textcircled{=} \ 3 \times (18 \div 6)$
$54 \div 6 \qquad 3 \times 3$
$9 \qquad 9$

25. **−14**

26.
$$\begin{array}{r} 3 \\ 2\overline{)6} \\ 6 \\ \hline 0 \end{array} \qquad \begin{array}{r} 3 \\ 20\overline{)60} \\ 60 \\ \hline 0 \end{array} \qquad \begin{array}{r} 3 \\ 4\overline{)12} \\ 12 \\ \hline 0 \end{array} \qquad \begin{array}{r} 3\frac{1}{8} \\ 8\overline{)25} \\ 24 \\ \hline 1 \end{array}$$

D. $\mathbf{\frac{25}{8}}$

27. $\frac{3}{10} \times \frac{7}{10} = \mathbf{\frac{21}{100}}$

28. $\mathbf{\frac{21}{100}}$**; 0.21**

29.
$$\begin{array}{r} \mathbf{8} \\ 50\overline{)400} \\ 400 \\ \hline 0 \end{array} \qquad \begin{array}{r} \mathbf{8} \\ 100\overline{)800} \\ 800 \\ \hline 0 \end{array}$$

Solutions

30. $4 \cdot r = 50$

$$\begin{array}{r} 12\frac{2}{4} = 12\frac{1}{2} \text{ inches} \\ 4\overline{)50} \\ \underline{4} \\ 10 \\ \underline{8} \\ 2 \end{array}$$

Possible answer: If you cut the ribbon in half, you have two pieces 25 inches long. If you cut each piece in half, you have four pieces $12\frac{1}{2}$ inches long.

Practice Set 36

a.

$$\begin{array}{r} 3 \\ -\,2\frac{1}{2} \\ \hline \end{array} \xrightarrow{2\,+\,\frac{2}{2}} \begin{array}{r} 2\frac{2}{2} \\ -\,2\frac{1}{2} \\ \hline \mathbf{\frac{1}{2}} \end{array}$$

b.

$$\begin{array}{r} 2 \\ -\,\frac{1}{4} \\ \hline \end{array} \xrightarrow{1\,+\,\frac{4}{4}} \begin{array}{r} 1\frac{4}{4} \\ -\,\frac{1}{4} \\ \hline \mathbf{1\frac{3}{4}} \end{array}$$

c.

$$\begin{array}{r} 4 \\ -\,2\frac{1}{4} \\ \hline \end{array} \xrightarrow{3\,+\,\frac{4}{4}} \begin{array}{r} 3\frac{4}{4} \\ -\,2\frac{1}{4} \\ \hline \mathbf{1\frac{3}{4}} \end{array}$$

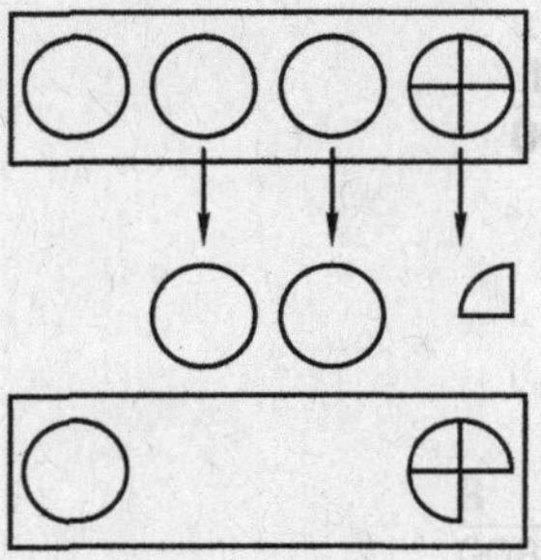

$$4 = 3\frac{4}{4}$$

$$\begin{array}{r} -\,2\frac{1}{4} \\ \hline 1\frac{3}{4} \end{array}$$

d.

$$\begin{array}{r} 3 \\ -\,\frac{5}{12} \\ \hline \end{array} \xrightarrow{2\,+\,\frac{12}{12}} \begin{array}{r} 2\frac{12}{12} \\ -\,\frac{5}{12} \\ \hline \mathbf{2\frac{7}{12}} \end{array}$$

e.

$$\begin{array}{r} 10 \\ -\,2\frac{1}{2} \\ \hline \end{array} \xrightarrow{9\,+\,\frac{2}{2}} \begin{array}{r} 9\frac{2}{2} \\ -\,2\frac{1}{2} \\ \hline \mathbf{7\frac{1}{2}} \end{array}$$

f.

$$\begin{array}{r} 6 \\ -\,1\frac{3}{10} \\ \hline \end{array} \xrightarrow{5\,+\,\frac{10}{10}} \begin{array}{r} 5\frac{10}{10} \\ -\,1\frac{3}{10} \\ \hline \mathbf{4\frac{7}{10}} \end{array}$$

g. Drawing: Answers will vary. See student work. Sample answer (for c.):

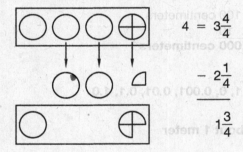

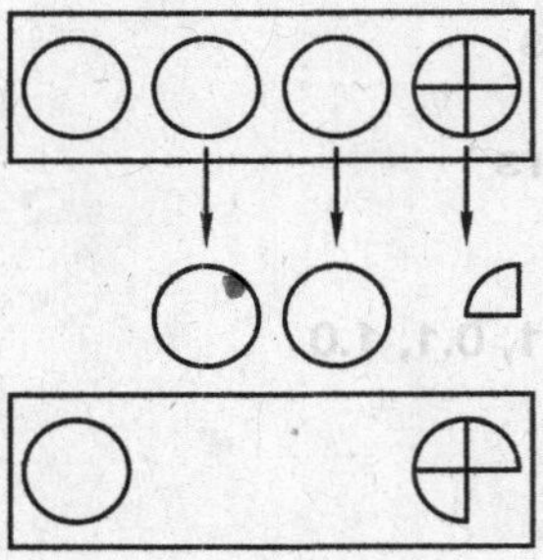

$$4 = 3\frac{4}{4}$$

$$\begin{array}{r} -\,2\frac{1}{4} \\ \hline 1\frac{3}{4} \end{array}$$

h. Word problem: Answers will vary. See student work. Sample answer (for e.): Sam cut $2\frac{1}{2}$ feet from a 10 foot long board. How long is the board now?

i.

$$\begin{array}{r} 4 \\ -\,1\frac{5}{6} \\ \hline \end{array} \xrightarrow{3\,+\,\frac{6}{6}} \begin{array}{r} 3\frac{6}{6} \\ -\,1\frac{5}{6} \\ \hline \mathbf{2\frac{1}{6}} \end{array} \textbf{ pies}$$

j. **Answers may vary. See student work. Sample answer: There are two pies on the shelf. The little boy ate $\frac{2}{3}$ of a pie. How many pies are left on the shelf?**

$$\begin{array}{r} 2 \\ -\ \frac{2}{3} \\ \hline \end{array} \xrightarrow{1 + \frac{3}{3}} \begin{array}{r} 1\frac{3}{3} \\ -\ \frac{2}{3} \\ \hline \mathbf{1\frac{1}{3}} \end{array} \textbf{ pies}$$

Written Practice 36

1. $\frac{25}{100}$

$\frac{25 \div 25}{100 \div 25} = \mathbf{\frac{1}{4}}$

2.
$$\begin{array}{r} 1 \\ -\ \frac{3}{4} \\ \hline \end{array} \xrightarrow{1 - \frac{4}{4}} \begin{array}{r} \frac{4}{4} \\ -\ \frac{3}{4} \\ \hline \mathbf{\frac{1}{4}} \end{array}$$

3. **1760 yards**
$$3\overline{)5280}$$
```
   3
   22
   21
    18
    18
     00
     00
      0
```

4. **3**

5. **One and three tenths**

6. **0.05**

7. **a.** $\mathbf{\frac{31}{100}}$

b. **0.31**

8. 400 + 3 = **403**

9. **3**

10. **a.** **3 inches**

b.
$$\begin{array}{r} 3 \text{ inches} \\ \times\ 4 \\ \hline \mathbf{12 \text{ inches}} \end{array}$$

11. **∠*AMB*** (or **∠*BMA***) and **∠*DMC*** (or **∠*CMD***)

12. $3\frac{1}{4} + 2\frac{1}{4} = 5\frac{2}{4} = \mathbf{5\frac{1}{2}}$

13.
$$\begin{array}{r} 3 \\ -\ 1\frac{1}{4} \\ \hline \end{array} \xrightarrow{2 + \frac{4}{4}} \begin{array}{r} 2\frac{4}{4} \\ -\ 1\frac{1}{4} \\ \hline \mathbf{1\frac{3}{4}} \end{array}$$

14. $3\frac{1}{3} + 2\frac{2}{3} = 5\frac{3}{3} = \mathbf{6}$

15. $\frac{3}{4} \times \frac{28}{1} = \frac{84}{4}$

21
$$4\overline{)84}$$
```
 8
 04
  4
  0
```

16. $\frac{3}{4} \times \frac{4}{6} = \frac{12}{24}$

$\frac{12 \div 12}{24 \div 12} = \mathbf{\frac{1}{2}}$

17.

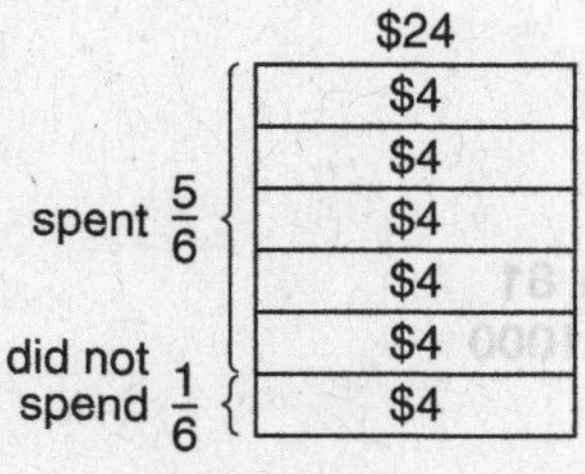

$20

18.
$$\begin{array}{r} \overset{1}{4}2 \\ 57 \\ +\ 63 \\ \hline 162 \end{array} \qquad \begin{array}{r} \mathbf{54} \\ 3\overline{)162} \end{array}$$
```
 15
  12
  12
   0
```


Solutions

19. **1, 2, 4, 5, 10, 20**

20. (a) Multiples of 9
9, (18), 27, 36, 45
Multiples of 6
6, 12, (18), 24, 30
LCM is **18**

(b) Factors of 9
1, (3), 9
Factors of 6
1, 2, (3), 6
GCF is **3**

21. $\begin{array}{r} 12 \\ \times\ 6 \\ \hline 72 \end{array}$ check: $\begin{array}{r} 6 \\ 12\overline{)72} \\ 72 \\ \hline 0 \end{array}$

$m = $ **72**

22. $\begin{array}{r} 2 \\ 6\overline{)12} \\ 12 \\ \hline 0 \end{array}$ check: $\begin{array}{r} 6 \\ 2\overline{)12} \\ 12 \\ \hline 0 \end{array}$

$n = $ **2**

23. **59,000,000**

24. $\begin{array}{r} 800 \\ \times\ 700 \\ \hline \mathbf{560{,}000} \end{array}$

25. **50 mm**

26. $\mathbf{\frac{1}{6} + \frac{1}{3} = \frac{1}{2}}$
$\mathbf{\frac{1}{2} - \frac{1}{3} = \frac{1}{6}}$
$\mathbf{\frac{1}{2} - \frac{1}{6} = \frac{1}{3}}$

27. $\frac{9}{10} \times \frac{9}{100} = \mathbf{\frac{81}{1000}}$

28. **0.081**

29. a. $\mathbf{\frac{4}{3}}$

b. $\frac{4}{3} + \frac{4}{3} + \frac{4}{3} = \mathbf{\frac{12}{3} = 4}$

30. radius = 12 ft
diameter = 12 ft × 2 = 24 ft
$\frac{\text{radius}}{\text{diameter}} = \frac{12 \div 12}{24 \div 12} = \mathbf{\frac{1}{2}}$

Practice Set 37

a. $\begin{array}{r} 3.46 \\ +\ 0.2 \\ \hline \mathbf{3.66} \end{array}$

b. $\begin{array}{r} 8.28 \\ -\ 6.1 \\ \hline \mathbf{2.18} \end{array}$

c. $\begin{array}{r} 0.735 \\ +\ 0.21 \\ \hline \mathbf{0.945} \end{array}$

d. $\begin{array}{r} 0.543 \\ -\ 0.21 \\ \hline \mathbf{0.333} \end{array}$

e. $\begin{array}{r} 0.43 \\ 0.1 \\ +\ 0.413 \\ \hline \mathbf{0.943} \end{array}$

f. $\begin{array}{r} 0.\,\overset{2}{\not3}\,{}^{1}0 \\ -\ 0.\,2\,7 \\ \hline \mathbf{0.\,0\,3} \end{array}$

g. $\begin{array}{r} \overset{1}{0}.6 \\ +\ 0.7 \\ \hline \mathbf{1.3} \end{array}$

h. $\begin{array}{r} \overset{0}{\not1}.\,\overset{9}{\not0}\,{}^{1}0 \\ -\ 0.\,2\,4 \\ \hline \mathbf{0.\,7\,6} \end{array}$

i. $\begin{array}{r} \overset{1}{0}.9 \\ +\ 0.12 \\ \hline \mathbf{1.02} \end{array}$

j. $\begin{array}{r} \overset{0}{\not1}.\,{}^{1}2\,3 \\ -\ 0.\,4 \\ \hline \mathbf{0.\,8\,3} \end{array}$

Written Practice 37

1. $\frac{60}{100}$

$\frac{60 \div 20}{100 \div 20} = \mathbf{\frac{3}{5}}$

2. $8 + 4 =$ **12 pencils**

3. **375 + *n* = 1000**

$$\begin{array}{r} \overset{0}{\not1}\,\overset{9}{\not0}\,\overset{9}{\not0}\,{}^{1}0 \\ -\quad 3\;7\;5 \\ \hline \mathbf{6\;2\;5} \end{array}$$

4.
$$\begin{array}{r} \overset{1}{3}.4 \\ 0.62 \\ +\ 0.3 \\ \hline \mathbf{4.32} \end{array}$$

5.
$$\begin{array}{r} 4.56 \\ -\ 3.2 \\ \hline \mathbf{1.36} \end{array}$$

6.
$$\begin{array}{r} \$0.\overset{1}{3}\overset{1}{7} \\ \$0.23 \\ +\ \$0.48 \\ \hline \mathbf{\$1.08} \end{array}$$

7.
$$\begin{array}{r} \$\overset{4}{\not5}.\,\overset{9}{\not0}\,{}^{1}0 \\ -\quad \$0.\ 0\ 5 \\ \hline \mathbf{\$4.\ 9\ 5} \end{array}$$

8. **10,000**

9. a. **10 feet**

b.
$$\begin{array}{r} 10 \text{ feet} \\ \times\quad 4\phantom{\text{ feet}} \\ \hline \mathbf{40 \text{ feet}} \end{array}$$

10. **3**

11. **D. 0.01; Choices A and B are both one tenth and choice C reduces to one tenth, so $\frac{1}{10}$, 0.1, and $\frac{10}{100}$ are equal to each other but not equal to 0.01.**

12. $\underbrace{30 \times 40}_{1200} \times 40$

1200×40

48,000

13.
$$\begin{array}{r} \mathbf{1070} \\ 3\overline{)3210} \\ 3 \\ \hline 02 \\ 00 \\ \hline 21 \\ 21 \\ \hline 00 \\ 00 \\ \hline 0 \end{array}$$

14.
$$\begin{array}{r} \mathbf{1,070} \\ 30\overline{)32,100} \\ 30 \\ \hline 2\ 1 \\ 0\ 0 \\ \hline 2\ 10 \\ 2\ 10 \\ \hline 00 \\ 00 \\ \hline 0 \end{array}$$

15.
$$\begin{array}{r} \$\overset{0}{\not1}\,\overset{9}{\not0},\,\overset{9}{\not0}\,\overset{9}{\not0}\,{}^{1}0 \\ -\qquad \$3\ 4\ 5 \\ \hline \mathbf{\$9\ 6\ 5\ 5} \end{array}$$

16. $\frac{3}{4} + \frac{3}{4} = \frac{6}{4}$

$$\begin{array}{r} 1\frac{2}{4} = \mathbf{1\frac{1}{2}} \\ 4\overline{)6} \\ 4 \\ \hline 2 \end{array}$$

17.
$$\begin{array}{r} 3 \\ -\ 1\frac{3}{5} \\ \hline \end{array} \xrightarrow{2\ +\ \frac{5}{5}} \begin{array}{r} 2\frac{5}{5} \\ -\ 1\frac{3}{5} \\ \hline \mathbf{1\frac{2}{5}} \end{array}$$

18. $\frac{3}{3} - \frac{2}{2}$

$1 - 1 = \mathbf{0}$

19. $1\frac{1}{3} + 2\frac{1}{3} + 3\frac{1}{3} = 6\frac{3}{3} = \mathbf{7}$

20. $\frac{1}{4} + \frac{3}{4}$ ⓧ $\frac{1}{4} \times \frac{3}{4}$

$\frac{4}{4}$ $\qquad$ $\frac{3}{16}$

1

(The circled symbol is >: $\frac{1}{4} + \frac{3}{4} > \frac{1}{4} \times \frac{3}{4}$.)

21.
$$\begin{array}{r} \mathbf{14\tfrac{2}{7}} \\ 7\overline{)100} \\ \underline{7} \\ 30 \\ \underline{28} \\ 2 \end{array}$$

22.
$$\begin{array}{r} 90 \text{ lb} \\ {}_1 84 \text{ lb} \\ + \ 102 \text{ lb} \\ \hline 276 \text{ lb} \end{array} \qquad \begin{array}{r} \mathbf{92 \text{ lb}} \\ 3\overline{)276 \text{ lb}} \\ \underline{27\phantom{6 \text{ lb}}} \\ 06\phantom{\text{ lb}} \\ \underline{06\phantom{\text{ lb}}} \\ 0\phantom{\text{ lb}} \end{array}$$

23. Multiples of 4
4, 8, 12, 16, (20), 24, 28
Multiples of 5
5, 10, 15, (20), 25, 30
LCM is **20**

24.
$$\begin{array}{r} \$38.50 \\ - \ \$34.00 \\ \hline 4.50 \end{array} \qquad \mathbf{-\ 4.50}$$

25. $\mathbf{10\frac{1}{10}}$

26. $\frac{3}{10} \times \frac{9}{10} = \frac{27}{100} = \mathbf{0.27}$

27. Fractions may vary but must include such numbers as $\frac{2}{2}$, $\frac{3}{3}$, and $\frac{4}{4}$. If the numerator and denominator of a fraction are equal (but not zero), the fraction equals 1.

28. If we multiply the dividend and divisor by the same number, the resulting problem has the same quotient as the original problem. Here the dividend and divisor were both doubled (that is, multiplied by 2), so the quotients of the 2 problems are the same.

29.
$$\begin{array}{r} \overset{3:\,83}{\cancel{4}:\cancel{23}} \text{ p.m.} \\ - \ 2:50 \text{ p.m.} \\ \hline 1:33\phantom{\text{ p.m.}} \end{array}$$
1 hr 33 min

30. 25 students

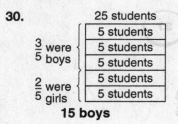

$\frac{3}{5}$ were boys	5 students
	5 students
	5 students
$\frac{2}{5}$ were girls	5 students
	5 students

15 boys

Early Finishers Solutions

a. $90 \text{ in.} \cdot \frac{1 \text{ yd}}{36 \text{ in.}} = 2.5$ yards of fabric

b. Chamile will have to purchase 3 yards of fabric and she will have $\frac{1}{2}$ yard of fabric left over.

Practice Set 38

a.
$$\begin{array}{r} 4 \\ + \ 2.1 \\ \hline \mathbf{6.1} \end{array}$$

b.
$$\begin{array}{r} 4.3 \\ - \ 2 \\ \hline \mathbf{2.3} \end{array}$$

c.
$$\begin{array}{r} 3 \\ + \ 0.4 \\ \hline \mathbf{3.4} \end{array}$$

d.
$$\begin{array}{r} \overset{3}{\cancel{4}}{}^{1}3.2 \\ - \ 5 \\ \hline \mathbf{38.2} \end{array}$$

e.
$$\begin{array}{r} 0.23 \\ 4 \\ + \ 3.7 \\ \hline \mathbf{7.93} \end{array}$$

f.
$$\begin{array}{r} 6.3 \\ - \ 6 \\ \hline \mathbf{0.3} \end{array}$$

g.
$$\begin{array}{r} 12.5 \\ + \ 10 \\ \hline \mathbf{22.5} \end{array}$$

h.
$$\begin{array}{r} 75.25 \\ - \ 25 \\ \hline \mathbf{50.25} \end{array}$$

i. $9 \times 9 = \mathbf{81}$

j. **9**

k. $6^2 + 8^2 = 36 + 64 = \mathbf{100}$

l. $\sqrt{100} - \sqrt{49} = 10 - 7 = \mathbf{3}$

m. $15 \times 15 = \mathbf{225}$

n. **12**

o. $(6 \cdot 6)(\text{ft} \cdot \text{ft}) = \mathbf{36\ ft^2}$

p. **8 m**

q. $5 \times 5 = 25$
$6 \times 6 = 36$
$7 \times 7 = 49$
$8 \times 8 = 64$
25, 36, 49, 64; 25, 36, 49, and 64 are perfect squares because they are the products of 5 × 5, 6 × 6, 7 × 7, and 8 × 8, respectively.

Written Practice 38

1. Factors of 54
1, 2, 3, 6, (9), 18, 27, 54
Factors of 45
1, 3, 5, (9), 15, 45
GCF is **9**

2. $3 \cdot w = 126$

$$\begin{array}{r} \mathbf{42}\ \textbf{weeks} \\ 3\overline{)126} \\ 12 \\ \hline 06 \\ 06 \\ \hline 0 \end{array}$$

3. $1948 - 1869 = d$

$$\begin{array}{r} {}^{8\,13}\quad \\ 1\,\not{9}\,\not{4}\,{}^{1}8 \\ -\ 1\,8\,6\,9 \\ \hline \mathbf{7\,9}\ \textbf{years old} \end{array}$$

4.
$$\begin{array}{r} 3 \\ +\ 1.2 \\ \hline \mathbf{4.2} \end{array}$$

5.
$$\begin{array}{r} 3.6 \\ +\ 4 \\ \hline \mathbf{7.6} \end{array}$$

6.
$$\begin{array}{r} 5.63 \\ -\ 1.2 \\ \hline \mathbf{4.43} \end{array}$$

7.
$$\begin{array}{r} {}^{1}\quad \\ 5.376 \\ +\ 0.24 \\ \hline \mathbf{5.616} \end{array}$$

8.
$$\begin{array}{r} 4.75 \\ -\ 0.6 \\ \hline \mathbf{4.15} \end{array}$$

9. $4 - 3 = \mathbf{1}$

10. a. $\mathbf{\frac{47}{100}}$

b. **0.47**

11. **9043**

12. **5**

13. a. $\sqrt{81} = \mathbf{9}$ **inches**

b.
$$\begin{array}{r} 9 \\ \times\ 4 \\ \hline \mathbf{36}\ \textbf{inches} \end{array}$$

14. Multiples of 2
2, 4, 6, 8, 10, (12), 14, 16
Multiples of 3
3, 6, 9, (12), 15, 18, 21
Multiples of 4
4, 8, (12), 16, 20, 24, 28
LCM is **12**

15. $1\frac{2}{3} + 2\frac{2}{3} = 3\frac{4}{3} = \mathbf{4\frac{1}{3}}$

16.
$$\begin{array}{r} 9 \\ -\ 1\frac{1}{4} \\ \hline \end{array} \xrightarrow{8 + \frac{4}{4}} \begin{array}{r} 8\frac{4}{4} \\ -\ 1\frac{1}{4} \\ \hline \mathbf{7\frac{3}{4}} \end{array}$$

17. $\frac{3}{4} \times \frac{4}{5} = \frac{12}{20}$

$\frac{12 \div 4}{20 \div 4} = \mathbf{\frac{3}{5}}$

18. $\frac{7}{10} \times \frac{11}{10} = \mathbf{\frac{77}{100}}$

19. **a.** $\mathbf{\frac{3}{2}}$

b. $\frac{3}{2} \times \frac{2}{1} = \frac{6}{2} = \mathbf{3}$

20. $\frac{6 \div 3}{9 \div 3} = \mathbf{\frac{2}{3}}$

21. **1, 2, 3, 5, 6, 10, 15, 30**

22. **a.** $\frac{35 \div 5}{100 \div 5} = \mathbf{\frac{7}{20}}$

b. $\frac{65 \div 5}{100 \div 5} = \mathbf{\frac{13}{20}}$

23. **186,000**

24. $\frac{3}{1} = 3$

m = 3

25. $\frac{22 + 23 + 24}{3} = \frac{69}{3}$

$$\begin{array}{r} \mathbf{23} \\ 3\overline{)69} \\ \underline{6} \\ 09 \\ \underline{09} \\ 0 \end{array}$$

26. $\underset{3}{24 \div 8} \; \textcircled{=} \; \underset{3}{240 \div 80}$

27. $\frac{7}{10} \times \frac{21}{100} = \frac{147}{1000} = \mathbf{0.147;}$

20 × 7 is 140, and 1 × 7 is 7, so 21 × 7 is 147. 10 × 100 is 1000. If two fractions are multiplied, the product will be less than the smaller fraction. 0.147 is less than 0.21.

28.
$$\begin{array}{r} \mathbf{\$0.08} \\ 10\overline{)\$0.80} \\ \underline{0\,0} \\ 80 \\ \underline{80} \\ 0 \end{array}$$

29. **D.** $\mathbf{\frac{4}{5}}$

30. **First divide the perimeter by 4 to find the length of each side. Then square the length of a side (multiply the length by itself) to find the area.**

Practice Set 39

a.
$$\begin{array}{r} 15 \\ \times\ 0.3 \\ \hline \mathbf{4.5} \end{array}$$

b.
$$\begin{array}{r} 1.5 \\ \times\ 3 \\ \hline \mathbf{4.5} \end{array}$$

c.
$$\begin{array}{r} 1.5 \\ \times\ 0.3 \\ \hline \mathbf{0.45} \end{array}$$

d.
$$\begin{array}{r} 0.15 \\ \times\ 3 \\ \hline \mathbf{0.45} \end{array}$$

e.
$$\begin{array}{r} 1.5 \\ \times\ 1.5 \\ \hline 75 \\ 150 \\ \hline \mathbf{2.25} \end{array}$$

f.
$$\begin{array}{r} 0.15 \\ \times\ 10 \\ \hline \mathbf{1.50} \end{array}$$ or **1.5**

g.
$$\begin{array}{r} 0.25 \\ \times\ 0.5 \\ \hline \mathbf{0.125} \end{array}$$

h.
$$\begin{array}{r} 0.025 \\ \times\ 100 \\ \hline \mathbf{2.500} \end{array}$$ or **2.5**

i.
$$\begin{array}{r} 0.8 \\ \times\ 0.8 \\ \hline \mathbf{0.64} \end{array}$$

j.
$$\begin{array}{r} 1.2 \\ \times\ 1.2 \\ \hline 24 \\ 120 \\ \hline \mathbf{1.44} \end{array}$$

k. **The non-zero digits in the problem numbers are the same. The number of decimal places in the factors and products are different.**

Written Practice 39

1. **29,029 feet**

2.
$$\begin{array}{r} 9{,}676 \\ 3\overline{)29{,}029} \\ \underline{27} \\ 20 \\ \underline{18} \\ 22 \\ \underline{21} \\ 19 \\ \underline{18} \\ 1 \end{array}$$

9,676 $\frac{1}{3}$ yards

3.
$$\begin{array}{r} 12\frac{4}{8} = 12\frac{1}{2}¢ \text{ in 1 bit} \\ 8\overline{)100} \\ \underline{8} \\ 20 \\ \underline{16} \\ 4 \end{array}$$

$$\begin{array}{r} \overset{1\,3}{12.5} \\ \times\quad 6 \\ \hline \mathbf{75.0¢} \text{ or } \mathbf{75¢} \end{array}$$

4.
$$\begin{array}{r} 0.\overset{2}{2}5 \\ \times\ 0.5 \\ \hline \mathbf{0.125} \end{array}$$

5.
$$\begin{array}{r} \$1.80 \\ \times\quad 10 \\ \hline \mathbf{\$18.00} \end{array}$$

6.
$$\begin{array}{r} \overset{2}{6}3 \\ \times\ 0.7 \\ \hline \mathbf{44.1} \end{array}$$

7.
$$\begin{array}{r} 1.23 \\ 4 \\ +\ 0.5 \\ \hline \mathbf{5.73} \end{array}$$

8.
$$\begin{array}{r} \overset{0}{\not{1}}\,\overset{1}{\not{2}}.{}^{1}3\,4 \\ -\quad 5.\,6 \\ \hline \mathbf{6.\,7\,4} \end{array}$$

9.
$$\begin{array}{r} 1.1 \\ \times\ 1.1 \\ \hline 11 \\ 110 \\ \hline \mathbf{1.21} \end{array}$$

10. a. **10.3**

b. **10 $\frac{3}{10}$**

11. **Answers will vary, but the product will be the smallest number of the three (so it will be listed first).**

12. **0.123**

13. 600 + 40 = **640**

14.
$$\begin{array}{r} 10 \\ 4\overline{)40} \end{array}$$

$$\begin{array}{r} 10 \text{ tiles in a row} \\ \times\ 10 \text{ rows} \\ \hline \mathbf{100 \text{ tiles}} \end{array}$$

15. Multiples of 2
2, 4, ⑥, 8, 10, 12
Multiples of 3
3, ⑥, 9, 12, 15, 18
Multiples of 6
⑥, 12, 18, 24, 30, 36
LCM is **6**

16.
$$\begin{array}{r} 2\frac{4}{8} = \mathbf{2\frac{1}{2}} \\ 8\overline{)20} \\ \underline{16} \\ 4 \end{array}$$

17. $\left(\frac{1}{3} + \frac{2}{3}\right) - 1$

$\left(\frac{3}{3}\right) - 1$

$\frac{3}{3} - \frac{3}{3} = \frac{0}{3} = \mathbf{0}$

18. $\frac{3}{5} \times \frac{2}{3} = \frac{6}{15}$

$\frac{6 \div 3}{15 \div 3} = \mathbf{\frac{2}{5}}$

19. $\frac{8}{9} \times \frac{9}{8} = \frac{72}{72} = \mathbf{1}$

20. $\frac{4 \div 2}{6 \div 2} = \mathbf{\frac{2}{3}}$

21. $\overset{12:60}{\cancel{1}:\cancel{00}}$ a.m.
 − 2:30
 10:30 p.m.

22. **27 correct answers;**

$\begin{array}{r} {}^{2}\,26 \\ 29 \\ 28 \\ +\ 25 \\ \hline 108 \end{array}$ $\quad$ $\begin{array}{r} 27 \\ 4\overline{)108} \\ 8 \\ \hline 28 \\ 28 \\ \hline 0 \end{array}$

I added 26, 29, 28, and 25. Then I divided that sum (108) by 4 (the number of assignments) and found that the average is 27.

23. $\begin{array}{r} \mathbf{200} \\ 40\overline{)8000} \\ 80 \\ \hline 00 \\ 00 \\ \hline 00 \\ 00 \\ \hline 0 \end{array}$

24. $\underset{1}{365 - 364}$ ⓶ $\underset{-1}{364 - 365}$ — $365 - 364 \; \textcircled{>} \; 364 - 365$; 1, -1

25. **3**

26. **$2\frac{3}{16}$ inches**

27. a. $\mathbf{\frac{5}{3}}$

b. $\frac{5}{3} \times \frac{2}{1} = \mathbf{\frac{10}{3}} = \mathbf{3\frac{1}{3}}$

$\begin{array}{r} 3\frac{1}{3} \\ 3\overline{)10} \\ 9 \\ \hline 1 \end{array}$

28. $\begin{array}{r} \mathbf{26} \\ 15\overline{)390} \\ 30 \\ \hline 90 \\ 90 \\ \hline 0 \end{array}$ $\quad$ $\begin{array}{r} \mathbf{26} \\ 5\overline{)130} \\ 10 \\ \hline 30 \\ 30 \\ \hline 0 \end{array}$ $\quad$ $\begin{array}{r} \mathbf{26} \\ 10\overline{)260} \\ 20 \\ \hline 60 \\ 60 \\ \hline 0 \end{array}$

29. $\begin{array}{r} 0.5 \text{ m} \\ \times\ 0.3 \text{ m} \\ \hline \mathbf{0.15 \ m^2} \end{array}$

30. $\frac{60 \div 60}{120 \div 60} = \mathbf{\frac{1}{2}}$

Early Finishers Solutions

November 3 + 2 days = November 5. If the process started at 9:00 a.m. + 30 minutes to prepare + $2\frac{1}{2}$ hours (2 hours 30 minutes) of cooking time, the turkey would be ready to eat at 12:00 p.m. on November 5.

Practice Set 40

a. $\begin{array}{r} 0.2 \\ \times\ 0.3 \\ \hline \mathbf{0.06} \end{array}$

b. $\begin{array}{r} 4.\overset{5}{\cancel{6}}{}^{1}0 \\ -\ 0.46 \\ \hline \mathbf{4.14} \end{array}$

c. $\begin{array}{r} 0.1 \\ \times\ 0.01 \\ \hline \mathbf{0.001} \end{array}$

d. $\begin{array}{r} 0.\overset{3}{\cancel{4}}{}^{1}0 \\ -\ 0.32 \\ \hline \mathbf{0.08} \end{array}$

e.
$$\begin{array}{r} 0.12 \\ \times\ \ 0.4 \\ \hline \mathbf{0.048} \end{array}$$

f.
$$\begin{array}{r} \overset{0}{\not1}.\overset{9}{\not0}{}^{1}0 \\ -\ 0.\,9\,8 \\ \hline \mathbf{0.\,0\,2} \end{array}$$

g.
$$\begin{array}{r} 0.3 \\ \times\ 0.3 \\ \hline \mathbf{0.09} \end{array}$$

h.
$$\begin{array}{r} 0.12 \\ \times\ 0.12 \\ \hline 24 \\ 120 \\ \hline \mathbf{0.0144} \end{array}$$

i. **10.011**

j. $\frac{8 \div 8}{32 \div 8} = \frac{1}{4} = \mathbf{25\%}$

Written Practice 40

1. $\frac{4 \div 4}{32 \div 4} = \frac{1}{8} = \mathbf{12\frac{1}{2}\%}$

2. $\mathbf{1920 - 1788 = \mathit{d}}$
$$\begin{array}{r} 1\,\overset{8}{\not9}\,\overset{11}{\not2}{}^{1}0 \\ -\ 1\,7\,8\,8 \\ \hline \mathbf{1\,3\,2 \text{ years}} \end{array}$$

3.
$$\begin{array}{r} \overset{12:120}{\not2:\not00} \text{ p.m.} \\ -\ 3:30 \\ \hline 9:90 \text{ a.m.} \\ \mathbf{10:30 \text{ a.m.}} \end{array}$$

4.
$$\begin{array}{r} \overset{2}{\not3}.{}^{1}0 \\ -\ 0.\,3 \\ \hline \mathbf{2.\,7} \end{array}$$

5.
$$\begin{array}{r} 1.\,\overset{1}{\not2}{}^{1}0 \\ -\ 0.\,1\,2 \\ \hline \mathbf{1.\,0\,8} \end{array}$$

6.
$$\begin{array}{r} 1.0 \\ -\ 0.1 \\ \hline \mathbf{0.9} \end{array}$$

7.
$$\begin{array}{r} 0.12 \\ \times\ \ \ 0.2 \\ \hline \mathbf{0.024} \end{array}$$

8.
$$\begin{array}{r} 0.1 \\ \times\ 0.1 \\ \hline \mathbf{0.01} \end{array}$$

9.
$$\begin{array}{r} 4.8 \\ \times\ 0.23 \\ \hline 14 \\ 960 \\ \hline \mathbf{1.104} \end{array}$$

10. **1.02**

11. $60{,}000 + 800 = \mathbf{60{,}800}$

12.
$$\begin{array}{r} 8 \\ 4\overline{)32} \\ 32 \\ \hline 0 \end{array}$$
$$\begin{array}{r} 8 \text{ tiles in a row} \\ \times\ 8 \text{ rows} \\ \hline \mathbf{64 \text{ tiles}} \end{array}$$

13. Multiples of 2
2, 4, 6, ⑧, 10, 12
Multiples of 4
4, ⑧, 12, 16, 20, 24
Multiples of 8
⑧, 16, 24, 32, 40
LCM is **8**

14. $6\frac{2}{3} + 4\frac{2}{3} = 10\frac{4}{3} = \mathbf{11\frac{1}{3}}$

15.
$$5 \xrightarrow{4 + \frac{8}{8}} 4\frac{8}{8}$$
$$\begin{array}{r} 5 \\ -\ 3\frac{3}{8} \\ \hline \end{array} \qquad \begin{array}{r} 4\frac{8}{8} \\ -\ 3\frac{3}{8} \\ \hline \mathbf{1\frac{5}{8}} \end{array}$$

16. $\frac{5}{8} \times \frac{2}{3} = \frac{10}{24}$

$\frac{10 \div 2}{24 \div 2} = \mathbf{\frac{5}{12}}$

17. $2\frac{5}{6} + 5\frac{2}{6} = 7\frac{7}{6} = \mathbf{8\frac{1}{6}}$

18. $\frac{1}{2} \times \frac{2}{2} \text{ (=) } \frac{1}{2} \times \frac{3}{3}$

$\frac{2}{4}$ $\quad$ $\frac{3}{6}$

$\frac{1}{2}$ $\quad$ $\frac{1}{2}$

19. $\begin{array}{r} \overset{0}{\not1}\,\overset{9}{\not0}\,\overset{9}{\not0}\,{}^{1}0 \\ -\ \ 567 \\ \hline 433 \end{array}$

$w = \mathbf{433}$

20. **2, 4, 5, 10, 20, 25, 50**

21. 81 + 3 = **84**

22. **$4200**

23. a. 15 students + 10 students + 5 students = **30 students**

b. $\frac{5 \div 5}{30 \div 5} = \mathbf{\frac{1}{6}}$

c. $\frac{15 \div 15}{30 \div 15} = \frac{1}{2} = \mathbf{50\%}$

24. $\frac{1}{5} + \frac{1}{5} = \frac{2}{5}$

$\frac{5}{5} - \frac{2}{5} = \mathbf{\frac{3}{5}}$

$\frac{3}{5} \times \frac{\$5.00}{1} = \frac{\$15.00}{5} = \mathbf{\$3.00}$

25. **Answers will vary. See student work.**

26. $0.3 \times 0.2 = \mathbf{0.06}$
$0.06 \div 0.3 = \mathbf{0.2}$
$0.06 \div 0.2 = \mathbf{0.3}$

27. $\begin{array}{r} \mathbf{16} \\ 15\overline{)240} \\ \underline{15} \\ 90 \\ \underline{90} \\ 0 \end{array}$ $\quad$ $\begin{array}{r} \mathbf{16} \\ 5\overline{)80} \\ \underline{5} \\ 30 \\ \underline{30} \\ 0 \end{array}$ $\quad$ $\begin{array}{r} \mathbf{16} \\ 10\overline{)160} \\ \underline{10} \\ 60 \\ \underline{60} \\ 0 \end{array}$

28. $\frac{40 \div 20}{100 \div 20} = \frac{2}{5}$

$\mathbf{\frac{2}{5}} \times \frac{25}{1} = \frac{50}{5} = 10 \text{ boys}$

$\begin{array}{r} 25 \\ -\ 10 \\ \hline 15 \end{array}$ $\quad$ $\frac{\text{girls}}{\text{boys}} = \frac{15 \div 5}{10 \div 5} = \mathbf{\frac{3}{2}}$

29. $\mathbf{5\frac{9}{10}}$

30. **Answers will vary. See student work.**

Investigation 4

1. **Number of items, quantitative**

2. **Color, qualitative**

3. **Time of bus trip, quantitative**

4. **Holiday, qualitative**

5. **Team, qualitative**

6. **Answers will vary. See student work.**

7. **Pet store shoppers are more likely to own pets than people from the general population. Support for a leash law might be lower among those surveyed than among the general population.**

8. **Orchestra members are more likely to have a high interest in music than students in general. Thus, movies preferred by orchestra members might be more musically oriented than movies preferred by students in general.**

9. People generally prefer to be considered "sensible" over being considered "not sensible." So a "yes" answer would be more likely due to the bias.

10. Discuss as a class. Politeness toward their host should be considered as a reason that the children might be less likely to give a "yes" answer.

Extensions

a. Answers will vary. See student work.

b. Answers will vary. See student work.

c. Answers will vary. See student work.

d. Answers will vary. See student work.

Practice Set 41

a. $\frac{50}{100} = \frac{1}{2}$

b. $\frac{10}{100} = \frac{1}{10}$

c. $\frac{25}{100} = \frac{1}{4}$

d. $\frac{75}{100} = \frac{3}{4}$

e. $\frac{20}{100} = \frac{1}{5}$

f. $\frac{1}{100}$

g. $\frac{65}{100} = 0.65$

h. $\frac{7}{100} = 0.07$

i. $\frac{30}{100} = 0.30$ or 0.3

j. $\frac{8}{100} = 0.08$

k. $\frac{60}{100} = 0.60$ or 0.6

l. $\frac{1}{100} = 0.01$

m. 35; 10% of 350 is $\frac{1}{10}$ of 350. Divide 350 by 10 to get 35.

n. 12; 25% of 48 is $\frac{1}{4}$ of 48. Divide 48 by 4 to get 12.

o.
$$\begin{array}{r} 15.00 \\ \times\ 0.08 \\ \hline \$1.2000 \end{array}$$
$1.20

p. \$1; $9\frac{1}{2}$% rounds to 10% and \$9.98 rounds to \$10. Find 10% $\left(\frac{1}{10}\right)$ of \$10, which is \$1.

q.
$$\begin{array}{r} 3\,0 \text{ baseball cards} \\ \times\ 0.80 \\ \hline 24.00 \end{array}$$
24 baseball cards

Written Practice 41

1.
$$\begin{array}{r} 2\,0 \text{ questions} \\ \times\ 0.80 \\ \hline 16.00 \end{array}$$
16 questions

2.
$$\begin{array}{r} \$8.50 \\ \times\ 0.08 \\ \hline \$0.68\,00 \end{array}$$
\$0.68; Possible answer: An 8% sales tax means 8 cents per dollar, so the tax on \$8 is 64¢ and the tax on half a dollar is 4¢. 64¢ + 4¢ = 68¢.

3.
$$\begin{array}{r} 220 \text{ yards} \\ \times\ 4 \\ \hline 880 \text{ yards} \end{array}$$

4. Convert 20% to a fraction $\left(\frac{1}{5}\right)$ or a decimal (0.20), and multiply that number by 30.

5. $20.00 - 9.18 = b$

$$\begin{array}{r} \overset{1}{\cancel{2}}\overset{9}{\cancel{0}}.\overset{9}{\cancel{0}}{}^{1}0 \\ -\ \$\quad 9.18 \\ \hline \$10.82 \end{array}$$

(The top number is $20.00.)

6. $16 \cdot C = 288$

18 chairs

$$\begin{array}{r} 18 \\ 16\overline{)288} \\ 16 \\ \hline 128 \\ 128 \\ \hline 0 \end{array}$$

7.

$$\begin{array}{r} 126 \\ 102 \\ +\ 141 \\ \hline 369 \end{array} \qquad \begin{array}{r} \mathbf{123} \\ 3\overline{)369} \\ 3 \\ \hline 06 \\ 6 \\ \hline 09 \\ 9 \\ \hline 0 \end{array}$$

8.

$$\begin{array}{r} 2.5\text{ m} \\ \times\quad 2\text{ m} \\ \hline 5.0\text{ m}^2 \end{array}$$

5 m^2

9. $-1, 0, \frac{2}{3}, \frac{3}{2}$

10. 2, 3, 5, 7, 11, 13, 17, 19

11. D. 9; the sum of the digits is not divisible by 9.

12.

$$\begin{array}{r} \overset{5}{\cancel{6}}{}^{1}0 \\ -\ 15 \\ \hline 45 \end{array}\text{ losses}$$

$$\frac{\text{win}}{\text{loss}} = \frac{\mathbf{15}}{\mathbf{45}} = \frac{\mathbf{1}}{\mathbf{3}}$$

13.

$$\begin{array}{r} \overset{1}{2}8\text{ inches} \\ \times\quad 2 \\ \hline \mathbf{56\text{ inches}} \end{array}$$

14. a. Ivy

b. Main

15. B. 45°

16.

$$\begin{array}{r} 2.5 \\ \times\ 2.5 \\ \hline 125 \\ 500 \\ \hline \mathbf{6.25} \end{array}$$

17. 9

18. $\frac{40}{100} = \frac{\mathbf{2}}{\mathbf{5}}$

19. 0.09

$$\begin{array}{r} 0.09 \\ \times\quad 10 \\ \hline \mathbf{\$0.90} \end{array}$$

20. $\frac{\mathbf{3}}{\mathbf{2}}$

21.

$$\begin{array}{r} 500 \\ 7\overline{)3500} \\ 35 \\ \hline 00 \\ 00 \\ \hline 00 \\ 00 \\ \hline 0 \end{array}$$

check:

$$\begin{array}{r} 500 \\ \times\quad 7 \\ \hline 3500 \end{array}$$

$\boldsymbol{m = 500}$

22.

$$\begin{array}{r} \$\overset{0}{\cancel{1}}\overset{9}{\cancel{0}}.\overset{9}{\cancel{0}}{}^{1}0 \\ -\quad \$6.25 \\ \hline \$3.75 \end{array}$$

check:

$$\begin{array}{r} \overset{1}{\$6}.\overset{1}{2}5 \\ +\ \$3.75 \\ \hline \$10.00 \end{array}$$

$\boldsymbol{w = \$3.75}$

23. $n = \frac{\mathbf{3}}{\mathbf{2}}$ check: $\frac{2}{3} \times \frac{3}{2} = \frac{6}{6} = 1$

24.

$$\begin{array}{r} \overset{1}{3}7 \\ +\ 76 \\ \hline 113 \end{array}$$

check:

$$\begin{array}{r} \overset{0}{\cancel{1}}\overset{0}{\cancel{1}}{}^{1}3 \\ -\ 37 \\ \hline 76 \end{array}$$

$\boldsymbol{x = 113}$

25.

$$\begin{array}{r} \overset{3}{\cancel{4}}.{}^{1}0 \\ -\ 2.5 \\ \hline 1.5 \end{array} \qquad \begin{array}{r} 6.25 \\ +\ 1.5 \\ \hline \mathbf{7.75} \end{array}$$

26. $3\frac{3}{4} + 2\frac{3}{4} = 5\frac{6}{4} = 6\frac{2}{4} = \mathbf{6\frac{1}{2}}$

27. $1 - 1 = \mathbf{0}$

28. $\frac{5}{6} \cdot \frac{3}{5} = \frac{15}{30} = \mathbf{\frac{1}{2}}$

29. $\frac{3}{4} \times \frac{48}{1} = \frac{144}{4} = \mathbf{36}$

$$\begin{array}{r} 36 \\ 4\overline{)144} \\ 12 \\ \hline 24 \\ 24 \\ \hline 0 \end{array}$$

30. **$3; Round 9% to 10% and $32.17 to $30. Then find 10% ($\frac{1}{10}$) of $30.**

Practice Set 42

a. $\frac{1}{3} \times \frac{4}{4} = \frac{4}{12}$ **4**

b. $\frac{2}{3} \times \frac{2}{2} = \frac{4}{6}$ **4**

c. $\frac{3}{4} \times \frac{2}{2} = \frac{6}{8}$ **6**

d. $\frac{3}{4} \times \frac{3}{3} = \frac{9}{12}$ **9**

e.

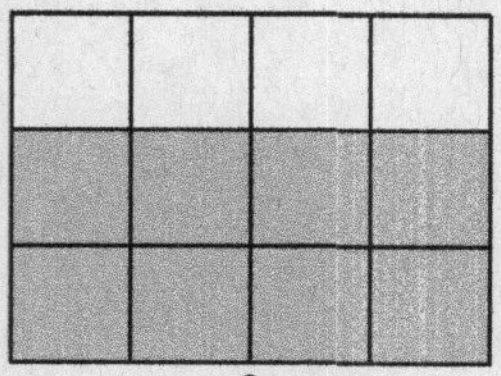

$\frac{8}{12}$

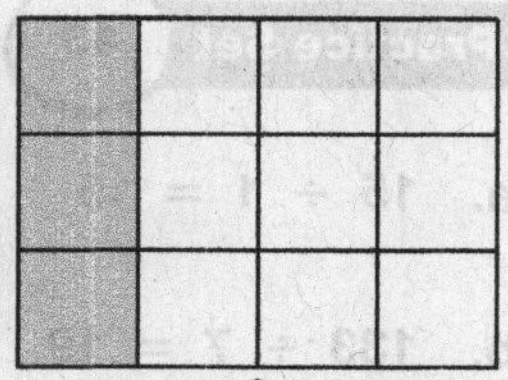

$\frac{3}{12}$

f. $\frac{2}{3} \times \frac{4}{4} = \frac{8}{12}$

$\frac{1}{4} \times \frac{3}{3} = \frac{3}{12}$

$\mathbf{\frac{8}{12} + \frac{3}{12} = \frac{11}{12}}$

g. **Sample answer: The shaded rectangles show the number of twelfths in $\frac{2}{3}$ and $\frac{1}{4}$. I can count the total number of shaded twelfths to find the sum of the fractions.**

h. $\frac{1}{6} \times \frac{2}{2} = \mathbf{\frac{2}{12}}$

$\mathbf{\frac{5}{12} - \frac{2}{12} = \frac{3}{12} = \frac{1}{4}}$

Written Practice 42

1. $\frac{1}{2} \times \frac{3}{3} = \frac{3}{6} \quad \frac{2}{3} \times \frac{2}{2} = \frac{4}{6}$

$\mathbf{\frac{3}{6} + \frac{4}{6} = \frac{7}{6} = 1\frac{1}{6}}$

2. **200,000,000,000 stars**

3.
$$\begin{array}{r} 120 \text{ yards} \\ \times \quad 40 \text{ yards} \\ \hline \end{array}$$
4800 square yards; Sample answer: Twelve times 4 is 48 so 120 times 40 would be 4800.

4.
$$\begin{array}{r} 0.40 \\ \times \quad 30 \\ \hline 12.00 \end{array}$$
12

5. $\frac{1}{2} \times \frac{4}{4} = \frac{4}{8}$ **4**

6. $\frac{1}{2} \times \frac{5}{5} = \frac{5}{10}$ **5**

7. $\sqrt{81} = 9$
$$\begin{array}{r} 4.32 \\ 0.6 \\ + \quad 9 \\ \hline \mathbf{13.92} \end{array}$$

8.
$$\begin{array}{r} \overset{5}{\cancel{6}}.\overset{12}{\cancel{3}}\overset{1}{0} \\ -\ 0.54 \\ \hline \mathbf{5.76} \end{array}$$

9.
$$\begin{array}{r} 0.15 \\ \times\ 0.15 \\ \hline 75 \\ 150 \\ \hline \mathbf{0.0225} \end{array}$$

10. $\mathbf{\frac{7}{6}}$

11. **4**

12. Multiples of 3
3, 6, 9, (12), 15, 18
Multiples of 4
4, 8, (12), 16, 20, 24
Multiples of 6
6, (12), 18, 24, 30, 36
LCM is **12**

13. $5\frac{3}{5} + 4\frac{4}{5} = 9\frac{7}{5} = \mathbf{10\frac{2}{5}}$

14. $\sqrt{36} = 6$

$$\begin{array}{r} 6 \\ -\ 4\frac{2}{3} \\ \hline \end{array} \xrightarrow{5 + \frac{3}{3}} \begin{array}{r} 5\frac{3}{3} \\ -\ 4\frac{2}{3} \\ \hline \mathbf{1\frac{1}{3}} \end{array}$$

15. $\frac{8}{3} \times \frac{1}{2} = \frac{8}{6} = 1\frac{2}{6} = \mathbf{1\frac{1}{3}}$

16. $\frac{6}{5} \times \frac{3}{1} = \frac{18}{5} = \mathbf{3\frac{3}{5}}$

17. $1 = \frac{4}{4} \qquad \frac{4}{4} - \frac{1}{4} = \mathbf{\frac{3}{4}}$

18.

$$\begin{array}{r} \frac{10}{10} \longrightarrow 1 \\ -\ \frac{5}{5} \longrightarrow 1 \\ \hline 0 \end{array} \qquad 1 - 1 = \mathbf{0}$$

19. Answers may vary but should include fractions such as $\frac{2}{6}$, $\frac{3}{9}$, and $\frac{4}{12}$.

20. 2 and 17

21. Round the scores to 12,000, 10,000, and 14,000. Add the scores and get 36,000; then divide by 3 to find the average (12,000 points).

22. 200; Round 8176 to 8000, and round 41 to 40. Then divide 8000 by 40.

23.

	12 eggs
$\frac{2}{3}$ of 12	4 eggs
	4 eggs
$\frac{1}{3}$ of 12	4 eggs

8 eggs

24. $\frac{3}{4} \times \frac{2}{2} = \mathbf{\frac{6}{8}}$

$\mathbf{\frac{7}{8}} - \mathbf{\frac{6}{8}} = \mathbf{\frac{1}{8}}$

25.

$$\begin{array}{r} \overset{1}{0}.4\text{ m} \\ 0.2\text{ m} \\ 0.4\text{ m} \\ +\ 0.2\text{ m} \\ \hline \mathbf{1.2\text{ m}} \end{array}$$

26.

$$\begin{array}{r} 0.4\text{ m} \\ \times\ 0.2\text{ m} \\ \hline \mathbf{0.08\text{ m}^2} \end{array}$$

27. $\mathbf{r - s = d}$
$\mathbf{s + d = r}$
$\mathbf{d + s = r}$

28. Divisor is 4; dividend is 20; quotient is 5

29.

$$\begin{array}{r} 11{:}45\text{ a.m.} \\ +\ 2{:}30 \\ \hline 13{:}75 \\ = 14{:}15 \end{array} \qquad \begin{array}{r} 14{:}15 \\ -\ 12{:}00 \\ \hline \mathbf{2{:}15\text{ p.m.}} \end{array}$$

30. a. $\mathbf{\frac{6}{5}}$

b. $\frac{6}{5} \times \frac{3}{1} = \mathbf{\frac{18}{5} = 3\frac{3}{5}}$

Practice Set 43

a. **15 ÷ 1 = 15**

b. **133 ÷ 7 = 19**

$$\begin{array}{r} 19 \\ 7\overline{)133} \\ 7 \\ \hline 63 \\ 63 \\ \hline 0 \end{array}$$

c.

$$\begin{array}{r} \overset{4}{\cancel{5}}.{}^{1}0 \\ -\ 3.\ 2 \\ \hline 1.\ 8 \end{array} \qquad \text{check: } \begin{array}{r} \overset{4}{\cancel{5}}.{}^{1}0 \\ -\ 1.\ 8 \\ \hline 3.\ 2 \end{array}$$

$d = \mathbf{1.8}$

d. $\frac{4}{5} + \frac{1}{5} = \frac{5}{5}$ check: $\frac{5}{5} - \frac{1}{5} = \frac{4}{5}$

$f = \mathbf{1}$

e.
$$\begin{array}{lcr} 4 & \xrightarrow{3\,+\,\frac{5}{5}} & 3\frac{5}{5} \\ -\ 1\frac{1}{5} & & -\ 1\frac{1}{5} \\ \hline & & m = \mathbf{2\frac{4}{5}} \end{array}$$

check:
$$\begin{array}{r} 2\frac{4}{5} \\ +\ 1\frac{1}{5} \\ \hline 3\frac{5}{5} = 4 \end{array}$$

f. $\frac{3}{8} \times \frac{8}{3} = \frac{24}{24} = 1$

$w = \mathbf{\frac{8}{3}}$

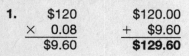

Written Practice 43

1.
$$\begin{array}{r} \$120 \\ \times\ \ 0.08 \\ \hline \$9.60 \end{array} \qquad \begin{array}{r} \$120.00 \\ +\ \ \$9.60 \\ \hline \mathbf{\$129.60} \end{array}$$

2. **150 − 128 = *d***
$$\begin{array}{r} 1\overset{4}{\cancel{5}}{}^{1}0 \\ -\ 1\ 2\ 8 \\ \hline \mathbf{2\ 2} \end{array}$$
empty places

3.
$$\begin{array}{r} 19.73 \text{ seconds} \\ -\ 19.32 \text{ seconds} \\ \hline \mathbf{0.41 \text{ second}} \end{array}$$

4. $\frac{2}{3} \times \frac{2}{2} = \frac{4}{6}$ **4**

5. $\frac{1}{2} \times \frac{3}{3} = \frac{3}{6}$ **3**

6. $n = \mathbf{\frac{3}{2}}$ check: $\frac{2}{3} \times \frac{3}{2} = \frac{6}{6} = 1$

7.
$$\begin{array}{lcr} 6 & \xrightarrow{5\,+\,\frac{5}{5}} & 5\frac{5}{5} \\ -\ 1\frac{4}{5} & & -\ 1\frac{4}{5} \\ \hline & & w = \mathbf{4\frac{1}{5}} \end{array}$$

check:
$$\begin{array}{lcr} 6 & \xrightarrow{5\,+\,\frac{5}{5}} & 5\frac{5}{5} \\ -\ 4\frac{1}{5} & & -\ 4\frac{1}{5} \\ \hline & & 1\frac{4}{5} \end{array}$$

8. $4\frac{1}{4} + 6\frac{3}{4} = 10\frac{4}{4} = 11$

$m = \mathbf{11}$

check:
$$\begin{array}{lcr} 11 & \xrightarrow{10\,+\,\frac{4}{4}} & 10\frac{4}{4} \\ -\ 4\frac{1}{4} & & -\ 4\frac{1}{4} \\ \hline & & 6\frac{3}{4} \end{array}$$

9.
$$\begin{array}{r} 2.45 \\ +\ 3 \\ \hline 5.45 \end{array} \qquad \text{check:} \quad \begin{array}{r} 5.45 \\ -\ 2.45 \\ \hline 3.00 \end{array}$$
$c = \mathbf{5.45}$

10.
$$\begin{array}{r} 1\overset{1}{\cancel{2}}.\overset{9}{\cancel{0}}{}^{1}0 \\ -\ \ 1.\ 4\ 3 \\ \hline 1\ 0.\ 5\ 7 \end{array} \qquad \text{check:} \quad \begin{array}{r} 1\overset{1}{\cancel{2}}.\overset{9}{\cancel{0}}{}^{1}0 \\ -\ 1\ 0.\ 5\ 7 \\ \hline 1.\ 4\ 3 \end{array}$$
$d = \mathbf{10.57}$

11. $\frac{5}{8} \times \frac{1}{5} = \frac{5}{40} = \mathbf{\frac{1}{8}}$

12. $\frac{3}{4} \times \frac{5}{1} = \frac{15}{4} = \mathbf{3\frac{3}{4}}$

13. $3\frac{7}{8} - 1\frac{3}{8} = 2\frac{4}{8} = \mathbf{2\frac{1}{2}}$

14. **B. 33**

15.
$$\begin{array}{ccc} \frac{2}{2} & \textcircled{=} & \frac{2}{2} \times \frac{2}{2} \\ 1 & & 1 \times 1 \\ & & 1 \end{array}$$

16. **−12**

17. **9.12**

18. **67,000,000**

19. 0.37×100

$$\begin{array}{r} 0.37 \\ \times \quad 100 \\ \hline \mathbf{37.00} \end{array}$$ or **37**

20.

$$\begin{array}{r} 0.6 \\ \times\ 0.4 \\ \hline 0.24 \end{array} \qquad \begin{array}{r} 0.24 \\ \times\ 0.2 \\ \hline \mathbf{0.048} \end{array}$$

21. $4\overline{)80}$ feet = 20 (8, 00, 00, 0)

$$\begin{array}{r} 20 \\ \times\ 20 \\ \hline \mathbf{400} \end{array}$$ **square feet**

22. $16\overline{)100}$ = $6\frac{4}{16} = \mathbf{6\frac{1}{4}}$ (96, 4)

23. a. $\mathbf{25 \div 4 = 6\frac{1}{4}}$

$4\overline{)25}$ = $6\frac{1}{4}$ (24, 1)

b. $\mathbf{9 \div 1 = 9}$

24. Multiples of 4
4, 8, 12, 16, 20, (24), 28
Multiples of 6
6, 12, 18, (24), 30, 36
Multiples of 8
8, 16, (24), 32, 40
LCM is **24**

25. $\mathbf{\frac{1}{2}, \frac{9}{16}, \frac{5}{8}}$

26. $\mathbf{1\frac{5}{8}}$ **inches**

27. $\mathbf{4\frac{7}{10}}$

28. $\frac{1}{2} \times \frac{5}{5} = \frac{5}{10} \qquad \frac{1}{5} \times \frac{2}{2} = \frac{2}{10}$

$\frac{5}{10} + \frac{2}{10} = \mathbf{\frac{7}{10}}$

29. 20 seats

	20 seats
$\frac{2}{5}$ were occupied	4 seats
	4 seats
$\frac{3}{5}$ were not occupied	4 seats
	4 seats
	4 seats

8 seats $\qquad \frac{40}{100} = \mathbf{\frac{2}{5}}$

30. a. **Right**
b. **Acute**
c. **Obtuse**
d. **Right**

Practice Set 44

a. **0.05**

b. **50**

c. **1.25**

d. **4**

e. 0.2 (>) 0.15

f. 12.5 (>) 1.25

g. 0.012 (<) 0.12

h. 0.31 (>) 0.039

i. 0.4 (=) 0.40

j. **0.015, 0.12, 0.125, 0.2**

Written Practice 44

1. 4, 8, (12)
5, 10, (15)
12 + 15 = **27**

2.

$$\begin{array}{r} 5280 \text{ feet} \\ \times \qquad 5 \\ \hline \mathbf{26{,}400 \text{ feet}} \end{array}$$

3. $\begin{array}{r} 2\overset{8}{\cancel{9}},\overset{9}{\cancel{0}}{}^{1}3\,5 \\ -\ 1\,4,\,4\,9\,5 \\ \hline \end{array}$ **14,540 feet**

4. $\begin{array}{r} 2\,\overset{8}{\cancel{9}},{}^{1}0\,3\,5 \text{ feet} \\ -\ 2\,6,\,4\,0\,0 \text{ feet} \\ \hline \end{array}$ **2635 feet**

5. $5\frac{1}{3} - 4$; $w = \mathbf{1\frac{1}{3}}$

check: $5\frac{1}{3} - 1\frac{1}{3} = 4$

6. $6\frac{4}{5} + 1\frac{3}{5} = 7\frac{7}{5} = 8\frac{2}{5}$

$m = \mathbf{8\frac{2}{5}}$

check: $7\frac{7}{5} - 6\frac{4}{5} = 1\frac{3}{5}$

7. $\begin{array}{r} \overset{1\,1}{6.74} \\ +\ 0.285 \\ \hline 7.025 \end{array}$

check: $\begin{array}{r} \overset{1\,1}{6.74} \\ 0.285 \\ +\ 4 \\ \hline 11.025 \end{array}$

$\begin{array}{r} \overset{0}{\cancel{1}}{}^{1}1.\,0\,2\,5 \\ -\ 7.\,0\,2\,5 \\ \hline 4.\,0\,0\,0 \end{array}$

$f = \mathbf{4}$

8. $\begin{array}{r} 0.\,\overset{3}{\cancel{4}}{}^{1}0 \\ -\ 0.\,3\,3 \\ \hline 0.\,0\,7 \end{array}$

$d = \mathbf{0.07}$

check: $\begin{array}{r} 0.\,\overset{3}{\cancel{4}}{}^{1}0 \\ -\ 0.\,0\,7 \\ \hline 0.\,3\,3 \end{array}$

9. $67\frac{3}{4} - 1\frac{1}{4} = 66\frac{2}{4} = \mathbf{66\frac{1}{2}}$ **inches**

10. **17 ÷ 1 = 17**

11. **0.032**

12. $\frac{1}{6} \times \frac{24{,}042}{1} = \frac{24{,}042}{6}$

$\begin{array}{r} \mathbf{4{,}007} \\ 6\overline{)24{,}042} \\ 24 \\ \hline 0\,0 \\ 0\,0 \\ \hline 04 \\ 00 \\ \hline 42 \\ 42 \\ \hline 0 \end{array}$

13. a. 0.25 ⓥ> 0.125

b. 25% > 12.5%

14. 600 + 4 = **604**

15. **\$3.60; 10% of \$36 is $\frac{1}{10}$ of \$36. Find $\frac{1}{10}$ of \$36 by dividing \$36 by 10.**

16. a. $\mathbf{\frac{8}{5}}$

b. $\frac{8}{5} \times \frac{3}{1} = \mathbf{\frac{24}{5}} = \mathbf{4\frac{4}{5}}$

17. Multiples of 2
2, 4, 6, 8, 10, ⑫, 14
Multiples of 3
3, 6, 9, ⑫, 15, 18
Multiples of 4
4, 8, ⑫, 16, 20, 24
Multiples of 6
6, ⑫, 18, 24, 30, 36
LCM is **12**

18. $\begin{array}{r} 1.3 \\ \times\ 1.3 \\ \hline 39 \\ 130 \\ \hline \mathbf{1.69} \end{array}$

19. $\frac{3}{4} \times \frac{3}{3} = \frac{9}{12}$ **9**

20. $\frac{2}{3} \times \frac{4}{4} = \frac{8}{12}$ **8**

21.
$$\begin{array}{r} \overset{1}{26} \\ 37 \\ 42 \\ +\ 43 \\ \hline 148 \end{array} \qquad \begin{array}{r} 37 \\ 4\overline{)148} \\ \underline{12} \\ 28 \\ \underline{28} \\ 0 \end{array}$$

22. **365,000**

23.
$$\begin{array}{r} \overset{2}{\not{3}}{}^{1}0 \\ -\ 1\ 2 \\ \hline 1\ 8 \end{array} \text{ boys} \qquad \frac{\text{boys}}{\text{girls}} = \frac{18}{12} = \mathbf{\frac{3}{2}}$$

24. a. **1, 2, 4, 5, 10, 20, 25, 50, 100**

b. **2 and 5**

25. $\mathbf{\frac{9}{100}}$**; 0.09**

26. $\frac{3}{4} \times \frac{3}{3} = \frac{9}{12} \qquad \frac{2}{3} \times \frac{4}{4} = \frac{8}{12}$

$\mathbf{\frac{9}{12} + \frac{8}{12} = \frac{17}{12} = 1\frac{5}{12}}$

27. **B. 40%. Nearly half of the rectangle is shaded. Since $\frac{1}{2}$ equals 50%, the shaded part is close to but less than 50%.**

28.
$$\begin{array}{rl} \overset{12:\,135}{\not{2}:\not{1}\not{5}} & \text{p.m.} \\ -\ 10:30 & \text{a.m.} \\ \hline 2:105 & \\ = 3:45 & \end{array}$$

3 hours 45 minutes

29. **C. 1.1**

30. $\mathbf{10\frac{1}{10}}$

Practice Set 45

a.
$$\begin{array}{r} \mathbf{1.8} \\ 2\overline{)3.6} \\ \underline{2} \\ 1\ 6 \\ \underline{1\ 6} \\ 0 \end{array} \text{ miles}$$

1.8 miles

b.
$$\begin{array}{r} \mathbf{1.6} \\ 4\overline{)6.4} \\ \underline{4} \\ 2\ 4 \\ \underline{2\ 4} \\ 0 \end{array} \text{ meters}$$

1.6 meters; I can multiply 1.6 by 4 or add 1.6 + 1.6 + 1.6 + 1.6.

c.
$$\begin{array}{r} \mathbf{1.5} \\ 3\overline{)4.5} \\ \underline{3} \\ 1\ 5 \\ \underline{1\ 5} \\ 0 \end{array}$$

d.
$$\begin{array}{r} \mathbf{0.15} \\ 4\overline{)0.60} \\ \underline{4} \\ 20 \\ \underline{20} \\ 0 \end{array}$$

e.
$$\begin{array}{r} \mathbf{0.07} \\ 2\overline{)0.14} \\ \underline{0\ 0} \\ 14 \\ \underline{14} \\ 0 \end{array}$$

f.
$$\begin{array}{r} \mathbf{0.08} \\ 5\overline{)0.40} \\ \underline{0\ 0} \\ 40 \\ \underline{40} \\ 0 \end{array}$$

g.
$$\begin{array}{r} \mathbf{0.075} \\ 4\overline{)0.300} \\ \underline{0\ 0} \\ 30 \\ \underline{28} \\ 20 \\ \underline{20} \\ 0 \end{array}$$

h.
$$\begin{array}{r} \mathbf{0.002} \\ 6\overline{)0.012} \\ \underline{00} \\ 12 \\ \underline{12} \\ 0 \end{array}$$

i.
$$\begin{array}{r} 0.14 \\ 10\overline{)1.40} \\ \underline{1\,0} \\ 40 \\ \underline{40} \\ 0 \end{array}$$

j.
$$\begin{array}{r} 0.14 \\ 5\overline{)0.70} \\ \underline{5} \\ 20 \\ \underline{20} \\ 0 \end{array}$$

k.
$$\begin{array}{r} 0.025 \\ 4\overline{)0.100} \\ \underline{0} \\ 10 \\ \underline{8} \\ 20 \\ \underline{20} \\ 0 \end{array}$$

Written Practice 45

1. $\mathbf{\frac{3}{5}}$

2.
$$\begin{array}{r} 50 \\ 20\overline{)1000} \\ \underline{100} \\ 00 \\ \underline{00} \\ 0 \end{array}$$

50 $20 bills

3. $\frac{2}{3} \times \frac{24}{1} = \frac{48}{3}$

$$\begin{array}{r} 16 \text{ shots made} \\ 3\overline{)48} \\ \underline{3} \\ 18 \\ \underline{18} \\ 0 \end{array}$$

$16 \times 2 =$ **32 points**

4.
$$\begin{array}{r} 1.5 \\ 3\overline{)4.5} \\ \underline{3} \\ 1\,5 \\ \underline{1\,5} \\ 0 \end{array}$$

5.
$$\begin{array}{r} 0.03 \\ 8\overline{)0.24} \\ \underline{0\,0} \\ 24 \\ \underline{24} \\ 0 \end{array}$$

6.
$$\begin{array}{r} 0.16 \\ 5\overline{)0.80} \\ \underline{5} \\ 30 \\ \underline{30} \\ 0 \end{array}$$

7. Multiples of 2
2, 4, 6, 8, 10, 12, 14, 16, 18, 20, 22, (24)
Multiples of 4
4, 8, 12, 16, 20, (24), 28
Multiples of 6
6, 12, 18, (24), 30
Multiples of 8
8, 16, (24), 32, 40
LCM is **24**

8. $\sqrt{36} = 6$

$$\begin{array}{r} 6 \\ \underline{-\ 2\frac{3}{10}} \end{array} \xrightarrow{5 + \frac{10}{10}} \begin{array}{r} 5\frac{10}{10} \\ \underline{-\ 2\frac{3}{10}} \\ m = \mathbf{3\frac{7}{10}} \end{array}$$

check:

$$\begin{array}{r} 6 \\ \underline{-\ 3\frac{7}{10}} \end{array} \xrightarrow{5 + \frac{10}{10}} \begin{array}{r} 5\frac{10}{10} \\ \underline{-\ 3\frac{7}{10}} \\ 2\frac{3}{10} \end{array}$$

9. $2\frac{2}{5} + 5\frac{4}{5} = 7\frac{6}{5} = 8\frac{1}{5}$

check: $7\frac{6}{5} - 2\frac{2}{5} = 5\frac{4}{5}$

$g = \mathbf{8\frac{1}{5}}$

10.
$$\begin{array}{r} \overset{1\,1}{1.56} \\ \underline{+\ 1.44} \\ 3.00 \end{array}$$

check:

$$\begin{array}{r} \overset{2\ \ 9}{\cancel{3}.\,\cancel{0}{}^{1}0} \\ \underline{-\ 1.\,5\,6} \\ 1.\,4\,4 \end{array}$$

$m = \mathbf{3}$

Solutions

11. $\begin{array}{r} \overset{8}{\not 9}.\overset{9}{\not 0}{}^{1}0 \\ -\ 5.\ 3\ 9 \\ \hline 3.\ 6\ 1 \end{array}$ check: $\begin{array}{r} \overset{8}{\not 9}.\overset{9}{\not 0}{}^{1}0 \\ -\ 3.\ 6\ 1 \\ \hline 5.\ 3\ 9 \end{array}$

$n = \mathbf{3.61}$

12. $4\frac{3}{8} - 2\frac{1}{8} = 2\frac{2}{8} = \mathbf{2\frac{1}{4}}$

13. $\frac{8}{3} \cdot \frac{5}{2} = \frac{40}{6}$

$\begin{array}{r} 6\frac{4}{6} \\ 6\overline{)40} \\ \underline{36} \\ 4 \end{array} = \mathbf{6\frac{2}{3}}$

14. $\begin{array}{r} 700 \\ \times\ \ 400 \\ \hline \mathbf{280{,}000} \end{array}$

15. $\begin{array}{r} 0.7 \\ \times\ 0.6 \\ \hline 0.42 \end{array}$ $\begin{array}{r} 0.42 \\ \times\ \ 0.5 \\ \hline 0.210 \end{array} = \mathbf{0.21}$

16. $\begin{array}{r} 0.46 \\ \times\ 0.17 \\ \hline 322 \\ \underline{460} \\ \mathbf{0.0782} \end{array}$

17. $\mathbf{8 \times a = 177.6}$

$\begin{array}{r} \mathbf{22.2} \\ 8\overline{)177.6} \\ \underline{16} \\ 17 \\ \underline{16} \\ 1\,6 \\ \underline{1\,6} \\ 0 \end{array}$ **miles per gallon**

18. $\frac{3}{8} \times \frac{6}{1} = \frac{18}{8}$

$\begin{array}{r} 2\frac{2}{8} \\ 8\overline{)18} \\ \underline{16} \\ 2 \end{array} = \mathbf{2\frac{1}{4}}$**; Multiplication**

19. \$10; 25% of \$40 is $\frac{1}{4}$ of \$40. Divide \$40 by 4 to find 25% of \$40.

20. $\frac{5}{6} \times \frac{2}{2} = \frac{10}{12}$

$\mathbf{\frac{10}{12} - \frac{7}{12} = \frac{3}{12} = \frac{1}{4}}$

21. a. $\sqrt{36\text{ ft}^2} = \mathbf{6\text{ ft}}$

b. 6 ft × 4 = **24 ft**

22. $\mathbf{\frac{27}{100}}$**; 0.27**

23. $\mathbf{1\frac{1}{8}}$ **inches**

24. $\frac{75}{100} = \mathbf{\frac{3}{4}}$

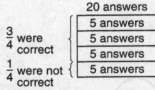

20 answers

$\frac{3}{4}$ were correct: 5 answers, 5 answers, 5 answers

$\frac{1}{4}$ were not correct: 5 answers

15 correct answers

25. $\mathbf{\frac{2}{3} \times \frac{1}{2} = \frac{1}{3}}$

$\mathbf{\frac{1}{3} \div \frac{1}{2} = \frac{2}{3}}$

$\mathbf{\frac{1}{3} \div \frac{2}{3} = \frac{1}{2}}$

26. B. 60%. Since a little more than half of the circle is shaded, a little more than 50% is shaded.

27. a. $\mathbf{\frac{9}{100}}$

b. 0.09

28. 15 ÷ 1 = 15

29. $\begin{array}{r} \overset{1}{2}4 \text{ students} \\ \times\ 3\qquad\quad \\ \hline \mathbf{72\ students} \end{array}$

30. $\begin{array}{r} 2640 \text{ feet} \\ 2\overline{)5280} \text{ feet} \\ \underline{4} \\ 12 \\ \underline{12} \\ 08 \\ \underline{8} \\ 00 \\ \underline{00} \\ 0 \end{array}$

$\begin{array}{r} \textbf{880 times} \\ 3\overline{)2640} \\ \underline{24} \\ 24 \\ \underline{24} \\ 00 \\ \underline{00} \\ 0 \end{array}$

Early Finishers Solutions

Estimate: 5% + 15% = 20%; Round the cost of the meal to $14. 10% of $14 is $1.40 so 20% of $14 is twice $1.40, or $2.80. The total cost of the meal, is $14 + $2.80 = $16.80. $16.80 divided by 2 is $8.40 which is what each person must pay.

Practice Set 46

a. $(2 \times 1) + \left(5 \times \frac{1}{100}\right)$

b. $(2 \times 10) + \left(5 \times \frac{1}{10}\right)$

c. $\left(2 \times \frac{1}{10}\right) + \left(5 \times \frac{1}{1000}\right)$

d. 70.8

e. 0.64

f. 3.5

g. 35

h. 25

i. 250

j. 1.25

k. 12.5

l. False

m. True

n. $\frac{15}{5} = 3$

o. $\frac{250}{5} = 50$

Written Practice 46

1. $\frac{30}{8} = 3\frac{6}{8} = 3\frac{3}{4}$

2. $100.2 - 98.6 = d$

$\begin{array}{r} \overset{0}{\not 1}\,\overset{9}{\not 0}\,\overset{9}{\not 0}.{}^{1}2°\text{F} \\ -98.6°\text{F} \\ \hline \textbf{1.6°F} \end{array}$

3. $\begin{array}{r} 20 \\ +\ 4 \\ \hline 24 \end{array}$ $\begin{array}{r} \textbf{2 dozen} \\ 12\overline{)24} \\ \underline{24} \\ 0 \end{array}$

4. 50.607

5. $\frac{21}{100}$; 0.21

6. $\frac{20}{100} = \frac{1}{5}$

7. $\begin{array}{r} 1.27 \\ 5\overline{)6.35} \\ \underline{5} \\ 1\,3 \\ \underline{1\,0} \\ 35 \\ \underline{35} \\ 0 \end{array}$

8.
$$\begin{array}{r} 0.125 \\ 4\overline{)0.500} \\ \underline{4} \\ 10 \\ \underline{8} \\ 20 \\ \underline{20} \\ 0 \end{array}$$

9.
$$\begin{array}{r} 0.125 \\ 8\overline{)1.000} \\ \underline{8} \\ 20 \\ \underline{16} \\ 40 \\ \underline{40} \\ 0 \end{array}$$

10.
$$9 \xrightarrow{8 + \frac{8}{8}} 8\frac{8}{8}$$
$$\begin{array}{r} 9 \\ \underline{-\ 3\frac{5}{8}} \end{array} \qquad \begin{array}{r} 8\frac{8}{8} \\ \underline{-\ 3\frac{5}{8}} \\ 5\frac{3}{8} \end{array}$$
$x = \mathbf{5\frac{3}{8}}$

11. $16\frac{1}{4} + 4\frac{3}{4} = 20\frac{4}{4} = 21$
$y = \mathbf{21}$

12.
$$\begin{array}{r} \overset{0}{\cancel{1}}.\overset{9}{\cancel{0}}\,\overset{9}{\cancel{0}}\,{}^{1}0 \\ \underline{-\ 0.\ 2\ 3\ 5} \\ 0.\ 7\ 6\ 5 \end{array}$$
$q = \mathbf{0.765}$

13.
$$\begin{array}{r} 26.9 \\ \underline{+\ 12.0} \\ 38.9 \end{array} \qquad \begin{array}{r} 4\ \overset{8}{\cancel{9}}.{}^{1}2\ 5 \\ \underline{-\ 3\ 8.\ 9} \\ 1\ 0.\ 3\ 5 \end{array}$$
$w = \mathbf{10.35}$

14.
$$\begin{array}{r} 2.5\text{ cm} \\ \underline{\times\ \ 4\text{ cm}} \\ 10.0\text{ cm}^2 \end{array} \qquad \begin{array}{r} \mathbf{5\text{ cm}^2} \\ 2\overline{)10\text{ cm}^2} \\ \underline{10\phantom{\text{ cm}^2}} \\ 0\phantom{\text{ cm}^2} \end{array}$$
; The area of the rectangle is 4 cm × 2.5 cm = 10 cm². Since 50% means $\frac{1}{2}$, the area of the shaded part is $\frac{1}{2}$ of 10 cm², which is 5 cm².

15. $\dfrac{\text{dime}}{\text{quarter}} = \dfrac{10}{25} = \mathbf{\dfrac{2}{5}}$

16.
$$\begin{array}{r} 0.25 \\ \underline{\times\ \ 3.7} \\ 175 \\ \underline{750} \\ \mathbf{0.925} \end{array}$$

17. $\dfrac{3}{4} \times \dfrac{3}{3} = \dfrac{9}{12}$ **9**

18. Multiples of 3
3, 6, 9, 12, 15, 18, 21, (24)
Multiples of 4
4, 8, 12, 16, 20, (24), 28
Multiples of 8
8, 16, (24), 32, 40
LCM is **24**

19. a. $\dfrac{1}{10}$ (=) 0.1
$\dfrac{1}{10}$

b. 0.1 (>) $(0.1)^2$
$$\begin{array}{r} 0.1 \\ \underline{\times\ 0.1} \\ 0.01 \end{array}$$

20. 7

21.
$$\begin{array}{r} 80 \\ 50\overline{)4000} \\ \underline{400} \\ 00 \\ \underline{00} \\ 0 \end{array}$$

22. $\sqrt{100\text{ cm}^2} = 10\text{ cm}$
$$\begin{array}{r} 10\text{ cm} \\ \underline{\times\ \ 4\phantom{\text{ cm}}} \\ \mathbf{40\text{ cm}} \end{array}$$

23.
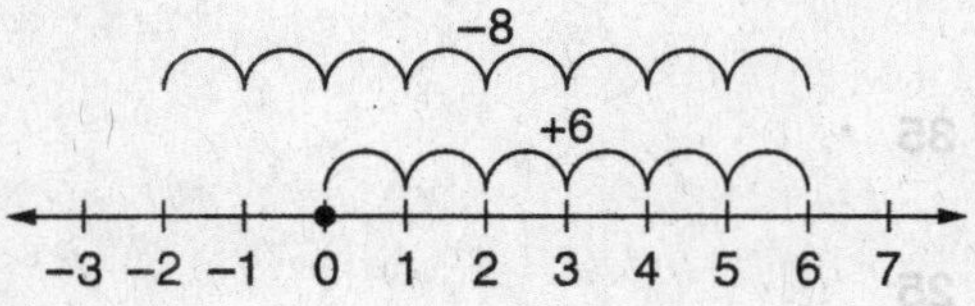

−2

24. $\dfrac{1}{2} \cdot \dfrac{4}{5} = \dfrac{4}{10} = \mathbf{\dfrac{2}{5}}$

25. $\left(\frac{3}{4}\right)\left(\frac{5}{3}\right) = \frac{15}{12} = 1\frac{3}{12} = \mathbf{1\frac{1}{4}}$

26. **Radius, diameter, circumference**

27.
$$\begin{array}{r} \$6.95 \\ \times\ 0.08 \\ \hline .5560 \end{array} \rightarrow \$0.56 \qquad \begin{array}{r} \$6.95 \\ +\ \$0.56 \\ \hline \$7.51 \end{array}$$

\$7.51; Round \$6.95 to \$7. 8% is a little less than 10%. 10% of \$7 is 70¢. Adding 70¢ to \$7 gives \$7.70, so \$7.51 is reasonable.

28. $\frac{6}{8}$ **inch** $\left(\text{or } \frac{3}{4} \textbf{ inch}\right)$

29. a. $\frac{8}{3}$

b. $\frac{8}{3} \times \frac{3}{1} = \frac{24}{3} = \frac{8}{1} = \mathbf{8}$

30. $\frac{1}{2} \times \frac{3}{3} = \frac{3}{6} \quad \frac{1}{3} \times \frac{2}{2} = \frac{2}{6}$

$\frac{3}{6} + \frac{2}{6} = \mathbf{\frac{5}{6}}$

Practice Set 47

a. **The product of "2 times *r*" in the second formula is equivalent to *d* in the first formula because 2 radii equal one diameter, so two radii times π equals one diameter times π.**

b. $C = \pi d$
$C \approx (3.14)(2 \text{ in.})$
$C \approx$ **6.28 in.**

c. $d = 3 \text{ cm} \times 2 = 6 \text{ cm}$
$C = \pi d$
$C \approx (3.14)(6 \text{ cm})$
$C \approx$ **18.84 cm**

d. $C = \pi d$
$C \approx (3.14)(0.75 \text{ in.})$
$C \approx$ **2.36 inches; If the diameter was one inch, the circumference would be about 3.14 inches. Since the diameter is a little less than an inch, the circumference should be a little less than 3.14 inches.**

e. $\mathbf{2\frac{3}{8}}$ **inches**

f. **C. 90 ft; The radius is about 15 ft, so the diameter is about 30 ft. Using 3 as a rough approximation for π, we calculate that the circumference is about 3 × 30 ft, or about 90 ft.**

g. $d = 5 \text{ in.} \times 2 = 10 \text{ in.}$
$C = \pi d$
$C \approx (3.14)(10 \text{ in.})$
$C \approx$ **31.4 inches**

Written Practice 47

1. 1, 3, 5, 7, 9, 11, 13, 15, 17, **(19)**

2. **600 × *h* = 3000**
$$\begin{array}{r} 5 \\ 600\overline{)3000} \\ \underline{3000} \\ 0 \end{array}$$
5 hours

3.
$$\begin{array}{r} 6 \\ 2\overline{)12} \\ \underline{12} \\ 0 \end{array}$$
6 months

4. $A = bh$
$A = (8)(4)$
$A =$ **32**

5. **2 · 2 · 3 · 3 · 3 · 5 · 5 · 7**

6. $\frac{4}{1} \times \frac{1}{2} = \frac{4}{2} = \mathbf{2}$

7. $\mathbf{(6 \times 1) + \left(2 \times \frac{1}{10}\right) + \left(5 \times \frac{1}{100}\right)}$

8. $\mathbf{\frac{99}{100}}$**; 0.99**

9.
$$\begin{array}{r} \mathbf{0.015} \\ 12\overline{)0.180} \\ \underline{0\,0} \\ 18 \\ \underline{12} \\ 60 \\ \underline{60} \\ 0 \end{array}$$

10.
$$10\overline{)12.30}\ \text{quotient } \mathbf{1.23}$$
$$\begin{array}{r} 10 \\ \hline 2\,3 \\ 2\,0 \\ \hline 30 \\ 30 \\ \hline 0 \end{array}$$

11. $w \div 6 = 36$
$$\begin{array}{r} 36 \\ \times\ 6 \\ \hline 216 \end{array}$$
$w = \mathbf{216}$

12.
$$5\overline{)1.25}\ \text{quotient } 0.25$$
$$\begin{array}{r} 1\,0 \\ \hline 25 \\ 25 \\ \hline 0 \end{array}$$
$y = \mathbf{0.25}$

13.
$$\begin{array}{r} 10 \\ -\ 5\frac{11}{12} \\ \hline \end{array} \xrightarrow{9\ +\ \frac{12}{12}} \begin{array}{r} 9\frac{12}{12} \\ -\ 5\frac{11}{12} \\ \hline 4\frac{1}{12} \end{array}$$
$n = \mathbf{4\frac{1}{12}}$

14. $6\frac{2}{5} + 3\frac{3}{5} = 9\frac{5}{5} = 10$
$m = \mathbf{10}$

15. $8\frac{3}{4} + 5\frac{3}{4} = 13\frac{6}{4} = 14\frac{2}{4} = \mathbf{14\frac{1}{2}}$

16. $\frac{5}{3} \times \frac{5}{4} = \frac{25}{12} = \mathbf{2\frac{1}{12}}$

17. $\frac{3}{4} \times \frac{5}{5} = \mathbf{\frac{15}{20}}$

18. $\frac{3}{5} \times \frac{4}{4} = \mathbf{\frac{12}{20}}$

19.
$$\begin{array}{r} {}^{1} \\ 18 \\ 20 \\ 18 \\ 20 \\ +\ 20 \\ \hline 96 \end{array} \qquad 5\overline{)96}\ \text{quotient } 19\tfrac{1}{5} \quad \begin{array}{r} 5 \\ \hline 46 \\ 45 \\ \hline 1 \end{array}$$
C. 19

20. $C = \pi d$
$C \approx (3.14)(20 \text{ in.})$
$C \approx$ **62.8 inches; The distance around a circle is a little more than three times the distance across the circle, so the distance around a 20-inch diameter tire is a little more than 3 × 20 inches.**

21. Factors of 20
①, ②, 4, ⑤, ⑩, 20
Factors of 30
①, ②, 3, ⑤, 6, ⑩, 15, 30
1, 2, 5, 10

22. **62.5; Since the problem is to multiply by 10, simply shift the decimal point in 6.25 one place to the right.**

23. $\frac{12.5}{5}$
$$5\overline{)12.5}\ \text{quotient } \mathbf{2.5}$$
$$\begin{array}{r} 10 \\ \hline 2\,5 \end{array}$$

24.
$$\begin{array}{r} 0.90 \\ \times\ \ 40 \\ \hline 36.00 \end{array}$$
36

25.
$$\begin{array}{r} 687 \\ -\ 365 \\ \hline 322 \end{array}$$
322 more days

26.
$$200\overline{)700}\ \text{quotient } 3$$
$$\begin{array}{r} 600 \\ \hline 100 \end{array}$$
About 3 times

27. **Length = 1 inch**

Width = $\frac{3}{4}$ inch

28. $1 \text{ in.} + 1 \text{ in.} + \frac{3}{4} \text{ in.} + \frac{3}{4} \text{ in.}$

$2 \text{ in.} + \frac{6}{4} \text{ in.} = 2 \text{ in.} + 1\frac{2}{4} \text{ in.}$

$= 2 \text{ in.} + 1\frac{1}{2} \text{ in.} = \mathbf{3\frac{1}{2}}$ **inches**

29. $\frac{2}{5} \times \frac{2}{2} = \frac{4}{10}$

$\frac{9}{10} - \frac{4}{10} = \frac{5}{10} = \mathbf{\frac{1}{2}}$

30. **The numbers 1.5 and 1.50 are equivalent. Attaching a zero to a decimal number does not shift place values. To multiply 1.5 by 10, we can move the decimal point one place to the right, which shifts the place values and makes the product 15.**

Early Finishers Solutions

Estimate: \$12 + 2(\$15) + \$10 = \$52; Hassan does not have enough money.

Practice Set 48

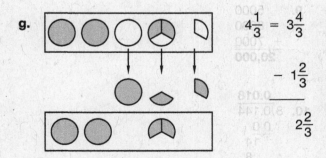

a.
$$\begin{array}{r} 4\frac{1}{3} \\ -\ 1\frac{2}{3} \\ \hline \end{array} \xrightarrow{3 + \frac{3}{3} + \frac{1}{3}} \begin{array}{r} 3\frac{4}{3} \\ -\ 1\frac{2}{3} \\ \hline \mathbf{2\frac{2}{3}} \end{array}$$

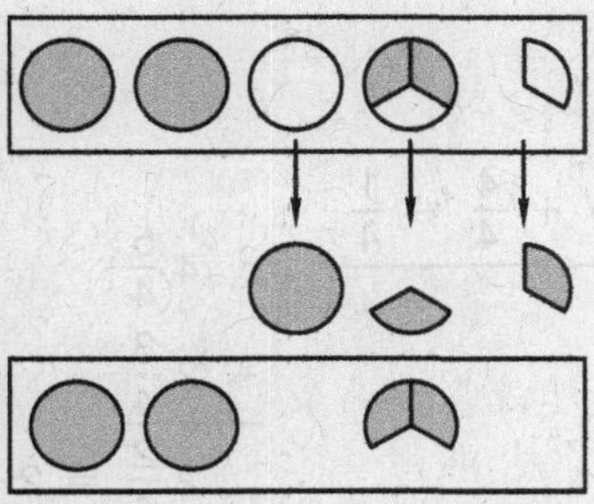

$4\frac{1}{3} = 3\frac{4}{3}$

$-\ 1\frac{2}{3}$

$2\frac{2}{3}$

b.
$$\begin{array}{r} 3\frac{2}{5} \\ -\ 2\frac{3}{5} \\ \hline \end{array} \xrightarrow{2 + \frac{5}{5} + \frac{2}{5}} \begin{array}{r} 2\frac{7}{5} \\ -\ 2\frac{3}{5} \\ \hline \mathbf{\frac{4}{5}} \end{array}$$

c.
$$\begin{array}{r} 5\frac{2}{4} \\ -\ 1\frac{3}{4} \\ \hline \end{array} \xrightarrow{4 + \frac{4}{4} + \frac{2}{4}} \begin{array}{r} 4\frac{6}{4} \\ -\ 1\frac{3}{4} \\ \hline \mathbf{3\frac{3}{4}} \end{array}$$

d.
$$\begin{array}{r} 5\frac{1}{8} \\ -\ 2\frac{4}{8} \\ \hline \end{array} \xrightarrow{4 + \frac{8}{8} + \frac{1}{8}} \begin{array}{r} 4\frac{9}{8} \\ -\ 2\frac{4}{8} \\ \hline \mathbf{2\frac{5}{8}} \end{array}$$

e.
$$\begin{array}{r} 7\frac{3}{12} \\ -\ 4\frac{10}{12} \\ \hline \end{array} \xrightarrow{6 + \frac{12}{12} + \frac{3}{12}} \begin{array}{r} 6\frac{15}{12} \\ -\ 4\frac{10}{12} \\ \hline \mathbf{2\frac{5}{12}} \end{array}$$

f.
$$\begin{array}{r} 6\frac{1}{4} \\ -\ 2\frac{3}{4} \\ \hline \end{array} \xrightarrow{5 + \frac{4}{4} + \frac{1}{4}} \begin{array}{r} 5\frac{5}{4} \\ -\ 2\frac{3}{4} \\ \hline 3\frac{2}{4} = \mathbf{3\frac{1}{2}} \end{array}$$

g.

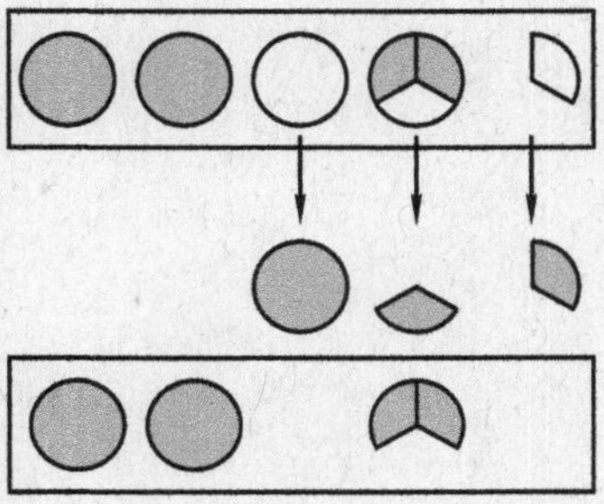

$4\frac{1}{3} = 3\frac{4}{3}$

$-\ 1\frac{2}{3}$

$2\frac{2}{3}$

h. **See student work. Sample answer: From the trailhead to the summit is $6\frac{1}{4}$ miles. After hiking $2\frac{3}{4}$ miles, how much farther is it to the summit?**

Written Practice 48

1. $\begin{array}{r} 10 \\ \times\ 2 \\ \hline \mathbf{20} \end{array}$

2. $\begin{array}{r} \$2.279 \\ \times\ \ 10.0 \\ \hline \$22.790\,0 \end{array} \longrightarrow \mathbf{\$22.79}$

3. $\begin{array}{rl} \overset{12:\,80}{\not{1}:\not{20}} & \text{p.m.} \\ -\ 11:45 & \text{a.m.} \\ \hline 1:35 & \end{array}$

   1 hour 35 minutes

4. **B. 0.2**

5. **−1, 0, 0.102, 0.12, 1.02, 1.20**

6. $\begin{array}{r} \overset{1}{0}.1 \\ 0.2 \\ 0.3 \\ +\ 0.4 \\ \hline \mathbf{1.0} \end{array}$ or **1**

7. $\begin{array}{r} 0.125 \\ \times\ \ \ \ 8 \\ \hline \mathbf{1.000} \end{array}$ or **1**

8. $3 - 2.1 = r$

   $\begin{array}{r} \overset{2}{\not{3}}.{}^{1}0 \\ -\ 2.\ 1 \\ \hline \mathbf{0.\ 9} \end{array}$ **mile**

9. $\begin{array}{r} 5000 \\ 8000 \\ +\ 7000 \\ \hline \mathbf{20{,}000} \end{array}$

10. $\begin{array}{r} \mathbf{0.018} \\ 8\overline{)0.144} \\ 0\,0 \\ \hline 14 \\ 8 \\ \hline 64 \\ 64 \\ \hline 0 \end{array}$

11. $\begin{array}{r} \mathbf{0.15} \\ 6\overline{)0.90} \\ 6 \\ \hline 30 \\ 30 \\ \hline 0 \end{array}$

12. $\begin{array}{r} \mathbf{0.225} \\ 4\overline{)0.900} \\ 8 \\ \hline 10 \\ 8 \\ \hline 20 \\ 20 \\ \hline 0 \end{array}$

13. $0.39 × 100

    $39.00

14. **50.64**

15. Multiples of 6
    6, 12, 18, (24), 30, 36
    Multiples of 8
    8, 16, (24), 32, 40
    LCM is **24**

16. $7\frac{7}{12} + 5\frac{5}{12} = 12\frac{12}{12} = \mathbf{13}$

    $w = \mathbf{13}$

17. $\begin{array}{r} 12 \\ -\ 5\frac{2}{3} \\ \hline \end{array} \xrightarrow{11 + \frac{3}{3}} \begin{array}{r} 11\frac{3}{3} \\ -\ 5\frac{2}{3} \\ \hline 6\frac{1}{3} \end{array}$

    $m = \mathbf{6\frac{1}{3}}$

18. $\begin{array}{r} 5\frac{1}{4} \\ -\ 2\frac{3}{4} \\ \hline \end{array} \xrightarrow{4 + \frac{4}{4} + \frac{1}{4}} \begin{array}{r} 4\frac{5}{4} \\ -\ 2\frac{3}{4} \\ \hline 2\frac{2}{4} \end{array} = 2\frac{1}{2}$

    $n = \mathbf{2\frac{1}{2}}$

19.
$$\begin{array}{r} \overset{3}{\cancel{4}}.\overset{9}{\cancel{0}}{}^{1}0 \\ -\ 3.2\,1 \\ \hline 0.7\,9 \end{array}$$
$x = \mathbf{0.79}$

20. $\frac{2}{3} \times \frac{3}{4} = \frac{6}{12} = \mathbf{\frac{1}{2}}$

21. $3 + 5 - 12$
$8 - 12$
$\mathbf{-4}$

22. $C = \pi d$
$C \approx (3.14)(2\text{ cm})$
$C \approx \mathbf{6.28\text{ cm}}$
π is a little more than 3, and 3 × 2 cm is 6 cm, so 6.28 cm is a reasonable answer.

23. $\frac{12}{8} = \mathbf{\frac{3}{2}}$

24.
$$\begin{array}{r} 12\text{ inches} \\ \times\ 4 \\ \hline \mathbf{48\text{ inches}} \end{array}$$

25.
$$\begin{array}{r} 12\text{ inches} \\ \times\ 12\text{ inches} \\ \hline 24 \\ 120 \\ \hline \mathbf{144\text{ square inches}} \end{array}$$

26. $d = rt$
$d = (60)(4)$
$d = \mathbf{240}$

27. $\frac{75}{100} = \frac{3}{4}$
$\frac{3}{4} \times \frac{32}{1} = \frac{96}{4} = \mathbf{24\text{ chairs}}$

28. $\frac{1}{3} \times \frac{4}{4} = \frac{4}{12}$ $\quad \frac{1}{4} \times \frac{3}{3} = \frac{3}{12}$
$\mathbf{\frac{4}{12} + \frac{3}{12} = \frac{7}{12}}$

29. $\frac{35}{7} = \mathbf{5}$

30. The server can cut one of the whole pies into sixths. Then there will be $2\frac{7}{6}$ pies on the shelf. The server can remove $1\frac{5}{6}$ pies, leaving $1\frac{2}{6}$ pies ($1\frac{1}{3}$ pies) on the shelf.

Early Finishers Solutions

4.0 – 0.5 – 0.09 – 1.25 = 2.16 pounds

Practice Set 49

a. **10**

b. **100**

c. $\mathbf{\frac{2.4}{4}}$
$$\begin{array}{r} \mathbf{0.6} \\ 4\overline{)2.4} \\ \underline{2.4} \\ 0 \end{array}$$

d. $\mathbf{\frac{90}{3}}$
$$\begin{array}{r} \mathbf{30} \\ 3\overline{)90} \\ \underline{9} \\ 00 \\ \underline{00} \\ 0 \end{array}$$

e.
$$\begin{array}{r} \mathbf{50} \\ 5\overline{)250} \\ \underline{25} \\ 00 \\ \underline{00} \\ 0 \end{array}$$

f.
$$\begin{array}{r} \mathbf{40} \\ 3\overline{)120} \\ \underline{12} \\ 00 \\ \underline{00} \\ 0 \end{array}$$

g. **2.4 ÷ 8**
$$\begin{array}{r} \mathbf{0.3} \\ 8\overline{)2.4} \\ \underline{2\,4} \\ 0 \end{array}$$

h. **30 ÷ 3**
$$\begin{array}{r} \mathbf{10} \\ 3\overline{)30} \\ \underline{3} \\ 00 \\ \underline{00} \\ 0 \end{array}$$

i. $5\overline{)40}$ = **8**

40
0

j. 2 ÷ 4

$4\overline{)2.0}$ = **0.5**

2 0
0

k. $5\overline{)325}$ = 65 **65 nickels**

30
25
25
0

Written Practice 49

1. (0.2 + 0.3) − (0.2 × 0.3)

0.5 − 0.06

0.44

2.

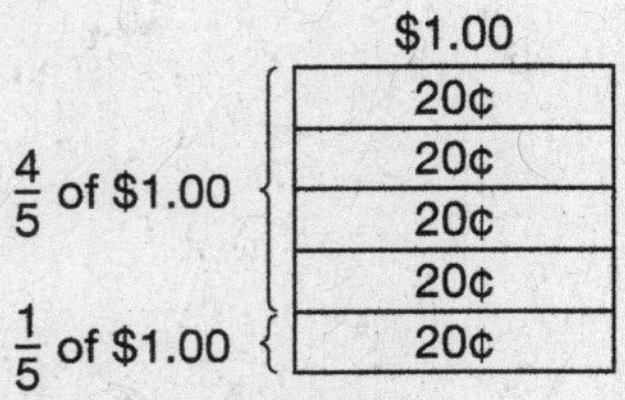

80¢

3.
$$\begin{array}{r} 2.6 \text{ inches} \\ \times\ 2.2 \text{ inches} \\ \hline 52 \\ 520 \\ \hline \mathbf{5.72 \text{ square inches}} \end{array}$$

4.
$$\begin{array}{r} \overset{1}{2}.6 \text{ in.} \\ 2.6 \text{ in.} \\ 2.2 \text{ in.} \\ +\ 2.2 \text{ in.} \\ \hline \mathbf{9.6 \text{ in.}} \end{array}$$

5. **a.** 0.31 ⓶> 0.301

b. 31% ⓶> 30.1%

6.
$$\begin{array}{r} \overset{1\,1}{0.67} \\ 2 \\ +\ 1.33 \\ \hline 4.00 \end{array}$$ or **4**

7.
$$\begin{array}{r} 12 \\ \times\ 0.25 \\ \hline 60 \\ 240 \\ \hline 3.00 \end{array}$$ or **3**

8. $7\overline{)350}$ = **50**

35
00
00
0

9. $5\overline{)120}$ = **24**

10
20
20
0

10. $8\overline{)0.1400}$ = **0.0175**

0 0
14
8
60
56
40
40
0

11.
$$\begin{array}{r} 0.012 \\ \times\ \ 1.5 \\ \hline 0060 \\ 00120 \\ \hline 0.0180 \end{array}$$ or **0.018**

12. $6\frac{1}{8} + 4\frac{3}{8} = 10\frac{4}{8} = 10\frac{1}{2}$

$\boldsymbol{n = 10\frac{1}{2}}$

13. $\frac{4}{5} \times \frac{20}{20} = \frac{80}{100}$

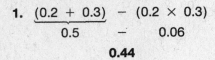

$\boldsymbol{x = 80}$

14.
$$\begin{array}{r} \overset{4}{\cancel{5}}.\overset{9}{\cancel{0}}{}^{1}0 \\ -\ 1.37 \\ \hline 3.63 \end{array}$$
m = **3.63**

15.
$$\begin{array}{r} 15 \\ -\ 7\frac{1}{4} \\ \hline \end{array} \xrightarrow{14 + \frac{4}{4}} \begin{array}{r} 14\frac{4}{4} \\ -\ 7\frac{1}{4} \\ \hline \end{array}$$
$m = \mathbf{7\frac{3}{4}}$

16. **1.012**

17. $5\frac{7}{10} + 4\frac{9}{10} = 9\frac{16}{10} = 10\frac{6}{10} = \mathbf{10\frac{3}{5}}$

18. $\frac{5}{2} \times \frac{5}{3} = \frac{25}{6} = \mathbf{4\frac{1}{6}}$

19.
$$\begin{array}{r} \$25.00 \\ \times\quad 0.4 \\ \hline \$10.000 \end{array}$$
or **$10.00**

20. a. $\frac{8}{24} = \mathbf{\frac{1}{3}}$

b. $\mathbf{\frac{1}{3}}$

c.
$$\begin{array}{r} \overset{1}{\cancel{2}}{}^{1}4 \\ -\ 8 \\ \hline 16 \end{array} \qquad \frac{16}{24} = \mathbf{\frac{2}{3}}$$

21. Factors of 12
①, ②, ③, 4, ⑥, 12
Factors of 18
①, ②, ③, ⑥, 9, 18
1, 2, 3, 6

22.
$$\begin{array}{r} \overset{1}{1}.2 \\ 1.3 \\ +\ 1.7 \\ \hline 4.2 \end{array} \qquad \begin{array}{r} \mathbf{1.4} \\ 3\overline{)4.2} \\ 3 \\ \hline 1\,2 \\ 1\,2 \\ \hline 0 \end{array}$$

23. **$25; Round 51% to 50% and round $49.78 to $50. Since 50% equals $\frac{1}{2}$, find $\frac{1}{2}$ of $50.**

24. a. $\mathbf{\frac{4}{3}}$

b. $\frac{4}{3} \times \frac{4}{1} = \frac{16}{3} = \mathbf{5\frac{1}{3}}$

25. a. ***y***

b. ***x***

c. ***z***

26. $\frac{420}{70}$
$$\begin{array}{r} \mathbf{6} \\ 70\overline{)420} \\ 420 \\ \hline 0 \end{array}$$

27. $\frac{\$3.00}{\$0.25} \times \frac{100}{100} = \frac{\$300}{\$25} = 12$ (all bold)

28. **Side = $\frac{3}{4}$ in.**
$\frac{3}{4} \times \frac{4}{1} = \frac{12}{4} = 3$ in.
Perimeter = 3 in.

29. $C = \pi d$
$C \approx (3.14)(4 \text{ cm})$
$C \approx$ **12.56 cm**

30. **Yes, Sam found the correct answer. Both $\frac{10}{10}$ and $\frac{100}{100}$ are equal to 1. When we multiply by different fraction names for 1, we get numbers that are equal even though they may look different. So $\frac{2.5}{0.5}$, $\frac{25}{5}$, and $\frac{250}{50}$ are three equivalent division problems with the same quotient.**

Early Finishers Solutions

a. The total cost for each bucket of popcorn is \$0.05 + \$0.02 + \$0.25 = \$0.32. Since each bucket of popcorn sells for \$3.00, the profit per bucket is \$3.00 − \$0.32 = \$2.68. When \$2.68 is multiplied by 115 buckets, the profit is \$308.20.

b. \$365.70 ÷ 115 = \$3.18 profit on each bucket. Add the cost per bucket to find the amount you should charge for each bucket. \$3.18 + \$0.32 = \$3.50 per bucket.

Solutions

Practice Set 50

a. $\frac{1}{10} = \mathbf{0.1}$

b. $\frac{5}{10} = \mathbf{0.5}$

c. $\frac{9}{10} = \mathbf{0.9}$

d. $1\frac{2}{10} = \mathbf{1.2}$

e. $1\frac{6}{10} = \mathbf{1.6}$

f. $1\frac{8}{10} = \mathbf{1.8}$

g. $4 \div \frac{1}{4}$

$1 \div \frac{1}{4} = \frac{4}{1} = 4$

$4 \times 4 = 16$

h. $12 \div \frac{3}{8}$ in.

$1 \div \frac{3}{8} = \frac{8}{3}$

$12 \times \frac{8}{3} = \frac{12}{1} \times \frac{8}{3} = \frac{96}{3} =$ **32 pads**

Written Practice 50

1. Sum of first 3 odd numbers: 1 + 3 + 5 = 9 OR 3 × 3 = 9
Sum of first 5 odd numbers: 1 + 3 + 5 + 7 + 9 = 25 OR 5 × 5 = 25
Sum of first 10 odd numbers: 1 + 3 + 5 + 7 + 9 + 11 + 13 + 15 + 17 + 19 = **100** OR 10 × 10 = **100**
Strategy used: Find the sum by adding. OR Find the sum by recognizing the pattern.

2. $6 \div \frac{3}{8}$ in.

$1 \div \frac{3}{8} = \frac{8}{3}$

$\frac{6}{1} \times \frac{8}{3} = \frac{48}{3} =$ **16 boxes**

3.

$$\begin{array}{r} 11 \text{ rounds} \\ \times\ \ 3 \text{ minutes} \\ \hline 33 \text{ minutes} \end{array} \qquad \begin{array}{r} 33 \text{ minutes} \\ +\ \ 2 \text{ minutes} \\ \hline \mathbf{35 \text{ minutes}} \end{array}$$

4. a. 3.4 $\bigcirc\!\!\!\!>$ 3.389

b. 0.60 $\bigcirc\!\!\!\!=$ 0.600

5. $9.25 + w = 10$

$$\begin{array}{r} \overset{0}{\cancel{1}}\overset{9}{\cancel{0}}.\overset{9}{\cancel{0}}{}^{1}0 \\ -\ \ 9.\,2\,5 \\ \hline 0.\,7\,5 \end{array}$$

$w = \mathbf{0.75}$

6.

$$\begin{array}{r} 0.024 \\ 6\overline{)0.144} \\ \underline{0\,0} \\ 14 \\ \underline{12} \\ 24 \\ \underline{24} \\ 0 \end{array}$$

$w = \mathbf{0.024}$

7. $\frac{12}{12} - \frac{5}{12} = \frac{7}{12}$

$w = \mathbf{\frac{7}{12}}$

8.

$$\begin{array}{r} 6\frac{1}{8} \\ -\ 1\frac{7}{8} \\ \hline \end{array} \xrightarrow{\ 5 + \frac{8}{8} + \frac{1}{8}\ } \begin{array}{r} 5\frac{9}{8} \\ -\ 1\frac{7}{8} \\ \hline 4\frac{2}{8} = 4\frac{1}{4} \end{array}$$

$x = \mathbf{4\frac{1}{4}}$

9.

$$\begin{array}{r} \$20.00 \\ \times\ \ \ .07 \\ \hline \$1.4000 \end{array} \qquad \begin{array}{r} \$20.00 \\ +\ \ \$1.40 \\ \hline \mathbf{\$21.40} \end{array}$$

10.

$$\begin{array}{r} \overset{0}{\cancel{1}}.\overset{9}{\cancel{0}}{}^{1}0 \\ -\ 0.9\,7 \\ \hline \mathbf{0.0\,3} \end{array}$$

11.
```
     60
12)720
   72
    00
    00
     0
```

12.
```
  17.5
4)70.0
  4
  30
  28
   20
   20
    0
```

13.
```
 0.023
6)0.138
  00
   13
   12
    18
    18
     0
```

14.
```
   3.75
 × 2.4
  1500
  7500
 9.000
```
9.000 or **9**

15. $\frac{3}{4} \times \frac{6}{6} = \frac{18}{24}$ **18**

16. **6**

17.
```
   100 cm
 × 100 cm
```
10,000 square centimeters

18. Multiples of 6
6, 12, (18), 24, 30, 36
Multiples of 9
9, (18), 27, 36, 45
LCM is **18**

19. $6\frac{5}{8} + 4\frac{5}{8} = 10\frac{10}{8} = 11\frac{2}{8} = \mathbf{11\frac{1}{4}}$

20. $\frac{8}{3} \times \frac{3}{1} = \frac{24}{3} = \mathbf{8}$

21. $\frac{2}{3} \cdot \frac{3}{4} = \frac{6}{12} = \mathbf{\frac{1}{2}}$

22. $\frac{7}{1} \times \frac{22}{7} = \frac{154}{7} =$ **22 cm**
π is a little more than 3, and 3 × 7 cm is 21 cm, so 22 cm is reasonable.

23.
```
   1
  2.4          4.8
  6.3       3)14.4
+ 5.7         12
 14.4          24
               24
                0
```

24.
```
    35
25)875
   75
   125
   125
     0
```
35 quarters

25. $5\frac{3}{10} = \mathbf{5.3}$

26. $\frac{210}{10} = \mathbf{21}$

27. **37.5**

28. $\frac{1}{3} \times \frac{2}{2} = \mathbf{\frac{2}{6}}$
$\mathbf{\frac{5}{6} - \frac{2}{6} = \frac{3}{6} = \frac{1}{2}}$

29. a. ***y***
b. ***z***
c. ***x***

30. 552; No, last digit is not 5 or 0.
255; No, last digit is not even.
250; Yes, last digit is even and 5 or 0.
525; No, last digit is not even.
C. 250

Early Finishers Solutions

a. 13 miles per hour $\times$ 5 hours = 65 miles

b. Yes, 65 miles per day $\times$ 3 days = 195 miles

Investigation 5

1.

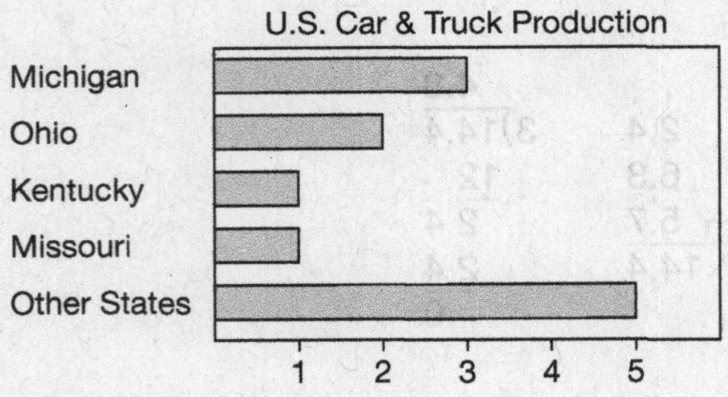

2. $\dfrac{\text{Michigan's production}}{\text{Total production}} = \dfrac{3}{12} = \mathbf{\dfrac{1}{4}}$

3. Michigan: $\dfrac{3}{12} \times 360° = \mathbf{90°}$

Ohio: $\dfrac{2}{12} \times 360° = \mathbf{60°}$

Kentucky: $\dfrac{1}{12} \times 360° = \mathbf{30°}$

Missouri: $\dfrac{1}{12} \times 360° = \mathbf{30°}$

Other States: $\dfrac{5}{12} \times 360° = \mathbf{150°}$

4.

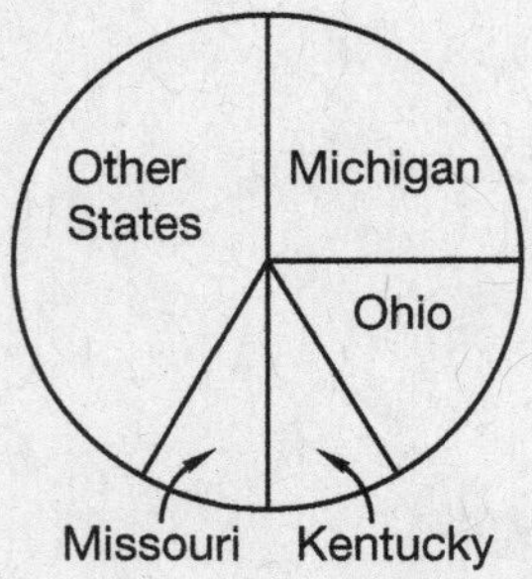

5. **The pictograph illustrates the topic of the graph and shows the comparison between states. The bar graph also shows the comparison, but without the pictures. In the circle graph we see that the four states produce the majority of cars and trucks in the United States.**

6. 47, 48, 49, 50, 51, 52, 53, 53, 53, 56, 56, 57, 58, 58, 60, 60, 60, 62, 62, 63

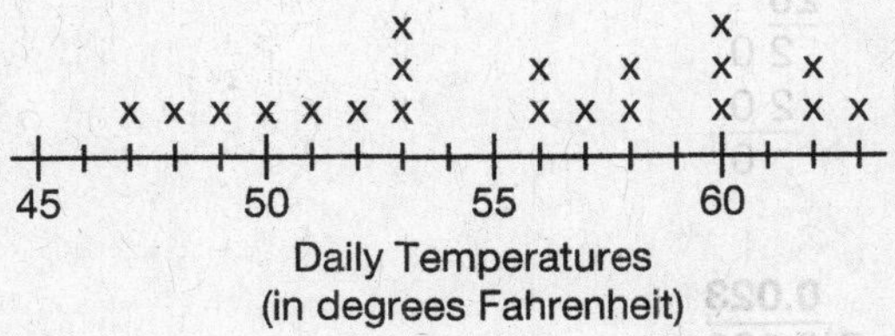

7. 47, 48, 49, 50, 51, 52, 53, 53, 53, <u>56, 56,</u> 57, 58, 58, 60, 60, 60, 62, 62, 63

Median: **56°**

8. 47, 48, 49, 50, 51, 52, <u>53, 53, 53,</u> 56, 56, 57, 58, 58, <u>60, 60, 60,</u> 62, 62, 63

Modes: **53° and 60°**

9. $\begin{array}{r} \overset{5}{\not 6}{}^{1}3° \\ -\ 4\,7° \\ \hline 1\,6 \end{array}$ **degrees**

10.

stem	leaves
4	7 8 9
5	0 1 2 3 3 3 6 6 7 8 8
6	0 0 0 2 2 3

11. **Discuss with students. Both the line plot and the stem-and-leaf plot show individual data points. In a line plot, the range and mode can be easily identified due to the visual representation. In a stem-and-leaf plot, individual data points can be easily read.**

Extension

Answers will vary. See student work.

Practice Set 51

a. **$6.67**

b. **$0.46**

c. **$0.08**

d. **0.1**

e. **12.3**

f. **2.4**

g. **17**

h. **5**

i. **$73**

j.
$$\begin{array}{r} \$3.79 \\ \times \quad .06 \\ \hline \$0.2274 \\ \mathbf{\$0.23} \end{array}$$

k. **Round 7.75% to 8% and round $7.89 to $8. Find 8% of $8 (or 8¢ per dollar) is 64¢. Since both numbers were rounded up, the tax should be a little less than 64¢.**

Written Practice 51

1. 8, 16, (24)
6, 12, 18, (24)
24 − 24 = **0**

2.
$$\begin{array}{r} 3.5 \text{ miles} \\ \times \quad 2 \\ \hline 7.0 \end{array}$$ or **7 miles**

3. **1804 − 1769 = *d***
$$\begin{array}{r} 1\,\overset{7}{\cancel{8}}\,\overset{9}{\cancel{0}}\,{}^{1}4 \\ -\ 1\,7\,6\,9 \\ \hline 3\,5 \end{array}$$ **years old**

4. a.
$$\begin{array}{r} \$12.89 \\ \times \quad .08 \\ \hline \$1.0312 \\ \mathbf{\$1.03} \end{array}$$

b.
$$\begin{array}{r} \overset{1}{\$12.89} \\ +\ \$1.03 \\ \hline \mathbf{\$13.92} \end{array}$$

5. a. 3 × 2 = **6 inches**

b. $C = \pi d$
$C \approx (3.14)(6 \text{ inches})$
$C \approx 18.84$ inches
$C \approx$ **19 inches**

6. **The whole-number part of 12.75 is 12. The next digit, 7, is greater than or equal to 5, so round up to the next whole number, 13.**

7.
$$\begin{array}{r} \overset{1\,1}{0.125} \\ 0.25 \\ +\ 0.375 \\ \hline \mathbf{0.750} \end{array}$$ or **0.75**

8.
$$\begin{array}{r} 0.\,\overset{3}{\cancel{4}}\,\overset{9}{\cancel{0}}\,{}^{1}0 \\ -\ 0.\,3\,9\,9 \\ \hline 0.\,0\,0\,1 \end{array}$$
w = **0.001**

9.
$$\begin{array}{r} \mathbf{16} \\ 25\overline{)400} \\ \underline{25} \\ 150 \\ \underline{150} \\ 0 \end{array}$$

10.
$$\begin{array}{r} \mathbf{0.125} \\ 4\overline{)0.500} \\ \underline{4} \\ 10 \\ \underline{8} \\ 20 \\ \underline{20} \\ 0 \end{array}$$

11.
$$\begin{array}{r} \mathbf{0.325} \\ 10\overline{)3.250} \\ \underline{3\,0} \\ 25 \\ \underline{20} \\ 50 \\ \underline{50} \\ 0 \end{array}$$

12.

$$3\frac{5}{12} \xrightarrow{2 + \frac{12}{12} + \frac{5}{12}} 2\frac{17}{12}$$

$$-1\frac{7}{12} \qquad -1\frac{7}{12}$$

$$1\frac{10}{12} = \mathbf{1\frac{5}{6}}$$

13. $\frac{5}{8} \times \frac{3}{3} = \frac{15}{24} = \mathbf{15}$

14.

$$25 \xrightarrow{24 + \frac{4}{4}} 24\frac{4}{4}$$

$$-17\frac{3}{4} \qquad -17\frac{3}{4}$$

$$\mathbf{7\frac{1}{4}}$$

15.

$$\begin{array}{r} 0.19 \\ \times\ 0.21 \\ \hline 19 \\ 380 \\ \hline \mathbf{0.0399} \end{array}$$

16. $\mathbf{\frac{1}{100}}$

17. **60.07**

18. $\sqrt{64 \text{ cm}^2} = 8 \text{ cm}$

$8 \text{ cm} \times 4 = \mathbf{32 \text{ cm}}$

19. Multiples of 2

2, 4, 6, 8, 10, (12), 14

Multiples of 3

3, 6, 9, (12), 15, 18

Multiples of 4

4, 8, (12), 16, 20, 24

LCM is **12**

20. $5\frac{3}{10} + 6\frac{9}{10} = 11\frac{12}{10} = 12\frac{2}{10} = \mathbf{12\frac{1}{5}}$

21. $\frac{10}{3} \times \frac{1}{2} = \frac{10}{6} = 1\frac{4}{6} = \mathbf{1\frac{2}{3}}$

22. $12 \div \frac{3}{4}$ in.

$1 \div \frac{3}{4} = \frac{4}{3}$

$\frac{12}{1} \times \frac{4}{3} = \frac{48}{3} =$ **16 books**

23.

$$\begin{array}{r} \mathbf{50} \\ 100\overline{)5000} \\ 500 \\ \hline 00 \\ 00 \\ \hline 0 \end{array}$$

24. Factors of 16

(1), (2), (4), (8), 16

Factors of 24

(1), (2), 3, (4), 6, (8), 12, 24

1, 2, 4, 8

25. $12 \times 4 = \mathbf{48}$

Rounded 11.8 to 12 and 3.89 to 4; then multiplied 12 by 4.

26. $\frac{7}{10} + 1\frac{3}{10} = 1\frac{10}{10} = 2$

$2 \div 2 = \mathbf{1}$

27. $\frac{180}{60} = \mathbf{3}$

28. **$7.90; Since the problem is to multiply by 10, shift the decimal point in $0.79 one place to the right.**

29. $\frac{2}{3} \times \frac{4}{4} = \frac{8}{12} \qquad \frac{3}{4} \times \frac{3}{3} = \frac{9}{12}$

$\mathbf{\frac{8}{12} + \frac{9}{12} = \frac{17}{12} = 1\frac{5}{12}}$

30. a. 75, 80, 80, 85, 85, 90, 90, 90, 100

Median: 85

Mode: 90

b.

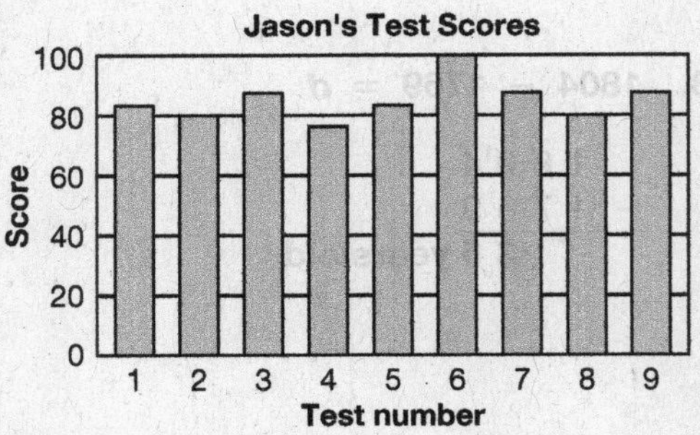

Practice Set 52

a. **0.25**

b. **0.025**

c. **8.75**

d. **0.875**

e. **0.05**

f. **0.005**

g. **2.5**

h. **0.25**

i. **0.15 cm, 1.5 mm**

Written Practice 52

1. $\frac{1}{2} \times \frac{2}{3} = \frac{2}{6} = \mathbf{\frac{1}{3}}$

2. $88 - 52 = 36$ black keys

   $\overset{4}{\cancel{5}}{}^{1}2 - 36 = \mathbf{16}$ **more white keys**

3. **28,232 feet**

4. a. **37.5; To multiply 3.75 by 10, shift the decimal point one place to the right.**

   b. **0.375; To divide 3.75 by 10, shift the decimal point one place to the left.**

5. $\frac{\text{student}}{\text{teacher}} = \frac{320}{16} = \mathbf{\frac{20}{1}}$

6. **32**

7. $0.125 \times 4 = 0.500$ or **0.5**

8. $150 \div 12 = 12\frac{6}{12} = \mathbf{12\frac{1}{2}}$

   $$\begin{array}{r} 12\tfrac{6}{12} \\ 12\overline{)150} \\ \underline{12} \\ 30 \\ \underline{24} \\ 6 \end{array}$$

9. $\frac{(1 + 0.2)}{(1 - 0.2)} = \frac{1.2}{0.8}$

   $$\begin{array}{r} \mathbf{0.15} \\ 8\overline{)1.20} \\ \underline{8} \\ 40 \\ \underline{40} \\ 0 \end{array}$$

10. $\frac{5}{2} \times \frac{4}{1} = \frac{20}{2} = \mathbf{10}$

11. $5\frac{1}{3} \xrightarrow{4 + \frac{3}{3} + \frac{1}{3}} 4\frac{4}{3}$

    $4\frac{4}{3} - 1\frac{2}{3}$

    $m = \mathbf{3\frac{2}{3}}$

12. $5\frac{1}{3} + 1\frac{2}{3} = 6\frac{3}{3} = 7$

    $m = \mathbf{7}$

13. $\$\overset{0}{\cancel{1}}\,\overset{9}{\cancel{0}}.{}^{1}00 - \$0.10 = \$9.90$

    $w = \mathbf{\$9.90}$

14. $\$8.59 \times .06 = \$0.5154$

    52¢

15. $C = \pi d$

    $C \approx (3.14)(24 \text{ inches})$

    $C \approx 75.36$ inches

    $C \approx$ **75 inches**

16. **0.201, 0.21, 1.02, 1.2**

17. **16**

18.
$$\begin{array}{r} 20 \text{ feet} \\ 4\overline{)80} \text{ feet} \\ \underline{8} \\ 00 \\ \underline{00} \\ 0 \end{array}$$

$$\begin{array}{r} 20 \text{ tiles in a row} \\ \underline{\times\ 20 \text{ rows}} \\ \textbf{400 tiles} \end{array}$$

19. 1 foot = 12 inches

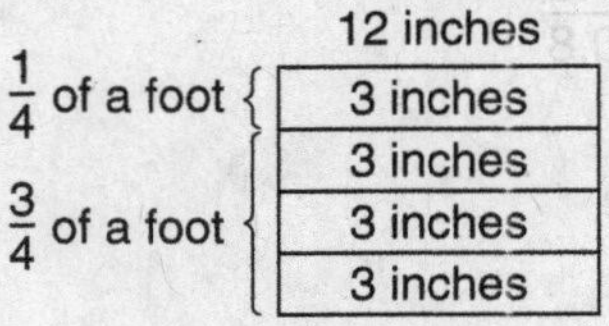

$\mathbf{\frac{1}{4}}$

20. 1 dollar = 100 cents

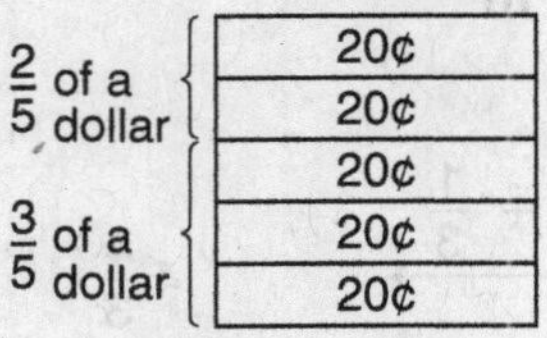

40¢

21. $12 \div \frac{3}{4}$ in.

$1 \div \frac{3}{4} = \frac{4}{3}$

$\frac{12}{1} \times \frac{4}{3} = \frac{48}{3} =$ **16 pennies;**

One method is to divide 12 by $\frac{3}{4}$.

22. Multiples of 2
2, 4, 6, 8, 10, (12), 14
Multiples of 4
4, 8, (12), 16, 20, 24
Multiples of 6
6, (12), 18, 24, 30
LCM is **12**

23. **a.** $1 - 1 = \mathbf{0}$

b. $2 - 4 = \mathbf{-2}$

24. **About 2 meters in most classrooms**

25. **1.8**

26. $\frac{1}{2} \times \frac{3}{3} = \frac{3}{6}$ $\quad \frac{2}{3} \times \frac{2}{2} = \frac{4}{6}$

$\mathbf{\frac{3}{6} + \frac{4}{6} = \frac{7}{6} = 1\frac{1}{6}}$

27. Sample Answer:

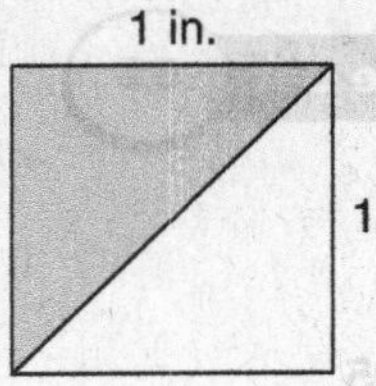

28. **a.** **78%**

b. $\mathbf{\frac{78}{100}}$, **0.78**

29. **a.** **20%**

b. $\frac{20 \div 20}{100 \div 20} = \mathbf{\frac{1}{5}}$

30. **Students should choose a circle graph:**

Gases in Earth's Atmosphere

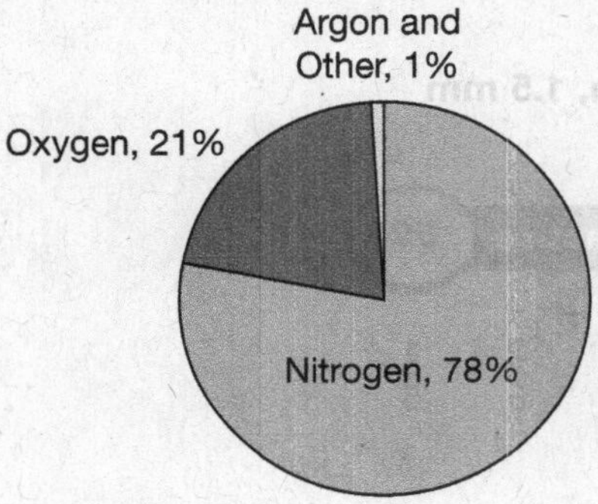

Practice Set 53

a. Sample Answer:

5 − 4.2	0.4 × 0.2
line up	multiply; then count
0.12 ÷ 3	5 ÷ 0.4
up	over, over, up

b. **Decimal Arithmetic Reminders**

Operation	+ or −	×	÷ by whole (*W*)	÷ by decimal (*D*)
Memory cue	line up ± .	×; then count × .	up *W*) .	over, over, up *D*.) .

You may need to…
- Place a decimal point to the right of a whole number.
- Fill empty places with zeros.

c.

$$\frac{5}{6} \times \frac{2}{2} = \frac{10}{12}$$
$$+ \frac{5}{12} = \frac{5}{12}$$
$$\frac{15}{12} = \frac{5}{4} = \mathbf{1\frac{1}{4}}$$

d.

$$\frac{9}{10} = \frac{9}{10}$$
$$+ \frac{3}{5} \times \frac{2}{2} = \frac{6}{10}$$
$$\frac{15}{10} = \frac{3}{2} = \mathbf{1\frac{1}{2}}$$

e.

$$\frac{2}{3} \times \frac{4}{4} = \frac{8}{12}$$
$$+ \frac{7}{12} = \frac{7}{12}$$
$$\frac{15}{12} = \frac{5}{4} = \mathbf{1\frac{1}{4}}$$

Written Practice 53

1. **We add or subtract only digits that have the same place value. When we line up the decimal points, digits with the same place value are automatically aligned.**

2. 3:00 p.m. (regrouped as 12:180)
   − 4:45
   8:135
   10:15 a.m.

3. 7 seconds $\div \frac{1}{4}$

   $1 \div \frac{1}{4} = \frac{4}{1}$

   7 seconds $\times$ 4 = **28 seconds**

4. 47 + 52 + 63 + 66 = 228

   $228 \div 4 = 57$ points (4)228: 20, 28, 28, 0)

   Mean = **57 points**

   66 − 47 = 19 points (6 regrouped as 5, 16)

   Range = **19 points**

5. $37500 \div 375 = 100$ (375)37500: 375, 00, 00, 00, 00, 0)

   x = **100**

6. $1.25 \times 10 = 12.5$

   m = **12.5**

7. $\mathbf{\frac{1}{100}}$**; 0.01**

8. 3.6
   4
   + 0.39
   7.99

9. $3600 \div 12 = $ **300** (12)3600: 36, 00, 00, 00, 00, 0)

10. $0.1500 \div 4 = $ **0.0375** (4)0.1500: 12, 30, 28, 20, 20, 0)

11. $6\frac{1}{4} \xrightarrow{5 + \frac{4}{4} + \frac{1}{4}} 5\frac{5}{4}$

    $$5\frac{5}{4} - 3\frac{3}{4} = 2\frac{2}{4} = \mathbf{2\frac{1}{2}}$$

12. $\frac{2}{3} \times \frac{3}{5} = \frac{6}{15} = \mathbf{\frac{2}{5}}$

13. $5\frac{5}{8} + 7\frac{7}{8} = 12\frac{12}{8} = 12\frac{3}{2} = \mathbf{13\frac{1}{2}}$

14. **5**

15. **a.**
$$\begin{array}{r} \$5.20 \\ \times \quad .08 \\ \hline \$0.4160 \end{array}$$
42¢

b.
$$\begin{array}{r} \$5.20 \\ + \ \$0.42 \\ \hline \mathbf{\$5.62} \end{array}$$

16. **B. 0.9**

17. $C = \pi d$
$C \approx (3.14)(40 \text{ feet})$
$C \approx 125.6 \text{ feet}$
$C \approx$ **126 feet**

18. $\frac{3}{8} \text{ in.} \times \frac{4}{1} = \frac{12}{8} = 1\frac{4}{8} = \mathbf{1\frac{1}{2} \text{ in.}}$

19. $\frac{3}{36} = \mathbf{\frac{1}{12}}$

20. **a.** Factors of 11: **1, 11**

b. **Prime number**

21. $16 - 2 = \mathbf{14}$

22. Multiple of 6
6, 12, (18), 24, 30
Multiple of 9
9, (18), 36, 45
LCM is **18**

23. $\mathbf{\frac{3}{2} \cdot \frac{2}{3} = 1}$

$\mathbf{1 \div \frac{2}{3} = \frac{3}{2}}$

$\mathbf{1 \div \frac{3}{2} = \frac{2}{3}}$

24. $\frac{600}{100} = \mathbf{6}$

25. $\frac{5}{6} \times \frac{4}{4} = \frac{20}{24}$ **20**

26. **Answers may vary. See student work. Sample answer:**

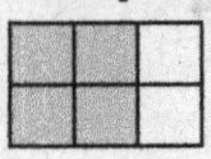

27.

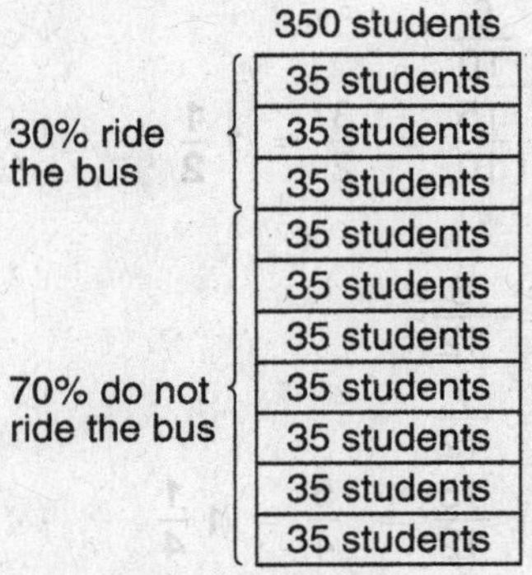

105 students

28. $\frac{1}{4} \times \frac{3}{3} = \frac{3}{12}$ $\frac{1}{6} \times \frac{2}{2} = \frac{2}{12}$

$\mathbf{\frac{3}{12} + \frac{2}{12} = \frac{5}{12}}$

29.
$$\begin{array}{r} 8.7 \\ - \ 7.4 \\ \hline \mathbf{1.3} \end{array}$$

30. $24 \div \frac{3}{4} \text{ in.}$

$1 \div \frac{3}{4} = \frac{4}{3}$

$\frac{24}{1} \times \frac{4}{3} = \frac{96}{3} =$ **32 books**

Early Finishers Solutions

Line plot; A line plot is the most appropriate display because it shows individual data points. Every bid begins with the digit 1, so a stem-and-leaf plot would not be a good choice as there would only be one stem.

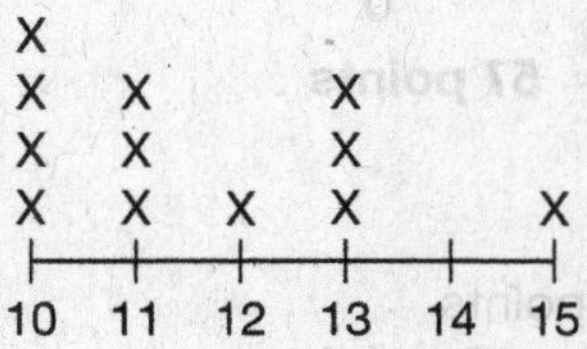

Practice Set 54

a. $\dfrac{2 \cdot 2 \cdot 5 \cdot 3}{2 \cdot 2 \cdot 5} = 1 \cdot 1 \cdot 1 \cdot 3 = \mathbf{3}$

b. $\dfrac{2 \cdot 2 \cdot 3 \cdot 3 \cdot 5}{2 \cdot 2 \cdot 3 \cdot 5 \cdot 5} = 1 \cdot 1 \cdot 1 \cdot \dfrac{3}{5} \cdot 1 = \mathbf{\dfrac{3}{5}}$

c. $\dfrac{1}{2} \div \dfrac{3}{8}$

$1 \div \dfrac{3}{8} = \dfrac{8}{3}$

$\dfrac{1}{2} \times \dfrac{8}{3} = \dfrac{8}{6} = 1\dfrac{2}{6} = \mathbf{1\dfrac{1}{3}}$

d. $\dfrac{3}{8} \div \dfrac{1}{2}$

$1 \div \dfrac{1}{2} = 2$

$\dfrac{3}{8} \times \dfrac{2}{1} = \dfrac{6}{8} = \mathbf{\dfrac{3}{4}}$

Written Practice 54

1. **Decimal Arithmetic Reminders**

Operation	+ or −	×	÷ by whole (*W*)	÷ by decimal (*D*)
Memory cue	line up $\pm$.	×; then count × .	up $W\overline{)\;.\;}$	over, over, up $D.\overline{)\;.\;}$

You may need to...
- Place a decimal point to the right of a whole number.
- Fill empty places with zeros.

2.
$$4\overline{)0.4} = \mathbf{0.1}$$
$$\begin{array}{r} 4 \\ \hline 0 \end{array}$$

3.
$$\begin{array}{r} \overset{0}{\cancel{1}}\,\overset{14}{\cancel{5}}\,{}^{1}1{,}000{,}000 \\ -\ 76{,}000{,}000 \\ \hline \mathbf{75{,}000{,}000} \end{array}$$

4. $61\dfrac{1}{4} - 59\dfrac{3}{4} = d$

$$\begin{array}{r} 61\dfrac{1}{4} \\ -\ 59\dfrac{3}{4} \\ \hline \end{array} \xrightarrow{60 \;+\; \frac{4}{4} \;+\; \frac{1}{4}} \begin{array}{r} 60\dfrac{5}{4} \\ -\ 59\dfrac{3}{4} \\ \hline 1\dfrac{2}{4} \end{array} = \mathbf{1\dfrac{1}{2}\ inches}$$

5. $1000 - (100 - 1)$
$1000 - 99$
$\mathbf{901}$

6.
$$24\overline{)1000} = 41\tfrac{16}{24} = \mathbf{41\tfrac{2}{3}}$$
$$\begin{array}{r} 96 \\ \hline 40 \\ 24 \\ \hline 16 \end{array}$$

7.
$$\begin{array}{r} 1\,\overset{3}{\cancel{4}}\,{}^{1}3 \\ -\ \ 3\,7 \\ \hline 1\,0\,6 \end{array} \qquad 2\overline{)106} = 53 \quad \begin{array}{r} 10 \\ \hline 06 \\ 06 \\ \hline 0 \end{array} \qquad \begin{array}{r} \overset{1}{3}7 \\ +\ 53 \\ \hline \mathbf{90} \end{array}$$

8.
$$\begin{array}{r} \$\overset{2}{\cancel{3}}.\,\overset{9}{\cancel{0}}\,{}^{1}0 \\ -\ \$0.\,2\,4 \\ \hline \$2.\,7\,6 \end{array}$$
$n = \mathbf{\$2.76}$

9.
$$\begin{array}{r} 6\dfrac{2}{5} \\ -\ 3\dfrac{4}{5} \\ \hline \end{array} \xrightarrow{5 \;+\; \frac{5}{5} \;+\; \frac{2}{5}} \begin{array}{r} 5\dfrac{7}{5} \\ -\ 3\dfrac{4}{5} \\ \hline \end{array}$$
$m = \mathbf{2\dfrac{3}{5}}$

10. $4.2 \div 100 = \mathbf{0.042}$

11. $(1.2 \div 0.12)(1.2)$
$$12\overline{)120} = 10 \quad \begin{array}{r} 12 \\ \hline 00 \\ 00 \\ \hline 0 \end{array}$$
$10(1.2) = \mathbf{12}$

12. $\dfrac{4}{3} \times \dfrac{4}{3} = \dfrac{16}{9} = \mathbf{1\dfrac{7}{9}}$

13. $3 + 4 = \mathbf{7}$

14. **4**

15. $\begin{array}{r} \$289.90 \\ \times\quad .08 \\ \hline \$23.1920 \end{array}$
\$23.19

16. Two centimeters $<$ one inch

17. $12 \times 2 = 24 - 1 = \mathbf{23}$

18. $\begin{array}{r} 14\text{ ft} \\ \times\ 12\text{ ft} \\ \hline 28 \\ 140 \end{array}$
168 square feet of tile

19. a. $\frac{9}{30} = \mathbf{\frac{3}{10}}$

b. $\frac{9}{21} = \mathbf{\frac{3}{7}}$

20. a. $\frac{5}{6} \times \frac{4}{4} = \mathbf{\frac{20}{24}}$

b. $\frac{5}{8} \times \frac{3}{3} = \mathbf{\frac{15}{24}}$

21. Multiples of 3
3, 6, 9, (12), 15, 18
Multiples of 4
4, 8, (12), 16, 20, 24
Multiples of 6
6, (12), 18, 24, 30
LCM is **12**

22. $\frac{2}{3} \div \frac{1}{2}$

$1 \div \frac{1}{2} = 2$

$\frac{2}{3} \times \frac{2}{1} = \frac{4}{3} = \mathbf{1\frac{1}{3}}$

23.

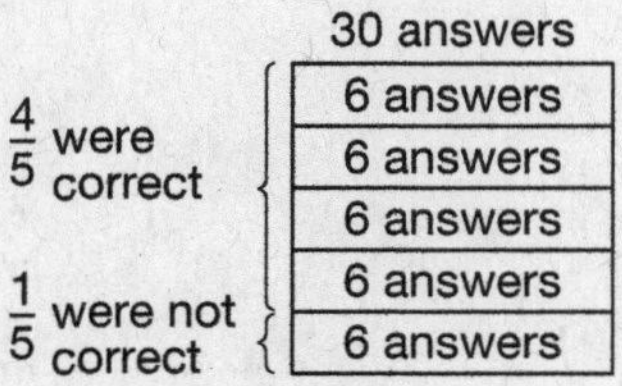

24 answers

24. $2.54\text{ cm} \times 100 = \mathbf{254\ centimeters}$

25. $\frac{2 \cdot 3 \cdot 5 \cdot 2 \cdot 3}{2 \cdot 3 \cdot 5 \cdot 2} = 1 \cdot 1 \cdot 1 \cdot 1 \cdot 3 = \mathbf{3}$

26. $\frac{2 \cdot 3 \cdot 5 \cdot 3}{2 \cdot 3 \cdot 5 \cdot 2 \cdot 2} = 1 \cdot 1 \cdot 1 \cdot \frac{3}{4} = \mathbf{\frac{3}{4}}$

27. $\frac{2}{3} \times \frac{2}{2} = \frac{4}{6} \qquad \frac{1}{2} \times \frac{3}{3} = \frac{3}{6}$

$\mathbf{\frac{4}{6} + \frac{3}{6} = \frac{7}{6} = 1\frac{1}{6}}$

28. $C = \pi d$
$C \approx (3.14)(15\text{ in.})$
$C \approx 47.1\text{ in.}$
$C \approx$ **47 inches**
π is a little more than 3, and 3 × 15 inches is 45 inches. So 47 inches is reasonable.

29.

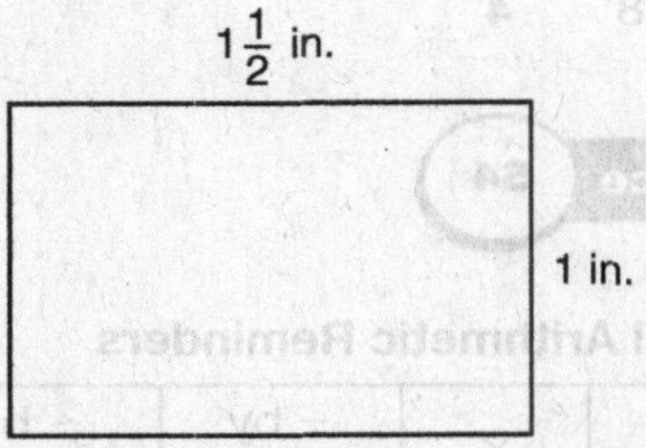

a. $1\frac{1}{2}\text{ in.} + 1\frac{1}{2}\text{ in.} + 1\text{ in.} + 1\text{ in.}$
$= 4\frac{2}{2}\text{ in.} = \mathbf{5\ inches}$

b. $1\frac{1}{2}\text{ in.} \times 1\text{ in.} = \mathbf{1\frac{1}{2}\ square\ inches}$

30. $\left(2\frac{1}{2} \times 2\right) \div \left(\frac{1}{2} \times 2\right)$
$\mathbf{5 \div 1 = 5}$

Early Finishers Solutions

Strategy: Act it out. Jenna is not correct. 50% of 12 is 6 and 12 + 6 = 18, Brooke needs about 24 tulip bulbs, so she needs 100% more.

Practice Set 55

a. $\frac{1}{2} \times \frac{4}{4} = \frac{4}{8}$

$+\ \frac{3}{8} = \frac{3}{8}$

$\mathbf{\frac{7}{8}}$

b. $\frac{3}{8} = \frac{3}{8}$

$+\ \frac{1}{4} \times \frac{2}{2} = \frac{2}{8}$

$\mathbf{\frac{5}{8}}$

c. $\frac{3}{4} \times \frac{2}{2} = \frac{6}{8}$

$+\ \frac{1}{8} = \frac{1}{8}$

$\mathbf{\frac{7}{8}}$

d. $\frac{1}{2} \times \frac{2}{2} = \frac{2}{4}$

$-\ \frac{1}{4} = \frac{1}{4}$

$\mathbf{\frac{1}{4}}$

e. $\frac{5}{8} = \frac{5}{8}$

$-\ \frac{1}{4} \times \frac{2}{2} = \frac{2}{8}$

$\mathbf{\frac{3}{8}}$

f. $\frac{3}{4} \times \frac{2}{2} = \frac{6}{8}$

$-\ \frac{3}{8} = \frac{3}{8}$

$\mathbf{\frac{3}{8}}$

g. **We can round to benchmark fractions such as $\frac{1}{2}$ and $\frac{1}{4}$ and add these fractions. Then we can check our written answers to see if the results are close.**

Written Practice 55

1. **When we divide a decimal number by a whole number using a division box, we place a decimal point in the quotient directly "up" from the decimal point in the dividend.**

2. $12 \div \frac{3}{8}$ in.

$1 \div \frac{3}{8} = \frac{8}{3}$

$\frac{12}{1} \times \frac{8}{3} = \frac{96}{3} =$ **32 CD cases**

3. $6\overline{)324}$ = **54 average pumpkins**

30
24
24
0

4. $\frac{1}{8} = \frac{1}{8}$

$+\ \frac{1}{2} \times \frac{4}{4} = \frac{4}{8}$

$\mathbf{\frac{5}{8}}$

5. $\frac{1}{2} \times \frac{4}{4} = \frac{4}{8}$

$-\ \frac{1}{8} = \frac{1}{8}$

$\mathbf{\frac{3}{8}}$

6. $\frac{2}{3} \times \frac{2}{2} = \frac{4}{6}$

$-\ \frac{1}{6} = \frac{1}{6}$

$\frac{3}{6} = \mathbf{\frac{1}{2}}$

7. 6.28
4
+ 0.13
10.41

Solutions

8.
$$\begin{array}{r} \mathbf{90} \\ 9\overline{)810} \\ \underline{81} \\ 00 \\ \underline{00} \\ 0 \end{array}$$

9.
$$\begin{array}{r} \mathbf{0.02} \\ 10\overline{)0.20} \\ \underline{20} \\ 0 \end{array}$$

10. **17**

11. $\frac{3}{4} + 3\frac{1}{4} = 3\frac{4}{4} = \mathbf{4}$

12. $\frac{5}{6} \cdot \frac{2}{3} = \frac{10}{18} = \mathbf{\frac{5}{9}}$

13. $\frac{5}{8} \times \frac{3}{3} = \frac{15}{24}$ **15**

14. **20,320 feet**

15.
$$\begin{array}{r} 0.14 \\ \underline{\times\ \ 0.8} \\ 0.112 \\ \mathbf{0.11} \end{array}$$

16. $\frac{2}{3} \ominus \frac{2}{3} \times \frac{2}{2}$

$\frac{2}{3} \times 1$

$\frac{2}{3}$

17. $C = \pi d$

$C \approx (3.14)(93 \text{ km})$

$C \approx 292.2 \text{ km} \approx$ **290 km**

18.
$$\begin{array}{r} 5 \text{ feet} \\ 4\overline{)20 \text{ feet}} \\ \underline{20} \\ 0 \end{array} \qquad \begin{array}{r} 5 \text{ feet} \\ \underline{\times\ 5 \text{ feet}} \\ \mathbf{25 \text{ square feet}} \end{array}$$

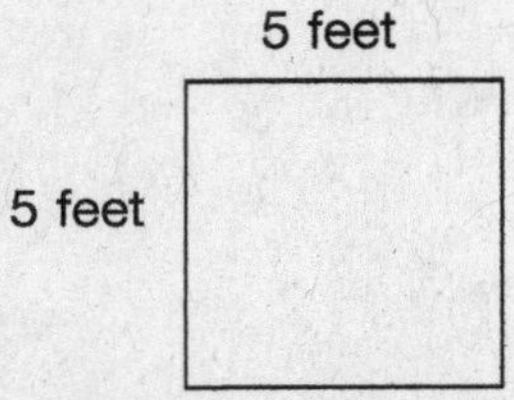

19. $\frac{60}{100} = \mathbf{\frac{3}{5}}$

20. Multiples of 3
3, 6, 9, (12), 15, 18
Multiples of 4
4, 8, (12), 16, 20
LCM is **12**

21. **a.** Factors of 23
1, 23

b. **Prime number**

22. $\mathbf{\frac{5}{2}}$

23. $9 + 16 \ominus 25$

24. $\frac{1}{2} \div \frac{2}{5}$

$1 \div \frac{2}{5} = \frac{5}{2}$

$\frac{1}{2} \times \frac{5}{2} = \frac{5}{4} = \mathbf{1\frac{1}{4}}$

25.
$$\begin{array}{r} 101 \\ 12\overline{)1212} \\ \underline{12} \\ 01 \\ \underline{00} \\ 12 \\ \underline{12} \\ 0 \end{array}$$

26. $\frac{36}{48} = \mathbf{\frac{3}{4}}$

27. $\mathbf{\frac{1}{3}}$

28. $\frac{2 \cdot 3 \cdot 2 \cdot 5 \cdot 3 \cdot 7}{2 \cdot 3 \cdot 2 \cdot 5 \cdot 5 \cdot 5}$

$= 1 \cdot 1 \cdot 1 \cdot 1 \cdot \frac{21}{25} = \mathbf{\frac{21}{25}}$

29.
$$\begin{array}{r} \overset{9}{\cancel{10}}\text{: } \overset{85}{\cancel{25}} \text{ p.m.} \\ \underline{-\ \ 7\text{: } 45 \text{ p.m.}} \\ 2\text{: } 40 \end{array}$$

2 hours 40 minutes

30. **a.** Triangle *GHI*

b. Triangle *DEF*

Practice Set 56

a.
$$\begin{array}{r} \frac{2}{3} \times \frac{2}{2} = \frac{4}{6} \\ -\ \frac{1}{2} \times \frac{3}{3} = \frac{3}{6} \\ \hline \mathbf{\frac{1}{6}} \end{array}$$

b.
$$\begin{array}{r} \frac{1}{4} \times \frac{5}{5} = \frac{5}{20} \\ +\ \frac{2}{5} \times \frac{4}{4} = \frac{8}{20} \\ \hline \mathbf{\frac{13}{20}} \end{array}$$

c.
$$\begin{array}{r} \frac{3}{4} \times \frac{3}{3} = \frac{9}{12} \\ -\ \frac{1}{3} \times \frac{4}{4} = \frac{4}{12} \\ \hline \mathbf{\frac{5}{12}} \end{array}$$

d.
$$\begin{array}{r} \frac{2}{3} \times \frac{4}{4} = \frac{8}{12} \\ +\ \frac{1}{4} \times \frac{3}{3} = \frac{3}{12} \\ \hline \mathbf{\frac{11}{12}} \end{array}$$

e.
$$\begin{array}{r} \frac{1}{3} \times \frac{4}{4} = \frac{4}{12} \\ -\ \frac{1}{4} \times \frac{3}{3} = \frac{3}{12} \\ \hline \mathbf{\frac{1}{12}} \end{array}$$

f.
$$\begin{array}{r} \frac{1}{2} \times \frac{5}{5} = \frac{5}{10} \\ -\ \frac{1}{10} \qquad = \frac{1}{10} \\ \hline \end{array}$$
$$\frac{4 \div 2}{10 \div 2} = \mathbf{\frac{2}{5}}$$

g.
$$\frac{3}{2} \bigcirc \frac{1}{2}$$
$$\frac{2}{3} \times \frac{2}{2} \qquad \frac{1}{2} \times \frac{3}{3}$$
$$\mathbf{\frac{4}{6} > \frac{3}{6}}$$

h.
$$\frac{4}{6} \bigcirc \frac{3}{4}$$
$$\frac{4}{6} \times \frac{2}{2} \qquad \frac{3}{4} \times \frac{3}{3}$$
$$\mathbf{\frac{8}{12} < \frac{9}{12}}$$

i.
$$\frac{2}{3} \bigcirc \frac{3}{5}$$
$$\frac{2}{3} \times \frac{5}{5} \qquad \frac{3}{5} \times \frac{3}{3}$$
$$\mathbf{\frac{10}{15} > \frac{9}{15}}$$

Written Practice 56

1.
$$\begin{array}{r} \frac{1}{4} \times \frac{3}{3} = \frac{3}{12} \\ +\ \frac{1}{3} \times \frac{4}{4} = \frac{4}{12} \\ \hline \mathbf{\frac{7}{12}} \end{array}$$

2.
$$\begin{array}{r} \frac{1}{2} \times \frac{3}{3} = \frac{3}{6} \\ -\ \frac{1}{3} \times \frac{2}{2} = \frac{2}{6} \\ \hline \mathbf{\frac{1}{6}} \end{array}$$

3. **a.** $\frac{52}{88} = \mathbf{\frac{13}{22}}$

b.
$$\begin{array}{r} 88 \\ -\ 52 \\ \hline 36 \end{array}$$
36 black keys

$\frac{\text{black keys}}{\text{white keys}} = \frac{36}{52} = \mathbf{\frac{9}{13}}$

4.
$$\begin{array}{r} 7.5 \\ \times\ 2 \\ \hline 15.0 \end{array}$$
15.0 or **15 apples**

5.
$$\begin{array}{r} \frac{2}{3} \times \frac{4}{4} = \frac{8}{12} \\ -\ \frac{1}{4} \times \frac{3}{3} = \frac{3}{12} \\ \hline \mathbf{\frac{5}{12}} \end{array}$$

6. $\frac{1}{3} \times \frac{2}{2} = \frac{2}{6}$

$+ \frac{1}{6} = \frac{1}{6}$

$\frac{3}{6} = \mathbf{\frac{1}{2}}$

7. $\frac{5}{6} = \frac{5}{6}$

$- \frac{1}{2} \times \frac{3}{3} = \frac{3}{6}$

$\frac{2}{6} = \mathbf{\frac{1}{3}}$

8.
```
   1
  $3 1
  $1.75
+ $0.65
  $5.40
```
$5.40

9.
```
  0.625
×   0.4
 0.2500  or  0.25
```
0.2500 or **0.25**

10. 36 ÷ 0.08
```
   450
8)3600
  32
   40
   40
    00
    00
     0
```
450

11. $3\frac{1}{8} - 1\frac{7}{8}$; $3\frac{1}{8} \xrightarrow{2 + \frac{8}{8} + \frac{1}{8}} 2\frac{9}{8}$

$2\frac{9}{8} - 1\frac{7}{8} = 1\frac{2}{8} = \mathbf{1\frac{1}{4}}$

12. $\frac{5}{8} \cdot \frac{2}{3} = \frac{10}{24} = \mathbf{\frac{5}{12}}$

13. a. $\frac{40}{100} = \mathbf{\frac{2}{5}}$

b. $\mathbf{\frac{2}{5}}$ OR

$\frac{2}{5} \times \frac{100}{1} = \frac{200}{5} =$ **40 students**

14. 80.65

15. 3600 + 4200 = **7800**

16. Yes. To estimate the distance the bike traveled, Molly found the circumference of the tire. She multiplied the diameter of the tire by 3, which is a very rough approximation for π. If Molly had used 3.14 for π, she would have calculated 6.28 ft for the circumference, which is about 6 ft 3 in.

17.
```
   1
   1.2         1.35
   1.3      4)5.40
   1.4        4
 + 1.5        1 4
   5.4        1 2
                20
                20
                 0
```
1.35

18.
```
   9 inches
4)36 inches
  36
   0
```
9 inches × 9 inches = **81 square inches**

19. 2 · 3 · 5

20. $0 \div \frac{2}{3} = 0$

$w = \mathbf{0}$

21. $m = \mathbf{\frac{3}{2}}$

22. $0 + \frac{2}{3} = \frac{2}{3}$

$n = \mathbf{\frac{2}{3}}$

23.
```
  $100
−  $40
   $60
```
$60

24.
```
  $45
− $25
  $20
```
$20

25. $\frac{25}{100} = \mathbf{\frac{1}{4}}$

26. **Answers will vary. See student work.**

27. $\frac{2 \cdot 3 \cdot 5}{2 \cdot 3 \cdot 5 \cdot 7} = 1 \cdot 1 \cdot 1 \cdot \frac{1}{7} = \mathbf{\frac{1}{7}}$

28. $\frac{1}{2} \div \frac{2}{3}$

$1 \div \frac{2}{3} = \frac{3}{2}$

$\frac{1}{2} \times \frac{3}{2} = \mathbf{\frac{3}{4}}$

29.

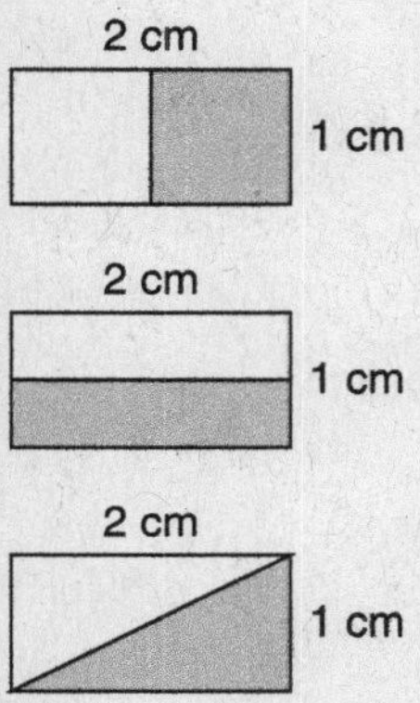

30. $\mathbf{\frac{2}{3}} \text{ ⓒ } \mathbf{\frac{5}{6}}$ (<)

$\frac{2}{3} \times \frac{2}{2}$

$\frac{4}{6}$

<u>**Early Finishers Solutions**</u>

$\frac{1}{2}$ of $\frac{1}{4} = \frac{1}{2} \cdot \frac{1}{4} = \frac{1}{8}$ of the pizza

Practice Set 57

a.
$$\begin{array}{r} \frac{1}{2} \times \frac{3}{3} = \frac{3}{6} \\ + \quad \frac{1}{6} \qquad = \frac{1}{6} \\ \hline \frac{4}{6} = \mathbf{\frac{2}{3}} \end{array}$$

b.
$$\begin{array}{r} \frac{2}{3} \times \frac{4}{4} = \frac{8}{12} \\ + \quad \frac{3}{4} \times \frac{3}{3} = \frac{9}{12} \\ \hline \frac{17}{12} = \mathbf{1\frac{5}{12}} \end{array}$$

c.
$$\begin{array}{r} \frac{1}{5} \times \frac{2}{2} = \frac{2}{10} \\ + \quad \frac{3}{10} \qquad = \frac{3}{10} \\ \hline \frac{5}{10} = \mathbf{\frac{1}{2}} \end{array}$$

d.
$$\begin{array}{r} \frac{5}{6} \qquad = \frac{5}{6} \\ - \quad \frac{1}{2} \times \frac{3}{3} = \frac{3}{6} \\ \hline \frac{2}{6} = \mathbf{\frac{1}{3}} \end{array}$$

e.
$$\begin{array}{r} \frac{7}{10} \qquad = \frac{7}{10} \\ - \quad \frac{1}{2} \times \frac{5}{5} = \frac{5}{10} \\ \hline \frac{2}{10} = \mathbf{\frac{1}{5}} \end{array}$$

f.
$$\begin{array}{r} \frac{5}{12} \qquad = \frac{5}{12} \\ - \quad \frac{1}{6} \times \frac{2}{2} = \frac{2}{12} \\ \hline \frac{3}{12} = \mathbf{\frac{1}{4}} \end{array}$$

Written Practice 57

1. $\frac{1}{2} + \frac{1}{2} = \frac{2}{2} = 1 \qquad \frac{1}{2} \times \frac{1}{2} = \frac{1}{4}$

$\frac{4}{4} - \frac{1}{4} = \mathbf{\frac{3}{4}}$

2. **1800 − 1743 = *d***

$$\begin{array}{r} 1\,\overset{7}{\cancel{8}}\,\overset{9}{\cancel{0}}\,{}^{1}0 \\ -\ 1\,7\,4\,3 \\ \hline \mathbf{5\,7} \end{array}$$ **years old**

3.
$$\begin{array}{r} \frac{5}{6} \times \frac{2}{2} = \frac{10}{12} \\ - \quad \frac{3}{4} \times \frac{3}{3} = \frac{9}{12} \\ \hline \mathbf{\frac{1}{12}} \end{array}$$

4. $\frac{1}{2} \times \frac{3}{3} = \frac{3}{6}$
$+\ \frac{2}{3} \times \frac{2}{2} = \frac{4}{6}$
$\frac{7}{6} = \mathbf{1\frac{1}{6}}$

5. $\frac{1}{2} \times \frac{3}{3} = \frac{3}{6}$
$+\ \frac{1}{6} = \frac{1}{6}$
$\frac{4}{6} = \mathbf{\frac{2}{3}}$

6. $\frac{5}{6} = \frac{5}{6}$
$+\ \frac{2}{3} \times \frac{2}{2} = \frac{4}{6}$
$\frac{9}{6} = 1\frac{3}{6} = \mathbf{1\frac{1}{2}}$

7. $\frac{3}{4} \div \frac{3}{5}$
$1 \div \frac{3}{5} = \frac{5}{3}$
$\frac{3}{4} \times \frac{5}{3} = \frac{15}{12} = 1\frac{3}{12} = \mathbf{1\frac{1}{4}}$

8. **$3.25**

9. $\sqrt{4} - (1 - 0.2)$
$2 - 0.8$
1.2

10. $12\overline{)600}$ = **50**
60
00
00
0

11. $5\frac{3}{8} \xrightarrow{4 + \frac{8}{8} + \frac{3}{8}} 4\frac{11}{8}$
$-\ 2\frac{5}{8} \qquad -\ 2\frac{5}{8}$
$2\frac{6}{8} = \mathbf{2\frac{3}{4}}$

12. $\frac{3}{4} \cdot \frac{5}{3} = \frac{15}{12} = 1\frac{3}{12} = \mathbf{1\frac{1}{4}}$

13. $\frac{50}{100} = \mathbf{\frac{1}{2}}$
20 mm
× 10 mm
200 sq. mm

$2\overline{)200}$ = **100 sq. mm**
2
00
00
00
00
0

14. **Thousandths**

15. $4\overline{)0.500}$ = 0.125
4
10
8
20
20
0
0.1

16. **0.03, 0.3, 3.0**

17. 20 × 2 = **40**

18. $\mathbf{\frac{4}{52}} = \mathbf{\frac{1}{13}}$

19. a. $\frac{1}{4} = \frac{1}{4}$ in.
$\frac{1}{4} = \frac{1}{4}$ in.
$\frac{1}{2} \times \frac{2}{2} = \frac{2}{4}$ in.
$+\ \frac{1}{2} \times \frac{2}{2} = \frac{2}{4}$ in.
$\frac{6}{4}$ in. $= 1\frac{2}{4}$ in. $= \mathbf{1\frac{1}{2}}$ **in.**

b. $\frac{1}{4}$ in. × $\frac{1}{2}$ in. = $\mathbf{\frac{1}{8}}$ **in.^{2}**

20. $\frac{5}{8} \times \frac{80}{1} = \frac{400}{8} = \mathbf{50}$

21. Factors of 29: **1, 29**

22. Multiples of 12
12, 24, (36), 48
Multiples of 18
18, (36), 54, 72
LCM is **36**

23. $\frac{5}{8} \; \text{(<)} \; \frac{7}{10}$

$\frac{5}{8} \times \frac{5}{5}$ $\qquad$ $\frac{7}{10} \times \frac{4}{4}$

$\frac{25}{40}$ $\qquad$ $\frac{28}{40}$

24. **−4°F**

25. **16°F**

26. $\frac{2 \cdot 2 \cdot 5 \cdot 7 \cdot 3 \cdot 3}{2 \cdot 2 \cdot 5 \cdot 7 \cdot 5 \cdot 7} = \mathbf{\frac{9}{35}}$

27. $\mathbf{\frac{1}{3}}$

28. $9 \div \frac{3}{8}$ in.

$1 \div \frac{3}{8} = \frac{8}{3}$

$\frac{9}{1} \times \frac{8}{3} = \frac{72}{3} =$ **24 CDs; $\frac{3}{8}$ in. is a little than $\frac{1}{2}$ in. If the CDs were $\frac{1}{2}$ in. thick, then there would be 18 CDs. 18 is a little less than 24, so the answer is reasonable.**

29. $\frac{4}{5} \times \frac{2}{2} = \frac{8}{10}$

$-\frac{1}{2} \times \frac{5}{5} = \frac{5}{10}$

$\mathbf{\frac{3}{10}}$

30. $C = \pi d$
$C \approx (3.14)(18 \text{ inches})$
$C \approx$ **56.52 inches**

Early Finishers Solutions

$\frac{3}{4} + 1 + 2 + 3 + \frac{1}{2} + 1$

$= 7 + \frac{3}{4} + \frac{2}{4} = 8\frac{1}{4}$ cups

Practice Set 58

a. $\frac{40}{100} = \frac{4}{10} = \mathbf{\frac{2}{5}}$
$\frac{40}{100} = 0.40 = \mathbf{0.4}$

b. $1 - \frac{2}{5} = \frac{5}{5} - \frac{2}{5} = \mathbf{\frac{3}{5}}$
$1 - 0.4 = \mathbf{0.6}$

c. **Complementary**

d. **Sample space = {1, 2, 3, 4, 5, 6}**

e. $\frac{3}{6} = \frac{1}{2}$**; The possible odd numbers are 1, 3, and 5, so three of the six possible outcomes are odd, and $\frac{3}{6}$ reduces to $\frac{1}{2}$.**

f. $\mathbf{\frac{5}{6}}$

g. **The probability the number rolled is not less than 6 is $\frac{1}{6}$.**

h. Blue: $\mathbf{\frac{1}{2}}$

Black: $\mathbf{\frac{1}{6}}$

White: $\mathbf{\frac{1}{3}}$

i. $\mathbf{\frac{2}{3}}$

j. **The probability of landing on white is $\frac{1}{3}$.**

k. Blue: $30 \div 2 =$ **15 times**
White: $30 \div 3 =$ **10 times**
Black: $30 \div 6 =$ **5 times**

Solutions

l. Answers may vary. See student work.
Sample Answer:

1	II
2	IIII
3	III
4	III
5	~~IIII~~ I
6	~~IIII~~ I

I rolled 5 and 6 more times than I expected.

Written Practice 58

1.
$$\frac{1}{2} \times \frac{3}{3} = \frac{3}{6} \qquad \frac{1}{2} \times \frac{1}{3} = \frac{1}{6}$$
$$+\ \frac{1}{3} \times \frac{2}{2} = \frac{2}{6}$$
$$\frac{5}{6}$$
$$\frac{5}{6} - \frac{1}{6} = \frac{4}{6} = \mathbf{\frac{2}{3}}$$

2.
$$\begin{array}{r} 12 \\ \times\ 2.5 \\ \hline 60 \\ 240 \\ \hline 30.0 \end{array}$$
30 eggs

3.
$$\begin{array}{r} \mathbf{\$14{,}800} \\ 3\overline{)\$44{,}400} \\ 3 \\ \hline 14 \\ 12 \\ \hline 24 \\ 24 \\ \hline 00 \\ 00 \\ \hline 00 \\ 00 \\ \hline 0 \end{array}$$

4. $\frac{5}{8}$ ⓪ $\frac{1}{2}$ — $\frac{5}{8} > \frac{1}{2}$
$$\frac{1}{2} \times \frac{4}{4}$$
$$\frac{4}{8}$$

5. 36 + 64 ⊜ 100
100

6.
$$\frac{1}{2} \times \frac{4}{4} = \frac{4}{8}$$
$$-\ \frac{3}{8} = \frac{3}{8}$$
$$\frac{1}{8}$$
$$m = \mathbf{\frac{1}{8}}$$

7.
$$\frac{2}{3} \times \frac{4}{4} = \frac{8}{12}$$
$$+\ \frac{3}{4} \times \frac{3}{3} = \frac{9}{12}$$
$$\frac{17}{12} = 1\frac{5}{12}$$
$$n = \mathbf{1\frac{5}{12}}$$

8.
$$3 \xrightarrow{2 + \frac{6}{6}} 2\frac{6}{6}$$
$$-\ \frac{5}{6} \qquad -\ \frac{5}{6}$$
$$2\frac{1}{6}$$
$$f = \mathbf{2\frac{1}{6}}$$

9. $325.00

10.
$$\begin{array}{r} 6.2 \\ \times\ 0.48 \\ \hline 496 \\ 2480 \\ \hline \mathbf{2.976} \end{array}$$

11.
$$\begin{array}{r} \mathbf{1.25} \\ 8\overline{)10.00} \\ 8 \\ \hline 2\,0 \\ 1\,6 \\ \hline 40 \\ 40 \\ \hline 0 \end{array}$$

12.
$$\begin{array}{r} \mathbf{240} \\ 5\overline{)1200} \\ 10 \\ \hline 20 \\ 20 \\ \hline 00 \\ 00 \\ \hline 0 \end{array}$$

13. $\frac{7}{8} \cdot \frac{8}{7} = \frac{56}{56} = \mathbf{1}$

14. $\frac{5}{6} \cdot \frac{3}{4} = \frac{15}{24} = \mathbf{\frac{5}{8}}$

15. **15 ÷ 3 = 5**

16.
$$\begin{array}{r} \$9.79 \\ \times \quad .07 \\ \hline \$0.6853 \end{array} \qquad \begin{array}{r} {}^{1\,1} \\ \$9.79 \\ + \ \$0.69 \\ \hline \mathbf{\$10.48} \end{array}$$

17. **1.0** or **1**

18.
4 cm ÷ 4 = 1 cm
1 cm × 1 cm = **1 cm^2**

19. $\frac{3}{4} \div \frac{3}{5}$

$1 \div \frac{3}{5} = \frac{5}{3}$

$\frac{3}{4} \times \frac{5}{3} = \frac{15}{12} = 1\frac{3}{12} = \mathbf{1\frac{1}{4}}$

20.
$$\begin{array}{r} 100 \\ 32\overline{)3200} \\ \underline{32} \\ 00 \\ \underline{00} \\ 00 \\ \underline{00} \\ 0 \end{array}$$
w = **100**

21.
$$\begin{array}{r} \overset{4}{\not 5}.{}^{1}0 \\ -\ 3.\ 4 \\ \hline 1.\ 6 \end{array}$$
x = **1.6**

22. $\frac{3}{6} = \mathbf{\frac{1}{2}}$

23. **20 mm, 1 in., 3 cm**

24. a. Less than half; 50% equals $\frac{1}{2}$ and Larry answered less than 50% correctly.

b. $\frac{45}{100} = \mathbf{\frac{9}{20}}$

25. Finding $\frac{1}{10}$ of $12.50 is the same as dividing $12.50 by 10. We shift the decimal point in $12.50 one place to the left, which makes $1.250. Then we remove the trailing zero. The answer is $1.25.

26. $\frac{2 \cdot 5 \cdot 2 \cdot 7 \cdot 3 \cdot 3}{2 \cdot 5 \cdot 2 \cdot 7 \cdot 2 \cdot 5} = \mathbf{\frac{9}{10}}$

27. $1\frac{6}{10} + 2\frac{4}{10} = 3\frac{10}{10} = \mathbf{4}$

28. One possibility:

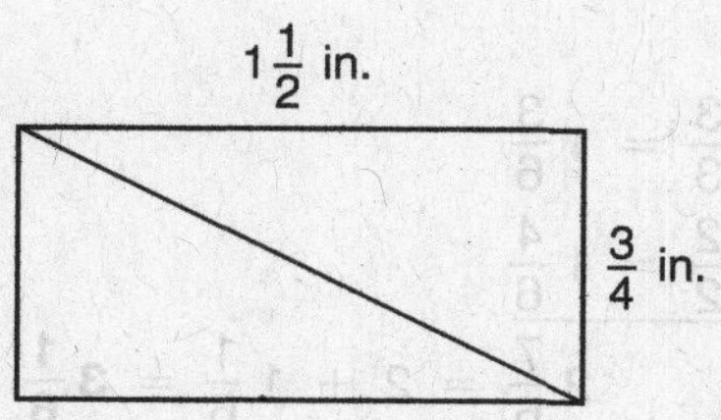

29.
$$\begin{array}{rcl} 1\frac{1}{2} \times \frac{2}{2} & = & 1\frac{2}{4} \\ 1\frac{1}{2} \times \frac{2}{2} & = & 1\frac{2}{4} \\ \frac{3}{4} & = & \frac{3}{4} \\ + \frac{3}{4} & = & \frac{3}{4} \\ \hline & & 2\frac{10}{4} \end{array}$$
$2\frac{10}{4} = 4\frac{2}{4} = \mathbf{4\frac{1}{2}}$ **inches**

30.
$A = lw$
$A = (1.5)(0.75)$
$A =$ **1.125**

$$\begin{array}{r} 0.75 \\ \times \ 1.5 \\ \hline 375 \\ 750 \\ \hline \mathbf{1.125} \end{array}$$

Early Finishers Solutions

Line graph; While a bar graph can be used to display comparisons, a line graph would be better because it clearly displays a change over time.

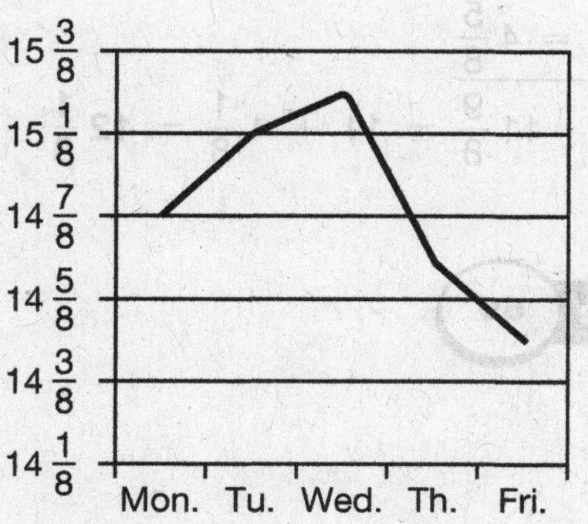

Solutions

Practice Set 59

a.

$$\begin{array}{r} 1\frac{1}{2} \times \frac{3}{3} = 1\frac{3}{6} \\ +\ 1\frac{1}{3} \times \frac{2}{2} = 1\frac{2}{6} \\ \hline \mathbf{2\frac{5}{6}} \end{array}$$

b.

$$\begin{array}{r} 1\frac{1}{2} \times \frac{3}{3} = 1\frac{3}{6} \\ +\ 1\frac{2}{3} \times \frac{2}{2} = 1\frac{4}{6} \\ \hline 2\frac{7}{6} = 2 + 1\frac{1}{6} = \mathbf{3\frac{1}{6}} \end{array}$$

c.

$$\begin{array}{r} 5\frac{1}{3} \times \frac{2}{2} = 5\frac{2}{6} \\ +\ 2\frac{1}{6} \qquad = 2\frac{1}{6} \\ \hline 7\frac{3}{6} = \mathbf{7\frac{1}{2}} \end{array}$$

d.

$$\begin{array}{r} 3\frac{3}{4} \times \frac{3}{3} = 3\frac{9}{12} \\ +\ 1\frac{1}{3} \times \frac{4}{4} = 1\frac{4}{12} \\ \hline 4\frac{13}{12} = 4 + 1\frac{1}{12} = \mathbf{5\frac{1}{12}} \end{array}$$

e.

$$\begin{array}{r} 5\frac{1}{2} \times \frac{3}{3} = 5\frac{3}{6} \\ +\ 3\frac{1}{6} \qquad = 3\frac{1}{6} \\ \hline 8\frac{4}{6} = \mathbf{8\frac{2}{3}} \end{array}$$

f.

$$\begin{array}{r} 7\frac{1}{2} \times \frac{4}{4} = 7\frac{4}{8} \\ +\ 4\frac{5}{8} \qquad = 4\frac{5}{8} \\ \hline 11\frac{9}{8} = 11 + 1\frac{1}{8} = \mathbf{12\frac{1}{8}} \end{array}$$

Written Practice 59

1.

$$\begin{array}{r} 0.04 \\ \times\ 0.4 \\ \hline \mathbf{0.016} \end{array}$$

2.

$$\begin{array}{r} \overset{11:\ \overset{5}{\cancel{6}}{}^{1}0}{\cancel{12}:\ \cancel{00}} \text{ a.m.} \\ -\ 9:45 \text{ p.m.} \\ \hline 2:15 \end{array} \qquad \begin{array}{r} 2:15 \\ +\ 8:30 \\ \hline 10:45 \end{array}$$

10 hours 45 minutes

3. **5,900,000,000 kilometers**

4.

$$\begin{array}{r} 2\frac{1}{2} \times \frac{3}{3} = 2\frac{3}{6} \\ +\ 1\frac{1}{6} \qquad -\ 1\frac{1}{6} \\ \hline 3\frac{4}{6} = \mathbf{3\frac{2}{3}} \end{array}$$

5.

$$\begin{array}{r} 1\frac{1}{2} \times \frac{3}{3} = 1\frac{3}{6} \\ +\ 2\frac{2}{3} \times \frac{2}{2} = 2\frac{4}{6} \\ \hline 3\frac{7}{6} = 3 + 1\frac{1}{6} = \mathbf{4\frac{1}{6}} \end{array}$$

6. $\frac{1}{2} \text{ (<) } \frac{3}{5}$

$\frac{1}{2} \times \frac{5}{5} \qquad \frac{3}{5} \times \frac{2}{2}$

$\frac{5}{10} \qquad \frac{6}{10}$

7. $\frac{2}{3} \text{ (=) } \frac{6}{9}$

$\frac{2}{3} \times \frac{3}{3}$

$\frac{6}{9}$

8.

$$\begin{array}{r} 8\frac{1}{5} \\ -\ 3\frac{4}{5} \end{array} \xrightarrow{7 + \frac{5}{5} + \frac{1}{5}} \begin{array}{r} 7\frac{6}{5} \\ -\ 3\frac{4}{5} \\ \hline \mathbf{4\frac{2}{5}} \end{array}$$

9. $\frac{3}{4} \times \frac{5}{2} = \frac{15}{8} = \mathbf{1\frac{7}{8}}$

10. $\frac{2}{5} \div \frac{1}{2}$

$1 \div \frac{1}{2} = \frac{2}{1}$

$\frac{2}{5} \times \frac{2}{1} = \mathbf{\frac{4}{5}}$

11. $0.875 \times 40 = $ **35.000** or **35**

12. $4\overline{)0.0700}$ = **0.0175**

$$\begin{array}{r} 4 \\ \hline 30 \\ 28 \\ \hline 20 \\ 20 \\ \hline 0 \end{array}$$

13. $6\overline{)300}$ = 50

$$\begin{array}{r} 30 \\ \hline 00 \\ 00 \\ \hline 0 \end{array}$$

d = **50**

14. $0.24 - 0.10 = 0.14$

$2\overline{)0.14}$ = 0.07; 14, 0

$0.10 + 0.07 = $ **0.17**

15. **36,000,000**

16. 8°F − 23°F = **−15°F**

17. $C = \pi d$

$C \approx (3.14)(10 \text{ inches})$

$C \approx 31.4$ inches

$C \approx$ **31 inches**

18. 12 inches × 12 inches

24

120

144 square inches

19. $\mathbf{\frac{1}{100}}$

20. a. **62.5; To multiply 6.25 by 10, shift the decimal point one place to the right.**

b. **0.625; To divide 6.25 by 10, shift the decimal point one place to the left.**

21. a. $\frac{2}{6} = \mathbf{\frac{1}{3}}$

b. **The probability of rolling a number not less than three is $\frac{2}{3}$.**

22. $(0.8)^2$ ⓐ< 0.8

0.64

23. $\overset{6}{\cancel{7}}{}^{1}2$°F − 64°F = **8°F**

24. **67°F**

25. **Sample Answer: How much warmer was it at noon on Wednesday than at noon on Tuesday?**

72°F − 70°F = 2°F

26. $15 \div \frac{6}{10}$

$1 \div \frac{6}{10} = \frac{10}{6}$

$\frac{15}{1} \times \frac{10}{6} = \frac{150}{6} =$ **25 bags**

27. $\overset{1}{1}2.5\% \times 3 = $ **37.5%** or **$37\frac{1}{2}\%$**

28. **\$22.99; To multiply \$2.299 by 10, shift the decimal point one place to the right.**

29. **$\frac{3}{4}$, 1, the reciprocal of $\frac{3}{4}$**

30. $P = 2l + 2w$
$P = 2(4) + 2(3)$
$P = 8 + 6$
$P = \mathbf{14}$

Early Finishers Solutions

a. {B, B, B}, {B, B, G}, {B, G, B}, {G, B, B}, {B, G, G}, {G, B, G}, {G, G, B}, {G, G, G}

b. P(2 boys, 1 girl)

$= \frac{|\{B,B,G\},\{B,G,B\},\{G,B,B\}|}{|\{B,B,B\},\{B,B,G\},\{B,G,B\},\{G,B,B\},\{B,G,G\},\{G,B,G\},\{G,G,B\},\{G,G,G\}|}$

$= \frac{3}{8}$

Practice Set 60

a. Hexagon

b. 5 sides

c. Yes

d. Vertex

e. Quadrilateral

Written Practice 60

1. $\mathbf{42 \cdot c = 1.26}$

$0.03 per ounce

$$\begin{array}{r} 0.03 \\ 42\overline{)1.26} \\ 1\ 26 \\ \hline 0\ 00 \end{array}$$

2.
$$\begin{array}{r} \$2.48 \\ \times\ \ 1.1 \\ \hline 248 \\ 2480 \\ \hline \$2.728 \end{array}$$

$2.73; Amy bought only a little more than a gallon, so the cost should be only a little more than 2.47\frac{9}{10}$. The answer $2.73 is reasonable.

3. 999

4.
$$\begin{array}{rcl} \frac{3}{4} \times \frac{2}{2} & = & \frac{6}{8} \\ + \frac{5}{8} & = & \frac{5}{8} \\ \hline & & \frac{11}{8} = \mathbf{1\frac{3}{8}} \end{array}$$

5.
$$\begin{array}{rcl} 1\frac{1}{2} \times \frac{3}{3} & = & 1\frac{3}{6} \\ + 3\frac{1}{6} & = & 3\frac{1}{6} \\ \hline & & 4\frac{4}{6} = \mathbf{4\frac{2}{3}} \end{array}$$

6. $1 \times (1 - 1)$
1×0
$\mathbf{0}$

7. $\frac{3}{5} \cdot \frac{1}{3} = \frac{3}{15} = \mathbf{\frac{1}{5}}$

8. $\frac{3}{5} \div \frac{1}{3}$

$1 \div \frac{1}{3} = 3$

$\frac{3}{5} \times \frac{3}{1} = \frac{9}{5} = \mathbf{1\frac{4}{5}}$

9.

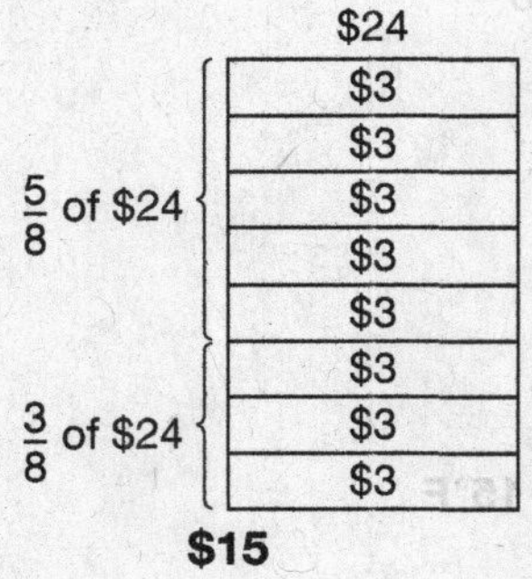

10.
$$\begin{array}{r} 0.65 \\ \times\ 0.14 \\ \hline 260 \\ 650 \\ \hline \end{array}$$
0.0910 or **0.091**

11.

$$\begin{array}{r} \mathbf{1300} \\ 5\overline{)6500} \\ \underline{5} \\ 15 \\ \underline{15} \\ 00 \\ \underline{00} \\ 00 \\ \underline{00} \\ 0 \end{array}$$

12. **4 sides**

13.

$$\begin{array}{r} 0.24 \\ \times\ 0.26 \\ \hline 144 \\ \underline{480} \\ .0624 \\ \mathbf{0.06} \end{array}$$

14.

$$\begin{array}{r} \overset{1}{1}.3 \\ 2 \\ \underline{0.81} \\ 4.11 \end{array} \qquad \begin{array}{r} \mathbf{1.37} \\ 3\overline{)4.11} \\ \underline{3} \\ 1\,1 \\ \underline{9} \\ 21 \\ \underline{21} \\ 0 \end{array}$$

15. $1 + 3 + 5 + 7 + 9 + 11 + 13 =$ **49**

16. 3 ft × 3 ft = **9 square feet**

17. $\frac{10}{100} = \mathbf{\frac{1}{10}}$

18. $3x = 3.6$

$$\begin{array}{r} 1.2 \\ 3\overline{)3.6} \\ \underline{3} \\ 06 \\ \underline{06} \\ 0 \end{array}$$

$x =$ **1.2**

19. $1 \div \frac{4}{3} = \frac{3}{4}$

$y = \mathbf{\frac{3}{4}}$

20.

$$\begin{array}{r} 5 \\ -\ 1\frac{3}{5} \\ \hline \end{array} \xrightarrow{4 + \frac{5}{5}} \begin{array}{r} 4\frac{5}{5} \\ -\ 1\frac{3}{5} \\ \hline 3\frac{2}{5} \end{array}$$

$m = \mathbf{3\frac{2}{5}}$

21.

$$\begin{array}{r} 6\frac{1}{8} \\ -\ 3\frac{5}{8} \\ \hline \end{array} \xrightarrow{5 + \frac{8}{8} + \frac{1}{8}} \begin{array}{r} 5\frac{9}{8} \\ -\ 3\frac{5}{8} \\ \hline 2\frac{4}{8} = 2\frac{1}{2} \end{array}$$

$w = \mathbf{2\frac{1}{2}}$

22. **41, 43, 47**

23. $C = \pi d$
$C \approx (3.14)(4\text{ cm})$
$C \approx 12.56$ cm
$C \approx$ **13 cm**

24. **a.** **5.4**

b. **5**

25. **Sample space = {1, 2, 3, 4} or {1, 1, 2, 2, 3, 3, 4, 4};** $\frac{2}{8} = \mathbf{\frac{1}{4}}$

26. $12 \div \frac{3}{8}$

$1 \div \frac{3}{8} = \frac{8}{3}$

$\frac{12}{1} \times \frac{8}{3} = \frac{96}{6} =$ **32 years old**

27. $\frac{12}{60} = \mathbf{\frac{1}{5}}$

28. **Possible Answers:**
200 ÷ 8 = 25
100 ÷ 4 = 25
50 ÷ 2 = 25

29.
$$\begin{array}{r} \$6.89 \\ \times \ \ 0.06 \\ \hline 0.4134 \end{array} \qquad \begin{array}{r} \overset{1\,1}{\$6.89} \\ +\ \$0.41 \\ \hline \mathbf{\$7.30} \end{array}$$

30. a. $3\frac{1}{2} \circledcirc\!\!= \frac{7}{2}$

$3\frac{1}{2}$

b. $\frac{5}{8} < \frac{3}{4}$ (circled)

$\frac{3}{4} \times \frac{2}{2} = \frac{6}{8}$

Investigation 6

1. Rectangular prism, box
2. Cylinder, can
3. Triangular prism, lean-to roof or half of a gable roof
4. Cone, cone
5. Sphere, ball
6. Pyramid, pyramid
7. 6 faces
8. 12 edges
9. 8 vertices
10. 5 faces
11. 8 edges
12. 5 vertices
13.

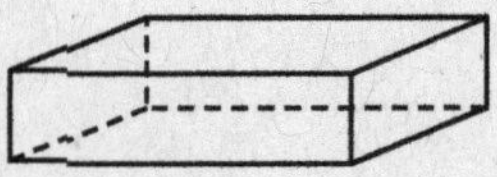

14.

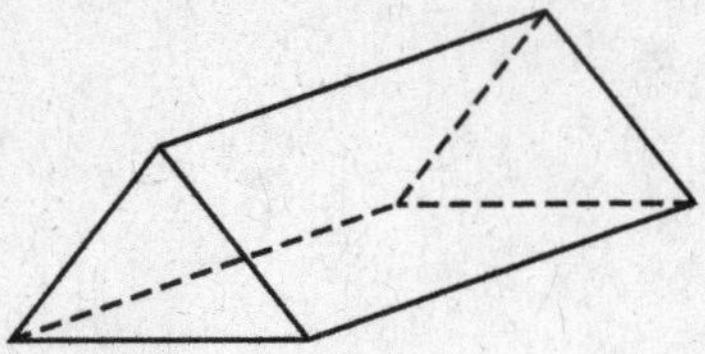

15.

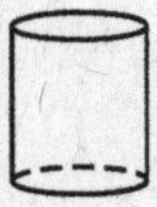

16. $5 \text{ in.} \times 5 \text{ in.} = 25 \text{ in.}^2$
17. $25 \text{ in.}^2 \times 6 = 150 \text{ in.}^2$
18. $10 \text{ in.} \times 7 \text{ in.} = 70 \text{ in.}^2$
19. $7 \text{ in.} \times 2 \text{ in.} = 14 \text{ in.}^2$
20. $10 \text{ in.} \times 2 \text{ in.} = 20 \text{ in.}^2$
21. $70 \text{ in.}^2 + 70 \text{ in.}^2 + 14 \text{ in.}^2 + 14 \text{ in.}^2 + 20 \text{ in.}^2 + 20 \text{ in.}^2 = 208 \text{ in.}^2$
22. C.

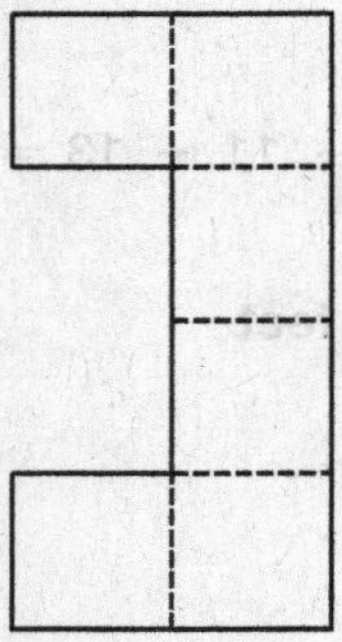

23. 12 cubes
24. 27 cubes
25. 18 cubes

Extension

1. Answers will vary. See student work.
2. Answers will vary. See student work.

Practice Set 61

a.
$$\frac{1}{2} \times \frac{4}{4} = \frac{4}{8}$$
$$\frac{3}{4} \times \frac{2}{2} = \frac{6}{8}$$
$$+\ \frac{1}{8} \times \frac{1}{1} = \frac{1}{8}$$
$$\frac{11}{8} = \mathbf{1\frac{3}{8}}$$

b.
$$\frac{1}{2} \times \frac{3}{3} = \frac{3}{6}$$
$$\frac{1}{3} \times \frac{2}{2} = \frac{2}{6}$$
$$+\ \frac{1}{6} \times \frac{1}{1} = \frac{1}{6}$$
$$\frac{6}{6} = \mathbf{1}$$

c.
$$1\frac{1}{2} \times \frac{6}{6} = 1\frac{6}{12}$$
$$1\frac{1}{3} \times \frac{4}{4} = 1\frac{4}{12}$$
$$+\ 1\frac{1}{4} \times \frac{3}{3} = 1\frac{3}{12}$$
$$3\frac{13}{12} = \mathbf{4\frac{1}{12}}$$

d.
$$\frac{1}{2} \times \frac{3}{3} = \frac{3}{6}$$
$$\frac{2}{3} \times \frac{2}{2} = \frac{4}{6}$$
$$+\ \frac{5}{6} \times \frac{1}{1} = \frac{5}{6}$$
$$\frac{12}{6} = \mathbf{2}$$

e.
$$\frac{1}{2} \times \frac{4}{4} = \frac{4}{8}$$
$$\frac{3}{4} \times \frac{2}{2} = \frac{6}{8}$$
$$+\ \frac{7}{8} \times \frac{1}{1} = \frac{7}{8}$$
$$\frac{17}{8} = \mathbf{2\frac{1}{8}}$$

f.
$$1\frac{1}{4} \times \frac{2}{2} = 1\frac{2}{8}$$
$$1\frac{1}{8} \times \frac{1}{1} = 1\frac{1}{8}$$
$$+\ 1\frac{1}{2} \times \frac{4}{4} = 1\frac{4}{8}$$
$$\mathbf{3\frac{7}{8}}$$

g.
$$\frac{5}{8} \times \frac{1}{1} = \frac{5}{8}$$
$$\frac{3}{8} \times \frac{1}{1} = \frac{3}{8}$$
$$+\ \frac{1}{2} \times \frac{4}{4} = \frac{4}{8}$$
$$\frac{12}{8} = 1\frac{4}{8} = \mathbf{1\frac{1}{2}\ in.}$$

h. **Answers will vary. See student work.**

Written Practice 61

1. $\frac{20}{6} = 3\frac{2}{6} = \mathbf{3\frac{1}{3}}$

2.
```
   2.5
×    6 feet
  15.0 = 15 feet
```
2.5×6 feet $= 15.0 =$ **15 feet**

3.
```
   923
3)2769     923 cars
  27
   06
    6
    09
     9
     0
```

4.
$$5\frac{1}{2} \times \frac{3}{3} = 5\frac{3}{6} \xrightarrow{4 + \frac{6}{6} + \frac{3}{6}} 4\frac{9}{6}$$
$$-\ 1\frac{2}{3} \times \frac{2}{2} = 1\frac{4}{6} \qquad -\ 1\frac{4}{6}$$
$$\mathbf{3\frac{5}{6}}$$

5.

$$\begin{array}{r} 5\frac{1}{3} \times \frac{2}{2} = 5\frac{2}{6} \\ -\ 2\frac{1}{2} \times \frac{3}{3} = 2\frac{3}{6} \\ \hline \end{array} \xrightarrow{4 + \frac{6}{6} + \frac{2}{6}} \begin{array}{r} 4\frac{8}{6} \\ -\ 2\frac{3}{6} \\ \hline \mathbf{2\frac{5}{6}} \end{array}$$

6.

$$\begin{array}{r} 1\frac{1}{2} \times \frac{6}{6} = 1\frac{6}{12} \\ 2\frac{1}{3} \times \frac{4}{4} = 2\frac{4}{12} \\ +\ 3\frac{1}{4} \times \frac{3}{3} = 3\frac{3}{12} \\ \hline 6\frac{13}{12} \end{array} = \mathbf{7\frac{1}{12}}$$

7.

$$\begin{array}{r} 3\frac{3}{4} \times \frac{3}{3} = 3\frac{9}{12} \\ +\ 3\frac{1}{3} \times \frac{4}{4} = 3\frac{4}{12} \\ \hline 6\frac{13}{12} \end{array} = \mathbf{7\frac{1}{12}}$$

8. **a.** $\frac{2}{3}$ (>) $\frac{3}{5}$

$\frac{2}{3} \times \frac{5}{5}$ $\qquad$ $\frac{3}{5} \times \frac{3}{3}$

$\frac{10}{15}$ $\qquad$ $\frac{9}{15}$

b. 16 (>) 12

9. $\frac{5}{6} \times \frac{36}{1} = \frac{180}{6} = \mathbf{30}$

10. $\frac{3}{8} \times \frac{2}{3} = \frac{6}{24} = \mathbf{\frac{1}{4}}$

11. $\frac{3}{8} \div \frac{2}{3}$

$1 \div \frac{2}{3} = \frac{3}{2}$

$\frac{3}{8} \times \frac{3}{2} = \mathbf{\frac{9}{16}}$

12. $(4 - 0.4) \div 4$

$3.6 \div 4$

0.9

13. $4 - (0.4 \div 4)$

$4 - 0.1$

3.9

14. 6

15.

$$\begin{array}{r} \$600.00 \\ +\ \$900.00 \\ \hline \mathbf{\$1500.00} \end{array}$$

Round $642.23 to $600 and $861.17 to $900. Then add $600 to $900.

16. **a.** 4 cm × 2 = **8 cm; The diameter is twice the radius.**

b. $C = \pi d$

$C \approx (3.14)(8\text{ cm})$

$C \approx$ **25.12 cm**

17. **0.1** or $\mathbf{\frac{1}{10}}$

18.

$$\begin{array}{r} 3\text{ inches} \\ 4\overline{)12\text{ inches}} \\ \underline{12} \\ 0 \end{array}$$

3 in. × 3 in. = **9 square inches**

19. $\frac{\text{dime}}{\text{quarter}} = \frac{10}{25} = \mathbf{\frac{2}{5}}$

20. $15m = 300$

$$\begin{array}{r} 20 \\ 15\overline{)300} \\ \underline{30} \\ 00 \\ \underline{00} \\ 0 \end{array}$$

m = **20**

21. $\frac{1}{10} \times \frac{10}{10} = \frac{10}{100}$

n = **10**

22. $\mathbf{\frac{5}{5}}$

23.

$$\begin{array}{r} 9{:}50\text{ a.m.} \\ +\ 5{:}15 \\ \hline 14{:}65 \end{array}$$

2:65 p.m. = **3:05 p.m.**

24. $\sqrt{16\text{ in.}^2} = 4\text{ in.}$

4 in. + 4 in. + 4 in. + 4 in. = **16 inches**

25. **Pentagon**

26.
$$\begin{array}{r} \overset{1\,1}{\$4.95} \\ +\ \$2.79 \\ \hline \$7.74 \end{array} \qquad \begin{array}{r} \$7.74 \\ \times\ \ .07 \\ \hline 0.5418 \end{array} \qquad \begin{array}{r} \$7.74 \\ +\ \$0.54 \\ \hline \mathbf{\$8.28} \end{array}$$

Round \$4.95 to \$5 and round \$2.79 to \$3. Add \$5 and \$3 to get \$8. Mentally multiply 7% and \$8 and get 56¢. Add 56¢ to \$8 and get \$8.56. Since we rounded the prices up to estimate, the answer of \$8.28 is reasonable.

27. $\$37 \div 100 =$ **\$0.37**

28. **One possibility:**

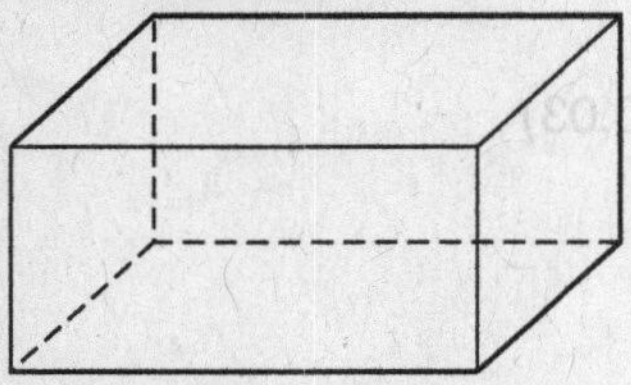

a. **6 faces**

b. **12 edges**

c. **8 vertices**

29. $3 \text{ cm} \times 3 \text{ cm} = \mathbf{9\ cm^2}$

30. $9 \text{ cm}^2 \times 6 = \mathbf{54\ cm^2}$

Early Finishers Solutions

921 ft × 5 sides = 4605 feet long ÷ 3 = 1535 yards

Practice Set 62

a. $\frac{10}{5} + \frac{4}{5} = \mathbf{\frac{14}{5}}$

b. $\frac{6}{2} + \frac{1}{2} = \mathbf{\frac{7}{2}}$

c. $\frac{4}{4} + \frac{3}{4} = \mathbf{\frac{7}{4}}$

d. $\frac{24}{4} + \frac{1}{4} = \mathbf{\frac{25}{4}}$

e. $\frac{6}{6} + \frac{5}{6} = \mathbf{\frac{11}{6}}$

f. $\frac{30}{10} + \frac{3}{10} = \mathbf{\frac{33}{10}}$

g. $\frac{6}{3} + \frac{1}{3} = \mathbf{\frac{7}{3}}$

h. $\frac{24}{2} + \frac{1}{2} = \mathbf{\frac{25}{2}}$

i. $\frac{18}{6} + \frac{1}{6} = \mathbf{\frac{19}{6}}$

j. $\frac{3}{2} \times \frac{10}{3} = \frac{30}{6} = \mathbf{5}$

Written Practice 62

1. a. $1 \div \frac{1}{4} = \frac{4}{1} =$ **4 quarter notes**

b. $\frac{1}{4} \div \frac{1}{8}$

$1 \div \frac{1}{8} = 8$

$\frac{1}{4} \times \frac{8}{1} = \frac{8}{4} =$ **2 eighth notes**

2.
$$\begin{array}{r} \overset{1}{1}2 \text{ inches} \\ \times\ \ 5 \quad\quad\ \ \\ \hline 60 \text{ inches} \end{array}$$

$60 + 2\frac{1}{2} = \mathbf{62\frac{1}{2}}$ **inches**

3. **B. 21**

4. $\frac{4}{3} \cdot \frac{3}{2} = \frac{12}{6} = \mathbf{2}$

5. **100% − 20% = 80%**

6.
$$\begin{array}{r} \overset{1\,1\;1}{\$36.25} \\ \$41.50 \\ +\ \$43.75 \\ \hline \$121.50 \end{array} \qquad \begin{array}{r} \$40.50 \\ 3\overline{)\$121.50} \\ 12 \\ \hline 01 \\ 00 \\ \hline 1\,5 \\ 1\,5 \\ \hline 00 \\ 00 \\ \hline 0 \end{array}$$

Each amount is close to $40, so $40 is about the average price.

7. $30 \div 5 = \mathbf{6}$

8.
$$\begin{array}{r} 4\frac{3}{8} \times \frac{1}{1} = 4\frac{3}{8} \\ +\ 3\frac{1}{4} \times \frac{2}{2} = 3\frac{2}{8} \\ \hline m = \mathbf{7\frac{5}{8}} \end{array}$$

9.
$$\begin{array}{r} \frac{3}{5} \times \frac{2}{2} = \frac{6}{10} \\ -\ \frac{3}{10} \qquad = \frac{3}{10} \\ \hline n = \mathbf{\frac{3}{10}} \end{array}$$

10.
$$\begin{array}{r} 0.076 \\ 6\overline{)0.456} \\ 42 \\ \hline 36 \\ 36 \\ \hline 0 \end{array}$$

$d = \mathbf{0.076}$

11.
$$\begin{array}{r} 37.5 \\ 4\overline{)150.0} \\ 12 \\ \hline 30 \\ 28 \\ \hline 2\,0 \\ 2\,0 \\ \hline 0 \end{array}$$

$w = \mathbf{37.5}$

12.
$$\begin{array}{r} \frac{1}{2} \times \frac{4}{4} = \frac{4}{8} \\ \frac{3}{4} \times \frac{2}{2} = \frac{6}{8} \\ +\ \frac{5}{8} \times \frac{1}{1} = \frac{5}{8} \\ \hline \frac{15}{8} = \mathbf{1\frac{7}{8}} \end{array}$$

13.
$$\begin{array}{r} \frac{5}{6} \times \frac{1}{1} = \frac{5}{6} \\ -\ \frac{1}{2} \times \frac{3}{3} = \frac{3}{6} \\ \hline \frac{2}{6} = \mathbf{\frac{1}{3}} \end{array}$$

14. $\frac{1}{2} \cdot \frac{4}{5} = \frac{4}{10} = \mathbf{\frac{2}{5}}$

15. $\frac{2}{3} \div \frac{1}{2}$

$1 \div \frac{1}{2} = \frac{2}{1}$

$\frac{2}{3} \times \frac{2}{1} = \frac{4}{3} = \mathbf{1\frac{1}{3}}$

16. $1 - (0.2 - 0.03)$

$1 - 0.17$

$\mathbf{0.83}$

17.
$$\begin{array}{r} 0.14 \\ \times\ 0.16 \\ \hline 84 \\ 140 \\ \hline \mathbf{0.0224} \end{array}$$

18. $2.5\text{ cm} \times 10 =$ **25 millimeters**

19. Factors of 18

①, ②, ③, ⑥, 9, 18

Factors of 24

①, ②, ③, 4, ⑥, 8, 12, 24

1, 2, 3, ⑥

20. a. $\frac{4}{10} = \mathbf{\frac{2}{5}}$

b. **The probability of not drawing red is $\frac{3}{5}$.**

c. **They sum to 1**

21.
$$\begin{array}{r} 10\text{ mm} \\ 4\overline{)40\text{ mm}} \\ 4 \\ \hline 00 \\ 00 \\ \hline 0 \end{array} \qquad \begin{array}{r} 10\text{ mm} \\ \times\ 10\text{ mm} \\ \hline \mathbf{100\text{ mm}^2} \end{array}$$

22. $14°\text{F} - (-6°\text{F}) = \mathbf{20°F}$

23. **a.** $1\frac{1}{2}$ inches $\times$ 2 = **3 inches**

b. $C = \pi d$
$C \approx (3.14)(3 \text{ inches})$
$C \approx$ **9.42 inches**

24.
$$\begin{array}{r} \overset{3}{\cancel{4}}\,{}^{1}0 \\ -\ 2\ 2 \\ \hline 1\ 8 \end{array}$$
1 8 more people

25. $\frac{40}{100} = \mathbf{\frac{2}{5}}$

26. **No. A majority of 100 people is at least 51 people. No sport was the favorite sport of 51 or more people.**

27. 22 out of 100 or **22%**

28.
$$\begin{array}{r} 200 \\ \times\ \ 0.40 \\ \hline 80.00 \end{array}$$
80

29. **2 · 2 · 5**

30. 8.9, 9.0, (9.1) 9.2, 9.2
9.1

Practice Set 63

a.
$$\begin{array}{rcl} 5\frac{1}{2} \times \frac{3}{3} &=& 5\frac{3}{6} \\ -\ 3\frac{1}{3} \times \frac{2}{2} &=& 3\frac{2}{6} \\ \hline && \mathbf{2\frac{1}{6}} \end{array}$$

b.
$$\begin{array}{rcl} 4\frac{1}{4} \times \frac{3}{3} &=& \overset{3}{\cancel{4}}\,\frac{\overset{15}{\cancel{3}}}{12} \\ -\ 2\frac{1}{3} \times \frac{4}{4} &=& 2\frac{4}{12} \\ \hline && \mathbf{1\frac{11}{12}} \end{array}$$

c.
$$\begin{array}{rcl} 6\frac{1}{2} \times \frac{2}{2} &=& \overset{5}{\cancel{6}}\,\frac{\overset{6}{\cancel{2}}}{4} \\ -\ 1\frac{3}{4} \times \frac{1}{1} &=& 1\frac{3}{4} \\ \hline && \mathbf{4\frac{3}{4}} \end{array}$$

d.
$$\begin{array}{rcl} 7\frac{2}{3} \times \frac{2}{2} &=& \overset{6}{\cancel{7}}\,\frac{\overset{10}{\cancel{4}}}{6} \\ -\ 3\frac{5}{6} \times \frac{1}{1} &=& 3\frac{5}{6} \\ \hline && \mathbf{3\frac{5}{6}} \end{array}$$

e.
$$\begin{array}{rcl} 6\frac{1}{6} \times \frac{1}{1} &=& \overset{5}{\cancel{6}}\,\frac{\overset{7}{\cancel{1}}}{6} \\ -\ 1\frac{1}{2} \times \frac{3}{3} &=& 1\frac{3}{6} \\ \hline && 4\frac{4}{6} = \mathbf{4\frac{2}{3}} \end{array}$$

f.
$$\begin{array}{rcl} 4\frac{1}{3} \times \frac{2}{2} &=& \overset{3}{\cancel{4}}\,\frac{\overset{8}{\cancel{2}}}{6} \\ -\ 1\frac{1}{2} \times \frac{3}{3} &=& 1\frac{3}{6} \\ \hline && \mathbf{2\frac{5}{6}} \end{array}$$

g.
$$\begin{array}{rcl} 4\frac{5}{6} \times \frac{1}{1} &=& 4\frac{5}{6} \\ -\ 1\frac{1}{3} \times \frac{2}{2} &=& 1\frac{2}{6} \\ \hline && 3\frac{3}{6} = \mathbf{3\frac{1}{2}} \end{array}$$

h.
$$\begin{array}{rcl} 6\frac{1}{2} \times \frac{3}{3} &=& \overset{5}{\cancel{6}}\,\frac{\overset{9}{\cancel{3}}}{6} \\ -\ 3\frac{5}{6} \times \frac{1}{1} &=& 3\frac{5}{6} \\ \hline && 2\frac{4}{6} = \mathbf{2\frac{2}{3}} \end{array}$$

i.
$$\begin{array}{rcl} 8\frac{2}{3} \times \frac{4}{4} &=& \overset{7}{\cancel{8}}\,\frac{\overset{20}{\cancel{8}}}{12} \\ -\ 5\frac{3}{4} \times \frac{3}{3} &=& 5\frac{9}{12} \\ \hline && \mathbf{2\frac{11}{12}} \end{array}$$

j. **Answers will vary. See student work.**

Solutions

Written Practice 63

1. $(0.6 + 0.4) - (0.6 \times 0.4)$
$1 - 0.24$
0.76

2. $\begin{array}{r} \overset{1}{1}4{,}494 \text{ feet} \\ +\ 282 \text{ feet} \\ \hline \textbf{14,776 feet} \end{array}$

3. $\begin{array}{r} 39° \\ -\ 11° \\ \hline \end{array}$ **28°; Fahrenheit**

4. $\mathbf{\frac{14}{3}}$

5. **\$680; \$678.25 is more than \$670 but less than \$680. It is closer to \$680 because it is more than \$675, which is halfway between \$670 and \$680.**

6. 10:15 a.m. + 2:30
12:45 p.m.; Possible answer: I added 2 hours to 10:15 a.m. and got 12:15 p.m. Then I added half an hour (30 minutes) to 12:15 p.m. and got 12:45 p.m.

7. $(30 \times 15) \div (30 - 15)$
$450 \div 15$
30

8. $\frac{5}{8} \text{ ⓘ} \frac{2}{3}$ → $\frac{5}{8} < \frac{2}{3}$
$\frac{5}{8} \times \frac{3}{3} \qquad \frac{2}{3} \times \frac{8}{8}$
$\frac{15}{24} \qquad \frac{16}{24}$

9. $3\frac{2}{3} \times \frac{2}{2} = 3\frac{4}{6}$
$+\ 1\frac{1}{2} \times \frac{3}{3} = 1\frac{3}{6}$
$4\frac{7}{6} = 5\frac{1}{6}$
$w = \mathbf{5\frac{1}{6}}$

10. $\frac{6}{8} \times \frac{1}{1} = \frac{6}{8}$
$-\ \frac{3}{4} \times \frac{2}{2} = \frac{6}{8}$
$\frac{0}{8} = \mathbf{0}$

11. $6\frac{1}{4} \times \frac{2}{2} = \overset{5}{\cancel{6}}\frac{\overset{10}{\cancel{2}}}{8}$
$-\ 5\frac{5}{8} \times \frac{1}{1} = 5\frac{5}{8}$
$\mathbf{\frac{5}{8}}$

12. $\frac{3}{4} \times \frac{2}{5} = \frac{6}{20} = \mathbf{\frac{3}{10}}$

13. $\frac{3}{4} \div \frac{2}{5}$
$1 \div \frac{2}{5} = \frac{5}{2}$
$\frac{3}{4} \times \frac{5}{2} = \frac{15}{8} = \mathbf{1\frac{7}{8}}$

14. $(1 - 0.4)(1 + 0.4)$
$(0.6)(1.4)$
0.84

15. $\begin{array}{r} \$45 \\ \times\ 0.60 \\ \hline \textbf{\$27.00} \end{array}$

16. $8\overline{)0.40}$ = **0.05**
40
0

17. $4\overline{)80}$ = **20**
8
00
00
0

18. **1.0** or **1**

19. 2, 3, 5, 7, 11, 13, 17, 19, 23, 29
29

20.
$$\begin{array}{rl} & 1\frac{1}{8}\text{ in.} \times \frac{1}{1} = 1\frac{1}{8}\text{ in.} \\ & 1\frac{1}{8}\text{ in.} \times \frac{1}{1} = 1\frac{1}{8}\text{ in.} \\ & \frac{3}{4}\text{ in.} \times \frac{2}{2} = \frac{6}{8}\text{ in.} \\ + & \frac{3}{4}\text{ in.} \times \frac{2}{2} = \frac{6}{8}\text{ in.} \\ \hline & 2\frac{14}{8}\text{ in.} = 3\frac{6}{8}\text{ in.} = \mathbf{3\frac{3}{4}\text{ in.}} \end{array}$$

21. **a.** **5 faces**
b. **9 edges**
c. **6 vertices**

22. $\frac{5}{2} \cdot \frac{6}{5} = \frac{30}{10} = 3$

23.
$$\begin{array}{r} 30\text{ cm} \\ \times\ 10\text{ cm} \\ \hline 300\text{ cm}^2 \end{array} \qquad \begin{array}{r} \mathbf{150\text{ cm}^2} \\ 2\overline{)300\text{ cm}^2} \\ 2 \\ \hline 10 \\ 10 \\ \hline 00 \\ 00 \\ \hline 0 \end{array}$$

24.
$$\begin{array}{r} \overset{1}{2}.5 \\ \times\ 2000\text{ pounds} \\ \hline \mathbf{5000.0\text{ pounds}} \end{array}$$

25. ***C***

26. **a.** $C = \pi d$
$C \approx (3.14)(7\text{ cm})$
$C \approx 21.98$
$C \approx$ **22 cm**

b. $C = \pi d$
$C \approx (3.14)(5\text{ cm})$
$C \approx 15.70$
$C \approx$ **16 cm**

27. $\frac{30}{100} = \frac{3}{10}$
$\frac{3}{10} \times \frac{240}{1} = \frac{720}{10} =$ **72 hits**

28.
$$\begin{array}{r} 2\ \overset{5}{\cancel{6}}\,{}^{1}2\text{ mi} \\ -\ 1\ 1.\ 5\text{ mi} \\ \hline \mathbf{1\ 4.\ 7\text{ mi}} \end{array}$$

29.
$$\begin{array}{r} \overset{1}{\$1}\overset{1}{5}.49 \\ \times\qquad 2 \\ \hline \$30.98 \end{array} \qquad \begin{array}{r} \$30.98 \\ \times\quad 0.07 \\ \hline \$2.1686 \end{array} \qquad \begin{array}{r} \$\overset{1}{3}\overset{1}{0}.98 \\ +\quad \$2.17 \\ \hline \mathbf{\$33.15} \end{array}$$

30.
$$\begin{array}{rl} & \frac{1}{2}\text{ tsp} \times \frac{2}{2} = \frac{2}{4}\text{ tsp} \\ + & \frac{3}{4}\text{ tsp} \times \frac{1}{1} = \frac{3}{4}\text{ tsp} \\ \hline & \frac{5}{4} = \mathbf{1\frac{1}{4}\text{ teaspoons}} \end{array}$$

Early Finishers Solutions

$\frac{1}{4} + \frac{1}{2} + \frac{5}{12} = \frac{3}{12} + \frac{6}{12} + \frac{5}{12} = \frac{14}{12} = 1\frac{2}{12}$
$= 1\frac{1}{6}$ leftover pizza.

Practice Set 64

a. **A quadrilateral is a four-sided polygon.**

b. **A parallelogram has two pairs of parallel sides; a trapezoid has only one pair of parallel sides.**

c.

d.
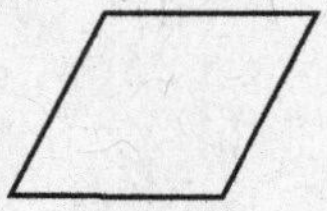

e. **True**

f. **True**

Written Practice 64

1. (1.3 + 1.2) ÷ (1.3 − 1.2)
2.5 ÷ 0.1
25

Solutions

2.

$$\begin{array}{r} 1\,\overset{5}{\cancel{6}}\,{}^{1}1\,6 \text{ years} \\ -\ 1\,5\,6\,4 \text{ years} \\ \hline \mathbf{5\,2 \text{ years}} \end{array}$$

3.

$$\begin{array}{r} \overset{1}{4}5 \text{ feet} \\ \times\ 3 \quad\quad \\ \hline \mathbf{135 \text{ feet}} \end{array}$$

4. **A square is a four-sided polygon, so it is a quadrilateral. The four sides of a square have the same length, and the four angles have the same measure, so a square is "regular."**

5.

$$\begin{array}{r} \mathbf{6 \text{ inches}} \\ 6\overline{)36} \text{ inches} \\ \underline{36} \\ 00 \end{array}$$

6. $\frac{1}{4} \times \frac{25}{25} = \frac{25}{100}$ **25**

7. $\frac{8 \times 8}{8 + 8} = \frac{64}{16} = \frac{4}{1} =$ **4**

8.

$$\begin{array}{r} 5\frac{2}{3} \times \frac{4}{4} = 5\frac{8}{12} \\ +\ 3\frac{3}{4} \times \frac{3}{3} = 3\frac{9}{12} \\ \hline 8\frac{17}{12} = \mathbf{9\frac{5}{12}} \end{array}$$

9.

$$\begin{array}{r} \frac{1}{2} \times \frac{6}{6} = \frac{6}{12} \\ \frac{2}{3} \times \frac{4}{4} = \frac{8}{12} \\ +\ \frac{1}{4} \times \frac{3}{3} = \frac{3}{12} \\ \hline \frac{17}{12} = \mathbf{1\frac{5}{12}} \end{array}$$

10.

$$\begin{array}{r} \frac{9}{10} \times \frac{1}{1} = \frac{9}{10} \\ -\ \frac{1}{2} \times \frac{5}{5} = \frac{5}{10} \\ \hline \frac{4}{10} = \mathbf{\frac{2}{5}} \end{array}$$

11.

$$\begin{array}{r} 6\frac{1}{2} \times \frac{4}{4} = \overset{5}{\cancel{6}}\,\frac{\overset{12}{\cancel{4}}}{8} \\ -\ 2\frac{7}{8} \times \frac{1}{1} = 2\frac{7}{8} \\ \hline \mathbf{3\frac{5}{8}} \end{array}$$

12. 2×0.4 (<) $2 + 0.4$

$\quad 0.8 \qquad\quad 2.4$

13.

$$\begin{array}{r} 4.8 \\ \times\ 0.35 \\ \hline 240 \\ 1440 \\ \hline 1.680 \end{array} = \mathbf{1.68}$$

14.

$$\begin{array}{r} \mathbf{2.5} \\ 4\overline{)10.0} \\ \underline{8}\ \ \ \\ 2\,0 \\ \underline{2\,0} \\ 0 \end{array}$$

15.

$$\begin{array}{r} \mathbf{40 \text{ pencils}} \\ 12\overline{)480} \\ \underline{48}\ \\ 00 \\ \underline{00} \\ 0 \end{array}$$

16.

$$\begin{array}{r} 0.33 \\ \times\ 0.38 \\ \hline 264 \\ 990 \\ \hline 0.1254 \\ \mathbf{0.13} \end{array}$$

17. $\frac{1}{2}$ in. $\times \frac{3}{4}$ in. $=$ **$\frac{3}{8}$ sq. in.**

18. **Yes**

19. 2, 3, 5, 7, 11, 13, 17, 19, 23, 29, 31, 37
37

20. **a.** $\sqrt{9 \text{ cm}^2} =$ **3 cm**

b. 3 cm $\times$ 4 = **12 cm**

21. **One possibility:**

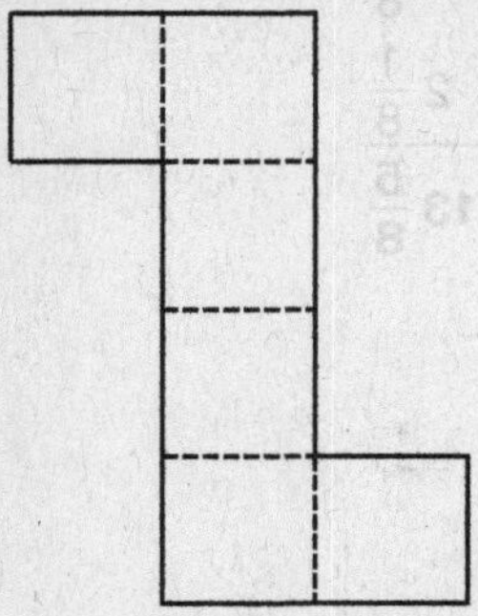

6 faces

22. **a.** 10 in. × 10 in. = **100 in.^{2}**

b. 100 in.^{2} × 6 = **600 in.^{2}**

23. 2.5 × 100 cm = **250 centimeters**

24. $\frac{3}{2} \cdot \frac{5}{2} = \frac{15}{4} = 3\frac{3}{4}$

25.
9 = 3 · 3
10 = 2 · 5
12 = 2 · 2 · 3

26. $\frac{75}{100}$; **0.75**

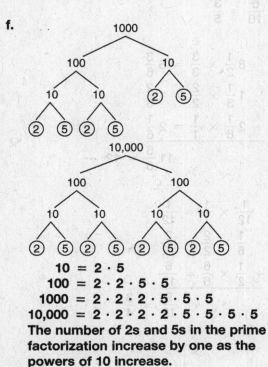

27. $\frac{2 \cdot 2 \cdot 3 \cdot 2 \cdot 3}{2 \cdot 2 \cdot 3 \cdot 5 \cdot 5} = 1 \cdot 1 \cdot 1 \cdot \frac{6}{25} = \frac{6}{25}$

28.
$\overset{1}{\cancel{2}}\ \overset{15}{\cancel{6}}.{}^{1}2$ miles
− 1 6. 6 miles
9.6 miles
d = **9.6 miles**

29. **a.** 4° − (−6°C)
4°C
+ 6°C
10°C

b. 16° − (−6°C)
$\overset{1}{1}$6°C
+ 6°C
22°C

30. **It probably dropped about 5 degrees. The graph's lines seem to be following each other closely, about 10–12 degrees apart.**

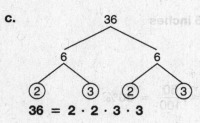

Practice Set 65

a. **20, 21, 22**

b.
20 = 2 · 2 · 5
21 = 3 · 7
22 = 2 · 11

c.

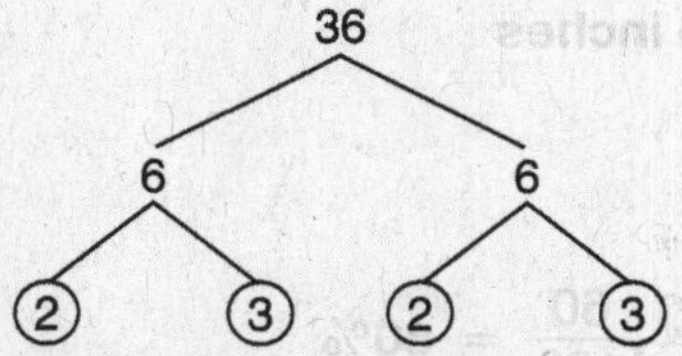

36 = 2 · 2 · 3 · 3

d.
$$\begin{array}{r} 1 \\ 3\overline{)3} \\ 2\overline{)6} \\ 2\overline{)12} \\ 2\overline{)24} \\ 2\overline{)48} \end{array}$$
48 = 2 · 2 · 2 · 2 · 3

e.

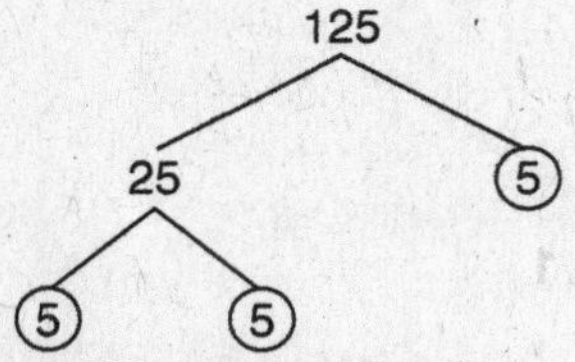

125 = 5 · 5 · 5

f.

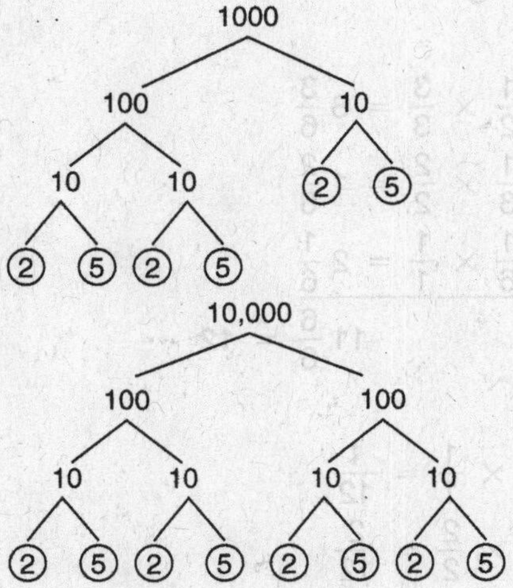

10 = 2 · 5
100 = 2 · 2 · 5 · 5
1000 = 2 · 2 · 2 · 5 · 5 · 5
10,000 = 2 · 2 · 2 · 2 · 5 · 5 · 5 · 5
The number of 2s and 5s in the prime factorization increase by one as the powers of 10 increase.

Solutions

Written Practice 65

1. **57,506,000 square miles**

2.
$$\begin{array}{r} 5.5 \\ \times\ 12 \text{ inches} \\ \hline 110 \\ 550 \\ \hline 66.0 \end{array}$$
66.0 or **66 inches**

3. $\frac{6}{10} = \frac{3}{5}$

$\frac{6}{10} \times \frac{10}{10} = \frac{60}{100} = \mathbf{60\%}$

4. **One possibility:**

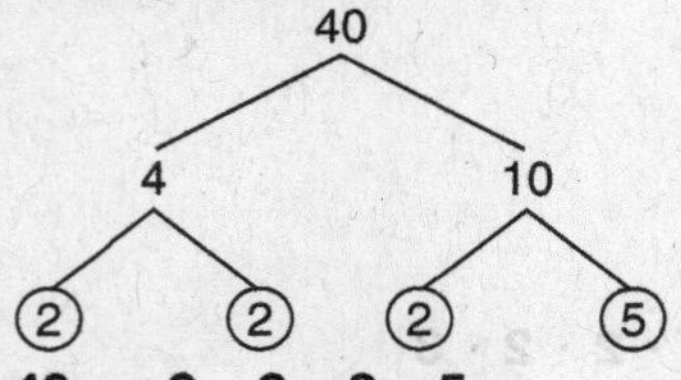

40 = 2 · 2 · 2 · 5

5. **A. 21**

6. $\frac{8}{3} \cdot \frac{3}{8} = \frac{24}{24} = \mathbf{1}$

7. $\frac{6}{10} = \frac{3}{5}$

8.
$$\begin{array}{rcl} 8\frac{1}{2} \times \frac{3}{3} &=& 8\frac{3}{6} \\ 1\frac{1}{3} \times \frac{2}{2} &=& 1\frac{2}{6} \\ +\ 2\frac{1}{6} \times \frac{1}{1} &=& 2\frac{1}{6} \\ \hline && 11\frac{6}{6} = \mathbf{12} \end{array}$$

9.
$$\begin{array}{rcl} \frac{1}{12} \times \frac{1}{1} &=& \frac{1}{12} \\ \frac{1}{6} \times \frac{2}{2} &=& \frac{2}{12} \\ +\ \frac{1}{2} \times \frac{6}{6} &=& \frac{6}{12} \\ \hline && \frac{9}{12} = \mathbf{\frac{3}{4}} \end{array}$$

10.
$$\begin{array}{rcl} 15\frac{3}{4} \times \frac{2}{2} &=& 15\frac{6}{8} \\ -\ 2\frac{1}{8} \times \frac{1}{1} &=& 2\frac{1}{8} \\ \hline m &=& \mathbf{13\frac{5}{8}} \end{array}$$

11. $\frac{4}{25} \times \frac{4}{4} = \frac{16}{100}$

$n = \mathbf{16}$

12.
$$\begin{array}{r} 0.0012 \\ 12\overline{)0.0144} \\ 12 \\ \hline 24 \\ 24 \\ \hline 0 \end{array}$$
$w = \mathbf{0.0012}$

13. $\frac{3}{8} \times \frac{1}{3} = \frac{3}{24} = \frac{1}{8}$

$y = \mathbf{\frac{1}{8}}$

14. $\frac{1}{2} - \frac{1}{3} \ \textcircled{=}\ \frac{2}{3} - \frac{1}{2}$

$$\begin{array}{rcl} \frac{1}{2} \times \frac{3}{3} &=& \frac{3}{6} \\ -\ \frac{1}{3} \times \frac{2}{2} &=& \frac{2}{6} \\ \hline && \frac{1}{6} \end{array} \qquad \begin{array}{rcl} \frac{2}{3} \times \frac{2}{2} &=& \frac{4}{6} \\ -\ \frac{1}{2} \times \frac{3}{3} &=& \frac{3}{6} \\ \hline && \frac{1}{6} \end{array}$$

15. $1 - (0.2 + 0.48)$

$1 - 0.68$

0.32

16. 50¢ × 24 = $12

8¢ × 12 = 96¢

$12 + $0.96 = **$12.96**

Two dozen is 24. The price is 50¢ each, which is half a dollar each. So 24 erasers cost $12. 8% of $12 is 8¢ for each dollar. Twelve times 8¢ is 96¢. Add $12 and 96¢ and get $12.96.

17.
$$\begin{array}{r} \textbf{80 quarters} \\ 25\overline{)2000} \\ 200 \\ \hline 00 \\ 00 \\ \hline 0 \end{array}$$

18. a. **5 faces**

b. **8 edges**

c. **5 vertices**

19.
$$\begin{array}{r} 1 \\ 5\overline{)5} \\ 5\overline{)25} \\ 2\overline{)50} \end{array}$$
$$\mathbf{50 = 2 \cdot 5 \cdot 5}$$

20. **Hexagon; 6 vertices**

21. $\mathbf{\dfrac{25}{7}}$

22. a. $\sqrt{36 \text{ in.}^2} = \mathbf{6 \text{ in.}}$

b. $6 \text{ in.} \times 4 = \mathbf{24 \text{ in.}}$

23. $\dfrac{16}{100} = \mathbf{\dfrac{4}{25}}$

24. **50 mm**

25. **About 4 meters**

26.

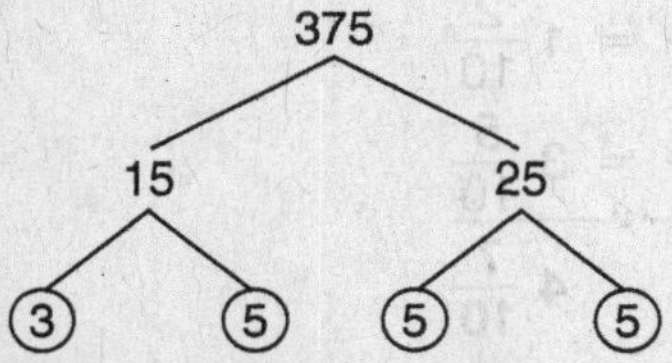

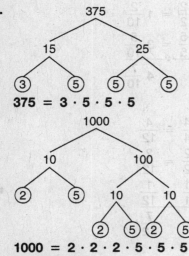

$\mathbf{375 = 3 \cdot 5 \cdot 5 \cdot 5}$

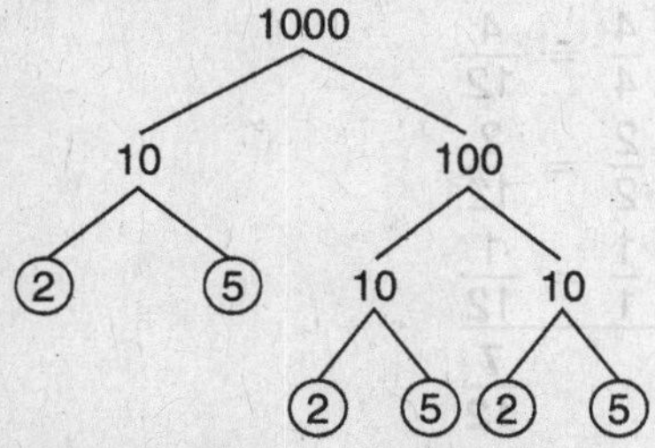

$\mathbf{1000 = 2 \cdot 2 \cdot 2 \cdot 5 \cdot 5 \cdot 5}$

Factor trees

27. $\dfrac{5 \cdot 5 \cdot 5 \cdot 3}{5 \cdot 5 \cdot 5 \cdot 2 \cdot 2 \cdot 2} = 1 \cdot 1 \cdot 1 \cdot \dfrac{3}{8} = \mathbf{\dfrac{3}{8}}$

28.
$$C = \pi d$$
$$C \approx (3.14)(30 \text{ feet})$$
$$C \approx 94.2$$
$$C \approx \mathbf{94 \text{ feet}}$$

The radius is 15 ft, so the diameter is 30 ft. π is a little more than 3, and 3 times 30 ft is 90 ft, so 94 ft is reasonable.

29. $\dfrac{80}{100} \times \dfrac{20}{1} = \dfrac{1600}{100} = \mathbf{16 \text{ answers}}$

30. **A rectangle is a four-sided polygon with four right angles. Since every square is four-sided with four right angles, every square is a rectangle. (A rectangle need not be longer than it is wide.)**

Practice Set 66

a. $\dfrac{3}{2} \times \dfrac{2}{3} = \dfrac{6}{6} = \mathbf{1}$

b. $\dfrac{5}{3} \times \dfrac{3}{4} = \dfrac{15}{12} = 1\dfrac{3}{12} = \mathbf{1\dfrac{1}{4}}$

c. $\dfrac{3}{2} \times \dfrac{5}{3} = \dfrac{15}{6} = 2\dfrac{3}{6} = \mathbf{2\dfrac{1}{2}}$

d. $\dfrac{5}{3} \times \dfrac{3}{1} = \dfrac{15}{3} = \mathbf{5}$

e. $\dfrac{5}{2} \times \dfrac{8}{3} = \dfrac{40}{6} = 6\dfrac{4}{6} = \mathbf{6\dfrac{2}{3}}$

f. $\dfrac{3}{1} \times \dfrac{7}{4} = \dfrac{21}{4} = \mathbf{5\dfrac{1}{4}}$

g. $\dfrac{10}{3} \times \dfrac{5}{3} = \dfrac{50}{9} = \mathbf{5\dfrac{5}{9}}$

h. $\dfrac{11}{4} \times \dfrac{2}{1} = \dfrac{22}{4} = 5\dfrac{2}{4} = \mathbf{5\dfrac{1}{2}}$

i. $\dfrac{2}{1} \times \dfrac{7}{2} = \dfrac{14}{2} = \mathbf{7}$

j.

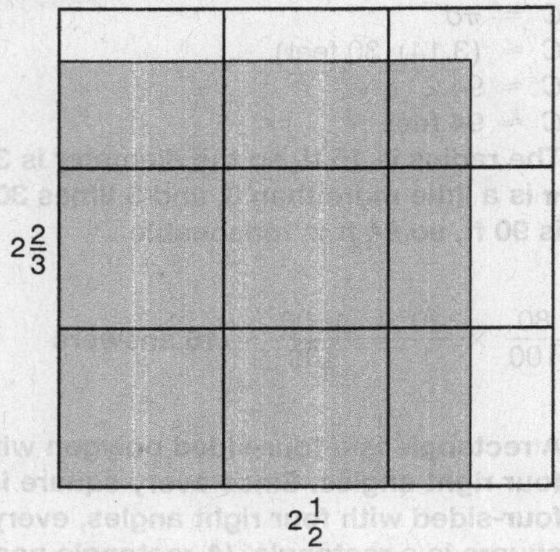

Area is more than 6 and near 7.

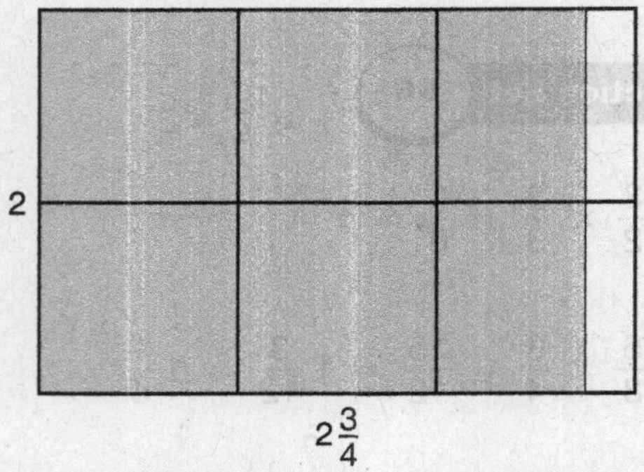

Area is more than 5 but less than 6.

k. Answers will vary. See student work.

Written Practice 66

1.
$$\begin{array}{r} 60 \\ \times\ 0.50 \\ \hline 30.00 \end{array}$$ or **30 questions**

2. a.
$$\begin{array}{r} \overset{2}{\cancel{3}}{}^{1}0 \\ -\ 12 \\ \hline 18 \end{array}$$ girls

$$\frac{\text{boys}}{\text{girls}} = \frac{12}{18} = \mathbf{\frac{2}{3}}$$

b. $\frac{18}{30} = \mathbf{\frac{3}{5}}$

3.
$$\begin{array}{r} 11 \text{ yards} \\ 3\overline{)33} \\ 3 \\ \hline 03 \\ 03 \\ \hline 0 \end{array}$$

$$\begin{array}{r} 155 \\ \times\ 11 \\ \hline 155 \\ 1550 \\ \hline \mathbf{1705} \end{array}$$ **1705 pounds**

4. $\frac{3}{2} \times \frac{8}{3} = \frac{24}{6} = \mathbf{4}$

5. $\frac{8}{3} \times \frac{2}{1} = \frac{16}{3} = \mathbf{5\frac{1}{3}}$

6.
$$\begin{array}{r} \mathbf{40} \\ 5\overline{)200} \\ 20 \\ \hline 00 \\ 00 \\ \hline 0 \end{array}$$

7. $\frac{175}{25} = \mathbf{7}$

8.
$$\begin{array}{r} 1\frac{1}{5} \times \frac{2}{2} = 1\frac{2}{10} \\ +\ 3\frac{1}{2} \times \frac{5}{5} = 3\frac{5}{10} \\ \hline \mathbf{4\frac{7}{10}} \end{array}$$

9.
$$\begin{array}{r} \frac{1}{3} \times \frac{4}{4} = \frac{4}{12} \\ \frac{1}{6} \times \frac{2}{2} = \frac{2}{12} \\ +\ \frac{1}{12} \times \frac{1}{1} = \frac{1}{12} \\ \hline \mathbf{\frac{7}{12}} \end{array}$$

10.
$$\begin{array}{r} 35\frac{1}{4} \times \frac{1}{1} = \overset{34}{\cancel{35}}\frac{\overset{5}{\cancel{1}}}{4} \\ -\ 12\frac{1}{2} \times \frac{2}{2} = 12\frac{2}{4} \\ \hline \mathbf{22\frac{3}{4}} \end{array}$$

11. $\frac{4}{5} \times \frac{1}{2} = \frac{4}{10} = \mathbf{\frac{2}{5}}$

12. $\frac{4}{5} \div \frac{1}{2}$

$1 \div \frac{1}{2} = \frac{2}{1}$

$\frac{4}{5} \times \frac{2}{1} = \frac{8}{5} = \mathbf{1\frac{3}{5}}$

13. $5\overline{)0.25}$ = **0.05**

$\begin{array}{r} 25 \\ \hline 00 \end{array}$

14. $25\overline{)500}$ = **20**

$\begin{array}{r} 50 \\ \hline 00 \\ 00 \\ \hline 0 \end{array}$

15. $\begin{array}{r} 0.05 \\ \times\ 20 \\ \hline 1.00 \end{array}$ or **1**

16. $\frac{1}{2} + \frac{1}{2} = \frac{2}{2} = 1$

a. $\frac{1}{2} - \frac{1}{2} = \frac{0}{2} = 0$

b. $\frac{1}{2} \times \frac{1}{2} = \frac{1}{4}$

c. $\frac{1}{2} \div \frac{1}{2}$

$1 \div \frac{1}{2} = \frac{2}{1}$

$\frac{1}{2} \times \frac{2}{1} = \frac{2}{2} = 1$

(C) $\mathbf{\frac{1}{2} \div \frac{1}{2}}$

17. **One possibility:**

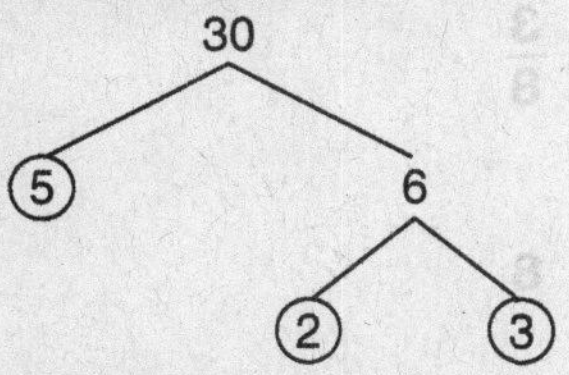

30 = 2 · 3 · 5

18. $\begin{array}{r} \overset{1}{7}5¢ \\ \times\ \ 2 \\ \hline 150¢ \end{array}$ or **\$1.50**

19. 0.075 × \$10 = **\$0.75**

20. $\begin{array}{r} 0.8 \text{ meters} \\ \times\ 5 \quad\quad \\ \hline 4.0 \quad\quad \end{array}$ or **4 meters**

21. $\frac{20}{60} = \mathbf{\frac{1}{3}}$

22. 12°C − (−8°C)

$\begin{array}{r} 12°C \\ +\ \ 8°C \\ \hline \mathbf{20°C} \end{array}$

23. $\begin{array}{r} 18 \text{ ounces} \\ -\ 11 \text{ ounces} \\ \hline \mathbf{7 \text{ ounces}} \end{array}$

24. $\begin{array}{r} 18 \text{ ounces} \\ 16 \text{ ounces} \\ +\ 11 \text{ ounces} \\ \hline 45 \text{ ounces} \end{array}$

$3\overline{)45 \text{ ounces}}$ = **15 ounces**

$\begin{array}{r} 3 \\ \hline 15 \\ 15 \\ \hline 0 \end{array}$

25. **Answers will vary. See student work. Sample answer: The flakes cereal weighs how much more than the puffed cereal?**

$\begin{array}{r} 16 \text{ ounces} \\ -\ 11 \text{ ounces} \\ \hline \mathbf{5 \text{ ounces}} \end{array}$

26. $\begin{array}{r} 1 \\ 5\overline{)5} \\ 5\overline{)25} \\ 2\overline{)50} \\ 2\overline{)100} \\ 2\overline{)200} \\ 2\overline{)400} \end{array}$

400 = 2 · 2 · 2 · 2 · 5 · 5

27. $\sqrt{144}$ = **12 tiles**

28. 2.2 pounds × 100 = **220 pounds**

29. $\frac{5 \cdot 5 \cdot 5 \cdot 7}{5 \cdot 5 \cdot 5 \cdot 2 \cdot 2 \cdot 2} = 1 \cdot 1 \cdot 1 \cdot \frac{7}{8} = \mathbf{\frac{7}{8}}$

30. **B.**

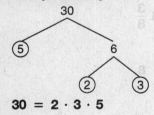

Solutions

Practice Set 67

a. $\dfrac{\overset{1}{\cancel{5}} \cdot \overset{1}{\cancel{5}} \cdot \overset{1}{\cancel{5}} \cdot 7}{2 \cdot 2 \cdot 2 \cdot \underset{1}{\cancel{5}} \cdot \underset{1}{\cancel{5}} \cdot \underset{1}{\cancel{5}}} = \mathbf{\dfrac{7}{8}}$

b. $\dfrac{\overset{1}{\cancel{2}} \cdot \overset{1}{\cancel{2}} \cdot \overset{1}{\cancel{2}} \cdot \overset{1}{\cancel{2}} \cdot 3}{\underset{1}{\cancel{2}} \cdot \underset{1}{\cancel{2}} \cdot \underset{1}{\cancel{2}} \cdot \underset{1}{\cancel{2}} \cdot 5 \cdot 5} = \mathbf{\dfrac{3}{25}}$

c. $\dfrac{\overset{1}{\cancel{5}} \cdot \overset{1}{\cancel{5}} \cdot \overset{1}{\cancel{5}}}{2 \cdot 2 \cdot \underset{1}{\cancel{5}} \cdot \underset{1}{\cancel{5}} \cdot \underset{1}{\cancel{5}}} = \mathbf{\dfrac{1}{4}}$

d. $\dfrac{2 \cdot 2 \cdot \overset{1}{\cancel{3}} \cdot \overset{1}{\cancel{3}}}{\underset{1}{\cancel{3}} \cdot \underset{1}{\cancel{3}} \cdot 3 \cdot 3} = \mathbf{\dfrac{4}{9}}$

Written Practice 67

1.
$$\begin{aligned} 2 &= 2 \\ \frac{1}{2} \times \frac{2}{2} &= \frac{2}{4} \\ + \frac{3}{4} \times \frac{1}{1} &= \frac{3}{4} \\ \hline 2\frac{5}{4} &= 3\frac{1}{4} \text{ yards} \end{aligned}$$

$\dfrac{13}{4} \times \dfrac{2}{1} = \dfrac{26}{4} = 6\dfrac{2}{4} = 6\dfrac{1}{2}$

$6.50

2.
$$\begin{array}{r} \overset{5}{\cancel{6}}{}^{1}0\,8\,0 \text{ ft} \\ -\ 5\,2\,8\,0 \text{ ft} \\ \hline \end{array}$$
About 8 0 0 feet

3. **$150 ÷ $5**

$$\begin{array}{r} 30 \\ \$5\overline{)\$150} \\ 15 \\ \hline 00 \\ 00 \\ \hline 0 \end{array}$$

4.
$$\begin{array}{r} 11 \text{ cm} \\ -\ 6 \text{ cm} \\ \hline 5 \text{ cm} \end{array}$$
k = **5 cm**

5.
$$\begin{array}{r} 1.2 \\ 8\overline{)9.6} \\ 8 \\ \hline 1\,6 \\ 1\,6 \\ \hline 0 \end{array}$$
g = **1.2**

6.
$$\begin{aligned} \frac{7}{10} \times \frac{1}{1} &= \frac{7}{10} \\ - \frac{1}{2} \times \frac{5}{5} &= \frac{5}{10} \\ \hline \frac{2}{10} &= \frac{1}{5} \end{aligned}$$

$w = \mathbf{\dfrac{1}{5}}$

7. $\dfrac{3}{5} \times \dfrac{20}{20} = \dfrac{60}{100}$

n = **60**

8.
$$\begin{array}{r} \mathbf{43 \text{ inches}}; \\ 4\overline{)172 \text{ inches}} \\ 16 \\ \hline 12 \\ 12 \\ \hline 0 \end{array}$$
From the given information, we cannot know what type of quadrilateral the figure is. Many combinations of four side lengths total 172 inches and can form a quadrilateral.

9. $100.00 − ($46.75 + $9.68)
$100.00 − $56.43
$43.57

10. (2 × 0.3) − (0.2 × 0.3)
(0.6) − (0.06)
0.54

11.
$$\begin{aligned} 4\frac{1}{4} \times \frac{2}{2} &= \overset{3}{\cancel{4}}\frac{\overset{10}{\cancel{2}}}{8} \\ - 2\frac{7}{8} \times \frac{1}{1} &= 2\frac{7}{8} \\ \hline & \mathbf{1\frac{3}{8}} \end{aligned}$$

12. $\dfrac{8}{3} \times \dfrac{3}{1} = \dfrac{24}{3} = \mathbf{8}$

13.
$$\begin{aligned} 3\frac{1}{3} \times \frac{4}{4} &= 3\frac{4}{12} \\ + 2\frac{3}{4} \times \frac{3}{3} &= 2\frac{9}{12} \\ \hline 5\frac{13}{12} &= \mathbf{6\frac{1}{12}} \end{aligned}$$

14. $\frac{4}{3} \times \frac{9}{4} = \frac{36}{12} = \mathbf{3}$

15.
$$\begin{array}{r} \mathbf{0.024} \\ 60\overline{)1.440} \\ \underline{1\,20} \\ 240 \\ \underline{240} \\ 0 \end{array}$$

16.
$$\begin{array}{r} \mathbf{40} \\ 15\overline{)600} \\ \underline{60} \\ 00 \\ \underline{00} \\ 0 \end{array}$$

17.
$$\begin{array}{r} \mathbf{\$1.25} \\ 4\overline{)\$5.00} \\ \underline{4} \\ 1\,0 \\ \underline{8} \\ 20 \\ \underline{20} \\ 0 \end{array}$$

18. $\sqrt{100 \text{ in.}^2} = 10$ in.
10 in. $\times$ 4 $=$ **40 in.; Square**

19. $\frac{\overset{1}{\cancel{5}} \cdot \overset{1}{\cancel{5}} \cdot \overset{1}{\cancel{5}} \cdot 5}{2 \cdot 2 \cdot 2 \cdot \underset{1}{\cancel{5}} \cdot \underset{1}{\cancel{5}} \cdot \underset{1}{\cancel{5}}} = \mathbf{\frac{5}{8}}$

20. $\frac{3}{2}$ in. $\times$ $\frac{3}{4}$ in. $= \frac{9}{8}$ in.^{2} $=$ $\mathbf{1\frac{1}{8}}$ **in.^{2}**

21. $\frac{36}{88} = \mathbf{\frac{9}{22}}$

22. One possibility:

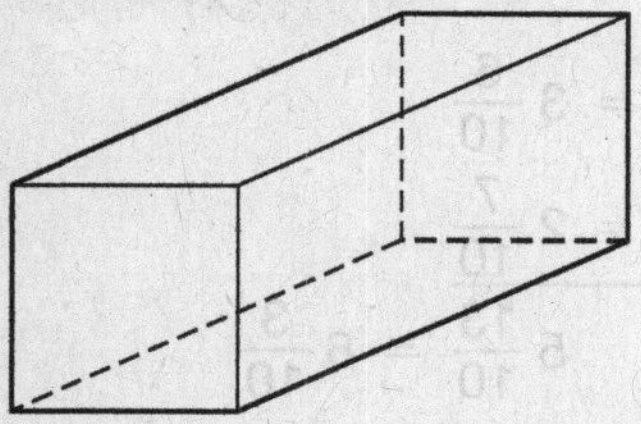

23. $\frac{3}{2} \times \frac{2}{3} = 1$
$\mathbf{\frac{2}{3}}$

24. 2.5 km $\times$ 1000 $=$ **2500 meters**

25. ***C***

26. $C = \pi d$
$C \approx (3.14)(12 \text{ in.})$
$C \approx 37.68$
$C \approx$ **38 inches**

27. Sphere

28. $\mathbf{\frac{51}{100}}$**; 0.51**

29. The probability of rolling a 2, 3, or 5 is $\frac{3}{6}$ or $\frac{1}{2}$.

30. Trapezoid

Practice Set 68

a. $\frac{8}{5} \div \frac{4}{1}$
$1 \div \frac{4}{1} = \frac{1}{4}$
$\frac{8}{5} \times \frac{1}{4} = \frac{8}{20} = \mathbf{\frac{2}{5}}$

b. $\frac{1}{4} \times \frac{8}{5} = \frac{8}{20} = \mathbf{\frac{2}{5}}$

c. $\frac{12}{5} \div \frac{3}{1}$
$1 \div \frac{3}{1} = \frac{1}{3}$
$\frac{12}{5} \times \frac{1}{3} = \frac{12}{15} = \mathbf{\frac{4}{5}}$

d. $\frac{1}{3} \times \frac{12}{5} = \frac{12}{15} = \mathbf{\frac{4}{5}}$

e. Division is the opposite of multiplication so dividing by 4 is the same as multiplying by the inverse of 4 or $\frac{1}{4}$.

f. $\frac{5}{3} \div \frac{5}{2}$

$1 \div \frac{5}{2} = \frac{2}{5}$

$\frac{5}{3} \times \frac{2}{5} = \frac{10}{15} = \mathbf{\frac{2}{3}}$

g. $\frac{5}{2} \div \frac{5}{3}$

$1 \div \frac{5}{3} = \frac{3}{5}$

$\frac{5}{2} \times \frac{3}{5} = \frac{15}{10} = 1\frac{5}{10} = \mathbf{1\frac{1}{2}}$

h. $\frac{3}{2} \div \frac{3}{2}$

$1 \div \frac{3}{2} = \frac{2}{3}$

$\frac{3}{2} \times \frac{2}{3} = \frac{6}{6} = \mathbf{1}$

i. $\frac{7}{1} \div \frac{7}{4}$

$1 \div \frac{7}{4} = \frac{4}{7}$

$\frac{7}{1} \times \frac{4}{7} = \frac{28}{7} = \mathbf{4}$

j. $\frac{9}{4} \div 3$

$1 \div 3 = \frac{1}{3}$

$\frac{9}{4} \times \frac{1}{3} = \frac{9}{12} = \mathbf{\frac{3}{4}}$ **hour**

Written Practice 68

1. $\frac{1}{2} \times \frac{2}{2} = \frac{2}{4}$ $\qquad \frac{1}{2} \times \frac{1}{4} = \frac{1}{8}$

$$\begin{array}{r} \frac{2}{4} \\ + \frac{1}{4} \\ \hline \frac{3}{4} \end{array}$$

$\frac{3}{4} \times \frac{2}{2} = \frac{6}{8}$

$$\begin{array}{r} \frac{6}{8} \\ - \frac{1}{8} \\ \hline \mathbf{\frac{5}{8}} \end{array}$$

2. 60 seconds × 2 = 120 seconds

$$\begin{array}{r} 120 \text{ seconds} \\ + \ 55 \text{ seconds} \\ \hline \mathbf{175 \text{ seconds}} \end{array}$$

3.
$$\begin{array}{r} 12 \text{ in.} \\ \times \ 4 \\ \hline 48 \text{ in.} \end{array} \qquad \begin{array}{r} \overset{1}{4}8 \text{ inches} \\ + \ 8.5 \text{ inches} \\ \hline \mathbf{56.5 \text{ inches}} \end{array}$$

4. $\frac{3}{2} \div \frac{8}{3}$

$1 \div \frac{8}{3} = \frac{3}{8}$

$\frac{3}{2} \times \frac{3}{8} = \mathbf{\frac{9}{16}}$

5. $\frac{4}{3} \div \frac{4}{1}$

$1 \div \frac{4}{1} = \frac{1}{4}$

$\frac{4}{3} \times \frac{1}{4} = \frac{4}{12} = \mathbf{\frac{1}{3}}$

6.
$$\begin{array}{r} \mathbf{18} \text{ \textbf{points per game}} \\ 6\overline{)108} \\ \underline{6} \\ 48 \\ \underline{48} \\ 0 \end{array}$$

7. $\frac{\overset{1}{\cancel{2}} \cdot \overset{1}{\cancel{2}} \cdot \overset{1}{\cancel{2}} \cdot 3}{\underset{1}{\cancel{2}} \cdot \underset{1}{\cancel{2}} \cdot \underset{1}{\cancel{2}} \cdot 5 \cdot 5} = \mathbf{\frac{3}{25}}$

8.
$$\begin{array}{rcl} 5\frac{3}{8} \times \frac{2}{2} & = & 5\frac{6}{16} \\ + \ 1\frac{3}{16} \times \frac{1}{1} & = & 1\frac{3}{16} \\ \hline & m = & \mathbf{6\frac{9}{16}} \end{array}$$

9.
$$\begin{array}{rcl} 3\frac{3}{5} \times \frac{2}{2} & = & 3\frac{6}{10} \\ + \ 2\frac{7}{10} \times \frac{1}{1} & = & 2\frac{7}{10} \\ \hline & & 5\frac{13}{10} = 6\frac{3}{10} \end{array}$$

$n = \mathbf{6\frac{3}{10}}$

10. $25\overline{)0.375}$ = 0.015

$$\begin{array}{r} 0.015 \\ 25\overline{)0.375} \\ \underline{25} \\ 125 \\ \underline{125} \\ 0 \end{array}$$

d = **0.015**

11. $\frac{3}{4} \times \frac{25}{25} = \frac{75}{100}$

w = **75**

12.
$$\begin{array}{r} 5\frac{1}{8} \times \frac{1}{1} = \overset{4}{\cancel{5}}\frac{\overset{9}{\cancel{1}}}{8} \\ -\ 1\frac{1}{2} \times \frac{4}{4} = 1\frac{4}{8} \\ \hline \mathbf{3\frac{5}{8}} \end{array}$$

13. $\frac{10}{3} \times \frac{3}{2} = \frac{30}{6} = \mathbf{5}$

14. $\frac{10}{3} \div \frac{3}{2}$

$1 \div \frac{3}{2} = \frac{2}{3}$

$\frac{10}{3} \times \frac{2}{3} = \frac{20}{9} = \mathbf{2\frac{2}{9}}$

15. $\frac{4}{1}$ in. $\times \frac{7}{4}$ in. $= \frac{28}{4} =$ **7 square inches**

16. $(3.2 + 1) - (0.6 \times 7)$

$4.2 - 4.2$

0

17.
$$\begin{array}{r} \mathbf{31.25} \\ 4\overline{)125.00} \\ \underline{12} \\ 05 \\ \underline{4} \\ 1\,0 \\ \underline{8} \\ 20 \\ \underline{20} \\ 0 \end{array}$$

18. $3.2 \times 10 = 32$

A $32 \div 10 = 3.2$

B $320 \div 10 = 32$

C $0.32 \div 10 = .032$

B. 320 ÷ 10

19.
$$\begin{array}{r} 6000 \\ 6000 \\ +\ 5000 \\ \hline \mathbf{17{,}000} \end{array}$$

20. $100 \div 3 = \mathbf{33\frac{1}{3}}$

21. a.
$$\begin{array}{r} 0.6 \text{ meter} \\ 4\overline{)2.4 \text{ meters}} \\ \underline{24\phantom{\text{ meters}}} \\ 0\phantom{\text{ meters}} \end{array}$$

b.
$$\begin{array}{r} 0.6 \text{ m} \\ \times\ 0.6 \text{ m} \\ \hline \mathbf{0.36 \text{ square meter}} \end{array}$$

22.
$$\begin{array}{r} \$18{,}000 \\ \times\ .08 \\ \hline \$1440.00 \\ \mathbf{\$1440} \end{array}$$

23. $\mathbf{\frac{999{,}999}{1{,}000{,}000}}$

24. **Polygons have straight sides. Since a circle is curved, it is not a polygon.**

25. $\frac{1}{3} \times 4\frac{1}{2}$ ⊜ $4\frac{1}{2} \div 3$

$\frac{1}{3} \times \frac{9}{2}$ $\qquad$ $\frac{9}{2} \div 3$

$\frac{9}{6} = 1\frac{3}{6} = 1\frac{1}{2}$ $\qquad$ $1 \div \frac{3}{1} = \frac{1}{3}$

$\frac{9}{2} \times \frac{1}{3} = \frac{9}{6}$

$= 1\frac{3}{6} = 1\frac{1}{2}$

26. $\mathbf{1\frac{7}{8}}$ **in.**

27. **∠*WMX*** or **∠*XMW***

28. $\mathbf{\frac{3}{100}}$**; 0.03**

29. **Rectangular prism**

30. $\overset{11:60}{\cancel{12:00}}$ p.m.
$-$ 6:20 a.m.
5:40

5:40
$+$ 5:45
10:85
11:25
11 hr 25 min

Early Finishers Solutions

Accept any answer that meets the criteria.
Examples:

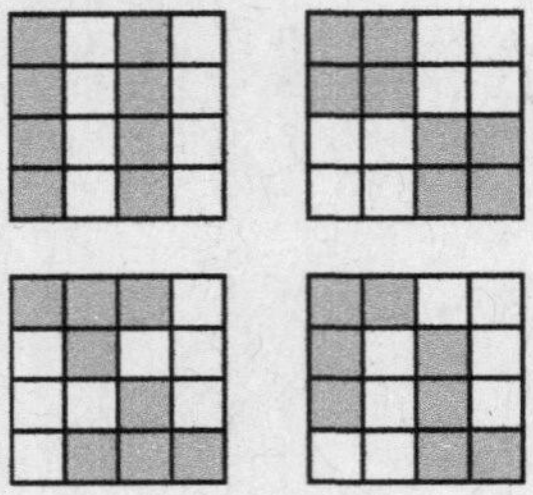

Practice Set 69

a. 26 mm + AB = 60 mm
$\overset{5}{\cancel{6}}{}^{1}0$ mm
$-$ 2 6 mm
3 4 mm

b. 90°
$-$ 60°
30°

c. 180°
$-$ 60°
120°

d. **No. Supplementary angles total 180°, but acute angles have measures less than 90°. Two angles with measures less than 90° cannot total 180°.**

e. **∠1 and ∠2**

f. **∠2 and ∠3**

Written Practice 69

1.

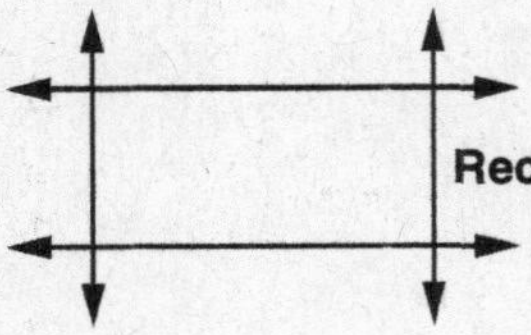

Rectangle

2. $\frac{1}{2} \div \frac{1}{8}$

$1 \div \frac{1}{8} = \frac{8}{1}$

$\frac{1}{2} \times \frac{8}{1} = \frac{8}{2} = \mathbf{4}$

3. 136°F − (−129°F)

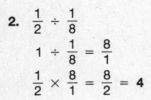

$\overset{1}{1}$36°F
$+$ 129°F
265°F

4. 6 × 1000 = 6000

$$\begin{array}{r} \mathbf{500} \\ 12\overline{)6000} \\ \underline{60} \\ 00 \\ \underline{00} \\ 00 \\ \underline{00} \\ 0 \end{array}$$

About 500 feet

5. $\frac{\overset{1}{\cancel{3}} \cdot \overset{1}{\cancel{3}} \cdot 5}{2 \cdot 2 \cdot 2 \cdot \underset{1}{\cancel{3}} \cdot \underset{1}{\cancel{3}}} = \mathbf{\frac{5}{8}}$

6. $\mathbf{\overline{QT}}$ or $\mathbf{\overline{TQ}}$

7. \$27.50 ÷ 10 = **\$2.75 per day**

8. $\frac{120}{15} = \mathbf{8}$

9. $3\frac{1}{2} \times \frac{4}{4} = 3\frac{4}{8}$

$2\frac{3}{4} \times \frac{2}{2} = 2\frac{6}{8}$

$+\ 1\frac{5}{8} \times \frac{1}{1} = 1\frac{5}{8}$

$6\frac{15}{8} = \mathbf{7\frac{7}{8}}$

10.
$$\begin{array}{rl} 5\frac{3}{8} \times \frac{1}{1} = & \overset{4}{\cancel{5}}\,\frac{\overset{11}{\cancel{3}}}{8} \\ -\ 1\frac{3}{4} \times \frac{2}{2} = & 1\frac{6}{8} \\ \hline & 3\frac{5}{8} \end{array}$$

$m = \mathbf{3\frac{5}{8}}$

11.
$$\begin{array}{rl} \frac{3}{4} \times \frac{3}{3} = & \frac{9}{12} \\ -\ \frac{1}{3} \times \frac{4}{4} = & \frac{4}{12} \\ \hline & \frac{5}{12} \end{array}$$

$f = \mathbf{\frac{5}{12}}$

12. $w = \mathbf{\frac{5}{2}}$

13. $\frac{8}{25} \times \frac{4}{4} = \frac{32}{100}$
$n = \mathbf{32}$

14. $\frac{5}{3} \div \frac{2}{1}$

$1 \div \frac{2}{1} = \frac{1}{2}$

$\frac{5}{3} \times \frac{1}{2} = \mathbf{\frac{5}{6}}$

15. $\frac{8}{3} \times \frac{6}{5} = \frac{48}{15} = 3\frac{3}{15} = \mathbf{3\frac{1}{5}}$

16.
$$\begin{array}{r} \mathbf{30} \\ 8\overline{)240} \\ \underline{24} \\ 00 \\ \underline{00} \\ 0 \end{array}$$

17. a.
$$\begin{array}{r} 2.5\text{ m} \\ \times\quad 4 \\ \hline 10.0\text{ m} \end{array} = \mathbf{10\text{ m}}$$

b.
$$\begin{array}{r} 2.5\text{ m} \\ \times\ 2.5\text{ m} \\ \hline 125 \\ 500 \\ \hline \mathbf{6.25\text{ sq. m}} \end{array}$$

18. If a counting number is divisible by a counting number other than itself or 1, then the number is composite.

19. One possibility:

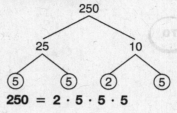

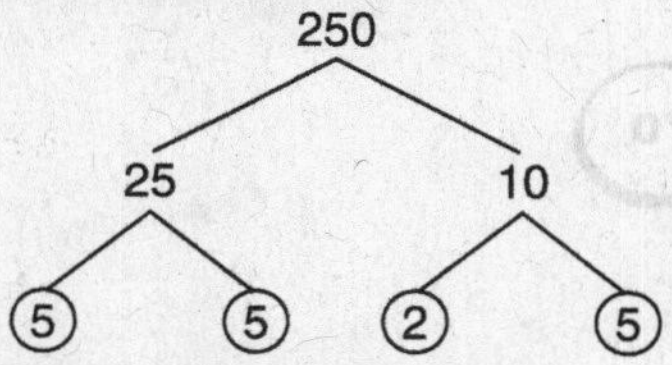

250 = 2 · 5 · 5 · 5

20. Octagon

21. a. $\frac{12}{27} = \mathbf{\frac{4}{9}}$

b. $\frac{15}{12} = \mathbf{\frac{5}{4}}$

22. 9 ÷ 3 = 3

23. $\mathbf{\frac{2}{5}}$

24. 2.25 kg × 1000 = **2250 grams**

25. 35 mm

26.
$$\begin{array}{r} 53\text{ mm} \\ +\ 35\text{ mm} \\ \hline \mathbf{88\text{ mm}} \end{array}$$

27.

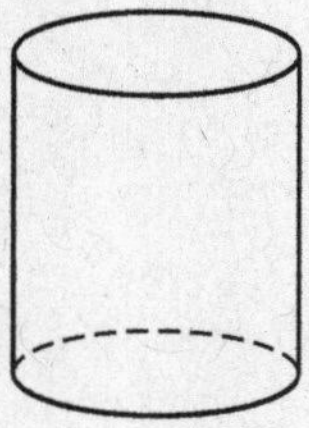

28. −1, 0, 0.1, 1

29.

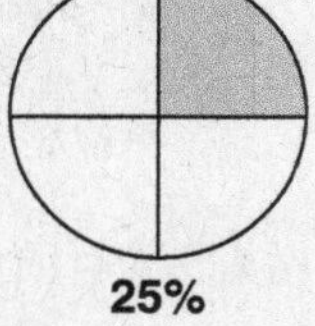

25%

30. 8 cubes

Early Finishers Solutions

25 yds × 36 inches = 900 inches; 900 ÷ $7\frac{1}{2}$ = 120 ribbons per roll; 2 rolls × 120 ribbons = 240 ribbons.

Practice Set 70

a. $\frac{3}{\underset{1}{\cancel{4}}} \cdot \frac{\overset{1}{\cancel{4}}}{5} = \mathbf{\frac{3}{5}}$

b. $\frac{\overset{1}{\cancel{2}}}{\underset{1}{\cancel{3}}} \cdot \frac{\overset{1}{\cancel{3}}}{\underset{2}{\cancel{4}}} = \mathbf{\frac{1}{2}}$

c. $\frac{\overset{4}{\cancel{8}}}{\underset{1}{\cancel{9}}} \cdot \frac{\overset{1}{\cancel{9}}}{\underset{5}{\cancel{10}}} = \mathbf{\frac{4}{5}}$

d. $\frac{9}{\underset{1}{\cancel{4}}} \times \frac{\overset{1}{\cancel{4}}}{1} = \frac{9}{1} = \mathbf{9}$

e. $\frac{\overset{1}{\cancel{3}}}{\underset{1}{\cancel{2}}} \times \frac{\overset{4}{\cancel{8}}}{\underset{1}{\cancel{3}}} = \frac{4}{1} = \mathbf{4}$

f. $\frac{\overset{5}{\cancel{10}}}{\underset{1}{\cancel{3}}} \times \frac{\overset{3}{\cancel{9}}}{\underset{2}{\cancel{4}}} = \frac{15}{2} = \mathbf{7\frac{1}{2}}$

g. $\frac{2}{5} \div \frac{2}{3}$

$1 \div \frac{2}{3} = \frac{3}{2}$

$\frac{\overset{1}{\cancel{2}}}{5} \times \frac{3}{\underset{1}{\cancel{2}}} = \mathbf{\frac{3}{5}}$

h. $\frac{8}{9} \div \frac{2}{3}$

$1 \div \frac{2}{3} = \frac{3}{2}$

$\frac{\overset{4}{\cancel{8}}}{\underset{3}{\cancel{9}}} \times \frac{\overset{1}{\cancel{3}}}{\underset{1}{\cancel{2}}} = \frac{4}{3} = \mathbf{1\frac{1}{3}}$

i. $\frac{9}{10} \div \frac{6}{5}$

$1 \div \frac{6}{5} = \frac{5}{6}$

$\frac{\overset{3}{\cancel{9}}}{\underset{2}{\cancel{10}}} \times \frac{\overset{1}{\cancel{5}}}{\underset{2}{\cancel{6}}} = \mathbf{\frac{3}{4}}$

Written Practice 70

1. **$7,200,000**

2. $\frac{1}{2} \div \frac{1}{8}$

$1 \div \frac{1}{8} = \frac{8}{1}$

$\frac{1}{\underset{1}{\cancel{2}}} \times \frac{\overset{4}{\cancel{8}}}{1} = \frac{4}{1} =$ **4 eighth notes**

3. **25 ÷ 5 = 5**

4. $\frac{\overset{1}{\cancel{5}}}{\underset{3}{\cancel{6}}} \cdot \frac{\overset{2}{\cancel{4}}}{\underset{1}{\cancel{5}}} = \mathbf{\frac{2}{3}}$

5. $\frac{5}{6} \div \frac{5}{2}$

$1 \div \frac{5}{2} = \frac{2}{5}$

$\frac{\overset{1}{\cancel{5}}}{\underset{3}{\cancel{6}}} \times \frac{\overset{1}{\cancel{2}}}{\underset{1}{\cancel{5}}} = \mathbf{\frac{1}{3}}$

6. $\frac{\overset{3}{\cancel{9}}}{\underset{2}{\cancel{10}}} \cdot \frac{\overset{1}{\cancel{5}}}{\underset{2}{\cancel{6}}} = \mathbf{\frac{3}{4}}$

7. 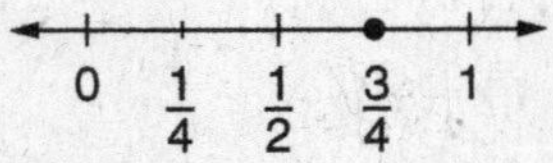

$\mathbf{\frac{3}{4}}$

8. 10 + 100 = **110**

9.
$$\begin{array}{r} 3\frac{2}{3}\times\frac{2}{2} = 3\frac{4}{6} \\ +\ 4\frac{5}{6}\times\frac{1}{1} = 4\frac{5}{6} \\ \hline 7\frac{9}{6} = 8\frac{3}{6} = \mathbf{8\frac{1}{2}} \end{array}$$

10.
$$\begin{array}{r} 7\frac{1}{8}\times\frac{1}{1} = \overset{6}{\cancel{7}}\,\frac{\overset{9}{\cancel{1}}}{8} \\ -\ 2\frac{1}{2}\times\frac{4}{4} = 2\frac{4}{8} \\ \hline \mathbf{4\frac{5}{8}} \end{array}$$

11.
$$\begin{array}{r} {}^{1}\overset{1}{4}.37 \\ 12.8 \\ +\ \ 6 \\ \hline \mathbf{23.17} \end{array}$$

12.
$$\begin{array}{r} \mathbf{0.092} \\ 5\overline{)0.460} \\ 45 \\ \hline 10 \\ 10 \\ \hline 0 \end{array}$$

13.
$$\begin{array}{r} \mathbf{75} \\ 8\overline{)600} \\ 56 \\ \hline 40 \\ 40 \\ \hline 0 \end{array}$$

14.
$$\begin{array}{r} \overset{1}{4}.5 \\ 5 \\ +\ 5.8 \\ \hline 15.3 \end{array} \qquad \begin{array}{r} \mathbf{5.1} \\ 3\overline{)15.3} \\ 15 \\ \hline 0\,3 \\ 0\,3 \\ \hline 0 \end{array}$$

15. **B. 150 ÷ 6**

16. 3.8 L × 1000 = **3800 milliliters**

17. $\frac{3}{3} - \frac{2}{3} = \frac{1}{3}$

$n = \mathbf{\frac{1}{3}}$

18. $m = \mathbf{\frac{3}{2}}$

19.
$$\begin{array}{r} \frac{5}{6}\times\frac{2}{2} = \frac{10}{12} \\ +\ \frac{3}{4}\times\frac{3}{3} = \frac{9}{12} \\ \hline \frac{19}{12} = 1\frac{7}{12} \end{array}$$

$f = \mathbf{1\frac{7}{12}}$

20. **a. 4 faces**

b. 6 edges

c. 4 vertices

21. $\frac{\overset{1}{\cancel{5}}}{\underset{1}{\cancel{3}}} \times \frac{\overset{2}{\cancel{6}}}{\underset{1}{\cancel{5}}} = \frac{2}{1} = \mathbf{2}$

22. $\frac{8}{9} \div \frac{8}{3}$

$1 \div \frac{8}{3} = \frac{3}{8}$

$\frac{\overset{1}{\cancel{8}}}{\underset{3}{\cancel{9}}} \times \frac{\overset{1}{\cancel{3}}}{\underset{1}{\cancel{8}}} = \mathbf{\frac{1}{3}}$

23.
$$\begin{array}{r} \overset{6}{\cancel{7}}{}^{1}0 \\ -\ 6\,3 \\ \hline \end{array}$$
7 beats per minute more

24.
$$\begin{array}{r} 65 \\ \times\ \ 3 \\ \hline \end{array}$$
195 times

25. **Answers will vary. See student work. Sample answer: One Wednesday John took his pulse for 2 minutes before marking the graph. How many times did his heart beat in those 2 minutes?**

$$\begin{array}{r} \mathbf{66} \\ \mathbf{\times\ 2} \\ \hline \end{array}$$
132 times

26. $\frac{\overset{1}{\cancel{2}} \cdot \overset{1}{\cancel{2}} \cdot 2 \cdot \overset{1}{\cancel{3}} \cdot 3}{\underset{1}{\cancel{2}} \cdot \underset{1}{\cancel{2}} \cdot \underset{1}{\cancel{3}} \cdot 5 \cdot 5} = \mathbf{\frac{6}{25}}$

27.
$$\begin{array}{r} \overset{2}{2}.5\text{ cm} \\ 2.5\text{ cm} \\ 1.5\text{ cm} \\ +\ 1.5\text{ cm} \\ \hline 8.0\text{ cm} \end{array}$$
8.0 cm or **8 cm**

28.
$$\begin{array}{r} 2.5\text{ cm} \\ \times\ 1.5\text{ cm} \\ \hline 125 \\ 250 \\ \hline \mathbf{3.75\ cm^2} \end{array}$$

29. $\overline{AD}$ (or $\overline{DA}$) and $\overline{BC}$ (or $\overline{CB}$)

30.
$$\begin{array}{r} \mathbf{1.875\ cm^2} \\ 2\overline{)3.750} \\ 2 \\ \hline 1\,7 \\ 1\,6 \\ \hline 15 \\ 14 \\ \hline 10 \\ 10 \\ \hline 0 \end{array}$$

Early Finishers Solutions

\$8.97 + \$2.89 + \$1.59 = \$13.45; \$47.83 − \$13.45 = \$34.38; \$34.38 ÷ 2 = \$17.19
It costs \$17.19 for each gallon of paint.

Investigation 7

1. **(3, 1)**
2. **Point C**
3. **(−3, −1)**
4. **Point G**
5. **(−3, 1)**
6. **Point H**
7. a.

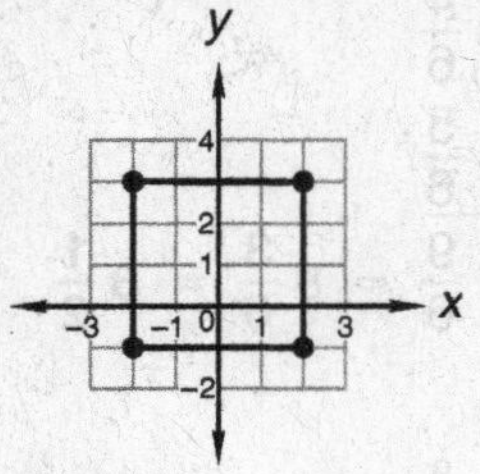

   b. **16 units**

   c. **16 sq. units**

8. a. **Origin**

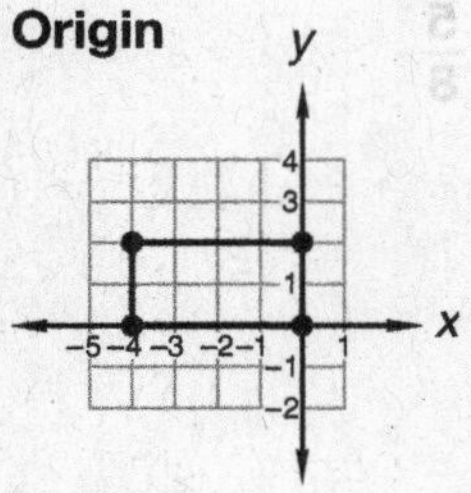

   b. **12 units**

   c. **8 sq. units**

9. a. **(3, −3)**

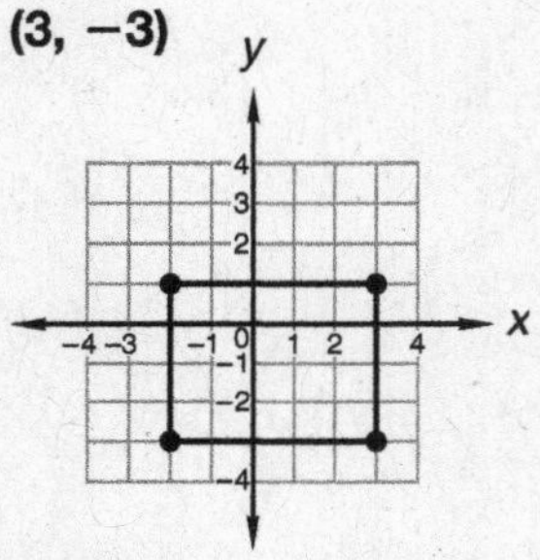

   b. **18 units**

   c. **20 sq. units**

10. **See student work.**
11. **See student work. The figure should look like a space shuttle.**
12. **See student work.**

Practice Set 71

a. $\angle S$

b. $\angle R$

c. $\angle S$ and $\angle Q$

d. $180° - 100° = \mathbf{80°}$

e. $P = 12\text{ m} + 12\text{ m} + 8\text{ m} + 8\text{ m} = \mathbf{40\text{ m}}$
$A = 10\text{ m} \times 8\text{ m} = \mathbf{80\text{ m}^2}$

f. $P = 6\text{ in.} + 6\text{ in.} + 8\text{ in.} + 8\text{ in.} = \mathbf{28\text{ in.}}$
$A = 5\text{ in.} \times 8\text{ in.} = \mathbf{40\text{ sq. in.}}$

g. $12\text{ cm} \times 6\text{ cm} = 72\text{ cm}^2$
$9\text{ cm} \times h = 72\text{ cm}^2$
$h = 72\text{ cm}^2 \div 9\text{ cm}$
$h = \mathbf{8\text{ cm}}$

Written Practice 71

1. Multiples of 6
6, 12, 18, 24, (30), 36
Multiples of 10
10, 20, (30), 40, 50
LCM is **30**

2. $29{,}035\text{ ft} + 1{,}371\text{ ft} = \mathbf{30{,}406\text{ ft}}$

3. 1:15 p.m. + 1:45 = 2:60 p.m.
3:00 p.m.

4. $\frac{\not{2}^1}{\not{3}_1} \cdot \frac{\not{3}^1}{\not{8}_4} = \mathbf{\frac{1}{4}}$

5. $\frac{5}{\not{4}_1} \cdot \frac{\not{8}^2}{3} = \frac{10}{3} = \mathbf{3\frac{1}{3}}$

6. $\frac{3}{4} \div \frac{3}{8}$
$1 \div \frac{3}{8} = \frac{8}{3}$
$\frac{\not{3}^1}{\not{4}_1} \cdot \frac{\not{8}^2}{\not{3}_1} = \frac{2}{1} = \mathbf{2}$

7. $\frac{9}{2} \div \frac{6}{1}$
$1 \div \frac{6}{1} = \frac{1}{6}$
$\frac{\not{9}^3}{2} \times \frac{1}{\not{6}_2} = \mathbf{\frac{3}{4}}$

8.
$6 = 6$
$3\frac{3}{4} = 3\frac{3}{4}$
$+ 2\frac{1}{2} \times \frac{2}{2} = 2\frac{2}{4}$
$11\frac{5}{4} = \mathbf{12\frac{1}{4}}$

9. $5 \xrightarrow{4 + \frac{8}{8}} 4\frac{8}{8}$
$4\frac{8}{8} - 3\frac{1}{8} = \mathbf{1\frac{7}{8}}$

10.
$5\frac{1}{4} \times \frac{2}{2} = \not{5}^4\frac{\not{2}^{10}}{8}$
$- 1\frac{7}{8} \times \frac{1}{1} = 1\frac{7}{8}$
$\mathbf{3\frac{3}{8}}$

11.
```
   3.5
 × 3.5
   175
  1050
 12.25
```
12.25

12.
```
    $5.00
15)$75.00
    75
     0 0
     0 0
      00
      00
       0
```
$5.00

Solutions

13. $(1 + 0.6) \div (1 - 0.6)$
$1.6 \div 0.4$
4

14. a.
$$\begin{array}{r} \$4.50 \\ \times\ 0.075 \\ \hline 2250 \\ 31500 \\ \hline 0.33750 \end{array} \longrightarrow \textbf{\$0.34}$$

b.
$$\begin{array}{r} \$4.50 \\ +\ \$0.34 \\ \hline \textbf{\$4.84} \end{array}$$

c.
$$\begin{array}{r} \$\overset{1}{\cancel{2}}\,\overset{9}{\cancel{0}}.\,\overset{9}{\cancel{0}}{}^{1}0 \\ -\ \$4.\,8\,4 \\ \hline \textbf{\$1\,5.\,1\,6} \end{array}$$

15. **Origin**

16. a. **Point *D***

b. **Point *G***

c. **(3, −3)**

d. **(−3, 0)**

17.
$$\begin{array}{r} \textbf{100} \\ 12\overline{)1200} \\ \underline{12} \\ 00 \\ \underline{00} \\ 00 \\ \underline{00} \\ 0 \end{array}$$

18.
$$\begin{array}{r} \textbf{100} \\ 12\overline{)1200} \\ \underline{12} \\ 00 \\ \underline{00} \\ 00 \\ \underline{00} \\ 0 \end{array}$$

19. $\dfrac{\overset{1}{\cancel{2}} \cdot \overset{1}{\cancel{2}} \cdot \overset{1}{\cancel{2}} \cdot \overset{1}{\cancel{2}} \cdot \overset{1}{\cancel{2}} \cdot 2}{\underset{1}{\cancel{2}} \cdot \underset{1}{\cancel{2}} \cdot \underset{1}{\cancel{2}} \cdot \underset{1}{\cancel{2}} \cdot \underset{1}{\cancel{2}} \cdot 7} = \mathbf{\dfrac{2}{7}}$

20.
$$\begin{array}{r} 1.6\text{ m} \\ 4\overline{)6.4} \\ \underline{4} \\ 2\,4 \\ \underline{2\,4} \\ 0 \end{array} \qquad \begin{array}{r} 1.6\text{ m} \\ \times\ 1.6\text{ m} \\ \hline 96 \\ 160 \\ \hline \end{array}$$
2.56 square meters

21. $\dfrac{6}{8} = \mathbf{\dfrac{3}{4}}$

22. $C = \pi d$
$C \approx (3.14)(2\text{ cm})$
$C \approx$ **6.28 cm; Sample answer: I multiplied the radius by 2 to find the diameter. Then I multiplied the diameter by 3.14.**

23. **Answers will vary but should be close to 5 cm.**

24. **4°F**

25. $\dfrac{20}{100} = \mathbf{\dfrac{1}{5}}$

$\dfrac{1}{\underset{1}{\cancel{5}}} \cdot \dfrac{\overset{12}{\cancel{60}}}{1}\text{ min} = \dfrac{12}{1} =$ **12 minutes**

26. **Cone**

27.
$$\begin{array}{r} 6\text{ cm} \\ 4\overline{)24} \\ \underline{24} \\ 0 \end{array}$$
6 cm × 3 = **18 cm**

28. **C. Square miles**

29. a. 8 cm + 8 cm + 10 cm + 10 cm
= **36 cm**

b. 10 cm × 7 cm = **70 cm²**

30. a. **∠AMB** (or **∠BMA**) and **∠BMC** (or **∠CMB**); *or* **∠CMD** (or **∠DMC**) and **∠DMA** (or **∠AMD**)

b. **∠BMC** (or **∠CMB**) and **∠CMD** (or **∠DMC**)

Practice Set 72

a. **See student work.**

b. **Step 1: Write the fractions so the denominators are the same.**
Step 2: Add the numerators but not the denominators.
Step 3: Simplify the answer if possible.

c. **Step 1: Write any mixed numbers in fraction form.**
Step 2: Rewrite the division problem as a multiplication problem by changing the divisor to its reciprocal. Cancel terms; then multiply the fractions.
Step 3: Simplify the answer if possible.

d. $\frac{\cancel{2}^{1}}{\cancel{3}_{1}} \cdot \frac{\cancel{4}^{1}}{5} \cdot \frac{\cancel{3}^{1}}{\cancel{8}_{\cancel{2}_{1}}} = \mathbf{\frac{1}{5}}$

e. $\frac{\cancel{5}^{1}}{\cancel{2}_{1}} \cdot \frac{11}{\cancel{10}_{\cancel{2}_{1}}} \cdot \frac{\cancel{4}^{\cancel{2}^{1}}}{1} = \frac{11}{1} = \mathbf{11}$

Written Practice 72

1. $$\begin{array}{r} \overset{1}{4}.2 \\ 2.61 \\ +\ 3.6 \\ \hline 10.41 \end{array} \qquad \begin{array}{r} \mathbf{3.47} \\ 3\overline{)10.41} \\ \underline{9} \\ 1\,4 \\ \underline{1\,2} \\ 21 \\ \underline{21} \\ 0 \end{array}$$

2. 4 T × 4 T = **16 tablespoons**

3. 130°C − (−110°C)
$$\begin{array}{r} 130°\text{C} \\ +\ 110°\text{C} \\ \hline \mathbf{240°C} \end{array}$$

4. (a) $\frac{4}{12} = \mathbf{\frac{1}{3}}$
(b) $\frac{8}{12} = \mathbf{\frac{2}{3}}$
(c) **Complementary**

5. $C = \pi d$
$C \approx (3.14)(100 \text{ cm})$
$C \approx$ **314 centimeters**

6. $\frac{5}{100} = \mathbf{\frac{1}{20}}$

7. $$\begin{array}{rcl} \frac{3}{5} \times \frac{2}{2} &=& \frac{6}{10} \\ +\ \frac{1}{2} \times \frac{5}{5} &=& \frac{5}{10} \\ \hline && \frac{11}{10} = 1\frac{1}{10} \end{array}$$
$n = \mathbf{1\frac{1}{10}}$

8. $\frac{12}{12} - \frac{7}{12} = \frac{5}{12}$
$w = \mathbf{\frac{5}{12}}$

9. $$\begin{array}{rcl} 3\frac{1}{3} \times \frac{2}{2} &=& \cancel{3}^{2}\frac{\cancel{2}^{8}}{6} \\ -\ 2\frac{1}{2} \times \frac{3}{3} &=& 2\frac{3}{6} \\ \hline && \frac{5}{6} \end{array}$$
$w = \mathbf{\frac{5}{6}}$

10. $$\begin{array}{r} \overset{0}{\cancel{1}}.\overset{9}{\cancel{0}}{}^{1}0 \\ -\ 0.2\,3 \\ \hline 0.7\,7 \end{array}$$
$w =$ **0.77**

11. **60.43**

12. **B. 0.1**

13. **97**

14. **C.**

15. a. $$\begin{array}{r} \textbf{6 inches} \\ 4\overline{)24} \\ \underline{24} \\ 0 \end{array}$$
b. 6 in. × 6 in. = **36 square inches**

16. a. **∠*MCB*** or **∠*BCM***
b. **∠*CMB*** (or **∠*BMC***) or **∠*DCM*** (or **∠*MCD***)

17.

$$\begin{array}{r} {}^{2\ 5} \\ \$3.49 \\ \$3.49 \\ \$3.29 \\ \$0.89 \\ \$1.09 \\ +\ \$1.09 \\ \hline \mathbf{\$13.34} \end{array}$$

18.

$$\begin{array}{r} \$13.34 \\ \times\ \ 0.07 \\ \hline \$0.9338 \end{array} \longrightarrow \mathbf{\$0.93}$$

$$\begin{array}{r} \$13.34 \\ +\ \ \$0.93 \\ \hline \$14.27 \end{array}$$

$$\begin{array}{r} {}^{1\ 9\ \ 9} \\ \$\not{2}\ \not{0}.\ \not{0}{}^{1}0 \\ -\ \$1\ 4.\ 2\ 7 \\ \hline \mathbf{\$5.\ 7\ 3} \end{array}$$

19. Answers will vary. See student work. Sample answer:

1 Pasta Salad	$\overset{2\ 3}{\mathbf{\$2.89}}$
1 Green Salad	**$3.29**
1 Small juice	**$0.89**
1 Large juice	**+ $1.29**
	$8.36

20. $A = (2.5)(0.4)$
$A = \mathbf{1}$

21. $\dfrac{\overset{1}{\not{2}} \cdot \overset{1}{\not{2}} \cdot \overset{1}{\not{2}} \cdot \overset{1}{\not{3}} \cdot 3}{\underset{1}{\not{2}} \cdot \underset{1}{\not{2}} \cdot \underset{1}{\not{2}} \cdot \underset{1}{\not{3}} \cdot 5} = \mathbf{\dfrac{3}{5}}$

22. a. (−3, 4)

b. (0, −3)

23. a. Point *E*

b. Point *I*

24.

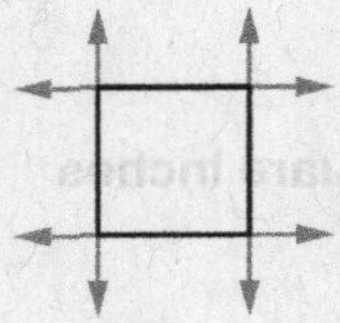

; yes

25. $\dfrac{1}{2} \cdot \dfrac{\overset{1}{\not{5}}}{\underset{2}{\not{6}}} \cdot \dfrac{\overset{1}{\not{3}}}{\underset{1}{\not{5}}} = \mathbf{\dfrac{1}{4}}$

26. $\dfrac{3}{1} \cdot \dfrac{\overset{1}{\not{3}}}{\underset{1}{\not{2}}} \cdot \dfrac{\overset{4}{\not{8}}}{\underset{1}{\not{3}}} = \dfrac{12}{1} = \mathbf{12}$

27. $\dfrac{3}{4} \div \dfrac{2}{1}$

$1 \div \dfrac{2}{1} = \dfrac{1}{2}$

$\dfrac{3}{4} \cdot \dfrac{1}{2} = \mathbf{\dfrac{3}{8}}$

28. $\dfrac{3}{2} \div \dfrac{5}{3}$

$1 \div \dfrac{5}{3} = \dfrac{3}{5}$

$\dfrac{3}{2} \cdot \dfrac{3}{5} = \mathbf{\dfrac{9}{10}}$

29.

$$\begin{array}{r} 0.12 \\ \times\ 0.24 \\ \hline 48 \\ 240 \\ \hline \mathbf{0.0288} \end{array}$$

30.

$$\begin{array}{r} \mathbf{2.4} \\ 25\overline{)60.0} \\ \underline{50\ \ \ } \\ 10\ 0 \\ \underline{10\ 0} \\ 0 \end{array}$$

Early Finishers Solutions

a. 20 + 10 + 5 + 30 = 65 minutes

b. 65 − 10 = 55 minutes; 55 ÷ 3 = $18\frac{1}{3}$ three minute intervals. Since it costs $0.05 per 3 minute interval, she will need to purchase at least 19 intervals. 19 × $0.05 = $0.95

Practice Set 73

a. $10 \times 10 \times 10 \times 10 = \mathbf{10{,}000}$

b. $2 \cdot 2 \cdot 2 + 2 \cdot 2 \cdot 2 \cdot 2$
$8 + 16 = \mathbf{24}$

c. $2 \cdot 2 \cdot 5 \cdot 5 = \mathbf{100}$

d.

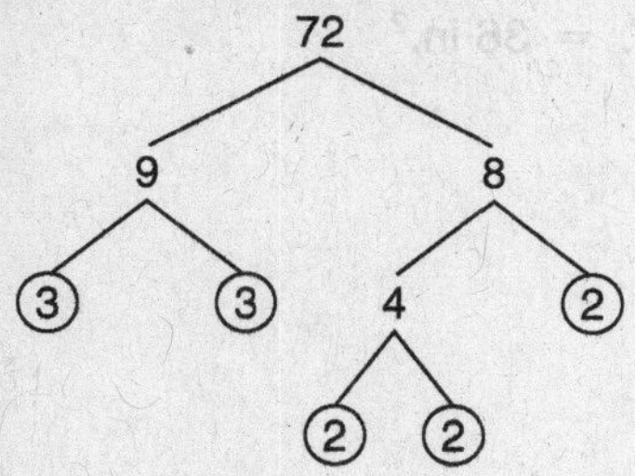

$$\mathbf{72 = 2^3 \cdot 3^2}$$

e. $12\frac{5}{10} = \mathbf{12\frac{1}{2}}$

f. $1\frac{25}{100} = \mathbf{1\frac{1}{4}}$

g. $\frac{125}{1000} = \mathbf{\frac{1}{8}}$

h. $\frac{5}{100} = \mathbf{\frac{1}{20}}$

i. $\frac{24}{100} = \mathbf{\frac{6}{25}}$

j. $10\frac{2}{10} = \mathbf{10\frac{1}{5}}$

Written Practice 73

1. **102°F − 98.6°F = *d***

$$\begin{array}{r} \overset{0}{\cancel{1}}\,\overset{9}{\cancel{0}}\,\overset{1}{\cancel{2}}.{}^{1}0\text{°F} \\ -\quad 9\,8.\,6\text{°F} \\ \hline \mathbf{3.\,4\text{°F}} \end{array}$$

2. **180 − 42 = *d***

$$\begin{array}{r} 1\,\overset{7}{\cancel{8}}{}^{1}0 \\ -\quad 4\,2 \\ \hline \mathbf{1\,3\,8 \text{ pages}} \end{array}$$

3. **3*p* = 138**

46 pages per day

$$\begin{array}{r} 46 \\ 3\overline{)138} \\ \underline{12} \\ 18 \\ \underline{18} \\ 0 \end{array}$$

4. $2\frac{5}{10} = \mathbf{2\frac{1}{2}}$

5. $\frac{35}{100} = \mathbf{\frac{7}{20}}$

6.

$$\begin{array}{r} \$12.60 \\ \times \quad .075 \\ \hline 6300 \\ \underline{88200} \\ \$0.94500 \end{array} \longrightarrow \mathbf{\$0.95}$$

$$\begin{array}{r} \$12.60 \\ + \quad \$0.95 \\ \hline \mathbf{\$13.55} \end{array}$$

7. $\frac{\overset{1}{\cancel{3}}}{\underset{1}{\cancel{4}}} \times \frac{2}{1} \times \frac{\overset{1}{\cancel{4}}}{\underset{1}{\cancel{3}}} = \frac{2}{1} = \mathbf{2}$

8. (100 − 100) ÷ 25

0 ÷ 25

0

9.

$$\begin{array}{rcl} 3 & = & 3 \\ 2\frac{1}{3} \times \frac{4}{4} & = & 2\frac{4}{12} \\ +\ 1\frac{3}{4} \times \frac{3}{3} & = & 1\frac{9}{12} \\ \hline & & 6\frac{13}{12} = \mathbf{7\frac{1}{12}} \end{array}$$

10.

$$\begin{array}{rcl} 5\frac{1}{6} \times \frac{1}{1} & = & \overset{4}{\cancel{5}}\,\frac{\overset{7}{\cancel{1}}}{6} \\ -\ 3\frac{1}{2} \times \frac{3}{3} & = & 3\frac{3}{6} \\ \hline & & 1\frac{4}{6} = \mathbf{1\frac{2}{3}} \end{array}$$

11. $\frac{3}{4} \div \frac{3}{2}$

$1 \div \frac{3}{2} = \frac{2}{3}$

$\frac{\overset{1}{\cancel{3}}}{\underset{2}{\cancel{4}}} \times \frac{\overset{1}{\cancel{2}}}{\underset{1}{\cancel{3}}} = \mathbf{\frac{1}{2}}$

12.

$$\begin{array}{r} \mathbf{17.5} \\ 4\overline{)70.0} \\ \underline{4} \\ 30 \\ \underline{28} \\ 2\,0 \\ \underline{2\,0} \\ 0 \end{array}$$

13. a. 5^2 ◯< 2^5

$5 \cdot 5$ $2 \cdot 2 \cdot 2 \cdot 2 \cdot 2$

25 32

b. 0.3 ◯> 0.125

14. a. $C = \pi d$

$C \approx (3.14)(2.4 \text{ cm})$

$C \approx$ **7.536 cm**

b. $\frac{1.2}{2.4} = \mathbf{\frac{1}{2}}$

15.
$$\begin{array}{r} 0.007 \\ 25\overline{)0.175} \\ 175 \\ \hline 0 \end{array}$$

$m =$ **0.007**

16. $5.45 + y = 7$

$$\begin{array}{r} \overset{6}{\cancel{7}}.\overset{9}{\cancel{0}}{}^{1}0 \\ -\ 5.45 \\ \hline 1.55 \end{array}$$

$y =$ **1.55**

17. 2

18. 0, $\frac{1}{10}$, $\frac{1}{4}$, $\frac{1}{2}$, 1

19.

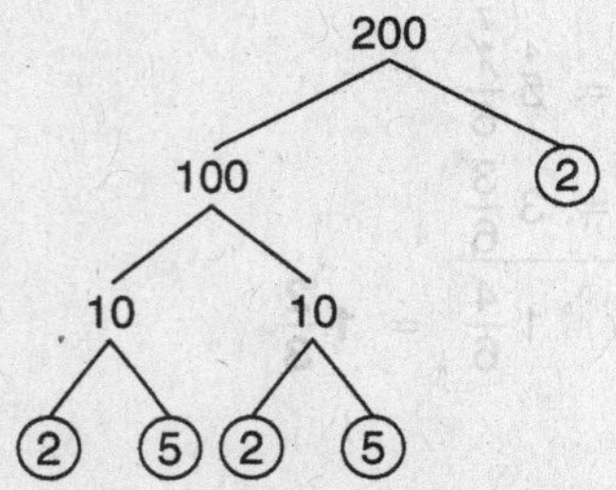

200 = $2^3 \cdot 5^2$

20. a.
$$\begin{array}{r} \$18.00 \\ \times\ 0.20 \\ \hline \$3.6000 \end{array}$$

$3.60

b.
$$\begin{array}{r} \$1\overset{7}{\cancel{8}}.{}^{1}00 \\ -\ \$3.60 \\ \hline \mathbf{\$14.40} \end{array}$$

21.
$$\begin{array}{r} \overset{4}{\cancel{5}}{}^{1}0 \text{ mm} \\ -\ 16 \text{ mm} \\ \hline \mathbf{34 \text{ mm}} \end{array}$$

22. 6 in. × 6 in. = 36 in.^{2}

$$\begin{array}{r} \mathbf{18 \text{ in.}^2} \\ 2\overline{)36} \\ 2 \\ \hline 16 \\ 16 \\ \hline 0 \end{array}$$

23. Yes

24. $\frac{4 + 8}{2} = \frac{12}{2} = \mathbf{6}$

25. Before we multiply fractions, we write any mixed numbers and any whole numbers as improper fractions.

26. a. (−4, −3)

b. (0, 3)

27. a. Point *J*

b. Point *C*

28. 9 × 9 = **81**

29. Answers will vary.

30. a. 180° − 75° = **105°**

b. 75°

<u>Early Finishers Solutions</u>

stem-and-leaf plot; A stem-and-leaf plot is the most appropriate display because it can be used to display individual data points. A line graph usually displays a change over time.

3	5, 9
4	1
5	1, 2, 4, 5, 6, 7, 8
6	1, 3, 4, 5, 6, 6, 7
7	0, 1, 3
8	0, 3, 6

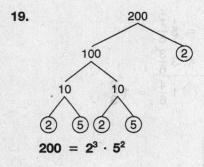

Practice Set 74

a. $4\overline{)3.00}$ = **0.75**

```
   0.75
4)3.00
  2 8
    20
    20
     0
```

b. $5\overline{)1.0}$ = 0.2 **4.2**

```
  0.2
5)1.0
  1 0
    0
```

c. $8\overline{)1.000}$ = **0.125**

```
   0.125
8)1.000
   8
   20
   16
    40
    40
     0
```

d. $20\overline{)7.00}$ = **0.35**

```
    0.35
20)7.00
   6 0
   1 00
   1 00
      0
```

e. $10\overline{)3.0}$ = 0.3 **3.3**

```
    0.3
10)3.0
   3 0
     0
```

f. $25\overline{)7.00}$ = **0.28**

```
    0.28
25)7.00
   5 0
   2 00
   2 00
      0
```

g. 0.6875

h. 0.96875

i. 3.375

j. $\mathbf{\frac{2}{5}}$**; 0.4**

```
  0.4
5)2.0
  2 0
    0
```

Written Practice 74

1. $4^3 - 5^2$
$64 - 25$
39

2. 10 miles × 3 = **30 miles**

3. $4\overline{)3.00}$ = 0.75 **2.75**

```
  0.75
4)3.00
  2 8
    20
    20
     0
```

4. **a. Sample space = {1, 2, 3, 4, 5}**

b. $\mathbf{\frac{4}{5}}$; $5\overline{)4.0}$ = **0.8**

```
  0.8
5)4.0
  4 0
    0
```

5. $\frac{24}{100} = \mathbf{\frac{6}{25}}$

6. 300 × 3 feet = 900 feet
900 − 400 = *d*
***d* = 500 feet**

7. $A = (12)(8)$
$A = \mathbf{96}$

8. 3^2 (>) $3 + 3$
9 6

9.
$$\frac{1}{2} \times \frac{3}{3} = \frac{3}{6}$$
$$\frac{2}{3} \times \frac{2}{2} = \frac{4}{6}$$
$$+\ \frac{1}{6} \times \frac{1}{1} = \frac{1}{6}$$
$$\frac{8}{6} = 1\frac{2}{6} = \mathbf{1\frac{1}{3}}$$

10.
$$3\frac{1}{4} \times \frac{2}{2} = \overset{2}{\cancel{3}}\,\frac{\overset{10}{\cancel{2}}}{8}$$
$$-\ 1\frac{7}{8} \times \frac{1}{1} = 1\frac{7}{8}$$
$$\mathbf{1\frac{3}{8}}$$

11. $\frac{\overset{1}{\cancel{5}}}{\underset{2}{\cancel{8}}} \cdot \frac{3}{\underset{1}{\cancel{5}}} \cdot \frac{\overset{1}{\cancel{4}}}{5} = \mathbf{\frac{3}{10}}$

12. $\frac{10}{\underset{1}{\cancel{3}}} \cdot \frac{\overset{1}{\cancel{3}}}{1} = \frac{10}{1} = \mathbf{10}$

13. $\frac{3}{4} \div \frac{3}{2}$

$1 \div \frac{3}{2} = \frac{2}{3}$

$\frac{\overset{1}{\cancel{3}}}{\underset{2}{\cancel{4}}} \times \frac{\overset{1}{\cancel{2}}}{\underset{1}{\cancel{3}}} = \mathbf{\frac{1}{2}}$

14. $(7.2) - 0.01 = \mathbf{7.19}$

15.

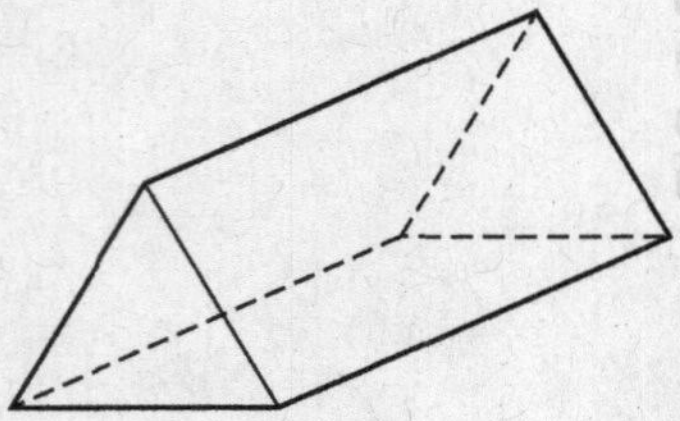

16. **12*g* = 10.44**

$$\begin{array}{r} \mathbf{\$0.87} \\ 12\overline{)10.44} \\ \underline{9\,6} \\ 84 \\ \underline{84} \\ 0 \end{array}$$

17.

$$\begin{array}{r} 80 \\ \underline{\times\ 40} \\ \mathbf{3200} \end{array}$$

18.

$$\begin{array}{r} 42 \text{ pages} \\ 46 \text{ pages} \\ 35 \text{ pages} \\ \underline{+\ 57 \text{ pages}} \\ 180 \text{ pages} \end{array} \qquad \begin{array}{r} \mathbf{45 \text{ pages per day}} \\ 4\overline{)180} \\ \underline{16} \\ 20 \\ \underline{20} \\ 0 \end{array}$$

19. Multiples of 6
6, 12, 18, (24), 30
Multiples of 8
8, 16, (24), 32
Multiples of 12
12, (24), 36, 48
LCM is **24**

20. $120 + c = 150$

$$\begin{array}{r} 150 \\ \underline{-\ 120} \\ \mathbf{30} \end{array}$$

21. $\frac{\overset{1}{\cancel{2}} \cdot \overset{1}{\cancel{2}} \cdot \overset{1}{\cancel{2}} \cdot 5}{\underset{1}{\cancel{2}} \cdot \underset{1}{\cancel{2}} \cdot \underset{1}{\cancel{2}} \cdot 2 \cdot 2 \cdot 3} = \mathbf{\frac{5}{12}}$

22. a.

$$\begin{array}{r} \mathbf{10 \text{ centimeters}} \\ 4\overline{)40 \text{ centimeters}} \\ \underline{4}\phantom{0 \text{ centimeters}} \\ 00\phantom{\text{ centimeters}} \\ \underline{00}\phantom{\text{ centimeters}} \\ 0\phantom{\text{ centimeters}} \end{array}$$

b. $C = \pi d$
$C \approx (3.14)(10 \text{ cm})$
$C \approx$ **31.4 centimeters**

23. $\frac{24}{36} = \mathbf{\frac{2}{3}}$

24. **All four sides of a square are the same length. Some rectangles are longer than they are wide, so not all the sides are the same length.**

25. ***B***

26. a. $\mathbf{\overline{SR}}$ or $\mathbf{\overline{RS}}$

b. $\mathbf{\overline{PS}}$ or $\mathbf{\overline{SP}}$

27. a. $3 \text{ ft} \times 3 \text{ ft} = \mathbf{9 \text{ ft}^2}$

b.

$$\begin{array}{r} 9 \text{ ft}^2 \\ \underline{\times\ 6\phantom{\text{ ft}^2}} \\ \mathbf{54 \text{ ft}^2} \end{array}$$

28. a. **(−3, −2)**

b. **(0, 0)**

29. $\mathbf{\overline{DA}}$ (or $\mathbf{\overline{AD}}$) and $\mathbf{\overline{CB}}$ (or $\mathbf{\overline{BC}}$)

30.

$$\begin{array}{r} 300 \text{ acres} \\ \underline{\times\ 0.60\phantom{\text{ acres}}} \\ 180.00\phantom{\text{ acres}} \end{array}$$

180 acres

Practice Set 75

a. **31%**

b. **1%**

c. $\frac{1}{10} \times \frac{10}{10} = \frac{10}{100}$ **10%**

d. $\frac{3}{50} \times \frac{2}{2} = \frac{6}{100}$ **6%**

e. $\frac{7}{25} \times \frac{4}{4} = \frac{28}{100}$ **28%**

f. $\frac{2}{5} \times \frac{20}{20} = \frac{40}{100}$ **40%**

g. $\frac{12}{30} = \frac{2}{5}$

$\frac{2}{5} \times \frac{20}{20} = \frac{40}{100}$ **40%**

h. $\frac{18}{20} = \frac{9}{10}$

$\frac{9}{10} \times \frac{10}{10} = \frac{90}{100}$ **90%**

i. $\frac{25}{100} =$ **25%**

j. $0.30 = \frac{30}{100} =$ **30%**

k. $\frac{5}{100} =$ **5%**

l. $1.0 =$ **100%**

m. $0.70 = \frac{70}{100} =$ **70%**

n. $\frac{15}{100} =$ **15%**

Written Practice 75

1. $2\frac{3}{5} = \frac{13}{5}$

$\mathbf{\frac{5}{13}}$

2.
```
    2:30 p.m.
  + 1:35
    3:65 p.m.
```
4:05 p.m.

3.
```
     $0.25 per ounce
16)$4.00
    3 2
      80
      80
       0
```

4.
```
   $4.00
   $0.94           $11.29        $11.29
 + $6.35      ×     $0.08      +  $0.90
  $11.29          $0.9032        $12.19
```
$12.19

Round 94¢ to $1 and round $6.35 to $6. Add $4, $1, and $6 and get $11. Tax is 8¢ per dollar, which comes to about 88¢ for the meal. So the estimated total is $11.88. Since $6.35 was rounded down more than 94¢ was rounded up, the answer $12.19 is reasonable.

5. $100\% - 50\% =$ **50%**

6. 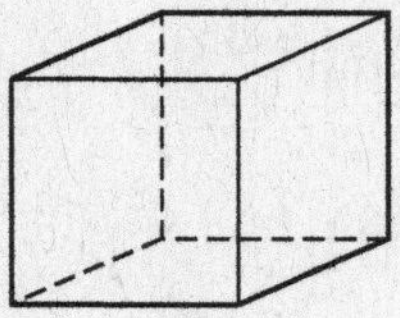

12 edges

7. a. $\frac{3}{4} \times \frac{25}{25} = \frac{75}{100} =$ **0.75**

b. **75%**

8. a. $\frac{3}{20} \times \frac{5}{5} = \mathbf{\frac{15}{100}}$

b. **15%**

9. $\dfrac{12}{100} = \dfrac{3}{25}$

$\dfrac{3}{25} \times \dfrac{4}{4} = \dfrac{12}{100} = \mathbf{12\%}$

10. $\dfrac{7}{10} \times \dfrac{10}{10} = \dfrac{70}{100}$

$n = \mathbf{70}$

11.

$$\begin{array}{r} 5 \\ -\ 3\frac{1}{8} \\ \hline \end{array} \xrightarrow{4\frac{8}{8}} \begin{array}{r} 4\frac{8}{8} \\ -\ 3\frac{1}{8} \\ \hline 1\frac{7}{8} \end{array}$$

$m = \mathbf{1\frac{7}{8}}$

12.

$$\begin{array}{r} \overset{0}{\cancel{1}}.\overset{9}{\cancel{0}}{}^{1}0 \\ -\ 0.\ 9\ 5 \\ \hline 0.\ 0\ 5 \end{array}$$

$w = \mathbf{0.05}$

13.

$$\begin{array}{r} 3\frac{1}{6} \times \frac{1}{1} = \overset{2}{\cancel{3}}\frac{\overset{7}{\cancel{1}}}{6} \\ -\ 1\frac{2}{3} \times \frac{2}{2} = 1\frac{4}{6} \\ \hline 1\frac{3}{6} = 1\frac{1}{2} \end{array}$$

$m = \mathbf{1\frac{1}{2}}$

14.

$$\begin{array}{r} \frac{1}{2} \times \frac{3}{3} = \frac{3}{6} \\ +\ \frac{1}{3} \times \frac{2}{2} = \frac{2}{6} \\ \hline \frac{5}{6} \end{array}$$

$\dfrac{5}{6} - \dfrac{1}{6} = \dfrac{4}{6} = \mathbf{\dfrac{2}{3}}$

15. $\dfrac{7}{\underset{1}{\cancel{2}}} \times \dfrac{\overset{\overset{1}{\cancel{2}}}{\cancel{4}}}{\underset{1}{\cancel{3}}} \times \dfrac{\overset{1}{\cancel{3}}}{\underset{1}{\cancel{2}}} = \dfrac{7}{1} = \mathbf{7}$

16.

$$\begin{array}{r} 0.43 \\ \times\ \ 2.6 \\ \hline 258 \\ 860 \\ \hline \mathbf{1.118} \end{array}$$

17.

$$\begin{array}{r} \mathbf{0.052} \\ 5\overline{)0.260} \\ 25 \\ \hline 10 \\ 10 \\ \hline 0 \end{array}$$

18. $\dfrac{17}{20} \times \dfrac{5}{5} = \dfrac{85}{100} = \mathbf{85\%}$

19. $C = \pi d$

$C \approx (3.14)(5 \text{ ft})$

$C \approx 15.7 \text{ ft.}$

About 16 feet

20. **7**

21. $\dfrac{\overset{1}{\cancel{2}} \cdot \overset{1}{\cancel{3}} \cdot 3}{\underset{1}{\cancel{2}} \cdot \underset{1}{\cancel{3}} \cdot 5} = \mathbf{\dfrac{3}{5}}$

22. Factors of 18

1, 2, 3, (6), 9, 18

Factors of 30

1, 2, 3, 5, (6), 10, 15, 30

GCF is **6**

23. **B. Reciprocals**

24. **A quadrilateral is a four-sided polygon, and every rectangle has four sides.**

25. $\dfrac{8 \cdot 6}{2} = \dfrac{48}{2} = \mathbf{24}$

26. **One possibility:**

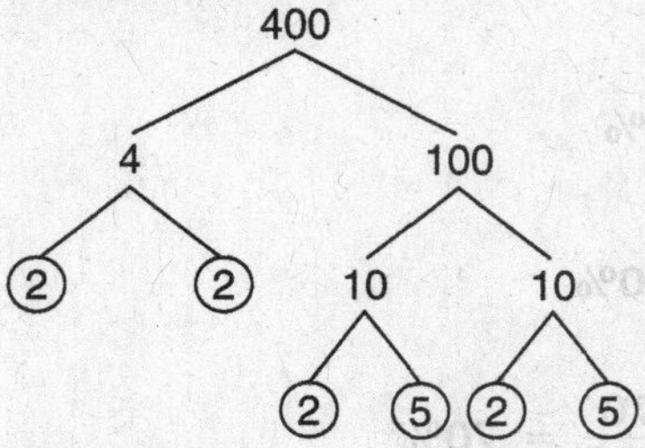

$400 = 2 \cdot 2 \cdot 2 \cdot 2 \cdot 5 \cdot 5$

$400 = \mathbf{2^4 \cdot 5^2}$

27.

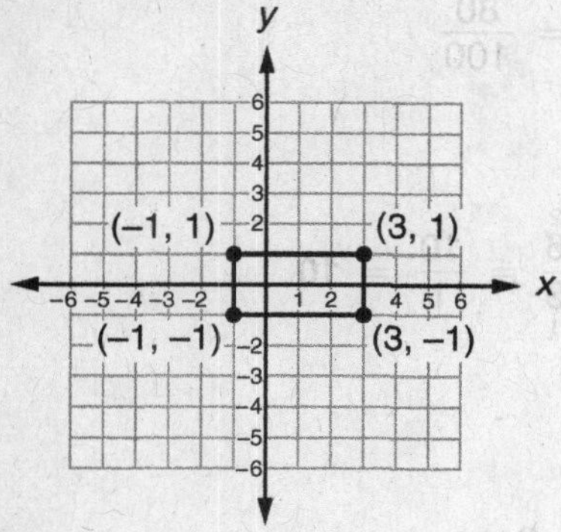

28. a. 4 units + 2 units + 4 units + 2 units = **12 units**

b. 4 units × 2 units = **8 sq. units**

29. a. 15 cm + 20 cm + 15 cm + 20 cm = **70 cm**

b. 12 cm × 20 cm = **240 cm²** ($12\text{ cm} \times 20\text{ cm} = 240\text{ cm}^2$)

30. **One possibility:**

; no

Early Finishers Solutions

a. 620 × 620 = 384,400 km

b. 384,400 km ÷ 30 = 12813.3 which rounds to 12813 km.

Practice Set 76

a. $\frac{3}{20} > \frac{1}{8}$

20)3.00 = 0.15: 2 0, 1 00, 1 00, 0

8)1.000 = 0.125: 8, 20, 16, 40, 40, 0

b. $\frac{3}{8} < \frac{2}{5}$

8)3.000 = 0.375: 2 4, 60, 56, 40, 40, 0

5)2.0 = 0.4: 2 0, 0

c. $\frac{15}{25} = \frac{3}{5}$

25)15.0 = 0.6: 15 0, 0

5)3.0 = 0.6: 3 0, 0

d. $0.7 < \frac{4}{5}$

5)4.0 = 0.8: 4 0, 0

e. $\frac{2}{5} < 0.5$

5)2.0 = 0.4: 2 0, 0

f. $\frac{3}{8} > 0.325$

8)3.000 = 0.375: 2 4, 60, 56, 40, 40, 0

Written Practice 76

1. $10^2 \times 2^3$

100 × 8

800

2. 6.7 − 4.5 = 2.2

2)2.2 = 1.1

4.5 + 1.1 = **5.6**

3. **13 · 7 = *y***

13 × 7 = **91 years old**

4. $\frac{2}{5}$ ⓥ $\frac{1}{4}$ (circled $>$)

$$\begin{array}{r} 0.4 \\ 5\overline{)2.0} \\ \underline{2\ 0} \\ 0 \end{array} \qquad \begin{array}{r} 0.25 \\ 4\overline{)1.00} \\ \underline{8} \\ 20 \\ \underline{20} \\ 0 \end{array}$$

5. **a.** $\mathbf{\frac{3}{4}}$

b. $$\begin{array}{r} \mathbf{0.75} \\ 4\overline{)3.00} \\ \underline{2\ 8} \\ 20 \\ \underline{20} \\ 0 \end{array}$$

c. $\frac{75}{100} = \mathbf{75\%}$

6. **A. Centimeters**

7. **a.** $$\begin{array}{r} 0.5 \\ 2\overline{)1.0} \\ \underline{1\ 0} \\ 0 \end{array}$$ **2.5**

b. $3\frac{75}{100} = \mathbf{3\frac{3}{4}}$

8. **a.** $\frac{4}{100} = \mathbf{\frac{1}{25}}$

b. **4%**

9. $$\begin{array}{r} \mathbf{11\frac{1}{9}} \\ 9\overline{)100} \\ \underline{9} \\ 10 \\ \underline{9} \\ 1 \end{array}$$

10.
$$\begin{array}{rcl} 6\frac{1}{3} \times \frac{4}{4} & = & 6\frac{4}{12} \\ 3\frac{1}{4} \times \frac{3}{3} & = & 3\frac{3}{12} \\ + \ 2\frac{1}{2} \times \frac{6}{6} & = & 2\frac{6}{12} \\ \hline & & 11\frac{13}{12} = \mathbf{12\frac{1}{12}} \end{array}$$

11. $\frac{4}{5} \times \frac{20}{20} = \frac{80}{100}$

$? = 80$

12. $\frac{\overset{1}{\cancel{5}}}{\underset{1}{\cancel{2}}} \cdot \frac{\overset{5}{\cancel{10}}}{\underset{1}{\cancel{3}}} \cdot \frac{\overset{2}{\cancel{6}}}{\underset{1}{\cancel{5}}} = \frac{10}{1} = \mathbf{10}$

13. $\frac{5}{1} \div \frac{5}{2}$

$1 \div \frac{5}{2} = \frac{2}{5}$

$\frac{\overset{1}{\cancel{5}}}{1} \cdot \frac{2}{\underset{1}{\cancel{5}}} = \frac{2}{1} = \mathbf{2}$

14. $7.18 + n = 8$

$$\begin{array}{r} \overset{7}{\cancel{8}}.\ \overset{9}{\cancel{0}}\,{}^{1}0 \\ -\ 7.\ 1\ 8 \\ \hline 0.\ 8\ 2 \end{array}$$

$n = \mathbf{0.82}$

15.
$$\begin{array}{r} \overset{0}{\cancel{1}}\,\overset{11}{\cancel{2}}.\ \overset{9}{\cancel{0}}\,{}^{1}0 \\ -\quad 4.\ 7\ 5 \\ \hline 7.\ 2\ 5 \end{array}$$

$d = \mathbf{7.25}$

16.
$$\begin{array}{r} 0.35 \\ \times\ 0.45 \\ \hline 175 \\ 1400 \\ \hline \mathbf{0.1575} \end{array}$$

17. $4.3 \div 100 = \mathbf{0.043}$

18. 0.2, 0.25, (0.27), 0.3, 0.313
0.27

19. $4000 + 5000 = \mathbf{9000}$

20. **41, 43, 47**

21. $\frac{12}{25} \times \frac{4}{4} = \frac{48}{100} = \mathbf{48\%}$

22. 20 mm + 16 mm + 12 mm = **48 mm**

23. $\begin{array}{r} \overset{8}{\cancel{9}}{}^{1}0° \\ -\ 5\ 3° \\ \hline \mathbf{3\ 7°} \end{array}$

24. **About 45 mm**

25. **a.** 20 cm × 10 cm = **200 cm²**

b. 200 cm² ÷ 2 = **100 cm²**

26. **12 cubes**

27. **Triangle:**

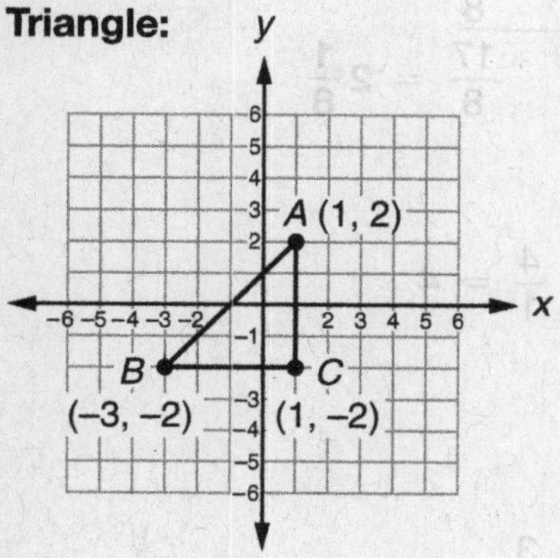

28. **a.** $\overline{BC}$ **or** $\overline{CB}$

b. **∠C**

29. $\frac{(12)(9)}{2} = \frac{108}{2} = \mathbf{54}$

30. **One possibility:**

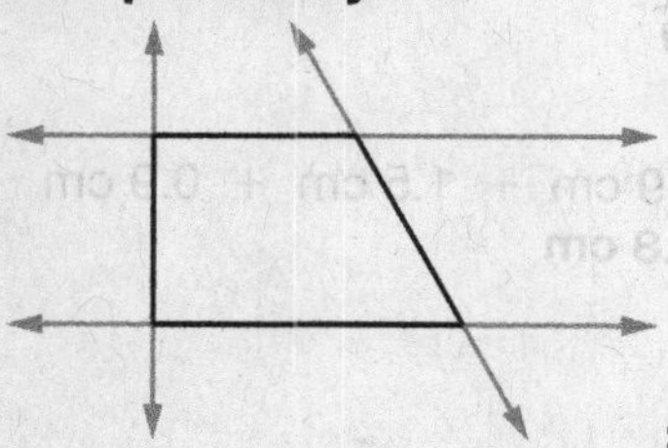

; No

Practice Set 77

40 engines

$\frac{3}{8}$ could climb the hill.	5 engines
	5 engines
	5 engines
$\frac{5}{8}$ could not climb the hill.	5 engines
	5 engines
	5 engines
	5 engines
	5 engines

a. **8 parts**

b. **5 engines**

c. **3 parts**

d. **15 engines**

e. **5 parts**

f. **25 engines**

g. $\frac{1}{\cancel{4}_1} \times \frac{\overset{3}{\cancel{12}}}{1} = \mathbf{3\ sectors}$

h. 12 − 3 = **9 sectors**

i. $\frac{9}{12} = \mathbf{\frac{3}{4}}$

j. $\frac{1}{4} + \frac{3}{4} = \frac{4}{4} = \mathbf{1}$

The events are complementary.

Written Practice 77

1. $\frac{\overset{19}{\cancel{114}}\text{ pounds}}{1} \cdot \frac{1}{\cancel{6}_1} = \frac{19}{1} = \mathbf{19\ pounds}$

2. **Answers will vary. See student work.**

3. **a.** $\frac{6}{24} = \mathbf{\frac{1}{4}}$

b. $\frac{1}{4} \times \frac{25}{25} = \frac{25}{100} = \mathbf{25\%}$

4.

30 students

$\frac{3}{5}$ are boys.	6 students
	6 students
	6 students
$\frac{2}{5}$ are girls.	6 students
	6 students

a. **5 parts**

b. **6 students**

c. **18 boys**

d. **12 girls**

5. a. $\frac{4}{10} = \mathbf{\frac{2}{5}}$

b. $\frac{4}{10} = \mathbf{0.4}$

c. $\frac{4}{10} \times \frac{10}{10} = \frac{40}{100} = \mathbf{40\%}$

6. $3\frac{6}{10} = \mathbf{3\frac{3}{5}}$

7.
$$\begin{array}{r} \overset{3}{\cancel{4}}.{}^{1}1\,5 \\ -\ 3.\,6 \\ \hline 0.\,5\,5 \end{array}$$
$a = \mathbf{0.55}$

8. $x = \mathbf{\frac{5}{2}}$

9. **If the chance of rain is 60%, then the chance that it will not rain is 40%. It is more likely to rain because 60% is greater than 40%.**

10. $\frac{3}{5} \times \frac{20}{20} = \frac{60}{100} = \mathbf{60\%}$

11. $32°F - (-3°F)$
$$\begin{array}{r} 32°F \\ +\ \ 3°F \\ \hline \mathbf{35°F} \end{array}$$

12. a. $0.35 \ \textcircled{=}\ \frac{7}{20}$
$$\begin{array}{r} 0.35 \\ 20\overline{)7.00} \\ 6\,0 \\ \hline 1\,00 \\ 1\,00 \\ \hline 0 \end{array}$$

b. $3^2 \ \textcircled{>}\ 2^3$
$9 \qquad 8$

13.
$$\begin{array}{r} \frac{1}{2} \times \frac{3}{3} = \frac{3}{6} \\ +\ \frac{2}{3} \times \frac{2}{2} = \frac{4}{6} \\ \hline \frac{7}{6} = \mathbf{1\frac{1}{6}} \end{array}$$

14.
$$\begin{array}{r} \overset{2}{\cancel{3}}\,\frac{\overset{6}{\cancel{1}}}{5} \\ -\ 1\frac{3}{5} \\ \hline \mathbf{1\frac{3}{5}} \end{array}$$

15.
$$\begin{array}{r} \frac{1}{2} \times \frac{4}{4} = \frac{4}{8} \\ \frac{3}{4} \times \frac{2}{2} = \frac{6}{8} \\ +\ \frac{7}{8} \times \frac{1}{1} = \frac{7}{8} \\ \hline \frac{17}{8} = \mathbf{2\frac{1}{8}} \end{array}$$

16. $\frac{\overset{1}{\cancel{3}}}{1} \times \frac{4}{\underset{1}{\cancel{3}}} = \frac{4}{1} = \mathbf{4}$

17. $\frac{3}{1} \div \frac{4}{3}$

$1 \div \frac{4}{3} = \frac{3}{4}$

$\frac{3}{1} \times \frac{3}{4} = \frac{9}{4} = \mathbf{2\frac{1}{4}}$

18. $\frac{4}{3} \div \frac{3}{1}$

$1 \div \frac{3}{1} = \frac{1}{3}$

$\frac{4}{3} \times \frac{1}{3} = \mathbf{\frac{4}{9}}$

19. 1.5 cm + 0.9 cm + 1.5 cm + 0.9 cm = **4.8 cm**

20.
$$\begin{array}{r} 1.5 \text{ cm} \\ \times\ 0.9 \text{ cm} \\ \hline \mathbf{1.35 \text{ cm}^2} \end{array}$$

21.

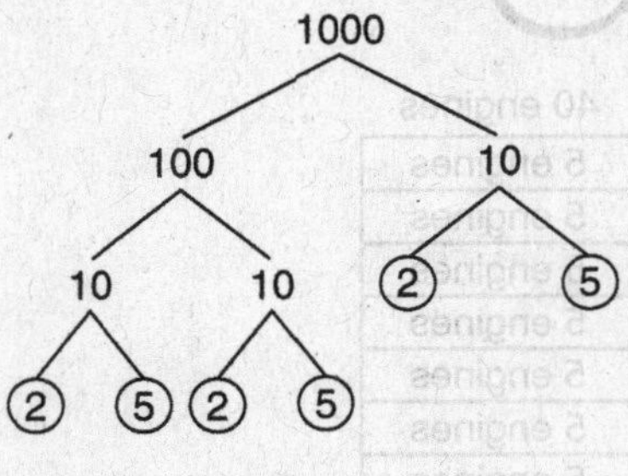

$1000 = 2^3 \times 5^3$

22. a. $80
× 0.40
$32.00

b. $80 (8 crossed out, 7 above; 0 becomes 10)
− $3 2
$4 8

23. a. $38.80
× 0.07
2.7160 ⟶ **$2.72**

b. $38.80
+ $2.72
$41.52

24. **Yes**

25. 12:00 p.m. (12:00 crossed out, 11 : 60 above)
− 1:14
10:46 a.m.

26. **B. 40%**

27.

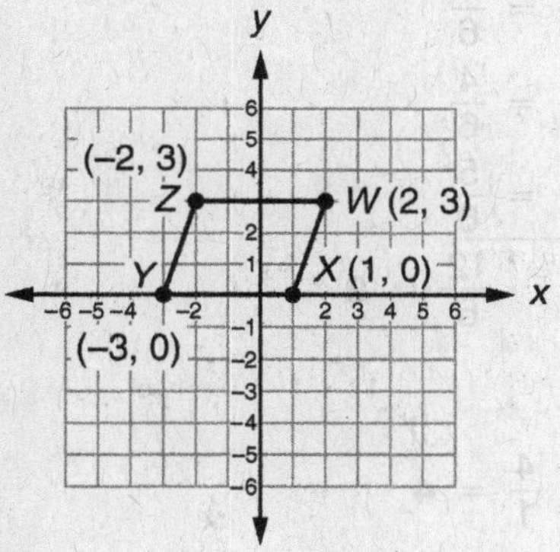

28. a. $\overline{ZY}$ or $\overline{YZ}$

b. $\overline{WZ}$ or $\overline{ZW}$

29. $\dfrac{\cancel{2}^{1} \cdot 3 \cdot \cancel{5}^{1} \cdot \cancel{7}^{1}}{\cancel{2}_{1} \cdot \cancel{5}_{1} \cdot 5 \cdot \cancel{7}_{1}} = \mathbf{\dfrac{3}{5}}$

30. a. **Sphere**

b. $C = \pi d$
$C \approx (3.14)(2160 \text{ miles})$
$C \approx 6782.4$
$C \approx$ **6780 miles**

Early Fnishers Solutions

$3^2 \times 2^3 = 72$
$2^2 \times 3^3 \times 5 = 540$
$2^2 \times 3^3 \times 5^2 = 900$
$3^5 = 243$
$2^4 \times 7^2 = 784$

Answers can vary. Examples: All of the numbers are divisible by 3 except 784 so it does not belong. All of the numbers are even except 243 so it does not belong. Check to see if student answer is appropriate.

Practice Set 78

a. 1 gallon = 4 quarts
$\mathbf{\dfrac{1}{4}}$

b. 2 × 1000 mL = **2000 mL**

c. $\dfrac{1}{2}$ gallon = 2 quarts
1 quart = 4 cups
$\dfrac{1}{2}$ gallon = **8 cups**

d. **The half-gallon carton will overflow because 2 liters is a little more than half of a gallon.**

Written Practice 78

1. $\left(\dfrac{1}{2} + \dfrac{1}{2}\right) - \left(\dfrac{1}{2} \times \dfrac{1}{2}\right)$

$\dfrac{2}{2} \times \dfrac{2}{2} = \dfrac{4}{4}$

$- \quad \dfrac{1}{4} \times \dfrac{1}{1} = \dfrac{1}{4}$

$\mathbf{\dfrac{3}{4}}$

2. 10 × 10 millimeters = **100 millimeters**

3. 41, no
42, no
43, no
44, no **48**
45, no
46, no
47, no
48, yes
49, no

4.

	60 lights
$\frac{4}{5}$ were on.	12 lights
	12 lights
	12 lights
	12 lights
$\frac{1}{5}$ were off.	12 lights

a. **5 parts**
b. **12 lights**
c. **48 lights**
d. **12 lights**

5. 1

6. $m = \mathbf{\frac{5}{4}}$

7. $\frac{5}{5} - \frac{4}{5} = \frac{1}{5}$
$w = \mathbf{\frac{1}{5}}$

8. $x = \mathbf{\frac{4}{5}}$

9. $\frac{3}{4} \times \frac{25}{25} = \frac{75}{100}$
n = 75

10. a. $\frac{4}{16} = \mathbf{\frac{1}{4}}$
b. $\frac{1}{4} \times \frac{25}{25} = \frac{25}{100} = \mathbf{0.25}$
c. **25%**

11. $1\frac{15}{100} = \mathbf{1\frac{3}{20}}$

12. a. $\frac{3}{5}$ ⓶ 0.35 — $\frac{3}{5}$ (>) 0.35

$$5\overline{)3.0} = 0.6;\quad 3\,0;\quad 0$$

b. $\sqrt{100}$ (>) $1^4 + 2^3$
10 $\quad 1 + 8$
$\quad 9$

13.
$$\frac{5}{6} \times \frac{1}{1} = \frac{5}{6}$$
$$-\ \frac{1}{2} \times \frac{3}{3} = \frac{3}{6}$$
$$\frac{2}{6} = \mathbf{\frac{1}{3}}$$

14.
$$4\frac{1}{4} \times \frac{3}{3} = \cancel{4}^{3}\,\frac{\cancel{3}^{15}}{12}$$
$$-\ 3\frac{1}{3} \times \frac{4}{4} = 3\frac{4}{12}$$
$$\mathbf{\frac{11}{12}}$$

15.
$$\frac{1}{2} \times \frac{3}{3} = \frac{3}{6}$$
$$\frac{2}{3} \times \frac{2}{2} = \frac{4}{6}$$
$$+\ \frac{5}{6} \times \frac{1}{1} = \frac{5}{6}$$
$$\frac{12}{6} = \mathbf{2}$$

16. $\frac{\cancel{3}^{1}}{\cancel{2}_{1}} \times \frac{\cancel{8}^{4}}{\cancel{3}_{1}} = \frac{4}{1} = \mathbf{4}$

17. $\frac{3}{2} \div \frac{8}{3}$
$1 \div \frac{8}{3} = \frac{3}{8}$
$\frac{3}{2} \cdot \frac{3}{8} = \mathbf{\frac{9}{16}}$

18. $\frac{8}{3} \div \frac{3}{2}$
$1 \div \frac{3}{2} = \frac{2}{3}$
$\frac{8}{3} \times \frac{2}{3} = \frac{16}{9} = \mathbf{1\frac{7}{9}}$

19. a. $\frac{1}{\cancel{2}_1}\text{ in.} \times \frac{\cancel{4}^2}{1} = \frac{2}{1} = \textbf{2 in.}$

b. $\frac{1}{2}\text{ in.} \times \frac{1}{2}\text{ in.} = \mathbf{\frac{1}{4}\text{ in.}^2}$

20. **True**

21.
$$\begin{array}{r} \overset{1}{2}7 \\ +\ 25 \\ \hline 52 \end{array} \qquad \begin{array}{r} \mathbf{26} \\ 2\overline{)52} \\ 4 \\ \hline 12 \\ 12 \\ \hline 0 \end{array}$$

22.
$$\frac{22}{7} = 7\overline{)22.000}\ \text{with quotient } 3.142 \quad \rightarrow \mathbf{3.14}$$
$$\begin{array}{r} 21 \\ \hline 10 \\ 7 \\ \hline 30 \\ 28 \\ \hline 20 \\ 14 \\ \hline 6 \end{array}$$

23. $\frac{5}{\cancel{2}_1} \times \frac{\cancel{12}^6\text{ inches}}{1} = \frac{30}{1} = \textbf{30 inches}$

24. **C**

25. **See student work. Figure should have four sides and no more than two right angles.**

26. **One possibility:**

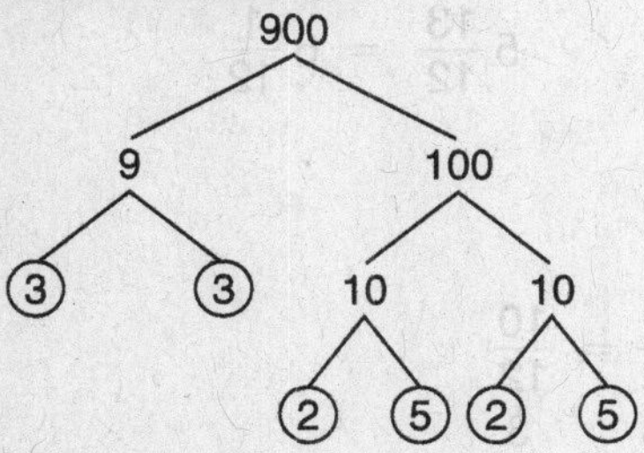

$\mathbf{2^2 \times 3^2 \times 5^2}$

27.

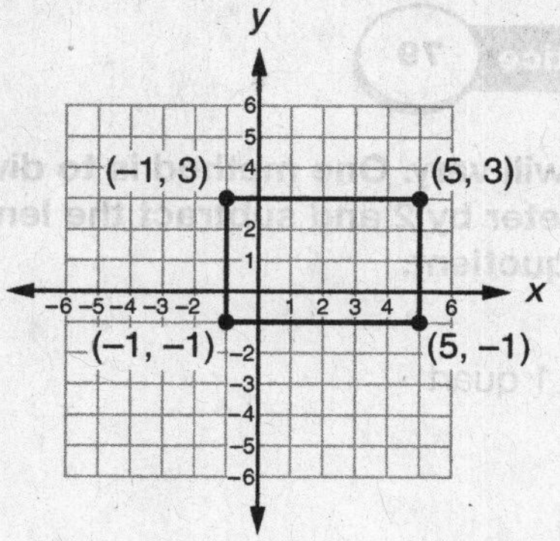

(−1, 3)

28. a. 3 teaspoons = 1 tablespoon

$\mathbf{\frac{1}{3}}$

b. 4 quarts = 1 gallon
4 quarts = 8 pints
8 pints = 16 cups
1 gallon = **16 cups**

29. **B. Quart**

30. 1 pint = 2 cups
2 cups = **16 ounces**
1 pint = **16 ounces**

Practice Set 79

a. $A = \frac{(10\text{ ft})(6\text{ ft})}{2}$

$A = \mathbf{30\ ft^2}$

b. $A = \frac{(8\text{ in.})(6\text{ in.})}{2}$

$A = \mathbf{24\ in.^2}$

c. $A = \frac{(56\text{ mm})(15\text{ mm})}{2}$

$A = \mathbf{420\ mm^2}$

d. $A = \frac{(5\text{ cm})(6\text{ cm})}{2}$

$A = \mathbf{15\ cm^2}$

e. $A = \frac{(30\text{ mm})(56\text{ mm})}{2}$

$A = 840\text{ mm}^2$

Yes, the area would be 840 mm², which is twice 420 mm².

Solutions

Written Practice 79

1. **Answers will vary. One method is to divide the perimeter by 2 and subtract the length from the quotient.**

2. 1 liter ⓪ 1 quart — 1 liter $\textcircled{>}$ 1 quart

3.
$$\begin{array}{r} \overset{1}{3}8 \\ +\ 33 \\ \hline \textbf{71} \end{array}$$
71 years old

4. a. **False**

   b. **True**

5. a. $\dfrac{\overset{9}{\cancel{90}}}{\underset{\underset{1}{\cancel{10}}}{\cancel{100}}} \cdot \dfrac{\overset{3}{\cancel{30}}}{1}$ students $= \dfrac{27}{1} =$ **27 trees**

   b. $\dfrac{27}{3} = \mathbf{\dfrac{9}{1}}$

6. a. $\dfrac{18}{24} = \mathbf{\dfrac{3}{4}}$

   b. $\dfrac{4}{4} - \dfrac{3}{4} = \mathbf{\dfrac{1}{4}}$

   c. $\dfrac{1}{4} \times \dfrac{25}{25} = \dfrac{25}{100} =$ **25%**

7. $A = 20\text{ mm} \times 12\text{ mm} = 240\text{ mm}^2$

$$\begin{array}{r} \mathbf{120\ mm^2} \\ 2\overline{)240\ mm^2} \\ \underline{2} \\ 04 \\ \underline{04} \\ 00 \\ \underline{00} \\ 0 \end{array}$$

8. $1000 \div 100 =$ **10**

9.
$$\begin{array}{r} {}_{1}\overset{1}{6}.42 \\ 12.7 \\ +\ \ 8 \\ \hline \mathbf{27.12} \end{array}$$

10.
$$\begin{array}{r} 1.2 \\ \times\ 0.12 \\ \hline 24 \\ \underline{120} \\ \mathbf{0.144} \end{array}$$

11.
$$\begin{array}{r} \mathbf{800} \\ 8\overline{)6400} \\ \underline{64} \\ 00 \\ \underline{00} \\ 00 \\ \underline{00} \\ 0 \end{array}$$

12. $\dfrac{\overset{\overset{1}{\cancel{2}}}{\cancel{10}}}{\underset{1}{\cancel{3}}} \times \dfrac{1}{\underset{1}{\cancel{5}}} \times \dfrac{\overset{1}{\cancel{3}}}{\underset{2}{\cancel{4}}} = \mathbf{\dfrac{1}{2}}$

13. $\dfrac{5}{2} \div \dfrac{3}{1}$

   $1 \div \dfrac{3}{1} = \dfrac{1}{3}$

   $\dfrac{5}{2} \times \dfrac{1}{3} = \mathbf{\dfrac{5}{6}}$

14.
$$\begin{array}{r} \overset{0}{\cancel{1}}\,\overset{9}{\cancel{0}}\,.\,\overset{9}{\cancel{0}}{}^{1}0 \\ -\quad 9\,.\,8\,7 \\ \hline 0\,.\,1\,3 \end{array}$$
$q =$ **0.13**

15.
$$\begin{array}{r} 0.012 \\ 24\overline{)0.288} \\ \underline{24} \\ 48 \\ \underline{48} \\ 0 \end{array}$$
$m =$ **0.012**

16.
$$\begin{array}{rcl} 2\dfrac{3}{4} \times \dfrac{3}{3} & = & 2\dfrac{9}{12} \\ +\ 3\dfrac{1}{3} \times \dfrac{4}{4} & = & 3\dfrac{4}{12} \\ \hline & & 5\dfrac{13}{12} = 6\dfrac{1}{12} \end{array}$$
$n = \mathbf{6\dfrac{1}{12}}$

17.
$$\begin{array}{rcl} \dfrac{5}{6} \times \dfrac{2}{2} & = & \dfrac{10}{12} \\ -\ \dfrac{1}{4} \times \dfrac{3}{3} & = & \dfrac{3}{12} \\ \hline & & \dfrac{7}{12} \end{array}$$
$w = \mathbf{\dfrac{7}{12}}$

18. $4\overline{)80\text{ cm}}$ = **20 cm**
8
00
00
0

$20\text{ cm} \times 20\text{ cm} =$ **400 sq. cm**

19. **96.03**

20. $C = \pi d$
$C \approx (3.14)(20\text{ cm})$
$C \approx$ **62.8 cm**

21. **B. 0.2**

22. $7 \times 7 =$ **49**
Round 6.7 to 7 and round 7.3 to 7. Then multiply 7 by 7.

23. $3 \cdot 3 \cdot 3 \cdot 3 =$ **81**

24. $0.3 + 0.2 = 0.5$

$2\overline{)0.50}$ = **0.25**
4
10
10
0

25. **10.2**

26. **Trapezoid**

27.

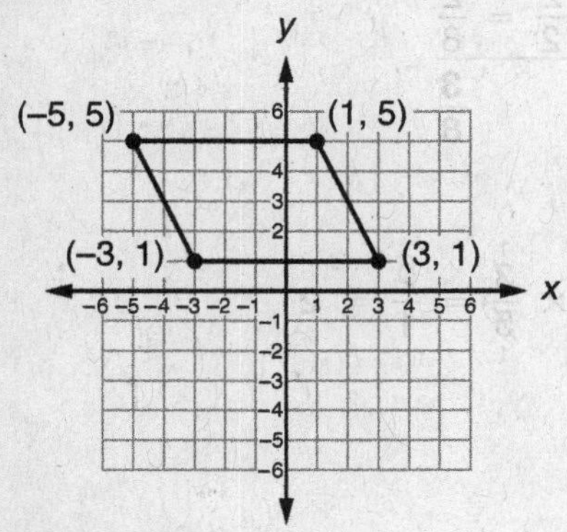

Parallelogram

28. a. $\sqrt{100\text{ cm}^2} =$ **10 cm**

b. $10\text{ cm} \times 4 =$ **40 cm**

29. a. **10 cm**

b. $10\text{ cm} \times 6 =$ **60 cm**

30. $\dfrac{\cancel{2}^{1} \cdot \cancel{2}^{1} \cdot \cancel{2}^{1} \cdot \cancel{2}^{1} \cdot 2}{\cancel{2}_{1} \cdot \cancel{2}_{1} \cdot \cancel{2}_{1} \cdot \cancel{2}_{1} \cdot 3} = \mathbf{\dfrac{2}{3}}$

Early Finishers Solutions

One gallon = 16 cups; Each day the children drink $(4 \times 4) + (4 \times 2) = 24$ cups of milk.
24 cups × 4 days = 96 cups of milk;
96 cups ÷ 16 cups per gallon = 6 gallons.

Practice Set 80

a.

	Ratio	Actual Count
Boys	6	*b*
Girls	5	60

$60 \div 5 = 12$
$6 \times 12 = 72$
72 boys

b.

	Ratio	Actual Count
Ants	8	*a*
Flies	3	24

$24 \div 3 = 8$
$8 \times 8 = 64$
64 ants

Written Practice 80

1. $96 + 49 + 68 + 75 = 288$

$4\overline{)288}$ = 72
28
08
08
0

Mean is **72**

$96 - 49 = 47$

Range is **47**

2. $\dfrac{5}{\cancel{2}_{1}} \cdot \dfrac{\cancel{5280}^{2640}\text{ ft}}{1} = \dfrac{13{,}200}{1} =$ **13,200 ft**

3. $12p = 168$

$$\begin{array}{r} \mathbf{14} \textbf{ players} \\ 12\overline{)168} \\ \underline{12} \\ 48 \\ \underline{48} \\ 0 \end{array}$$

4. **a.** 5 in. + 5 in. + 3 in. + 3 in. = **16 in.**

b. 3 in. × 4 in. = **12 in.²**

5. **a.** 3 in. + 4 in. + 5 in. = **12 in.**

b. $A = \frac{3 \text{ in.} \times 4 \text{ in.}}{2} = \frac{12 \text{ in.}^2}{2} = \mathbf{6 \text{ in.}^2}$

6. **Trapezoid**

7. **True**

8. $\frac{4}{\cancel{5}_1} \cdot \frac{\cancel{30}^{6} \text{ students}}{1} = \frac{24}{1}$

= 24 students were present

30 − 24 = **6 students were absent**

9.

	Ratio	Actual Count
Dogs	2	10
Cats	5	*c*

$$\begin{array}{r} 5 \\ 2\overline{)10} \\ \underline{10} \\ 0 \end{array}$$

5 × 5 = **25 cats**

10. **a.** $\frac{19}{20} \times \frac{5}{5} = \frac{95}{100} = \mathbf{95\%}$

b. $\frac{6}{10} \times \frac{10}{10} = \frac{60}{100} = \mathbf{60\%}$

11. **a.** $\frac{1}{4} \times \frac{25}{25} = \frac{25}{100} = \mathbf{25\%}$

b. $\frac{\text{side}}{\text{perimeter}} = \mathbf{\frac{1}{4}}$

$\frac{1}{4} \times \frac{25}{25} = \frac{25}{100} = \mathbf{25\%}$

12. **a.** $0.5 \text{ ⓒ} \frac{3}{4}$ (0.5 < 3/4, circled)

$$\begin{array}{r} 0.75 \\ 4\overline{)3.00} \\ \underline{2\,8} \\ 20 \\ \underline{20} \\ 0 \end{array}$$

b. 3 quarts < 1 gallon
4 quarts

13. $4\frac{4}{10} = \mathbf{4\frac{2}{5}}$

14.
$$\begin{array}{r} \mathbf{0.125} \\ 8\overline{)1.000} \\ \underline{8} \\ 20 \\ \underline{16} \\ 40 \\ \underline{40} \\ 0 \end{array}$$

15.
$$\begin{array}{r} \frac{5}{6} \times \frac{1}{1} = \frac{5}{6} \\ + \frac{1}{2} \times \frac{3}{3} = \frac{3}{6} \\ \hline \frac{8}{6} = 1\frac{2}{6} = \mathbf{1\frac{1}{3}} \end{array}$$

16.
$$\begin{array}{r} \frac{5}{8} \times \frac{1}{1} = \frac{5}{8} \\ - \frac{1}{4} \times \frac{2}{2} = \frac{2}{8} \\ \hline \mathbf{\frac{3}{8}} \end{array}$$

17. $\frac{\cancel{5}^1}{\cancel{2}_1} \times \frac{\cancel{4}^2}{\cancel{3}_1} \times \frac{\cancel{3}^1}{\cancel{5}_1} = \frac{2}{1} = \mathbf{2}$

18.
$$\begin{array}{r} \overset{3}{\cancel{4}}.{}^{1}0 \\ -\ 2.\ 6 \\ \hline 1.\ 4 \end{array}$$

$a = \mathbf{1.4}$

19. $\frac{3}{2} \div \frac{3}{1}$

$1 \div \frac{3}{1} = \frac{1}{3}$

$\frac{\overset{1}{\cancel{3}}}{2} \cdot \frac{1}{\underset{1}{\cancel{3}}} = \frac{1}{2}$

$n = \mathbf{\frac{1}{2}}$

20.
$$\begin{array}{r} 0.072 \\ 5\overline{)0.360} \\ \underline{35} \\ 10 \\ \underline{10} \\ 0 \end{array}$$

$x = \mathbf{0.072}$

21.
$$\begin{array}{r} 70 \\ 9\overline{)630} \\ \underline{63} \\ 00 \\ \underline{00} \\ 0 \end{array}$$

$y = \mathbf{70}$

22. 0.43

23. About 35 grams

24. 40 grams ÷ 2 = **about 20 grams**

25. Answers will vary. See student work. Sample answer: About how many grams of sugar, per 100 grams of cereal, does Oat Squares contain? About 10 grams

26. 1 quart = 2 pints
2 pints = 4 cups
1 quart = 4 cups
4 cups − 1 cup = **3 cups**

27.

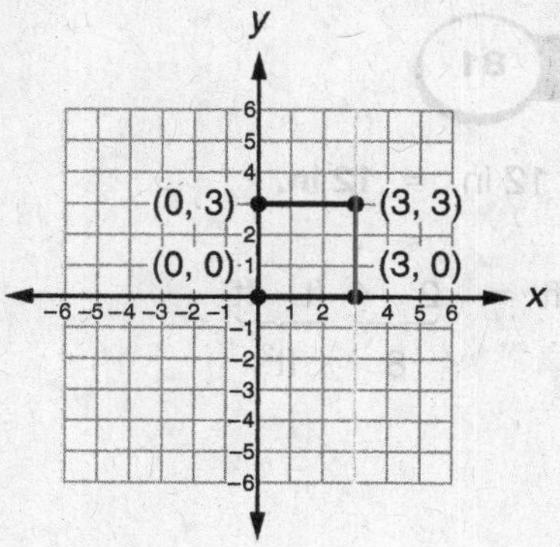

a. (0, 0)

b. 3 units × 3 units = **9 units^2**

28. 90° − 30° = 60°
A. ∠

29. $A = \frac{1}{2}(6)(8)$

$A = \frac{48}{2}$

$A = \mathbf{24}$

30. Possibilities include:

yes

Investigation 8

Activity 1. Answers will vary. See student work.

Activity 2. Answers will vary. See student work.

Activity 3. Answers will vary. See student work.

Solutions

Practice Set 81

a. 24 in. − 12 in. = **12 in.**

b. $2 \text{ ft} \times 4 \text{ ft} = \underbrace{2 \cdot 4}_{8}\ \underbrace{\text{ft} \cdot \text{ft}}_{\text{ft}^2}$

8 ft²

c. $\dfrac{\overset{4}{\cancel{12}}}{\underset{1}{\cancel{3}}}\ \dfrac{\cancel{\text{cm}} \cdot \text{cm}}{\cancel{\text{cm}}}$

4 cm

d. $\dfrac{\overset{60}{\cancel{300}}}{\underset{1}{\cancel{5}}}\ \dfrac{\text{mi}}{\text{hr}}$

$\mathbf{60\ \dfrac{mi}{hr}}$

Written Practice 81

1. 1 gallon = 4 quarts
2 gallons = 8 quarts
8 quarts − 2 quarts = **6 quarts**

2. 1 quart ⓧ 1 liter — 1 quart $<$ 1 liter
945 mL 1000 mL

3. $\dfrac{5}{2}\text{ inches} \cdot \dfrac{3}{1} = \dfrac{15}{2} = \mathbf{7\frac{1}{2}\ inches}$

4. $\dfrac{\overset{400}{\cancel{1200}}\text{ miles}}{\underset{1}{\cancel{3}}\text{ hours}} = \mathbf{400\ \dfrac{miles}{hour}}$

5. $\dfrac{2 \cdot \overset{1}{\cancel{3}} \cdot \overset{1}{\cancel{3}} \cdot \overset{1}{\cancel{3}}}{\underset{1}{\cancel{3}} \cdot \underset{1}{\cancel{3}} \cdot \underset{1}{\cancel{3}} \cdot 5} = \mathbf{\dfrac{2}{5}}$

6. $\dfrac{60}{100} = \mathbf{\dfrac{3}{5}}$

$\dfrac{3}{\underset{1}{\cancel{5}}} \cdot \dfrac{\overset{16}{\cancel{80}}}{1} = $ **48 points**

7.
$$\begin{array}{r} 25\text{ m} \\ \times\ 24\text{ m} \\ \hline 100 \\ 500 \\ \hline \mathbf{600\ m^2} \end{array}$$

8. 26 m + 26 m + 24 m + 24 m = **100 m**

9. **False**

10.

	Ratio	Actual Count
red	3	r
blue	4	24

$$\begin{array}{r} 6 \\ 4\overline{)24} \\ 24 \\ \hline 0 \end{array} \qquad 6 \times 3 = 18$$

18 red marbles

11. $\mathbf{\dfrac{1}{5},\ 0.4,\ \dfrac{1}{2}}$

12. a. $\dfrac{4}{25} \times \dfrac{4}{4} = \dfrac{16}{100} = \mathbf{0.16}$

b. **16%**

13.
$$\begin{array}{r} 9.9 \\ \times\ 0.1 \\ \hline \mathbf{0.99} \end{array}$$

14.
$$\begin{array}{r} \mathbf{1.7} \\ 2\overline{)3.4} \\ 2 \\ \hline 1\ 4 \\ 1\ 4 \\ \hline 0 \end{array}$$

15.
$$\begin{array}{r} \dfrac{5}{8} \times \dfrac{1}{1} = \dfrac{5}{8} \\ +\ \dfrac{3}{4} \times \dfrac{2}{2} = \dfrac{6}{8} \\ \hline \dfrac{11}{8} = \mathbf{1\frac{3}{8}} \end{array}$$

16.
$$\begin{array}{r} \dfrac{3}{1} \times \dfrac{8}{8} = \dfrac{24}{8} \\ -\ \dfrac{9}{8} \times \dfrac{1}{1} = \dfrac{9}{8} \\ \hline \dfrac{15}{8} = \mathbf{1\frac{7}{8}} \end{array}$$

17. $4\frac{1}{2} \times \frac{2}{2} = \overset{3}{\cancel{4}}\frac{\overset{6}{\cancel{2}}}{4}$

$-\ 1\frac{3}{4} \times \frac{1}{1} = 1\frac{3}{4}$

$\mathbf{2\frac{3}{4}}$

18. $\frac{\overset{1}{\cancel{5}}}{\underset{2}{\cancel{6}}} \cdot \frac{\overset{1}{\cancel{4}}}{\underset{1}{\cancel{5}}} \cdot \frac{\overset{1}{\cancel{3}}}{\underset{2}{\cancel{8}}} = \mathbf{\frac{1}{4}}$

19. $\frac{\overset{3}{\cancel{9}}}{\underset{1}{\cancel{2}}} \times \frac{\overset{2}{\cancel{4}}}{\underset{1}{\cancel{3}}} = \frac{6}{1} = \mathbf{6}$

20. $\frac{10}{3} \div \frac{5}{3}$

$1 \div \frac{5}{3} = \frac{3}{5}$

$\frac{\overset{2}{\cancel{10}}}{\underset{1}{\cancel{3}}} \cdot \frac{\overset{1}{\cancel{3}}}{\underset{1}{\cancel{5}}} = \frac{2}{1} = \mathbf{2}$

21.
```
   50 cm
4)200 cm
  20
   00
   00
    0
```

22. **a.** **50 cm**

b. $C = \pi d$
$C \approx (3.14)(50 \text{ cm})$
$C \approx$ **157 cm**

23.
```
   $12.80
 ×   0.06
  $0.7680  ⟶  77¢
```
(**77¢**)

24.
```
  10:40 a.m.
+  2:30
  12:70 p.m.
   1:10 p.m.
```
(**1:10 p.m.**)

25. $2\frac{10}{16}$ in. $=$ $\mathbf{2\frac{5}{8}}$ **in.**

26.

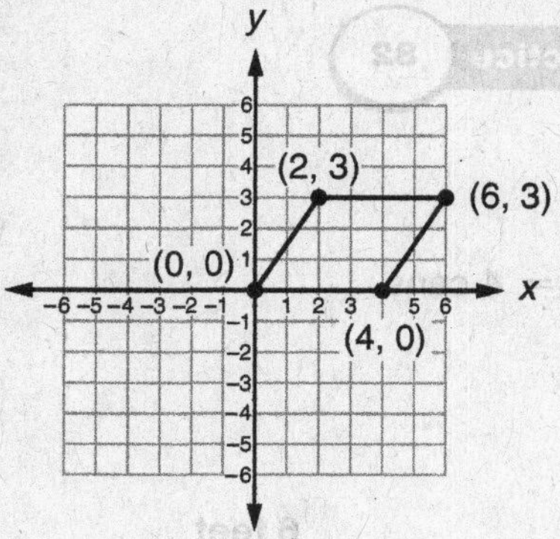

$A = bh$
$A = (4 \text{ units})(3 \text{ units})$
$A =$ **12 sq. units**

27. **Cone**

28. $\sqrt{1 \text{ sq. foot}} = 1 \text{ ft}$
$1 \text{ ft} \times 4 =$ **4 ft**

29. **a.** 2 yd + 1 yd = **3 yd**

b. 5 m · 3 m = **15 m²** ($\mathbf{15 \text{ m}^2}$)

c. $\frac{\overset{6}{\cancel{36}}}{\underset{1}{\cancel{6}}} \quad \frac{\cancel{\text{ft}} \times \text{ft}}{\cancel{\text{ft}}} =$ **6 ft**

d. $\frac{\overset{20}{\cancel{400}}}{\underset{1}{\cancel{20}}} \frac{\text{miles}}{\text{gallons}} = \mathbf{20 \frac{miles}{gallon}}$

30. One possibility:

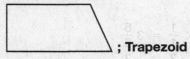

; **Trapezoid**

Practice Set 82

a. 4 × 4 = 16 cubes

16 × 4 = **64 cubes**

b. $V = lwh$
$V = (5 \text{ ft})(3 \text{ ft})(2 \text{ ft})$
$V =$ $\mathbf{30 \text{ ft}^3}$

c. 10 × 6 = **60 cubes**
60 × 4 = **240 cubes**

d. **B. Cubic feet**

Solutions

Written Practice 82

1. **21.05**

2. $12 \div 3 = 4$ cans
$$\begin{array}{r} \$2.49 \\ \times \quad 4 \\ \hline \mathbf{\$9.96} \end{array}$$

3. $$\begin{array}{r} 18 \text{ in.} \\ \times\ 4 \text{ in.} \\ \hline 72 \text{ inches} \end{array} \qquad \begin{array}{r} \textbf{6 feet} \\ 12\overline{)72} \\ \underline{72} \\ 0 \end{array}$$

4. a. **7%**

   b. $\frac{7}{10} \times \frac{10}{10} = \frac{70}{100} = \mathbf{70\%}$

5. $\frac{90}{100} = \mathbf{\frac{9}{10}}$
   0.9

6. $\frac{23}{50} \times \frac{2}{2} = \frac{46}{100} = \mathbf{46\%}$

7. $\frac{9}{25} \times \frac{4}{4} = \frac{36}{100} = \mathbf{36\%}$

8. **Rectangular prism**

9. $$\begin{array}{rcl} 3\frac{5}{6} \times \frac{1}{1} &=& 3\frac{5}{6} \\ +\ 2\frac{1}{3} \times \frac{2}{2} &=& 2\frac{2}{6} \\ \hline && 5\frac{7}{6} = 6\frac{1}{6} \end{array}$$
   $w = \mathbf{6\frac{1}{6}}$

10. $$\begin{array}{rcl} 3\frac{1}{4} \times \frac{2}{2} &=& \overset{2}{\cancel{3}}\frac{\overset{10}{\cancel{2}}}{8} \\ -\ 1\frac{5}{8} \times \frac{1}{1} &=& 1\frac{5}{8} \\ \hline && 1\frac{5}{8} \end{array}$$
   $y = \mathbf{1\frac{5}{8}}$

11. $$\begin{array}{r} 0.02 \\ 6\overline{)0.12} \\ \underline{12} \\ 0 \end{array}$$
   $n = \mathbf{0.02}$

12. $$\begin{array}{r} 50 \\ 12\overline{)600} \\ \underline{60\ } \\ 00 \\ \underline{00} \\ 0 \end{array}$$
   $m = \mathbf{50}$

13. $$\begin{array}{r} 20 \\ 5\overline{)100} \\ \underline{10\ } \\ 00 \\ \underline{00} \\ 0 \end{array}$$
   $n = \mathbf{20}$

14. $\frac{6}{1} \div \frac{3}{2}$

   $1 \div \frac{3}{2} = \frac{2}{3}$

   $\frac{\overset{2}{\cancel{6}}}{1} \cdot \frac{2}{\underset{1}{\cancel{3}}} = \frac{4}{1} = 4$

   $w = \mathbf{4}$

15. a. $\frac{6}{10} = \mathbf{\frac{3}{5}}$

   b. $\frac{3}{5} \times \frac{20}{20} = \frac{60}{100} = \mathbf{60\%}$

16. $0.5 + 1 + 0.25 = \mathbf{1.75}$

17. $$\begin{array}{rcl} \frac{1}{2} \times \frac{5}{5} &=& \frac{5}{10} \\ \frac{1}{5} \times \frac{2}{2} &=& \frac{2}{10} \\ +\ \frac{1}{10} \times \frac{1}{1} &=& \frac{1}{10} \\ \hline && \frac{8}{10} = \mathbf{\frac{4}{5}} \end{array}$$

18. $\frac{\overset{3}{\cancel{9}}}{\underset{1}{\cancel{5}}} \times \frac{\overset{1}{\cancel{5}}}{\underset{1}{\cancel{3}}} = \frac{3}{1} = \mathbf{3}$

19. **6**

20. $40 \times 40 =$ **1600**

21. a. $\frac{12}{36} = \mathbf{\frac{1}{3}}$

b. $\frac{12}{48} = \mathbf{\frac{1}{4}}$

$\frac{1}{4} \times \frac{25}{25} = \frac{25}{100}$

$= \mathbf{0.25}$

22.
$$\begin{array}{r} 25 \text{ mm} \\ \times\ 20 \text{ mm} \\ \hline \mathbf{500\ mm^2} \end{array}$$

23. $25 \text{ mm} + 25 \text{ mm} + 22 \text{ mm} + 22 \text{ mm}$
$=$ **94 mm**

24.

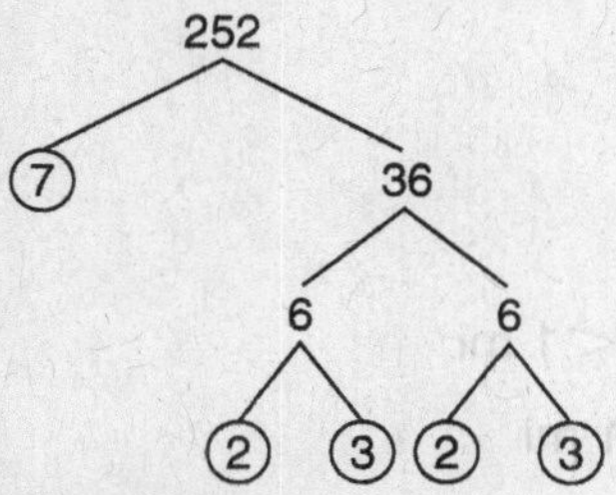

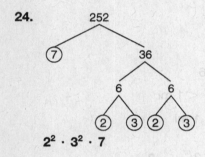

$\mathbf{2^2 \cdot 3^2 \cdot 7}$

25. **False. Quadrilaterals have four sides, but triangles have three sides.**

26.

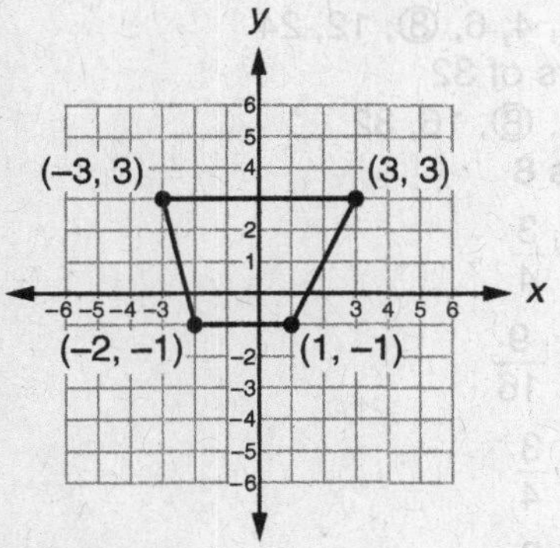

Trapezoid

27. $V = lwh$
$V = (2 \text{ in.})(2 \text{ in.})(2 \text{ in.})$
$V =$ **8 in.³**

28. a. 2 pints = 1 quart
3 quarts + 1 quart = **4 quarts**

b. $\frac{\overset{7}{\cancel{49}}\ \cancel{m} \cdot m}{\underset{1}{\cancel{7}}\ \cancel{m}} =$ **7 m**

c. $\frac{\overset{50}{\cancel{400}} \text{ miles}}{\underset{1}{\cancel{8}} \text{ hours}} = \mathbf{50 \frac{miles}{hour}}$

29. $\frac{3}{12} = \frac{1}{4} \times \frac{25}{25} = \frac{25}{100} =$ **25%**

30. 1 gallon = 4 quarts
4 quarts = 8 pints
1 gallon = 8 pints
About 8 pounds

Practice Set 83

a. **C.** $\mathbf{\frac{15}{6}}$

b. $\mathbf{\frac{6}{8} = \frac{9}{12}}$

c. $\mathbf{\frac{4}{3} = \frac{12}{n}}$

$\frac{4}{3} \times \frac{3}{3} = \frac{12}{9}$

$n =$ **9; Possible answer: I copied the proportion the way it was described and found that 4 × 3 = 12, so I multiplied $\frac{4}{3}$ by $\frac{3}{3}$ to complete the proportion.**

d. $\mathbf{\frac{6}{9} = \frac{n}{36}}$

$\frac{6}{9} \times \frac{4}{4} = \frac{24}{36}$

$n =$ **24; Possible answer: Ratios are equal if they reduce to the same ratio. Both $\frac{6}{9}$ and $\frac{24}{36}$ reduce to $\frac{2}{3}$ so they are equal.**

Written Practice 83

1. $(0.2 + 0.2) \times (0.2 - 0.2)$
$(0.4) \times (0)$
0

2. $\frac{3}{2} \times \frac{3}{1} = \frac{9}{2} =$ **$4\frac{1}{2}$ miles per hour**

Solutions

3.
$$\begin{array}{r} 4{:}45 \text{ p.m.} \\ -\ 1{:}45 \text{ p.m.} \\ \hline 3{:}00 \end{array} \qquad \begin{array}{r} \$4 \text{ per hour} \\ \times\ \ 3 \text{ hours} \\ \hline \mathbf{\$12} \end{array}$$
3 hours

4. $\frac{55}{100} = \mathbf{\frac{11}{20}}$

5. **a.** **9%**

b. $\frac{9}{10} \times \frac{10}{10} = \frac{90}{100} = \mathbf{90\%}$

6. **100%**

7. **a.** $\frac{10}{100} = \mathbf{\frac{1}{10}}$

b. $\frac{10}{100} = \mathbf{10\%}$

8. **a.** $\frac{48}{100} = \mathbf{\frac{12}{25}}$

b. $\frac{48}{100} = \mathbf{48\%}$

9.
$$\begin{array}{r} \mathbf{0.875} \\ 8\overline{)7.000} \\ 6\,4 \\ \hline 60 \\ 56 \\ \hline 40 \\ 40 \\ \hline 0 \end{array}$$

10.
$$\begin{array}{r} 1\frac{1}{3} \times \frac{2}{2} = 1\frac{2}{6} \\ +\ 1\frac{1}{6} \times \frac{1}{1} = 1\frac{1}{6} \\ \hline 2\frac{3}{6} = 2\frac{1}{2} \end{array}$$

$$\begin{array}{r} 2\frac{1}{2} \times \frac{3}{3} = \overset{1}{\cancel{2}}\frac{\overset{9}{\cancel{3}}}{6} \\ -\ 1\frac{2}{3} \times \frac{2}{2} = 1\frac{4}{6} \\ \hline \mathbf{\frac{5}{6}} \end{array}$$

11. $\frac{\overset{1}{\cancel{3}}}{\underset{1}{\cancel{2}}} \cdot \frac{\overset{1}{\cancel{3}}}{1} \cdot \frac{\overset{5}{\cancel{10}}}{\underset{1}{\cancel{\underset{\cancel{3}}{\cancel{9}}}}} = \frac{5}{1} = \mathbf{5}$

12. $\frac{14}{3} \div \frac{7}{6}$

$1 \div \frac{7}{6} = \frac{6}{7}$

$\frac{\overset{2}{\cancel{14}}}{\underset{1}{\cancel{3}}} \cdot \frac{\overset{2}{\cancel{6}}}{\underset{1}{\cancel{7}}} = \frac{4}{1} = \mathbf{4}$

13. $0.1 + 0.99$
1.09

14. $\mathbf{\frac{3}{4} = \frac{9}{n}}$

$\frac{3}{4} \times \frac{3}{3} = \frac{9}{12}$

$n = 12$

15. **C.** $\mathbf{\frac{12}{20}}$

16. **80,420**

17. **a.** 2^4 ⊜ 4^2
16   16

b. 1 km **<** 1 mi

0.621 mi 1 mi

18. $\frac{\overset{1}{\cancel{2}} \cdot \overset{1}{\cancel{2}} \cdot \overset{1}{\cancel{2}} \cdot 3}{\underset{1}{\cancel{2}} \cdot \underset{1}{\cancel{2}} \cdot \underset{1}{\cancel{2}} \cdot 2 \cdot 2} = \mathbf{\frac{3}{4}}$

19. **a.** Factors of 24
1, 2, 3, 4, 6, ⑧, 12, 24
Factors of 32
1, 2, 4, ⑧, 16, 32
GCF is **8**

b. $\frac{24}{32} = \frac{3}{4}$

$\frac{9}{16} = \frac{9}{16}$

$\frac{9}{12} = \frac{3}{4}$

$\frac{12}{18} = \frac{2}{3}$

$\mathbf{\frac{24}{32}}$ **and** $\mathbf{\frac{9}{12}}$

20. $C = \pi d$
$C \approx (3.14)(4 \text{ ft})$
$C \approx 12.56$ ft.
C. $\mathbf{12\frac{1}{2}}$ **ft.**

21. 10 mm + 13 mm + 20 mm + 13 mm
= **56 mm**

22. 3.1 cm ≈ 3 cm
$V = lwh$
$V = (3 \text{ cm})(3 \text{ cm})(3 \text{ cm})$
$V = 27 \text{ cm}^3$
about 27 cm³

23. a. $A = bh$
$A = (6 \text{ in.})(4 \text{ in.})$
$A = \mathbf{24 \text{ in.}^2}$

b. $24 \text{ in.}^2 \div 2 = \mathbf{12 \text{ in.}^2}$

24. $\frac{1}{\cancel{4}_1} \cdot \frac{\cancel{120}^{30}}{1} = 30$ students took wood shop

$$\begin{array}{r} 120 \\ -\ 30 \\ \hline 90 \end{array}$$ **students did not take wood shop**

25. 2.5 × 10 millimeters = **25 millimeters**

26. a. Pyramid

b.

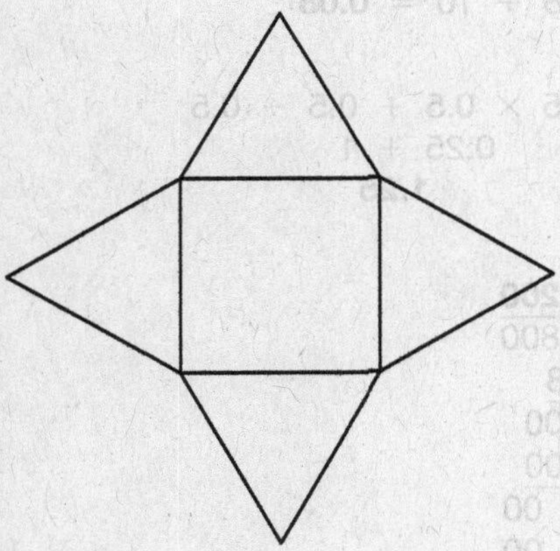

27. a. 1 quart = 2 pints
3 quarts = 6 pints
6 pints + 2 pints = **8 pints**

b. $\frac{\cancel{64}^{8} \cancel{\text{cm}} \cdot \text{cm}}{\cancel{8}_1 \cancel{\text{cm}}} = \mathbf{8 \text{ cm}}$

c. $\frac{\cancel{60}^{20} \text{ students}}{\cancel{3}_1 \text{ teachers}} =$ **20 students per teacher**

28. $\frac{20}{25} \times \frac{4}{4} = \frac{80}{100} = \mathbf{80\%}$

29. One possibility:

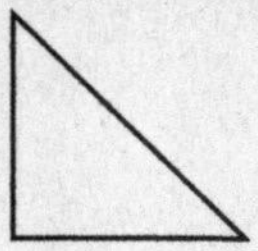

30. a.
$$\begin{array}{r} \mathbf{15} \text{ nickels} \\ 5\overline{)75} \\ \underline{5} \\ 25 \\ \underline{25} \\ 0 \end{array}$$

b. $\frac{2}{3} = \frac{d}{15}$
$\frac{2}{3} \times \frac{5}{5} = \frac{10}{15}$
10 dimes

c.
$$\begin{array}{r} \$0.75 \\ +\ \$1.00 \\ \hline \mathbf{\$1.75} \end{array}$$

Early Finishers Solutions

∠*ABF*	45°; acute	∠*ABE*	90°; right
∠*ABD*	165°; obtuse	∠*ABC*	180°; straight
∠*FBE*	45°; acute	∠*FBD*	120°; obtuse
∠*CBD*	15°; acute	∠*CBE*	90°; right
∠*CBF*	135°; obtuse	∠*DBE*	75°; acute

Practice Set 84

a. 5 + 5 × 5 − 5 ÷ 5
5 + 25 − 1 = **29**

b. 32 + 1.8(20)
32 + 36 = **68**

c. 5 + 4 × 3 ÷ 2 − 1
5 + 12 ÷ 2 − 1
5 + 6 − 1 = **10**

d. 2(10) + 2(6)
20 + 12 = **32**

e. 3 + 3 × 3 − 3 ÷ 3
3 + 9 − 1 = **11**

f. 2(10 + 6)
2(16) = **32**

Solutions

Written Practice 84

1. $\dfrac{\text{Prime numbers}}{\text{Composite numbers}} = \mathbf{\dfrac{4}{5}}$

2. 1 gallon = 4 quarts
   4 quarts = 8 pints
   8 pints = 16 cups
   $\frac{1}{2}$ gallon = 8 cups
   8 cups − 4 cups = **4 cups**

3. 6 + 6 × 6 − 6 ÷ 6
   6 + 36 − 1 = **41**

4. $\dfrac{30}{100} = \mathbf{\dfrac{3}{10}}$**; 0.3**

5. $A = \dfrac{9\text{ cm} \times 4\text{ cm}}{2}$
   $A = \dfrac{36\text{ cm}^2}{2}$
   $A = \mathbf{18\text{ cm}^2}$

6. $A = \dfrac{6\text{ cm} \times 6\text{ cm}}{2}$
   $A = \dfrac{36\text{ cm}^2}{2}$
   $A = \mathbf{18\text{ cm}^2}$

7. **a.** $\dfrac{1}{20} \times \dfrac{5}{5} = \dfrac{5}{100} = \mathbf{0.05}$
   b. 5%

8. **True**

9. $A = 16\text{ cm} \times 24\text{ cm}$
   $A = \mathbf{384\text{ cm}^2}$

10. 16 cm + 16 cm + 25 cm + 25 cm = **82 cm**

11. $3\frac{1}{8} \times \frac{1}{1} = 3\frac{1}{8}$
    $+\ 2\frac{1}{4} \times \frac{2}{2} = 2\frac{2}{8}$
    $= 5\frac{3}{8}$

    $5\frac{3}{8} \times \frac{1}{1} = \cancel{5}^{4}\,\frac{\cancel{3}^{11}}{8}$
    $-\ 1\frac{1}{2} \times \frac{4}{4} = 1\frac{4}{8}$
    $\mathbf{3\frac{7}{8}}$

12. $\dfrac{5}{\cancel{6}_{3}} \times \dfrac{\cancel{8}^{4}}{\cancel{3}_{1}} \times \dfrac{\cancel{3}^{1}}{1} = \dfrac{20}{3} = \mathbf{6\dfrac{2}{3}}$

13. $\dfrac{25}{3} \div \dfrac{100}{1}$
    $\dfrac{1}{1} \div \dfrac{100}{1} = \dfrac{1}{100}$
    $\dfrac{\cancel{25}^{1}}{3} \times \dfrac{1}{\cancel{100}_{4}} = \mathbf{\dfrac{1}{12}}$

14. 0.8 ÷ 10 = **0.08**

15. 0.5 × 0.5 + 0.5 ÷ 0.5
    0.25 + 1
    1.25

16. **200**
    4)800
    8
    00
    00
    00
    00
    0

17. **4**

18. **The mixed number $5\frac{1}{8}$ is more than 5 but less than 6. Since $\frac{1}{8}$ is less than $\frac{1}{2}$, $5\frac{1}{8}$ is closer to 5 than to 6. Thus $5\frac{1}{8}$ rounds to 5.**

19.

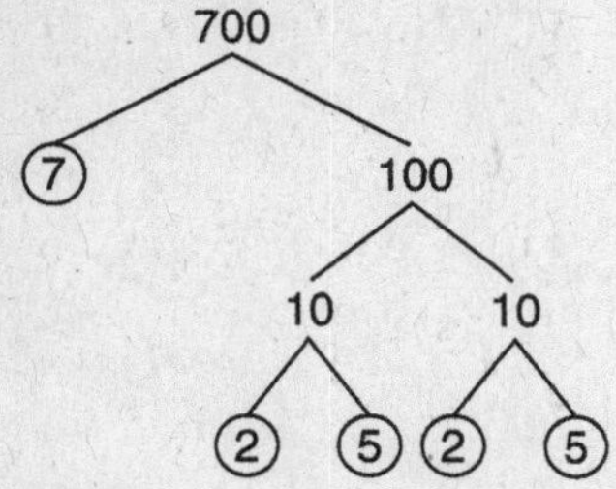

$2^2 \cdot 5^2 \cdot 7$

20. $\frac{15}{12} = \frac{5}{4}$

$\frac{15}{9} = \frac{5}{3}$

$\frac{25}{10} = \frac{5}{2}$

$\frac{35}{21} = \frac{5}{3}$

$\mathbf{\frac{15}{9}}$ **and** $\mathbf{\frac{35}{21}}$

21.
$$\begin{array}{r} \mathbf{25\ cm} \\ 4\overline{)100\ cm} \\ \underline{8\ \ } \\ 20 \\ \underline{20} \\ 0 \end{array}$$

22. a. $\frac{9}{45} = \mathbf{\frac{1}{5}}$

b. $\frac{1}{5} \times \frac{20}{20} = \frac{20}{100} = \mathbf{20\%}$

23.
$$\begin{array}{r} \overset{1}{9}\text{:30 p.m.} \\ \underline{+\ 5\text{:30}\ \ \ \ \ \ \ } \\ 15\text{:00}\ \ \ \ \ \ \ \end{array}$$
3:00 a.m.

24. $\frac{6}{4} = \frac{n}{8}$

$\frac{6}{4} \times \frac{2}{2} = \frac{12}{8}$

$n = \mathbf{12}$

25. **m∠A = 70°**
m∠B = 180° − 70° = **110°**
m∠C = m∠A = 70°
m∠D = m∠B = 110°

26. 40 × 1 cm^3 = **40 cm^3**

27. 24 in. + 24 in. = **48 in.**

28. a. $\frac{\overset{10}{\cancel{100}}}{\underset{1}{\cancel{10}}}\ \frac{\cancel{cm} \cdot cm}{\cancel{cm}} = \mathbf{10\ cm}$

b. $\frac{\overset{45}{\cancel{180}}}{\underset{1}{\cancel{4}}}\ \frac{\text{pages}}{\text{days}} = \textbf{45 pages per day}$

29.

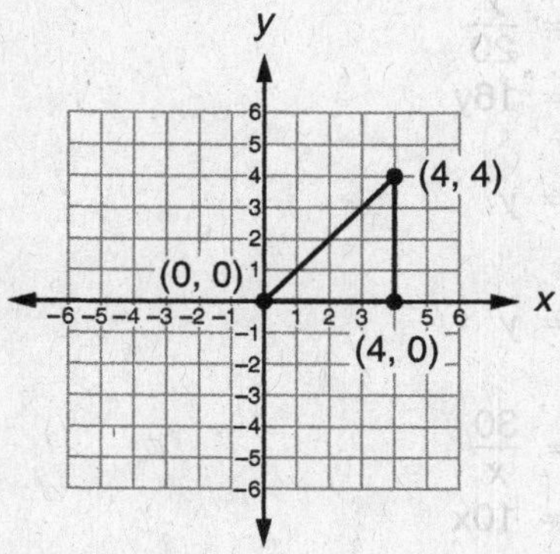

a. 6 full squares

b. 4 half squares

30.
$$\begin{array}{r} \overset{1}{\cancel{2}}{}^{1}4 \\ \underline{-\ 1\ 6} \\ 8\ \text{fiction} \end{array}$$

$\frac{\text{fiction}}{\text{non-fiction}} = \frac{8}{16} = \mathbf{\frac{1}{2}}$

<u>Early Finishers Solutions</u>

$A = \frac{1}{2}bh$; Area of the land she owns now:
$\frac{1}{2}(16\text{ km})(12\text{ km}) = 96\text{ km}^2$
Area of the land she hopes to buy:
$\frac{1}{2}(10\text{ km})(12\text{ km}) = 60\text{ km}^2$

Practice Set 85

a.

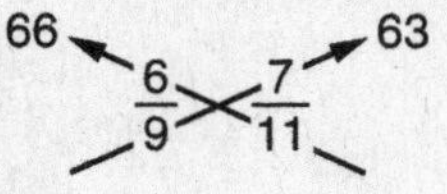

No

b.

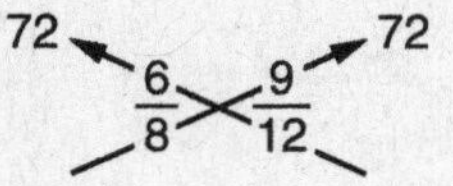

Yes

c. $\dfrac{6}{10} = \dfrac{9}{x}$

$9 \cdot 10 = 6x$

$\dfrac{\overset{3}{\cancel{9}} \cdot \overset{5}{\cancel{10}}}{\underset{\underset{1}{\cancel{2}}}{\cancel{6}}} = x$

$\mathbf{15} = x$

d. $\dfrac{12}{16} = \dfrac{y}{20}$

$12 \cdot 20 = 16y$

$\dfrac{\overset{3}{\cancel{12}} \cdot \overset{5}{\cancel{20}}}{\underset{\underset{1}{\cancel{4}}}{\cancel{16}}} = y$

$\mathbf{15} = y$

e. $\dfrac{10}{15} = \dfrac{30}{x}$

$15 \cdot 30 = 10x$

$\dfrac{\overset{3}{\cancel{15}} \cdot \overset{15}{\cancel{30}}}{\underset{\underset{1}{\cancel{2}}}{\cancel{10}}} = x$

$\mathbf{45} = x$

Written Practice 85

1. $\dfrac{21}{25} \times \dfrac{4}{4} = \dfrac{84}{100} =$ **84%**

2. 17°F − (−6°F)

$$\begin{array}{r} \overset{1}{1}7°F \\ +\ 6°F \\ \hline \mathbf{23°F} \end{array}$$

3.

$$\begin{array}{r} \$1.50 \\ +\ \$4.00 \\ \hline \mathbf{\$5.50} \end{array}$$

4. $\dfrac{5}{7} = \dfrac{350}{x}$

$7 \cdot 350 = 5x$

$\dfrac{7 \cdot \overset{70}{\cancel{350}}}{\underset{1}{\cancel{5}}} = x$

490 walkers

5. 90° − 55° = **35°**

6. a.

$$\begin{array}{r} \$55 \\ \times\ 0.20 \\ \hline \mathbf{\$11.00} \end{array}$$

b.

$$\begin{array}{r} \$55 \\ -\ \$11 \\ \hline \mathbf{\$44} \end{array}$$

7. a.

$$\begin{array}{r} \$39.60 \\ \times\ 0.08 \\ \hline \$3.1680 \end{array}$$

$3.17

b.

$$\begin{array}{r} \$\overset{1}{3}9.60 \\ +\ \$\ 3.17 \\ \hline \mathbf{\$42.77} \end{array}$$

8. a. $\dfrac{1}{25} \times \dfrac{4}{4} = \dfrac{4}{100}$ **0.04**

b. **4%**

9. 65 ← $\dfrac{5}{11}$ ╳ $\dfrac{6}{13}$ → 66

No

10. $\dfrac{\mathbf{4}}{\mathbf{6}} = \dfrac{\mathbf{10}}{\boldsymbol{w}}$

$6 \cdot 10 = 4w$

$\dfrac{\overset{3}{\cancel{6}} \cdot \overset{5}{\cancel{10}}}{\underset{\underset{1}{\cancel{2}}}{\cancel{4}}} = w$

15 = *w*; One possibility: I multiplied 4 times *w* and 6 times 10, which equals 60. Then I divided both sides by 4. 60 divided by 4 equals 15, so *w* equals 15.

11. $\dfrac{10}{1} \div \dfrac{5}{2}$

$1 \div \dfrac{5}{2} = \dfrac{2}{5}$

$\dfrac{\overset{2}{\cancel{10}}}{1} \cdot \dfrac{2}{\underset{1}{\cancel{5}}} = \dfrac{4}{1} = \mathbf{4}$

12. 6.5 − 3.68

2.82

13.
$$\begin{array}{r} 6.25 \\ \times \quad 1.6 \\ \hline 3750 \\ 6250 \\ \hline 10.000 \end{array}$$
10

14.
$$\begin{array}{r} \mathbf{0.005} \\ 12\overline{)0.060} \\ \underline{60} \\ 0 \end{array}$$

15.
$$\begin{array}{rcl} 3\frac{1}{4} \times \frac{1}{1} & = & \overset{2}{\cancel{3}}\,\frac{\overset{5}{\cancel{1}}}{4} \\ -\ 2\frac{1}{2} \times \frac{2}{2} & = & 2\frac{2}{4} \\ \hline & & \frac{3}{4} \end{array}$$
$x = \mathbf{\frac{3}{4}}$

16.
$$\begin{array}{rcl} 4\frac{1}{8} \times \frac{1}{1} & = & \overset{3}{\cancel{4}}\,\frac{\overset{9}{\cancel{1}}}{8} \\ -\ 1\frac{1}{2} \times \frac{4}{4} & = & 1\frac{4}{8} \\ \hline & & 2\frac{5}{8} \end{array}$$
$y = \mathbf{2\frac{5}{8}}$

17.
$$\frac{9}{12} = \frac{n}{20}$$
$$9 \cdot 20 = 12n$$
$$\frac{\overset{3}{\cancel{9}} \cdot \overset{5}{\cancel{20}}}{\underset{1}{\cancel{\cancel{12}}}} = n$$
$$\mathbf{15} = n$$

18. **30%, 0.4, $\mathbf{\frac{1}{2}}$**

19. $\frac{300}{15} = \mathbf{\frac{20}{1}}$

20. **The probability of rolling a 4 or a 6 is $\frac{2}{6}$ or $\frac{1}{3}$.**

21. $\frac{1}{\underset{1}{\cancel{4}}} \cdot \frac{\overset{8}{\cancel{32}}}{1} = 8$ have pets

$$\begin{array}{r} \overset{2}{\cancel{3}}{}^{1}2 \\ -\ \ 8 \\ \hline \end{array}$$
2 4 do not have pets

22.

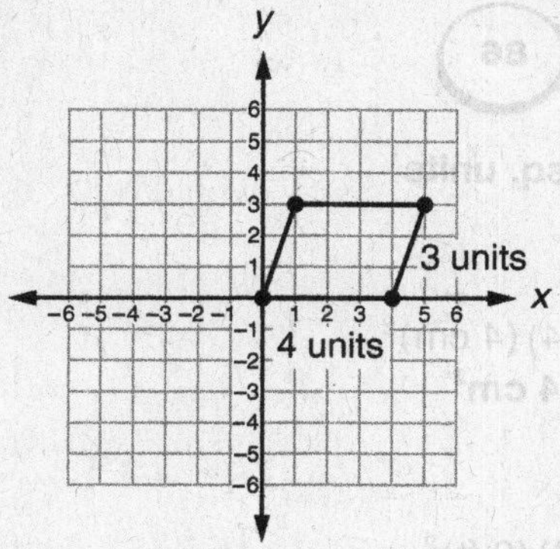

4 units × 3 units = **12 sq. units**

23. $2 + 2 \times 2 - 2 \div 2$
$2 + 4 - 1 = \mathbf{5}$

24.
$$\begin{array}{r} \overset{8\,:\,69}{\cancel{9}\text{:}0\cancel{9}} \text{ a.m.} \\ -\ \ 8\text{:}22 \text{ a.m.} \\ \hline \mathbf{47 \text{ min.}} \end{array}$$

25. $10 \times 0.621 = 6.21 \rightarrow$ **6 miles**

26. **a.** $4 \times 5 =$ **20 boxes**

b. $4 \times 5 \times 3 =$ **60 boxes**

27. **a.** 2 ft + 2 ft = **4 ft**

b. 3 yd · 3 yd = **9 yd^2**

28. 1 gallon = 4 quarts
$\frac{1}{4} \times \frac{25}{25} = \frac{25}{100} =$ **25%**

29. **a.** 10 cm × 10 cm = **100 cm^2**

b. 100 cm^2 ÷ 2 = **50 cm^2**

30. **A guess might be about 75 cm^2. Students will learn to calculate the area of a circle in Lesson 86.**

Early Finishers Solutions

$50\frac{1}{4} - 26\frac{1}{4} = 24$ ounces given to the neighbors;
$24 \div 2 = 12$ ounces of syrup

Solutions

Practice Set 86

a. **About 50 sq. units**

b.
$A = \pi r^2$
$A \approx (3.14)(4\text{ cm})^2$
$A \approx \mathbf{50.24\ cm^2}$

c.
$A = \pi r^2$
$A \approx (3.14)(2\text{ ft})^2$
$A \approx \mathbf{12.56\ ft^2}$

d.
$A = \pi r^2$
$A \approx (3.14)(1\text{ ft})^2$
$A \approx \mathbf{3.14\ ft^2}$

e.
$A = \pi r^2$
$A \approx (3.14)(5\text{ in.})^2$
$A \approx \mathbf{78.5\ in.^2}$

Written Practice 86

1.
$$\begin{array}{r} 265 \\ 4\overline{)1060} \\ \underline{8} \\ 26 \\ \underline{24} \\ 20 \\ \underline{20} \\ 0 \end{array}$$

2.
$$\begin{array}{rl} \overset{12:75}{\cancel{1}:\cancel{15}} & \text{p.m.} \\ -\ 3:00 & \\ \hline 9:75 & \text{a.m.} \end{array}$$
10:15 a.m.

3.
$$\begin{array}{r} 12 \\ \times\ \$0.75 \\ \hline 60 \\ \underline{840} \\ \$9.00 \end{array} \qquad \begin{array}{r} \$10.00 \\ -\ \ \$9.00 \\ \hline \mathbf{\$1.00} \end{array}$$

4.
$32 + 1.8(50)$
$32 + \quad 90$
122

5. **16 in.^{3}**

6.
$$\frac{5}{2} = \frac{600}{n}$$
$$2 \cdot 600 = 5n$$
$$\frac{2 \cdot \overset{120}{\cancel{600}}}{\underset{1}{\cancel{5}}} = n$$
240 paperbacks

7. $\dfrac{3}{20} \times \dfrac{5}{5} = \dfrac{15}{100} = \mathbf{15\%}$

8.
$$\begin{array}{r} 0.015 \\ \times\ \$2000 \\ \hline \$30.000 \end{array}$$
$30

9. **a.** $\dfrac{4}{5} \times \dfrac{20}{20} = \dfrac{80}{100} = \mathbf{0.8}$

b. **80%**

10. $\mathbf{\dfrac{1}{4}}$

11.
$$\begin{array}{rcl} 5\frac{1}{2} \times \frac{4}{4} & = & 5\frac{4}{8} \\ +\ 3\frac{7}{8} \times \frac{1}{1} & = & 3\frac{7}{8} \\ \hline & & 8\frac{11}{8} = \mathbf{9\frac{3}{8}} \end{array}$$

12.
$$\begin{array}{rcl} 3\frac{1}{4} \times \frac{2}{2} & = & \overset{2}{\cancel{3}}\frac{\overset{10}{\cancel{2}}}{8} \\ -\ \frac{5}{8} \times \frac{1}{1} & = & \frac{5}{8} \\ \hline & & \mathbf{2\frac{5}{8}} \end{array}$$

13. $\dfrac{\overset{3}{\cancel{9}}}{\underset{1}{\cancel{2}}} \cdot \dfrac{\overset{1}{\cancel{2}}}{\underset{1}{\cancel{3}}} = \dfrac{3}{1} = \mathbf{3}$

14.
$$\frac{25}{2} \div \frac{100}{1}$$
$$1 \div \frac{100}{1} = \frac{1}{100}$$
$$\frac{\overset{1}{\cancel{25}}}{2} \cdot \frac{1}{\underset{4}{\cancel{100}}} = \mathbf{\frac{1}{8}}$$

15. $\frac{5}{1} \div \frac{3}{2}$

$1 \div \frac{3}{2} = \frac{2}{3}$

$\frac{5}{1} \cdot \frac{2}{3} = \frac{10}{3} = \mathbf{3\frac{1}{3}}$

16. $\frac{5}{\not{6}_1} \cdot \frac{\not{30}^5}{1} = \frac{25}{1} = \mathbf{\$25}$

17. $16.72 + n = 50.4$

$$\begin{array}{r} 50.40 \\ -\ 16.72 \\ \hline 33.68 \end{array}$$

$n = \mathbf{33.68}$

18.

$$\begin{array}{r} \$10.00 \\ -\ \$\ 9.87 \\ \hline \$\ 0.13 \end{array}$$

$m = \mathbf{\$0.13}$

19.

$$\begin{array}{r} 0.16 \\ 3\overline{)0.48} \\ 3 \\ \hline 18 \\ 18 \\ \hline 0 \end{array}$$

$n = \mathbf{0.16}$

20. $\frac{w}{8} = \frac{25}{20}$

$25 \cdot 8 = 20w$

$\frac{\not{25}^5 \cdot \not{8}^2}{\not{20}_{\not{4}_1}} = w$

$\mathbf{10} = w$

21. **121, 144, 169**

22. **a.** $A = 15 \text{ cm} \times 10 \text{ cm}$

$A = \mathbf{150\ cm^2}$

b.

$$\begin{array}{r} \mathbf{75\ cm^2} \\ 2\overline{)150\ cm^2} \\ 14 \\ \hline 10 \\ 10 \\ \hline 0 \end{array}$$

23. $A = \pi r^2$

$A \approx (3.14)(10 \text{ cm})^2$

$A \approx \mathbf{314\ cm^2}$

24. **B. Square feet**

25. $\frac{7}{12} = \frac{7}{12}$

$\frac{8}{14} = \frac{4}{7}$

$\frac{12}{21} = \frac{4}{7}$

$\frac{20}{36} = \frac{5}{9}$

$\frac{8}{14}$ and $\frac{12}{21}$; Both ratios reduce to the same fraction, or the cross products are equal.

26. $C = \pi d$

$\frac{C}{\pi} = d;\ \pi \approx 3.14 \approx 3$

$\frac{12 \text{ feet}}{3} = 4 \text{ feet}$

B. 4 feet

27.

$$\begin{array}{r} \mathbf{58\ mph} \\ 6\text{ hours}\overline{)348\text{ miles}} \\ 30 \\ \hline 48 \\ 48 \\ \hline 0 \end{array}$$

28. **m∠*Y* = 180° − 110° = 70°**

m∠*Z* = 110°

29. $C = \pi d$

$C \approx (3.14)(10 \text{ in.})$

$C \approx 31.4$

$C \approx$ **31 inches**

30.

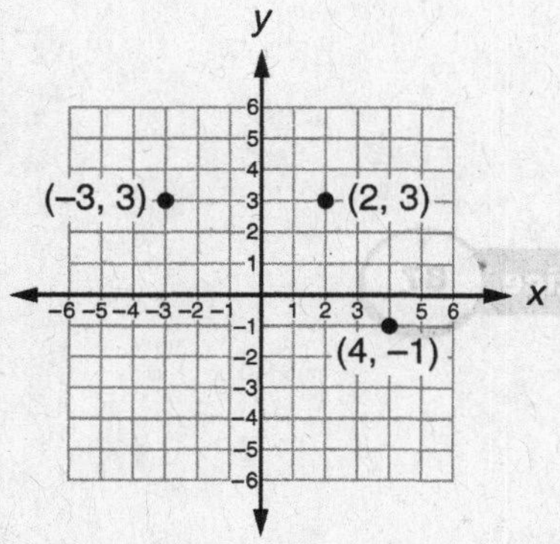

(−1, −1) or (−5, 7) or (9, −1)

Solutions

Early Finishers Solutions

$\frac{3 \text{ pounds}}{6 \text{ feet}} = \frac{4 \text{ pounds}}{x \text{ feet}}$; $3x = 24$; $x = 8$ feet

Practice Set 87

a. $6\overline{)21}$ with quotient $3\frac{3}{6} = 3\frac{1}{2}$

$$\begin{array}{r} 21 \\ \underline{18} \\ 3 \end{array}$$

$w = \mathbf{3\frac{1}{2}}$

b. $3\overline{)50}$ with quotient $16\frac{2}{3}$ $\quad f = \mathbf{16\frac{2}{3}}$

$$\begin{array}{r} 50 \\ \underline{3} \\ 20 \\ \underline{18} \\ 2 \end{array}$$

c. $5\overline{)36}$ with quotient $7\frac{1}{5}$ $\quad n = \mathbf{7\frac{1}{5}}$

$$\begin{array}{r} 36 \\ \underline{35} \\ 1 \end{array}$$

d. $3\overline{)2.4}$ with quotient 0.8 $\quad t = \mathbf{0.8}$

$$\begin{array}{r} 2.4 \\ \underline{2\,4} \\ 0 \end{array}$$

e. $8\overline{)3.2}$ with quotient 0.4 $\quad m = \mathbf{0.4}$

$$\begin{array}{r} 3.2 \\ \underline{3\,2} \\ 0 \end{array}$$

f. $5\overline{)8.0}$ with quotient 1.6 $\quad x = \mathbf{1.6}$

$$\begin{array}{r} 8.0 \\ \underline{5} \\ 3\,0 \\ \underline{3\,0} \\ 0 \end{array}$$

Written Practice 87

1.
$$\begin{array}{r} 12 \\ \times\ 24 \\ \hline 48 \\ \underline{240} \\ \mathbf{288} \end{array}$$

2. $\frac{\overset{35}{\cancel{140}} \text{ tons}}{1} \cdot \frac{1}{\underset{1}{\cancel{4}}} = \frac{35}{1} = \mathbf{35\ tons}$

3.
$$\begin{array}{r} \overset{2}{\cancel{3}}{}^{1}2 \\ -\ 1\,4 \\ \hline 1\,8 \text{ girls} \end{array}$$

$\frac{\text{boys}}{\text{girls}} = \frac{14}{18} = \mathbf{\frac{7}{9}}$

4. $3\overline{)2.7}$ with quotient 0.9 $\quad m = \mathbf{0.9}$

$$\begin{array}{r} 2.7 \\ \underline{2\,7} \\ 0 \end{array}$$

5. $5\overline{)31}$ with quotient $6\frac{1}{5}$ $\quad n = \mathbf{6\frac{1}{5}}$

$$\begin{array}{r} 31 \\ \underline{30} \\ 1 \end{array}$$

6. $3\overline{)36}$ with quotient 12 $\quad n = \mathbf{12}$

$$\begin{array}{r} 36 \\ \underline{3} \\ 06 \\ \underline{06} \\ 0 \end{array}$$

7. $4\overline{)0.3500}$ with quotient 0.0875 $\quad n = \mathbf{0.0875}$

$$\begin{array}{r} 0.3500 \\ \underline{32} \\ 30 \\ \underline{28} \\ 20 \\ \underline{20} \\ 0 \end{array}$$

8. $\frac{25}{100} = \frac{1}{4}$

$$\begin{array}{r} 3\frac{1}{4} \\ +\ \frac{1}{4} \\ \hline 3\frac{2}{4} \end{array} = \mathbf{3\frac{1}{2}}$$

9. $\frac{3}{5} \times \frac{20}{20} = \frac{60}{100} = 0.60$

$$\begin{array}{r} \overset{1}{6}.5 \\ +\ 0.6 \\ \hline \mathbf{7.1} \end{array}$$

10. $\frac{1}{50} \times \frac{2}{2} = \frac{2}{100} = \mathbf{0.02;\ 2\%}$

11.

$$\begin{array}{r} \overset{11}{\cancel{12}}\frac{\overset{6}{\cancel{1}}}{5} \\ -\ 3\frac{4}{5} \\ \hline \mathbf{8\frac{2}{5}} \end{array}$$

12. $\frac{\overset{4}{\cancel{20}}}{\underset{1}{\cancel{3}}} \times \frac{\overset{2}{\cancel{6}}}{\underset{1}{\cancel{5}}} = \frac{8}{1} = \mathbf{8}$

13. $\frac{100}{9} \div \frac{100}{1}$

$1 \div \frac{100}{1} = \frac{1}{100}$

$\frac{\overset{1}{\cancel{100}}}{9} \cdot \frac{1}{\underset{1}{\cancel{100}}} = \mathbf{\frac{1}{9}}$

14.

$$\begin{array}{r} \overset{1}{4}.75 \\ 12.6 \\ +\ 10 \\ \hline \mathbf{27.35} \end{array}$$

15. $35 - (0.35 \times 100)$

$35 - 35$

0

16. $\frac{12}{m} = \frac{18}{9}$

$12 \cdot 9 = 18m$

$\frac{\overset{6}{\cancel{12}} \cdot \overset{1}{\cancel{9}}}{\underset{1}{\cancel{\underset{2}{\cancel{18}}}}} = m$

$\mathbf{6} = m$

17. **12.05**

18. $V = lwh$

$V = 10 \text{ in.} \times 5 \text{ in.} \times 5 \text{ in.}$

$V = \mathbf{250\ in.^3}$

19. $2(15) - 5$

$30 - 5$

25

20. $A = (25 \text{ mm})(18 \text{ mm})$

$A = \mathbf{450\ mm^2}$

21. 25 mm + 25 mm + 20 mm + 20 mm

= **90 mm**

22. **True**

23. $\frac{1}{\underset{1}{\cancel{10}}} \cdot \frac{\overset{10}{\cancel{100}}}{1} = 10$ shillings

100 − 10 = **90 shillings**

24. 18°F − (−19°F)

$$\begin{array}{r} \overset{1}{1}8°F \\ -\ 19°F \\ \hline \mathbf{37°F} \end{array}$$

25. **4 cm**

26. 2 liter = 2000 milliliters

2000 mL − 500 mL = **1500 mL**

27. **Triangular prism**

28. **a.** 2 m + 1 m = **3 m**

b. 2 m × 4 m = $\mathbf{8\ m^2}$

29. 4 + 4 × 4 − 4 ÷ 4

4 + 16 − 1

19

30.

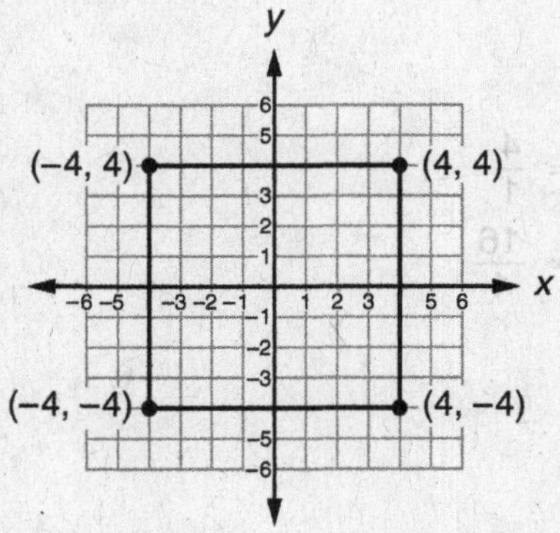

8 units + 8 units + 8 units + 8 units

= **32 units**

Early Finishers Solutions

a. 986 ÷ 17 = 58 miles per hour

b. 986 ÷ 29 = 34 gallons

Practice Set 88

a.

	Ratio	A. C.
DVDs	5	d
CDs	4	60

$$\frac{5}{4} = \frac{d}{60}$$

$$5 \cdot 60 = 4d$$

$$\frac{5 \cdot \overset{15}{\cancel{60}}}{\underset{1}{\cancel{4}}} = d$$

$$75 = d$$

75 DVDs

b.

	Ratio	A. C.
Home	5	30
Away	3	g

$$\frac{5}{3} = \frac{30}{g}$$

$$5g = 3 \cdot 30$$

$$g = \frac{3 \cdot \overset{6}{\cancel{30}}}{\underset{1}{\cancel{5}}}$$

$$g = 18$$

18 fans

Written Practice 88

1. $\frac{12}{20} = \frac{3}{5}$

$\frac{3}{5} \times \frac{20}{20} = \frac{60}{100} =$ **60%**

2. $\frac{4}{1} \div \frac{1}{4}$

$1 \div \frac{1}{4} = \frac{4}{1}$

$\frac{4}{1} \times \frac{4}{1} = \frac{16}{1}$

16 hours

3.

$$\begin{array}{r} \$\,\overset{4}{\cancel{5}}{}^{1}0 \\ -\ \$\,1\,4 \\ \hline \$\,3\,6 \end{array}$$

$$\begin{array}{r} 6 \\ \$6\overline{)\$36} \\ 36 \\ \hline 0 \end{array}$$

6 hours

4. $A = \frac{\overset{8}{\cancel{16}} \cdot 8}{\underset{1}{\cancel{2}}}$

$A =$ **64 mm²**

5.

	Ratio	A. C.
Adults	3	b
Students	5	15

$$\frac{3}{5} = \frac{b}{15}$$

$$3 \cdot 15 = 5b$$

$$\frac{3 \cdot \overset{3}{\cancel{15}}}{\underset{1}{\cancel{5}}} = b$$

$$9 = b$$

9 adults

6. $V = 10 \text{ in.} \times 6 \text{ in.} \times 8 \text{ in.}$

$V =$ **480 in.³**

7.

$$\begin{array}{r} 2\tfrac{5}{10} = 2\tfrac{1}{2} \\ 10\overline{)25} \\ 20 \\ \hline 5 \end{array}$$

$w =$ $\mathbf{2\frac{1}{2}}$

8.

$$\begin{array}{r} 2\tfrac{2}{9} \\ 9\overline{)20} \\ 18 \\ \hline 2 \end{array}$$

$m =$ $\mathbf{2\frac{2}{9}}$

9. **a.** 10 in. + 6 in. + 8 in. = **24 in.**

b. $A = \frac{8 \text{ in.} \times 6 \text{ in.}}{2}$

$A = \frac{48 \text{ in.}^2}{2}$

$A =$ **24 in.²**

10. **a.** $\frac{5}{100} =$ **0.05**

b. $\frac{5}{100} = \mathbf{\frac{1}{20}}$

11. $\begin{array}{r} 0.4 \\ 5\overline{)2.0} \\ \underline{2\,0} \\ 0 \end{array}$

$\begin{array}{r} 2.5 \\ \times\ 0.4 \\ \hline 1.00 \end{array}$

1

12. $\frac{2}{3} + \frac{3}{2}$ ⓹ $\frac{2}{3} \cdot \frac{3}{2}$

$\frac{4}{6} + \frac{9}{6} = \frac{13}{6}$ $\qquad \frac{6}{6} = 1$

$2\frac{1}{6}$

13. $\frac{1}{3} \times \frac{100}{1} = \frac{100}{3} = \mathbf{33\frac{1}{3}}$

14. $\frac{6}{1} \div \frac{3}{2}$

$1 \div \frac{3}{2} = \frac{2}{3}$

$\frac{\overset{2}{\cancel{6}}}{1} \cdot \frac{2}{\underset{1}{\cancel{3}}} = \mathbf{4}$

15. $\begin{array}{r} \mathbf{48} \\ 25\overline{)1200} \\ \underline{100} \\ 200 \\ \underline{200} \\ 0 \end{array}$

16. $0.025 \times 100 = \mathbf{2.5}$

17. $\begin{array}{r} \$24.90 \\ \times\ \ 0.07 \\ \hline 1.7430 \end{array} \longrightarrow \mathbf{\$1.74}$

18. $4 \cdot 9 \cdot 25 = \mathbf{900}$

19. C. 81

20. $1.23 \longrightarrow \mathbf{1.2}$

21. $\frac{\overset{5}{\cancel{60}}}{1} \cdot \frac{7}{\underset{1}{\cancel{12}}} = 35$ muffins

$\begin{array}{r} \overset{5}{\cancel{6}}{}^{1}0 \\ -\ 3\,5 \\ \hline \mathbf{2\,5} \end{array}$ **muffins**

22. $6 \times 3 - 6 \div 3$

$18 - 2$

$\mathbf{16}$

23. 4 milliliters × 1000 = **4000 milliliters**

24. See student work.

$\frac{9}{4} \div \frac{2}{1}$

$1 \div \frac{2}{1} = \frac{1}{2}$

$\frac{9}{4} \cdot \frac{1}{2} = \frac{9}{8} = 1\frac{1}{8}$ in.

$\mathbf{AB = BC = 1\frac{1}{8}}$ **in.**

25.

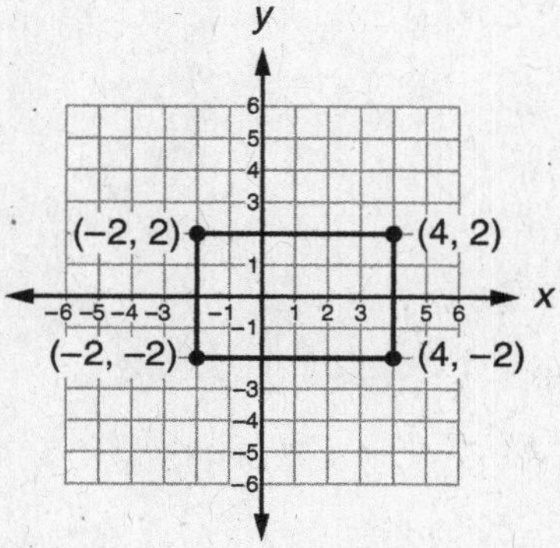

$A = 6 \text{ units} \times 4 \text{ units}$

$A = \mathbf{24\ units^2}$

26. $\frac{\text{length}}{\text{width}} = \frac{6}{4} = \mathbf{\frac{3}{2}}$

27. One method is to multiply the base by the height of the triangle and then divide the product by 2.

28. a. $180° - 45° = \mathbf{135°}$

b. $\frac{45}{135} = \mathbf{\frac{1}{3}}$

29. a. $20 \text{ cm} \times 20 \text{ cm} = \mathbf{400\ cm^2}$

b. $A = \pi r^2$

$A \approx (3.14)(10 \text{ cm})^2$

$A \approx \mathbf{314\ cm^2}$

30. **One possibility: The ratio of fiction books to non-fiction books sold at the book fair is 6 to 8. If 100 non-fiction books were sold, how many fiction books were sold?**

$$\frac{6}{8} = \frac{w}{100}$$

$$6 \cdot 100 = 8w$$

$$\frac{\overset{3}{\cancel{6}} \cdot \overset{25}{\cancel{100}}}{\underset{1}{\cancel{\underset{\cancel{4}}{\cancel{8}}}}} = w$$

$$\mathbf{75} = w$$

Practice Set 89

a. $\sqrt{169}$

$$\begin{array}{r} 13 \\ \times\ 13 \\ \hline 39 \\ 130 \\ \hline 169 \end{array}$$

13

b. $\sqrt{484}$

$$\begin{array}{r} 22 \\ \times\ 22 \\ \hline 44 \\ 440 \\ \hline 484 \end{array}$$

22

c. $\sqrt{961}$

$$\begin{array}{r} 31 \\ \times\ 31 \\ \hline 31 \\ 930 \\ \hline 961 \end{array}$$

31

d. The number 2 is between the perfect squares 1 and 4, so $\sqrt{2}$ is between $\sqrt{1}$ and $\sqrt{4}$. Since $\sqrt{1}$ is 1 and $\sqrt{4}$ is 2, $\sqrt{2}$ is between 1 and 2.
$\sqrt{2}$
1 and 2

e. The number 15 is between the perfect squares 9 and 16, so $\sqrt{15}$ is between $\sqrt{9}$ and $\sqrt{16}$. Since $\sqrt{9}$ is 3 and $\sqrt{16}$ is 4, $\sqrt{15}$ is between 3 and 4.
$\sqrt{15}$
3 and 4

f. The number 40 is between the perfect squares 36 and 49, so $\sqrt{40}$ is between $\sqrt{36}$ and $\sqrt{49}$. Since $\sqrt{36}$ is 6 and $\sqrt{49}$ is 7, $\sqrt{40}$ is between 6 and 7.
$\sqrt{40}$
6 and 7

g. The number 60 is between the perfect squares 49 and 46, so $\sqrt{60}$ is between $\sqrt{49}$ and $\sqrt{64}$. Since $\sqrt{49}$ is 7 and $\sqrt{64}$ is 8, $\sqrt{60}$ is between 7 and 8.
$\sqrt{60}$
7 and 8

h. The number 70 is between the perfect squares 64 and 81, so $\sqrt{70}$ is between $\sqrt{64}$ and $\sqrt{81}$. Since $\sqrt{64}$ is 8 and $\sqrt{81}$ is 9, $\sqrt{70}$ is between 8 and 9.
$\sqrt{70}$
8 and 9

i. The number 80 is between the perfect squares 64 and 81, so $\sqrt{80}$ is between $\sqrt{64}$ and $\sqrt{81}$. Since $\sqrt{64}$ is 8 and $\sqrt{81}$ is 9, $\sqrt{80}$ is between 8 and 9.
$\sqrt{80}$
8 and 9

j. The display on the calculator will show 1.732050808. This number rounded to two decimal places is 1.73.
$\sqrt{3}$
1.73

k. The display on the calculator will show 3.162277660. This number rounded to two decimal places is 3.16.
$\sqrt{10}$
3.16

l. The display on the calculator will show 7.071067812. This number rounded to two decimal places is 7.07.
$\sqrt{50}$
7.07

Written Practice 89

1. $\left(\frac{1}{4} + \frac{1}{4}\right) - \left(\frac{1}{2} \times \frac{1}{2}\right)$

$\frac{2}{4} \quad - \quad \frac{1}{4}$

$\mathbf{\frac{1}{4}}$

2. 4 gallons = 16 quarts
16 quarts = 64 cups
64 cups

3. $\frac{3}{\cancel{4}_{2}}$ cup $\times \frac{\cancel{2}^{1}}{1} = \frac{3}{2} = \mathbf{1\frac{1}{2}}$ **cups**

4.

	Ratio	A. C.
Sugar	2	*s*
Flour	9	18

$\frac{2}{9} = \frac{s}{18}$

$2 \cdot 18 = 9s$

$\frac{2 \cdot \cancel{18}^{2}}{\cancel{9}_{1}} = s$

$4 = s$

4 pounds

5. **C.** $\mathbf{\sqrt{45}}$

6. $7\overline{)30}$ = $4\frac{2}{7}$
28
2

$n = \mathbf{4\frac{2}{7}}$

7. a. 2×4 in. = **8 in.**

b. $C = \pi d$
$C \approx (3.14)(8 \text{ in.})$
$C \approx$ **25.12 in.**

8. $A = \pi r^2$
$A \approx (3.14)(16 \text{ in.})^2$
$A \approx$ **50.24 in²**

9. $A = \frac{8 \text{ in.} \times 5 \text{ in.}}{2}$
$A = \frac{40 \text{ in.}^2}{2}$
$A = \mathbf{20 \text{ in.}^2}$

10. a. $A = 8 \text{ in.} \times 5 \text{ in.}$
$A = \mathbf{40 \text{ in.}^2}$

b. 6 in. + 8 in. + 6 in. + 8 in. = **28 in.**

11. $\frac{5}{10} = \frac{1}{2}$

$3\frac{1}{4} \times \frac{1}{1} = \cancel{3}^{2}\frac{\cancel{1}^{5}}{4}$

$-\ \frac{1}{2} \times \frac{2}{2} = \frac{2}{4}$

$\mathbf{2\frac{3}{4}}$

12. $\frac{3}{4} \times \frac{25}{25} = \frac{75}{100}$; 0.75

$0.75 \times 0.6 = 0.450$

0.45

13. $2 \times 15 + 2 \times 12$
$30 + 24$
54

14. $\sqrt{900}$

$30 \times 30 = 900$

30

15. $8\overline{)\$6.00}$ = \$0.75
5 6
40
40
0

\$0.75

16. $\frac{\cancel{8}^{2}}{\cancel{5}_{1}} \times \frac{\cancel{10}^{2}}{1} \times \frac{1}{\cancel{4}_{1}} = \frac{4}{1} = \mathbf{4}$

17. $\frac{75}{2} \div \frac{100}{1}$

$1 \div \frac{100}{1} = \frac{1}{100}$

$\frac{\overset{3}{\cancel{75}}}{2} \times \frac{1}{\underset{4}{\cancel{100}}} = \mathbf{\frac{3}{8}}$

18. $\frac{3}{1} \div \frac{15}{2}$

$1 \div \frac{15}{2} = \frac{2}{15}$

$\frac{\overset{1}{\cancel{3}}}{1} \times \frac{2}{\underset{5}{\cancel{15}}} = \mathbf{\frac{2}{5}}$

19. Thousands

20. 510.05

21. $90 + m = 180$
$m = 180 - 90$
$m = \mathbf{90}$

22. $\frac{\overset{16}{\cancel{32}}}{1} \cdot \frac{1}{\underset{1}{\cancel{2}}} = 16$ girls

$\frac{\overset{8}{\cancel{16}}}{1} \cdot \frac{1}{\underset{1}{\cancel{2}}} = 8$ brown hair

$\frac{\overset{4}{\cancel{8}}}{1} \cdot \frac{1}{\underset{1}{\cancel{2}}} = \mathbf{4}$ **students**

23. $4 \times 3 =$ **12 books**

24. $20 - 14 =$ **6 more books**

25. Answers will vary. See student work. Sample answer: How many books has Pat read? 14 books

26. $\frac{12}{8} = \frac{21}{m}$

$8 \cdot 21 = 12m$

$\frac{\overset{2}{\cancel{8}} \cdot \overset{7}{\cancel{21}}}{\underset{\underset{1}{\cancel{3}}}{\cancel{12}}} = m$

$\mathbf{14} = m$

27. $\frac{2}{12} = \mathbf{\frac{1}{6}}$

$$\begin{array}{r} 0.166... \\ 6\overline{)1.000...} \\ \underline{6} \\ 40 \\ \underline{36} \\ 40 \\ \underline{36} \\ 4 \end{array}$$

0.17

28. A. Acute

29. a. $200 \text{ cm} = \mathbf{2 \text{ m}}$

b. $\frac{40 \text{ in.}^2}{2} = \mathbf{20 \text{ in.}^2}$

30. $64 \times 1 \text{ in.}^3 = \mathbf{64 \text{ in.}^3}$

Practice Set 90

a.

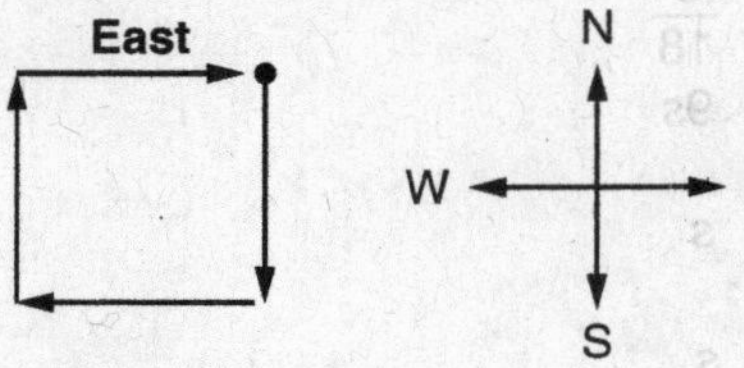

b. $\mathbf{2 \times 360° = 720°}$

c.

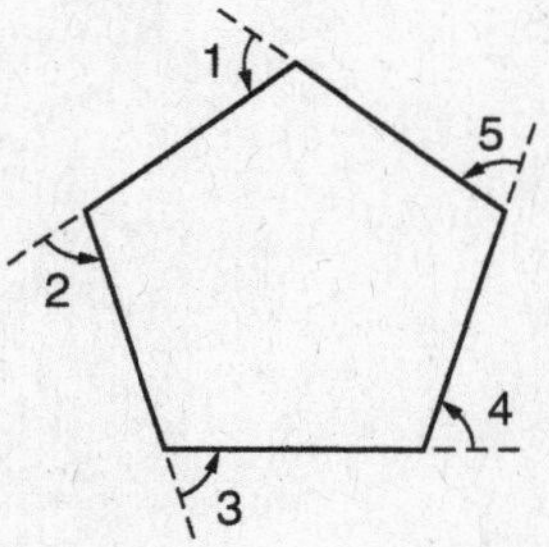

$\frac{\mathbf{360°}}{\mathbf{5}} = \mathbf{72°}$

Written Practice 90

1.
$$\begin{array}{r} 4.2 \\ 4.8 \\ +\ 5.1 \\ \hline 14.1 \end{array} \qquad \begin{array}{r} \mathbf{4.7} \\ 3\overline{)14.1} \\ \underline{12} \\ 2\ 1 \\ \underline{2\ 1} \\ 0 \end{array}$$

2.
$$\begin{array}{r} \text{7:15 p.m.} \\ +\ \ \text{2:00} \\ \hline \textbf{9:15 p.m.} \end{array}$$

3. $\frac{15}{25} \times \frac{4}{4} = \frac{60}{100} = \mathbf{60\%}$

4. 9 edges and 6 vertices
3 more edges

5. a. 12 inches $\div$ 2 = **6 inches**

b. $A = \pi r^2$
$A \approx (3.14)(6 \text{ in.})^2$
$A \approx \mathbf{113.04\ in.^2}$

6. **A trapezoid is a polygon with four sides. Two of the sides are parallel. The other two sides are not parallel.**

7. $\mathbf{-4, -2, 0, \frac{1}{2}, 1}$

8.
$$\begin{array}{r} 2\,\frac{20}{25} = 2\,\frac{4}{5} \\ 25\overline{)70} \\ \underline{50} \\ 20 \end{array}$$

$n = \mathbf{2\frac{4}{5}}$

9. $A = \frac{20 \text{ mm} \times 15 \text{ mm}}{2}$

$A = \frac{300 \text{ mm}^2}{2}$

$A = \mathbf{150\ mm^2}$

10. 25 mm + 20 mm + 15 mm = **60 mm**

11. $\frac{15}{25} = \frac{3}{5}$

$\frac{3}{5} \times \frac{20}{20} = \frac{60}{100} = \mathbf{0.6}$

12. $6\frac{25}{100} = 6\frac{1}{4}$

$$\begin{array}{rcl} 6\frac{1}{4} \times \frac{2}{2} & = & \overset{5}{\cancel{6}}\,\frac{\overset{10}{\cancel{2}}}{8} \\ -\ \frac{5}{8} \times \frac{1}{1} & = & \frac{5}{8} \\ \hline & & \mathbf{5\frac{5}{8}} \end{array}$$

13. 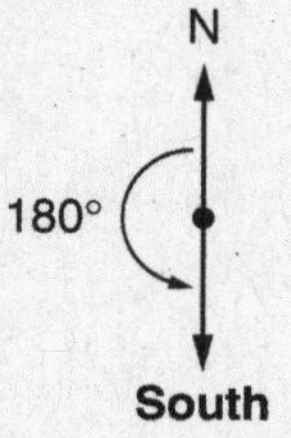

14. $\frac{28}{100} = \mathbf{\frac{7}{25}}$

15. $\frac{n}{12} = \frac{20}{30}$

$12 \cdot 20 = 30n$

$\frac{\overset{4}{\cancel{12}} \cdot \overset{2}{\cancel{20}}}{\underset{\underset{1}{\cancel{3}}}{\cancel{30}}} = n$

$\mathbf{8} = n$

16. 0.625 $\div$ 10 = **0.0625**

17.
$$\begin{array}{r} \mathbf{31.25} \\ 8\overline{)250.00} \\ \underline{24} \\ 10 \\ \underline{8} \\ 2\,0 \\ \underline{1\,6} \\ 40 \\ \underline{40} \\ 0 \end{array}$$

18.
$$\begin{array}{rcl} 3\frac{3}{8} \times \frac{1}{1} & = & 3\frac{3}{8} \\ +\ 3\frac{3}{4} \times \frac{2}{2} & = & 3\frac{6}{8} \\ \hline & & 6\frac{9}{8} = \mathbf{7\frac{1}{8}} \end{array}$$

19.
$$\begin{array}{r} \overset{4}{\cancel{5}}\,\frac{\overset{9}{\cancel{1}}}{8} \\ -\ 1\frac{7}{8} \\ \hline 3\frac{2}{8} = \mathbf{3\frac{1}{4}} \end{array}$$

20. $\frac{\overset{2}{\cancel{20}}}{\underset{1}{\cancel{3}}} \times \frac{\overset{1}{\cancel{3}}}{\underset{1}{\cancel{10}}} \times \frac{4}{1} = \frac{8}{1} = \mathbf{8}$

Solutions

21. $\frac{1}{\cancel{3}_{1}} \cdot \frac{\cancel{24}^{8}}{1} = 8$

$$\begin{array}{r} \overset{1}{\cancel{2}}\,{}^{1}4 \\ -\quad 8 \\ \hline 1\,6 \end{array}$$ **knights**

22.
$$\begin{array}{r} 38 \text{ ounces} \\ +\ 26 \text{ ounces} \\ \hline 64 \text{ ounces} \end{array} \qquad \begin{array}{r} 32 \text{ ounces} \\ 2\overline{)64 \text{ ounces}} \\ \underline{6}\phantom{4 \text{ ounces}} \\ 04\phantom{\text{ ounces}} \\ \underline{04}\phantom{\text{ ounces}} \\ 0\phantom{\text{ ounces}} \end{array}$$

38 ounces − 32 ounces = 6

6 ounces

23. $27 \times 1 \text{ cm}^3 = \mathbf{27\ cm^3}$

24. $0.48 \longrightarrow$ **0.5**

25. $12 - 11 =$ **1**

26. $\frac{\text{cats}}{\text{dogs}} = \mathbf{\frac{5}{6}}$

27. $10 + 10 \times 10 - 10 \div 10$

$10 + 100 - 1$

109

28. 1 gallon = 4 quarts

4 quarts = 8 pints

$$\begin{array}{r} 2 \text{ pints in 2 days} \\ 4\overline{)8}\phantom{\text{ pints in 2 days}} \\ \underline{8}\phantom{\text{ pints in 2 days}} \\ 0\phantom{\text{ pints in 2 days}} \end{array}$$

1 pint per day; One possibility: One gallon equals 4 quarts. Four quarts equals 8 pints. Eight pints divided by four people is 2 pints in 2 days. So on one day, each person drinks an average of 1 pint of milk.

29. a. 100 mm + 100 mm = **200 mm**

b. $\frac{\cancel{300}^{10} \text{ books}}{\cancel{30}_{1} \text{ students}}$

10 books per student

30.

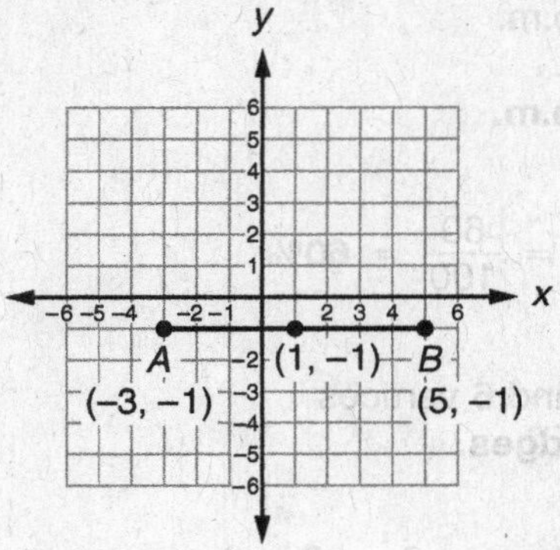

(1, −1)

Early Finishers Solutions

58 students ÷ 2 = She needs to buy ingredients for 28 pairs.

$1\frac{3}{4} \times 28 = \frac{7}{4} \times \frac{28}{1} = 49$ cups of all-purpose flour,

$1 \times 28 = 28$ teaspoons of baking soda,

$1 \times 28 = 28$ sticks of butter and

$1\frac{1}{4} \times 28 = 35$ cups of milk.

Investigation 9

1.

	Freq.	Relative Frequency
Bob's Market	30	$\frac{30}{80} = 0.375$
Corner Grocery	12	$\frac{12}{80} = 0.15$
Express Grocery	14	$\frac{14}{80} = 0.175$
Fine Foods	24	$\frac{24}{80} = 0.30$

2. $\frac{14}{80} =$ **0.175**

3. $\frac{30}{80} = \mathbf{\frac{3}{8}}$

4. $\frac{24}{80} = 0.30 =$ **30%**

5. $\frac{12}{80} = 0.15$

$$\begin{array}{r} 4000 \\ \times\ 0.15 \\ \hline 20000 \\ 40000 \\ \hline 600.00 \end{array}$$

About 600 adults

6. **Answers will vary. See student work.**

7. **Answers will vary. See student work.**

8. **Answers will vary. See student work. Theoretical probability is $\frac{2}{5}$, which equals 0.4.**

Extensions

a. **Answers will vary. See student work.**

b. **Answers will vary. See student work.**

c. **Answers will vary. See student work.**

Practice Set 91

a. $A = lw$
$A = (8\text{ cm})(5\text{ cm})$
$A = \mathbf{40\text{ cm}^2}$

b. $P = 2b + 2s$
$P = 2(10\text{ cm}) + 2(6\text{ cm})$
$P = \mathbf{32\text{ cm}}$

Written Practice 91

1. $\frac{4}{8} = \mathbf{\frac{1}{2}}$

2. $\overset{17}{\cancel{5}}$:45 p.m.
− 6:15 a.m.
11:30
11 hr. 30 min.

3.

	Ratio	A.C.
Leapers	3	12
Duckers	2	d

$\frac{3}{2} = \frac{12}{d}$

$2 \cdot 12 = 3d$

$\frac{2 \cdot \overset{4}{\cancel{12}}}{\underset{1}{\cancel{3}}} = d$

8 duckers

4. 6 faces − 5 faces = 1 face
1 more face

5. $A = bh$
$A = (15\text{ cm})(4\text{ cm})$
$A = \mathbf{60\text{ cm}^2}$

6. $\frac{4}{5} = \frac{d}{360}$
$5d = 4 \cdot 360$
$d = \frac{4 \cdot \overset{72}{\cancel{360}}}{\underset{1}{\cancel{5}}}$
$d = \mathbf{288}$

7. a. **4 faces**
b. **6 edges**
c. **4 vertices**

8. a. $P = 2b + 2s$
$P = 2(12\text{ in.}) + 2(10\text{ in.})$
$P = \mathbf{44\text{ in.}}$

b. $A = bh$
$A = (12\text{ in.})(9\text{ in.})$
$A = \mathbf{108\text{ in.}^2}$

9. a. $\frac{7}{20} \times \frac{5}{5} = \frac{35}{100} = \mathbf{0.35}$

b. $\frac{7}{20} \cdot \frac{5}{5} = \frac{35}{100} = \mathbf{35\%}$

10. $P = 2l + 2w$
$P = 2(5\text{ ft}) + 2(3\text{ ft})$
$P = \mathbf{16\text{ ft}}$

11.
$$6\frac{2}{3} \times \frac{4}{4} = 6\frac{8}{12}$$
$$+\ 1\frac{3}{4} \times \frac{3}{3} = 1\frac{9}{12}$$
$$7\frac{17}{12} = \mathbf{8\frac{5}{12}}$$

12.
$$5 = 4\frac{5}{5}$$
$$-\ 1\frac{2}{5} = 1\frac{2}{5}$$
$$\mathbf{3\frac{3}{5}}$$

13.
$$4\frac{1}{4} \times \frac{2}{2} = \overset{3}{\cancel{4}}\,\frac{\overset{10}{\cancel{2}}}{8}$$
$$-\ 3\frac{5}{8} \times \frac{1}{1} = 3\frac{5}{8}$$
$$\mathbf{\frac{5}{8}}$$

14. $\frac{3}{1} \times \frac{\cancel{3}^{1}}{\cancel{4}_{1}} \times \frac{\cancel{8}^{2}}{\cancel{3}_{1}} = \frac{6}{1} = \mathbf{6}$

15. $\frac{20}{3} \div \frac{100}{1}$

$1 \div \frac{100}{1} = \frac{1}{100}$

$\frac{\cancel{20}^{1}}{3} \times \frac{1}{\cancel{100}_{5}} = \mathbf{\frac{1}{15}}$

16. $\frac{5}{2} \div \frac{15}{4}$

$1 \div \frac{15}{4} = \frac{4}{15}$

$\frac{\cancel{5}^{1}}{\cancel{2}_{1}} \times \frac{\cancel{4}^{2}}{\cancel{15}_{3}} = \mathbf{\frac{2}{3}}$

17. $\frac{9}{20}$ ⓧ 50% (circled: $<$)

$\frac{9}{20} \times \frac{5}{5} \qquad \frac{50}{100}$

$\frac{45}{100}$

18. a. $\mathbf{\frac{1}{4}}$

b. $\frac{1}{4} \times \frac{25}{25} = \frac{25}{100} = \mathbf{25\%}$

19. $\frac{5}{\cancel{6}_{1}} \cdot \frac{\cancel{300}^{50} \text{ seeds}}{1} = \frac{250}{1} = 250$

$300 - 250 =$ **50 seeds**

20. $6\overline{)10}$ quotient $1\frac{4}{6} = \mathbf{1\frac{2}{3}}$

$\underline{6}$

4

21. $20 \cdot 12 = 15w$

$\frac{\cancel{20}^{4} \cdot \cancel{12}^{4}}{\cancel{15}_{\cancel{5}_{1}}} = w$

$\mathbf{16} = w$

22. $A = \frac{1}{2}bh$

$A = \frac{1}{2}(6 \text{ ft})(4 \text{ ft})$

$A = \frac{1}{2}(24 \text{ ft}^2)$

$A = \mathbf{12 \text{ ft}^2}$

23. $V = (12 \text{ in.})(12 \text{ in.})(12 \text{ in.})$

$V = \mathbf{1728 \text{ in.}^3}$

24.

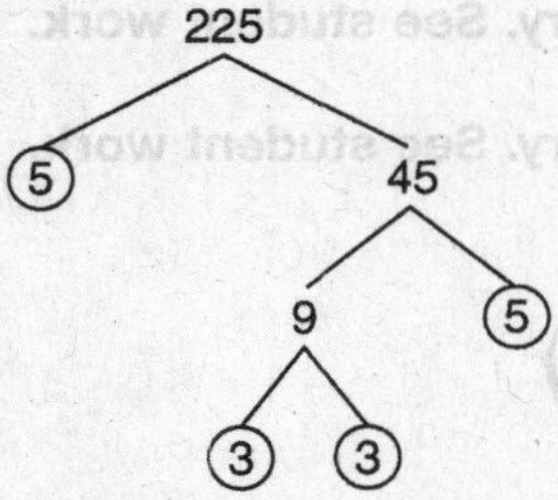

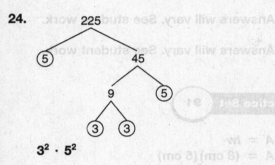

$\mathbf{3^2 \cdot 5^2}$

25. $\begin{array}{r} 56 \text{ mm} \\ -\ 26 \text{ mm} \\ \hline \mathbf{30 \text{ mm}} \end{array}$

26. The number 60 is between the perfect squares 49 and 64, so $\sqrt{60}$ is between $\sqrt{49}$ and $\sqrt{64}$. Since $\sqrt{49}$ is 7 and $\sqrt{64}$ is 8, $\sqrt{60}$ is between **7 and 8.**

27. $\begin{array}{r} 15 \\ \times\ 15 \\ \hline 75 \\ 150 \\ \hline 225 \end{array}$

15

28.

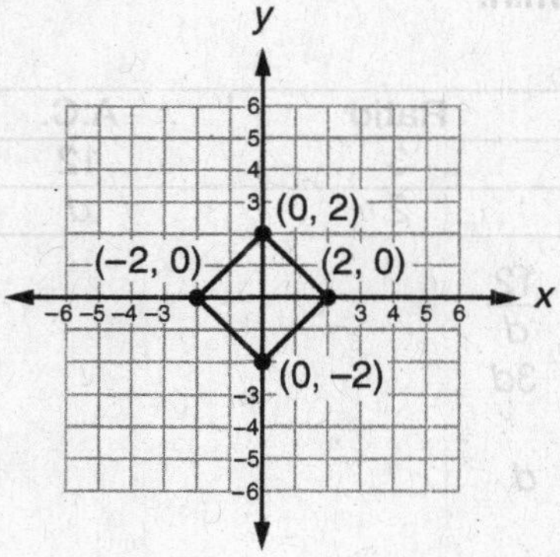

29. a. **4 whole squares**

b. **8 half squares**

c. 8 half squares = 4 whole squares
Total area = 4 whole squares
+ 4 whole squares
= **8 square units**

30. $\frac{1}{2} \times \frac{1}{2} \times \frac{1}{2} = \mathbf{\frac{1}{8}}$

Early Finishers Solutions

a. $A = s^2$, so $820 = s^2$ and $s = \sqrt{820}$. Since $\sqrt{784} = 28$ and $\sqrt{841} = 29$, $\sqrt{820}$ is between 28 and 29. 28 yd × 4 = 112 yd and 29 yd × 4 = 116 yd. Thus the distance Raul runs to warm up is between 112 and 116 yards.

b. (2 × 112) × 3 = 672 yards and (2 × 116) × 3 = 696 yards. Raul will run between 672 and 696 yards next week.

Practice Set 92

a. $\mathbf{(2 \times 10^6) + (5 \times 10^5)}$

b. **5,200,000,000**

c. $10 + 2^3 \times 3 - (7 + 2) \div \sqrt{9}$
$10 + 2^3 \times 3 - 9 \div \sqrt{9}$
$10 + 8 \times 3 - 9 \div 3$
$10 + 24 - 3$
31

d. $\frac{1}{2} \cdot \frac{1}{2} \cdot \frac{1}{2} = \mathbf{\frac{1}{8}}$

e. $0.1 \times 0.1 = \mathbf{0.01}$

f. $\frac{3}{2} \cdot \frac{3}{2} = \frac{9}{4} = \mathbf{2\frac{1}{4}}$

g. $(2 + 3)^2 - (2^2 + 3^2)$
$(5)^2 - (4 + 9)$
$25 - 13$
12

Written Practice 92

1. **It is more likely not to rain. If the chance of rain is 40%, then the chance that it will not rain is 60%. So the chance that it will not rain is greater than the chance that it will rain.**

2. $\frac{9 \text{ squares}}{36 \text{ cards}} = \mathbf{\frac{1}{4}}$
$\frac{1}{4} \times \frac{25}{25} = \frac{25}{100} = \mathbf{0.25}$

3. $144 \div 3 = \mathbf{48}$
12
24
24
0

4. **True**

5. 21 × 21: 21, 420, 441
21

6. $2 \cdot 3^2 - \sqrt{9} + (3 - 1)^3$
$2 \cdot 3^2 - \sqrt{9} + (2)^3$
$2 \cdot 9 - 3 + 8$
$18 - 3 + 8$
23

7. $\mathbf{P = 2l + 2w}$
P = 2(12 in.) + 2(6 in.)
P = 24 in. + 12 in.
P = 36 in.

8. **−1, 0, 0.1, 1**

9. $\frac{5}{\cancel{6}_1} \times \frac{\cancel{30}^5 \text{ members}}{1} = 25 \text{ members}$
30 − 25 = **5 members**

10. $\frac{(\cancel{24}^1)(\cancel{36}^{18})}{\cancel{48}_{\cancel{2}_1}} = \frac{18}{1} = \mathbf{18}$

11. $\frac{10}{5} = \mathbf{2}$

12.
$$\begin{array}{r} 12\frac{5}{6} \times \frac{1}{1} = 12\frac{5}{6} \\ +\ 15\frac{1}{3} \times \frac{2}{2} = 15\frac{2}{6} \\ \hline 27\frac{7}{6} = \mathbf{28\frac{1}{6}} \end{array}$$

13.
$$\begin{array}{r} \overset{0}{\not1}\,\overset{9}{\not0}\,\overset{9}{\not0}.{}^{1}0 \\ -\quad 9.\,9 \\ \hline \mathbf{9\,0.\,1} \end{array}$$

14. $\frac{4}{7} \times \frac{100}{1} = \frac{400}{7} = \mathbf{57\frac{1}{7}}$

15. $\frac{5}{8} = \frac{w}{48}$

$5 \cdot 48 = 8w$

$\frac{5 \cdot \overset{6}{\not{48}}}{\underset{1}{\not8}} = w$

$\mathbf{30} = w$

16.
$$\begin{array}{r} \$4.60 \\ \times\ 0.25 \\ \hline 2300 \\ 9200 \\ \hline \$1.1500 \end{array} \longrightarrow \mathbf{\$1.15}$$

17. $A = \pi r^2$

$A \approx (3.14)(3 \text{ in.})^2$

$A \approx (3.14)(9 \text{ in.}^2)$

$A \approx 28.26 \text{ in.}^2$

$A \approx \mathbf{28 \text{ in.}^2}$

18. $\frac{15}{4} \times \frac{25}{25} = \frac{375}{100} = 3.75$

$$\begin{array}{r} \overset{6}{\not7}.\overset{13}{\not4}{}^{1}0 \\ -\ 3.\,7\,5 \\ \hline \mathbf{3.\,6\,5} \end{array}$$

19. *A*, B, C, D, *E*, F, G, H, *I*, J

$\frac{3}{10} \times \frac{10}{10} = \frac{30}{100} = \mathbf{30\%}$

20.

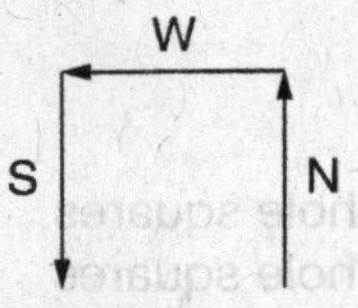

South

21. $7 \times 12 = \mathbf{84}$

22. $\frac{16}{10} = \frac{w}{25}$

$16 \cdot 25 = 10w$

$\frac{\overset{8}{\not{16}} \cdot \overset{5}{\not{25}}}{\underset{1}{\underset{2}{\not{10}}}} = w$

$\mathbf{40 = w}$

23. $A = \frac{1}{2}bh$

$A = \frac{1}{2}(8 \text{ cm})(6 \text{ cm})$

$A = \frac{1}{2}(48 \text{ cm}^2)$

$\mathbf{A = 24 \text{ cm}^2}$

24. **a. 6 faces**

b. 12 edges

25. $\mathbf{\frac{5}{16}, \frac{3}{8}, \frac{7}{16}, \frac{1}{2}}$

26. $P = 2l + 2w$

$P = 2\left(\frac{3}{4} \text{ in.}\right) + 2\left(\frac{1}{2} \text{ in.}\right)$

$P = \left(\frac{6}{4} \text{ in.}\right) + \left(\frac{2}{2} \text{ in.}\right)$

$P = \left(\frac{3}{2} \text{ in.}\right) + \left(\frac{2}{2} \text{ in.}\right)$

$P = \frac{5}{2} \text{ in.}$

$P = \mathbf{2\frac{1}{2} \text{ in.}}$

27. $A = lw$

$A = \left(\frac{3}{4} \text{ in.}\right)\left(\frac{1}{2} \text{ in.}\right)$

$A = \mathbf{\frac{3}{8} \text{ in.}^2}$

28.

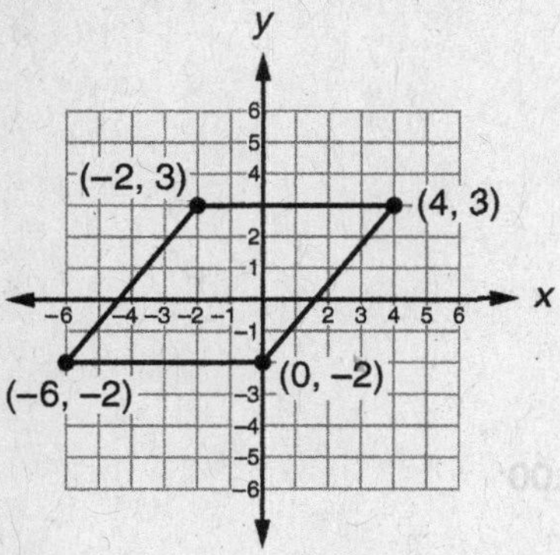

$A = bh$
$A = (6 \text{ units})(5 \text{ units})$
$A = \textbf{30 units}^2$

29. a. $(12 \text{ cm})(8 \text{ cm}) = \textbf{96 cm}^2$

b. $\dfrac{\overset{9}{\cancel{36}}}{\underset{1}{\cancel{4}}} \dfrac{\cancel{ft} \cdot ft}{\cancel{ft}} = \textbf{9 ft}$

30. 3 gallon = 12 quarts
12 quarts = 24 pints
24 pints

Early Finishers Solutions

$\dfrac{1000 \text{ people}}{1 \text{ sq. mile}} = \dfrac{x \text{ people}}{3.5 \text{ sq. mile}}; x = 1000 \times 3.5 = $
3500; there are about 3500 people living in
a 3.5 square mile area.

Practice Set 93

a. $15 \text{ cm} \times 3 = \textbf{45 cm}$

b. True

c. False

d. Isosceles (also acute) triangle

e. False

Written Practice 93

1.

	Ratio	A.C.
Length	5	l
Width	2	60

$\dfrac{5}{2} = \dfrac{l}{60}$
$5 \cdot 60 = 2l$
$\dfrac{5 \cdot \overset{30}{\cancel{60}}}{\underset{1}{\cancel{2}}} = l$
150 ft $= l$

2. $\dfrac{1}{4} \times \dfrac{1}{4} = \dfrac{1}{16}$

3.
$$\begin{array}{r} 36 \\ 4\overline{)144} \\ 12 \\ \hline 24 \\ 24 \\ \hline 0 \end{array}$$

4. $V = lwh$
$V = (4 \text{ cm})^3$
$V = \textbf{64 cm}^3$

5. $\dfrac{9}{25} \times \dfrac{4}{4} = \dfrac{36}{100}$
0.36, 36%

6. $\dfrac{16}{5} \times \dfrac{20}{20} = \dfrac{320}{100} = 3.20$

$$\begin{array}{r} 3.5 \\ + \ 3.20 \\ \hline 6.70 \end{array}$$
6.7

7. $\dfrac{\overset{9}{\cancel{45}}}{\underset{\underset{1}{\cancel{5}}}{\cancel{100}}} \times \dfrac{\overset{4}{\cancel{80}}}{1} = \dfrac{36}{1} = \textbf{36}$

8.
$$\begin{array}{r} 0.3 \\ \times \ 0.3 \\ \hline 0.09 \end{array} \qquad \begin{array}{r} 0.09 \\ \times \ 0.3 \\ \hline \textbf{0.027} \end{array}$$

9. $\dfrac{5}{2} \times \dfrac{5}{2} = \dfrac{25}{4} = 6\dfrac{1}{4}$

    277

10. $3 \cdot 10 = \mathbf{30}$

11. $\frac{20}{24} = \mathbf{\frac{5}{6}}$

12. $\frac{4}{20} = \mathbf{\frac{1}{5}}$

13.
$$\begin{array}{r} 9\frac{1}{3} \times \frac{4}{4} = \overset{8}{\cancel{9}}\,\frac{\overset{16}{\cancel{4}}}{12} \\ -\;4\frac{3}{4} \times \frac{3}{3} = 4\frac{9}{12} \\ \hline w = \mathbf{4\frac{7}{12}} \end{array}$$

14. $6 \cdot 30 = 5m$

$\frac{6 \cdot \overset{6}{\cancel{30}}}{\underset{1}{\cancel{5}}} = m$

$\mathbf{36} = m$

15. Equilateral triangle

16. $\frac{3}{\underset{2}{\cancel{8}}} \times \frac{\overset{25}{\cancel{100}}}{1} = \frac{75}{2} = \mathbf{37\frac{1}{2}}$

17. $10 + 6^2 \div 3 - \sqrt{9} \times 3$

$10 + 36 \div 3 - 3 \times 3$

$10 + 12 - 9$

13

18. 5 faces

19. $2\frac{1}{2}$ gallons = **10 quarts**

20. One possiblity:

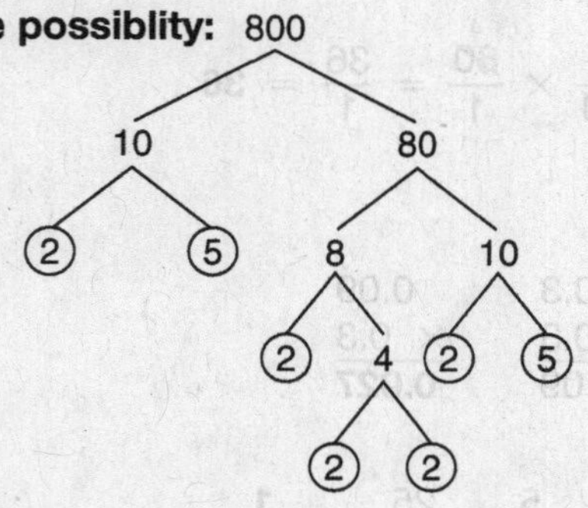

$\mathbf{2^5 \times 5^2}$

21. 0.125
0.1

22.
$$\begin{array}{r} \$15 \\ 8\overline{)\$120} \\ \underline{8} \\ 40 \\ \underline{40} \\ 0 \end{array}$$

$n = \mathbf{\$15.00}$

23.
$A = lw$
$A = (26\text{ mm})(18\text{ mm})$
$A = 468\text{ mm}^2$
$468\text{ mm}^2 \div 2 = \mathbf{234\text{ mm}^2}$

24. $\frac{17}{20} \times \frac{5}{5} = \frac{85}{100} = \mathbf{85\%}$

25. B. $\mathbf{\sqrt{2}}$

26. 7,250,000,000

27. a. $\mathbf{\frac{1}{6}}$

b. $\mathbf{\frac{5}{6}}$

28.

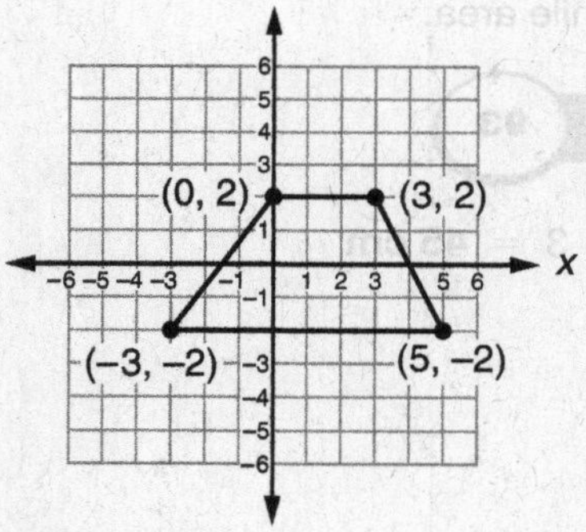

Trapezoid

29. $A = \frac{bh}{2}$

$A = \frac{(20\text{ cm})(15\text{ cm})}{2}$

$A =$ **150 cm²; Possible answer: I used the formula for the area of a triangle,** $A = \frac{bh}{2}$**. I substituted 20 cm for *b* and 15 cm for *h*.**

30. $\frac{7}{16}, \frac{1}{2}, \frac{9}{16}, \frac{5}{8}$; **Possible answer: The rule is add $\frac{1}{16}$ to the preceding number.**

Early Finishers Solutions

a. Stem-and-leaf plot; A stem-and-leaf plot is the most appropriate display because a circle graph is used to display parts of a whole.

5	0
6	6
7	0, 5, 5, 7
8	0, 4, 5
9	0, 1
10	0

b. Accept any answer that is supported by sensible reasoning. Sample based on hint: Any answer that is 20% more or less than 85 seems reasonable. Since 20% of 85 = 17, and 85 − 17 = 68 and 85 + 17 = 102, any answer between 68 and 102 is reasonable. Using plus or minus 20%, all answers except two—50 and 66—were reasonable guesses.

Practice Set 94

a. $0.5 \times 100\% = \mathbf{50\%}$

b. $0.06 \times 100\% = \mathbf{6\%}$

c. $0.125 \times 100\% = \mathbf{12.5\%}$

d. $0.45 \times 100\% = \mathbf{45\%}$

e. $1.3 \times 100\% = \mathbf{130\%}$

f. $0.025 \times 100\% = \mathbf{2.5\%}$

g. $0.09 \times 100\% = \mathbf{9\%}$

h. $1.25 \times 100\% = \mathbf{125\%}$

i. $0.625 \times 100\% = \mathbf{62.5\%}$

j. $\frac{2}{3} \times \frac{100\%}{1} = \frac{200\%}{3} = \mathbf{66\frac{2}{3}\%}$

k. $\frac{1}{6} \times \frac{100\%}{1} = \frac{100\%}{6} = 16\frac{4}{6}\% = \mathbf{16\frac{2}{3}\%}$

l. $\frac{1}{\cancel{8}_{2}} \times \frac{\cancel{100\%}^{25}}{1} = \frac{25\%}{2} = \mathbf{12\frac{1}{2}\%}$

m. $\frac{5}{\cancel{4}_{1}} \times \frac{\cancel{100\%}^{25}}{1} = \frac{125\%}{1} = \mathbf{125\%}$

n. $\frac{14}{\cancel{5}_{1}} \times \frac{\cancel{100\%}^{20}}{1} = \frac{280\%}{1} = \mathbf{280\%}$

o. $\frac{4}{3} \times \frac{100\%}{1} = \frac{400\%}{3} = \mathbf{133\frac{1}{3}\%}$

p. $\frac{5}{\cancel{6}_{3}} \times \frac{\cancel{100\%}^{50}}{1} = \frac{250\%}{3} = \mathbf{83\frac{1}{3}\%}$

q. $\frac{1}{3} \times \frac{100\%}{1} = \frac{100\%}{3} = \mathbf{33\frac{1}{3}\%}$

Written Practice 94

1. $\frac{10}{30} = \frac{1}{3}$

$\frac{1}{3} \times 100\% = \frac{100\%}{3} = \mathbf{33\frac{1}{3}\%}$

2. $100°C \div 2 = \mathbf{50°C}$

3. $\frac{1}{\cancel{3}_{1}} \times \frac{\cancel{12}^{4}}{1}\text{ cm} = \frac{4}{1} = 4\text{ cm}$

$12\text{ cm} - 4\text{ cm} = \mathbf{8\text{ cm}}$

4. $\frac{2}{\cancel{5}_{1}} \times \frac{\cancel{100\%}^{20}}{1} = \frac{40\%}{1} = \mathbf{40\%}$

5. $\frac{5}{3} \times \frac{100\%}{1} = \frac{500\%}{3} = \mathbf{166\frac{2}{3}\%}$

6. $1.5 \times 100\% = \mathbf{150\%}$

7. $\dfrac{25}{4} \times \dfrac{25}{25} = \dfrac{625}{100} = 6.25$

$$\begin{array}{r} 6.\overset{3}{\cancel{4}}{}^{1}0 \\ -\ 6.2\ 5 \\ \hline \mathbf{0.1\ 5} \end{array}$$

8. $10{,}000 - 1000 = \mathbf{9000}$

9. $\dfrac{3}{\underset{1}{\cancel{4}}} \times \dfrac{\overset{90}{\cancel{360}}}{1} = \dfrac{270}{1} = \mathbf{270}$

10. $C = \pi d$
$C \approx (3.14)(8 \text{ cm})$
$C \approx \mathbf{25.12\ cm}$

11. $A = \pi r^2$
$A \approx (3.14)(4 \text{ cm})^2$
$A \approx \mathbf{50.24\ cm^2}$

12.
$$\begin{array}{rcl} 3\frac{1}{2} \times \frac{4}{4} &=& 3\frac{4}{8} \\ 1\frac{3}{4} \times \frac{2}{2} &=& 1\frac{6}{8} \\ +\ 4\frac{5}{8} \times \frac{1}{1} &=& 4\frac{5}{8} \\ \hline && 8\frac{15}{8} = \mathbf{9\frac{7}{8}} \end{array}$$

13. $\dfrac{\overset{1}{\cancel{9}}}{\underset{\underset{1}{2}}{\cancel{10}}} \cdot \dfrac{\overset{1}{\cancel{5}}}{\underset{3}{\cancel{6}}} \cdot \dfrac{\overset{\overset{2}{4}}{\cancel{8}}}{\underset{1}{\cancel{9}}} = \mathbf{\dfrac{2}{3}}$

14. $\mathbf{(2 \times 10^5) + (5 \times 10^4)}$

15.
$$\begin{array}{r} \$8.47 \\ \$12.00 \\ +\ \$0.95 \\ \hline \mathbf{\$21.42} \end{array}$$

16. $37.5 \div 100 = \mathbf{0.375}$

17. $\dfrac{3}{7} = \dfrac{21}{x}$
$7 \cdot 21 = 3x$
$\dfrac{7 \cdot \overset{7}{\cancel{21}}}{\underset{1}{\cancel{3}}} = x$
$\mathbf{49} = x$

18. $\dfrac{100}{3} \div \dfrac{100}{1}$
$1 \div \dfrac{100}{1} = \dfrac{1}{100}$
$\dfrac{\overset{1}{\cancel{100}}}{3} \times \dfrac{1}{\underset{1}{\cancel{100}}} = \mathbf{\dfrac{1}{3}}$

19. $100\% - 90\% = \mathbf{10\%}$

20. **120.03**

21. $\mathbf{-5.2,\ -2.5,\ \frac{2}{5},\ \frac{5}{2}}$

22. **8 edges**

23. $A = bh$
$A = (10 \text{ in.})(8 \text{ in.})$
$A = \mathbf{80\ in.^2}$

24. **C. Obtuse**

25.
$$\begin{array}{r} 103°\text{F} \\ +\ 37°\text{F} \\ \hline \mathbf{140°F} \end{array}$$

26.

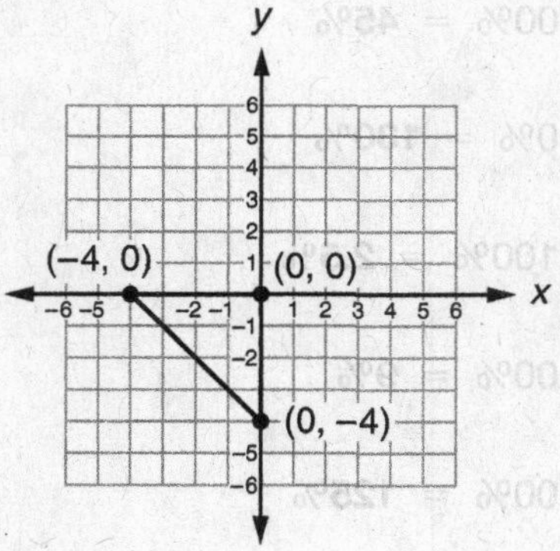

$A = \dfrac{bh}{2}$

$A = \dfrac{4 \text{ units} \times 4 \text{ units}}{2} = \dfrac{16}{2} = \mathbf{8\ sq.\ units}$

27. **a.** Mode = **22**
b. 19, 20, 21, 22, (22), 22, 24, 24, 25,
Median = **22**

28. $2^3 + \sqrt{25} \times 3 - 4^2 \div \sqrt{4}$

$8 + 5 \times 3 - 16 \div 2$

$8 + 15 - 8$

15

29. 1 gallon = 4 quarts

6 gallons = 24 quarts

6 gallons

30. $\frac{2}{52} = \frac{\mathbf{1}}{\mathbf{26}}$

$$\begin{array}{r} 0.0384 \\ 26\overline{)1.0000} \\ \underline{78} \\ 220 \\ \underline{208} \\ 120 \\ \underline{104} \\ 16 \end{array} \longrightarrow \mathbf{0.04}$$

Practice Set 95

a. $\frac{3 \text{ dollars}}{1 \cancel{\text{hour}}} \times \frac{8 \cancel{\text{hours}}}{1} = \mathbf{24\ dollars}$

b. $\frac{6 \text{ baskets}}{\underset{1}{\cancel{10}} \cancel{\text{shots}}} \times \frac{\overset{10}{\cancel{100}} \cancel{\text{shots}}}{1} = \mathbf{60\ baskets}$

c. $\frac{10 \text{ cents}}{1 \cancel{\text{kwh}}} \times \frac{26.3 \cancel{\text{kwh}}}{1} = \mathbf{263\ cents}$

d. $\frac{\overset{80}{\cancel{160}} \text{ km}}{\underset{1}{\cancel{2}} \cancel{\text{hours}}} \cdot \frac{10 \cancel{\text{hours}}}{1} = \mathbf{800\ km}$

e. $\frac{18 \cancel{\text{teachers}}}{1} \times \frac{29 \text{ students}}{1 \cancel{\text{teacher}}} = \mathbf{522\ students}$

f. $\frac{2.3 \cancel{\text{meters}}}{1} \times \frac{100 \text{ centimeters}}{1 \cancel{\text{meter}}} = \mathbf{230\ cm}$

g. $\frac{6 \cancel{\text{hours}}}{1} \times \frac{45 \text{ miles}}{\cancel{\text{hour}}} = \mathbf{270\ miles}$

Written Practice 95

1.
$$\begin{array}{r} \$45.79 \\ \times\ \ \ 0.07 \\ \hline \$3.2053 \end{array} \longrightarrow \$3.21$$

$$\begin{array}{r} \overset{1\ 1}{}\\ \$45.79 \\ +\ \ \$\ 3.21 \\ \hline \mathbf{\$49.00} \end{array}$$

2. $\frac{1.67 \cancel{\text{m}}}{1} \times \frac{100 \text{ cm}}{1 \cancel{\text{m}}} = \mathbf{167\ cm}$

3. $\frac{5}{\underset{1}{\cancel{8}}} \times \frac{\overset{5}{\cancel{40}}}{1} = 25$ sprouted

$$\begin{array}{r} \overset{3}{\cancel{4}}{}^{1}0 \\ -\ 2\ 5 \\ \hline 1\ 5 \end{array}$$ **seeds did not sprout**

4. **560.73**

5. $\frac{1}{\underset{3}{\cancel{6}}} \times \frac{\overset{50}{\cancel{100}}\%}{1} = \frac{50\%}{3} = \mathbf{16\frac{2}{3}\%}$

6. $2.5 \times 100\% = \mathbf{250\%}$

7.
$$\begin{array}{r} \$12.00 \\ \times\ \ \ \ 0.30 \\ \hline \$3.6000 \end{array} \longrightarrow \mathbf{\$3.60}$$

8. 180° is a half turn

$\frac{1}{2}$ of 60 minutes = **30 minutes**

9.
$$\begin{array}{r} \mathbf{5\ turns} \\ 6\overline{)30} \\ \underline{30} \\ 0 \end{array}$$

10. $V = lwh$

$V = (4 \text{ ft})(3 \text{ ft})(3 \text{ ft})$

$V = \mathbf{36\ ft^3}$

11.
$$\begin{array}{r} \frac{3}{4} \times \frac{5}{5} = \frac{15}{20} \\ + \frac{3}{5} \times \frac{4}{4} = \frac{12}{20} \\ \hline \frac{27}{20} = \mathbf{1\frac{7}{20}} \end{array}$$

12.
$$\begin{array}{r} 18\frac{1}{8} \times \frac{1}{1} = \cancel{18}^{17}\frac{\cancel{1}^{9}}{8} \\ -12\frac{1}{2} \times \frac{4}{4} = 12\frac{4}{8} \\ \hline \mathbf{5\frac{5}{8}} \end{array}$$

13. $\dfrac{\cancel{15}^{\cancel{5}^{1}}}{\cancel{4}_{1}} \times \dfrac{\cancel{8}^{\cancel{2}^{1}}}{\cancel{3}_{1}} \times \dfrac{11}{\cancel{10}_{\cancel{2}_{1}}} = \dfrac{11}{1} = \mathbf{11}$

14. $\dfrac{\cancel{2} \cdot \cancel{2} \cdot \cancel{2} \cdot 2 \cdot 2}{\cancel{2} \cdot \cancel{2} \cdot \cancel{2}} = \dfrac{4}{1} = \mathbf{4}$

15. $\dfrac{5}{2} \div \dfrac{1}{4}$

$1 \div \dfrac{1}{4} = \dfrac{4}{1}$

$\dfrac{5}{\cancel{2}_{1}} \times \dfrac{\cancel{4}^{2}}{1} = \dfrac{10}{1} = \mathbf{10}$

16.
$$\begin{array}{r} 12 \\ 8.75 \\ + \ 6.8 \\ \hline \mathbf{27.55} \end{array}$$

17.
$$\begin{array}{r} 1.5 \\ \times \ 1.5 \\ \hline 75 \\ 150 \\ \hline \mathbf{2.25} \end{array}$$

18. $\dfrac{32}{5} = 6.4$

$$\begin{array}{r} \mathbf{8} \\ 8\overline{)64} \\ 64 \\ \hline 0 \end{array}$$

19. $\dfrac{25}{4} = 6.25$

$6 + 5 + 8 = \mathbf{19}$

Round $6\frac{1}{4}$ to 6, round 4.95 to 5, and round 8.21 to 8. Then add 6, 5, and 8.

20. a. 60 inches $\div$ 2 = **30 inches**

b. $A = \pi r^2$
$A \approx (3.14)(30 \text{ inches})^2$
$A \approx$ **2826 in.**

21. **4%, $\frac{1}{4}$, 0.4**

22.
$$\begin{array}{r} \cancel{5}^{4}.{}^{1}0 \\ - \ 3.\ 4 \\ \hline 1.\ 6 \end{array}$$

$y = \mathbf{1.6}$

23. $\dfrac{4}{8} = \dfrac{x}{12}$

$4 \cdot 12 = 8x$

$\dfrac{\cancel{4}^{1} \cdot \cancel{12}^{6}}{\cancel{8}_{\cancel{2}_{1}}} = x$

$\mathbf{6} = x$

24. a. $A = lw$
$A = 6 \text{ cm} \times 6 \text{ cm}$
$A = \mathbf{36\ cm^2}$

b. $V = lwh$
$V = (6 \text{ cm})(6 \text{ cm})(6 \text{ cm})$
$V = \mathbf{216\ cm^3}$

c. Surface area $= 6 \times 36 \text{ cm}^2 = \mathbf{216\ cm^2}$

25.
$$\begin{array}{r} \cancel{4}^{3}\,{}^{1}2 \text{ mm} \\ - \ 2\ 4 \text{ mm} \\ \hline \mathbf{1\ 8\ mm} \end{array}$$

26. $6^2 \div \sqrt{9} + 2 \times 2^3 - \sqrt{400}$
$36 \div 3 + 2 \times 8 - 20$
$12 + 16 - 20$
$\mathbf{8}$

27. 1 quart = 2 pints

$\mathbf{\frac{1}{2}}$

28. $A = bh$

$A = (1.2 \text{ m})(0.9 \text{ m})$

$A =$ **1.08 m^2; 1.2 m rounds to 1 m. 0.9 m rounds to 1 m. 1 m × 1 m is 1 m^2, so the answer 1.08 m^2 is reasonable.**

29. $\frac{2.5 \text{ liters}}{1} \times \frac{1000 \text{ milliliters}}{1 \text{ liter}} =$ **2500 milliliters**

30. $\frac{2}{4} = \mathbf{\frac{1}{2}}$

$\frac{1}{2} \times \frac{50}{50} = \frac{50}{100} =$ **0.5**

__Early Finishers Solutions__

a. $(4.85 \times 10^4) \times 2.25 = 10.9125 \times 10^4$
$= 1.09125 \times 10^2$

b. $\frac{(6 \times 10^4) \times 2.25}{1 \times 10^3} = \frac{1.35 \times 10^5}{1 \times 10^3} =$
$1.35 \times 10^2 = 135$; 135 boxes of cups will be needed.

Practice Set 96

a. $x - 2 = y$
$10 - 2 = 8$
$y =$ **8**

b. $a + 5 = b$
$10 + 5 = 15$
$a =$ **10**

c. $3(8) + 1 =$ **25**

d. $3(4) - 1 =$ **11**

e.

Q	P
1	2
2	4
3	6
4	8

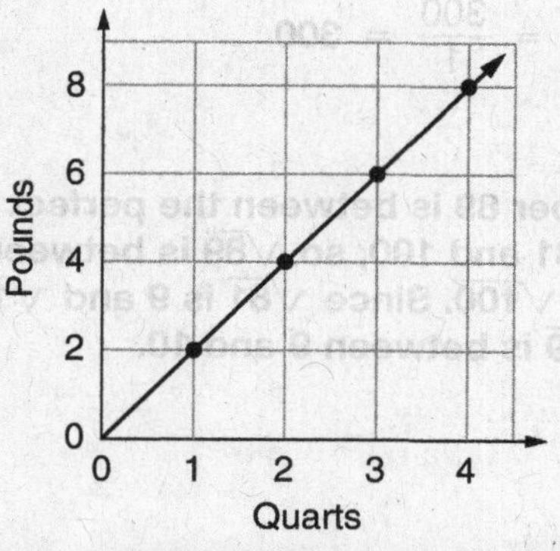

It is appropriate to use a ray, because any portion of a quart may be weighed.

Written Practice 96

1. $(2.0 \times 2.0) - (2.0 + 2.0)$
$4.0 - 4.0$
0

2. $42\overline{)420}$ = **10 objects**
42
00
00
0

3. 12 × 8 = **96**

4. **Trapezoid**

5. **a.** $0.15 \times 100\% =$ **15%**

b. $1.5 \times 100\% =$ **150%**

6. $\frac{5}{\cancel{6}_3} \times \frac{\cancel{100}^{50}\%}{1} = \frac{250\%}{3} =$ **$83\frac{1}{3}\%$**

Solutions

7. **C. 0.1**

8. $11 \times 11 \times 11 = \mathbf{1331}$

9. $\dfrac{5}{\not{6}_{1}} \times \dfrac{\not{360}^{60}}{1} = \dfrac{300}{1} = \mathbf{300}$

10. **The number 89 is between the perfect squares 81 and 100, so $\sqrt{89}$ is between $\sqrt{81}$ and $\sqrt{100}$. Since $\sqrt{81}$ is 9 and $\sqrt{100}$ is 10, $\sqrt{89}$ is between 9 and 10.**

11.
$$\begin{array}{r} \mathbf{120^\circ} \\ 3\overline{)360^\circ} \\ \underline{3} \\ 06 \\ \underline{06} \\ 00 \\ \underline{00} \\ 0 \end{array}$$

12. $2(13) - 1 = \mathbf{25}$

13. $\dfrac{(\not{3}^{1} \cdot \not{3}^{1} \cdot 5) \cdot (2 \cdot \not{3}^{1} \cdot \not{3}^{1} \cdot 3)}{\not{3}_{1} \cdot \not{3}_{1} \cdot \not{3}_{1} \cdot \not{3}_{1}} = \dfrac{30}{1} = \mathbf{30}$

14.
$$\begin{array}{r} \mathbf{375} \\ 8\overline{)3000} \\ \underline{24} \\ 60 \\ \underline{56} \\ 40 \\ \underline{40} \\ 0 \end{array}$$

15. $\dfrac{50}{3} \div \dfrac{100}{1}$

$1 \div \dfrac{100}{1} = \dfrac{1}{100}$

$\dfrac{\not{50}^{1}}{3} \times \dfrac{1}{\not{100}_{2}} = \mathbf{\dfrac{1}{6}}$

16.
$$\begin{array}{rl} 2\frac{1}{2} \times \frac{3}{3} = & 2\frac{3}{6} \\ 3\frac{1}{3} \times \frac{2}{2} = & 3\frac{2}{6} \\ +\ 4\frac{1}{6} \times \frac{1}{1} = & 4\frac{1}{6} \\ \hline & 9\frac{6}{6} = \mathbf{10} \end{array}$$

17. $\dfrac{6}{1} \times \dfrac{\not{16}^{2}}{\not{3}_{1}} \times \dfrac{\not{3}^{1}}{\not{8}_{1}} = \dfrac{12}{1} = \mathbf{12}$

18. $\dfrac{2}{5} \times \dfrac{\$12}{1} = \dfrac{\$24}{5}$

$$\begin{array}{r} \mathbf{\$4.80} \\ 5\overline{)\$24.00} \\ \underline{20} \\ 4\ 0 \\ \underline{4\ 0} \\ 00 \\ \underline{00} \\ 0 \end{array}$$

19.
$$\begin{array}{r} \$6.50 \\ \times\ 0.12 \\ \hline 1300 \\ 6500 \\ \hline \$0.7800 \end{array} \longrightarrow \mathbf{\$0.78}$$

20. $\dfrac{15}{4} = 3.75$

$$\begin{array}{r} \not{5}^{4}.\ \not{3}^{12}{}^{1}0 \\ -\ \ 3.\ 7\ 5 \\ \hline \mathbf{1.\ 5\ 5} \end{array}$$

21. $\dfrac{10}{25} = \mathbf{\dfrac{2}{5}}$

22. $4n = 6 \cdot 14$

$n = \dfrac{\not{6}^{3} \cdot \not{14}^{7}}{\not{4}_{\not{2}_{1}}}$

$n = \mathbf{21}$

23. $3\overline{)120}$ = 40
12
00
00
0

n = **40**

24. See student work.

$\frac{7}{4} \div \frac{2}{1}$

$1 \div \frac{2}{1} = \frac{1}{2}$

$\frac{7}{4} \times \frac{1}{2} = \frac{7}{8}$ inch

***RS* = *ST* = $\frac{7}{8}$ inch**

25. $\frac{6}{9} = \frac{36}{w}$

$6w = 9 \cdot 36$

$w = \frac{9 \cdot \overset{6}{\cancel{36}}}{\underset{1}{\cancel{6}}}$

w = **54**

26. $\frac{4 \cancel{\text{hours}}}{1} \times \frac{6 \text{ dollars}}{1 \cancel{\text{hour}}}$ = **24 dollars**

27.

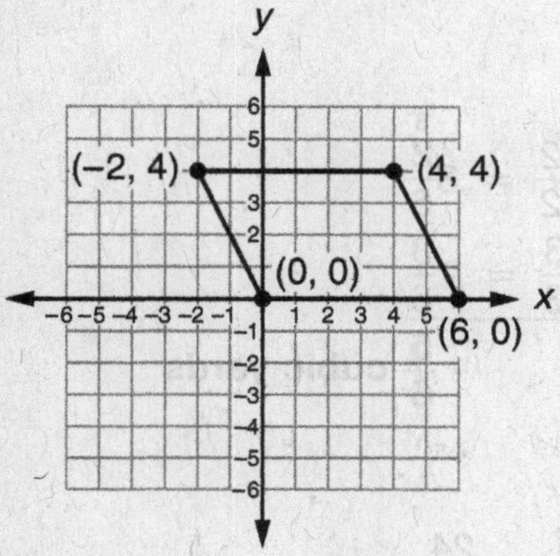

$A = bh$
A = (6 units)(4 units)
A = **24 units²**

28. 1 gallon = 4 quarts
4 quarts = 8 pints
1 gallon = 8 pints
About 8 pounds

29. $3^2 + 2^3 - \sqrt{4} \times 5 + 6^2 \div \sqrt{16}$
$9 + 8 - 2 \times 5 + 36 \div 4$
$9 + 8 - 10 + 9$
16

30. $\frac{3}{6} = \frac{1}{2}$

$\frac{1}{2} \times \frac{50}{50} = \frac{50}{100}$ = **0.5**

Practice Set 97

a. **Line *c***

b. **∠5**

c. **∠4**

d. **∠1**

e. **Angle 3, ∠5, and ∠7 each measure 105°. Angle 2, ∠4, ∠6, and ∠8 each measure 75°.**

Written Practice 97

1. $\frac{100}{1} \div \frac{1}{4}$

$1 \div \frac{1}{4} = \frac{4}{1}$

$\frac{100}{1} \cdot \frac{4}{1} = \frac{400}{1} = 400$

400 hamburgers

2. $\overset{1}{2}{}^{1}12$°F − 32°F = 180°F

$2\overline{)180°F}$ = 90°F
18
00
00
0

32°F + 90°F = **122°F**

3. 1.8(30) + 32
86
1.8(100) + 32 = 212
The boiling point of water is 100°C and 212°F.

4. $\frac{5}{8} \bigcirc\!\!\!< \; 0.675$

$$\begin{array}{r} 0.625 \\ 8\overline{)5.000} \\ \underline{4\,8} \\ 20 \\ \underline{16} \\ 40 \\ \underline{40} \\ 0 \end{array}$$

5. $\frac{9}{4} \times \frac{25}{25} = \frac{225}{100} = \mathbf{225\%}$

6. $\frac{7}{5} \times \frac{20}{20} = \frac{140}{100} = \mathbf{140\%}$

7. $\frac{7}{10} \times \frac{10}{10} = \frac{70}{100} = \mathbf{70\%}$

8. $\frac{7}{\cancel{8}_2} \times \frac{\cancel{100}^{25}\%}{1} = \frac{175}{2} = \mathbf{87\frac{1}{2}\%}$

9.
$$\begin{array}{r} 1 \\ 5\overline{)5} \\ 2\overline{)10} \\ 2\overline{)20} \\ 2\overline{)40} \\ 2\overline{)80} \\ 2\overline{)160} \\ 2\overline{)320} \end{array}$$
$\mathbf{2^6 \cdot 5}$

10. $\frac{360°}{60} = \mathbf{6°}$

11.
$$\begin{array}{r} \mathbf{90°} \\ 4\overline{)360} \\ \underline{36} \\ 00 \\ \underline{00} \\ 0 \end{array}$$

12.
$$\begin{array}{rcl} 6\frac{3}{4} \times \frac{2}{2} & = & 6\frac{6}{8} \\ +\ 5\frac{7}{8} \times \frac{1}{1} & = & 5\frac{7}{8} \\ \hline & & 11\frac{13}{8} = \mathbf{12\frac{5}{8}} \end{array}$$

13.
$$\begin{array}{rcl} 6\frac{1}{3} \times \frac{2}{2} & = & \cancel{6}^{5}\frac{\cancel{2}^{8}}{6} \\ -\ 2\frac{1}{2} \times \frac{3}{3} & = & 2\frac{3}{6} \\ \hline & & \mathbf{3\frac{5}{6}} \end{array}$$

14. $\frac{5}{2} \div \frac{100}{1}$

$1 \div \frac{100}{1} = \frac{1}{100}$

$\frac{\cancel{5}^{1}}{2} \times \frac{1}{\cancel{100}_{20}} = \mathbf{\frac{1}{40}}$

15.
$$\begin{array}{r} 6.93 \\ 8.429 \\ +\ 12 \\ \hline \mathbf{27.359} \end{array}$$

16. $(1 - 0.1)(1 \div 0.1)$

$(0.9)(10)$

$\mathbf{9}$

17. $\frac{7}{8} = 0.875$
$$\begin{array}{r} 4.2 \\ +\ 0.875 \\ \hline \mathbf{5.075} \end{array}$$

18.
$$\begin{array}{rcl} 3\frac{1}{3} \times \frac{2}{2} & = & \cancel{3}^{2}\frac{\cancel{2}^{8}}{6} \\ -\ 2\frac{1}{2} \times \frac{3}{3} & = & 2\frac{3}{6} \\ \hline & & \mathbf{\frac{5}{6}} \end{array}$$
cubic yards

19. $\frac{\cancel{80}^{8}}{\cancel{100}_{\cancel{10}_{1}}} \times \frac{\cancel{30}^{3}}{1} = \frac{24}{1} = 24$

$30 - 24 = \mathbf{6\ students}$

20. $\frac{1}{2} \div \frac{1}{3} \bigcirc\!\!\!> \; \frac{1}{3} \div \frac{1}{2}$

$1 \div \frac{1}{3} = \frac{3}{1}$ $\qquad$ $1 \div \frac{1}{2} = \frac{2}{1}$

$\frac{1}{2} \times \frac{3}{1} = \frac{3}{2}$ $\qquad$ $\frac{1}{3} \cdot \frac{2}{1} = \frac{2}{3}$

21. **Since each number in the sequence is $\frac{1}{10}$ of the previous term, the next number is $\frac{1}{10}$ of 1, which is $\frac{1}{10}$ or 0.1.**

22. $a + 130 = 180$

$$\begin{array}{r} 180 \\ -\ 130 \\ \hline 50 \end{array}$$

$a = \mathbf{50}$

23. $\frac{7}{4} = \frac{w}{44}$

$4w = 7 \cdot 44$

$w = \frac{7 \cdot \overset{11}{\cancel{44}}}{\underset{1}{\cancel{4}}}$

$w = \mathbf{77}$

24. $b = h = \frac{48 \text{ in.}}{4} = 12 \text{ in.}$

$A = \frac{1}{2}bh$

$A = \frac{1}{2}(12 \text{ in.})(12 \text{ in.})$

$A = \mathbf{72 \text{ in.}^2}$

25. 5:00 ÷ 2 = **2:30**

26. **B. 11:00**

27. **Answers will vary. See student work. Sample answer: If Mark continued his $\frac{1}{2}$ mile record pace while running a 1-mile race, what would his 1-mile time be?**

$$\begin{array}{r} \mathbf{2{:}20} \\ \times\ \ \mathbf{2} \\ \hline \mathbf{4{:}40} \end{array}$$

28. a. **∠6**

b. m∠5 = 180° − 78° = **102°**

m∠8 = m∠2 = **78°**

29. $10^2 - \sqrt{49} - (10 + 8) \div 3^2$

$100 - 7 - 18 \div 9$

$100 - 7 - 2$

$\mathbf{91}$

30. $\frac{2}{6} = \mathbf{\frac{1}{3}}$

Practice Set 98

a. **Since the sum of the interior angles of a triangle is 180°, the sum of m∠1, m∠2, and m∠3, is 180°.**

b. m∠4 + m∠5 + m∠6 = **180°**

c. (m∠1 + m∠2 + m∠3) + (m∠4 + m∠5 + m∠6)

180° + 180°

360°

d. m∠P + 75° + 30° = 180°

m∠P + 105° = 180°

m∠P = **75°**

e. **90°**

f.

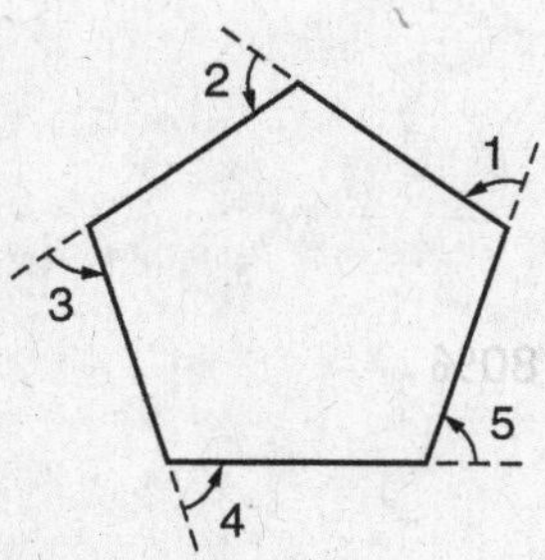

$\frac{\mathbf{360°}}{\mathbf{5}} = \mathbf{72°}$

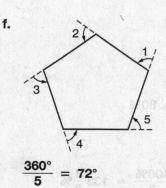

Written Practice 98

1. $\frac{1}{2} \times \frac{2}{2} = \frac{2}{4}$ $\qquad \frac{1}{2} \times \frac{1}{4} = \frac{1}{8}$

$+\ \frac{1}{4} \times \frac{1}{1} = \frac{1}{4}$

$\frac{3}{4}$

$\frac{3}{4} \div \frac{1}{8}$

$1 \div \frac{1}{8} = \frac{8}{1}$

$\frac{3}{\underset{1}{\cancel{4}}} \times \frac{\overset{2}{\cancel{8}}}{1} = \mathbf{6}$

2. $\frac{11}{\cancel{2}_1} \times \frac{\cancel{12}^{6}\text{ inches}}{1} = $ **66 inches**

3. $\frac{4}{\cancel{5}_1} \times \frac{\cancel{200}^{40}}{1} = 160$

$200 - 160 = $ **40 runners**

4. **a.** **∠8**

b. m∠6 = **85°**
m∠7 = 180° − 85° = **95°**

5. **$(2 \times 10^4) + (5 \times 10^3)$ miles**

6. **$\frac{15}{16}$ inch; Divide by 2 to find the radius; multiply by π to find the circumference.**

7. **C. tire**

8. 13 + 8 = **21**

9. 100% − 20% = 80%
0.8 or $\frac{4}{5}$

10. $\frac{4}{3} \times \frac{100\%}{1} = \frac{400\%}{3} = $ **$133\frac{1}{3}\%$**

11.
```
   $7.50
8)$60.00
  56
   4 0
   4 0
     00
     00
      0
```
$w = $ **$7.50**

12. $\frac{0.999}{0.03} = $ **33.3**

13. $\frac{10}{3} \div \frac{100}{1}$

$1 \div \frac{100}{1} = \frac{1}{100}$

$\frac{\cancel{10}^{1}}{3} \times \frac{1}{\cancel{100}_{10}} = $ **$\frac{1}{30}$**

14. $V = lwh$
$V = (5\text{ in.})(2\text{ in.})(3\text{ in.})$
$V = $ **30 cubic inches**

15.
```
   6.5
+  4.95
  11.45
```
(**11.45**)

16. $2\frac{1}{6} \times \frac{1}{1} = \cancel{2}^{1}\frac{\cancel{1}^{7}}{6}$

$-\ 1\frac{1}{2} \times \frac{3}{3} = 1\frac{3}{6}$

$\frac{4}{6} = $ **$\frac{2}{3}$**

17.
```
  $19.79        $19.79
×   0.06      +  $1.19
  1.1874        $20.98
```
$19.79 is close to $20.00. If you estimate the 6% sales-tax as 5% of $20.00, you get $1.00. $20.00 + $1.00 = $21.00, which is close to the actual answer of $20.98.

18. $\frac{3}{12} = $ **$\frac{1}{4}$**

19. $\frac{3}{100} = $ **3%**

20. $\frac{5}{3} = \frac{45}{a}$
$5a = 3 \cdot 45$
$a = \frac{3 \cdot \cancel{45}^{9}}{\cancel{5}_1}$
$a = 27$
27 adults

21. **$-1, -\frac{1}{2}, 0, \frac{1}{2}, 1$**

22. **Trapezoid**

23. **Not congruent**

24. **a.** 40° + 110° + m∠A = 180°
150° + m∠A = 180°
m∠A = **30°**

b. 180° − 110° = x
70° = x

25. a. $\frac{40}{100} = \mathbf{\frac{2}{5}}$

b. $0.40 = \mathbf{0.4}$

26. $A = \pi r^2$
$A \approx (3.14)(10\text{ mm})^2$
$A \approx \mathbf{314\ mm^2}$

27. $2^3 + \sqrt{81} \div 3^2 + \left(\frac{1}{2}\right)^2$
$8 + 9 \div 9 + \frac{1}{4}$
$8 + 1 + \frac{1}{4}$
$\mathbf{9\frac{1}{4}}$

28. $\frac{\overset{10}{\cancel{120}}\text{ in.}}{1} \times \frac{1\text{ ft}}{\underset{1}{\cancel{12}}\text{ in.}} = \mathbf{10\ ft}$

29. a. $\frac{20}{15} = \mathbf{\frac{4}{3}}$

b. $\frac{15}{35} = \mathbf{\frac{3}{7}}$

30. **Isosceles triangle**

Practice Set 99

a. $\frac{3}{5} \times \frac{20}{20} = \frac{60}{100} = \mathbf{0.6}$

b. $\frac{3}{5} \times \frac{100\%}{1} = \frac{300\%}{5} = \mathbf{60\%}$

c. $0.8 = \frac{8}{10} = \mathbf{\frac{4}{5}}$

d. $\frac{80}{100} = \mathbf{80\%}$

e. $\frac{20}{100} = \mathbf{\frac{1}{5}}$

f. $20\% = 0.20 = \mathbf{0.2}$

g. $\frac{3}{4} \times \frac{25}{25} = \frac{75}{100} = \mathbf{0.75}$

h. $\frac{3}{4} \times 100\% = \mathbf{75\%}$

i. $\frac{12}{100} = \mathbf{\frac{3}{25}}$

j. $\frac{12}{100} = \mathbf{12\%}$

k. $\frac{5}{100} = \mathbf{\frac{1}{20}}$

l. $\frac{5}{100} = \mathbf{0.05}$

Written Practice 99

1. $12 \div 1\frac{1}{2}\text{ lengths} = \frac{12}{1} \div \frac{3}{2}$
$1 \div \frac{3}{2} = \frac{2}{3}$
$\frac{\overset{4}{\cancel{12}}}{1} \times \frac{2}{\underset{1}{\cancel{3}}} = \frac{8}{1} = \mathbf{8\ lengths}$

2. **Cylinder**

3. $\frac{3}{8} + \frac{3}{8} = \frac{6}{8}$
$\frac{8}{8} - \frac{6}{8} = \frac{2}{8} = \mathbf{\frac{1}{4}}$

4. a. $\frac{9}{12} = \mathbf{\frac{3}{4}}$

b. $\frac{3}{\underset{1}{\cancel{4}}} \times \frac{\overset{25}{\cancel{100\%}}}{1} = \mathbf{75\%}$

5. $V = lwh$
$V = (4\text{ ft})(3\text{ ft})(4\text{ ft})$
$V = \mathbf{48\ ft^3}$

Solutions

6. 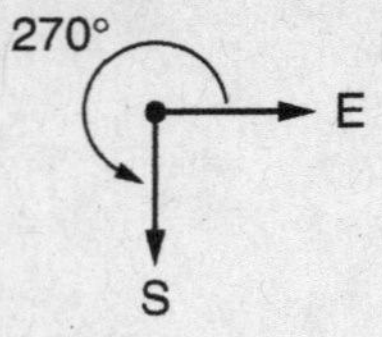

South

7. $\frac{1}{5} \times \frac{20}{20} = \frac{20}{100} = 20\%$

$100\% - 20\% = \mathbf{80\%}$

8. $\frac{1}{7} \times \frac{100\%}{1} = \frac{100\%}{7} = \mathbf{14\frac{2}{7}\%}$

9. $\begin{array}{r} 6.75 \\ -\ 6.2 \\ \hline \mathbf{0.55} \end{array}$

10. $5 \cdot 4 \cdot 3 \cdot 2 \cdot 1 \cdot 0$
$20 \cdot 3 \cdot 2 \cdot 1 \cdot 0$
$60 \cdot 2 \cdot 1 \cdot 0$
$120 \cdot 1 \cdot 0$
$120 \cdot 0$
$\mathbf{0}$

11. $\begin{array}{r} \mathbf{25} \\ 18\overline{)450} \\ \underline{36} \\ 90 \\ \underline{90} \\ 0 \end{array}$

12. $\begin{array}{r} 40 \\ \times\ 40 \\ \hline 1600 \end{array}$ $\sqrt{1600} = \mathbf{40}$

13. $\sqrt{64} + 5^2 - \sqrt{25} \times (2 + 3)$
$8 + 25 - 5 \times 5$
$8 + 25 - 25$
$\mathbf{8}$

14. $\frac{15}{20} = \frac{24}{n}$
$15n = 20 \cdot 24$
$n = \frac{\overset{4}{\cancel{20}} \cdot \overset{8}{\cancel{24}}}{\underset{\underset{1}{\cancel{3}}}{\cancel{15}}}$
$n = \mathbf{32}$

15. $\frac{25}{\underset{1}{\cancel{2}}} \times \frac{\overset{4}{\cancel{8}}}{\underset{1}{\cancel{5}}} \times \frac{\overset{1}{\cancel{5}}}{1} = \frac{100}{1} = \mathbf{100}$

16. $0.21 \div 7 = \mathbf{0.03}$

17. $\begin{array}{r} \$111.11 \\ \times\ \ 0.07 \\ \hline \$7.7777 \end{array} \longrightarrow \mathbf{\$7.78}$

18. a. Mode = **46%**

b. Italy 43%, Peru 44%, Poland 46%, Chile 46%, Greece 51%, Luxembourg 53%, Iceland 57%

Median = 46%, **Poland or Chile**

c. **It is called the median. The median may be the same as the mode, but will not always be the same. The mode is the number that appears the most often. The median is the number in the middle.**

19. 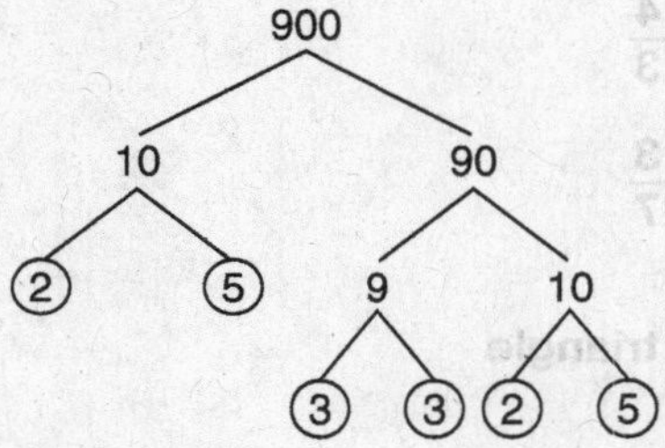

$\mathbf{2^2 \cdot 3^2 \cdot 5^2}$

20. **The GCF is 1.**

21. $\begin{array}{r} \mathbf{50\ cm} \\ 4\overline{)200\ cm} \\ \underline{20} \\ 00 \\ \underline{00} \\ 0 \end{array}$

50 centimeters; $P = 4s$, 2 meters = 200 cm, 200 cm = $4s$, 200 ÷ 4 = s, s = 50 cm

22. a. $A = \frac{bh}{2}$

$A = \frac{(\overset{4}{\cancel{8}}\text{ cm})(5\text{ cm})}{\underset{1}{\cancel{2}}}$

$A = \mathbf{20\ cm^2}$

b. **Obtuse triangle**

23. **a.** $110° + 90° + 75° + m\angle B = 360°$
$m\angle B = \mathbf{85°}$

b. $180° - 110° = 70°$
Exterior angle measure is **70°**

24. **a.** $\frac{6}{10} = \mathbf{\frac{3}{5}}$

b. $\frac{6}{10} \times \frac{10}{10} = \frac{60}{100} = \mathbf{60\%}$

25. **a.** $\frac{15}{100} = \mathbf{\frac{3}{20}}$

b. $\frac{15}{100} = \mathbf{0.15}$

26. **a.** $\frac{3}{10} = \mathbf{0.3}$

b. $\frac{3}{10} \times \frac{10}{10} = \frac{30}{100} = \mathbf{30\%}$

27. A ——— B ——— C

$1\frac{1}{4}$ inches $\div 2 = \frac{5}{4} \div \frac{2}{1}$

$1 \div \frac{2}{1} = \frac{1}{2}$

$\frac{5}{4} \cdot \frac{1}{2} = \frac{5}{8}$

$\boldsymbol{AB = BC = \frac{5}{8}}$ **inch**

28. $\frac{8}{32} = \frac{1}{4}$

$\frac{1}{4} \times \frac{25}{25} = \frac{25}{100} = \mathbf{25\%}$

29. 1 gallon = 4 quarts
1 quart < 1 liter
So, 4 quarts < 4 liters
and **1 gallon < 4 liters**

30. $2\overline{)5.0}$ = **2.5**

$$\begin{array}{r} 2.5 \\ 2\overline{)5.0} \\ \underline{4} \\ 1\,0 \\ \underline{1\,0} \\ 0 \end{array}$$

To find *d*, multiply *r* by 2 (*d* = 2*r*).

Early Finishers Solutions

$4 \times (6 - 2) = 16$

Practice Set 100

a.

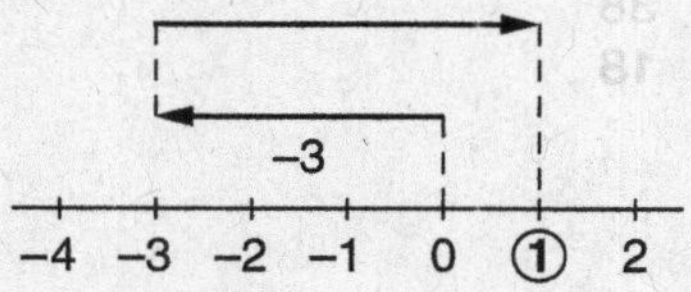

+1

b.

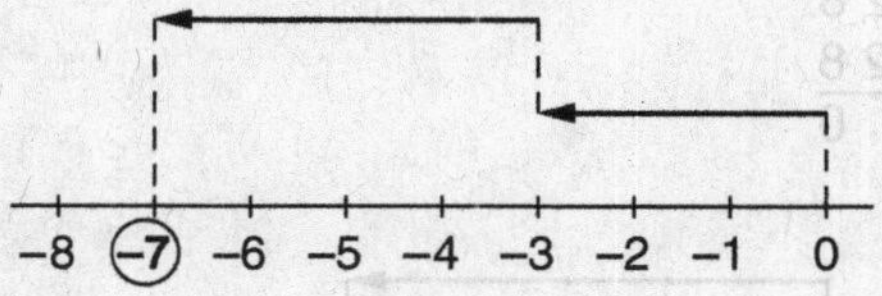

–7

c. **0**

d. **+1**

e. **–1**

f. **+5**

g. **–15**

h. **–5**

i. **+8**

j. **–4**

k. **0**

l. –3 + +4 = **+1**

m. –4 + –2 = **–6**

n. +3 + +6 = **+9**

o. –2 + +4 = **+2**

Solutions

Written Practice 100

1. $\begin{array}{r} 1.2 \\ \times\ 0.6 \\ \hline \mathbf{0.72} \end{array}$

2. $50 - 12 = 38$
   $38 - 20 = \mathbf{18}$

3. $4\overline{)14.8}$ = **3.7**
   $\begin{array}{r} 12 \\ \hline 2\,8 \\ 2\,8 \\ \hline 0 \end{array}$

4. 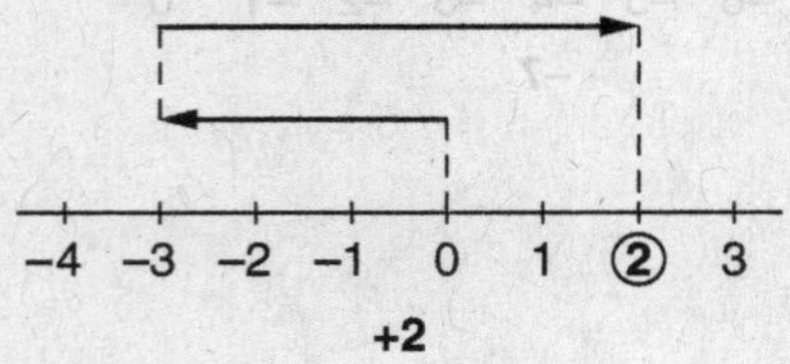

5. a. **0**
   b. **−5**
   c. **−2**
   d. **−5**

6. a. $-2 + +5 = \mathbf{+3}$
   b. $-3 + +3 = \mathbf{0}$
   c. $+2 + +3 = \mathbf{+5}$
   d. $-2 + -3 = \mathbf{-5}$

7. $3\overline{)180°}$ = **60°**
   $\begin{array}{r} 18 \\ \hline 00 \\ 00 \\ \hline 0 \end{array}$

8. $m\angle B = 180° - 70° = \mathbf{110°}$
   $m\angle C = m\angle A$, so $m\angle C = \mathbf{70°}$
   $m\angle B = 180° - m\angle A$, so $m\angle B = \mathbf{110°}$
   $m\angle D = 180° - m\angle A$, so $m\angle D = \mathbf{110°}$

9. a. $\frac{1}{3}$**; There are two sectors with the number 2. Each sector has an area of $\frac{1}{6}$. So, $\frac{1}{6} + \frac{1}{6} = \frac{2}{6} = \frac{1}{3}$.**

   b. $\frac{1}{\cancel{6}_{1}} \times \frac{\cancel{30}^{5}}{1} = \frac{5}{1} =$ **5 times**

10. $V = lwh$
    $V = (7 \text{ in.})(5 \text{ in.})(6 \text{ in.})$
    $V = \mathbf{210\ in.^3}$

11. $\begin{array}{r} 27 \\ -\ 12 \\ \hline 15 \end{array}$ girls

    $\frac{15}{12} = \mathbf{\frac{5}{4}}$

12. $10^2 + (5^2 - 11) \div \sqrt{49} - 3^3$
    $100 + 14 \div 7 - 27$
    $100 + 2 - 27$
    75

13. $\frac{2}{3} \times \frac{100\%}{1} = \frac{200\%}{3} = \mathbf{66\frac{2}{3}\%}$

14. $100\% - 20\% = 80\%$
    $80\% = \frac{80}{100} = \mathbf{\frac{4}{5}}$

15. $\frac{16}{16} = \mathbf{1}$

16. $\begin{array}{rcl} 5\frac{7}{8} \times \frac{1}{1} & = & 5\frac{7}{8} \\ +\ 4\frac{3}{4} \times \frac{2}{2} & = & 4\frac{6}{8} \\ \hline & & 9\frac{13}{8} = \mathbf{10\frac{5}{8}} \end{array}$

17. $\frac{3}{2} \div \frac{5}{2}$

    $1 \div \frac{5}{2} = \frac{2}{5}$

    $\frac{3}{\cancel{2}_{1}} \times \frac{\cancel{2}^{1}}{5} = \mathbf{\frac{3}{5}}$

18. $5 - (3.2 + 0.4)$
$5 - 3.6$
$\mathbf{1.4}$

19. $A = \pi r^2$
$A \approx (3.14)(9\text{ ft}^2)$
$A \approx 28.26\text{ ft}^2$
About 28 square feet

20. **Volume is a measure of space. To measure space, we use units that take up space (cubes). We do not use squares to measure volume, because squares do not take up space.**

21. $\frac{9}{12} = \frac{15}{x}$

$9x = 12 \cdot 15$

$x = \frac{\overset{4}{\cancel{12}} \cdot \overset{5}{\cancel{15}}}{\underset{\underset{1}{\cancel{3}}}{\cancel{9}}}$

$x = \mathbf{20}$

22. $A = \frac{bh}{2}$

$A = \frac{(8\text{ cm})(6\text{ cm})}{2}$

$A = \mathbf{24\ cm^2}$

23. 8 cm + 6 cm + 10 cm
24 cm

24. **21 millimeters**

25. $C = \pi d$
$C \approx (3.14)(21\text{ mm})$
$C \approx 65.94\text{ mm}$
About 66 millimeters

26. $\frac{4}{12} = \mathbf{\frac{1}{3}}$

$$\begin{array}{r} 0.333 \\ 3\overline{)1.000} \\ \underline{9} \\ 10 \\ \underline{9} \\ 10 \\ \underline{9} \\ 1 \end{array} \rightarrow \mathbf{0.33}$$

27. **a.** $\frac{9}{10} = \mathbf{0.9}$

b. $\frac{9}{10} \times \frac{10}{10} = \frac{90}{100} = \mathbf{90\%}$

28. **a.** $1.5 = \mathbf{1\frac{1}{2}}$

b. $1.5 \times 100\% = \mathbf{150\%}$

29. **a.** $\frac{4}{100} = \mathbf{\frac{1}{25}}$

b. $\frac{4}{100} = \mathbf{0.04}$

30. 1 gallon = 4 quarts = 8 pints
8 pints − 2 pints = 6 pints
6 pints = **3 quarts**

Early Finishers Solutions

a. $2^2 \times 5^2 = 100$
$2^4 \times 5^4 = 10{,}000$
$2^5 \times 5^5 = 100{,}000$

b. $2^3 \times 5^3$

Investigation 10

1. $\frac{1}{\underset{1}{\cancel{2}}} \cdot \frac{\overset{1}{\cancel{2}}}{6} = \mathbf{\frac{1}{6}}$

2. $\frac{1}{\underset{1}{\cancel{4}}} \cdot \frac{\overset{1}{\cancel{4}}}{6} = \mathbf{\frac{1}{6}}$

3. $\frac{1}{\underset{2}{\cancel{4}}} \cdot \frac{\overset{1}{\cancel{2}}}{6} = \mathbf{\frac{1}{12}}$

4. $\frac{1}{\underset{1}{\cancel{4}}} \cdot \frac{\overset{1}{\cancel{4}}}{6} = \mathbf{\frac{1}{6}}$

5. $\frac{1}{\underset{2}{\cancel{4}}} \cdot \frac{\overset{1}{\cancel{2}}}{6} = \mathbf{\frac{1}{12}}$

6. $\frac{12}{12} = \mathbf{1}$

7.

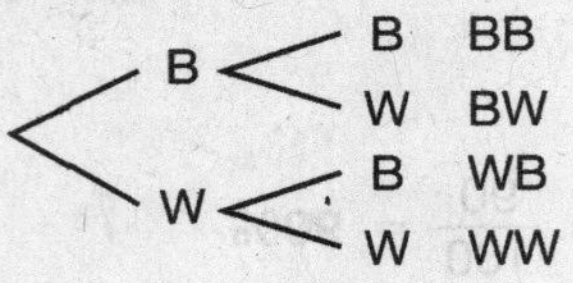

8.

Outcome	Probability
green, green	$\frac{\cancel{4}^{2}}{\cancel{6}_{\cancel{2}_{1}}} \cdot \frac{\cancel{3}^{1}}{5} = \frac{2}{5}$
green, white	$\frac{4}{\cancel{6}_{3}} \cdot \frac{\cancel{2}^{1}}{5} = \frac{4}{15}$
white, green	$\frac{2}{\cancel{6}_{3}} \cdot \frac{\cancel{4}^{2}}{5} = \frac{4}{15}$
white, white	$\frac{\cancel{2}^{1}}{\cancel{6}_{3}} \cdot \frac{1}{5} = \frac{1}{15}$
sum of all possibilities	$\frac{15}{15} = 1$

9. three white marbles: $\frac{2}{6} \cdot \frac{1}{5} \cdot \frac{0}{4} = \mathbf{0}$

three green marbles: $\frac{\cancel{4}^{1}}{\cancel{6}_{\cancel{2}_{1}}} \cdot \frac{\cancel{3}^{1}}{5} \cdot \frac{\cancel{2}^{1}}{\cancel{4}_{1}} = \mathbf{\frac{1}{5}}$

10.

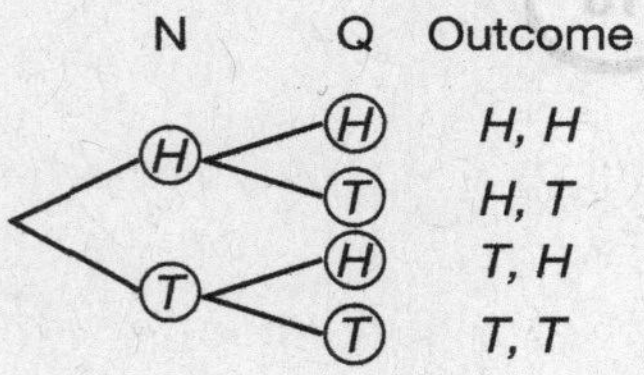

11.

Outcome	Probability
H, *H*	$\frac{1}{2} \cdot \frac{1}{2} = \frac{1}{4}$
H, *T*	$\frac{1}{2} \cdot \frac{1}{2} = \frac{1}{4}$
T, *H*	$\frac{1}{2} \cdot \frac{1}{2} = \frac{1}{4}$
T, *T*	$\frac{1}{2} \cdot \frac{1}{2} = \frac{1}{4}$

12. $\frac{1}{4} + \frac{1}{4} = \frac{2}{4} = \mathbf{\frac{1}{2}}$

13. $\frac{1}{4} + \frac{1}{4} + \frac{1}{4} = \mathbf{\frac{3}{4}}$

14. $\mathbf{\frac{1}{4}}$

Extensions

a. $\frac{4}{15} + \frac{4}{15} = \mathbf{\frac{8}{15}}$

b. $\frac{2}{5} + \frac{1}{15} = \mathbf{\frac{7}{15}}$

c. $1 - \frac{1}{3} = \frac{3}{3} - \frac{1}{3} = \mathbf{\frac{2}{3}}$

d. $\frac{1}{12} + \frac{1}{12} = \frac{2}{12} = \mathbf{\frac{1}{6}}$

e. **The outcomes in c. can include A and can include green, just not both. The outcomes in d. cannot include either A or green, so there are fewer possibilities.**

f.

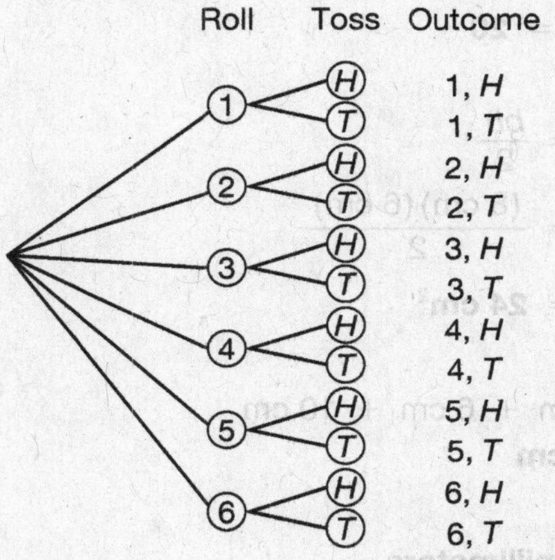

g. **The probability of each compound outcome is $\frac{1}{12}$.**

Practice Set 101

a.

	Ratio	A.C.
Sparrows	5	*s*
Crows	3	*c*
Total	8	72

$\frac{3}{8} = \frac{c}{72}$

$3 \cdot 72 = 8c$

$27 = c$

27 crows

b.

	Ratio	A.C.
Raisins	2	r
Nuts	3	n
Total	5	60

$$\frac{2}{5} = \frac{r}{60}$$
$$2 \cdot 60 = 5r$$
$$24 = r$$

24 ounces

c.

Ratio	A.C.
3	y
2	x
5	20

$$\frac{2}{5} = \frac{x}{20}$$
$$2 \cdot 20 = 5x$$
$$8 = x$$
$$\frac{3}{2} = \frac{y}{8}$$
$$3 \cdot 8 = 2y$$
$$12 = y$$

12 and 8

Written Practice 101

1.

	Ratio	A.C.
Boys	3	b
Girls	2	g
Total	5	30

$$\frac{2}{5} = \frac{g}{30}$$
$$2 \cdot 30 = 5g$$
$$12 = g$$

12 girls

2. **Rectangular prism**

3.
$$\begin{array}{r} 12 \\ \times\ 6 \\ \hline \mathbf{72} \end{array}$$

4. $1\frac{1}{2}$ inches $\div 2 = \frac{3}{2} \div \frac{2}{1}$

$\frac{3}{2} \times \frac{1}{2} = \mathbf{\frac{3}{4}}$ **inch**

5.
$$\begin{array}{r} \$1.65 \\ \times\ 2.6 \\ \hline 990 \\ 3300 \\ \hline \$4.290 \end{array} \longrightarrow \mathbf{\$4.29}$$

6. $\frac{\overset{3}{\cancel{12}}}{1} \cdot \frac{1}{\underset{1}{\cancel{4}}} = \frac{3}{1} = 3 \text{ cm}$

$12 \text{ cm} - 3 \text{ cm} = \mathbf{9\ cm}$

7. **a.** **−7**

b. **0**

c. **−3**

d. **+3**

8. **a.** $-3 + +4 = \mathbf{+1}$

b. $+5 + +5 = \mathbf{+10}$

c. $-6 + -3 = \mathbf{-9}$

d. $-6 + +6 = \mathbf{0}$

e. **Add the opposite of the number instead of subtracting the number.**

9. **There are four equally likely outcomes.**

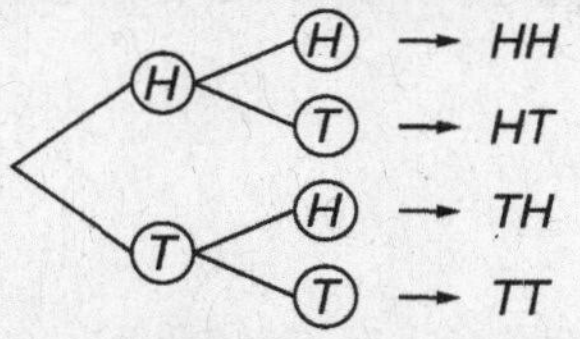

a. **One of the four outcomes is HH, so the probability is $\frac{1}{4}$.**

b. **Two of the four outcomes are HT and TH, so the probability is $\frac{1}{2}$.**

10. **a.** $\frac{3}{4} \times \frac{25}{25} = \frac{75}{100} = \mathbf{0.75}$

b. $\frac{75}{100} = \mathbf{75\%}$

11. **a.** $1\frac{6}{10} = \mathbf{1\frac{3}{5}}$

b. $\frac{8}{5} \times \frac{20}{20} = \frac{160}{100} = \mathbf{160\%}$

12. **a.** $\frac{5}{100} = \mathbf{\frac{1}{20}}$

b. $\frac{5}{100} = \mathbf{0.05}$

Solutions

13. $\frac{3}{\overset{}{\cancel{2}}_{1}} \times \frac{\overset{2}{\cancel{4}}}{1} = \frac{6}{1} = \mathbf{6}$

14. $\frac{6}{1} \div \frac{3}{2}$

$1 \div \frac{3}{2} = \frac{2}{3}$

$\frac{\overset{2}{\cancel{6}}}{1} \times \frac{2}{\cancel{3}_{1}} = \frac{4}{1} = \mathbf{4}$

15. $0.16 \div 8$

$$\begin{array}{r} \mathbf{0.02} \\ 8\overline{)0.16} \\ \underline{16} \\ 00 \end{array}$$

16.
$$\begin{array}{rcl} \frac{5}{1} \times \frac{2}{2} & = & \frac{10}{2} \\ -\ \frac{5}{2} \times \frac{1}{1} & = & \frac{5}{2} \\ \hline & & \frac{5}{2} = \mathbf{2\frac{1}{2}} \end{array}$$

$x = \mathbf{2\frac{1}{2}}$

17. $\frac{8}{5} = \frac{40}{x}$

$40 \cdot 5 = 8x$

$\frac{\overset{5}{\cancel{40}} \cdot 5}{\cancel{8}} = x$

$\mathbf{25} = x$

18.
$$\begin{array}{r} \$2.50 \\ 6\overline{)\$15.00} \\ \underline{12} \\ 3\,0 \\ \underline{3\,0} \\ 00 \\ \underline{00} \\ 0 \end{array}$$

$n = \mathbf{\$2.50}$

19. $6n = 84$

$$\begin{array}{r} 14 \\ 6\overline{)84} \\ \underline{6} \\ 24 \\ \underline{24} \\ 0 \end{array}$$

$n = \mathbf{14}$

20. a. $20 \times 20 =$ **400 boxes**

b. $400 \times 8 =$ **3200 boxes**

21. $C = \pi d$
$C \approx (3.14)(2.5 \text{ in.})$
$C \approx 7.85$ in.

C. $7\frac{3}{4}$ in.

22. $9^2 - \sqrt{9} \times 10 - 2^4 \times 2$
$81 - 3 \times 10 - 16 \times 2$
$81 - 30 - 32$
19

23. **Pentagon**

24. **180°**

25.
$$\begin{array}{r} 15°\text{F} \\ +\ 8°\text{F} \\ \hline \mathbf{23°F} \end{array}$$

26. **8.8**

27. **The probability of rolling 1 or 4 is $\frac{2}{6}$ or $\frac{1}{3}$.**

28.

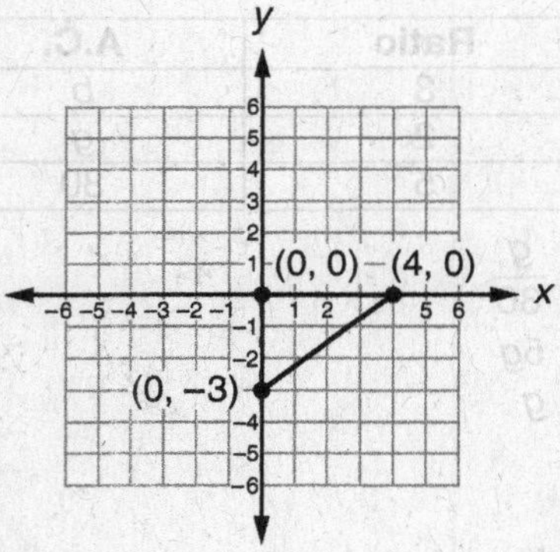

$A = \frac{bh}{2}$

$A = \frac{4 \text{ units} \cdot 3 \text{ units}}{2}$

$A = \mathbf{6\ units^2}$

29. **We set up 18 feet as a fraction and multiply by the number of feet in one yard: $\frac{18 \text{ feet}}{1} \times \frac{1 \text{ yard}}{3 \text{ feet}}$. Then we simplify by canceling: $\frac{18 \text{ feet}}{3 \text{ feet}} = \frac{6}{1}$. Finally, we multiply the numerators: 6×1 yd $= 6$ yd.**

30. 1 gallon = 4 quarts

$$\begin{array}{r} \$0.95 \\ 4\overline{)\$3.80} \\ \underline{3\,6} \\ 20 \\ \underline{20} \\ 0 \end{array}$$

$0.95 per quart

Early Finishers Solutions

9588 m; −408 m − 330 m = 738 m;
8850 m − (−738 m) = 9588 m

Practice Set 102

a. 1000 g = 1 kg

$\frac{1}{2}$ kg = **500 grams**

b. 1 liter = 1 kg
2 liters = 2 kg
2 kg = **2000 grams**

c.

$$\begin{array}{rr} & 5\text{ lb } 10\text{ oz} \\ + & 1\text{ lb } 9\text{ oz} \\ \hline & 6\text{ lb } 19\text{ oz} \\ & \mathbf{7\text{ lb } 3\text{ oz}} \end{array}$$

d.

$$\begin{array}{rr} & \overset{8}{\cancel{9}}\text{ lb } \overset{24}{\cancel{8}}\text{ oz} \\ - & 6\text{ lb } 10\text{ oz} \\ \hline & \mathbf{2\text{ lb } 14\text{ oz}} \end{array}$$

e. 1 ton = 2000 pounds

$\frac{1}{2}$ ton = **1000 pounds**

Written Practice 102

1. **a.** Mode = **92%**

b. Range = 96% − 84% = **12%**

2.

$$\begin{array}{r} \overset{1}{9}0\% \\ 92\% \\ 96\% \\ 92\% \\ 84\% \\ +\ 92\% \\ \hline 546\% \end{array} \qquad \begin{array}{r} \mathbf{91\%} \\ 6\overline{)546\%} \\ \underline{54} \\ 06 \\ \underline{06} \\ 0 \end{array}$$

3. 96 − 18 − 18 = 60 points
30 two-point baskets

First I found the number of points from one-point baskets and three-point baskets. There were 18 points from one-point baskets and 18 points from three-point baskets (6 × 3 = 18). Then I subtracted 36 (18 + 18 = 36) from 96, getting 60 points left from two-point baskets. I then divided 60 by 2 and got 30 two-point baskets.

4. **C.** $\mathbf{\frac{12}{21}}$

5.

$$\frac{4}{5} = \frac{x}{20}$$

$$4 \cdot 20 = 5x$$

$$\frac{4 \cdot \overset{4}{\cancel{20}}}{\underset{1}{\cancel{5}}} = x$$

$$\mathbf{16} = x$$

6. **−1, −0.1, 0, 0.1, 1**

7. **C.** $\mathbf{10^5}$

8. **a.** $\sqrt{100\text{ mm}^2}$ = **10 mm**

b. 10 mm × 2 = **20 mm**

c. $A = \pi r^2$
$A \approx (3.14)(10\text{ mm})^2$
$A \approx$ **314 mm²**

9. **a.** $\frac{4}{25} \times \frac{4}{4} = \frac{16}{100} =$ **0.16**

b. $\frac{16}{100}$ = **16%**

10. **a.** $\mathbf{\frac{1}{100}}$

b. $\frac{1}{100}$ = **1%**

11. **a.** $\frac{90}{100} = \mathbf{\frac{9}{10}}$

b. $\frac{9}{10}$ = **0.9**

12. $1\frac{2}{3} \times \frac{2}{2} = 1\frac{4}{6}$

$3\frac{1}{2} \times \frac{3}{3} = 3\frac{3}{6}$

$+\,4\frac{1}{6} \times \frac{1}{1} = 4\frac{1}{6}$

$8\frac{8}{6} = 9\frac{2}{6} = \mathbf{9\frac{1}{3}}$

13. $\frac{\cancel{5}^{1}}{\cancel{6}_{\cancel{3}_{1}}} \times \frac{\cancel{3}^{1}}{\cancel{10}_{\cancel{2}_{1}}} \times \frac{\cancel{4}^{\cancel{2}^{1}}}{1} = \frac{1}{1} = \mathbf{1}$

14. $\frac{25}{4} \div \frac{100}{1}$

$1 \div \frac{100}{1} = \frac{1}{100}$

$\frac{\cancel{25}^{1}}{4} \times \frac{1}{\cancel{100}_{4}} = \mathbf{\frac{1}{16}}$

15.
$$\begin{array}{r} 6.437 \\ 12.8 \\ +\ \ 7 \\ \hline \mathbf{26.237} \end{array}$$

16.
$$\begin{array}{r} 0.142 \\ 7\overline{)1.000} \\ \underline{7} \\ 30 \\ \underline{28} \\ 20 \\ \underline{14} \\ 6 \end{array}$$

0.14

17. 8 sides − 5 sides = 3 sides
3 more sides

18. $4 \times 5^2 - 50 \div \sqrt{4} + (3^2 - 2^3)$
$4 \times 25 - 50 \div 2 + 1$
$100 - 25 + 1$
$\mathbf{76}$

19. $\frac{1}{4} \cdot \frac{1}{4} = \mathbf{\frac{1}{16}}$

20. $\frac{3}{4} \cdot 100 = 75$
About 75 times

21. 4 in. × 4 in. × 4 in. = **64 in.^{3}**

22. 4 × 5 = **20**

23.
$$\begin{array}{rr} \cancel{10}^{9} \text{ pounds} & \cancel{1}^{17} \text{ ounce} \\ -\ \ 8 \text{ pounds} & 4 \text{ ounce} \\ \hline \mathbf{1\ pound} & \mathbf{13\ ounces} \end{array}$$

24. a. **∠3**

b. **m∠1 = m∠5 = 76°**
m∠2 = 180° − 76° = **104°**

25. 3(5) − 5 = **10**

26. 6 cm + 9 cm + 12 cm + 4 cm
+ 6 cm + 5 cm = **42 cm**

27. a. $A = bh$
$A = (6\text{ in.})(4\text{ in.})$
$A = \mathbf{24\ in.^2}$

b. $A = \frac{bh}{2}$
$A = \frac{(3\text{ in.})(4\text{ in.})}{2}$
$A = \mathbf{6\ in.^2}$

c. 24 in.^{2} + 6 in.^{2} = **30 in.^{2}**

28. 1000 mg = 1 g
$\frac{1}{2}$ g = **500 milligrams**

29.

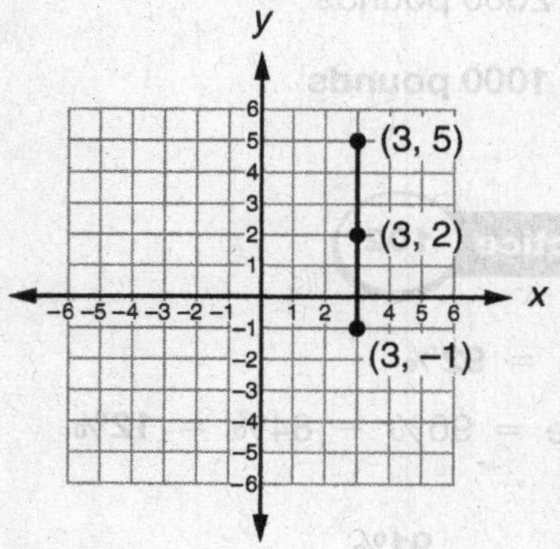

(3, 2)

30.

$$\begin{array}{r} 3.1 \\ 10\overline{)31.0} \\ \underline{30} \\ 1\,0 \\ \underline{1\,0} \\ 0 \end{array}$$

About 3.1 diameters

Practice Set 103

a.

$$\begin{aligned} 3\text{ cm} + x &= 8\text{ cm} \\ x &= 5\text{ cm} \\ 5\text{ cm} + y &= 12\text{ cm} \\ y &= 7\text{ cm} \end{aligned}$$

$$12\text{ cm} + 8\text{ cm} + 5\text{ cm} + 5\text{ cm} + 7\text{ cm} + 3\text{ cm} = \mathbf{40\text{ cm}}$$

b.

$$\begin{aligned} 16\text{ mm} + x &= 20\text{ mm} \\ x &= 4\text{ mm} \\ 7\text{ mm} + y &= 15\text{ mm} \\ y &= 8\text{ mm} \end{aligned}$$

$$20\text{ mm} + 7\text{ mm} + 4\text{ mm} + 8\text{ mm} + 16\text{ mm} + 15\text{ mm} = \mathbf{70\text{ mm}}$$

Written Practice 103

1.

$$\frac{1}{2} \times \frac{3}{3} = \frac{3}{6} \qquad \frac{1}{2} \times \frac{1}{3} = \frac{1}{6}$$

$$+\ \frac{1}{3} \times \frac{2}{2} = \frac{2}{6}$$

$$\frac{5}{6}$$

$$\frac{5}{6} \div \frac{1}{6}$$

$$1 \div \frac{1}{6} = \frac{6}{1}$$

$$\frac{5}{\cancel{6}_1} \times \frac{\cancel{6}^1}{1} = \frac{5}{1} = \mathbf{5}$$

2. a.

$$\begin{array}{r} \overset{1}{2}4 \\ \times\ 3 \\ \hline \end{array}$$

72 years

b.

$$\begin{aligned} 22 + 22 + y &= 72 \\ 72 - 44 &= y \end{aligned}$$

28 years old

3. a.

$$\begin{array}{r} \mathbf{9\text{ in.}} \\ 4\overline{)36} \\ \underline{36} \\ 0 \end{array}$$

b. $9\text{ in.} \times 9\text{ in.} = \mathbf{81\text{ in.}^2}$

4.

$$\begin{aligned} \frac{5}{3} &= \frac{30}{m} \\ 5m &= 3 \cdot 30 \\ m &= \frac{3 \cdot \cancel{30}^{6}}{\cancel{5}_{1}} \\ m &= \mathbf{18} \end{aligned}$$

5.

$$\begin{array}{r} \overset{2}{\cancel{3}}\,{}^{1}0 \\ -\ 1\,4 \\ \hline 1\,6 \end{array}\ \text{non-mysteries}$$

$$\frac{14}{16} = \frac{\mathbf{7}}{\mathbf{8}}$$

6.

	Ratio	A.C.
Boys	4	b
Girls	7	g
Total	11	33

$$\begin{aligned} \frac{7}{11} &= \frac{g}{33} \\ 7 \cdot 33 &= 11g \\ \frac{7 \cdot \cancel{33}^{3}}{\cancel{11}_{1}} &= g \end{aligned}$$

21 girls

7.

$$100 \div 10^2 + 3 \times (2^3 - \sqrt{16})$$
$$100 \div 100 + 3 \times 4$$
$$1 + 12$$
$$\mathbf{13}$$

8. a. 2000 pounds

b. Close to zero

9. a. $\frac{1}{100} = \mathbf{0.01}$

b. $\frac{1}{100} = \mathbf{1\%}$

10. a. $0.4 = \frac{4}{10} = \mathbf{\frac{2}{5}}$

b. $\frac{4}{10} \times \frac{10}{10} = \frac{40}{100} = \mathbf{40\%}$

11. a. $\frac{8}{100} = \mathbf{\frac{2}{25}}$

b. $\frac{8}{100} = \mathbf{0.08}$

12. $\frac{21}{2} \div \frac{7}{2}$

$1 \div \frac{7}{2} = \frac{2}{7}$

$\frac{\overset{3}{\cancel{21}}}{\underset{1}{\cancel{2}}} \times \frac{\overset{1}{\cancel{2}}}{\underset{1}{\cancel{7}}} = \frac{3}{1} = \mathbf{3}$

13. $8.4 \div 0.04$

$$\begin{array}{r} \mathbf{210} \\ 4\overline{)840} \\ \underline{8} \\ 04 \\ \underline{04} \\ 00 \\ \underline{00} \\ 0 \end{array}$$

14.
$$\begin{array}{rcl} 7\frac{1}{2} \times \frac{2}{2} = 7\frac{2}{4} \\ + \ 6\frac{3}{4} \times \frac{1}{1} = 6\frac{3}{4} \\ \hline 13\frac{5}{4} = 14\frac{1}{4} \end{array}$$

$$\begin{array}{r} 15\frac{3}{8} \times \frac{1}{1} = 15\frac{3}{8} \\ - \ 14\frac{1}{4} \times \frac{2}{2} = 14\frac{2}{8} \\ \hline n = \mathbf{1\frac{1}{8}} \end{array}$$

15.
$$\begin{array}{r} 7\frac{1}{2} \times \frac{2}{2} = 7\frac{2}{4} \\ + \ 1\frac{3}{4} \times \frac{1}{1} = 1\frac{3}{4} \\ \hline x = 8\frac{5}{4} = \mathbf{9\frac{1}{4}} \end{array}$$

16. **21 ÷ 7 = 3**

17.
$$\begin{array}{r} 3.18\phantom{\text{ in.}} \\ 11\overline{)35.00\text{ in.}} \\ \underline{33}\phantom{.00\text{ in.}} \\ 2\,0\phantom{0\text{ in.}} \\ \underline{1\,1}\phantom{0\text{ in.}} \\ 90\phantom{\text{ in.}} \\ \underline{88}\phantom{\text{ in.}} \\ 2\phantom{\text{ in.}} \end{array}$$

About 3.2 diameters

18. $\mathbf{(2 \times 10^7) + (5 \times 10^5)}$

19. **41, 43, 47**

20. **a. −11**

b. +5

c. −5

d. −11

21. $180° - 40° = 140°$

$$\begin{array}{r} \mathbf{70°} \\ 2\overline{)140°} \\ \underline{14} \\ 00 \\ \underline{00} \\ 0 \end{array}$$

22. **a.** 20 mm + 15 mm + 25 mm = **60 mm**

b. $A = \frac{bh}{2}$

$A = \frac{\overset{10}{\cancel{20}}\text{ mm} \times 15\text{ mm}}{\underset{1}{\cancel{2}}}$

$A = \mathbf{150\ mm^2}$

c. $\frac{20}{25} = \mathbf{\frac{4}{5}}$

$\frac{4}{5} \times \frac{20}{20} = \frac{80}{100} = \mathbf{0.8}$

23. $V = lwh$

$V = 8\text{ ft.} \times 5\text{ ft.} \times 3\text{ ft.}$

$V = 120\text{ ft}^3$

120 boxes

24. $\frac{\text{number of outcomes in the event}}{\text{number of possible outcomes}} = \mathbf{\frac{1}{52}}$

25. **a. −8°F**

b. −8°F + 12°F = **4°F**

26. 10 mm + x = 20 mm

x = 10 mm

30 mm + y = 50 mm

y = 20 mm

10 mm + 20 mm + 10 mm + 30 mm + 20 mm + 50 mm = **140 mm**

27. **a.** A = 10 mm × 8 mm = $\mathbf{80\ mm^2}$

b. A = 7 mm × 20 mm = $\mathbf{140\ mm^2}$

c. $A = 80\text{ mm}^2 + 140\text{ mm}^2 = \mathbf{220\ mm^2}$

28.
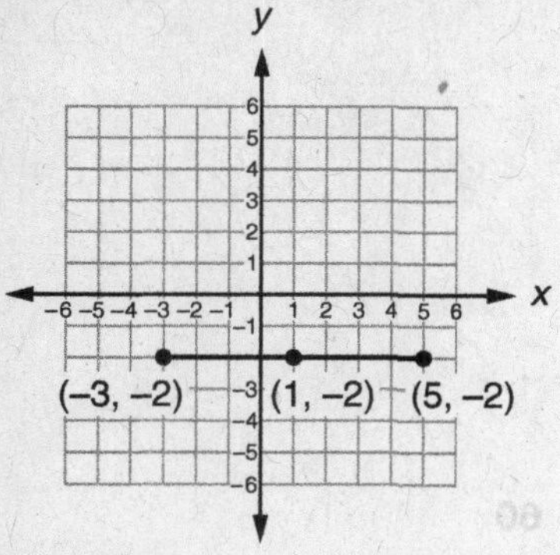

(1, − 2)

29. $\frac{1}{2}$ gallon = 2 quarts

2 quarts = 4 pints

1 pint = 16 oz

16 oz = 1 pound

About 4 pounds

30. a. $\frac{360°}{5} = $ **72°**

b. 180° − 72° = **108°**

Practice Set 104

a. −2 − 3 + 4 − 5

−10 + 4

−6

b. −3 + 2 − 5 + 6

−8 + 8

0

c. +3 − 4 − 6 + 7 + 1

+11 − 10

+1

d. +2 − 3 + 9 − 7 + 1

−10 + 12

+2

e. +3 + 5 − 4 − 2 + 8

+16 − 6

+10

f. −10 − 20 + 30 − 40

−70 + 30

−40

Written Practice 104

1. 8 edges and 5 vertices

3 more edges

2.

$$\begin{array}{r} \overset{11}{\cancel{12}}\text{ lb} \quad \overset{22}{\cancel{6}}\text{ oz} \\ -\ 7\text{ lb} \quad 8\text{ oz} \\ \hline \mathbf{4\text{ lb}} \quad \mathbf{14\text{ oz}} \end{array}$$

3. $\frac{6}{10} = \mathbf{\frac{3}{5}}$

4.

	Ratio	A.C.
Win	3	*w*
Loss	2	*l*
Total	5	20

$\frac{3}{5} = \frac{w}{20}$

$3 \cdot 20 = 5w$

$\frac{3 \cdot \overset{4}{\cancel{20}}}{\underset{1}{\cancel{5}}} = w$

12 games

5. $\frac{1}{2} \cdot \frac{1}{6} = \mathbf{\frac{1}{12}}$

6. a. 7 cm + 7 cm + 8 cm + 8 cm = **30 cm**

b. $A = bh$

$A = 8\text{ cm} \times 6\text{ cm}$

$A = \mathbf{48\text{ cm}^2}$

7. 180° − 59° = **121°**

8. a. **Answers will vary, but should be in the vicinity of 12 to 14 sq. units.**

b. $A = \pi r^2$

$A \approx (3.14)\,(2\text{ units})^2$

$A \approx$ **12.56 sq. units**

9. **C.** $\mathbf{\frac{4}{6}}$

10. $\frac{6}{8} = \frac{a}{12}$

$6 \cdot 12 = 8a$

$\frac{\overset{3}{\cancel{6}} \cdot \overset{3}{\cancel{12}}}{\underset{\underset{1}{\cancel{4}}}{\cancel{8}}} = a$

$9 = a$

11. $5 \text{ cm} + x = 13 \text{ cm}$

$x = 8 \text{ cm}$

$6 \text{ cm} + y = 12 \text{ cm}$

$y = 6 \text{ cm}$

$12 \text{ cm} + 5 \text{ cm} + 6 \text{ cm} + 8 \text{ cm}$
$+ 6 \text{ cm} + 13 \text{ cm} = \mathbf{50 \text{ cm}}$

12. a. $\frac{3}{20} \times \frac{5}{5} = \frac{15}{100} = \mathbf{0.15}$

b. $\frac{15}{100} = \mathbf{15\%}$

13. a. $1\frac{2}{10} = \mathbf{1\frac{1}{5}}$

b. $\frac{12}{10} \times \frac{10}{10} = \frac{120}{100} = \mathbf{120\%}$

14. a. $\frac{10}{100} = \mathbf{\frac{1}{10}}$

b. $\frac{1}{10} = \mathbf{0.1}$

15.

$$\begin{array}{r} \$6.95 \\ \times \quad 0.40 \\ \hline \$2.7800 \end{array}$$

$$\begin{array}{r} \$6.\overset{8}{\cancel{9}}{}^{1}5 \\ - \ \$2.7\,8 \\ \hline \mathbf{\$4.1\,7} \end{array}$$

16. The number 200 is between the perfect squares 196 and 225, so $\sqrt{200}$ is between $\sqrt{196}$ and $\sqrt{225}$. Since $\sqrt{196}$ is 14 and $\sqrt{225}$ is 15, $\sqrt{200}$ is between 14 and 15.

14 and 15

17. $\left(\frac{1}{2}\right)^3 = \frac{1}{2} \cdot \frac{1}{2} \cdot \frac{1}{2} = \frac{1}{8}$

The probability of 3 consecutive "heads" coin tosses $= \frac{1}{2} \cdot \frac{1}{2} \cdot \frac{1}{2} = \frac{1}{8}$.

So, $\left(\frac{1}{2}\right)^3$ = the probability of 3 consecutive "heads" coin tosses.

18.

$$\begin{array}{r} 12.4 \\ 5\overline{)62.4} \\ \underline{5} \\ 12 \\ \underline{10} \\ 24 \\ \underline{20} \\ 4 \end{array}$$

12

19. $20 \times 3 = \mathbf{60}$

20.

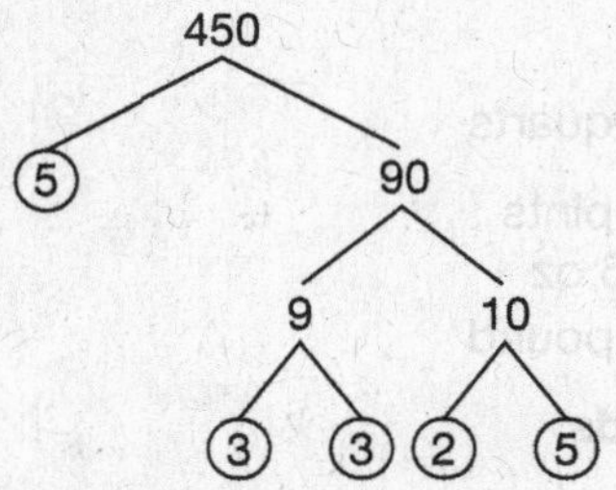

$\mathbf{2 \cdot 3^2 \cdot 5^2}$

21. $-3 - 5 + 4 - 2$

$-10 + 4$

$\mathbf{-6}$

22. $81 + 25 \times 4 - 10 \times 8$

$81 + 100 - 80$

101

23. $V = lwh$

$V = 12 \text{ in.} \times 6 \text{ in.} \times 5 \text{ in.}$

$V = 360 \text{ in.}^3$

360 blocks

24. $\frac{3}{\underset{1}{\cancel{4}}} \times \frac{\overset{15}{\cancel{60}}}{1} = 45$ athletes played

$60 - 45 =$ **15 athletes**

25. $\frac{88 \text{ km}}{1 \cancel{\text{hr}}} \times \frac{4 \cancel{\text{hr}}}{1} = \mathbf{352 \text{ km}}$

26. a. $A = 5 \text{ cm} \times 12 \text{ cm} = \mathbf{60 \text{ cm}^2}$

b. $A = 8 \text{ cm} \times 6 \text{ cm} = \mathbf{48 \text{ cm}^2}$

c. $A = 60 \text{ cm}^2 + 48 \text{ cm}^2 = \mathbf{108 \text{ cm}^2}$

27.

$$\begin{array}{r} 3.12 \\ 3.2 \\ 3.15 \\ +\ 3.1 \\ \hline 12.57 \end{array} \qquad \begin{array}{r} 3.142 \\ 4\overline{)12.570} \\ \underline{12} \\ 0\,5 \\ \underline{4} \\ 17 \\ \underline{16} \\ 10 \\ \underline{8} \\ 2 \end{array}$$

3.14

28. There are 90 two-digit counting numbers. Since Hector was thinking of only one number, the probability of correctly guessing the number in one try is $\frac{1}{90}$.

29.

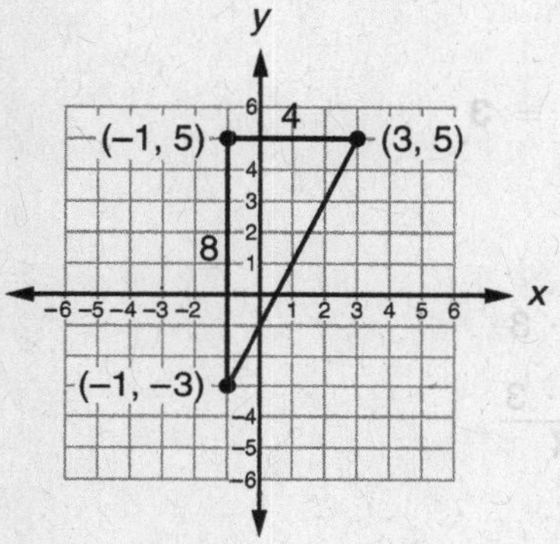

$A = \frac{bh}{2}$

$A = \frac{4 \text{ units} \times \overset{4}{\cancel{8}} \text{ units}}{\underset{1}{\cancel{2}}}$

$A =$ **16 sq. units**

30. $\frac{2 \cancel{\text{gal}}}{1} \times \frac{4 \cancel{\text{qt}}}{1 \cancel{\text{gal}}} \times \frac{2 \text{ pt}}{1 \cancel{\text{qt}}} =$ **16 pt**

Practice Set 105

a.

	%	A.C.
Digital	40	*a*
Not Digital	60	24
Total	100	*t*

$\frac{60}{100} = \frac{24}{t}$

$60t = 100 \cdot 24$

$t = \frac{\overset{10}{\cancel{100}} \cdot \overset{4}{\cancel{24}}}{\underset{1}{\cancel{\underset{10}{\cancel{60}}}}}$

$t =$ **40 cameras**

b.

	%	A.C.
Played	70	21
Did not play	30	*d*
Total	100	*t*

$\frac{70}{30} = \frac{21}{d}$

$70d = 30 \cdot 21$

$d = \frac{\overset{3}{\cancel{30}} \cdot \overset{3}{\cancel{21}}}{\underset{1}{\cancel{\underset{10}{\cancel{70}}}}}$

$d =$ **9 team members**

c. $\frac{\mathbf{70}}{\mathbf{100}} = \frac{\mathbf{21}}{\mathbf{t}}$

d. $\frac{0.6}{10} = \frac{d}{25}$

$10d = 0.6 \cdot 25$

$d = \frac{0.6 \cdot \overset{5}{\cancel{25}}}{\underset{2}{\cancel{10}}}$

$d =$ **1.5 miles**

e. See student work.

Written Practice 105

1. $\frac{50 \text{ mi}}{1 \cancel{\text{hr}}} \times \frac{2.5 \cancel{\text{hr}}}{1} =$ **125 mi**

2. 1 inch = 50 miles
4 inches = **200 miles**

3. $\frac{2}{1} = \frac{900}{o}$

$2o = 900$

$o =$ **450 orcas**

4. $V = lwh$

$V = 7 \text{ in.} \times 3.5 \text{ in.} \times 5 \text{ in.}$

$V =$ **122.5 in.³**

5. a. 0

b. 0

c. $+6 - 5 + 4$
$10 - 5$
5

6. $\begin{array}{r} 2.2 \text{ pounds} \\ \times \ 50 \\ \hline 110.0 \end{array}$

About 110 pounds

7.

	Ratio	A.C.
Dimes	3	*d*
Nickels	5	*n*
Total	8	120

$$\frac{3}{8} = \frac{d}{120}$$
$$8d = 3 \cdot 120$$
$$d = \frac{3 \cdot \cancel{120}^{15}}{\cancel{8}_{1}}$$
$d =$ **45 dimes**

8.

	%	A.C.
Discount	25	45
Not at discount	75	*n*
Total	100	*t*

$$\frac{25}{100} = \frac{45}{t}$$
$$25t = 100 \cdot 45$$
$$t = \frac{\cancel{100}^{4} \cdot 45}{\cancel{25}_{1}}$$
$t =$ **180 seats; One possibility: I know my answer is correct because 25% of 180 is 45. 180 × 0.25 = 45.**

9. a. $\frac{3}{50} \times \frac{2}{2} = \frac{6}{100} =$ **0.06**

b. $\frac{6}{100} =$ **6%**

10. a. $\frac{4}{100} = \mathbf{\frac{1}{25}}$

b. $\frac{4}{100} =$ **4%**

11. a. $\frac{150}{100} = \frac{3}{2} = \mathbf{1\frac{1}{2}}$

b. $\frac{150}{100} =$ **1.5**

12.
$$4\frac{1}{12} \times \frac{1}{1} = 4\frac{1}{12}$$
$$5\frac{1}{6} \times \frac{2}{2} = 5\frac{2}{12}$$
$$+\ 2\frac{1}{4} \times \frac{3}{3} = 2\frac{3}{12}$$
$$11\frac{6}{12} = \mathbf{11\frac{1}{2}}$$

13. $\frac{4}{\cancel{8}_{1}} \times \frac{\cancel{10}^{2}}{\cancel{3}_{1}} \times \frac{\cancel{3}^{1}}{1} = \frac{8}{1} =$ **8**

14. $\begin{array}{r} 0.125 \\ \times \quad 80 \\ \hline 10.000 \end{array}$

10

15. $1.5 \div 0.5 =$ **3**

16.
$$\frac{c}{12} = \frac{3}{4}$$
$$4c = 12 \cdot 3$$
$$c = \frac{\cancel{12}^{3} \cdot 3}{\cancel{4}_{1}}$$
$c =$ **9**

17. $\begin{array}{r} \$8.75 \\ \times \ 0.08 \\ \hline \$0.7000 \end{array}$ $\quad$ $\begin{array}{r} \overset{1}{\$8.75} \\ +\ \$0.70 \\ \hline \mathbf{\$9.45} \end{array}$

18. **105.05**

19. m∠*B* = 180° − 115° = **65°**
m∠*C* = **90°**

20.

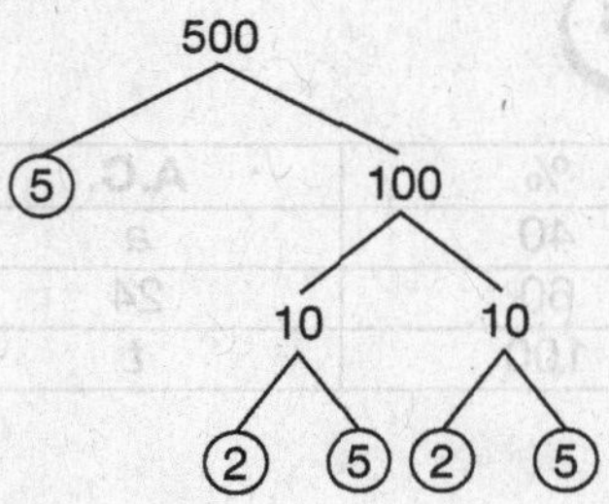

$\mathbf{2^2 \times 5^3}$

21. 1 gallon = 4 quarts
4 liters

22. $\frac{1}{4} \times \frac{1}{4} = \mathbf{\frac{1}{16}}$

23. 18 cm − 5 cm − 5 cm = **8 cm**

24. $A = \frac{bh}{2}$

$A = \frac{\overset{4}{\cancel{8}} \text{ cm} \times 3 \text{ cm}}{\underset{1}{\cancel{2}}}$

$A = \mathbf{12\ cm^2}$

25. −5°F + 12°F = **7°F**

26. 100% − 30% = 70%

$70\% = \frac{70}{100} = 0.70 = \mathbf{0.7}$

27. 6 + *x* = 12
x = 6
6 + *y* = 12
y = 6
12 in. + 6 in. + 6 in. + 6 in.
+ 6 in. + 12 in. = **48 in.**

28. **Multiply *x* by 3 to find *y*.**

29. a. **5 yards long and 4 yards wide.**

b. *A* = 5 yards × 4 yards = **20 sq. yards**

30. **The probability is $\frac{1}{6}$ because the past outcome does not affect the future outcome.**

Practice Set 106

a. **3*n* + 1 = 16** check: 3(5) + 1 = 16
3*n* = 15 15 + 1 = 16
***n* = 5** 16 = 16

b. **2*x* − 1 = 9** check: 2(5) − 1 = 9
2*x* = 10 10 − 1 = 9
***x* = 5** 9 = 9

c. **3*y* − 2 = 22** check: 3(8) − 2 = 22
3*y* = 24 24 − 2 = 22
***y* = 8** 22 = 22

d. **5*m* + 3 = 33** check: 5(6) + 3 = 33
5*m* = 30 30 + 3 = 33
***m* = 6** 33 = 33

e. **4*w* − 1 = 35** check: 4(9) − 1 = 35
4*w* = 36 36 − 1 = 35
***w* = 9** 35 = 35

f. **7*a* + 4 = 25** check: 7(3) + 4 = 25
7*a* = 21 21 + 4 = 25
***a* = 3** 25 = 25

Written Practice 106

1. 20 × 3 = 60   60 − 28 − 15 = **17**

2. $\frac{2\frac{1}{2} \cancel{\text{in.}}}{1} \times \frac{10 \text{ mi}}{1 \cancel{\text{in.}}} = \mathbf{25\ mi}$

3. $\frac{1}{\underset{1}{\cancel{4}}} \times \frac{\overset{90}{\cancel{360}}}{0} = \frac{90}{1} = \mathbf{90}$

4. $\frac{5}{25} \times \frac{4}{4} = \frac{20}{100} = \mathbf{20\%}$

5. Possibilities: 1, 10, 11, 12, 13, 14, 15, 16, 17, 18, 19, 21

$\frac{12}{30} = \mathbf{\frac{2}{5}}$

$\frac{2}{5} \times \frac{20}{20} = \frac{40}{100} = \mathbf{0.4}$

6. 8*x* + 1 = 25 check: 8(3) + 1 = 25
8*x* = 24 24 + 1 = 25
x = **3** 25 = 25

7. 3*w* − 5 = 25 check: 3(10) − 5 = 25
3*w* = 30 30 − 5 = 25
w = **10** 25 = 25

8. a. **+5**

b. −15 − 20 = **−35**

c. −3 − 2 + 1 = **−4**

9. 1 ton = 2000 pounds
4000 pounds = **2 tons**

10. 4 quarts − 1 quart = 3 quarts
3 quarts = **6 pints**

11. $\frac{9}{5} = \frac{414}{k}$
$9k = 414 \cdot 5$
$k = \frac{\overset{46}{\cancel{414}} \cdot 5}{\underset{1}{\cancel{9}}}$
$k =$ **230 koalas**

12. a. $8\overline{)1.000}$ = **0.125**
8
20
16
40
40
0

b. 0.125 × 100% = **12.5%**

13. a. $1\frac{8}{10} = \mathbf{1\frac{4}{5}}$

b. $\frac{18}{10} \times \frac{10}{10} = \frac{180}{100} =$ **180%**

14. a. $\mathbf{\frac{3}{100}}$

b. $\frac{3}{100} =$ **0.03**

15. $8\frac{1}{3} \times \frac{2}{2} = \overset{7}{\cancel{8}}\frac{\overset{8}{\cancel{2}}}{6}$
$-\ 3\frac{1}{2} \times \frac{3}{3} = 3\frac{3}{6}$
$\mathbf{4\frac{5}{6}}$

16. $\frac{5}{2} \div \frac{100}{1}$
$\frac{100}{1} \div 1 = \frac{1}{100}$
$\frac{\overset{1}{\cancel{5}}}{2} \times \frac{1}{\underset{20}{\cancel{100}}} = \mathbf{\frac{1}{40}}$

17. $5\overline{)0.140}$ = **0.028**
10
40
40
0

18. **60,907**

19. $\mathbf{2^6 \cdot 5^6}$

20. $12 = 11\frac{4}{4}$
$-\ 5\frac{1}{4} = 5\frac{1}{4}$
$\mathbf{6\frac{3}{4}}$ **inches**

21. 6 + 9(5 − 2)
6 + 9(3)
6 + 27
33

22. $V = lwh$
$V =$ (4 cm) (2 cm) (3 cm)
$V =$ **24 cubic centimeters**

23. $\frac{3}{12} = \frac{1}{4} \times \frac{25}{25} = \frac{25}{100} =$ **25%**

24. a. A = 3 cm × 2 cm = **6 cm²**

b. A = 4 cm × 7 cm = **28 cm²**

c. A = 6 cm² + 28 cm² = **34 cm²**

25. 4 cm + 2 cm = x
6 cm = x
3 cm + y = 7 cm
y = 4 cm
4 cm + 7 cm + 6 cm + 3 cm
+ 2 cm + 4 cm = **26 cm**

26. $C = \pi d$
$C \approx$ (3.14) (2 ft)
$C \approx$ 6.28 ft
B. 6 ft 3 in.

27. $A = \frac{bh}{2}$
$A = \frac{7\text{ cm} \times \overset{2}{\cancel{4}}\text{ cm}}{\underset{1}{\cancel{2}}}$
$A =$ **14 cm²**

28. Miles: 3, 4, 5, ⑥, 7, 7, 10
6 miles

29. $7 + 3 + 6 + 10 + 5 + 4 + 7 = 42$

$$\begin{array}{r} \textbf{6 miles} \\ 7\overline{)42 \text{ miles}} \\ \underline{42} \\ 0 \end{array}$$

30. **Answers may vary. See student work. Sample answer: How many more miles did Celina ride on Wednesday compared to Monday?**
10 miles − 3 miles = 7 miles

Practice Set 107

a.

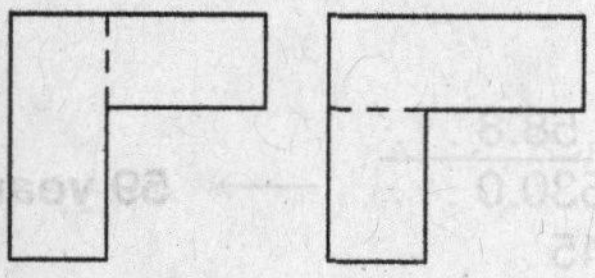

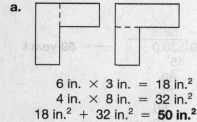

$6 \text{ in.} \times 3 \text{ in.} = 18 \text{ in.}^2$
$4 \text{ in.} \times 8 \text{ in.} = 32 \text{ in.}^2$
$18 \text{ in.}^2 + 32 \text{ in.}^2 = \mathbf{50 \text{ in.}^2}$

$10 \text{ in.} \times 3 \text{ in.} = 30 \text{ in.}^2$
$5 \text{ in.} \times 4 \text{ in.} = 20 \text{ in.}^2$
$30 \text{ in.}^2 + 20 \text{ in.}^2 = \mathbf{50 \text{ in.}^2}$

b. $10 \text{ cm} \times 6 \text{ cm} = 60 \text{ cm}^2$

$$A = \frac{(6 \text{ cm})(\overset{2}{\cancel{4}} \text{ cm})}{\underset{1}{\cancel{2}}}$$

$A = 12 \text{ cm}^2$
$60 \text{ cm}^2 + 12 \text{ cm}^2 = \mathbf{72 \text{ cm}^2}$

Written Practice 107

1. $\dfrac{0.48}{0.8}$

$$\begin{array}{r} \mathbf{0.6} \\ 8\overline{)4.8} \\ \underline{4\,8} \\ 0 \end{array}$$

2. $\dfrac{1 \text{ inch}}{2 \text{ feet}} = \dfrac{4 \text{ inches}}{t}$
$t = \mathbf{8 \text{ feet}}$

3. $\dfrac{800}{600} = \mathbf{\dfrac{4}{3}}$

4. $\dfrac{1}{5} \times \dfrac{20}{20} = \dfrac{20}{100} = \mathbf{20\%}$

5. $\mathbf{\dfrac{1}{1000}}$

6. a. $\mathbf{+5}$

b. $-15 + 10 = \mathbf{-5}$

c. $+3 - 5 + 2 - 4 = \mathbf{-4}$

7. $1000 - (100 - 10) - 1000 \div 100$
$1000 - 90 - 10$
$\mathbf{900}$

8. $\dfrac{6}{n} = \dfrac{8}{1.2}$
$8n = 6 \cdot 1.2$
$n = \dfrac{7.2}{8}$
$n = \mathbf{0.9}$

9. a. **1.1**

b. $\dfrac{11}{10} \times \dfrac{10}{10} = \dfrac{110}{100} = \mathbf{110\%}$

10. a. $\dfrac{45}{100} = \mathbf{\dfrac{9}{20}}$

b. $\dfrac{45}{100} = \mathbf{45\%}$

11. a. $\dfrac{80}{100} = \mathbf{\dfrac{4}{5}}$

b. $\dfrac{80}{100} = \mathbf{0.8}$

12.
$$\begin{array}{r} 5\frac{3}{8} \times \frac{1}{1} = 5\frac{3}{8} \\ 4\frac{1}{4} \times \frac{2}{2} = 4\frac{2}{8} \\ + \; 3\frac{1}{2} \times \frac{4}{4} = 3\frac{4}{8} \\ \hline 12\frac{9}{8} = \mathbf{13\frac{1}{8}} \end{array}$$

13. $\dfrac{\overset{1}{\cancel{\overset{4}{\cancel{8}}}}}{\underset{1}{\cancel{3}}} \cdot \dfrac{\overset{1}{\cancel{5}}}{\underset{1}{\cancel{\underset{4}{\cancel{12}}}}} \cdot \dfrac{\overset{1}{\cancel{\overset{3}{\cancel{9}}}}}{\underset{1}{\cancel{\underset{2}{\cancel{10}}}}} = \dfrac{1}{1} = \mathbf{1}$

14.
$$\begin{array}{r} 64.8 \\ 8.42 \\ +\ 24 \\ \hline \mathbf{97.22} \end{array}$$

15. $90° - 55° = \mathbf{35°}$

16. $\frac{1}{2}$ pint = 1 cup
1 cup = 8 ounces
8 ounces

17. $3m + 8 = 44$ check: $3(12) + 8 = 44$
$3m = 36$ $\quad 36 + 8 = 44$
$m = \mathbf{12}$ $\quad 44 = 44$

18. $\mathbf{(1 \times 10^8) + (1 \times 10^7)}$

19. Factors of 30
1, 2, 3, 5, 6, 10, (15), 30
Factors of 45
1, 3, 5, 9, (15), 45
GCF is **15.**

20. **a.** $\frac{1}{2}$ in. $\times$ $\frac{1}{4}$ in. $=$ $\mathbf{\frac{1}{8}}$ **in.²**

b. $\mathbf{\frac{1}{8}}$

21. $3\text{ ft} \times 3\text{ ft} \times 3\text{ ft} = 27\text{ ft}^3$
27 blocks

22.
$$\begin{array}{r} \mathbf{\$21.30} \\ 3\overline{)\$63.90} \\ 6 \\ \hline 03 \\ 3 \\ \hline 09 \\ 09 \\ \hline 00 \\ 00 \\ \hline 0 \end{array}$$
$n = \mathbf{\$21.30}$

23. $2\text{ cm} + x = 7\text{ cm}$
$x = 5\text{ cm}$
$5\text{ cm} + y = 8\text{ cm}$
$y = 3\text{ cm}$
$5\text{ cm} + 5\text{ cm} + 3\text{ cm} + 2\text{ cm}$
$+ 8\text{ cm} + 7\text{ cm} = \mathbf{30\text{ cm}}$

24. $7\text{ cm} \times 5\text{ cm} = 35\text{ cm}^2$
$3\text{ cm} \times 2\text{ cm} = 6\text{ cm}^2$
$A = 35\text{ cm}^2 + 6\text{ cm}^2 = \mathbf{41\text{ cm}^2}$

25. $A_1 = \dfrac{\overset{3}{\cancel{6}}\text{ cm} \times 10\text{ cm}}{\underset{1}{\cancel{2}}}$

$A_1 = 30\text{ cm}^2$

$A_2 = \dfrac{\overset{7}{\cancel{14}}\text{ cm} \times 6\text{ cm}}{\underset{1}{\cancel{2}}}$

$A_2 = 42\text{ cm}^2$

$A = A_1 + A_2 = 30\text{ cm}^2 + 42\text{ cm}^2 = \mathbf{72\text{ cm}^2}$

26. **a.** **57 years**

b. 54, 57, 57, 57, <u>57</u>, 58, 61, 61, 68
57 years

c.
$$\begin{array}{r} {}^{5} \\ 57 \\ 61 \\ 57 \\ 57 \\ 58 \\ 57 \\ 61 \\ 54 \\ +\ 68 \\ \hline 530 \end{array} \qquad \begin{array}{r} 58.8\ldots \\ 9\overline{)530.0\ldots} \\ 45 \\ \hline 80 \\ 72 \\ \hline 80 \\ 72 \\ \hline 8 \end{array} \longrightarrow \mathbf{59\ years}$$

d. **Mode; b. Median; c. Mean**

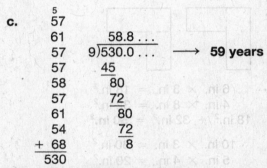

27.

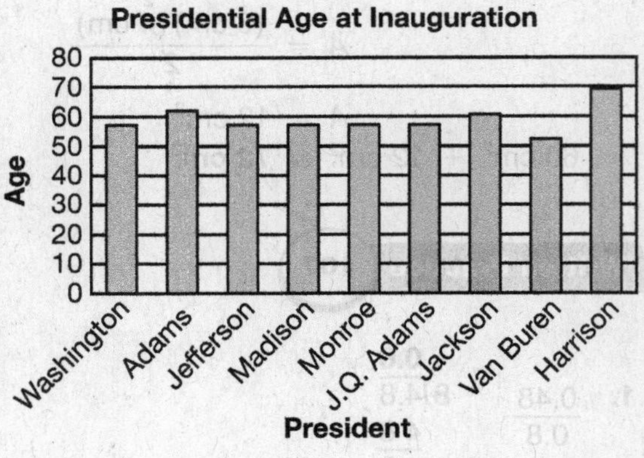

28.
$$\begin{array}{rr} \overset{11}{\cancel{12}}\text{ lb} & \overset{19}{\cancel{3}}\text{ oz} \\ -8\text{ lb} & 7\text{ oz} \\ \hline \mathbf{3\text{ lb}} & \mathbf{12\text{ oz}} \end{array}$$

29. **See student work.**

a. 10 cm ÷ 2 = **5 cm**

b. $C = \pi d$
$C \approx (3.14)(10\text{ cm})$
$C \approx$ **31.4 cm**

30. $\dfrac{10\ \cancel{\text{gallons}}}{1} \times \dfrac{31.5\text{ miles}}{1\ \cancel{\text{gallon}}} =$ **315 miles**

Practice Set 108

a. **Reflection**

b. **Translation**

c. **Rotation**

d. **Translation and reflection**

e. **Rotation and reflection**

f. **A (−2, 4)** **A′ (2, 4)**
B (−1, 1) **B′ (1, 1)**
C (−4, 2) **C′ (4, 2)**

Written Practice 108

1. 2 + 4 + 6 + 8 + 10 = **30**

2. $\dfrac{4}{3} = \dfrac{12}{l}$
$4l = 3 \cdot 12$
$l = \dfrac{3 \cdot \overset{3}{\cancel{12}}}{\underset{1}{\cancel{4}}}$
$l =$ **9 games**

3.

	%	A.C.
Correct	80	c
Incorrect	20	5
Total	100	t

$\dfrac{80}{20} = \dfrac{c}{5}$
$20c = 80 \cdot 5$
$c = \dfrac{\overset{4}{\cancel{80}} \cdot 5}{\underset{1}{\cancel{20}}}$

$c =$ **20 questions; One possibility: Five students is 20%, or $\frac{1}{5}$ of the class. So $\frac{4}{5}$ must be 4 × 5, or 20 students.**

4. $A = \pi r^2$
$A \approx (3.14)(6\text{ in.})^2$
$A \approx 113.04\text{ in.}^2$
$A \approx$ **113 in.²**

5. $\dfrac{3}{\underset{1}{\cancel{8}}} \times \dfrac{\overset{6}{\cancel{48}}}{1} = \dfrac{18}{1} = 18$
18 woodwind players

6. Multiples of 6
6, 12, 18, (24), 30
Multiples of 8
8, 16, (24), 32, 40
Multiples of 12
12, (24), 36, 48, 60
LCM is **24.**

7. **Answers may vary.**
Sample answer: Rotate triangle I until its orientation matches triangle II's. Then translate triangle I until it is positioned on triangle II.

8. $\dfrac{0.7}{20} = \dfrac{n}{100}$
$20n = 0.7 \cdot 100$
$n = \dfrac{0.7 \cdot \overset{5}{\cancel{100}}}{\underset{1}{\cancel{20}}}$
$n =$ **3.5**

9. a. $1\dfrac{2}{5} = 1\dfrac{4}{10} =$ **1.4**

b. $\dfrac{14}{10} \times \dfrac{10}{10} = \dfrac{140}{100} =$ **140%**

10. **a.** $\frac{24}{100} = \mathbf{\frac{6}{25}}$

b. $\frac{24}{100} = \mathbf{24\%}$

11. **a.** $\frac{35}{100} = \mathbf{\frac{7}{20}}$

b. $\frac{35}{100} = \mathbf{0.35}$

12.

$$2\frac{1}{4} \times \frac{2}{2} = \overset{1}{\cancel{2}}\frac{\overset{10}{\cancel{2}}}{8}$$
$$-\ \frac{7}{8} \times \frac{1}{1} = \frac{7}{8}$$
$$1\frac{3}{8}$$

$$4\frac{3}{4} \times \frac{2}{2} = 4\frac{6}{8}$$
$$+\ 1\frac{3}{8} \times \frac{1}{1} = 1\frac{3}{8}$$
$$5\frac{9}{8} = \mathbf{6\frac{1}{8}}$$

13. $\frac{2}{1} \div \frac{5}{3}$

$1 \div \frac{5}{3} = \frac{3}{5}$

$\frac{2}{1} \times \frac{3}{5} = \frac{6}{5}$

$\frac{6}{5} \div \frac{6}{5} = \mathbf{1}$

14.

$$\overset{8}{\cancel{9}}.\overset{9}{\cancel{0}}{}^{1}0 - 2.79 = 6.21$$
$$6.2 + 6.21 = \mathbf{12.41}$$

15. $-3 + 7 - 8 + 1$

$-11 + 8$

$\mathbf{-3}$

16. $\$2.89 \times 0.06 = \$0.1734 \longrightarrow$ **$0.17**

17. $\mathbf{\frac{1}{1000}}$

18. **0.3, 0.305, 0.31**

19. $V = lwh$

$V = 10\text{ cm} \times 10\text{ cm} \times 10\text{ cm}$

$V = \mathbf{1000\ cm^3}$

20. $32 - 25 + 5 \times 2$

$32 - 25 + 10$

$\mathbf{17}$

21. $8a - 4 = 60$

$8a = 64$

$a = \mathbf{8}$

check: $8(8) - 4 = 60$

$64 - 4 = 60$

$60 = 60$

22. $\frac{1}{\underset{1}{\cancel{3}}} \cdot \frac{\overset{30}{\cancel{90}}}{1} = \frac{30}{1} = \mathbf{30°}$

23. $20\text{ mm} + x = 30\text{ mm}$

$x = 10\text{ mm}$

$15\text{ mm} + y = 20\text{ mm}$

$y = 5\text{ mm}$

$20\text{ mm} + 20\text{ mm} + 30\text{ mm} + 15\text{ mm} + 10\text{ mm} + 5\text{ mm} = \mathbf{100\ mm}$

24. $15\text{ mm} \times 10\text{ mm} = 150\text{ mm}^2$

$20\text{ mm} \times 20\text{ mm} = 400\text{ mm}^2$

$A = 150\text{ mm}^2 + 400\text{ mm}^2 = \mathbf{550\ mm^2}$

25. 2 gallons = 8 quarts

8 quarts = 16 pints

1 pint = 1 lb

About 16 pounds

26. $A = \frac{bh}{2}$

$A_1 = \frac{\overset{10}{\cancel{20}}\text{ mm} \times 10\text{ mm}}{\underset{1}{\cancel{2}}}$

$A_1 = 100\text{ mm}^2$

$A_2 = \frac{\overset{6}{\cancel{12}}\text{ mm} \times 10\text{ mm}}{\underset{1}{\cancel{2}}}$

$A_2 = 60\text{ mm}^2$

$A = A_1 + A_2 = 100\text{ mm}^2 + 60\text{ mm}^2$

$= \mathbf{160\ mm^2}$

27. **1000 milliliters**

28. $\frac{6}{10} \cdot \frac{5}{9} = \frac{30}{90} = \mathbf{\frac{1}{3}}$

29. 1 km = 1000 m

$\frac{1}{2}$ km = 500 m

1500 meters

30.

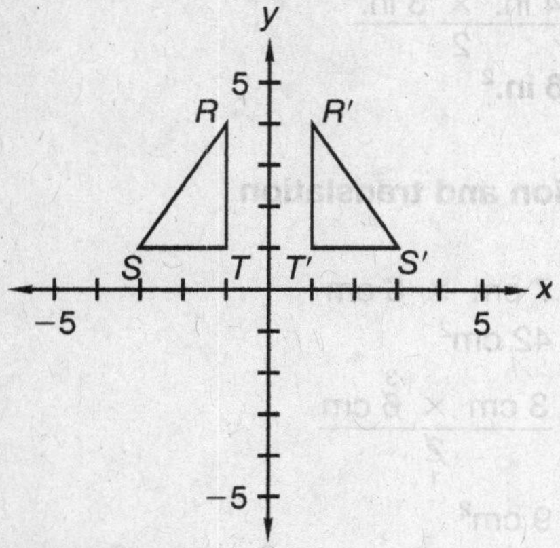

R′ (1, 4)
S′ (3, 1)
T′ (1, 1)

Practice Set 109

a. **True**

b. **False**

c. **True**

d. $\overline{QR}$ or $\overline{RQ}$

e. **I and II**

f. AE = **3 in.**
IJ = **3 in.**

Written Practice 109

1. $7 \times 11 \times 13 = \mathbf{1001}$

2. $\frac{2 \text{ cm}}{1 \text{ km}} = \frac{10 \text{ cm}}{x}$

$2x = 10 \cdot 1$

$x = \frac{\overset{5}{\cancel{10}} \cdot 1}{\underset{1}{\cancel{2}}}$

$x = \mathbf{5\ km}$

3. $\frac{8}{52} = \mathbf{\frac{2}{13}}$

4. a. **C.** 

b. **A.** 

5. $90° \div 2 = \mathbf{45°}$

6. $\frac{5}{50} = \mathbf{\frac{1}{10}}$

$\frac{1}{10} = \mathbf{0.1}$

7. $7w - 3 = 60$

$7w = 63$

$w = \mathbf{9}$

8. $\frac{8}{n} = \frac{4}{2.5}$

$4n = 8 \cdot 2.5$

$n = \frac{\overset{2}{\cancel{8}} \cdot 2.5}{\underset{1}{\cancel{4}}}$

$n = \mathbf{5}$

9. a.
```
    0.625
 8)5.000
   4 8
     20
     16
      40
      40
       0
```

b. $0.625 \times 100\% = \mathbf{62.5\%}$

10. a. $1\frac{25}{100} = \mathbf{1\frac{1}{4}}$

b. $\frac{125}{100} = \mathbf{125\%}$

11. a. $\frac{70}{100} = \mathbf{\frac{7}{10}}$

b. $\frac{7}{10} = \mathbf{0.7}$

12. a. **There are 3 numbers on the spinner that are less than 4. So the probability is $\frac{3}{4}$.**

b. **Two of the numbers (2 and 3) are prime. The spinner should land on a prime number about $\frac{1}{2}$ of the 100 spins.**

$\frac{1}{2} \cdot 100 = \mathbf{50\ times}$

13. $\frac{\cancelto{2}{200\text{ cm}}}{1} \cdot \frac{1\text{ m}}{\cancelto{1}{100\text{ cm}}} =$ **2 meters**

14.
$$\begin{array}{r} 1\overset{4}{\cancel{5}}.\overset{11}{\cancel{2}}{}^{1}0 \\ -\ \ 2.79 \\ \hline \mathbf{12.41} \end{array}$$

15. $1000 \div 100 - 10$
$10 - 10$
0

16. **Answers may vary. Sample answer:**

x	2	3	5	10
y	4	6	10	20

17.
$$\begin{array}{r} 0.666 \longrightarrow \mathbf{0.67} \\ 3\overline{)2.000} \\ 1\,8 \\ \hline 20 \\ 18 \\ \hline 20 \\ 18 \\ \hline 2 \end{array}$$

18. $V = lwh$
$V = 12\text{ ft} \times 10\text{ ft} \times 8\text{ ft}$
$V = 960\text{ ft}^2$
960 boxes

19. a. **The sides of the larger rectangle are three times larger than the sides of the smaller rectangle (3 ft × 3 = 9 ft and 1 ft × 3 = 3 ft). So the larger rectangle is larger than the smaller rectangle by a scale factor of 3.**

b. **Scale factor of $\frac{1}{3}$.**

20.
$$\begin{array}{r} \mathbf{\$35} \\ 12\overline{)\$420} \\ 36 \\ \hline 60 \\ 60 \\ \hline 0 \end{array}$$
\$35.00 $= m$

21. a. **−1**
b. **+1**
c. **−15**
d. **+1**

22. $A = \frac{4\text{ in.} \times 3\text{ in.}}{2}$
$A = \mathbf{6\ in.^2}$

23. **Rotation and translation**

24. $A_1 = 7\text{ cm} \times 6\text{ cm}$
$A_1 = 42\text{ cm}^2$
$A_2 = \frac{3\text{ cm} \times \cancelto{3}{6}\text{ cm}}{\cancelto{1}{2}}$
$A_2 = 9\text{ cm}^2$
$A = A_1 + A_2 = 42\text{ cm}^2 + 9\text{ cm}^2 = \mathbf{51\ cm^2}$

25. $C = \pi d$
$C \approx (3.14)(7\text{ cm})$
$C \approx 21.98\text{ cm}$
22 cm

26. **40°**

27. $\frac{9}{2} = \frac{p}{36}$
$2p = 36 \cdot 9$
$p = \frac{\cancelto{18}{36} \cdot 9}{\cancelto{1}{2}}$
$p =$ **162 peanuts**

28. a. **34 mm**
b. **3.4 cm**

29. $6\frac{2}{3} \div 100 = \frac{20}{3} \div \frac{100}{1}$

$1 \div \frac{100}{1} = \frac{1}{100}$

$\frac{\cancelto{1}{20}}{3} \cdot \frac{1}{\cancelto{5}{100}} = \mathbf{\frac{1}{15}}$

30. $\left(\frac{1}{10}\right)^2$ (=) 0.01
$\frac{1}{100}$
0.01

Early Finishers Solutions

No; $\frac{1}{5} + \frac{1}{2} = \frac{7}{10}$ ton; $\frac{7}{10} \cdot 2000 = 1400$, so Issam has a 1400 pound load. This exceeds the maximum load of his trailer so he cannot take the entire load in one trip.

Practice Set 110

a.

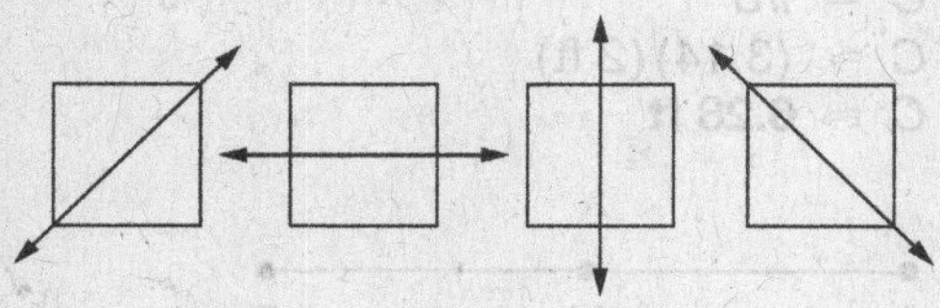

b. F

Written Practice 110

1. $99\overline{)9999}$ = **101**
$$\begin{array}{r} 99 \\ \hline 09 \\ 0 \\ \hline 99 \\ 99 \\ \hline 0 \end{array}$$

2.
$$\frac{x}{63} = \frac{5}{3}$$
$$3x = (5 \times 63)$$
$$3x = 315$$
$$x = \frac{315}{3}$$
$$x = \mathbf{105\ ft}$$

3. $V = lwh$
$V = 4\text{ in.} \times 4\text{ in.} \times 10\text{ in.}$
$V = \mathbf{160\ in.^3}$

4. $6\overline{)360°}$ = **60°**
$$\begin{array}{r} 36 \\ \hline 00 \\ 00 \\ \hline 0 \end{array}$$

5. **3 lines of symmetry**

6. $6\text{ cm} \times 3 = \mathbf{18\ cm}$

7. $A = \frac{\overset{2}{\cancel{4}}\text{ cm} \times 3\text{ cm}}{\underset{1}{\cancel{2}}}$

$A = \mathbf{6\ cm^2}$

8.

	%	A.C.
Boys	40	b
Girls	60	12
Total	100	t

$$\frac{60}{100} = \frac{12}{t}$$
$$60t = 12 \cdot 100$$
$$t = \frac{\overset{1}{\cancel{12}} \cdot \overset{20}{\cancel{100}}}{\underset{\underset{1}{\cancel{5}}}{\cancel{60}}}$$
$$t = \mathbf{20\ students}$$

9. **a.** $2\frac{3}{4} \times \frac{25}{25} = 2\frac{75}{100} = \mathbf{2.75}$

b. $\frac{275}{100} = \mathbf{275\%}$

10. **a.** $1.1 = \mathbf{1\frac{1}{10}}$

b. $\frac{11}{10} \times \frac{10}{10} = \frac{110}{100} = \mathbf{110\%}$

11. **a.** $\frac{64}{100} = \mathbf{\frac{16}{25}}$

b. $\frac{64}{100} = \mathbf{0.64}$

12.
$$\begin{array}{rcl} 24\frac{1}{6} \times \frac{1}{1} & = & 24\frac{1}{6} \\ 23\frac{1}{3} \times \frac{2}{2} & = & 23\frac{2}{6} \\ +\ 22\frac{1}{2} \times \frac{3}{3} & = & 22\frac{3}{6} \\ \hline & & 69\frac{6}{6} = \mathbf{70} \end{array}$$

13.
$$\frac{6}{5} \div \frac{2}{1} \qquad \frac{3}{5} \div \frac{5}{3}$$
$$1 \div \frac{2}{1} = \frac{1}{2} \qquad \frac{5}{3} \div 1 = \frac{3}{5}$$
$$\frac{\overset{3}{\cancel{6}}}{5} \times \frac{1}{\underset{1}{\cancel{2}}} = \frac{3}{5} \qquad \frac{3}{5} \times \frac{3}{5} = \frac{9}{25}$$
$$\mathbf{\frac{9}{25}}$$

14. $9 - 8.99 = \mathbf{0.01}$

15.

```
     $175
36)$6300
    36
    270
    252
     180
     180
       0
```

$175.00 $= m$

16.

```
    $24.89
  ×  0.065
     12445
    149340
  $1.61785  ⟶  $1.62
```

17.

```
   0.0162
4)0.0650
    4
    25
    24
     10
     08
      2
```

0.016

18.

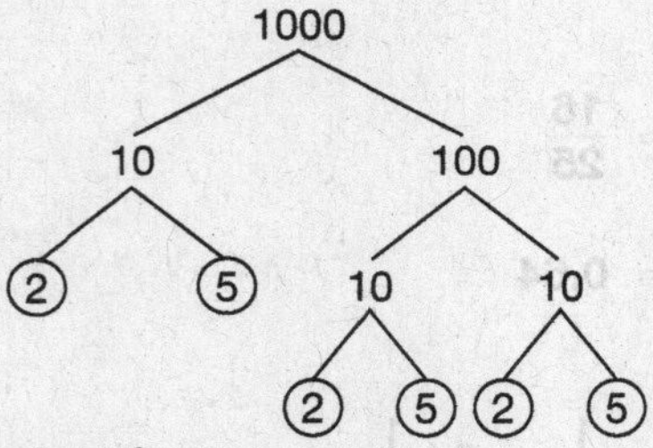

$2^3 \cdot 5^3$

19. **True**

20. $27 - 9 \div 3 - 3 \times 3$

$27 - 3 - 9$

15

21. $8\text{ m} + x = 10\text{ m}$

$x = 2\text{ m}$

$5\text{ m} + y = 12\text{ m}$

$y = 7\text{ m}$

$8\text{ m} + 12\text{ m} + 10\text{ m} + 5\text{ m} + 2\text{ m} + 7\text{ m} = \mathbf{44\text{ m}}$

22. $A_1 = 8\text{ m} \times 12\text{ m}$ $\quad A_2 = 2\text{ m} \times 5\text{ m}$

$A_1 = 96\text{ m}^2$ $\quad A_2 = 10\text{ m}^2$

$A = A_1 + A_2 = 96\text{ m}^2 + 10\text{ m}^2 = \mathbf{106\text{ m}^2}$

23. **Rotation, reflection, and translation**

24. $24\text{ cm} - 10\text{ cm} - 8\text{ cm} = \mathbf{6\text{ cm}}$

25. $C = \pi d$

$C \approx (3.14)(2\text{ ft})$

$C \approx \mathbf{6.28\text{ ft}}$

26.

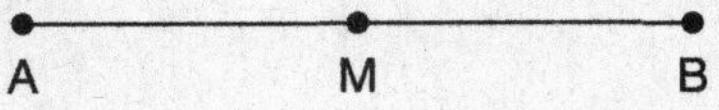

$1\frac{3}{4}\text{ inches} \div 2 = \frac{7}{4} \div \frac{2}{1}$

$1 \div \frac{2}{1} = \frac{1}{2}$

$\frac{7}{4} \times \frac{1}{2} = \mathbf{\frac{7}{8}}$ **inch**

27.

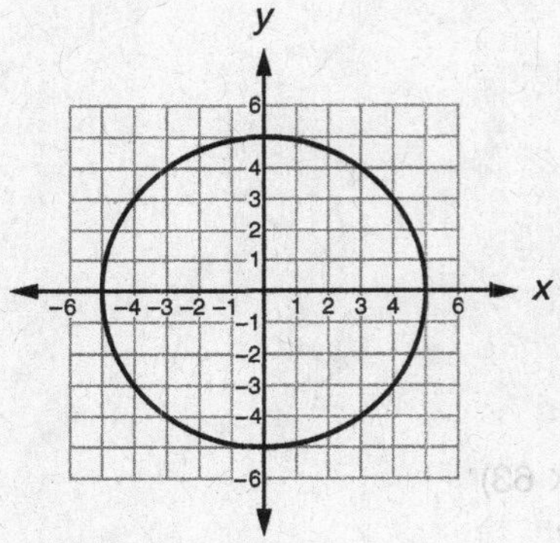

(5, 0) and (−5, 0)

28. $A = \pi r^2$

$A \approx (3.14)(5\text{ units})^2$

$A \approx$ **78.5 sq. units**

29. $-3 - 4 + 5 - 7$

$-14 + 5$

$\mathbf{-9}$

30. $\frac{1}{2} \times \frac{1}{2} \times \frac{1}{2} \times \frac{1}{2} = \mathbf{\frac{1}{16}}$

Investigation 11

1. kitchen in scale drawing: length = 1 inch; width = $\frac{1}{2}$ inch
   $\frac{1}{2}$ inch = 5 feet
   1 inch = 10 feet
   length = 10 feet; width = 5 feet

2. doorway = $\frac{1}{4}$ inch
   $\frac{1}{2}$ inch = 5 feet
   $\frac{1}{4}$ inch = **$2\frac{1}{2}$ feet**

3. 1 inch = 1.5 feet
   8 inches = 8(1.5 feet) = 12 feet
   10 inches = 10(1.5 feet) = 15 feet
   12 ft by 15 ft

4. 1 inch = 2 feet
   24 inches = 24(2 feet) = **48 feet**

5. $\frac{7}{3} = \frac{14}{w}$
   $7w = 3 \cdot 14$
   $w = \frac{3 \cdot \cancel{14}^{2}}{\cancel{7}_{1}}$
   $w =$ **6 feet**

6. $\frac{7}{h} = \frac{14}{4}$
   $14h = 7 \cdot 4$
   $h = \frac{\cancel{7}^{1} \cdot \cancel{4}^{2}}{\cancel{14}_{\cancel{2}_{1}}}$
   $h =$ **2 inches**
   One possibility: I know my answer is correct because $\frac{7}{2}$ and $\frac{14}{4}$ are equal ratios.

7. $\frac{3}{12} = \frac{F}{6}$
   $12F = 3 \cdot 6$
   $F = \frac{3 \cdot \cancel{6}^{1}}{\cancel{12}_{2}}$
   $F = \frac{3}{2}$ feet = **$1\frac{1}{2}$ feet**

8. $\frac{12 \text{ cm}}{6 \text{ ft}} = \frac{2 \text{ cm}}{1 \text{ ft}}$
   1 ft humerus is 2cm long on scale drawing.

9. a. **1 cm = 4 ft**
   b. bathroom in scale drawing:
   length = 2 cm; width = 1 cm
   length = 2 cm = 2(4 ft) = **8 feet**
   width = 1 cm = **4 feet**

10. **1 inch = 0.5 feet**

11. scale = $\frac{7 \text{ inches}}{14 \text{ feet}} = \frac{7 \text{ inches}}{168 \text{ inches}} =$ **$\frac{1}{24}$; 24**

12. 6-ft-8-in = 80 inches
    80 inches ÷ 10 = **8 inches**

13. scale factor = 6
    length = 6(3 feet) = 18 feet
    width = 6(1.5 feet) = 9 feet
    18 feet by 9 feet

Extensions

a. **Answers will vary. See student work.**
   Scale factor = $\frac{1 \text{ inch}}{3 \text{ feet}} = \frac{1 \text{ inch}}{36 \text{ inches}}$
   = **$\frac{1}{36}$ or 36**

b. **Answers will vary. See student work.**

c. 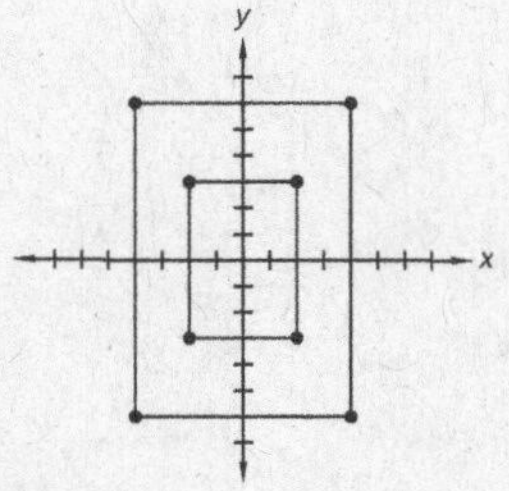

   (4, 6), (4, −6), (−4, −6), (−4, 6)

d. **Answers will vary. See student work.**
   Scale factor = $\frac{\frac{3}{4} \text{ in.}}{1 \text{ ft}} = \frac{\frac{3}{4} \text{ in.}}{12 \text{ in.}} =$ **$\frac{1}{16}$ or 16**
   Sides of model = $2\frac{1}{4}$ in., 3 in., $3\frac{3}{4}$ in.

Practice Set 111

a. $4\overline{)90}$ = 22 R 2
8
10
8
2
22, 22, 23, 23

b. $\frac{\$30}{\$9.50 \text{ per ticket}} = 3\frac{3}{19}$
3 tickets

c. $\frac{\overset{14}{\cancel{28}} \text{ children}}{\underset{3}{\cancel{6}} \text{ children per van}} = 4\frac{2}{3}$
5 vans

d. $8\frac{1}{2}$ in. ÷ 2 = $4\frac{1}{4}$ in.
11 in. ÷ 2 = $5\frac{1}{2}$ in.
$4\frac{1}{4}$ in. by $5\frac{1}{2}$ in.
I can check the answer by folding a paper and measuring it.

e.
$6.95
$7.95
$6.45
+ $8.85
$30.20

$4\overline{)\$30.20}$ = **$7.55**
28
22
20
20
20
0

Written Practice 111

1. $3\overline{)80}$ = 26 R 2
6
20
18
2
26, 27, 27

2. $\frac{\$45.00}{4 \text{ friends}} =$ **$11.25**

3. $39\overline{)1560}$ = 40
156
00
00
0
40 stamps

4. 3 cubes × 3 cubes × 3 cubes = **27 cubes**

5. **5043**

6. **30 cm or 31 cm (Accept either answer.) Twelve inches equals 30.48 cm, which is very near the midpoint of 30 cm and 31 cm.**

7. **Answers will vary. See student work.**

8. 180° − 80° − 70° = **30°**

9. **a.** $\frac{11}{20} \times \frac{5}{5} = \frac{55}{100} =$ **0.55**

b. $\frac{55}{100} =$ **55%**

10. **a.** $1\frac{5}{10} =$ **$1\frac{1}{2}$**

b. $\frac{15}{10} \times \frac{10}{10} = \frac{150}{100} =$ **150%**

11. **a.** **$\frac{1}{100}$**

b. $\frac{1}{100} =$ **0.01**

12. **a.** **−18**
b. **+6**
c. **−6**
d. **−18**

13. $\frac{25}{4} \div \frac{100}{1}$

$1 \div \frac{100}{1} = \frac{1}{100}$

$\frac{\overset{1}{\cancel{25}}}{4} \times \frac{1}{\underset{4}{\cancel{100}}} = \mathbf{\frac{1}{16}}$

14.
$$\begin{array}{r} \$14.70 \\ 3\overline{)\$44.10} \\ \underline{3} \\ 14 \\ \underline{12} \\ 2\,1 \\ \underline{2\,1} \\ 00 \\ \underline{00} \\ 0 \end{array}$$

$m = \mathbf{\$14.70}$

15.

	%	A.C.
Kim	30	15
Team	70	t
Total	100	T

$\frac{30}{100} = \frac{15}{T}$

$30T = 15 \cdot 100$

$T = \frac{\overset{1}{\cancel{15}} \cdot \overset{50}{\cancel{100}}}{\underset{\underset{1}{\cancel{2}}}{\cancel{30}}}$

$T = $ **50 points**

16. $6.7 + 6.6 + 6.7 + 6.7 + 6.8 = 33.5$

$33.5 \div 5 = \mathbf{6.7}$

17. **Answers will vary. See student work. Sample answer: What was the difference between the highest and lowest scores? 7.6 − 6.5 = 1.1**

18. $5\text{ m} \times 5\text{ m} = 25\text{ m}^2$

$\frac{\overset{3}{\cancel{6}}\text{ m} \times 5\text{ m}}{\underset{1}{\cancel{2}}} = 15\text{ m}^2$

$25\text{ m}^2 + 15\text{ m}^2 = \mathbf{40\text{ m}^2}$

19. 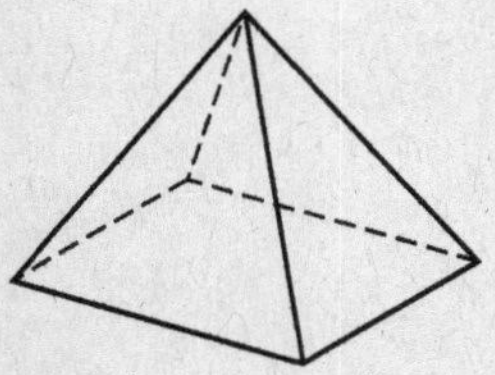 $\mathbf{\frac{5}{8}}$

20. **Line *t***

21. $3m + 1 = 100$ check: $3(33) + 1 = 100$

$3m = 99$ $\quad 99 + 1 = 100$

$m = \mathbf{33}$ $\quad 100 = 100$

22.

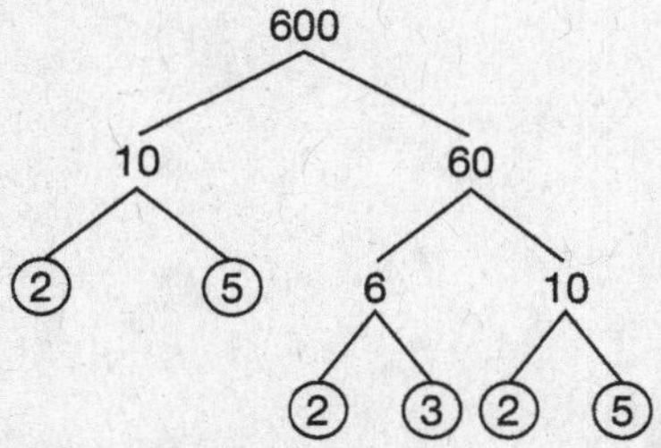

$\mathbf{2^3 \times 3 \times 5^2}$

23. **A rectangle and two same-size circles**

24.
$$\begin{array}{r} \$0.89 \\ \times\ \ 0.07 \\ \hline \$0.0623 \end{array} \qquad \begin{array}{r} \$0.89 \\ +\ \$0.06 \\ \hline \mathbf{\$0.95} \end{array}$$

25. $\mathbf{\frac{999{,}999}{1{,}000{,}000}}$

26. **Angle *B***

27. **Rotation and possibly translation**

28. $C = \pi d$

$C \approx (3.14)(10\text{ cm})$

$C \approx \mathbf{31.4\text{ cm}}$

29. $\frac{10}{16} = \frac{25}{y}$

$10y = 16 \cdot 25$

$y = \frac{\overset{8}{\cancel{16}} \cdot \overset{5}{\cancel{25}}}{\underset{\underset{1}{\cancel{2}}}{\cancel{10}}}$

$y = \mathbf{40}$

30. $d = \frac{50\text{ mi}}{1\ \cancel{\text{hr}}} \times \frac{5\ \cancel{\text{hr}}}{1}$

$d = \mathbf{250\text{ mi}}$

Solutions

Practice Set 112

Predictions: (b), (c), (f), and (h) will have positive answers; (a), (d), (e), and (g) will have negative answers.

a. **−20**

b. **+20**

c. **+20**

d. **−20**

e. **−6**

f. **+6**

g. **−6**

h. **+6**

Written Practice 112

1. $84\overline{)200}$ = 2 R 32
$$\begin{array}{r} 200 \\ \underline{168} \\ 32 \end{array}$$
3 buses

2. a. $\frac{25.2 \text{ in.}}{210 \text{ ft}} = \frac{25.2 \text{ in.}}{2520 \text{ in.}} = \mathbf{\frac{1}{100}}$

b. $\frac{25.2}{210} = \frac{28}{l}$

$25.2l = 5880$

$l = 233\frac{1}{3}$

about 233 feet

3. a. **+12**

b. **−3**

c. **+1**

d. **−12**

4. a. **−8**

b. **+4**

c. **−4**

d. **+8**

5.

	%	A.C.
Chopped	90	27
Not Chopped	10	i
Total	100	t

$\frac{90}{10} = \frac{27}{i}$

$90i = 10 \cdot 27$

$i = \frac{\overset{1}{\cancel{10}} \cdot \overset{3}{\cancel{27}}}{\underset{\underset{1}{\cancel{9}}}{\cancel{90}}}$

$i =$ **3 carrots**

6. **$(2 \times 10^7) + (5 \times 10^5) + (1 \times 10^4)$**

7.
$$\begin{array}{r} \$3.65 \\ \times \quad 0.08 \\ \hline \$0.2920 \end{array} \longrightarrow \mathbf{\$0.29}$$

8. $\frac{1}{2} \times \frac{1}{2} = \frac{1}{4}$

$\frac{1}{8} \div \frac{1}{2}$

$1 \div \frac{1}{2} = \frac{2}{1}$

$\frac{1}{\underset{4}{\cancel{8}}} \times \frac{\overset{1}{\cancel{2}}}{1} = \frac{1}{4}$

$\frac{1}{4} + \frac{1}{4} = \frac{2}{4} = \mathbf{\frac{1}{2}}$

9. a. $1\frac{4}{5} \times \frac{20}{20} = 1\frac{80}{100} = \mathbf{1.8}$

b. $\frac{180}{100} = \mathbf{180\%}$

10. a. $\frac{6}{10} = \mathbf{\frac{3}{5}}$

b. $\frac{6}{10} \times \frac{10}{10} = \frac{60}{100} = \mathbf{60\%}$

11. a. $\frac{2}{100} = \mathbf{\frac{1}{50}}$

b. $\frac{2}{100} = \mathbf{0.02}$

12. $5\frac{1}{2} \times \frac{3}{3} = \overset{4}{\cancel{5}}\frac{\overset{9}{\cancel{3}}}{6}$

$- 2\frac{5}{6} \times \frac{1}{1} = 2\frac{5}{6}$

$m = 2\frac{4}{6} = \mathbf{2\frac{2}{3}}$

13. $\frac{6}{10} = \frac{0.9}{n}$

$6n = 90$

$n = \mathbf{1.5}$

14. $9x - 7 = 92$

$9x = 99$

$x = \mathbf{11}$

15.
```
   160
5)800
  5
  30
  30
   00
   00
    0
```
$w = \mathbf{160}$

16. **a.** 6 lb ÷ 3 = **2 lb**

b. 2 lb × 8 = **16 lb**

17. $V = lwh$

$V = (8\text{ cm})(5\text{ cm})(2\text{ cm})$

$V = \mathbf{80\ cm^3}$

18. 1.2 × 1000 mm = **1200 mm**

19. $5\text{ mm} + x = 15\text{ mm}$

$x = 10\text{ mm}$

$5\text{ mm} + y = 12\text{ mm}$

$y = 7\text{ mm}$

$5\text{ mm} + 15\text{ mm} + 12\text{ mm} + 5\text{ mm} + 7\text{ mm} + 10\text{ mm} = \mathbf{54\ mm}$

20. $A_1 = 5\text{ mm} \times 15\text{ mm} = 75\text{ mm}^2$

$A_2 = 7\text{ mm} \times 5\text{ mm} = 35\text{ mm}^2$

$A = A_1 + A_2 = 75\text{ mm}^2 + 35\text{ mm}^2$

$= \mathbf{110\ mm^2}$

21. **Cube; One possibility: A cube has six faces that are squares.**

22. **D. 37**

23. $C = \pi d$

$C \approx (3.14)(12\text{ in.})$

$C \approx 37.68\text{ in.}$

38 inches

24. **a. H**

b. H

25. ***B***

26.

	Ratio	A.C.
Nonfiction	2	*n*
Fiction	3	*f*
Total	5	30

$\frac{2}{5} = \frac{n}{30}$

$5n = 2 \cdot 30$

$n = \frac{2 \cdot \overset{6}{\cancel{30}}}{\underset{1}{\cancel{5}}}$

$n =$ **12 nonfiction books**

27.

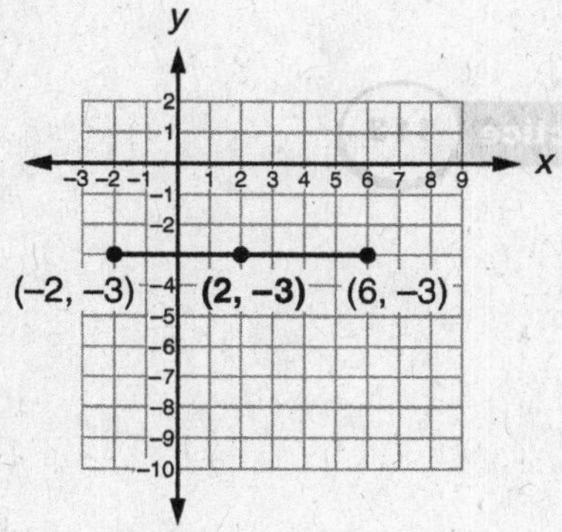

(2, –3)

28. $\mathbf{\frac{3}{39} = \frac{1}{13}}$

29. $A_1 = \frac{10\text{ in.} \times \overset{3}{\cancel{6}}\text{ in.}}{\underset{1}{\cancel{2}}}$

$A_1 = 30\text{ in.}^2$

$A_2 = \frac{\overset{3}{\cancel{6}}\text{ in.} \times 8\text{ in.}}{\underset{1}{\cancel{2}}}$

$A_2 = 24\text{ in.}^2$

$A = A_1 + A_2 = 30\text{ in.}^2 + 24\text{ in.}^2 = \mathbf{54\ in.^2}$

30. $9 + 2 \times 25 - 50 \div 5$

$9 + 50 - 10$

49

Solutions

Early Finishers Solutions

($20 + $25) ÷ 5 = $9 was spent at the bookstore.

Practice Set 113

a.

$$\begin{array}{rr} 6\text{ ft} & 5\text{ in.} \\ +\ 4\text{ ft} & 8\text{ in.} \\ \hline 10\text{ ft} & 13\text{ in.} \end{array}$$

11 ft 1 in.

b.

$$\begin{array}{rr} \overset{2}{\cancel{3}}\text{ hr} & \overset{75}{\cancel{15}}\text{ min} \\ -\ 1\text{ hr} & 40\text{ min} \\ \hline \mathbf{1\text{ hr}} & \mathbf{35\text{ min}} \end{array}$$

c. **12,000**

d. **1,500,000**

e. **2,500,000,000**

f. **250,000**

Written Practice 113

1.

$$\begin{array}{r} \mathbf{\$18.75} \\ 4\overline{)\$75.00} \\ \underline{4} \\ 35 \\ \underline{32} \\ 3\ 0 \\ \underline{2\ 8} \\ 20 \\ \underline{20} \\ 0 \end{array}$$

2. **B. 2 m**

3. $100\% - 80\% = 20\%$

$\frac{20}{100} = \mathbf{0.2}$

4.

	Ratio	A.C.
Walkers	5	*w*
Bus riders	3	*b*
Total	8	120

$$\frac{5}{8} = \frac{w}{120}$$

$$8w = 5 \cdot 120$$

$$w = \frac{5 \cdot \overset{15}{\cancel{120}}}{\underset{1}{\cancel{8}}}$$

$w =$ **75 students**

5. **4,500,000**

6. **a.** **−36**

b. **+36**

c. **−4**

d. **+4**

7. **a.** **−15**

b. **−9**

c. **−9**

d. **+15**

8. **A variety of methods are possible. One method is to convert each fraction to a decimal number, order the decimal numbers, and then place the corresponding fractions in the same order.**

9. **a.** $\frac{1}{50} \times \frac{2}{2} = \frac{2}{100} = \mathbf{0.02}$

b. $\frac{2}{100} = \mathbf{2\%}$

10. **a.** $1\frac{75}{100} = \mathbf{1\frac{3}{4}}$

b. $\frac{175}{100} = \mathbf{175\%}$

11. **a.** $\frac{25}{100} = \mathbf{\frac{1}{4}}$

b. $\frac{25}{100} = \mathbf{0.25}$

12.

$$\begin{array}{rcl} 12\frac{1}{4}\text{ in.} \times \frac{2}{2} & = & \overset{11}{\cancel{12}}\,\frac{\overset{10}{\cancel{2}}}{8}\text{ in.} \\ -\ 3\frac{5}{8}\text{ in.} \times \frac{1}{1} & = & 3\,\frac{5}{8}\text{ in.} \\ \hline & & \mathbf{8\frac{5}{8}\text{ in.}} \end{array}$$

13. $\frac{\overset{5}{\cancel{10}}}{\underset{1}{\cancel{3}}}\text{ ft} \times \frac{\overset{3}{\cancel{9}}}{\underset{2}{\cancel{4}}}\text{ ft} = \frac{15}{2}\text{ ft}^2 = \mathbf{7\frac{1}{2}\textbf{ ft}^2}$

14. 27 cm³

15. 0.3 m²

16. $25 + 32 =$ **57**

17. $A_1 = \frac{3\text{ ft} \times \overset{2}{\cancel{4}}\text{ ft}}{\underset{1}{\cancel{2}}} = 6\text{ ft}^2$

$A_2 = 7\text{ ft} \times 4\text{ ft} = 28\text{ ft}^2$

$A = A_1 + A_2 = 6\text{ ft}^2 + 28\text{ ft}^2 = \mathbf{34\textbf{ ft}^2}$

One possibility: I found the area of the triangle. Then I found the area of the rectangle. I added those two areas to find the area of the trapezoid.

18.
$$\begin{array}{r} \overset{1}{\cancel{2}}\text{ ft } \overset{15}{\cancel{3}}\text{ in.} \\ -\ 1\text{ ft }\ 9\text{ in.} \\ \hline \textbf{6 inches} \end{array}$$

19. a. Line *g*
b. Yes, the figure looks the same after a 180° turn.

20. 5 cm × 3 cm × 2 cm
30 cm³
30 cubes

21.
$$\begin{array}{r} \$80\text{ per day} \\ 3\overline{)\$240} \\ \underline{24} \\ 00 \\ \underline{00} \\ 0 \end{array}$$

$80.00 × 10 = **$800.00**

22.

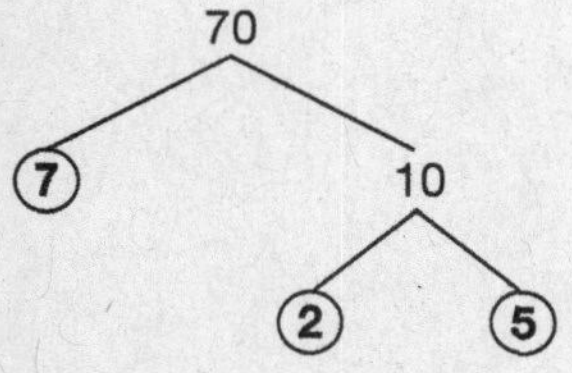

2 · 5 · 7

23. 900,000,000 miles

24. a. 8 in. × 4 = **32 in.**

b. $A = bh$
$A = (8\text{ in.})(7\text{ in.})$
$A =$ **56 in.²**

c. 180° − 61° = **119°**

25.

	Ratio	A.C.
Quarters	5	120
Dimes	8	*d*
Total	13	*t*

$\frac{5}{8} = \frac{120}{d}$

$5d = 8 \cdot 120$

$d = \frac{8 \cdot \overset{24}{\cancel{120}}}{\underset{1}{\cancel{5}}}$

$d =$ **192 dimes**

26. a.

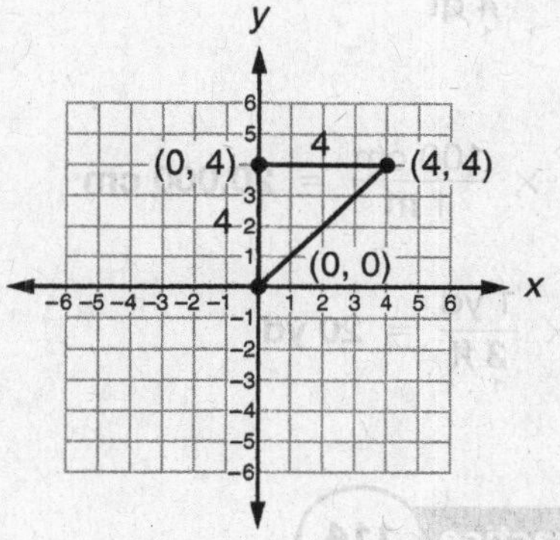

$A = \frac{4\text{ units} \times \overset{2}{\cancel{4}}\text{ units}}{\underset{1}{\cancel{2}}}$

$A =$ **8 sq. units**

b. (0, 0), (0, 4), and (−4, 4)

27. 7, 8, 8, 8, 9, 9, 11, 12, 12, 16
9

28.
$$\begin{array}{r} \mathbf{10} \\ 10\overline{)100} \\ \underline{10} \\ 00 \\ \underline{00} \\ 0 \end{array}$$

29. $C = \pi d$
$C \approx (3.14)(10\text{ in.})$
$C \approx$ **31.4 in.; Sample answer: I can multiply the diameter by 3 and find that the circumference is a little more than 30 in.**

30. $A = (10\text{ m})^2$
$A = \mathbf{100\ m^2}$

Practice Set 114

a. $\dfrac{1\text{ gal}}{4\text{ qt}}, \dfrac{4\text{ qt}}{1\text{ gal}}$

b. $\dfrac{4\text{ qt}}{1\text{ gal}}$

c. $\dfrac{1\text{ m}}{100\text{ cm}}, \dfrac{100\text{ cm}}{1\text{ m}}$

d. $\dfrac{1\text{ m}}{100\text{ cm}}$

e. $\dfrac{\overset{3}{\cancel{12}}\ \cancel{\text{qt}}}{1} \times \dfrac{1\text{ gal}}{\underset{1}{\cancel{4}}\ \cancel{\text{qt}}} = \mathbf{3\ gal}$

f. $\dfrac{200\ \cancel{\text{m}}}{1} \times \dfrac{100\text{ cm}}{1\ \cancel{\text{m}}} = \mathbf{20{,}000\ cm}$

g. $\dfrac{\overset{20}{\cancel{60}}\ \cancel{\text{ft}}}{1} \times \dfrac{1\text{ yd}}{\underset{1}{\cancel{3}}\ \cancel{\text{ft}}} = \mathbf{20\ yd}$

Written Practice 114

1.
```
     3 R 2
$6)$20
    18
     2
```
3 tickets

2.
```
   2 min
3)6
  6
  0
```
$2\text{ min} \times 4 = \mathbf{8\ minutes}$

3. $\dfrac{10}{25} = \mathbf{\dfrac{2}{5}}$

4. $\dfrac{2}{\underset{1}{\cancel{5}}} \times \dfrac{\overset{32}{\cancel{160}}}{1} = 64\text{ acres}$

$160 - 64 = \mathbf{96\ acres}$

5. **6**

6. **a.** $\dfrac{1\text{ gal}}{4\text{ qt}}, \dfrac{4\text{ qt}}{1\text{ gal}}$

b. $\dfrac{4\text{ qt}}{1\text{ gal}}$; **Sample answer: The units you are changing from should be in the denominator and the units you are changing to should be in the numerator.**

7. $\$36 + \$42 + \$27 = \mathbf{\$105}$

8. $4 + 16 \div 2 - 1$
$4 + 8 - 1$
$\mathbf{11}$

9.
$3\frac{1}{4} \times \frac{2}{2} = 3\frac{2}{8}$
$2\frac{1}{2} \times \frac{4}{4} = 2\frac{4}{8}$
$+\ 4\frac{5}{8} \times \frac{1}{1} = 4\frac{5}{8}$
$9\frac{11}{8} = \mathbf{10\frac{3}{8}\ in.}$

10. **a.**
```
   0.125
8)1.000
   8
   20
   16
    40
    40
     0
```

b. $0.125 \times 100\% = \mathbf{12.5\%}$

11. **a.** $\mathbf{\dfrac{9}{10}}$

b. $\dfrac{9}{10} \times \dfrac{10}{10} = \dfrac{90}{100} = \mathbf{90\%}$

12. **a.** $\dfrac{60}{100} = \mathbf{\dfrac{3}{5}}$

b. $\dfrac{60}{100} = \mathbf{0.6}$

13. $3\frac{1}{4} \div \frac{2}{3}$

$\frac{13}{4} \div \frac{2}{3}$

$1 \div \frac{2}{3} = \frac{3}{2}$

$\frac{13}{4} \times \frac{3}{2} = \frac{39}{8} = \mathbf{4\frac{7}{8}}$

14. $3m - 10 = 80$

$3m = 90$

$m = \mathbf{30}$

15. $\frac{3}{2} = \frac{1.8}{m}$

$3m = 3.6$

$m = \mathbf{1.2}$

16. **a.** **+100**

b. **−100**

c. **−4**

d. **+4**

17. **No;** $\frac{6\ \cancel{\text{hours}}}{1} \times \frac{55\ \text{miles}}{1\ \cancel{\text{hour}}}$

330 miles

18. $9\text{ m} + x = 15\text{ m}$

$x = 6\text{ m}$

$8\text{ m} + y = 10\text{ m}$

$y = 2\text{ m}$

$6\text{ m} \times 8\text{ m} = 48\text{ m}^2$

$9\text{ m} \times 10\text{ m} = 90\text{ m}^2$

$48\text{ m}^2 + 90\text{ m}^2 = \mathbf{138\ m^2}$

19. $15\text{ m} + 10\text{ m} + 9\text{ m} + 2\text{ m}$

$+ 6\text{ m} + 8\text{ m} = \mathbf{50\ m}$

20. **a.** **−25**

b. **−15**

c. **0**

d. **+25**

21. **a.** **∠5**

b. $180° - 45° = \mathbf{135°}$

22. $\frac{5}{100} = \frac{50}{x}$

$5x = 50 \cdot 100$

$x = \frac{\overset{10}{\cancel{50}} \cdot 100}{\underset{1}{\cancel{5}}}$

$x =$ **1000 surveys**

I set up a proportion between the equal ratios $\frac{5}{100}$ and $\frac{50}{x}$. Then, I used cross products to find the value of x.

23. **Selected pairs of prime numbers will differ.**
The LCM will be the product of the selected prime numbers.

24. **1,500,000**

25. $V = lwh$

$V = (30\text{ ft})(30\text{ ft})(10\text{ ft})$

$V = \mathbf{9000\ ft^3}$

26. $\frac{\overset{2}{\cancel{8}}\ \cancel{\text{qt}}}{1} \cdot \frac{1\text{ gal}}{\underset{1}{\cancel{4}}\ \cancel{\text{qt}}} = \mathbf{2\ gal}$

27.

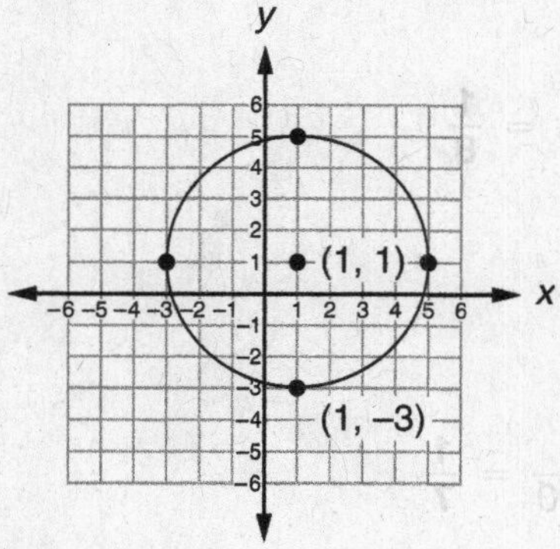

a. **4 units**

b. $A = \pi r^2$

$A \approx (3.14)(4\text{ units})^2$

$A \approx \mathbf{50.24\ units^2}$

28.

$$\begin{array}{r} 95 \\ -\ 35 \\ \hline \mathbf{60} \end{array}$$

29.

$$\begin{array}{rr} \overset{3}{\cancel{4}}\text{ ft} & \overset{15}{\cancel{3}}\text{ in.} \\ -\ 2\text{ ft} & 9\text{ in.} \\ \hline \mathbf{1\ ft} & \mathbf{6\ in.} \end{array}$$

Solutions

30. To find *A*, square *s*. I noticed a pattern between *s* and *A*. $s^2 = A$

Early Finishers Solutions

a. 2(16 ft + 14 ft + 8 ft + 3 ft + 8 ft + 11 ft) = 120 ft

b. 120 ft ÷ 8 ft = 15 sections

Practice Set 115

a. $\dfrac{66\frac{2}{3}}{100}$

$\dfrac{\overset{2}{\cancel{200}}}{3} \times \dfrac{1}{\underset{1}{\cancel{100}}} = \mathbf{\dfrac{2}{3}}$

b. $\dfrac{6\frac{2}{3}}{100}$

$\dfrac{\overset{1}{\cancel{20}}}{3} \times \dfrac{1}{\underset{5}{\cancel{100}}} = \mathbf{\dfrac{1}{15}}$

c. $\dfrac{12\frac{1}{2}}{100}$

$\dfrac{\overset{1}{\cancel{25}}}{2} \times \dfrac{1}{\underset{4}{\cancel{100}}} = \mathbf{\dfrac{1}{8}}$

d. $\dfrac{14\frac{2}{7}}{100}$

$\dfrac{\overset{1}{\cancel{100}}}{7} \times \dfrac{1}{\underset{1}{\cancel{100}}} = \mathbf{\dfrac{1}{7}}$

e. $\dfrac{83\frac{1}{3}}{100}$

$\dfrac{\overset{5}{\cancel{250}}}{3} \times \dfrac{1}{\underset{2}{\cancel{100}}} = \mathbf{\dfrac{5}{6}}$

Written Practice 115

1.

$$\begin{array}{r} \$12.60 \\ \times\ \ \ 0.07 \\ \hline \$0.8820 \end{array} \qquad \begin{array}{r} \overset{1}{\$12.60} \\ +\ \$\ 0.88 \\ \hline \mathbf{\$13.48} \end{array}$$

2. $\dfrac{16\frac{2}{3}}{100}$

$\dfrac{\overset{1}{\cancel{50}}}{3} \times \dfrac{1}{\underset{2}{\cancel{100}}} = \mathbf{\dfrac{1}{6}}$

3.

	%	A.C.
Correct	90	*c*
Not Correct	10	3
Total	100	*t*

$\dfrac{10}{100} = \dfrac{3}{t}$

$10t = 3 \cdot 100$

$t = \dfrac{3 \cdot \overset{10}{\cancel{100}}}{\underset{1}{\cancel{10}}}$

$t =$ **30 questions**

4. $\dfrac{331\text{ m}}{1\ \cancel{s}} \cdot \dfrac{60\ \cancel{s}}{1} =$ **19,860 m**

5. 50,600

6.

$$\begin{array}{r} 0.75\text{ meter} \\ \times\ \ \ \ \ 2\ \ \ \ \ \ \ \ \ \ \\ \hline 1.50\ \ \ \ \ \ \ \ \ \ \end{array}$$

1.5 meters

7. $\dfrac{11}{3} \cdot \dfrac{8}{3} = \dfrac{88}{9} = 9\dfrac{7}{9}$

10

8. $\dfrac{3}{6} \cdot \dfrac{2}{5} = \dfrac{6}{30} = \mathbf{\dfrac{1}{5}}$

9. a. $2\dfrac{2}{5} \times \dfrac{20}{20} = 2\dfrac{40}{100} =$ **2.4**

b. $\dfrac{240}{100} =$ **240%**

10. a. $\dfrac{85}{100} = \mathbf{\dfrac{17}{20}}$

b. $\dfrac{85}{100} =$ **85%**

11. $7x - 3 = 39$

$7x = 42$

$x = \mathbf{6}$

12. $\dfrac{x}{7} = \dfrac{35}{5}$

$5x = 35 \cdot 7$

$x = \dfrac{\overset{7}{\cancel{35}} \cdot 7}{\underset{1}{\cancel{5}}}$

$x = \mathbf{49}$

13. a. **+45**

b. **−5**

c. **+5**

d. **−45**

14. $-6 - 7 + 5 + 8$

0

15. $0.12 \div 30 = \mathbf{0.004}$

16.
```
    3.142
7)22.000
  21
   1 0
     7
    30
    28
     20
     14
      6
```
3.14

17. **100**

18.
$6 \text{ cm} + x = 10 \text{ cm}$

$x = 4 \text{ cm}$

$5 \text{ cm} + y = 8 \text{ cm}$

$y = 3 \text{ cm}$

$6 \text{ cm} \times 8 \text{ cm} = 48 \text{ cm}^2$

$4 \text{ cm} \times 5 \text{ cm} = 20 \text{ cm}^2$

$48 \text{ cm}^2 + 20 \text{ cm}^2 = \mathbf{68 \text{ cm}^2}$

19. $5 \text{ cm} + 10 \text{ cm} + 8 \text{ cm} + 6 \text{ cm} + 3 \text{ cm} + 4 \text{ cm} = \mathbf{36 \text{ cm}}$

20. $3 \text{ cm} \times 3 \text{ cm} \times 3 \text{ cm} = \mathbf{27 \text{ cm}^3}$

21. **31 days**

22.
```
   12 ounces per container
7)84 ounces
  7
  14
  14
   0
```
12 ounces × 10 = **120 ounces**

23. **4,500,000**

24. **59,000,000**

25. ***C***

26.

	$\overset{8}{\cancel{9}}$ pounds	$\overset{23}{\cancel{7}}$ ounces
−	7 pounds	9 ounces
	1 pound	**14 ounces**

27.

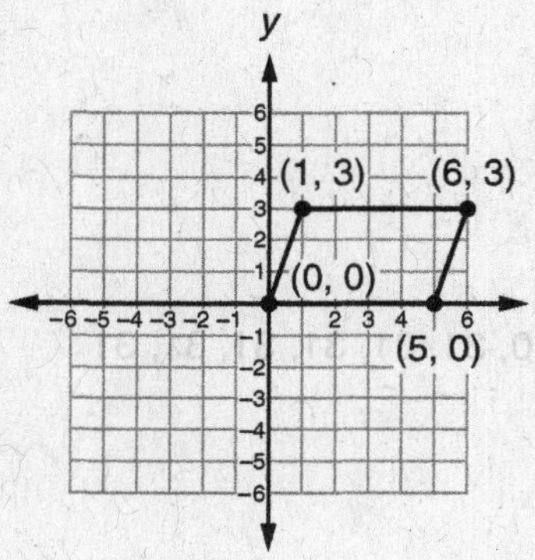

$A = bh$

$A = 5 \text{ units}(3 \text{ units})$

$A = \mathbf{15 \text{ sq. units}}$

28. **B. 6.4 lb**

29.

	2 gal	2 qt	1 pt
+	2 gal	2 qt	1 pt
	4 gal	4 qt	2 pt

5 gal 1 qt

30. **Gilbert can divide 323.4 miles by 14.2 gallons to calculate the miles per gallon.**

Early Finishers Solutions

a. Cars to trucks $= \dfrac{210}{125} = \dfrac{42}{25}$

Cars to motorcycles $= \dfrac{210}{14} = \dfrac{15}{1}$

Trucks to motorcycles $= \dfrac{125}{14}$

Solutions

b. $\frac{210}{349} = 0.602 = 60.2\%$

Practice Set 116

a. 1. **$5187.48**
2. **$13,455.00**

b. 1. **$2249.73**
2. **$2960.49**
3. **$4382.25**

c. 1. **$412.27**
2. **$2226.99**
3. **$9072.75**

Written Practice 116

1. $$\begin{array}{r} 30 \text{ R } 6 \\ 10\overline{)306} \\ \underline{30} \\ 06 \\ \underline{0} \\ 6 \end{array}$$
30, 30, 30, 30, 31, 31, 31, 31, 31, 31
4 rooms

2. $$\begin{array}{r} \$1.20 \\ \times \quad 2 \\ \hline \mathbf{\$2.40} \end{array}$$

3. a. $\frac{6}{15} = \mathbf{\frac{2}{5}}$

b. $\frac{\overset{2}{\cancel{6}}}{\underset{1}{\cancel{15}}\,(\cancel{3})} \times \frac{\overset{20}{\cancel{100}}\%}{1} = \mathbf{40\%}$

4. $\frac{1}{4} \times \frac{25}{25} = \frac{25}{100} = \mathbf{25\%}$

5. $\frac{2}{\underset{1}{\cancel{5}}} \times \frac{\overset{6}{\cancel{30}}}{1} = 12$ buy lunch
$30 - 12 = 18$ bring lunch
$\frac{12}{18} = \mathbf{\frac{2}{3}}$

6. **1,200,000,000**

7. $c = \frac{\$1.25}{\cancel{\text{pound}}} \times \frac{5 \cancel{\text{ pounds}}}{1}$
$c = \mathbf{\$6.25}$

8. **9.09, 9.9, 9.925, 9.95**

9. a. $$\begin{array}{r} 0.375 \\ 8\overline{)3.000} \\ \underline{2\,4} \\ 60 \\ \underline{56} \\ 40 \\ \underline{40} \\ 0 \end{array}$$
$3d = \mathbf{3.375}$

b. $3.375 \times 100\% = \mathbf{337.5\%}$

10. a. $\frac{15}{100} = \mathbf{\frac{3}{20}}$

b. $\frac{15}{100} = \mathbf{0.15}$

11. $9x + 17 = 80$
$9x = 63$
$x = \mathbf{7}$

12. $\frac{x}{3} = \frac{1.6}{1.2}$
$1.2x = 4.8$
$x = \mathbf{4}$

13. $-6 - 4 - 3 + 8$
$\mathbf{-5}$

14. $$\begin{array}{r} 6 \\ 3.75 \\ + \ 4.6 \\ \hline \mathbf{14.35} \end{array}$$

15. $$\begin{array}{r} 210 \\ \times \quad 3 \text{ feet} \\ \hline \mathbf{630 \text{ feet}} \end{array}$$

16. $$\begin{array}{r} 1 \\ 3\overline{)3} \\ 3\overline{)9} \\ 3\overline{)27} \\ 3\overline{)81} \\ 2\overline{)162} \\ 2\overline{)324} \\ 2\overline{)648} \end{array}$$
$\mathbf{2^3 \cdot 3^4}$

17. $\require{cancel}$
$$\begin{array}{r} \textbf{\$0.12 per ounce} \\ 32\overline{)\$3.84} \\ \underline{3\,2} \\ 64 \\ \underline{64} \\ 0 \end{array}$$

18. $A_1 = 6\text{ m} \times 4\text{ m} = 24\text{ m}^2$

$A_2 = \dfrac{\overset{1}{\cancel{2}}\text{ m} \times 4\text{ m}}{\underset{1}{\cancel{2}}} = 4\text{ m}^2$

$A = A_1 + A_2 = 24\text{ m}^2 + 4\text{ m}^2 = \mathbf{28\ m^2}$

19. **a.** $C = \pi d$
$\approx (3.14)(20\text{ cm})$
$\approx \mathbf{62.8\ cm}$

b. $A = \pi r^2$
$\approx (3.14)(10\text{ cm})^2$
$\approx \mathbf{314\ cm^2}$

20. $V = 3\text{ cm} \times 3\text{ cm} \times 3\text{ cm} = 27\text{ cm}^3$

$\dfrac{1}{\underset{1}{\cancel{3}}} \cdot \dfrac{\overset{9}{\cancel{27}}}{1} = \mathbf{9\ cm^3}$

21.
$$\begin{array}{r} 90 \\ 6\overline{)540} \\ \underline{54} \\ 00 \\ \underline{00} \\ 0 \end{array}$$

22. **a.** **+16**

b. **−16**

c. **−4**

d. **+4**

23.
$$\begin{array}{r} 10\text{R}6 \\ 30\overline{)306} \end{array}$$

Add 1 student to each of 6 rooms. The remaining 4 rooms each have 30 students.

24. **a.** $180° - 40° - 110° = \mathbf{30°}$

b. 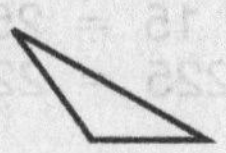

25. $\dfrac{1}{\underset{1}{\cancel{6}}} \cdot \dfrac{\overset{10}{\cancel{60}}}{1} = 10$ times

D. 10 times

26. $\sqrt{100\text{ mm}^2} = 10\text{ mm}$
$10\text{ mm} \times 3 = \mathbf{30\ mm}$

27. $\dfrac{\overset{1}{\cancel{100}}}{9} \cdot \dfrac{1}{\underset{1}{\cancel{100}}} = \mathbf{\dfrac{1}{9}}$

28. Mean:
181 cm + 177 cm + 189 cm + 158 cm + 195 cm = 900 cm
900 cm ÷ 5 = $\boxed{180\text{ cm}}$
Mean is 180 cm
Median:
158 cm, 177 cm, 181 cm, 189 cm, 195 cm
Median is 181 cm
Range:
195 cm − 158 cm = 37 cm
Range is 37 cm

29.
$$\begin{array}{rr} & 2\text{ lb}\ \ 12\text{ oz} \\ + & 3\text{ lb}\ \ \ \ 8\text{ oz} \\ \hline & 5\text{ lb}\ \ 20\text{ oz} \\ & \mathbf{6\ lb\ \ \ \ 4\ oz} \end{array}$$

30. **C. Scalene**

Early Finishers Solutions

a. $\dfrac{1488 - 372}{1488} = \dfrac{1116}{1488} = 0.75 = 75\%$

b. $\dfrac{372}{12} = 31$ points per game

Practice Set 117

a.

40	
8	
8	
8	
8	
8	$\frac{1}{5}$

b.

20	
4	
4	
4	
4	$\frac{2}{5}$
4	$\frac{2}{5}$

c.

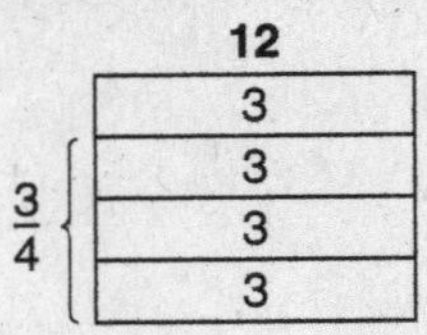

d.

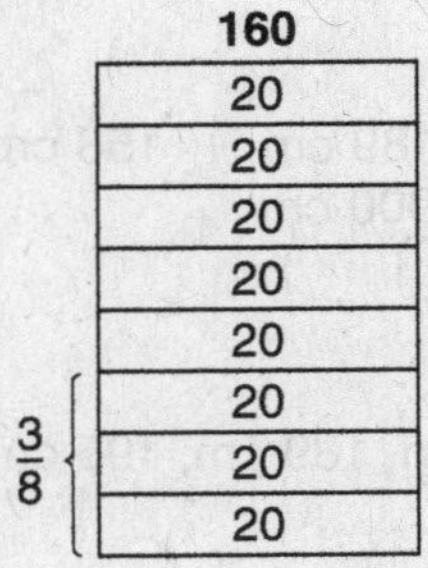

e.

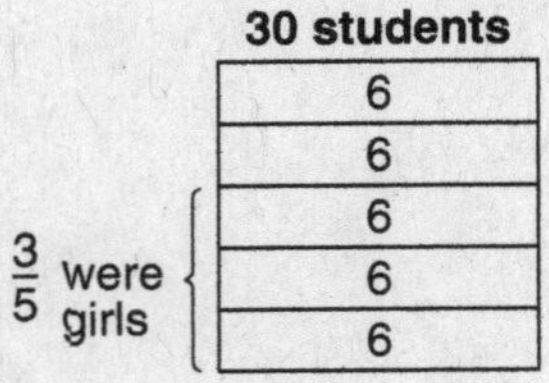

Written Practice 117

1.

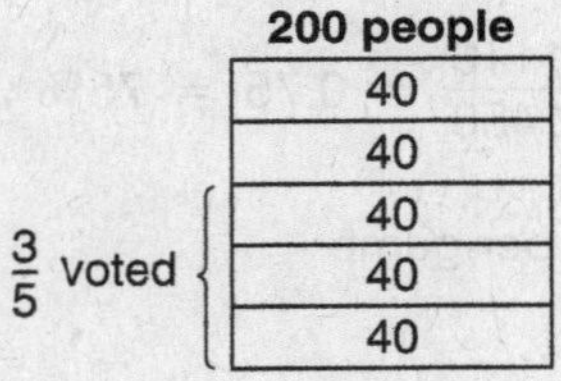

2. $4\overline{)130}$ = 32 R 2
12
10
8
2

32, 32, 33, 33

3. $\overset{14}{\cancel{2}}$:45 p.m. − 11:15 a.m. = 3:30 $1.25 × 7 = **$8.75**

4. $\sqrt{400 \text{ m}^2} = 20 \text{ m}$
$A = \pi r^2$
$A \approx (3.14)(20 \text{ m})^2$
$A \approx$ **1256 m²**

5. $\frac{46}{50} \times \frac{2}{2} = \frac{92}{100} =$ **92%**

6.

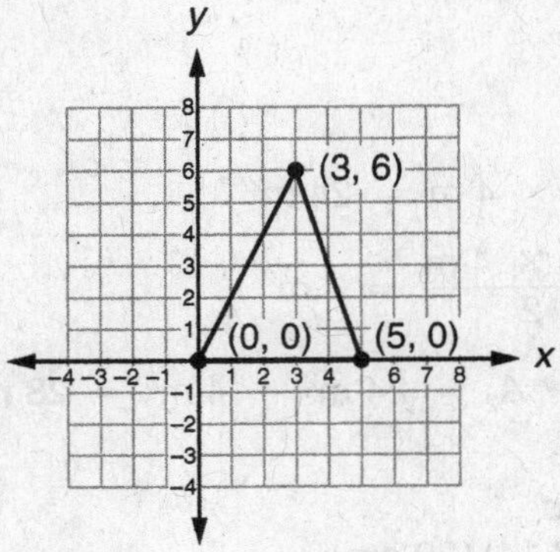

$A = \frac{5 \text{ units} \times \overset{3}{\cancel{6}} \text{ units}}{\underset{1}{\cancel{2}}}$

$A =$ **15 sq. units**

7. **0.105**

8. $9\overline{)\$7.000}$ = $0.777 ⟶ **$0.78**
6 3
70
63
70
63
7

9. $81\% = \frac{81}{100} = 0.81 = 0.810$
$\frac{4}{5} \cdot \frac{20}{20} = \frac{80}{100} = 0.80 = 0.800$
0.800, 0.810, 0.815
$\frac{4}{5}$, 81%, 0.815

10. $6x - 12 = 60$ check: $6(12) - 12 = 60$
$6x = 72$ $72 - 12 = 60$
$x =$ **12** $60 = 60$

11. $\frac{9}{15} = \frac{m}{25}$ check: $\frac{9}{15} = \frac{15}{25}$
$15m = 25 \cdot 9$ $15 \cdot 15 = 25 \cdot 9$
$225 = 225$
$m = \frac{\overset{5}{\cancel{25}} \cdot \overset{3}{\cancel{9}}}{\underset{1}{\cancel{\underset{3}{\cancel{15}}}}}$
$m =$ **15**

12.

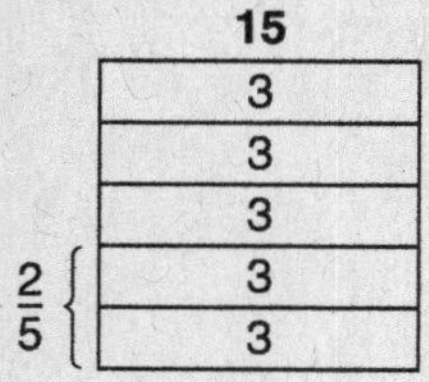

15
3
3
3
3
3

$\frac{2}{5}$

13.
$$4\frac{3}{3} - 1\frac{2}{3} = 3\frac{1}{3}$$
$$3\frac{1}{3} \times \frac{2}{2} = 3\frac{8}{6}$$
$$- 1\frac{1}{2} \times \frac{3}{3} = 1\frac{3}{6}$$
$$\overline{1\frac{5}{6}}$$

14.
$$\frac{12}{5} \div \frac{3}{2}$$
$$1 \div \frac{3}{2} = \frac{2}{3}$$
$$\frac{\overset{4}{\cancel{12}}}{5} \times \frac{2}{\underset{1}{\cancel{3}}} = \frac{8}{5} = 1\frac{3}{5}$$

15.
$$\begin{array}{r} 0.625 \\ \times \quad 2.4 \\ \hline 2500 \\ 12500 \\ \hline 1.5000 \end{array}$$
1.5

16. −15

17.
```
        36
       /  \
      6    6
     / \  / \
   (2)(3)(2)(3)
```
2² · 3²

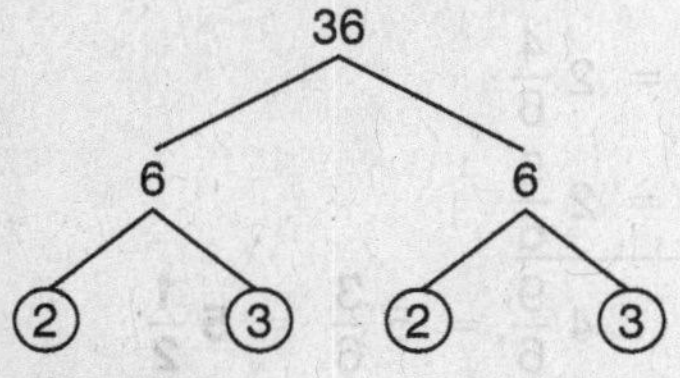

18.
$$\begin{array}{r} \$12.50 \\ \times \quad 0.06 \\ \hline \$0.7500 \end{array} \qquad \begin{array}{r} \$12.50 \\ + \ \$ 0.75 \\ \hline \mathbf{\$13.25} \end{array}$$

19. $A_1 = 8 \text{ in.} \times 9 \text{ in.} = 72 \text{ in.}^2$
$$A_2 = \frac{4 \text{ in.} \cdot 4 \text{ in.}}{2} = 8 \text{ in.}^2$$
$$A = A_1 + A_2 = 72 \text{ in.}^2 + 8 \text{ in.}^2 = \mathbf{80 \text{ in.}^2}$$

20. **600,000**

21. **a.** +5
b. −6
c. −24
d. +36

22. 5 in. × 3 in. × 4 in. = **60 in.³**

23. **One possibility:**

Acute triangle

24. 87

25. **a.** 1.065
b. $1207.95

26. $\frac{3}{4} \cdot \frac{3}{4} = \frac{9}{16}$

27. **B. Parallelogram**

28.

	Ratio	AC
Cattle	15	c
Horses	2	h
Total	17	1020

$$\frac{2}{17} = \frac{h}{1020}$$
$$17h = 2 \cdot 1020$$
$$h = \frac{2 \cdot \overset{60}{\cancel{1020}}}{\underset{1}{\cancel{17}}}$$
$$h = \mathbf{120 \text{ horses}}$$

29. $10 + 9 \times 5 - 9 \div 3$
$$10 + 45 - 3$$
52

30. **a. C.** ◯
b. All three figures have rotational symmetry.

Early Finishers Solutions

a. Track B; Track A costs ($7 × 2 hours) + $10 = $24 per person and Track B costs ($8 × 2) + $7 = $23 per person.

b. Track A; Track A costs ($7 × 4 hours) + $10 = $38 per person and Track B costs ($8 × 4) + $7 = $39 per person.

Practice Set 118

a. **14 (or 15) square units**

One possibility: I counted 9 entire or nearly entire squares within the paw print. I then counted 10 half squares, which makes 5 entire squares. So I estimated the area of the paw print to be 14 square units.

Written Practice 118

1.
$$7\overline{)52}\quad \text{7 R 3}$$
$$\begin{array}{r} 52 \\ \underline{49} \\ 3 \end{array}$$

3 students

2. **B. 18 cm**

3.

20 million

2 million
2 million
2 million
2 million
2 million
2 million
2 million
2 million
2 million
2 million

$\frac{3}{10}$ (bottom 3 rows)

About 20,000,000

4. **B.** $\mathbf{\frac{3}{4} \neq \frac{9}{16}}$

5.
$$\begin{array}{r} \$14.49 \\ \times\quad 0.07 \\ \hline \$1.0143 \end{array} \qquad \begin{array}{r} \$14.49 \\ +\quad \$1.01 \\ \hline \mathbf{\$15.50} \end{array}$$

6. $\frac{48}{84} = \mathbf{\frac{4}{7}}$

7. $17 + 24 + 27 + 28 = 96$

$96 \div 4 = \mathbf{24}$

8.
$$6.1 = 6.10$$
$$\sqrt{36} = 6 = 6.00$$
$$6\frac{1}{4} = 6.25$$

6.00, 6.10, 6.25

$\mathbf{\sqrt{36},\ 6.1,\ 6\frac{1}{4}}$

9.

30 cookies

3
3
3
3
3
3
3
3
3
3

$\frac{3}{10}$ (bottom 3 rows)

10. **Buz can divide the circumference by π (by 3.14) to calculate the diameter.**

11.

16

4
4
4
4

$\frac{3}{4}$ (bottom 3 rows)

12.
$$\begin{array}{rcl} 5\frac{1}{3} \times \frac{2}{2} & = & \overset{4}{\cancel{5}}\,\frac{\overset{8}{\cancel{2}}}{6} \\ -\ 2\frac{1}{2} \times \frac{3}{3} & = & 2\frac{3}{6} \\ \hline & & 2\frac{5}{6} \end{array}$$

$$\begin{array}{rcl} 2\frac{2}{3} \times \frac{2}{2} & = & 2\frac{4}{6} \\ +\ 2\frac{5}{6} \times \frac{1}{1} & = & 2\frac{5}{6} \\ \hline & & 4\frac{9}{6} = 5\frac{3}{6} = \mathbf{5\frac{1}{2}} \end{array}$$

13. $\frac{20}{3} \div \frac{25}{6}$

$1 \div \frac{25}{6} = \frac{6}{25}$

$\frac{\overset{4}{\cancel{20}}}{\underset{1}{\cancel{3}}} \times \frac{\overset{2}{\cancel{6}}}{\underset{5}{\cancel{25}}} = \frac{8}{5} = \mathbf{1\frac{3}{5}}$

14.
$$\begin{array}{r} 4.25 \\ +\ 3.2 \\ \hline \mathbf{7.45} \end{array}$$

15. $1 - 0.01 = \mathbf{0.99}$

16. **21**

17. $\frac{16 \text{ oz}}{1 \not{\text{lb}}} \times \frac{2.2 \not{\text{lb}}}{1}$
$= 35.2 \text{ ounces} \rightarrow \mathbf{35 \text{ ounces}}$

18. **a.** $A = bh$
$A = 6 \text{ cm} \times 4 \text{ cm}$
$A = \mathbf{24 \text{ cm}^2}$

b. $180° - 127° = \mathbf{53°}$

19. $1.8 \text{ cm} + x = 4 \text{ cm}$
$x = 2.2 \text{ cm}$
$1.4 \text{ cm} + y = 3 \text{ cm}$
$y = 1.6 \text{ cm}$
$1.8 \text{ cm} + 1.6 \text{ cm} + 2.2 \text{ cm} + 1.4 \text{ cm}$
$+ 4 \text{ cm} + 3 \text{ cm} = \mathbf{14 \text{ cm}}$

20. **4 lines of symmetry**

21. $4.11 \text{ feet} \rightarrow 4 \text{ feet}$
$V = 4 \text{ ft} \times 4 \text{ ft} \times 4 \text{ ft}$
$V = \mathbf{64 \text{ ft}^3}$

22. $\frac{f}{12} = \frac{12}{16}$
$16f = 12 \cdot 12$
$f = \frac{\overset{3}{\not{12}} \cdot \overset{3}{\not{12}}}{\underset{1}{\underset{\not{4}}{\not{16}}}}$
$f = \mathbf{9}$

23. $\mathbf{y = 5x}$
$40 = 5x$
$\mathbf{8} = x$

24. **12,500**

25. $-5 + 2 - 3 + 4 - 1$
$-9 + 6$
$\mathbf{-3}$

26. $\$4000 \times 1.025 = \$4100$
$\$4100 \times 1.025 = \mathbf{\$4202.50}$

27. $\frac{\frac{15}{2}}{100}$
$\frac{\overset{3}{\not{15}}}{2} \cdot \frac{1}{\underset{20}{\not{100}}} = \mathbf{\frac{3}{40}}$

28. $-3°\text{F} - 5°\text{F} = \mathbf{-8°F}$

29. $\mathbf{\frac{2}{8} = \frac{1}{4}}$

30. **a.** $\mathbf{8 \text{ units}^2}$

b. **B. Square feet**

Practice Set 119

a. $\mathbf{0.2n = 120}$
$2\overline{)1200}$ = 600
$n = \mathbf{600}$

b. $\mathbf{\frac{1}{2}n = 30}$
$30 \div \frac{1}{2} = \frac{30}{1} \cdot \frac{2}{1} = 60$
$n = \mathbf{60}$

c. $\mathbf{\frac{1}{4}n = 12}$
$12 \div \frac{1}{4} = \frac{12}{1} \times \frac{4}{1} = 48$
$n = \mathbf{48}$

d. $\mathbf{20 = 0.10n}$
$10\overline{)2000}$ = 200
$n = \mathbf{200}$

e. $\mathbf{12 = 1n}$
$1\overline{)12}$ = 12
$n = \mathbf{12}$

f. $\mathbf{15 = 0.15n}$
$15\overline{)1500}$ = 100
$n = \mathbf{100}$

Solutions

g. **Sample answer: Fifteen percent of what number is 12? Twelve sixth graders had parts in the school play. If 15% of the sixth graders were in the play, how many sixth graders are there in all? [80 sixth graders in all]**

Written Practice 119

1. a.

$$\begin{array}{r} \mathbf{46\ R\ 3} \\ 12\overline{)555} \\ \underline{48} \\ 75 \\ \underline{72} \\ 3 \end{array}$$

b. $46\frac{3}{12} = \mathbf{46\frac{1}{4}}$

2. $9.75 + 9.8 + 9.9 + 9.9 + 9.95 = \mathbf{49.3}$

3.

	%	A.C.
Trumpet	10	6
Not Trumpet	90	n
Total	100	t

$\frac{6}{t} = \frac{10}{100}$

$10t = 6 \cdot 100$

$t = \frac{6 \cdot \overset{10}{\cancel{100}}}{\underset{1}{\cancel{10}}}$

$t = \mathbf{60\ members}$

4. $8 = \frac{2}{3}n$

$8 \div \frac{2}{3} = \frac{\overset{4}{\cancel{8}}}{1} \times \frac{3}{\underset{1}{\cancel{2}}} = \mathbf{12}$

$n = \mathbf{12}$

5. **186,000**

6. $\frac{1\text{ inch}}{8\text{ feet}} = \frac{2\frac{1}{2}\text{ inches}}{x}$

$x = \mathbf{20\ feet}$

7. a. $180° - 45° - 45° = \mathbf{90°}$

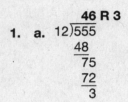

b.

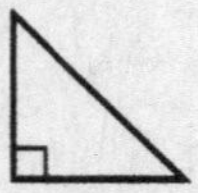

8. $\frac{\frac{25}{3}}{100}$

$\frac{\overset{1}{\cancel{25}}}{3} \times \frac{1}{\underset{4}{\cancel{100}}} = \mathbf{\frac{1}{12}}$

9. $\frac{9}{12} = \frac{3}{4}$

$\frac{3}{4} \times \frac{25}{25} = \frac{75}{100} = \mathbf{75\%}$

10. $.20x = 12$

$$\begin{array}{r} 60 \\ 20\overline{)1200} \end{array}$$

$x = \mathbf{60}$

11. $\frac{3}{10}x = 9$

$\frac{9}{1} \div \frac{3}{10} = \frac{\overset{3}{\cancel{9}}}{1} \times \frac{10}{\underset{1}{\cancel{3}}} = 30$

$x = \mathbf{30}$

12. $-5 - 6 - 7$

$\mathbf{-18}$

13. **+90**

14. $\frac{60}{84} = \mathbf{\frac{5}{7}}$

15.

$2\frac{1}{2} \times \frac{3}{3} = \overset{1}{\cancel{2}}\frac{\overset{9}{\cancel{3}}}{6}$

$-\ 1\frac{2}{3} \times \frac{2}{2} = 1\frac{4}{6}$

$\mathbf{\frac{5}{6}}$

16.

	Ratio	A.C.
Biking	5	b
Running	2	10
Total	7	t

$\frac{2}{7} = \frac{10}{t}$

$2t = 10 \cdot 7$

$t = \frac{\overset{5}{\cancel{10}} \cdot 7}{\underset{1}{\cancel{2}}}$

$t = \mathbf{35\ kilometers}$

17. $2.8\text{ cm}^2 \times 2 = \mathbf{5.6\ cm^2}$

18. $V = lwh$
$V = 10 \text{ in.} \times 3 \text{ in.} \times 4 \text{ in.}$
$V = \mathbf{120 \text{ in.}^3}$

19. **2 lines of symmetry**

20. **Pyramid**

21. $3m - 5 = 25$
$3m = 30$
$m = \mathbf{10}$

22. $\mathbf{y = 4x}$
$32 = 4x$
$\mathbf{8} = x$

23. 1 ton = 2000 pounds
10 tons = **20,000 pounds**

24. **B. pentagon**

25. Area of the square (>) area of the circle

26.

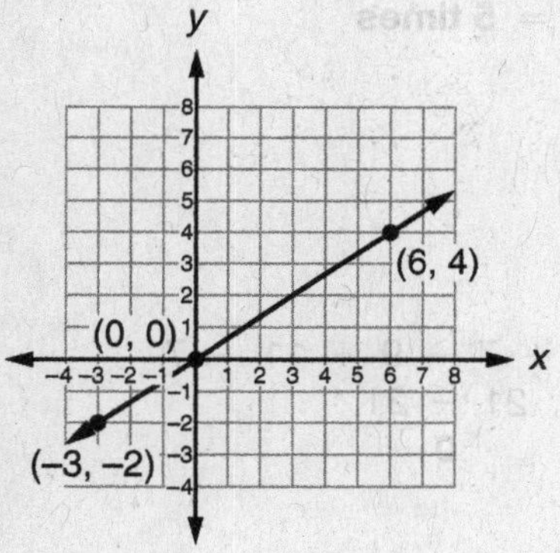

$x = \mathbf{6}$

27. $\mathbf{\frac{1}{2}}$

28. $\frac{1}{2} \times \frac{1}{2} \times \frac{1}{2} = \mathbf{\frac{1}{8}}$

29. **a.** $5 \text{ cm} \times 5 \text{ cm} = \mathbf{25 \text{ cm}^2}$

b. $A = \pi r^2$
$A \approx (3.14)(5 \text{ cm})^2$
$A \approx \mathbf{78.5 \text{ cm}^2}$

30. **Mode is 7; range is 10 − 2 = 8.**

Practice Set 120

$A = \pi r^2$
$A \approx (3.14)(4 \text{ cm})^2$
$A \approx 50.24 \text{ cm}^2$
$50.24 \text{ cm}^2 \times 12 \text{ cm} = 602.88 \text{ cm}^3$
$\mathbf{600 \text{ cm}^3}$

Written Practice 120

1.

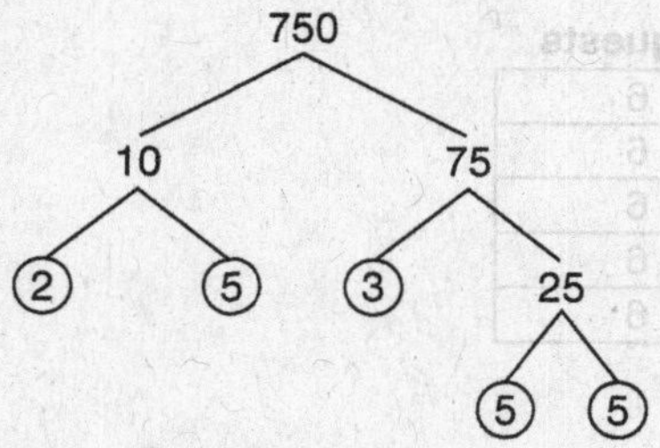

$\mathbf{2 \cdot 3 \cdot 5^3}$

2. **C. 50 mm**

3. $\frac{3}{24} = \frac{8}{x}$
$3x = 24 \cdot 8$
$x = \frac{\overset{8}{\cancel{24}} \cdot 8}{\underset{1}{\cancel{3}}}$
$x = \mathbf{64 \text{ grams}}$

4. $\frac{3}{24} = \frac{8}{w}$
$3w = 24 \cdot 8$
$w = \frac{\overset{8}{\cancel{24}} \cdot 8}{\underset{1}{\cancel{3}}}$
$w = \mathbf{64}$

5. **7004**

6. **205,056,000**

7. **a.** $17 + 23 + 25 + x = 100$
$65 + x = 100$
$x = \mathbf{35}$

b. $35 - 17 = 18$
The range is 18.

8. a. -2

b. -25

c. $+100$

9. $\dfrac{\frac{50}{3}}{100}$

$\dfrac{\overset{1}{\cancel{50}}}{3} \times \dfrac{1}{\underset{2}{\cancel{100}}} = \mathbf{\dfrac{1}{6}}$

10.

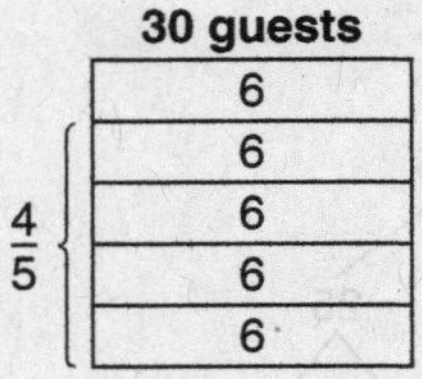

11.
$$1\frac{1}{3} \times \frac{4}{4} = 1\frac{4}{12}$$
$$3\frac{3}{4} \times \frac{3}{3} = 3\frac{9}{12}$$
$$+\ 1\frac{1}{6} \times \frac{2}{2} = 1\frac{2}{12}$$
$$5\frac{15}{12} = 6\frac{3}{12} = \mathbf{6\frac{1}{4}}$$

12. $\dfrac{5}{\underset{3}{\cancel{6}}} \times \dfrac{\overset{1}{\cancel{3}}}{1} \times \dfrac{\overset{4}{\cancel{8}}}{\underset{1}{\cancel{2}}} = \dfrac{20}{3} = \mathbf{6\dfrac{2}{3}}$

13.
$$\begin{array}{r} \overset{1}{5}.62 \\ 0.8 \\ +\ 4 \\ \hline \mathbf{10.42} \end{array}$$

14. $0.08 \div 2.5$

$$\begin{array}{r} \mathbf{0.032} \\ 25\overline{)0.800} \\ \underline{75} \\ 50 \\ \underline{50} \\ 0 \end{array}$$

15. $\mathbf{-6}$

16. $50 + 5$

55

17.
$$\begin{array}{r} \mathbf{\$0.07\ per\ ounce} \\ 16\overline{)\$1.12} \\ \underline{1\ 12} \\ 0 \end{array}$$

18. $C = \pi d$

$C \approx (3.14)(10\text{ m})$

$C \approx \mathbf{31.4\ m}$

19. $\sqrt{36\text{ cm}^2} = 6\text{ cm}$

$6\text{ cm} \times 4 = \mathbf{24\ cm}$

20. $V = 4\text{ cm} \times 3\text{ cm} \times 2\text{ cm}$

$V = \mathbf{24\ cm^3}$

21. $.60x = 18$

$$\begin{array}{r} 30 \\ 60\overline{)1800} \end{array}$$

$x = \mathbf{30\ votes}$

22. $\dfrac{1}{4} \times \dfrac{1}{4} \times \dfrac{1}{4} = \mathbf{\dfrac{1}{64}}$

23. $\dfrac{1}{\underset{1}{\cancel{4}}} \times \dfrac{\overset{5}{\cancel{20}}}{1} = \mathbf{5\ times}$

24. a. $\mathbf{-15}$

b. $\mathbf{-1}$

25. $+3 - 5 + 7 - 9 + 11 - 7$

$21 - 21$

0

26.

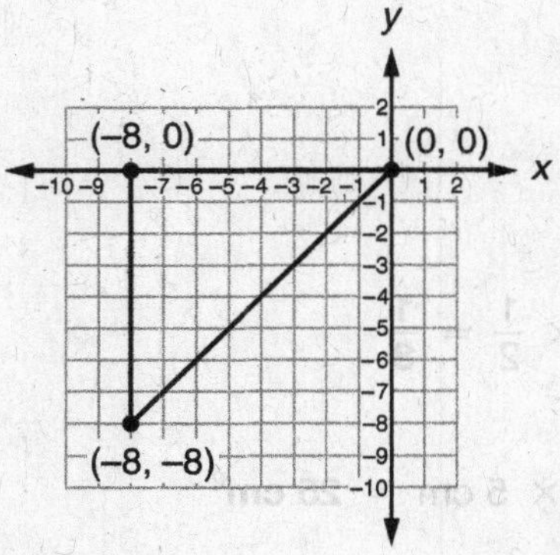

$A = \dfrac{\overset{4}{\cancel{8}}\text{ units} \times 8\text{ units}}{\underset{1}{\cancel{2}}}$

$A = \mathbf{32\ sq.\ units}$

27. $\frac{1}{2} \times \frac{1}{2} = \mathbf{\frac{1}{4}}$

28. $A = \pi r^2$
$A \approx (3.14)(4 \text{ cm})^2$
$A \approx 50.24 \text{ cm}^2$
$50.24 \text{ cm}^2 \times 7 \text{ cm} = \mathbf{351.68 \text{ cm}^3}$

29. **350 milliliters**

30.

	%	AC
Correct	90	c
Incorrect	10	4
Total	100	t

$$\frac{90}{10} = \frac{c}{4}$$
$$10c = 90 \cdot 4$$
$$c = \frac{\overset{9}{\cancel{90}} \cdot 4}{\underset{1}{\cancel{10}}}$$
$c =$ **36 questions**

Early Finishers Solutions

Strategy: Make a model, Act it out, or Draw a picture. Accept any answer that meets the criteria. Two possible answers are shown.

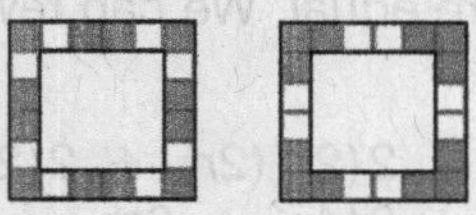

Investigation 12

1. $\text{Volume} = \frac{1}{3}(B \times h)$
$= \frac{1}{3}((6 \text{ ft} \times 5 \text{ ft}) \times 8 \text{ ft})$
$= \frac{1}{3}(240 \text{ ft}^3)$
$= \mathbf{80 \text{ ft}^3}$

2. $\text{Volume} = \frac{1}{3}(B \times h)$
$= \frac{1}{3}\left(\left(6 \text{ ft} \times 5\frac{1}{3} \text{ ft}\right) \times 12 \text{ ft}\right)$
$= \frac{1}{3}(384 \text{ ft}^3)$
$= \mathbf{128 \text{ ft}^3}$

3. $\text{Volume} = \frac{1}{3}(B \times h)$
$= \frac{1}{3}((3.1 \text{ m} \times 2.7 \text{ m}) \times 2.8 \text{ m})$
$\approx \frac{1}{3}(23.4 \text{ m}^3)$
$= \mathbf{7.8 \text{ m}^3}$

4. $\text{Volume} = \pi r^2 h$
$= \pi(5 \text{ cm})^2(5 \text{ cm})$
$= \mathbf{125\pi \text{ cm}^3}$

5. $\text{Volume} = \pi r^2 h$
$= \frac{22}{7}(7 \text{ ft})^2(9.9 \text{ ft})$
$\approx \frac{22}{7}(7 \text{ ft})^2(10 \text{ ft})$
$= \mathbf{1540 \text{ ft}^3}$

6. $\text{Volume} = \frac{1}{3}(\pi r^2 h)$
$= \frac{1}{3}(\pi(0.6 \text{ in.})^2(10 \text{ in.}))$
$= \frac{1}{3}(3.6\pi \text{ in.}^3)$
$= \mathbf{1.2\pi \text{ in.}^3}$

7. $\text{Surface Area} = 2lw + 2lh + 2wh$
$= 2(13 \text{ cm})(13 \text{ cm})$
$+ 2(13 \text{ cm})(13 \text{ cm})$
$+ 2(13 \text{ cm})(13 \text{ cm})$
$= 338 \text{ cm}^2 + 338 \text{ cm}^2$
$+ 338 \text{ cm}^2$
$= \mathbf{1014 \text{ cm}^2}$

8. $\text{Surface Area} = 2lw + 2lh + 2wh$
$= 2(11 \text{ units})(2 \text{ units})$
$+ 2(11 \text{ units})(2 \text{ units})$
$+ 2(2 \text{ units})(2 \text{ units})$
$= 44 \text{ units}^2 + 44 \text{ units}^2$
$+ 8 \text{ units}^2$
$= \mathbf{96 \text{ units}^2}$

9.

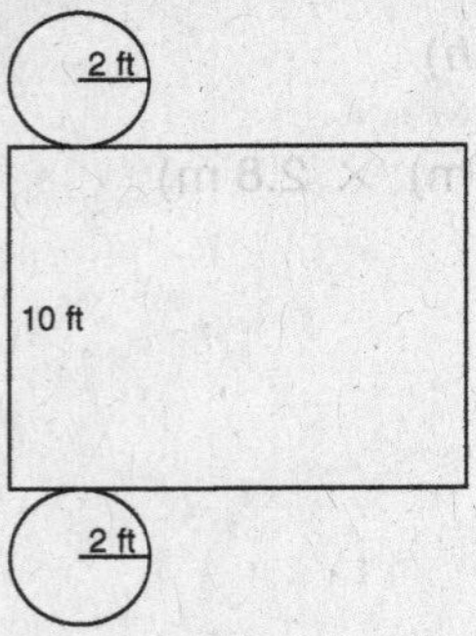

$$\begin{aligned}\text{Volume} &= \pi r^2 h \\ &= \pi(2\text{ ft})^2(10\text{ ft}) \\ &= \mathbf{40\pi\ ft^3}\end{aligned}$$

$$\begin{aligned}\text{Surface Area} &= 2\pi r^2 + 2\pi rh \\ &= 2\pi(2\text{ ft})^2 + 2\pi(2\text{ ft})(10\text{ ft}) \\ &= 8\pi\text{ ft}^2 + 40\pi\text{ ft}^2 \\ &= \mathbf{48\pi\ ft^2}\end{aligned}$$

10. $\text{Volume} = \frac{1}{3}(\pi r^2 h)$

$= \frac{1}{3}\left(\frac{22}{7}(7\text{ cm})^2(9\text{ cm})\right)$

$= \frac{1}{3}(1386\text{ cm}^3)$

$= \mathbf{462\ cm^3}$

11.

$$\begin{aligned}\text{Volume}_{\text{Cone}} &= \frac{1}{3}(\pi r^2 h) \\ &= \frac{1}{3}(\pi(5\text{ in.})^2(15\text{ in.})) \\ &= \mathbf{125\pi\ ft^3}\end{aligned}$$

$$\begin{aligned}\text{Surface Area}_{\text{Cylinder}} &= 2\pi r^2 + 2\pi rh \\ &= 2\pi(5\text{ in.})^2 \\ &\quad + 2\pi(5\text{ in.})(15\text{ in.}) \\ &= 50\pi\text{ in.}^2 + 150\pi\text{ in.}^2 \\ &= \mathbf{200\pi\ in.^2}\end{aligned}$$

12. $\text{Volume} = \frac{1}{3}(B \times h)$

$= \frac{1}{3}((4\text{ in.} \times 3.5\text{ in.}) \times 9\text{ in.})$

$= \mathbf{42\ in.^3}$

13. $\text{Surface Area} = 2(\text{area of base}) + \text{area of sides}$

$= 2\left(\frac{1}{2}(5.2\text{ ft})(13\text{ ft})\right) + (7\text{ ft})(14\text{ ft})$

$+ (7\text{ ft})(13\text{ ft}) + (7\text{ ft})(5.2\text{ ft})$

$\approx (5\text{ ft})(13\text{ ft}) + (7\text{ ft})(14\text{ ft})$

$+ (7\text{ ft})(13\text{ ft}) + (7\text{ ft})(5\text{ ft})$

$= 65\text{ ft}^2 + 98\text{ ft}^2 + 91\text{ ft}^2 + 35\text{ ft}^2$

$= \mathbf{289\ ft^2}$

(ext. a) $\text{Volume}_{\text{Prism}} = lwh$

$= (4\text{ m})\left(6\frac{3}{4}\text{ m}\right)\left(4\frac{1}{3}\text{ m}\right)$

$= \mathbf{117\ m^3}$

(ext. b) $\text{Volume}_{\text{Cone}} = \frac{1}{3}(\pi r^2 h)$

$= \frac{1}{3}(\pi(3\text{ units})^2(12\text{ units}))$

$= \mathbf{36\pi\ units^3}$

(ext. c) From the problem we know the volume of the cube $= 27\text{ in.}^3$
This means $s = 3$ in. since
(3 in.) (3 in.) (3 in.) $= 27\text{ in.}^3$

$$\begin{aligned}\text{Surface Area}_{\text{Cube}} &= 6s^2 \\ &= 6(3\text{ in.})^2 \\ &= \mathbf{54\ in.^2}\end{aligned}$$

(ext. d) $\text{Surface Area}_{\text{Cube}} = 6s^2$

$= 6(4\text{ cm})^2$

$= \mathbf{96\ cm^2}$

(ext. e) $\text{Surface Area}_{\text{Prism}} = 2lw + 2lh + 2wh$

$\text{Surface Area}_{\text{Cylinder}} = 2\pi r^2 + 2\pi rh$

To show: $2\pi r^2 + 2\pi rh \neq 2lw + 2lh + 2wh$

Assume they are equal. We can rewrite *l* and *w* as $2r$.

$$\begin{aligned}2\pi r^2 + 2\pi rh &= 2(2r)(2r) + 2(2r)h + 2(2r)h \\ 2(\pi r^2 + \pi rh) &= 2(4r^2 + 2rh + 2rh) \\ (\pi r^2 + \pi rh) &= (4r^2 + 4rh) \\ \pi r(r + h) &= 4r(r + h) \\ \pi r &= 4r \\ \pi &= 4\end{aligned}$$

This is false so our assumption that the surface areas are equal is false. Therefore, the surface areas are not equal.

Solutions

Cumulative Test 1A

1. **6 + 12 = 18** **12 + 6 = 18**
   18 − 12 = 6 **18 − 6 = 12**

2. **15 × 5 = 75** **5 × 15 = 75**
   75 ÷ 5 = 15 **75 ÷ 15 = 5**

3. $$\begin{array}{r} {}^{1\,1\,1} \\ 3675 \\ 285 \\ \times\ 1308 \\ \hline \mathbf{5268} \end{array}$$

4. $$\begin{array}{r} {}^{4\ \ 9\,1} \\ \$\not{5}.\not{0}0 \\ -\ \$2.85 \\ \hline \mathbf{\$2.15} \end{array}$$

5. $$\begin{array}{r} \$1.75 \\ \times\quad 4 \\ \hline \mathbf{\$7.00} \end{array}$$

6. 4 quarters × 10 = **40 quarters**

7. 240 ÷ 30 = **8 groups**

8. Three dozen (3 × 12) is 36.
   36 − 1 = **35 pencils**

9. $$\begin{array}{r} {}^{1}\quad \\ \$3.50 \\ \$0.95 \\ +\ \$12.00 \\ \hline \mathbf{\$16.45} \end{array}$$

10. 28 + 28 + 28 + 28 + 28 + 28
    $$\begin{array}{r} 28 \\ \times\ 6 \\ \hline \mathbf{168} \end{array}$$

11. $$\begin{array}{r} {}^{7\ 12} \\ 3\not{8}\not{2}6 \\ -\ 382 \\ \hline \mathbf{3444} \end{array}$$

12. $$\begin{array}{r} 563 \\ \times\ 48 \\ \hline 4504 \\ 2252\ \\ \hline \mathbf{27{,}024} \end{array}$$

13. $$\begin{array}{r} 408 \\ \times\ 67 \\ \hline 2856 \\ 2448\ \\ \hline \mathbf{27{,}336} \end{array}$$

14. $$\begin{array}{r} \mathbf{1202} \\ 8\overline{)9616} \\ \underline{8} \\ 16 \\ \underline{16} \\ 016 \\ \underline{16} \\ 0 \end{array}$$

15. $$\begin{array}{r} \mathbf{125} \\ 24\overline{)3000} \\ \underline{24} \\ 60 \\ \underline{48} \\ 120 \\ \underline{120} \\ 0 \end{array}$$

16. 20 − (10 − 5) = 20 − 5 = **15**

17. 36 ÷ (6 ÷ 2) = 36 ÷ 3 = **12**

18. $47 + m = 100$
    $$\begin{array}{r} 100 \\ -\ 47 \\ \hline \mathbf{53} \end{array}$$
    m = **53**
    Check: 47 + 53 = 100 ✓

19. $1000 - n = 258$
    $$\begin{array}{r} 1000 \\ -\ 258 \\ \hline \mathbf{742} \end{array}$$
    n = **742**
    Check: 1000 − 742 = 258 ✓

20. $5x = 85$
    $x = \frac{85}{5}$
    $$\begin{array}{r} \mathbf{17} \\ 5\overline{)85} \\ \underline{5} \\ 35 \\ \underline{35} \\ 0 \end{array}$$
    x = **17**
    Check: 5(17) = 85 ✓

Cumulative Test 1B

1. **5 + 11 = 16** **11 + 5 = 16**
   16 − 11 = 5 **16 − 5 = 11**

2. **4 × 16 = 64** **16 × 4 = 64**
   64 ÷ 4 = 16 **64 ÷ 16 = 4**

3. $$\begin{array}{r} \$1.25 \\ \$0.98 \\ +\ \$10.00 \\ \hline \mathbf{\$12.23} \end{array}$$

4. $\begin{array}{r} \$10.00 \\ -\ \$3.49 \\ \hline \mathbf{\$6.51} \end{array}$

5. $\begin{array}{r} \$0.29 \\ \times\ \ 12 \\ \hline 58 \\ 29\ \\ \hline \mathbf{\$3.48} \end{array}$

6. One quarter equals 5 nickels, so 3 quarters equals 3 × 5 = **15 nickels.**

7. 60 ÷ 5 = **12 players**

8. (4 × 7) + 3 = 28 + 3 = **31 days**

9. $\begin{array}{r} 5986 \\ 367 \\ +\ 1049 \\ \hline \mathbf{7402} \end{array}$

10. 365 + 365 + 365 + 365 $\begin{array}{r} 365 \\ \times\ \ 4 \\ \hline \mathbf{1460} \end{array}$

11. $\begin{array}{r} 4216 \\ -\ 377 \\ \hline \mathbf{3839} \end{array}$

12. $\begin{array}{r} 575 \\ \times\ 16 \\ \hline 3450 \\ 575\ \\ \hline \mathbf{9200} \end{array}$

13. $\begin{array}{r} 306 \\ \times\ 40 \\ \hline \mathbf{12{,}240} \end{array}$

14. $\begin{array}{r} \mathbf{1036} \\ 7\overline{)7252} \\ 7 \\ \hline 025 \\ 21 \\ \hline 42 \\ 42 \\ \hline 0 \end{array}$

15. $\begin{array}{r} \mathbf{144} \\ 25\overline{)3600} \\ 25 \\ \hline 110 \\ 100 \\ \hline 100 \\ 100 \\ \hline 0 \end{array}$

16. 56 − (23 + 12) = 56 − 35 = **21**

17. 48 ÷ (3 × 4) = 48 ÷ 12 = **4**

18. 67 + *m* = 114 $\begin{array}{r} 114 \\ -\ 67 \\ \hline 47 \end{array}$

m = **47**
Check: 67 + 47 = 114 ✓

19. 3000 − *n* = 1362 $\begin{array}{r} 3000 \\ -\ 1362 \\ \hline \mathbf{1638} \end{array}$

n = **1638**
Check: 3000 − 1638 = 1362 ✓

20. 4*x* = 72
$x = \frac{72}{4}$ $\begin{array}{r} \mathbf{18} \\ 4\overline{)72} \\ 4 \\ \hline 32 \\ 32 \\ \hline 0 \end{array}$

x = **18**
Check: 4(18) = 72 ✓

Cumulative Test 2A

1. $\begin{array}{r} \$0.49 \\ \$1.29 \\ +\ \$0.98 \\ \hline \mathbf{\$2.76} \end{array}$

2. $0.95 × 10 = **$9.50**

3. $\begin{array}{r} 3496 \\ 788 \\ +\ 1409 \\ \hline \mathbf{5693} \end{array}$

4. $\begin{array}{r} 4806 \\ -\ 1837 \\ \hline \mathbf{2969} \end{array}$

5. $\begin{array}{r} 47 \\ \times\ 36 \\ \hline 282 \\ 141\ \\ \hline \mathbf{1692} \end{array}$

6. $\begin{array}{r} \mathbf{28} \\ 15\overline{)420} \\ 30 \\ \hline 120 \\ 120 \\ \hline 0 \end{array}$

7.
$$\begin{array}{r} \$5.00 \\ \$3.49 \\ +\ \$0.28 \\ \hline \mathbf{\$8.77} \end{array}$$

8. 24 − (12 − 6) = 24 − 6 = **18**

9.
$$\begin{array}{r} \mathbf{506} \\ 8\overline{)4048} \\ \underline{40} \\ 048 \\ \underline{48} \\ 0 \end{array}$$

10. $67 + n = 130$
$$\begin{array}{r} 130 \\ -\ 67 \\ \hline \mathbf{63} \end{array}$$

11. $9m = 306$

$m = \frac{306}{9}$
$$\begin{array}{r} \mathbf{34} \\ 9\overline{)306} \\ \underline{27} \\ 36 \\ \underline{36} \\ 0 \end{array}$$

12. Three out of eight is $\mathbf{\frac{3}{8}}$.

13. 80 ÷ 2 = **40**

14. $\mathbf{2\frac{3}{4}}$ **in.**

15. **C. miles**

16. Perimeter = 10 mm + 20 mm + 10 mm + 20 mm = **60 mm**

17. 2, 6, 10, 14, **18**
Each number is 4 more than the preceding number.

18. **C. 4321** Note that it ends with an odd digit.

19. $\mathbf{4\overline{)20}}$ **20 ÷ 4** $\mathbf{\frac{20}{4}}$

20. **10 + 20 = 30** **20 + 10 = 30**
30 − 20 = 10 **30 − 10 = 20**

Cumulative Test 2B

1.
$$\begin{array}{r} \$20.00 \\ -\ \$14.37 \\ \hline \mathbf{\$5.63} \end{array}$$

2. Two dozen is 24.
24 ÷ 8 = 3
Each person will receive **3 pencils.**

3.
$$\begin{array}{r} 678 \\ 48 \\ +\ 1386 \\ \hline \mathbf{2112} \end{array}$$

4.
$$\begin{array}{r} 503 \\ -\ 86 \\ \hline \mathbf{417} \end{array}$$

5.
$$\begin{array}{r} 34 \\ \times\ 36 \\ \hline 204 \\ 102 \\ \hline \mathbf{1224} \end{array}$$

6.
$$\begin{array}{r} \mathbf{602} \\ 6\overline{)3612} \\ \underline{36} \\ 012 \\ \underline{12} \\ 0 \end{array}$$

7.
$$\begin{array}{r} \$6.25 \\ \$12.00 \\ +\ \$0.59 \\ \hline \mathbf{\$18.84} \end{array}$$

8. 18 − (9 + 6) = 18 − 15 = **3**

9.
$$\begin{array}{r} \mathbf{32} \\ 25\overline{)800} \\ \underline{75} \\ 50 \\ \underline{50} \\ 0 \end{array}$$

10. $46 + n = 81$
$$\begin{array}{r} 81 \\ -\ 46 \\ \hline \mathbf{35} \end{array}$$

11. $6m = 306$

$m = \frac{306}{6}$
$$\begin{array}{r} \mathbf{51} \\ 6\overline{)306} \\ \underline{30} \\ 06 \\ \underline{6} \\ 0 \end{array}$$

12. Three out of ten is $\mathbf{\frac{3}{10}}$.

13. 36 ÷ 2 = **18**

14. **27 mm**

15. **A. inches**

16. Perimeter = 10 mm × 4 = **40 mm**

17. 1, 2, 4, 8, 16, **32**
Each number is twice the preceding number.

18. **C. 7654** Note that it ends with an even digit.

19. $8\overline{)16}$ $16 \div 8$ $\frac{16}{8}$

20. $11 + 22 = 33$ $22 + 11 = 33$
$33 - 22 = 11$ $33 - 11 = 22$

Cumulative Test 3A

1. 1000 pennies ÷ 50 pennies in each roll
= **20 rolls**

2.
$$\begin{array}{r} 1776 \\ -\ 1215 \\ \hline \textbf{561} \end{array}$$ **561 years**

3. **ten thousands**

4. **ten million**

5. $(8 + 4) \div (8 - 4) = 12 \div 4 = \mathbf{3}$

6.
$$\begin{array}{r} 5020 \\ \times\ \ 86 \\ \hline 30120 \\ 40160\ \\ \hline \mathbf{431{,}720} \end{array}$$

7.
$$\begin{array}{r} 354 \\ -\ 189 \\ \hline \textbf{165} \end{array}$$ **165 steps**

8. **12°F** (*Note:* Tick marks are spaced 2° apart.)

9. Two out of 5 is $\mathbf{\frac{2}{5}}$.

10. $-7 \bigcirc\!\!\!\!< -4$

11.
$$\begin{array}{r} 5{,}874 \\ 36{,}287 \\ +\ \ \ 489 \\ \hline \mathbf{42{,}650} \end{array}$$

12.
$$\begin{array}{r} 48 \\ \times 67 \\ \hline 336 \\ 288\ \\ \hline \mathbf{3216} \end{array}$$

13.
$$\begin{array}{r} \$1.25 \\ \times\ \ \ \ 8 \\ \hline \mathbf{\$10.00} \end{array}$$

14.
$$\begin{array}{r} \mathbf{506} \\ 7\overline{)3542} \\ 35\ \ \\ \hline 042 \\ 42 \\ \hline 0 \end{array}$$

15.
$$\begin{array}{r} \mathbf{25} \\ 25\overline{)625} \\ 50\ \\ \hline 125 \\ 125 \\ \hline 0 \end{array}$$

16. $24 \div (12 \div 4) = 24 \div 3 = \mathbf{8}$

17. $1000 - m = 408$
$$\begin{array}{r} 1000 \\ -\ \ 408 \\ \hline \mathbf{592} \end{array}$$

18. $9n = 63$ $9\overline{)63}$ = **7**
$n = \frac{63}{9}$

19. Perimeter = 4 × 20 mm = **80 mm**

20. **8 × 15 = 120**   **15 × 8 = 120**
120 ÷ 8 = 15   **120 ÷ 15 = 8**

Cumulative Test 3B

1. 234 players ÷ 18 teams = **13 players per team**

2.
$$\begin{array}{r} 1776 \\ -\ 1620 \\ \hline \textbf{156} \end{array}$$ **156 years**

3. **thousands**

4. **four billion**

5. $(4 \times 5) - (4 + 5) = 20 - 9 = \mathbf{11}$

6. $12\overline{)240}$ = **20**

7.
$$\begin{array}{r} 354 \\ -\ 178 \\ \hline \textbf{176} \end{array}$$ **176 steps**

8. **2°F** (*Note:* Tick marks are spaced 2° apart.)

9. One out of 8 is $\mathbf{\frac{1}{8}}$.

10. $8 - 5 \textcircled{>} 5 - 8$

11.
$$\begin{array}{r} \$3.75 \\ \$0.48 \\ +\ \$5.00 \\ \hline \mathbf{\$9.23} \end{array}$$

12.
$$\begin{array}{r} 56 \\ \times\ 83 \\ \hline 168 \\ 448 \\ \hline \mathbf{4648} \end{array}$$

13.
$$\begin{array}{r} \$0.35 \\ \times\ \ \ 10 \\ \hline \mathbf{\$3.50} \end{array}$$

14.
$$\begin{array}{r} \mathbf{402} \\ 12\overline{)4824} \\ 48 \\ \hline 024 \\ 24 \\ \hline 0 \end{array}$$

15.
$$\begin{array}{r} \mathbf{\$4.17} \\ 3\overline{)\$12.51} \\ 12 \\ \hline 0\ 5 \\ 3 \\ \hline 21 \\ 21 \\ \hline 0 \end{array}$$

16. $24 \div (12 \div 6) = 24 \div 2 = \mathbf{12}$

17. $3000 - a = 1096$
$$\begin{array}{r} 3000 \\ -\ 1096 \\ \hline \mathbf{1904} \end{array}$$

18. $9m = 54$ $\quad m = \dfrac{54}{9}$
$$\begin{array}{r} \mathbf{6} \\ 9\overline{)54} \end{array}$$

19. Perimeter = 2 cm + 1 cm + 2 cm + 1 cm = **6 cm**

20. **8 + 15 = 23** **15 + 8 = 23**
23 − 8 = 15 **23 − 15 = 8**

Cumulative Test 4A

1. **(9 + 3) ÷ (9 − 3) = 12 ÷ 6 = 2**

2. **3**

3.
$$\begin{array}{r} \overset{2\ 10}{\cancel{3}\cancel{1}}\overset{1}{2} \\ -\ \ 9\ 6 \\ \hline \mathbf{216\ pages} \end{array}$$

4. From −5° to 4° is **9°**.

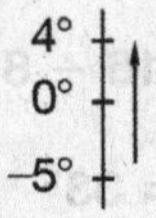

$5 + 4 = \mathbf{9}$

5. $Q - 40 = \mathbf{25}$
$$\begin{array}{r} 25 \\ +\ 40 \\ \hline \mathbf{65} \end{array}$$

6. $3n = 87$ $\quad n = \dfrac{87}{3}$
$$\begin{array}{r} \mathbf{29} \\ 3\overline{)87} \\ 6 \\ \hline 27 \\ 27 \\ \hline 0 \end{array}$$

7. Since the digit in the hundreds place is 5 or more, 37,542 rounds to **38,000.**

8. We estimate 51 × 48 by multiplying 50 × 50, which is **2500.**

9.
$$\begin{array}{r} \mathbf{41} \\ 3\overline{)123} \\ 12 \\ \hline 03 \\ 3 \\ \hline 0 \end{array}$$

10. $\dfrac{3 + 7 + 9 + 10 + 10 + 9}{6} = \dfrac{48}{6} = \mathbf{8}$

11. $\dfrac{24 + 98}{2} = \dfrac{122}{2} = \mathbf{61}$

12. **1, 2, 3, 6, 9, 18** are factors (divisors) of 18.

13.
$$\begin{array}{r} \$0.39 \\ \times\ \ \ 25 \\ \hline 195 \\ 78 \\ \hline \mathbf{\$9.75} \end{array}$$

14. Factors of 18: 1, 2, 3, 6, 9, 18
Factors of 24: 1, 2, 3, 4, 6, 8, 12, 24
The GCF of 18 and 24 is **6.**

15. **Friday**

16. **5 answers**

17. $3.50 ÷ 2 = **$1.75**

18. Perimeter = 12 mm + 18 mm + 12 mm + 18 mm = **60 mm**

19. 15, 30, 45, 60, **75**
Each number is 15 more than the preceding number.

20. $\mathbf{2\frac{1}{2}}$ **in.**

Cumulative Test 4B

1. (4 × 3) − (3 + 4) = 12 − 7 = 5

2. 5

3.
$$\begin{array}{r} \overset{1}{\cancel{2}}\overset{10}{\cancel{1}}\overset{1}{1} \\ -\ \ 94 \\ \hline \textbf{117 pages} \end{array}$$

4. From −8° to 10° is **18°**.

10°
0° — 8 + 10 = **18**
−8°

5. $R - 56 = 62$
$$\begin{array}{r} 62 \\ +\ 56 \\ \hline \textbf{118} \end{array}$$

6. $3m = 78$
$m = \frac{87}{3}$
$$\begin{array}{r} \textbf{26} \\ 3\overline{)78} \\ \underline{6} \\ 18 \\ \underline{18} \\ 0 \end{array}$$

7. The digit is the tens place (6) is 5 or more, so 4367 rounds to **4400.**

8. We estimate 5280 + 3910 by adding 5000 + 4000, which is **9000.**

9.
$$\begin{array}{r} \textbf{72} \\ 6\overline{)432} \\ \underline{42} \\ 12 \\ \underline{12} \\ 0 \end{array}$$

10. $\frac{6 + 10 + 8 + 7 + 9}{5} = \frac{40}{5} = \mathbf{8}$

11. $\frac{17 + 83}{2} = \frac{100}{2} = \mathbf{50}$

12. **1, 3, 7, 21,** are factors (divisors) of 21.

13.
$$\begin{array}{r} \$0.39 \\ \times\ \ \ \ 20 \\ \hline \mathbf{\$7.80} \end{array}$$

14. Factors of 16: 1, 2, 4, 8, 16
Factors of 24: 1, 2, 3, 4, 6, 8, 12, 24
The GCF of 16 and 24 is **8.**

15. 12 + 10 = 22
Maria and Susan together scored **22 points.**

16. 9 − 7 = 2
Tony scored **2 points** more than Rebert.

17. $7.50 ÷ 2 = **$3.75**

18. Perimeter = 4 × 8 mm = **32 mm**

19. 1, 3, 9, 27, **81**
Each number is 3 times the preceding number.

20. $\mathbf{1\frac{1}{2}}$ **in.**

Cumulative Test 5A

1. (20 × 10) − (20 + 10) = 200 − 30 = **170**

2.
$$\begin{array}{r} 28 \\ -\ 13 \\ \hline 15 \end{array} \qquad \frac{\text{boys}}{\text{girls}} = \mathbf{\frac{13}{15}}$$

3. **17,105,000**

4. 87 × 31 ≈ 91 × 30 = **2700**

5. 2 + 4 + 3 + 7 = 16
1 + 6 + 3 + 2 = 12
4 + 3 + 7 + 3 = 17
B. 1632

6.
$$\begin{array}{r} 2 \\ 5\overline{)12} \\ \underline{10} \\ 2 \end{array} \qquad \frac{12}{5} = \mathbf{2\frac{2}{5}}$$

7.
$$\begin{array}{r} 37 \\ 82 \\ 63 \\ +\ 58 \\ \hline 240 \end{array} \qquad \begin{array}{r} \textbf{60} \\ 4\overline{)240} \end{array}$$

8. **12**

9. Factors of 12: 1, 2, 3, 4, 6, 16
Factors of 18: 1, 2, 3, 6, 9, 18
The GCF of 12 and 18 is **6.**

10. $\mathbf{\frac{7}{12}}$

11. $\frac{12 \text{ miles}}{\cancel{\text{hour}}} \times \frac{3 \cancel{\text{hours}}}{1} = \textbf{36 miles}$

12. $3\overline{)12}$ = 4 $4 \times 2 = \mathbf{8}$

13. $\frac{2}{6} + \frac{3}{6} = \mathbf{\frac{5}{6}}$

14. $\frac{11}{12} - \frac{4}{12} = \mathbf{\frac{7}{12}}$

15. $1 - \frac{3}{5} = \frac{5}{5} - \frac{3}{5} = \mathbf{\frac{2}{5}}$

16. $\frac{3}{8} + \frac{5}{8} = \frac{8}{8} = \mathbf{1}$

17. $\frac{1}{2}$ of a circle is **50%** of a circle.

18. $\frac{1}{8} + \frac{1}{8} + \frac{1}{8} = \mathbf{\frac{3}{8}}$

19. $27.50 ÷ 10 = **$2.75**

20. $\frac{1}{2} \textcircled{>} \frac{1}{4}$

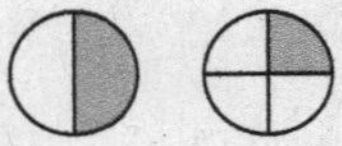

Cumulative Test 5B

1. (20 + 10) × (20 − 10) = 30 × 10 = **300**

2. $\begin{array}{r} 29 \\ -\ 13 \\ \hline 16 \end{array}$ $\frac{\text{boys}}{\text{girls}} = \mathbf{\frac{13}{16}}$

3. **21,286,000**

4. Since the tens digit (7) is 5 or more, 3875 rounds to **3900.**

5. 1 + 3 + 6 + 7 = 17
2 + 4 + 5 + 8 = 19
3 + 6 + 2 + 4 = 15
C. 3624

6. $\begin{array}{r} \mathbf{5} \\ 3\overline{)16} \\ 15 \\ \hline 1 \end{array}$ $\frac{16}{3} = \mathbf{5\frac{1}{3}}$

7. $\begin{array}{r} 3{,}742 \\ 4{,}918 \\ +\ 5{,}170 \\ \hline 13{,}830 \end{array}$ $\begin{array}{r} \mathbf{4610} \\ 3\overline{)13{,}830} \\ 12 \\ \hline 1\ 8 \\ 1\ 8 \\ \hline 03 \\ 3 \\ \hline 00 \end{array}$

8. **7**

9. Factors of 10: 1, 2, 5, 10
Factors of 15: 1, 3, 5, 15
The GCF of 10 and 15 is **5.**

10. $\mathbf{\frac{4}{15}}$

11. $\frac{60 \text{ miles}}{\cancel{\text{hour}}} \times \frac{4 \cancel{\text{hours}}}{1} = \textbf{240 miles}$

12. $4\overline{)24}$ = 6 $6 \times 3 = \mathbf{18}$

13. $\frac{1}{3} + \frac{1}{3} = \mathbf{\frac{2}{3}}$

14. $\frac{7}{8} - \frac{4}{8} = \mathbf{\frac{3}{8}}$

15. $1 - \frac{3}{8} = \frac{8}{8} - \frac{3}{8} = \mathbf{\frac{5}{8}}$

16. $\frac{5}{6} + \frac{1}{6} = \frac{6}{6} = \mathbf{1}$

17. $\frac{1}{4}$ of a circle is **25%** of a circle.

18. $\frac{1}{12} + \frac{2}{12} + \frac{4}{12} = \mathbf{\frac{7}{12}}$

19. $37.50 ÷ 10 = **$3.75**

20. $\frac{1}{2} \textcircled{<} \frac{3}{4}$

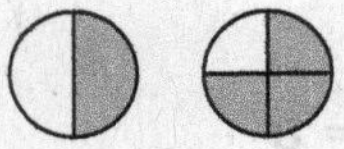

Cumulative Test 6A

1. $\begin{array}{r} 6 \\ 4\overline{)27} \\ \underline{24} \\ 3 \end{array}$ $\mathbf{6\frac{3}{4}}$ **inches**

2. $\begin{array}{r} 30 \\ \underline{-\ 16} \\ 14 \end{array}$ $\frac{\text{boys}}{\text{girls}} = \frac{14}{16} = \mathbf{\frac{7}{8}}$

3. $68 \times 21 \approx 70 \times 20 =$ **1400**

4. $\begin{array}{r} \mathbf{63} \\ 9\overline{)567} \\ \underline{54} \\ 27 \\ \underline{27} \\ 0 \end{array}$

5. $\begin{array}{r} 68 \\ 72 \\ \underline{+\ 82} \\ 222 \end{array}$ $\begin{array}{r} \mathbf{74} \\ 3\overline{)222} \\ \underline{21} \\ 12 \\ \underline{12} \\ 0 \end{array}$

6. The factors of 20 are **1, 2, 4, 5, 10, 20.**

7. Factors of 24: 1, 2, 3, 4, 6, 8, 12, 24
Factors of 16: 1, 2, 4, 8, 16
The GCF of 24 and 16 is **8.**

8. **B. diameter**

9. $\frac{3}{4} \times \frac{12}{1} = \frac{36}{4}$ which is **9 pencils.**

10. $\left(\frac{2}{7} + \frac{2}{7}\right) - \frac{4}{7} = \frac{4}{7} - \frac{4}{7} = \mathbf{0}$

11. $1 - \frac{1}{3} = \frac{3}{3} - \frac{1}{3} = \mathbf{\frac{2}{3}}$

12. $\frac{1}{2} \times \frac{3}{4} = \mathbf{\frac{3}{8}}$

13. $\begin{array}{r} 1\frac{4}{6} \\ 6\overline{)10} \\ \underline{6} \\ 4 \end{array}$ $1\frac{4}{6} = \mathbf{1\frac{2}{3}}$

14. $3\frac{2}{3} + 2\frac{2}{3} = 5\frac{4}{3} = \mathbf{6\frac{1}{3}}$

15. $\frac{3}{8} + \frac{3}{8} = \frac{6}{8} = \mathbf{\frac{3}{4}}$

16. Multiples of 4: 4, 8, 12, 16, 20, 24, ...
Multiples of 6: 6, 12, 18, 24, ...
The LCM of 4 and 6 is **12.**

17. 36 in. ÷ 4 = **9 in.**

18. $\frac{2}{3} \times \mathbf{\frac{3}{2}} = 1$

19. 8, 16, 24, 32, **40, 48, 56**
Each number is 8 more than the preceding number. Note that these numbers are the multiples of 8.

20. **∠*C*** or **∠*ACB*** or **∠*BCA***

Cumulative Test 6B

1. $\begin{array}{r} 7 \\ 4\overline{)29} \\ \underline{28} \\ 1 \end{array}$ $\mathbf{7\frac{1}{4}}$ **inches**

2. $\begin{array}{r} 30 \\ \underline{-\ 18} \\ 12 \end{array}$ $\frac{\text{boys}}{\text{girls}} = \frac{12}{18} = \mathbf{\frac{2}{3}}$

3. $6084 - 3973 \approx 6000 - 4000 =$ **2000**

4. $\begin{array}{r} \mathbf{24} \\ 18\overline{)432} \\ \underline{36} \\ 72 \\ \underline{72} \\ 0 \end{array}$

5. $\begin{array}{r} 143 \\ 98 \\ \underline{+\ 128} \\ 369 \end{array}$ $\begin{array}{r} \mathbf{123} \\ 3\overline{)369} \\ \underline{3} \\ 06 \\ \underline{6} \\ 09 \\ \underline{9} \\ 0 \end{array}$

6. The factors of 33 are **1, 3, 11, 33.**

7. Factors of 27: 1, 3, 9, 27
Factors of 45: 1, 3, 5, 9, 15, 45
The GCF of 27 and 45 is **9.**

8. **C. circumference**

9. $\frac{3}{4} \times \frac{20}{1} = \frac{60}{4} =$ **15 books**

10. $\left(\frac{3}{5} - \frac{2}{5}\right) + \frac{1}{5} = \frac{1}{5} + \frac{1}{5} = \mathbf{\frac{2}{5}}$

11. $1 - \frac{1}{4} = \frac{4}{4} - \frac{1}{4} = \mathbf{\frac{3}{4}}$

12. $\frac{1}{3} \times \frac{2}{5} = \mathbf{\frac{2}{15}}$

13. $8\overline{)12}$ → $1\frac{4}{8}$; $\frac{-8}{4}$ $\quad 1\frac{4}{8} = \mathbf{1\frac{1}{2}}$

14. $4\frac{4}{5} + 3\frac{3}{5} = 7\frac{7}{5} = \mathbf{8\frac{2}{5}}$

15. $\frac{5}{6} - \frac{1}{6} = \frac{4}{6} = \mathbf{\frac{2}{3}}$

16. Multiples of 6: 6, 12, 18, 24, 30, …
Multiples of 8: 8, 16, 24, 32, 40, …
The LCM of 6 and 8 is **24.**

17. 60 cm ÷ 4 = **15 cm**

18. $\frac{3}{4} \times \mathbf{\frac{4}{3}} = 1$

19. 7, 14, 21, 28, 35, 42, **49**
Each number is 7 more than the preceding number. Note that these numbers are the multiples of 7.

20. **∠*B* or ∠*ABC* or ∠*CBA***

Cumulative Test 7A

1. **1800**

2. $\mathbf{\frac{3}{2}}$

3. Perimeter = 4 × 8 in. = **32 in.**

4. 10 × 12 = **120 square tiles**

5. **3**

6. **0.012**

7. (5 × 100) + (6 × 1) = 500 + 6 = **506**

8. Radius = $\frac{\text{diameter}}{2} = \frac{24\text{ in.}}{2} = $ **12 in.**

9. $0.47 = \mathbf{\frac{47}{100}}$

10. $\frac{3}{4} \; \textcircled{<} \; \frac{4}{3}$

Note that $\frac{3}{4}$ is less than 1 and $\frac{4}{3}$ is greater than 1.

11. $\frac{35}{100} = \mathbf{0.35}$

12. $\frac{3}{5} + \frac{4}{5} = \frac{7}{5} = \mathbf{1\frac{2}{5}}$

13. $\frac{2}{3} \times \frac{3}{5} = \frac{6}{15} = \mathbf{\frac{2}{5}}$

14. 18 × 20 ÷ 12 = 360 ÷ 12 = **30**

15. $\frac{3}{4} \times \frac{36}{1} = \frac{108}{4} = \mathbf{27}$

16. $\frac{5}{8} - \frac{1}{8} = \frac{4}{8} = \mathbf{\frac{1}{2}}$

17. $w - 10 = 100$ $\quad 100 + 10 = \mathbf{110}$

18. $3 + N = 4\frac{1}{3}$

$N = 4\frac{1}{3} - 3 = \mathbf{1\frac{1}{3}}$

19. $80\% = \frac{80}{100} = \mathbf{\frac{4}{5}}$

20. $5\overline{)40}$ → 8; $\frac{40}{0}$ $\quad 8 \times 4 =$ **32 answers**

Cumulative Test 7B

1. **5300**

2. $\mathbf{\frac{6}{5}}$

3. Perimeter = 4 × 10 cm = **40 cm**

4. 10 × 15 = **150 square tiles**

5. **8**

6. **1.5**

7. (5 × 1000) + (7 × 10) = 5000 + 70 = **5070**

8. Radius = $\frac{\text{diameter}}{2} = \frac{28\text{ in.}}{2} = $ **14 in.**

9. $0.7 = \mathbf{\frac{7}{10}}$

10. $\frac{6}{5} \; \textcircled{>} \; \frac{5}{6}$

Note that $\frac{6}{5}$ is greater than 1 and $\frac{5}{6}$ is less than 1.

11. $\frac{3}{100} = \mathbf{0.03}$

12. $\frac{3}{7} + \frac{6}{7} = \frac{9}{7} = \mathbf{1\frac{2}{7}}$

13. $\frac{4}{5} \times \frac{3}{4} = \frac{12}{20} = \mathbf{\frac{3}{5}}$

14. $23 \times (500 \div 20) = 23 \times 25 = \mathbf{575}$

15. $\frac{5}{6} \times \frac{36}{1} = \frac{180}{6} = \mathbf{30}$

16. $\frac{5}{6} - \frac{1}{6} = \frac{4}{6} = \mathbf{\frac{2}{3}}$

17. $w - 50 = 500$ $\quad \begin{array}{r} 500 \\ +\ 50 \\ \hline \mathbf{550} \end{array}$

18. $3 + N = 5\frac{2}{3}$

$N = 5\frac{2}{3} - 3 = \mathbf{2\frac{2}{3}}$

19. $60\% = \frac{60}{100} = \mathbf{\frac{3}{5}}$

20. $\begin{array}{r} 10 \\ 4\overline{)40} \\ 40 \\ \hline 0 \end{array} \quad \begin{array}{r} 10 \\ \times\ 3 \\ \hline \mathbf{30} \end{array}$ **answers**

Cumulative Test 8A

1. $\angle \mathbf{BDC}$ or $\angle \mathbf{CDB}$

2. **5**

3. $\frac{16}{20} = \mathbf{\frac{4}{5}}$

4. $6107 - 2960 \approx 6000 + 3000 = \mathbf{9000}$

5. $4^2 + \sqrt{9} = 16 + 3 = \mathbf{19}$

6. $\begin{array}{r} 78 \\ 75 \\ +\ 90 \\ \hline 243 \end{array} \quad \begin{array}{r} \mathbf{81} \\ 3\overline{)243} \\ 24 \\ \hline 03 \\ 3 \\ \hline 0 \end{array}$ **pages**

7. Factors of 12: 1, 2, 3, 4, 6, 12
Factors of 20: 1, 2, 4, 5, 10, 20
The GCF of 12 and 20 is **4.**

8. $\frac{60}{100} = \frac{6}{10} = \mathbf{\frac{3}{5}}$

9. $1\frac{2}{3} + 2\frac{2}{3} = 3\frac{4}{3} = \mathbf{4\frac{1}{3}}$

10. $1 - \frac{5}{8} = \frac{8}{8} - \frac{5}{8} = \mathbf{\frac{3}{8}}$

11. $\frac{1}{3} \times \frac{3}{4} = \frac{3}{12} = \mathbf{\frac{1}{4}}$

12. **1 hr 53 min**

13. Multiples of 6: 6, 12, 18, 24, 30, …
Multiples of 8: 8, 16, 24, 32, 40, …
LCM of 6 and 8 is **24.**

14. $10 \times 10 =$ **100 square-inch tiles**

15. **3**

16. **10.05**

17. $\begin{array}{r} 0.7 \\ +\ 0.8 \\ \hline \mathbf{1.5} \end{array}$

18. $\begin{array}{r} 0.2 \\ 0.34 \\ +\ 5.0 \\ \hline \mathbf{5.54} \end{array}$

19. $\begin{array}{r} 0.15 \\ -\ 0.06 \\ \hline \mathbf{0.09} \end{array}$

20. $\begin{array}{r} 0.15 \\ \times\ 0.3 \\ \hline \mathbf{0.045} \end{array}$

Cumulative Test 8B

1. $\angle \mathbf{ADB}$ or $\angle \mathbf{BDA}$

2. **2**

3. $\frac{15}{20} = \mathbf{\frac{3}{4}}$

4. $8972 + 4106 \approx 9000 + 4000 = \mathbf{13{,}000}$

5. $5^2 + \sqrt{16} = 25 + 4 = \mathbf{29}$

6. $\begin{array}{r} 81 \\ 84 \\ +\ 84 \\ \hline 249 \end{array} \quad \begin{array}{r} \mathbf{83} \\ 3\overline{)249} \\ 24 \\ \hline 09 \\ 9 \\ \hline 0 \end{array}$ **pages**

Solutions

7. Factors of 21: 1, 3, 7, 21
Factors of 35: 1, 5, 7, 35
The GCF of 21 and 35 is **7.**

8. $\frac{40}{100} = \frac{4}{10} = \mathbf{\frac{2}{5}}$

9. $3\frac{3}{4} + 1\frac{1}{4} = 4\frac{4}{4} = \mathbf{5}$

10. $5 - 1\frac{1}{3} = 4\frac{3}{3} - 1\frac{1}{3} = \mathbf{3\frac{2}{3}}$

11. $\frac{1}{2} \times \frac{2}{3} = \frac{2}{6} = \mathbf{\frac{1}{3}}$

12. **6 hr 15 min**

13. Multiples of 3: 3, 6, 9, ...
Multiples of 6: 6, 12, 18, ...
LCM of 3 and 6 is **6.**

14. 6 × 8 = **48 square-inch tiles**

15. **4**

16. **3.12**

17.
$$\begin{array}{r} 0.3 \\ 0.4 \\ +\ 0.5 \\ \hline \mathbf{1.2} \end{array}$$

18.
$$\begin{array}{r} 6.0 \\ 4.2 \\ +\ 0.36 \\ \hline \mathbf{10.56} \end{array}$$

19.
$$\begin{array}{r} 0.23 \\ -\ 0.19 \\ \hline \mathbf{0.04} \end{array}$$

20.
$$\begin{array}{r} 0.12 \\ \times\ \ 0.4 \\ \hline \mathbf{0.048} \end{array}$$

Cumulative Test 9A

1. (10 × 6) − (7 + 8) = 60 − 15 = **45**

2. $\frac{3}{4} \times \frac{4}{3} = 1; \frac{4}{3} = \mathbf{1\frac{1}{3}}$

3. 36 in. ÷ 4 = **9 in.**

4. Area = 12 ft × 15 ft = **180 sq. ft**

5. **10.12**

6. $\frac{25}{100} = \frac{1}{4}$ $\quad \frac{1}{4} \times \frac{\$80}{1} = \mathbf{\$20}$

7. $\frac{3}{4} \times \frac{24}{1} = \frac{72}{4} = \mathbf{18}$

8. **C. 70%**

9. **4**

10. $7\% = \mathbf{\frac{7}{100}} = \mathbf{0.07}$

11. Factors of 12: 1, 2, 3, 4, 6, 12
Factors of 8: 1, 2, 4, 8
The GCF of 12 and 8 is **4.**

12. $2\frac{1}{3} + \sqrt{9} = 2\frac{1}{3} + 3 = \mathbf{5\frac{1}{3}}$

13. $\frac{1}{2} \times \frac{2}{3} = \frac{2}{6} = \mathbf{\frac{1}{3}}$

14.
$$\begin{array}{r} 0.43 \\ 6.7 \\ +\ 8.0 \\ \hline \mathbf{15.13} \end{array}$$

15.
$$\begin{array}{r} 5.00 \\ -\ 3.27 \\ \hline \mathbf{1.73} \end{array}$$

16.
$$\begin{array}{r} 0.34 \\ \times\ 0.26 \\ \hline 204 \\ 68 \\ \hline \mathbf{0.0884} \end{array}$$

17. $4\frac{2}{3} - 3\frac{1}{3} = \mathbf{1\frac{1}{3}}$

18. $\frac{2}{3} \times \frac{4}{4} = \mathbf{\frac{8}{12}}$

19.
$$\begin{array}{r} \mathbf{0.175} \\ 4\overline{)0.700} \\ 4 \\ \hline 30 \\ 28 \\ \hline 20 \\ 20 \\ \hline 0 \end{array}$$

20. **C.** $\overline{SR}$

Cumulative Test 9B

1. (8 + 2) × (8 − 2) = 10 × 6 = **60**

2. $\frac{2}{3} \times \frac{3}{2} = 1; \frac{3}{2} = \mathbf{1\frac{1}{2}}$

3. 100 cm ÷ 4 = **25 cm**

4. Area = 11 ft × 12 ft = **132 sq. ft**

5. **12.05**

6. $\frac{25}{100} = \frac{1}{4}$ $\quad \frac{1}{4} \times \frac{\$60}{1} = \mathbf{\$15}$

7. $\frac{2}{3} \times \frac{24}{1} = \frac{48}{3} = \mathbf{16}$

8. **A. 30%**

9. **7**

10. $9\% = \frac{9}{100} = \mathbf{0.09}$

11. Multiples of 12: 12, 24, 36, 48, …
Multiples of 8: 8, 16, 24, 32, 40, 48, …
The LCM of 12 and 8 is **24.**

12. $1\frac{3}{5} + \sqrt{4} = 1\frac{3}{5} + 2 = \mathbf{3\frac{3}{5}}$

13. $\frac{1}{3} \times \frac{3}{4} = \frac{3}{12} = \mathbf{\frac{1}{4}}$

14.
$$\begin{array}{r} 6.2 \\ 7.0 \\ +\ 0.48 \\ \hline \mathbf{13.68} \end{array}$$

15.
$$\begin{array}{r} 2.00 \\ -\ 0.34 \\ \hline \mathbf{1.66} \end{array}$$

16.
$$\begin{array}{r} 0.23 \\ \times\ 0.12 \\ \hline 46 \\ 23\ \\ \hline \mathbf{0.0276} \end{array}$$

17. $3\frac{3}{5} + 3\frac{2}{5} = 6\frac{5}{5} = \mathbf{7}$

18. $\frac{2}{3} \times \frac{3}{3} = \mathbf{\frac{6}{9}}$

19.
$$\begin{array}{r} \mathbf{0.375} \\ 8\overline{)3.000} \\ 2\ 4\ \ \ \\ \hline 60\ \ \\ 56\ \ \\ \hline 40\ \\ 40\ \\ \hline 0\ \end{array}$$

20. **D. $\overline{SQ}$**

Cumulative Test 10A

1. (0.3 + 0.4) − (0.3 × 0.4) = 0.7 − 0.12 = **0.58**

2. **3**

3. $8\% = \frac{8}{100} = 0.08$
$$\begin{array}{r} \$16 \\ \times\ 0.08 \\ \hline \mathbf{\$1.28} \end{array}$$

4. 5867 + 2106 ≈ 6000 + 2000 = **8000**

5.
$$\begin{array}{r} \mathbf{2005} \\ 20\overline{)40,100} \end{array}$$

6.
$$\begin{array}{r} 96 \\ 100 \\ +\ 92 \\ \hline 288 \end{array} \qquad \begin{array}{r} \mathbf{96} \\ 3\overline{)288} \\ 27\ \\ \hline 18 \\ 18 \\ \hline 0 \end{array}$$

7. $\frac{7}{24} + \frac{11}{24} = \frac{18}{24} = \mathbf{\frac{3}{4}}$

8. $\frac{5}{6} \times \frac{24}{1} = \frac{120}{6} = \mathbf{20}$

9. $\frac{1}{4} = \frac{2}{8}$ $\quad \frac{2}{8} + \frac{3}{8} = \mathbf{\frac{5}{8}}$

10. Multiples of 2: 2, 4, 6, 8, 10, 12, …
Multiples of 3: 3, 6, 9, 12, 15, 18, …
Multiples of 4: 4, 8, 12, 16, 20, 24, …
The LCM of 2, 3, and 4 is **12.**

11. Area = 100 cm × 100 cm = **10,000 sq. cm**

12. $C = \pi d$
$C = (3.14)(10)$
$$\begin{array}{r} 3.14 \\ \times\ \ 10 \\ \hline 0 \\ 3140\ \\ \hline \end{array}$$
31.40 in. or **31.4 in.**

13. **10.2**

14.
$$\begin{array}{r} 1.00 \\ -\ 0.23 \\ \hline \mathbf{0.77} \end{array}$$

15.
$$\begin{array}{r} 5.62 \\ 4.0\ \\ +\ 0.5\ \\ \hline \mathbf{10.12} \end{array}$$

16. $0.2 \times 0.3 \times 0.4 = \mathbf{0.024}$

17. $3\overline{)0.123}$ → **0.041**

18. $0.3\overline{)0.45}$ → **1.5**
$$\begin{array}{r} 3 \\ \hline 15 \\ 15 \\ \hline 0 \end{array}$$

19.
$$\begin{array}{r} 6\frac{1}{5} = 5\frac{6}{5} \\ -\ 1\frac{3}{5} = 1\frac{3}{5} \\ \hline \mathbf{4\frac{3}{5}} \end{array}$$

20. $12.5 \times 100 = \mathbf{1250}$

Cumulative Test 10B

1. $\left(\frac{1}{3} + \frac{2}{3}\right) - \left(\frac{1}{3} \times \frac{2}{3}\right) = 1 - \frac{2}{9} = \mathbf{\frac{7}{9}}$

2. **7**

3. $8\% = \frac{8}{100} = 0.08$
$$\begin{array}{r} \$14 \\ \times\ 0.08 \\ \hline \mathbf{\$1.12} \end{array}$$

4. $48 \times 21 \approx 50 \times 20 = \mathbf{1000}$

5. $12\overline{)2508}$ → **209**
$$\begin{array}{r} 24 \\ \hline 108 \\ 108 \\ \hline 0 \end{array}$$

6.
$$\begin{array}{r} 47 \\ 38 \\ 56 \\ +\ 43 \\ \hline 184 \end{array} \qquad 4\overline{)184} \rightarrow \mathbf{46} \qquad \begin{array}{r} 16 \\ \hline 24 \\ 24 \\ \hline 0 \end{array}$$

7. $\frac{11}{36} + \frac{13}{36} = \frac{24}{36} = \mathbf{\frac{2}{3}}$

8. $\frac{3}{4} \times \frac{48}{1} = \frac{144}{4} = \mathbf{36}$

9. $\frac{1}{4} = \frac{2}{8} \qquad \frac{2}{8} + \frac{5}{8} = \mathbf{\frac{7}{8}}$

10. Multiples of 2: 2, 4, 6, 8, 10, 12, …
Multiples of 4: 4, 8, 12, 16, 20, 24, …
Multiples of 8: 8, 16, 24, 32, 40, 48, …
The LCM of 2, 4, and 8 is **8.**

11. Area = 27 mm × 43 mm = **1161 sq. mm**

12. $C = \pi d$
$C = (3.14)(10)$
$$\begin{array}{r} 3.14 \\ \times\ 10 \\ \hline 0 \\ 3140 \\ \hline \end{array}$$
31.40 ft. or **31.4 ft.**

13. **21.05**

14.
$$\begin{array}{r} 1.00 \\ -\ 0.01 \\ \hline \mathbf{0.99} \end{array}$$

15.
$$\begin{array}{r} 4.6 \\ 0.47 \\ +\ 12.0 \\ \hline \mathbf{17.07} \end{array}$$

16.
$$\begin{array}{r} 0.12 \\ \times\ 0.13 \\ \hline 36 \\ 12 \\ \hline \mathbf{0.0156} \end{array}$$

17. $6\overline{)0.456}$ → **0.076**
$$\begin{array}{r} 42 \\ \hline 36 \\ 36 \\ \hline 0 \end{array}$$

18. $0.03\overline{)0.123}$ → **4.1**
$$\begin{array}{r} 12 \\ \hline 03 \\ 3 \\ \hline 0 \end{array}$$

19.
$$\begin{array}{r} 5\frac{1}{3} = 4\frac{4}{3} \\ -\ 2\frac{2}{3} = 2\frac{2}{3} \\ \hline \mathbf{2\frac{2}{3}} \end{array}$$

20. $3.5 \times 100 = \mathbf{350}$

Cumulative Test 11A

1. $d = 2r = 2(4) = 8$ cm
$C = \pi d$
$C = (3.14)(8)$
$$\begin{array}{r} 3.14 \\ \times\quad 8 \\ \hline \mathbf{25.12\ cm} \end{array}$$

2. $$\begin{array}{r} 1.5 \\ \times\ 0.025 \\ \hline 75 \\ 30 \\ \hline \mathbf{0.0375} \end{array}$$

3. Perimeter = 20 mm + 24 mm + 20 mm + 24 mm = **88 mm**

4. Area = 24 mm × 20 mm = **480 sq. mm**

5. $\frac{\text{length}}{\text{width}} = \frac{24}{20} = \mathbf{\frac{6}{5}}$

6. $30\% = \frac{30}{100} = \frac{3}{10}$
$\frac{3}{10} \times \frac{50}{1} = \frac{150}{10} = $ **15 dimes**

7. $7 - n = 4.7$
$$\begin{array}{r} 7.0 \\ -\ 4.7 \\ \hline \mathbf{2.3} \end{array}$$

8. 0.60 (=) 0.6

9. **80.08**

10. $2.8735 \approx$ **2.9**

11. $$\begin{array}{r} 3\frac{2}{3} \\ +\ 1\frac{2}{3} \\ \hline 4\frac{4}{3} = \mathbf{5\frac{1}{3}} \end{array}$$

12. $$\begin{array}{r} 6\frac{1}{3} = 5\frac{4}{3} \\ +\ 4\frac{2}{3} = 4\frac{2}{3} \\ \hline \mathbf{1\frac{2}{3}} \end{array}$$

13. $\frac{3}{8} \times \frac{4}{9} = \frac{12}{72} = \mathbf{\frac{1}{6}}$

14. $x = 1\frac{1}{3} - \frac{2}{3} = \frac{4}{3} - \frac{2}{3} = \mathbf{\frac{2}{3}}$

15. $3.75 \div 10^2 = 3.75 \div 100 =$ **0.0375**

16. $$\begin{array}{r} 0.0375 \\ 0.4\overline{)0.01500} \\ 12 \\ \hline 30 \\ 28 \\ \hline 20 \\ 20 \\ \hline 0 \end{array}$$

17. $\sqrt{36} \div 0.6 = 6 \div 0.6$ $\quad 0.6\overline{)6.0}$ = **10**

18. $$\begin{array}{r} \frac{3}{4} = \frac{6}{8} \\ +\ \frac{1}{8} = \frac{1}{8} \\ \hline \mathbf{\frac{7}{8}} \end{array}$$

19. $\frac{\cancel{2} \cdot 2 \cdot \cancel{3} \cdot 3 \cdot \cancel{5}}{\cancel{2} \cdot \cancel{3} \cdot \cancel{5} \cdot 7} = \frac{2 \cdot 3}{7} = \mathbf{\frac{6}{7}}$

20. **3.7**

Cumulative Test 11B

1. $d = 2r = 2(3\text{ cm}) = 6$ cm
$C = \pi d$
$C = (3.14)(6)$
$$\begin{array}{r} 3.14 \\ \times\quad 6 \\ \hline \mathbf{18.84\ cm} \end{array}$$

2. $$\begin{array}{r} 0.81 \\ \times\ 0.012 \\ \hline 162 \\ 81 \\ \hline \mathbf{0.00972} \end{array}$$

3. Perimeter = 20 mm + 15 mm + 20 mm + 15 mm = **70 mm**

4. Area = 15 mm × 20 mm = **300 sq. mm**

5. $\frac{\text{length}}{\text{width}} = \frac{20}{15} = \mathbf{\frac{4}{3}}$

6. $20\% = \frac{20}{100} = \frac{1}{5}$
$\frac{1}{5} \times \frac{50}{1} = \frac{50}{5} =$ **10 pennies**

7. $6 - w = 3.1$
$$\begin{array}{r} 6.0 \\ -\ 3.1 \\ \hline \mathbf{2.9} \end{array}$$

8. 1.23 (>) 0.140

9. **20.2**

10. $6.7347 \approx \mathbf{6.73}$

11. $$\begin{array}{r} 3\frac{3}{4} \\ +\ 2\frac{1}{4} \\ \hline 5\frac{4}{4} = \mathbf{6} \end{array}$$

12. $$\begin{array}{r} 5\frac{1}{5} = 4\frac{6}{5} \\ -\ 1\frac{3}{5} = 1\frac{3}{5} \\ \hline \mathbf{3\frac{3}{5}} \end{array}$$

13. $\frac{3}{4} \cdot \frac{2}{5} = \frac{6}{20} = \mathbf{\frac{3}{10}}$

14. $x = 1\frac{2}{5} - \frac{3}{5} = \frac{7}{5} - \frac{3}{5} = \mathbf{\frac{4}{5}}$

15. $0.45 \div 10^2 = 0.45 \div 100 = \mathbf{0.0045}$

16. $$\begin{array}{r} \mathbf{0.075} \\ 0.2\overline{)0.0150} \\ \underline{14} \\ 10 \\ \underline{10} \\ 0 \end{array}$$

17. $\sqrt{4} \div 0.4 = 2 \div 0.4 \qquad 0.4\overline{)2.0}$ with quotient $\mathbf{5}$

18. $$\begin{array}{r} \frac{1}{4} = \frac{2}{8} \\ +\ \frac{3}{8} = \frac{3}{8} \\ \hline \mathbf{\frac{5}{8}} \end{array}$$

19. $\frac{\cancel{2} \cdot \cancel{3} \cdot 3 \cdot \cancel{5}}{\cancel{2} \cdot 2 \cdot \cancel{3} \cdot \cancel{5} \cdot 5} = \frac{3}{2 \cdot 5} = \mathbf{\frac{3}{10}}$

20. **0.8**

Cumulative Test 12A

1. a. Sample space = **{1, 2, 3, 4, 5, 6}**

   b. Out of the six possible outcomes, only 5 and 6 are greater than 4.
   $\frac{2}{6} = \mathbf{\frac{1}{3}}$

2. Perimeter = 6 × 8 in. = **48 in.**

3. 24 cm × 4 cm = **96 sq. cm**

4. **3**

5. $$\begin{array}{r} 3.0 \\ 4.5 \\ +\ 0.23 \\ \hline \mathbf{7.73} \end{array}$$

6. $$\begin{array}{r} 1.00 \\ -\ 0.29 \\ \hline \mathbf{0.71} \end{array}$$

7. $$\begin{array}{r} 0.27 \\ \times\ \ 0.3 \\ \hline \mathbf{0.081} \end{array}$$

8. $C = \pi d$
   $C = (3.14)(30)$
   $$\begin{array}{r} 3.14 \\ \times\ \ 30 \\ \hline \mathbf{94.20} \end{array} \approx \mathbf{94\ inches}$$

9. **D. 9**

10. $\frac{\text{win}}{\text{loss}} = \frac{10}{20} = \mathbf{\frac{1}{2}}$

11. $$\begin{array}{r} 5 = 4\frac{3}{3} \\ -\ 2\frac{1}{3} = 2\frac{1}{3} \\ \hline \mathbf{2\frac{2}{3}} \end{array}$$

12. $9\overline{)0.45}$ with quotient $\mathbf{0.05}$

13. $0.04\overline{)1.20}$ with quotient $\mathbf{30}$

14. $12.34 \times 10 = \mathbf{123.4}$

15. $$\begin{array}{r} \frac{1}{2} = \frac{5}{10} \\ +\ \frac{3}{5} = \frac{6}{10} \\ \hline \frac{11}{10} = \mathbf{1\frac{1}{10}} \end{array}$$

16. $$\begin{array}{r} \frac{4}{5} = \frac{16}{20} \\ -\ \frac{1}{4} = \frac{5}{20} \\ \hline \mathbf{\frac{11}{20}} \end{array}$$

17. $\frac{3}{4} \textcircled{>} \frac{2}{3}$ because $\frac{9}{12} > \frac{8}{12}$

18. $3\frac{1}{2} = 3\frac{3}{6}$
$+\ 2\frac{2}{3} = 2\frac{4}{6}$
$5\frac{7}{6} = \mathbf{6\frac{1}{6}}$

19. $7\frac{1}{4} = 6\frac{5}{4}$
$-\ 1\frac{3}{4} = 1\frac{3}{4}$
$5\frac{2}{4} = \mathbf{5\frac{1}{2}}$

20. $8.29
$\times$ 0.08
0.6632
The tax was **$0.66.**

Cumulative Test 12B

1. a. Sample space = **{1, 2, 3, 4, 5, 6}**

   b. Out of the six possible outcomes, only 3 are less than 4.
   $\frac{3}{6} = \mathbf{\frac{1}{2}}$

2. Perimeter = 6 × 7 in. = **42 in.**

3. 9 cm × 12 cm = **108 sq. cm**

4. **8**

5. 6.2
0.56
+ 12.0
18.76

6. 2.50
− 0.25
2.25

7. 1.4
× 0.06
0.084

8. $C = \pi d$
$C = (3.14)(50)$
3.14
× 50
157.00 ≈ **157 inches**

9. **C. 4**

10. $\frac{\text{win}}{\text{loss}} = \frac{12}{18} = \mathbf{\frac{2}{3}}$

11. $1 = \frac{8}{8}$
$-\ \frac{5}{8} = \frac{5}{8}$
$\mathbf{\frac{3}{8}}$

12. $5\overline{)1.20}$ = **0.24**
1 0
20
20
0

13. $0.6\overline{)24.0}$ = **40**

14. 12.34 ÷ 10 = **1.234**

15. $\frac{3}{4} = \frac{9}{12}$
$+\ \frac{1}{3} = \frac{4}{12}$
$\frac{13}{12} = \mathbf{1\frac{1}{12}}$

16. $\frac{2}{3} = \frac{10}{15}$
$-\ \frac{1}{5} = \frac{3}{15}$
$\mathbf{\frac{7}{15}}$

17. $\frac{5}{8}$ Ⓢ<Ⓢ $\frac{3}{4}$ because $\frac{5}{8} < \frac{6}{8}$

18. $4\frac{3}{4} = 4\frac{3}{4}$
$+\ 2\frac{1}{2} = 2\frac{2}{4}$
$6\frac{5}{4} = \mathbf{7\frac{1}{4}}$

19. $8\frac{1}{3} = 7\frac{4}{3}$
$-\ 2\frac{2}{3} = 2\frac{2}{3}$
$\mathbf{5\frac{2}{3}}$

20. $9.49
× 0.08
0.7592
The tax was **$0.76.**

Solutions

Cumulative Test 13A

1. Side length = 8 ft ÷ 4 = 2 ft
   Area = 2 ft × 2 ft = **4 sq. ft**

2. $\frac{2}{3} \times \mathbf{\frac{4}{4}} = \frac{8}{12}$

3. **a.** $\frac{2}{6} = \mathbf{\frac{1}{3}}$
   b. $1 - \frac{1}{3} = \frac{3}{3} - \frac{1}{3} = \mathbf{\frac{2}{3}}$

4. $\frac{\text{radius}}{\text{diameter}} = \frac{21}{42} = \mathbf{\frac{1}{2}}$

5. **D.**

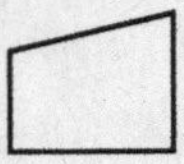

6. $\begin{array}{r} 1 \\ 5\overline{)5} \\ 2\overline{)10} \\ 2\overline{)20} \\ 2\overline{)40} \end{array}$ $\quad 40 = \mathbf{2 \cdot 2 \cdot 2 \cdot 5}$

7. $\frac{3}{5} \textcircled{<} \frac{2}{3}$ because $\frac{9}{15} < \frac{10}{15}$

8. $\begin{array}{r} \$12.95 \\ \times \quad 0.08 \\ \hline \$1.0360 \end{array}$ $\quad \begin{array}{r} \$12.95 \\ + \ \$1.04 \\ \hline \mathbf{\$13.99} \end{array}$

9. $\begin{array}{r} \$6.00 \\ - \ \$0.06 \\ \hline \mathbf{\$5.94} \end{array}$

10. $\begin{array}{r} 3.7 \\ 12.0 \\ + \ 4.31 \\ \hline \mathbf{20.01} \end{array}$

11. $\begin{array}{r} 7.40 \\ - \ 4.74 \\ \hline \mathbf{2.66} \end{array}$

12. $\begin{array}{r} 0.18 \\ \times \ 0.27 \\ \hline 126 \\ 36 \ \\ \hline \mathbf{0.0486} \end{array}$

13. $\begin{array}{r} \mathbf{.028} \\ 5\overline{)0.140} \\ 10 \\ \hline 40 \\ 40 \\ \hline 0 \end{array}$

14. $0.6\overline{)9.0}$ → **15**

15. $\begin{array}{r} 3\frac{5}{6} = 3\frac{5}{6} \\ -\ 1\frac{1}{2} = 1\frac{3}{6} \\ \hline 2\frac{2}{6} = \mathbf{2\frac{1}{3}} \end{array}$

16. $\begin{array}{r} 1\frac{2}{3} = 1\frac{4}{6} \\ +\ 1\frac{5}{6} = 1\frac{5}{6} \\ \hline 2\frac{9}{6} = 3\frac{3}{6} = \mathbf{3\frac{1}{2}} \end{array}$

17. $\begin{array}{r} \frac{1}{2} = \frac{4}{8} \\ \frac{3}{4} = \frac{6}{8} \\ +\ \frac{3}{8} = \frac{3}{8} \\ \hline \frac{13}{8} = \mathbf{1\frac{5}{8}} \end{array}$

18. $m = 6\frac{1}{3} - 3 = \mathbf{3\frac{1}{3}}$

19. **8 vertices**

20. $3\frac{3}{4} = \frac{15}{4} \qquad \frac{15}{4} \cdot \frac{1}{6} = \frac{15}{24} = \mathbf{\frac{5}{8}}$

Cumulative Test 13B

1. Side length = 16 in. ÷ 4 = 4 in.
   Area = 4 in. × 4 in. = **16 sq. in.**

2. $\frac{3}{4} \times \mathbf{\frac{3}{3}} = \frac{9}{12}$

3. **a.** $\frac{4}{6} = \mathbf{\frac{2}{3}}$
   b. $1 - \frac{2}{3} = \frac{3}{3} - \frac{2}{3} = \mathbf{\frac{1}{3}}$

4. $\frac{\text{radius}}{\text{diameter}} = \frac{18}{36} = \mathbf{\frac{1}{2}}$

5. **D.**

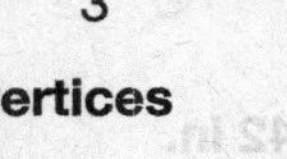

6. 50 → 5, 10; 10 → 2, 5   or   50 → 2, 25; 25 → 5, 5 $\quad 50 = \mathbf{2 \cdot 5 \cdot 5}$

7. $\frac{5}{6} \textcircled{>} \frac{5}{8}$ because $\frac{20}{24} > \frac{15}{24}$

8. $\begin{array}{r} \$14.85 \\ \times\ \ 0.07 \\ \hline \$1.0395 \end{array}$ $\begin{array}{r} \$14.85 \\ +\ \$1.04 \\ \hline \mathbf{\$15.89} \end{array}$

9. $\begin{array}{r} \$10.00 \\ -\ \ \$0.10 \\ \hline \mathbf{\$9.90} \end{array}$

10. $\begin{array}{r} 4.87 \\ 16.0 \\ +\ 12.8 \\ \hline \mathbf{33.67} \end{array}$

11. $\begin{array}{r} 4.70 \\ -\ 1.79 \\ \hline \mathbf{2.91} \end{array}$

12. $0.5 \times 0.6 \times 0.7 = 0.210 = \mathbf{0.21}$

13. $4\overline{)0.1500}$ = **0.0375**

$\begin{array}{r} 12 \\ \hline 30 \\ 28 \\ \hline 20 \\ 20 \\ \hline 0 \end{array}$

14. $0.6\overline{)15.0}$ = **25**

$\begin{array}{r} 12 \\ \hline 30 \\ 30 \\ \hline 0 \end{array}$

15. $\begin{array}{r} 4\frac{2}{3} = 4\frac{4}{6} \\ -\ 1\frac{1}{6} = 1\frac{1}{6} \\ \hline 3\frac{3}{6} = \mathbf{3\frac{1}{2}} \end{array}$

16. $\begin{array}{r} 3\frac{1}{2} = 3\frac{3}{6} \\ +\ 4\frac{5}{6} = 4\frac{5}{6} \\ \hline 7\frac{8}{6} = \mathbf{8\frac{1}{3}} \end{array}$

17. $\begin{array}{r} \frac{1}{2} = \frac{3}{6} \\ \frac{1}{3} = \frac{2}{6} \\ +\ \frac{1}{6} = \frac{1}{6} \\ \hline \frac{6}{6} = \mathbf{1} \end{array}$

18. $n = 5\frac{1}{4} - 2 = \mathbf{3\frac{1}{4}}$

19. **12 edges**

20. $2\frac{2}{3} = \frac{8}{3}$ $\frac{8}{3} \cdot \frac{1}{4} = \frac{8}{12} = \mathbf{\frac{2}{3}}$

Cumulative Test 14A

1. **9**

2. Side length = 44 cm ÷ 4 = 11 cm
Area = 11 cm × 11 cm = **121 sq. cm**

3. $10 - (0.25 + 1) = 10 - 1.25 = \mathbf{8.75}$

4. $\begin{array}{r} 0.12 \\ \times\ 0.12 \\ \hline 24 \\ 120 \\ \hline \mathbf{0.0144} \end{array}$

5. $\frac{11}{20} \cdot \frac{5}{5} = \mathbf{\frac{55}{100}}$

6. $0.45 \div \sqrt{36} = 0.45 \div 6$ $6\overline{)0.450}$ = **0.075**

$\begin{array}{r} 42 \\ \hline 30 \\ 30 \\ \hline 0 \end{array}$

7. **C.** 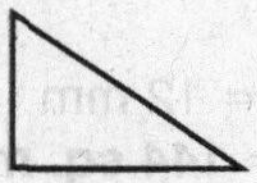

8. $0.2 + 0.2 \ \textcircled{>}\ 0.2 \times 0.2$ because $0.4 > 0.04$

9. $\begin{array}{r} \$24.94 \\ \times\ \ 0.06 \\ \hline \$1.4970 \end{array}$ $\begin{array}{r} \$24.95 \\ +\ \ \$1.50 \\ \hline \mathbf{\$26.45} \end{array}$

10. $4.5 \times 100 = \mathbf{450}$

11. $0.08\overline{)1.20}$ = **15**

$\begin{array}{r} 8 \\ \hline 40 \\ 40 \\ \hline 0 \end{array}$

12. $\begin{array}{r} 4\frac{1}{5} = 3\frac{12}{10} \\ -\ 3\frac{1}{2} = 3\frac{5}{10} \\ \hline \mathbf{\frac{7}{10}} \end{array}$

13. $1\frac{1}{2} = 1\frac{4}{8}$

$2\frac{1}{4} = 2\frac{2}{8}$

$+ 3\frac{3}{8} = 3\frac{3}{8}$

$6\frac{9}{8} = \mathbf{7\frac{1}{8}}$

14. $2 \times 2 \times 2 =$ **8 small cubes**

15. Perimeter = 12 mm × 6 = **72 mm**

16. $\frac{24}{30} = \frac{\mathbf{2 \cdot 2 \cdot 2 \cdot 3}}{\mathbf{2 \cdot 3 \cdot 5}} = \mathbf{\frac{4}{5}}$

17. $2\frac{1}{4} \times 1\frac{2}{3} = \frac{\overset{3}{\cancel{9}}}{4} \times \frac{5}{\underset{1}{\cancel{3}}} = \frac{15}{4} = \mathbf{3\frac{3}{4}}$

18. $1\frac{3}{4} \div 2 = \frac{7}{4} \times \frac{1}{2} = \mathbf{\frac{7}{8}}$

19. A line segment has two endpoints.
C. •————•

20. **a.** $\frac{\text{red}}{\text{total}} = \frac{3}{12} = \mathbf{\frac{1}{4}}$

b. $1 - \frac{1}{4} = \frac{4}{4} - \frac{1}{4} = \mathbf{\frac{3}{4}}$

Cumulative Test 14B

1. **4**

2. Side length = 48 mm ÷ 4 = 12 mm
Area = 12 mm × 12 mm = **144 sq. mm**

3. $2 - (0.6 + 0.7) = 2 - 1.3 = \mathbf{0.7}$

4.
```
  0.12
× 0.13
    36
   12
0.0156
```
(**0.0156**)

5. $\frac{9}{20} \cdot \frac{5}{5} = \mathbf{\frac{45}{100}}$

6. $0.28 \div \sqrt{64} = 0.28 \div 8$
```
   0.035
8)0.280
    24
     40
     40
      0
```
(**0.035**)

7. **C.**

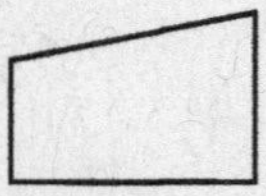

8. $0.2 + 0.2 \;\text{Ⓒ}\; 0.2 \div 0.2$ because $0.4 < 1$ (circled <)

9.
```
  $18.97        $18.97
×   0.08      + $1.52
$1.5176       $20.49
```
(**$20.49**)

10. $4.5 \div 100 = \mathbf{0.045}$

11.
```
     7.5
0.4)3.00
    2 8
      20
      20
       0
```
(**7.5**)

12. $5\frac{1}{8} = 4\frac{9}{8}$

$- 3\frac{1}{2} = 3\frac{4}{8}$

$\mathbf{1\frac{5}{8}}$

13. $6\frac{1}{3} = 6\frac{2}{6}$

$2\frac{1}{2} = 2\frac{3}{6}$

$+ 5\frac{1}{6} = 5\frac{1}{6}$

$13\frac{6}{6} = \mathbf{14}$

14. $3 \times 3 \times 3 =$ **27 small cubes**

15. 48 cm ÷ 8 = **6 cm**

16. $\frac{24}{60} = \frac{\mathbf{2 \cdot 2 \cdot 2 \cdot 3}}{\mathbf{2 \cdot 2 \cdot 2 \cdot 5}} = \mathbf{\frac{2}{5}}$

17. $1\frac{1}{3} \times 1\frac{3}{4} = \frac{\overset{1}{\cancel{4}}}{3} \times \frac{7}{\underset{1}{\cancel{4}}} = \frac{7}{3} = \mathbf{2\frac{1}{3}}$

18. $1\frac{1}{2} \div 2\frac{1}{2} = \frac{3}{2} \times \frac{2}{5} = \mathbf{\frac{3}{5}}$

19. A ray has one endpoint.
B. ←————•

20. **a.** $\frac{\text{white}}{\text{total}} = \frac{4}{12} = \mathbf{\frac{1}{3}}$

b. $1 - \frac{1}{3} = \frac{3}{3} - \frac{1}{3} = \mathbf{\frac{2}{3}}$

Cumulative Test 15A

1. 6 cm · 4 cm = **24 sq. cm**

2.
```
  $6.80       $6.80     $10.00
×  0.08     + $0.48   −  $7.28
$0.4760      $7.28      $2.72
```
(**$2.72**)

3. $\frac{3}{4} \textcircled{>} \frac{11}{16}$ because $\frac{12}{16} > \frac{11}{16}$

4. **Point *D***

5. **(3, −2)**

6. **B. pentagon**

7. $\frac{45}{54} = \frac{\mathbf{3 \cdot 3 \cdot 5}}{\mathbf{2 \cdot 3 \cdot 3 \cdot 3}} = \mathbf{\frac{5}{6}}$

8. $\frac{1}{4}$ $\quad 4\overline{)1.00}$ with quotient $\mathbf{0.25}$

9. $12\% = \frac{12}{100} = \mathbf{0.12} = \mathbf{\frac{3}{25}}$

10. Multiples of 6: 6, 12, 18, 24, 30, ...
Multiples of 8: 8, 16, 24, 32, 40, ...
Multiples of 12: 12, 24, 36, 48, 60, ...
The LCM of 6, 8, and 12 is **24.**

11. $6 - (3.7 + 0.48) = 6 - 4.18 = \mathbf{1.82}$

12.
$$\begin{array}{r} 1.2 \\ \times\ 0.3 \\ \hline \mathbf{0.36} \end{array}$$

13.
$$\begin{array}{r} \mathbf{12.5} \\ 0.4\overline{)5.00} \\ 4 \\ \hline 1\,0 \\ 8 \\ \hline 20 \\ 20 \\ \hline 0 \end{array}$$

14. $14.5 \div 100 = \mathbf{0.145}$

15.
$$\begin{array}{r} \frac{1}{2} = \frac{6}{12} \\ \frac{2}{3} = \frac{8}{12} \\ +\ \frac{3}{4} = \frac{9}{12} \\ \hline \frac{23}{12} = \mathbf{1\frac{11}{12}} \end{array}$$

16.
$$\begin{array}{r} 3\frac{3}{5} = 3\frac{6}{10} \\ +\ 6\frac{1}{2} = 6\frac{5}{10} \\ \hline 9\frac{11}{10} = \mathbf{10\frac{1}{10}} \end{array}$$

17.
$$\begin{array}{r} 6\frac{1}{4} = 5\frac{10}{8} \\ -\ 3\frac{7}{8} = 3\frac{7}{8} \\ \hline \mathbf{2\frac{3}{8}} \end{array}$$

18. $3\frac{1}{3} \times 1\frac{1}{5} = \frac{10}{3} \times \frac{6}{5} = \frac{60}{15} = \mathbf{4}$

19. $5 \div 1\frac{2}{3} = \frac{5}{1} \times \frac{3}{5} = \mathbf{3}$

20. $12.6 - w = 8.3$
$$\begin{array}{r} 12.6 \\ -\ 8.3 \\ \hline \mathbf{4.3} \end{array}$$

Cumulative Test 15B

1. 9 cm · 8 cm = **72 sq. cm**

2.
$$\begin{array}{r} \$5.90 \\ \times\ 0.08 \\ \hline \$0.4720 \end{array} \qquad \begin{array}{r} \$5.90 \\ +\ \$0.47 \\ \hline \$6.37 \end{array} \qquad \begin{array}{r} \$10.00 \\ -\ \$6.37 \\ \hline \mathbf{\$3.63} \end{array}$$

3. $\frac{3}{5} \textcircled{<} \frac{13}{20}$ because $\frac{12}{20} < \frac{13}{20}$

4. **Point *H***

5. **(2, −3)**

6. An octagon has **8 sides.**

7. $\frac{54}{81} = \frac{\mathbf{2 \cdot 3 \cdot 3 \cdot 3}}{\mathbf{3 \cdot 3 \cdot 3 \cdot 3}} = \mathbf{\frac{2}{3}}$

8. $\frac{4}{5}$ $\quad 5\overline{)4.0}$ with quotient $\mathbf{0.8}$

9. $15\% = \frac{15}{100} = \mathbf{0.15} = \frac{3}{20}$

10. Multiples of 4: 4, 8, 12, 16, 20, 24, ...
Multiples of 8: 8, 16, 24, 32, 40, 48, ...
Multiples of 12: 12, 24, 36, 48, 60, 72, ...
The LCM of 4, 8, and 12 is **24.**

11. $8 - (4.3 + 0.75) = 8 - 5.05 = \mathbf{2.95}$

12.
$$\begin{array}{r} 0.45 \\ \times\ 0.2 \\ \hline 0.090 = \mathbf{0.09} \end{array}$$

13. $0.5\overline{)4.0}$ with quotient $\mathbf{8}$

14. $12.5 \div 100 = \mathbf{0.125}$

15.

$$\frac{1}{2} = \frac{4}{8}$$
$$\frac{3}{4} = \frac{6}{8}$$
$$+\frac{3}{8} = \frac{3}{8}$$
$$\frac{13}{8} = 1\frac{5}{8}$$

16.

$$7\frac{1}{2} = 7\frac{3}{6}$$
$$+3\frac{5}{6} = 3\frac{5}{6}$$
$$10\frac{8}{6} = 11\frac{1}{3}$$

17.

$$5\frac{2}{3} = 4\frac{20}{12}$$
$$-1\frac{3}{4} = 1\frac{9}{12}$$
$$3\frac{11}{12}$$

18. $4\frac{1}{2} \times 2\frac{2}{3} = \frac{9}{2} \times \frac{8}{3} = \frac{72}{6} = $ **12**

19. $4 \div 1\frac{1}{3} = \frac{4}{1} \times \frac{3}{4} = \frac{12}{4} = $ **3**

20. $14.5 - m = 3.7$
$$\begin{array}{r} 14.5 \\ -\ 3.7 \\ \hline \mathbf{10.8} \end{array}$$

Cumulative Test 16A

1. $\frac{1}{4}$

2. $\frac{42}{50} = \frac{84}{100} = $ **84%**

3. $\frac{6\ cm \cdot 8\ cm}{2} = $ **24 sq. cm**

4. Perimeter $= 3 + 2 + 3 + 2 = $ **10 units**

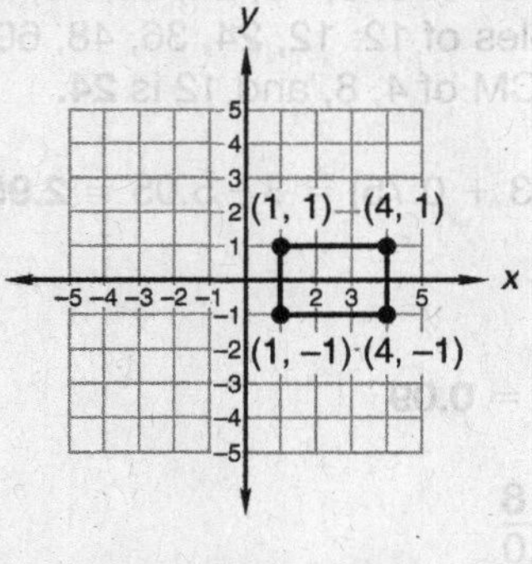

5. Area $= 3 \times 2 = $ **6 sq. units**

6. $\frac{4}{5}$ ⊘ 0.6   because $0.8 > 0.6$

7. $\frac{1}{3} \times \frac{12}{1} = 4$
$$\begin{array}{r} 12 \\ -\ 4 \\ \hline \mathbf{8\ months} \end{array}$$

8. False

9. $60\% = \frac{60}{100} = \frac{3}{5}$ $\frac{3}{5} \times \frac{30}{1} = $ **18 girls**

10.
$$\begin{array}{r} 1\ 0 \\ 0.5\overline{)5.0} \end{array}$$

11.
$$\begin{array}{r} 4.32 \\ 5.0 \\ +\ 6.7 \\ \hline \mathbf{16.02} \end{array}$$

12. $2.8 \div \sqrt{64} = 2.8 \div 8$
$$\begin{array}{r} 0.35 \\ 8\overline{)2.80} \\ \underline{2\ 4} \\ 40 \\ \underline{40} \\ 0 \end{array}$$

13. $3.6 \div 10^2 = 3.6 \div 100 = $ **0.036**

14.
$$\frac{2}{3} = \frac{4}{6}$$
$$-\frac{1}{6} = \frac{1}{6}$$
$$\frac{3}{6} = \frac{1}{2}$$

15.
$$4\frac{1}{2} = 4\frac{2}{4}$$
$$+2\frac{3}{4} = 2\frac{3}{4}$$
$$6\frac{5}{4} = 7\frac{1}{4}$$

16.
$$4\frac{1}{4} = 3\frac{5}{4}$$
$$-3\frac{3}{4} = 3\frac{3}{4}$$
$$\frac{2}{4} = \frac{1}{2}$$

17. $2\frac{1}{2} \times 1\frac{1}{5} = \frac{5}{2} \times \frac{6}{5} = 3$

18. $\frac{9}{25} \times \frac{4}{4} = \frac{36}{100}$

19. $2 \div 1\frac{2}{3} = \frac{2}{1} \times \frac{3}{5} = \frac{6}{5} = 1\frac{1}{5}$

20. $0.5678 \approx $ **0.57**

Cumulative Test 16B

1. **2 quarts**

2. $\frac{43}{50} = \frac{86}{100} = \mathbf{86\%}$

3. $\frac{3\text{ cm} \cdot 4\text{ cm}}{2} = \mathbf{6\text{ sq. cm}}$

4. Perimeter = 3 + 2 + 3 + 2 = **12 units**

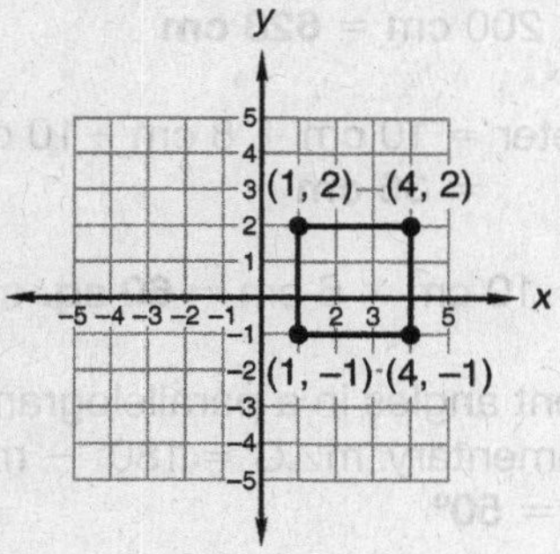

5. Area = 3 × 3 = **9 sq. units**

6. $\frac{1}{4}$ Ⓛ 0.3 because $0.25 < 0.3$

7. $\frac{1}{6} \times \frac{12}{1} = 2$
   12 − 2 = **10 muffins**

8. **True**

9. $40\% = \frac{40}{100} = \mathbf{\frac{2}{5}}$
   $\frac{2}{5} \times 60$ minutes = **24 minutes**

10. $0.4\overline{)4.0}$ = **10**

11.
$$\begin{array}{r} 12.0 \\ 4.87 \\ +\ 6.3 \\ \hline \mathbf{23.17} \end{array}$$

12. $3.4 \div \sqrt{25} = 3.4 \div 5$
$$\begin{array}{r} \mathbf{0.68} \\ 5\overline{)3.40} \\ \underline{3\,0} \\ 40 \\ \underline{40} \\ 0 \end{array}$$

13. $5.2 \div 10^2 = 5.2 \div 100 = \mathbf{0.052}$

14.
$$\begin{array}{r} \frac{5}{6} = \frac{5}{6} \\ -\ \frac{1}{3} = \frac{2}{6} \\ \hline \frac{3}{6} = \mathbf{\frac{1}{2}} \end{array}$$

15.
$$\begin{array}{r} 6\frac{5}{8} = 6\frac{5}{8} \\ +\ 1\frac{1}{2} = 1\frac{3}{4} \\ \hline 7\frac{9}{8} = \mathbf{8\frac{1}{8}} \end{array}$$

16.
$$\begin{array}{r} 6\frac{1}{2} = 5\frac{12}{8} \\ -\ 2\frac{7}{8} = 2\frac{7}{8} \\ \hline \mathbf{3\frac{5}{8}} \end{array}$$

17. $1\frac{1}{4} \times 2\frac{2}{5} = \frac{5}{4} \times \frac{12}{5} = \mathbf{3}$

18. $\frac{7}{12} \times \frac{4}{4} = \mathbf{\frac{28}{100}}$

19. $2 \div 2\frac{1}{3} = \frac{2}{1} \times \frac{3}{7} = \mathbf{\frac{6}{7}}$

20. $5.4638 \approx \mathbf{5.5}$

Cumulative Test 17A

1. $80\% = \frac{80}{100} = \mathbf{\frac{4}{5} = 0.80 = 0.8}$

2. $\frac{16\text{ cm} \cdot 6\text{ cm}}{2} = \frac{96\text{ cm}^2}{2} = \mathbf{48\text{ cm}^2}$

3. $\frac{3}{5} = \frac{60}{100} = \mathbf{60\%}$

4. $C = \pi d$
   3.14 × 100 cm = **314 cm**

5. Perimeter = 10 mm + 12 mm + 10 mm + 12 mm = **44 mm**

6. Area 10 mm × 9 mm = **90 sq. mm**

7. Opposite angles in a parallelogram are equal.
   $m\angle A = m\angle C =$ **50°**

8. $\frac{\text{chickens}}{\text{goats}} = \frac{12}{8} = \mathbf{\frac{3}{2}}$

9.

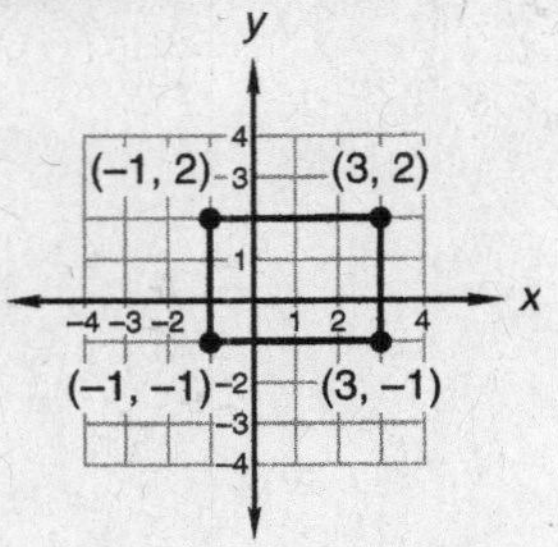

The fourth vertex is at **(−1, 2)**.

10. $\frac{3}{4} \times \frac{2000}{1} =$ **1500 tickets**

11. 3 ft = 36 in. 36 in. − 10 in. = **26 in.**

12. $3 \times 4 + 2 \times 5 = 12 + 10 =$ **22**

13. (12 in.)(6 in.)(5 in.) = **360 in.^{3}**

14. $\frac{6}{9} = \frac{10}{w}$
$6w = 9 \cdot 10$
$w = \frac{90}{6} =$ **15**

15. $10 - (0.1 + 1) = 10 - 1.1 =$ **8.9**

16. $3n = 0.45$
$n = \frac{0.45}{3}$

$$\begin{array}{r} 0.15 \\ 3\overline{)0.45} \\ \underline{3} \\ 15 \\ \underline{15} \\ 0 \end{array}$$

17.
$$\begin{array}{r} 3\frac{3}{4} = 3\frac{6}{8} \\ +\ 1\frac{5}{8} = 1\frac{5}{8} \\ \hline 4\frac{11}{8} = \mathbf{5\frac{3}{8}} \end{array}$$

18.
$$\begin{array}{r} 2\frac{1}{2} = 1\frac{6}{4} \\ -\ \frac{3}{4} = \frac{3}{4} \\ \hline \mathbf{1\frac{3}{4}} \end{array}$$

19. $2\frac{1}{4} \times 2 = \frac{9}{4} \times \frac{2}{1} = \frac{9}{2} = \mathbf{4\frac{1}{2}}$

20. $5 \div 3\frac{3}{4} = \frac{5}{1} \times \frac{4}{15} = \frac{4}{3} = \mathbf{1\frac{1}{3}}$

Cumulative Test 17B

1. $60\% = \frac{60}{100} = \frac{3}{5} =$ **0.60 = 0.6**

2. $\frac{12\text{cm} \cdot 8\text{cm}}{2} = \frac{96\text{cm}^2}{2} =$ **48 cm^2**

3. $\frac{4}{5} = \frac{80}{100} =$ **80%**

4. $C = \pi d$
3.14 × 200 cm = **628 cm**

5. Perimeter = 10 cm + 8 cm + 10 cm + 8 cm
= **36 cm**

6. Area = 10 cm × 6 cm = **60 sq. cm**

7. Adjacent angles in a parallelogram are supplementary. m∠C = 180° − m∠B = 180° − 130° = **50°**

8. $\frac{\text{children}}{\text{adults}} = \frac{80}{60} = \mathbf{\frac{4}{3}}$

9.

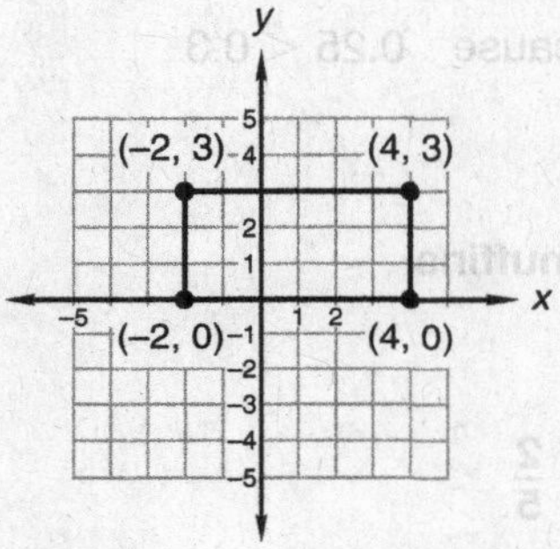

The fourth vertex is at **(−2, 3)**.

10. $\frac{4}{5} \times \frac{20}{1} =$ **16 questions**

11. 3 ft = 36 in. 36 in. − 6 in. = **30 in.**

12. $3 \times 4 - 2 \times 5 = 12 - 10 =$ **2**

13. (10 in.)(4 in.)(5 in.) = **200 in.^{3}**

14. $\frac{9}{m} = \frac{6}{10}$
$6m = 9 \cdot 10$
$m = \frac{90}{6} =$ **15**

15. $2 - (0.2 + 0.02) = 2 - 0.22 =$ **1.78**

16. $4n = 0.56$

$n = \frac{0.56}{4}$

$$\begin{array}{r} 0.14 \\ 4\overline{)0.56} \\ \underline{4} \\ 16 \\ \underline{16} \\ 0 \end{array}$$

17.
$$\begin{array}{r} 1\frac{3}{4} = 1\frac{3}{4} \\ + 1\frac{1}{2} = 1\frac{2}{4} \\ \hline 2\frac{5}{4} = \mathbf{3\frac{1}{4}} \end{array}$$

18.
$$\begin{array}{r} 4\frac{1}{2} = 3\frac{6}{4} \\ - 1\frac{3}{4} = 1\frac{3}{4} \\ \hline \mathbf{2\frac{3}{4}} \end{array}$$

19. $5 \times 1\frac{3}{5} = \frac{5}{1} \times \frac{8}{5} = \mathbf{8}$

20. $5 \div 6\frac{2}{3} = \frac{5}{1} \times \frac{3}{20} = \mathbf{\frac{3}{4}}$

Cumulative Test 18A

1. $\frac{3}{4} \times \frac{200}{1} = 150$ seeds sprouted

$200 - 150 =$ **50 seeds** did not sprout

2. $\frac{\text{boys}}{\text{girls}} = \frac{3}{2} = \frac{12}{g}$

$3g = 24$

$g =$ **8 girls**

3. Perimeter = 6 cm + 8 cm + 10 cm = **24 cm**

4. Area $= \frac{6\text{cm} \times 8\text{cm}}{2} =$ **24 sq. cm**

5.
$$\begin{array}{r} 5.00 \\ - 3.21 \\ \hline \mathbf{1.79} \end{array}$$

6.
$$\begin{array}{r} 2.7 \\ \times 0.03 \\ \hline \mathbf{0.081} \end{array}$$

7. $0.27 \div \sqrt{36} = 0.27 \div 6$

$$\begin{array}{r} \mathbf{0.045} \\ 6\overline{)0.270} \\ \underline{24} \\ 30 \\ \underline{30} \\ 0 \end{array}$$

8. $0.9\overline{)27.0}$ = **30**

9. $4^2 = 16$ and $5^2 = 25$

C. 4 and 5

10.
$$\begin{array}{r} \frac{5}{6} = \frac{5}{6} \\ + \frac{1}{2} = \frac{3}{6} \\ \hline \frac{8}{6} = \mathbf{1\frac{1}{3}} \end{array}$$

11.
$$\begin{array}{r} 3\frac{1}{3} = 2\frac{8}{6} \\ - 2\frac{1}{2} = 2\frac{3}{6} \\ \hline \mathbf{\frac{5}{6}} \end{array}$$

12. $3\frac{3}{4} \times 1\frac{3}{5} = \frac{15}{4} \times \frac{8}{5} = \mathbf{6}$

13. $5 \div 1\frac{1}{4} = \frac{5}{1} \times \frac{4}{5} = \mathbf{4}$

14. $5y = 9$

$y = \frac{9}{5} = \mathbf{1\frac{4}{5}}$

15. $C = \pi d$

3.14 × 20 cm = **62.8 cm**

16. $A = \pi r^2$

3.14 × 10 cm × 10 cm = **314 cm²**

17. $75\% = \frac{75}{100} = \mathbf{\frac{3}{4}} = \mathbf{0.75}$

18. (10 cm)(6 cm)(5 cm) = **300 cm³**

19. **6 faces**

20. **(−2, −2), (8, −2), or (2, 6)**

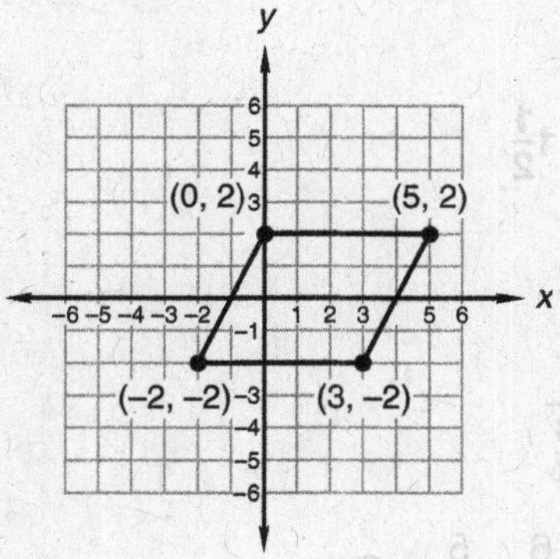

Cumulative Test 18B

1. $\dfrac{4}{5} \times \dfrac{200}{1} = 160$ seeds sprouted

   $200 - 160 =$ **40 seeds** did not sprout

2. $\dfrac{\text{boys}}{\text{girls}} = \dfrac{3}{2} = \dfrac{b}{12}$

   $2b = 36$

   $b =$ **18 boys**

3. Perimeter $= 5 \text{ cm} + 3 \text{ cm} + 4 \text{ cm} =$ **12 cm**

4. Area $= \dfrac{3 \text{ cm} \times 4 \text{ cm}}{2} =$ **6 sq. cm**

5. $\begin{array}{r} 6.0 \\ -\ 4.3 \\ \hline \mathbf{1.7} \end{array}$

6. $\begin{array}{r} 4.3 \\ \times\ 0.02 \\ \hline \mathbf{0.086} \end{array}$

7. $0.45 \div \sqrt{36} = 0.45 \div 6$

   $\begin{array}{r} 0.075 \\ 6\overline{)0.450} \\ \underline{42} \\ 30 \\ \underline{30} \\ 0 \end{array}$

8. $\begin{array}{r} 5\,0 \\ 0.9\overline{)45.0} \end{array}$

9. $5^2 = 25$ and $6^2 = 36$

   C. 5 and 6

10. $\begin{array}{r} \dfrac{2}{3} = \dfrac{4}{6} \\ +\ \dfrac{5}{6} = \dfrac{5}{6} \\ \hline \dfrac{9}{6} = 1\dfrac{1}{2} \end{array}$

11. $\begin{array}{r} 3\dfrac{1}{4} = 2\dfrac{5}{4} \\ -\ 2\dfrac{1}{2} = 2\dfrac{2}{4} \\ \hline \dfrac{3}{4} \end{array}$

12. $1\dfrac{1}{5} \times 1\dfrac{2}{3} = \dfrac{6}{5} \times \dfrac{5}{3} =$ **2**

13. $5 \div 1\dfrac{2}{3} = \dfrac{5}{1} \times \dfrac{3}{5} =$ **3**

14. $5y = 8$

    $y = \dfrac{8}{5} = \mathbf{1\dfrac{3}{5}}$

15. $C = \pi d$

    $3.14 \times 20 \text{ in.} =$ **62.8 in.**

16. $A = \pi r^2$

    $3.14 \times 10 \text{ in.} \times 10 \text{ in.} =$ **314 in.²**

17. $65\% = \dfrac{65}{100} = \dfrac{13}{20} =$ **0.65**

18. $(10 \text{ cm})(10 \text{ cm})(10 \text{ cm}) =$ **1000 cm³**

19. **12 edges**

20. **(1, 0), (–5, 0), or (5, 6)**

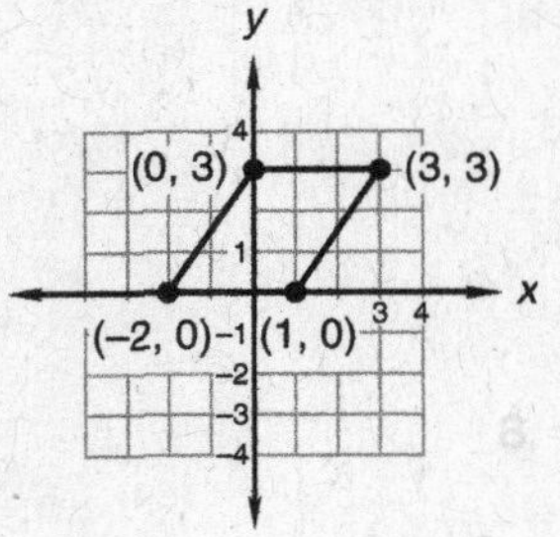

Cumulative Test 19A

1. $\dfrac{\text{favorable}}{\text{possible}} = \dfrac{3}{6} = \dfrac{1}{2}$

   $\dfrac{1}{2} \times \dfrac{5}{5} = \dfrac{5}{10} =$ **0.5**

2. 85, 85, 85, **90**, 90, 100, 100

3. $\dfrac{2}{8} = \dfrac{1}{4} = \dfrac{25}{100} =$ **25%**

4. **8 edges**

5. Area $= \dfrac{9 \text{ cm} \times 12 \text{ cm}}{2} =$ **54 sq. cm**

6. **C. right triangle**

7. $10 + 5 \times 4 - 2^2 = 10 + 20 - 4 =$ **26**

8. $\left(1\dfrac{1}{2}\right)^2 = \dfrac{3}{2} \cdot \dfrac{3}{2} = \dfrac{9}{4} = \mathbf{2\dfrac{1}{4}}$

9. $\dfrac{4}{6} = \dfrac{10}{w}$

   $4w = 60$

   $w = \dfrac{60}{4} =$ **15**

10. $4^2 - \sqrt{16} = 16 - 4 =$ **12**

11. $\dfrac{(15)(16)}{20} = \dfrac{240}{20} =$ **12**

12. $\dfrac{5}{8} \times \dfrac{56}{1} =$ **35**

13. $6 - (0.37 + 1.2) = 6 - 1.57 = \mathbf{4.43}$

14. $0.5\overline{)4.0}$ = **8**

15.
$$\begin{aligned} 6\tfrac{2}{3} &= 6\tfrac{4}{6} \\ 3 &= 3 \\ + 4\tfrac{1}{2} &= 4\tfrac{3}{6} \\ \hline 13\tfrac{7}{6} &= \mathbf{14\tfrac{1}{6}} \end{aligned}$$

16.
$$\begin{aligned} 3\tfrac{1}{3} &= 2\tfrac{16}{12} \\ - 2\tfrac{3}{4} &= 2\tfrac{9}{12} \\ \hline &\ \ \mathbf{\tfrac{7}{12}} \end{aligned}$$

17. $1\frac{4}{5} \div 3 = \frac{9}{5} \times \frac{1}{3} = \mathbf{\frac{3}{5}}$

18. $\frac{1}{3} \times 100\% = \frac{100\%}{3} = \mathbf{33\frac{1}{3}\%}$

19. $3\frac{3}{4} = \mathbf{3.75}$

$3.75 + 1.5 = \mathbf{5.25}$

20. Perimeter = 4 + 6 + 4 + 6 = **20 units**

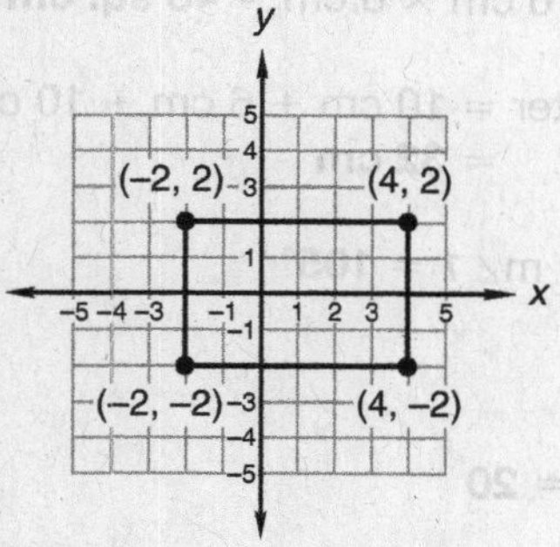

Cumulative Test 19B

1. $\frac{\text{favorable}}{\text{possible}} = \frac{3}{6} = \mathbf{\frac{1}{2}}$

$\frac{1}{2} \times \frac{5}{5} = \frac{5}{10} = \mathbf{0.5}$

2. 17, 18, 18, **19,** 19, 20, 20

3. $\frac{2}{5} = \frac{40}{100} = \mathbf{40\%}$

4. **5 faces**

5. Area = $\frac{5 \text{ cm} \times 12 \text{ cm}}{2}$ = **30 sq. cm**

6. **D. right triangle**

7. $8 + 4 \times 2 - 3^2 = 8 + 8 - 9 = \mathbf{7}$

8. $\left(2\frac{1}{2}\right)^2 = \frac{5}{2} \cdot \frac{5}{2} = \frac{25}{4} = \mathbf{6\frac{1}{4}}$

9. $\frac{6}{9} = \frac{8}{n}$

$6n = 72$

$n = \frac{72}{6} = \mathbf{12}$

10. $3^3 - \sqrt{9} = 27 - 3 = \mathbf{24}$

11. $\frac{(25)(18)}{15} = \frac{450}{15} = \mathbf{30}$

12. $\frac{3}{5} \times \frac{60}{1} = \mathbf{36}$

13. $6 + (1.2 - 0.37) = 6 + 0.83 = \mathbf{6.83}$

14. $0.5\overline{)3.0}$ = **6**

15.
$$\begin{aligned} 3\tfrac{3}{8} &= 3\tfrac{3}{8} \\ 4 &= 4 \\ + 2\tfrac{3}{4} &= 2\tfrac{6}{8} \\ \hline 9\tfrac{9}{8} &= \mathbf{10\tfrac{1}{8}} \end{aligned}$$

16.
$$\begin{aligned} 3\tfrac{2}{3} &= 2\tfrac{20}{12} \\ - 2\tfrac{3}{4} &= 2\tfrac{9}{12} \\ \hline &\ \ \mathbf{\tfrac{11}{12}} \end{aligned}$$

17. $5\frac{1}{3} \div 4 = \frac{16}{3} \times \frac{1}{4} = \frac{4}{3} = \mathbf{1\frac{1}{3}}$

18. $\frac{2}{3} \times 100\% = \frac{200\%}{3} = \mathbf{66\frac{2}{3}\%}$

19. $3\frac{3}{4} = \mathbf{3.75}$

$3.75 + 2.5 = \mathbf{6.25}$

20. Perimeter = 5 + 4 + 5 + 4 = **18 units**

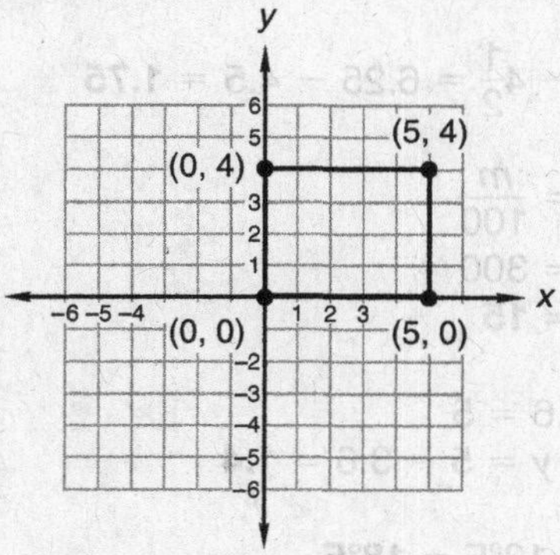

Solutions

Cumulative Test 20A

1. $\dfrac{\text{sparrows}}{\text{finches}} = \dfrac{3}{4} = \dfrac{12}{f}$
$\dfrac{3}{4} = \dfrac{12}{f}$
$3f = 48$
$f =$ **16 finches**

2. $\dfrac{1}{6} \times \dfrac{1}{6} = \mathbf{\dfrac{1}{36}}$

3. **a.** $0.6 = \dfrac{6}{10} = \mathbf{\dfrac{3}{5}}$
b. $0.6 = \dfrac{6}{10} = \dfrac{60}{100} =$ **60%**

4. **a.** $5\% = \dfrac{5}{100} = \mathbf{\dfrac{1}{20}}$
b. $5\% = \dfrac{5}{100} =$ **0.05**

5. $\dfrac{3}{5} \times 30 = 18$ students finished
$30 - 18 =$ **12 students** did not finish

6. Area = 12 mm × 15 mm = **180 sq. mm**

7. Perimeter = 13 mm + 15 mm + 13 mm + 15 mm = **56 mm**

8. $m\angle 6 = m\angle 2 =$ **80°**

9. **360°**

10. $\sqrt{900} =$ **30**

11. $-3 + -5 =$ **−8**

12. $-5 - (-7) = -5 + 7 =$ **2**

13. 5 cm × 4 cm × 3 cm = **60 cm³**

14. $12 - 8 =$ **4**

15. $2^3 - \sqrt{9} + 3 \times 2 = 8 - 3 + 6 =$ **11**

16. $6.25 - 4\frac{1}{2} = 6.25 - 4.5 =$ **1.75**

17. $\dfrac{3}{20} = \dfrac{m}{100}$
$20m = 300$
$m =$ **15**

18. $y + 3.6 = 5$
$y = 5 - 3.6 =$ **1.4**

19. 6°F + 12°F = **18°F**

20. $A = \pi r^2$
3.14 × 6 in. × 6 in. = **113.04 in.²**

Cumulative Test 20B

1. $\dfrac{\text{ducks}}{\text{geese}} = \dfrac{4}{3} = \dfrac{12}{g}$
$\dfrac{4}{3} = \dfrac{12}{g}$
$4g = 36$
$g =$ **9 geese**

2. $\dfrac{1}{6} \times \dfrac{1}{6} = \mathbf{\dfrac{1}{36}}$

3. **a.** $0.4 = \dfrac{4}{10} = \mathbf{\dfrac{2}{5}}$
b. $0.4 = \dfrac{4}{10} = \dfrac{40}{100} =$ **40%**

4. **a.** $4\% = \dfrac{4}{100} = \mathbf{\dfrac{1}{25}}$
b. $4\% = \dfrac{4}{100} =$ **0.04**

5. $\dfrac{2}{3} \times 30 = 20$ student finished
$30 - 20 =$ **10 students** did not finish

6. Area = 6 cm × 8 cm = **48 sq. cm**

7. Perimeter = 10 cm + 6 cm + 10 cm + 6 cm = **32 cm**

8. $m\angle 5 = m\angle 1 =$ **105°**

9. **360°**

10. $\sqrt{400} =$ **20**

11. $-2 + -5 =$ **−7**

12. $-3 - (-7) = -3 + 7 =$ **4**

13. 3 cm × 3 cm × 3 cm = **27 cm³**

14. $8 - 6 =$ **2**

15. $2^3 + \sqrt{9} - 3 \times 2 = 8 + 3 - 6 =$ **5**

16. $6\frac{1}{2} = 6.5$
$+ 4.25 = 4.25$
10.75

17. $\dfrac{3}{25} = \dfrac{m}{100}$
$25m = 300$
$m = 12$

18. $y + 2.7 = 5$
$y = 5 - 2.7 = \mathbf{2.3}$

19. $5°F + 8°F = \mathbf{13°F}$

20. $A = \pi r^2$
$3.14 \times 8 \text{ in.} \times 8 \text{ in.} = \mathbf{200.96 \text{ in.}^2}$

Cumulative Test 21A

1. $\$0.1625$ rounds to **$0.16**

$8\overline{)\$1.3000}$
8
50
48
20
16
40
40
0

2.

	Ratio	Actual Count
Adults	40%	20
Not adults	60%	n
Total	100%	p

$\frac{40}{100} = \frac{20}{p}$
$40p = 2000$
$p = $ **50 people**

3. (1, –2)

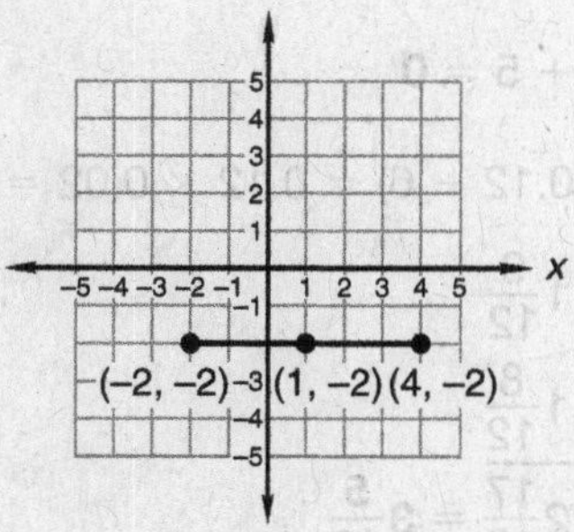

4. $10^2 - \sqrt{81} - 3 \times 10 = 100 - 9 - 30 = \mathbf{61}$

5. $4 \text{ in.} \times 2 \text{ in.} \times 3 \text{ in.} = 24 \text{ cu. in.}$
24 sugar cubes would be needed.

6. $7 \text{ cm} - 3 \text{ cm} = 4 \text{ cm}$
$5 \text{ cm} - 3 \text{ cm} = 2 \text{ cm}$
Perimeter $= 3 \text{ cm} + 5 \text{ cm} + 7 \text{ cm} + 3 \text{ cm} + 4 \text{ cm} + 2 \text{ cm} = \mathbf{24 \text{ cm}}$

7. $d = 2r = 2(10 \text{ cm}) = 20 \text{ cm}$
$C = \pi d$
$3.14 \times 20 \text{ cm} = \mathbf{62.8 \text{ cm}}$

8. $2 \text{ tons} \times \frac{2000 \text{ pound}}{1 \text{ ton}} = \mathbf{4000 \text{ pounds}}$

9. $\frac{6}{10} = \frac{a}{25}$
$10a = 6 \cdot 25$
$a = \frac{150}{10}$
$a = \mathbf{15}$

10.

	Ratio	Actual Count
Boys	5	b
Girls	4	g
Total	9	27

$\frac{5}{9} = \frac{b}{27}$
$9b = 135$
$b = \frac{135}{9} = $ **15 boys**

11. **a.** $1\frac{3}{5} = \frac{8}{5}$ $5\overline{)8.0}$ = **1.6**

b. $1\frac{3}{5} = 1.6 \times 100\% = \mathbf{160\%}$

12. **a.** $0.9 = \mathbf{\frac{9}{10}}$

b. $0.9 \times 100\% = \mathbf{90\%}$

13. **a.** $10\% = \frac{10}{100} = \mathbf{\frac{1}{10}}$

b. $10\% = 0.10 = \mathbf{0.1}$

14. $6.3 - (1.25 + 2) = 6.3 - 3.25 = \mathbf{3.05}$

15. $-3 - 2 + 4 = \mathbf{-1}$

16. $4 \div (0.2 \times 2) = 4 \div 0.4 = \mathbf{10}$

17. $6\frac{2}{3} = 6\frac{8}{12}$
$+ 3\frac{3}{4} = 3\frac{9}{12}$
$9\frac{17}{12} = \mathbf{10\frac{5}{12}}$

18. $6\frac{1}{4} \times 1\frac{3}{5} = \frac{25}{4} \times \frac{8}{5} = \mathbf{10}$

19. $2\frac{1}{3} \div 1\frac{5}{9} = \frac{7}{3} \times \frac{9}{14} = \frac{3}{2} = \mathbf{1\frac{1}{2}}$

20. $\text{Area} = \frac{6 \text{ cm} \cdot 8 \text{ cm}}{2} = \mathbf{24 \text{ sq. cm}}$

Cumulative Test 21B

1. $8\overline{)\$6.5000}$ = \$0.8125 rounds to **\$0.81**

$$\begin{array}{r} 6\,4 \\ \hline 10 \\ 8 \\ \hline 20 \\ 16 \\ \hline 40 \\ 40 \\ \hline 0 \end{array}$$

2.

	Ratio	Actual Count
Rode the bus	30%	9
Did not ride the bus	70%	n
Total	100%	s

$\frac{30}{100} = \frac{9}{s}$

$30s = 900$

$s =$ **30 students**

3. **(2, 3)**

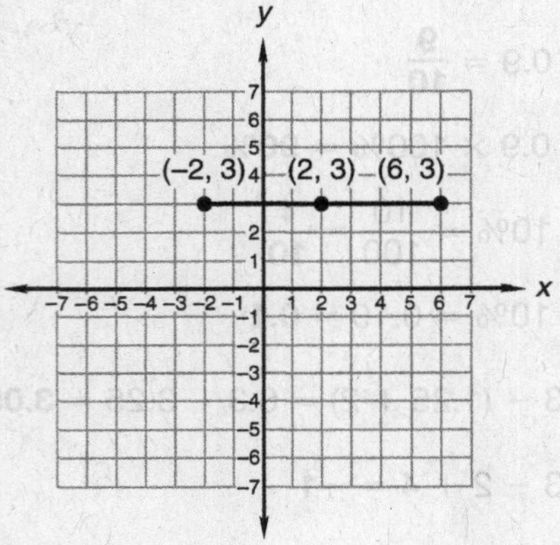

4. $10^2 + \sqrt{9} + 3 \times 10 = 100 + 3 + 30 = \mathbf{133}$

5. 3 cm × 3 cm × 3 cm = 27 cu. cm
27 sugar cubes would be needed.

6. 10 cm − 5 cm = 5 cm
7 cm − 4 cm = 3 cm
Perimeter = 4 cm + 10 cm + 7 cm + 5 cm + 3 cm + 5 cm = **34 cm**

7. $A = \pi r^2$
3.14 × 10 cm × 10 cm = **314 cm²**

8. $\frac{1}{2}$ ton × $\frac{2000 \text{ pounds}}{1 \text{ ton}}$ = **1000 pounds**

9. $\frac{8}{12} = \frac{12}{w}$

$8w = 12 \cdot 12$

$8w = 144$

$w = \frac{144}{8}$

$w = \mathbf{18}$

10.

	Ratio	Actual Count
Boys	4	b
Girls	5	g
Total	9	27

$\frac{4}{9} = \frac{b}{27}$

$9b = 108$

$b = \frac{108}{9} =$ **12 boys**

11. a. $2\frac{1}{5} = \frac{11}{5}$ $5\overline{)11.0}$ = **2.2**

b. $2\frac{1}{5} = 2.2 \times 100\% =$ **220%**

12. a. $0.7 = \mathbf{\frac{7}{10}}$

b. 0.7 × 100% = **70%**

13. a. $5\% = \frac{5}{100} = \mathbf{\frac{1}{20}}$

b. 5% = **0.05**

14. 4.2 + (3 − 1.75) = 4.2 + 1.25 = **5.45**

15. −2 − 3 + 5 = **0**

16. 0.12 × (0.12 ÷ 6) = 0.12 × 0.02 = **0.0024**

17.
$$\begin{array}{rl} 1\frac{3}{4} = & 1\frac{9}{12} \\ +\,1\frac{2}{3} = & 1\frac{8}{12} \\ \hline & 2\frac{17}{12} = \mathbf{3\frac{5}{12}} \end{array}$$

18. $8\frac{1}{3} \times 1\frac{4}{5} = \frac{25}{3} \times \frac{9}{5} = \mathbf{15}$

19. $2\frac{2}{5} \div 1\frac{4}{5} = \frac{12}{5} \times \frac{5}{9} = \frac{4}{3} = \mathbf{1\frac{1}{3}}$

20. Area = $\frac{6 \text{ cm} \cdot 10 \text{ cm}}{2}$ = **30 sq. cm**

Cumulative Test 22A

1. $180° - (70° + 70°) = \mathbf{40°}$

2.

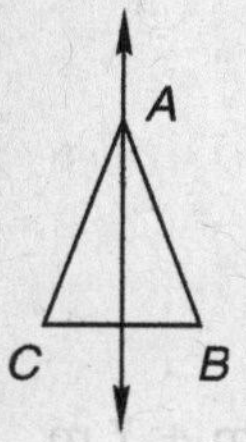

3. $$\begin{aligned} 4\tfrac{1}{2} &= 3\tfrac{9}{6} \\ -\,1\tfrac{5}{6} &= 1\tfrac{5}{6} \\ \hline 2\tfrac{4}{6} &= \mathbf{2\tfrac{2}{3}} \end{aligned}$$

4. $6\frac{2}{3} \div 1\frac{1}{4} = \frac{20}{3} \times \frac{4}{5} = \frac{16}{3} = \mathbf{5\frac{1}{3}}$

5. $3.75 + \frac{3}{8} = 3.75 + 0.375 = \mathbf{4.125}$

6. $\mathbf{-2, 0.2, \frac{1}{2}}$

7.

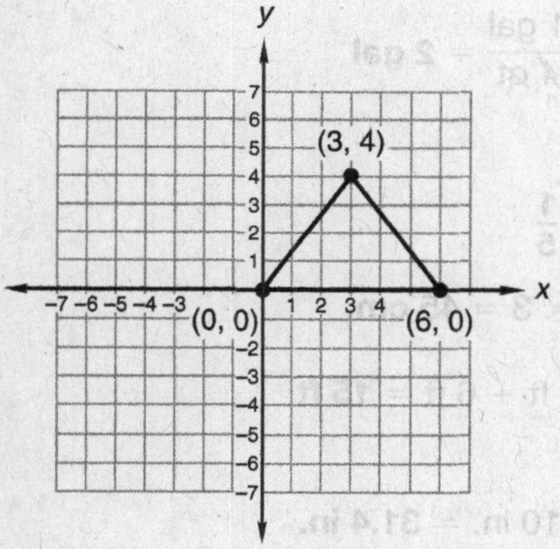

Area $= \frac{6 \cdot 4}{2} = \mathbf{12\ sq.\ units}$

8. $-6 - 4 - 3 = \mathbf{-13}$

9. $\frac{\overset{1}{\cancel{3}}}{\underset{5}{\cancel{10}}} \cdot \frac{\overset{1}{\cancel{2}}}{\underset{3}{\cancel{9}}} = \mathbf{\frac{1}{15}}$

10. $3^3 - 2^3 - 2 \times 3 = 27 - 8 - 6 = \mathbf{13}$

11. a. $1\frac{1}{5} = \frac{6}{5}$ $\quad 5\overline{)6.0}$ = **1.2**

b. $1\frac{1}{5} = 1.2 \times 100\% = \mathbf{120\%}$

12. a. $0.3 = \mathbf{\frac{3}{10}}$

b. $0.3 \times 100\% = \mathbf{30\%}$

13. a. $35\% = \frac{35}{100} = \mathbf{\frac{7}{20}}$

b. $35\% = \mathbf{0.35}$

14. 5 in. × 4 in. × 4 in. = **80 cu. in.**

15. $r = \frac{d}{2} = \frac{20\text{ in.}}{2} = 10\text{ in.}$

$A = \pi r^2$

3.14 × 10 in. × 10 in. = **314 in.²**

16. $\frac{\text{boy}}{\text{girl}} = \frac{14}{18} = \mathbf{\frac{7}{9}}$

17. $\frac{a}{1.2} = \frac{20}{30}$

$30a = 24$

$a = \frac{24}{30} = \mathbf{0.8}$

18. $3n + 2 = 35$

$3n = 33$

$n = \frac{33}{3} = \mathbf{11}$

19. 10 m − 4 m = 6 m

8 m − 3 m = 5 m

Perimeter = 4 m + 8 m + 10 m + 3 m + 6 m + 5 m = **36 m**

20. Area = (8 m × 4 m) + (6 m × 3 m)

= 32 sq. m + 18 sq. m = **50 sq. m**

Cumulative Test 22B

1. $180° - (75° + 75°) = \mathbf{30°}$

2.

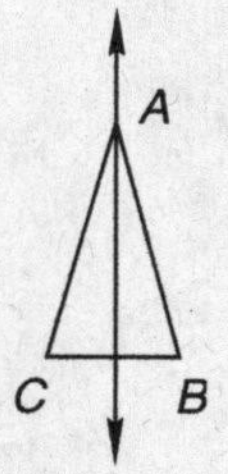

3. $$\begin{aligned} 5\tfrac{1}{3} &= 4\tfrac{8}{6} \\ -\,3\tfrac{1}{2} &= 3\tfrac{3}{6} \\ \hline &\mathbf{1\tfrac{5}{6}} \end{aligned}$$

4. $3\frac{3}{4} \div 1\frac{1}{4} = \frac{15}{4} \times \frac{4}{5} = \mathbf{3}$

5. $4.25 + \frac{3}{8} = 4.25 + 0.375 = \mathbf{4.625}$

6. $\mathbf{-3, 0.35, \frac{3}{4}}$

7.

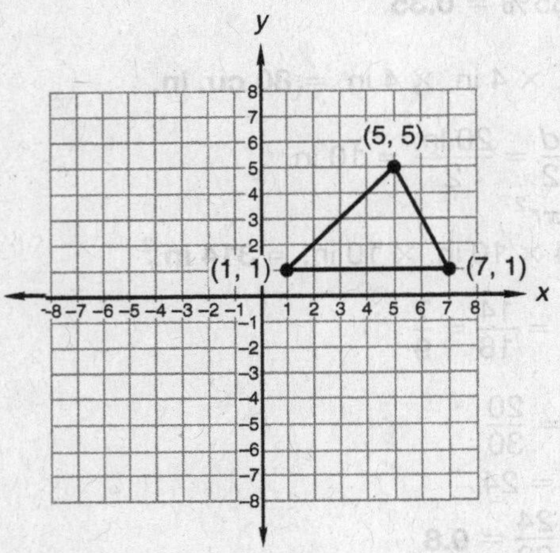

Area $= \frac{6 \cdot 4}{2} =$ **12 sq. units**

8. $-7 - 2 - 3 = \mathbf{-12}$

9. $\frac{\overset{1}{\cancel{5}}}{\underset{\underset{1}{\cancel{2}}}{\cancel{10}}} \cdot \frac{\overset{2}{\cancel{4}}}{9} = \mathbf{\frac{2}{9}}$

10. $3^2 - 2^3 + 2 \times 3 = 9 - 8 + 6 = \mathbf{7}$

11. a. $1\frac{1}{4} = \frac{5}{4}$ $\quad 4\overline{)5.00}$ with quotient **1.25**

b. $1\frac{1}{4} = 1.25 \times 100\% = \mathbf{125\%}$

12. a. $0.7 = \mathbf{\frac{7}{10}}$

b. $0.7 \times 100\% = \mathbf{70\%}$

13. a. $15\% = \frac{15}{100} = \mathbf{\frac{3}{20}}$

b. $15\% = \mathbf{0.15}$

14. $8 \times 3 \times 4 =$ **96 blocks**

15. $d = 2r = 2(16 \text{ in.}) = 32$ in.
$C = \pi d$
3.14×32 in. = **100.48 in.**

16. $\frac{\text{boy}}{\text{girl}} = \frac{18}{14} = \mathbf{\frac{9}{7}}$

17. $\frac{10}{a} = \frac{2.5}{3}$
$2.5a = 30$
$a = \frac{30}{2.5} = \mathbf{12}$

18. $4m + 4 = 40$
$4m = 36$
$m = \frac{36}{4} = \mathbf{9}$

19. 15 m − 7 m = 8m
10 m − 6 m = 4m
Perimeter = 6 m + 15 m + 10 m + 7 m
+ 4 m + 8 m = **50 m**

20. Area = (7 m × 10 m) + (6 m × 8 m)
= 70 sq. m + 48 sq. m = **118 sq. m**

Cumulative Test 23A

1. $\frac{110}{4} = 27 \text{ R } 2$
27, 27, 28, 28

2. $1\frac{1}{2}$ million = 1.5 million = **1,500,000**

3. $81 = 3 \cdot 3 \cdot 3 \cdot 3 = \mathbf{3^4}$

4. $\overset{2}{\cancel{8}}\ \cancel{\text{qt}} \times \frac{1 \text{ gal}}{\underset{1}{\cancel{4}}\ \cancel{\text{qt}}} =$ **2 gal**

5. **H**

6. $\frac{3}{6} \cdot \frac{2}{5} = \mathbf{\frac{1}{5}}$

7. 15 cm × 3 = **45 cm**

8. 4 ft + 5 ft + 6 ft = **15 ft**

9. $C = \pi d$
3.14 × 10 in. = **31.4 in.**

10. 4 m + 5 m = 9 m
12 m − 5 m = 7 m
Perimeter = 12 m + 5 m + 7 m + 4 m + 5 m
+ 9 m = **42 m**

11. Area = (5 m × 12 m) + (4 m × 5 m)
= 60 sq. m + 20 sq. m = **80 sq. m**

12. a. $4\overline{)3.00}$ with quotient **0.75**

b. $\frac{3}{4} = 0.75 \times 100\% = \mathbf{75\%}$

13. a. $0.02 = \frac{2}{100} = \mathbf{\frac{1}{50}}$

b. $0.02 \times 100\% = \mathbf{2\%}$

14. a. $120\% = \frac{120}{100} = \frac{6}{5} = \mathbf{1\frac{1}{5}}$

b. $120\% = 1.20 = \mathbf{1.2}$

15. $\begin{array}{r} 5.00 \\ -\,0.45 \\ \hline 4.55 \end{array}$ $\quad \begin{array}{r} 4.550 \\ +\,0.475 \\ \hline \mathbf{5.025} \end{array}$

16. $0.6 \div (0.4 \times 0.5) = 0.6 \div 0.2 = \mathbf{3}$

17. $(-4)(-7) = \mathbf{28}$

18. $\frac{-16}{+2} = \mathbf{-8}$

19. $\text{Area} = \frac{8\text{ cm} \times 10\text{ cm}}{2} = \mathbf{40\text{ sq. cm}}$

20. $100\% - 80\% = 20\%$
$\frac{20}{100} = \frac{\$5.00}{p}$
$20p = \$500.00$
$p = \mathbf{\$25.00}$

Cumulative Test 23B

1. $\frac{85}{3} = 28\text{ R }1$
28, 28, 29

2. 1.5 billion = **1,500,000,000**

3. $64 = 2 \cdot 2 \cdot 2 \cdot 2 \cdot 2 \cdot 2 = \mathbf{2^6}$

4. $8\text{ qt} \times \frac{2\text{ pt}}{1\text{ qt}} = \mathbf{16\text{ pt}}$

5. **S**

6. $\frac{3}{6} \cdot \frac{2}{5} = \mathbf{\frac{1}{5}}$

7. Perimeter = 36 in. ÷ 3 = **12 in.**

8. Side length = 20 cm ÷ 4 = 5 cm
Area = 5 cm × 5 cm = **25 sq. cm**

9. $d = 2r = 2(10\text{ in.}) = 20\text{ in.}$
$C = \pi d$
$C = (3.14)(20\text{ in.}) = \mathbf{62.8\text{ in.}}$

10. 10 cm − 6 cm = 4 cm
6 cm − 4 cm = 2 cm
Perimeter = 6 cm + 4 cm + 10 cm + 6 cm + 4 cm + 2 cm = **32 cm**

11. Area = (10 cm × 4 cm) + (2 cm × 4 cm)
= 40 sq. cm + 8 sq. cm = **48 sq. cm**

12. a. $4\overline{)1.00}$ = **0.25**

b. $\frac{1}{4} = 0.25 \times 100\% = \mathbf{25\%}$

13. a. $0.04 = \frac{4}{100} = \mathbf{\frac{1}{25}}$

b. $0.04 \times 100\% = \mathbf{4\%}$

14. a. $150\% = \frac{150}{100} = \frac{3}{2} = \mathbf{1\frac{1}{2}}$

b. $150\% = 1.50 = \mathbf{1.5}$

15. $6.23 + (4 - 0.5) = 6.23 + 3.5 = \mathbf{9.73}$

16. $6 \div (0.4 \times 0.5)$
$6 \div 0.2 = \mathbf{30}$

17. $(-9)(-4) = \mathbf{36}$

18. $\frac{-18}{+3} = \mathbf{-6}$

19. $\text{Area} = \frac{8\text{ mm} \times 12\text{ mm}}{2} = \mathbf{48\text{ sq. mm}}$

20. $100\% - 80\% = 20\%$
$\frac{20}{100} = \frac{\$6.00}{p}$
$20p = \$600.00$
$p = \mathbf{\$30.00}$

Name ______________________ Time __________

Power-Up Test 1

Math Course 1

Facts Add.

4 + 6 = 10	9 + 9 = 18	3 + 4 = 7	5 + 5 = 10	7 + 8 = 15	2 + 3 = 5	7 + 0 = 7	5 + 9 = 14	2 + 6 = 8	3 + 9 = 12
3 + 5 = 8	2 + 2 = 4	6 + 7 = 13	8 + 8 = 16	2 + 9 = 11	5 + 7 = 12	4 + 9 = 13	6 + 6 = 12	3 + 8 = 11	7 + 7 = 14
4 + 4 = 8	7 + 9 = 16	5 + 8 = 13	2 + 7 = 9	0 + 0 = 0	6 + 8 = 14	3 + 7 = 10	2 + 4 = 6	7 + 1 = 8	4 + 8 = 12
5 + 6 = 11	4 + 7 = 11	2 + 5 = 7	3 + 6 = 9	8 + 9 = 17	2 + 8 = 10	10 + 10 = 20	4 + 5 = 9	6 + 9 = 15	3 + 3 = 6

Problem Solving Answer the question below.

Problem: Brothers Josh and Wes take turns multiplying numbers. Josh starts with 4, which Wes then multiplies by 4 to get 16. Josh then multiplies 16 by 4 to get 64. Wes multiplies 64 by 4 to get 256. Back and forth they multiply until one of them arrives at 1,048,576. Which brother came up with the product 1,048,576?

Understand

I know there is a sequence of numbers that are multiples of 4 and 16. I need to find a pattern that helps determine a particular term in the sequence.

Plan

Strategy: Make an organized list; Find a pattern.

List a few numbers in each sequence of multiples to find a pattern. Then use the pattern to predict which brother (sequence) arrived at 1,048,576.

Solve

Josh's numbers include 4, 64 and 1024. Wes' numbers include 16, 256 and 4096. From this, a pattern emerges: Josh will always achieve a product that has a 4 as the ones digit, and Wes will always achieve a product that has a 6 as the ones digit. Therefore, Wes arrived at 1,048,576.

Check

Name ____________________ Time ______________ **Power-Up Test 2**

Math Course 1

Facts Subtract.

$8 - 5 = 3$	$10 - 4 = 6$	$12 - 6 = 6$	$6 - 3 = 3$	$8 - 4 = 4$	$14 - 7 = 7$	$20 - 10 = 10$	$11 - 5 = 6$	$7 - 4 = 3$	$13 - 6 = 7$
$7 - 2 = 5$	$15 - 8 = 7$	$9 - 7 = 2$	$17 - 9 = 8$	$10 - 5 = 5$	$8 - 1 = 7$	$16 - 7 = 9$	$6 - 0 = 6$	$12 - 3 = 9$	$9 - 5 = 4$
$13 - 5 = 8$	$11 - 7 = 4$	$14 - 8 = 6$	$10 - 7 = 3$	$5 - 3 = 2$	$15 - 6 = 9$	$6 - 4 = 2$	$10 - 8 = 2$	$18 - 9 = 9$	$15 - 7 = 8$
$12 - 4 = 8$	$11 - 2 = 9$	$16 - 8 = 8$	$9 - 9 = 0$	$13 - 4 = 9$	$11 - 8 = 3$	$9 - 6 = 3$	$14 - 9 = 5$	$8 - 6 = 2$	$12 - 5 = 7$

Problem Solving Answer the question below.

Problem: Six telephone poles are evenly spaced along a street. It takes Raul 60 seconds to walk from the first pole to the third pole. At this rate, how long will it take Raul to walk from the first pole to the sixth pole?

Understand

I know there are 6 evenly spaced poles, and it takes Raul 60 seconds to walk $\frac{2}{5}$ of the total distance. I need to find how long it takes him to walk the entire distance between the first and sixth poles.

Plan

Strategy: Draw a picture.

Solve

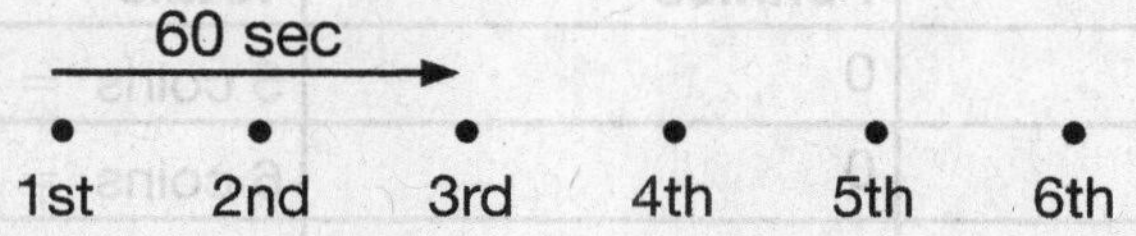

If it takes 60 seconds to walk from the first to the third pole, Raul takes an average of 30 seconds to walk the distance between two poles. The first and sixth poles are separated by 5 such distances, so 30 seconds $\times$ 5 $=$ 150 seconds, or $2\frac{1}{2}$ minutes.

Check

Name ____________________ Time ____________

Power-Up Test 3

Math Course 1

Facts Multiply.

$\begin{array}{r}7\\ \times 7\\ \hline 49\end{array}$	$\begin{array}{r}4\\ \times 6\\ \hline 24\end{array}$	$\begin{array}{r}8\\ \times 1\\ \hline 8\end{array}$	$\begin{array}{r}2\\ \times 2\\ \hline 4\end{array}$	$\begin{array}{r}0\\ \times 5\\ \hline 0\end{array}$	$\begin{array}{r}6\\ \times 3\\ \hline 18\end{array}$	$\begin{array}{r}8\\ \times 9\\ \hline 72\end{array}$	$\begin{array}{r}5\\ \times 8\\ \hline 40\end{array}$	$\begin{array}{r}6\\ \times 2\\ \hline 12\end{array}$	$\begin{array}{r}10\\ \times 10\\ \hline 100\end{array}$
$\begin{array}{r}9\\ \times 4\\ \hline 36\end{array}$	$\begin{array}{r}2\\ \times 5\\ \hline 10\end{array}$	$\begin{array}{r}9\\ \times 6\\ \hline 54\end{array}$	$\begin{array}{r}7\\ \times 3\\ \hline 21\end{array}$	$\begin{array}{r}5\\ \times 5\\ \hline 25\end{array}$	$\begin{array}{r}7\\ \times 2\\ \hline 14\end{array}$	$\begin{array}{r}6\\ \times 8\\ \hline 48\end{array}$	$\begin{array}{r}3\\ \times 5\\ \hline 15\end{array}$	$\begin{array}{r}9\\ \times 9\\ \hline 81\end{array}$	$\begin{array}{r}5\\ \times 4\\ \hline 20\end{array}$
$\begin{array}{r}3\\ \times 4\\ \hline 12\end{array}$	$\begin{array}{r}6\\ \times 5\\ \hline 30\end{array}$	$\begin{array}{r}8\\ \times 2\\ \hline 16\end{array}$	$\begin{array}{r}4\\ \times 4\\ \hline 16\end{array}$	$\begin{array}{r}6\\ \times 7\\ \hline 42\end{array}$	$\begin{array}{r}8\\ \times 8\\ \hline 64\end{array}$	$\begin{array}{r}2\\ \times 3\\ \hline 6\end{array}$	$\begin{array}{r}7\\ \times 4\\ \hline 28\end{array}$	$\begin{array}{r}5\\ \times 9\\ \hline 45\end{array}$	$\begin{array}{r}3\\ \times 6\\ \hline 18\end{array}$
$\begin{array}{r}3\\ \times 9\\ \hline 27\end{array}$	$\begin{array}{r}7\\ \times 8\\ \hline 56\end{array}$	$\begin{array}{r}2\\ \times 4\\ \hline 8\end{array}$	$\begin{array}{r}5\\ \times 7\\ \hline 35\end{array}$	$\begin{array}{r}3\\ \times 3\\ \hline 9\end{array}$	$\begin{array}{r}9\\ \times 7\\ \hline 63\end{array}$	$\begin{array}{r}4\\ \times 8\\ \hline 32\end{array}$	$\begin{array}{r}0\\ \times 0\\ \hline 0\end{array}$	$\begin{array}{r}9\\ \times 2\\ \hline 18\end{array}$	$\begin{array}{r}6\\ \times 6\\ \hline 36\end{array}$

Problem Solving Answer the question below.

Problem: Letha has an assortment of dimes, nickels, and pennies in her pocket. She selects 7 coins that total 50 cents. What are the coins, and how many of each has she selected?

Understand

Given 7 of a variety of coins, I need to determine which combination(s) and what quantities of coins will total 50 cents.

Plan

Strategy: Make or use a table, chart or graph; Guess-and-check.
Make a chart of coin combinations starting with the coins with the greatest value.

Solve

Dimes	Nickels	Pennies	Totals
5 = 50¢	0	0	5 coins = 50 cents
4 = 40¢	2 = 10¢	0	6 coins = 50 cents
4 = 40¢	1 = 5¢	5 = 5¢	10 coins = 50 cents
4 = 40¢	0	10 = 10¢	14 coins = 50 cents
3 = 30¢	4 = 20¢	0	7 coins = 50 cents

Letha has selected 3 dimes and 4 nickels.

Check

Name ______________________ Time __________

Power-Up Test 4

Math Course 1

Facts Multiply.

$7 \times 7 = 49$	$4 \times 6 = 24$	$8 \times 1 = 8$	$2 \times 2 = 4$	$0 \times 5 = 0$	$6 \times 3 = 18$	$8 \times 9 = 72$	$5 \times 8 = 40$	$6 \times 2 = 12$	$10 \times 10 = 100$
$9 \times 4 = 36$	$2 \times 5 = 10$	$9 \times 6 = 54$	$7 \times 3 = 21$	$5 \times 5 = 25$	$7 \times 2 = 14$	$6 \times 8 = 48$	$3 \times 5 = 15$	$9 \times 9 = 81$	$5 \times 4 = 20$
$3 \times 4 = 12$	$6 \times 5 = 30$	$8 \times 2 = 16$	$4 \times 4 = 16$	$6 \times 7 = 42$	$8 \times 8 = 64$	$2 \times 3 = 6$	$7 \times 4 = 28$	$5 \times 9 = 45$	$3 \times 6 = 18$
$3 \times 9 = 27$	$7 \times 8 = 56$	$2 \times 4 = 8$	$5 \times 7 = 35$	$3 \times 3 = 9$	$9 \times 7 = 63$	$4 \times 8 = 32$	$0 \times 0 = 0$	$9 \times 2 = 18$	$6 \times 6 = 36$

Problem Solving Answer the question below.

Problem: In one section of the school auditorium there are 12 rows of seats. In the first row there are 23 seats, in the second row there are 26 seats, and in the third row there are 29 seats. If the pattern continues, how many seats are in the twelfth row?

Understand

There are 12 rows of seats. The number of seats in each row increases by 3 as the row number increases by 1. I need to find the number of seats in the twelfth row.

Plan

Strategy: Find a pattern.

Compare rows and the number of chairs in each to find a pattern. Use the pattern to determine how many chairs are in the last row.

Solve

Three extra seats are added to each row. The twelfth term of the pattern is 56, so the twelfth row has 56 seats.

Check

Name ____________________ Time ____________

Power-Up Test 5

Math Course 1

Facts Multiply.

8 × 8 = 64	3 × 9 = 27	6 × 7 = 42	5 × 2 = 10	0 × 0 = 0	3 × 8 = 24	4 × 6 = 24	5 × 8 = 40	2 × 9 = 18	9 × 9 = 81
6 × 1 = 6	2 × 6 = 12	3 × 3 = 9	4 × 5 = 20	5 × 5 = 25	8 × 6 = 48	4 × 2 = 8	7 × 7 = 49	7 × 4 = 28	5 × 3 = 15
6 × 9 = 54	8 × 4 = 32	5 × 9 = 45	4 × 3 = 12	7 × 8 = 56	2 × 2 = 4	6 × 5 = 30	2 × 7 = 14	8 × 9 = 72	3 × 6 = 18
4 × 4 = 16	5 × 7 = 35	3 × 2 = 6	7 × 9 = 63	6 × 6 = 36	3 × 7 = 21	2 × 8 = 16	0 × 7 = 0	9 × 4 = 36	10 × 10 = 100

Problem Solving Answer the question below.

Problem: Bryan held a number cube between two fingers so that he covered opposite faces of the number cube. On two of the faces that Bryan could see were the numbers 3 and 5. What were the numbers on each of the two faces his fingers covered? (Reminder: Opposite faces on a number cube always total 7.)

Understand

I know there are 6 faces on a number cube. The numbers on opposite faces add up to 7. Given two numbers, 3 and 5, I need to find the two covered numbers.

Plan

Strategy: Use logical reasoning (*or,* Draw a picture or diagram; or Make a model).
Use the known numbers to find their opposites. The numbers left are the ones covered.

Solve

The 4 is opposite the 3, and the 2 is opposite the 5, so it is the 1 and the 6 that Bryan's two fingers are covering.

{Students might also make a net drawing of the cube to visualize which numbers are covered by process of elimination.}

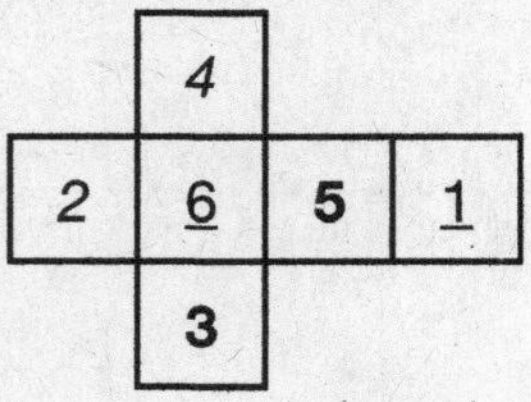

Check

Name ____________________ Time ____________

Power-Up Test 6

Math Course 1

Facts Multiply.

$\begin{array}{r} 8 \\ \times 8 \\ \hline 64 \end{array}$	$\begin{array}{r} 3 \\ \times 9 \\ \hline 27 \end{array}$	$\begin{array}{r} 6 \\ \times 7 \\ \hline 42 \end{array}$	$\begin{array}{r} 5 \\ \times 2 \\ \hline 10 \end{array}$	$\begin{array}{r} 0 \\ \times 0 \\ \hline 0 \end{array}$	$\begin{array}{r} 3 \\ \times 8 \\ \hline 24 \end{array}$	$\begin{array}{r} 4 \\ \times 6 \\ \hline 24 \end{array}$	$\begin{array}{r} 5 \\ \times 8 \\ \hline 40 \end{array}$	$\begin{array}{r} 2 \\ \times 9 \\ \hline 18 \end{array}$	$\begin{array}{r} 9 \\ \times 9 \\ \hline 81 \end{array}$
$\begin{array}{r} 6 \\ \times 1 \\ \hline 6 \end{array}$	$\begin{array}{r} 2 \\ \times 6 \\ \hline 12 \end{array}$	$\begin{array}{r} 3 \\ \times 3 \\ \hline 9 \end{array}$	$\begin{array}{r} 4 \\ \times 5 \\ \hline 20 \end{array}$	$\begin{array}{r} 5 \\ \times 5 \\ \hline 25 \end{array}$	$\begin{array}{r} 8 \\ \times 6 \\ \hline 48 \end{array}$	$\begin{array}{r} 4 \\ \times 2 \\ \hline 8 \end{array}$	$\begin{array}{r} 7 \\ \times 7 \\ \hline 49 \end{array}$	$\begin{array}{r} 7 \\ \times 4 \\ \hline 28 \end{array}$	$\begin{array}{r} 5 \\ \times 3 \\ \hline 15 \end{array}$
$\begin{array}{r} 6 \\ \times 9 \\ \hline 54 \end{array}$	$\begin{array}{r} 8 \\ \times 4 \\ \hline 32 \end{array}$	$\begin{array}{r} 5 \\ \times 9 \\ \hline 45 \end{array}$	$\begin{array}{r} 4 \\ \times 3 \\ \hline 12 \end{array}$	$\begin{array}{r} 7 \\ \times 8 \\ \hline 56 \end{array}$	$\begin{array}{r} 2 \\ \times 2 \\ \hline 4 \end{array}$	$\begin{array}{r} 6 \\ \times 5 \\ \hline 30 \end{array}$	$\begin{array}{r} 2 \\ \times 7 \\ \hline 14 \end{array}$	$\begin{array}{r} 8 \\ \times 9 \\ \hline 72 \end{array}$	$\begin{array}{r} 3 \\ \times 6 \\ \hline 18 \end{array}$
$\begin{array}{r} 4 \\ \times 4 \\ \hline 16 \end{array}$	$\begin{array}{r} 5 \\ \times 7 \\ \hline 35 \end{array}$	$\begin{array}{r} 3 \\ \times 2 \\ \hline 6 \end{array}$	$\begin{array}{r} 7 \\ \times 9 \\ \hline 63 \end{array}$	$\begin{array}{r} 6 \\ \times 6 \\ \hline 36 \end{array}$	$\begin{array}{r} 3 \\ \times 7 \\ \hline 21 \end{array}$	$\begin{array}{r} 2 \\ \times 8 \\ \hline 16 \end{array}$	$\begin{array}{r} 0 \\ \times 7 \\ \hline 0 \end{array}$	$\begin{array}{r} 9 \\ \times 4 \\ \hline 36 \end{array}$	$\begin{array}{r} 10 \\ \times 10 \\ \hline 100 \end{array}$

Problem Solving Answer the question below.

Problem: There are two routes that Tia can take to school. There are three routes Samantha can take to school. If Tia is going from her house to school and then on to Samantha's house, how many different routes is it possible for Tia to take?

Understand

Tia can take two routes to school and three routes to Samantha's house from school. I need to find how many routes Tia can take from her house to school and then to Samantha's house.

Plan

Strategy: Draw a picture or diagram; Use logical reasoning.
Start by drawing a diagram of the routes between the houses and school. Then count or calculate possible routes.

Solve

There are 3 ways to go to Samantha's house for *each* of the 2 routes Tia takes to school, so there are $2 \times 3 = 6$ different possible routes for Tia to take.

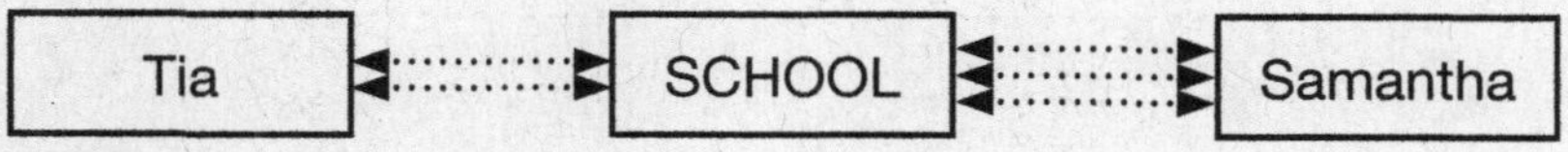

Check

Name ______________________ Time ______________

Power-Up Test 7

Math Course 1

Facts Divide.

$7\overline{)49}$ = 7	$9\overline{)27}$ = 3	$5\overline{)25}$ = 5	$4\overline{)12}$ = 3	$6\overline{)36}$ = 6	$7\overline{)21}$ = 3	$10\overline{)100}$ = 10	$5\overline{)10}$ = 2	$4\overline{)0}$ = 0	$4\overline{)16}$ = 4
$8\overline{)72}$ = 9	$4\overline{)28}$ = 7	$2\overline{)14}$ = 7	$7\overline{)35}$ = 5	$5\overline{)40}$ = 8	$2\overline{)8}$ = 4	$8\overline{)8}$ = 1	$3\overline{)9}$ = 3	$8\overline{)24}$ = 3	$4\overline{)24}$ = 6
$6\overline{)54}$ = 9	$3\overline{)18}$ = 6	$8\overline{)56}$ = 7	$3\overline{)6}$ = 2	$8\overline{)48}$ = 6	$5\overline{)20}$ = 4	$2\overline{)16}$ = 8	$7\overline{)63}$ = 9	$6\overline{)12}$ = 2	$1\overline{)6}$ = 6
$4\overline{)32}$ = 8	$9\overline{)45}$ = 5	$2\overline{)18}$ = 9	$8\overline{)64}$ = 8	$6\overline{)30}$ = 5	$5\overline{)15}$ = 3	$6\overline{)42}$ = 7	$3\overline{)24}$ = 8	$9\overline{)81}$ = 9	$4\overline{)36}$ = 9

Problem Solving Answer the question below.

Problem: If 12 glubs = 1 lorn, and 4 lorns = 1 dort, then how many glubs = $\frac{1}{2}$ dort?

Understand

I know that 1 dort is 4 lorns and each lorn is 12 glubs. I need to find the number of glubs that equal $\frac{1}{2}$ dort.

Plan

Strategy: Use logical reasoning.

Solve

Because 1 dort is equal to 4 lorns, and 1 lorn is equal to 12 glubs, then 1 dort is equal to 48 glubs. Therefore, $\frac{1}{2}$ dort is $\frac{1}{2}$ of 48 glubs, so 24 glubs is equal to $\frac{1}{2}$ dort.

Check

Name ______________________ Time ____________

Power-Up Test 8

Math Course 1

Facts Reduce each fraction to lowest terms.

$\frac{2}{8} = \frac{1}{4}$	$\frac{4}{6} = \frac{2}{3}$	$\frac{6}{10} = \frac{3}{5}$	$\frac{2}{4} = \frac{1}{2}$	$\frac{5}{100} = \frac{1}{20}$	$\frac{9}{12} = \frac{3}{4}$
$\frac{4}{10} = \frac{2}{5}$	$\frac{4}{12} = \frac{1}{3}$	$\frac{2}{10} = \frac{1}{5}$	$\frac{3}{6} = \frac{1}{2}$	$\frac{25}{100} = \frac{1}{4}$	$\frac{3}{12} = \frac{1}{4}$
$\frac{4}{16} = \frac{1}{4}$	$\frac{3}{9} = \frac{1}{3}$	$\frac{6}{9} = \frac{2}{3}$	$\frac{4}{8} = \frac{1}{2}$	$\frac{2}{12} = \frac{1}{6}$	$\frac{6}{12} = \frac{1}{2}$
$\frac{8}{16} = \frac{1}{2}$	$\frac{2}{6} = \frac{1}{3}$	$\frac{8}{12} = \frac{2}{3}$	$\frac{6}{8} = \frac{3}{4}$	$\frac{5}{10} = \frac{1}{2}$	$\frac{75}{100} = \frac{3}{4}$

Problem Solving Answer the question below.

Problem: The sum of five different single-digit whole numbers is 30. Two of the numbers are 1 and 8. If we multiply the same five numbers, the product is 2520. What are the other three numbers?

Understand

Given: the sum of 5 single-digit whole numbers is 30, their product is 2520, and 2 of the numbers are 1 and 8. I need to find the other three numbers.

Plan

Strategy: Use logical reasoning; Work backwards; Guess and check.
Use 2 known numbers and simple math, such as calculating products and sums, to find the remaining 3 numbers.

Solve

Since I know two of the numbers are 8 and 1, I can divide 2520 by 8 and 1 to find the product of the other three numbers: $2520 \div (8 \times 1) = 315$. One of the three numbers must be 5, because 315 is divisible by 5: $315 \div 5 = 63$. I also know that $30 - (8 + 1 + 5) = 16$, so the remaining two numbers are factors of 63 and total 16. Both 7 and 9 are factors of 63: $7 \times 9 = 63$. Also, $7 + 9 = 16$, so the five numbers are 1, 5, 7, 8, and 9.

Check

Facts Reduce each fraction to lowest terms.

$\frac{2}{8} = \frac{1}{4}$	$\frac{4}{6} = \frac{2}{3}$	$\frac{6}{10} = \frac{3}{5}$	$\frac{2}{4} = \frac{1}{2}$	$\frac{5}{100} = \frac{1}{20}$	$\frac{9}{12} = \frac{3}{4}$
$\frac{4}{10} = \frac{2}{5}$	$\frac{4}{12} = \frac{1}{3}$	$\frac{2}{10} = \frac{1}{5}$	$\frac{3}{6} = \frac{1}{2}$	$\frac{25}{100} = \frac{1}{4}$	$\frac{3}{12} = \frac{1}{4}$
$\frac{4}{16} = \frac{1}{4}$	$\frac{3}{9} = \frac{1}{3}$	$\frac{6}{9} = \frac{2}{3}$	$\frac{4}{8} = \frac{1}{2}$	$\frac{2}{12} = \frac{1}{6}$	$\frac{6}{12} = \frac{1}{2}$
$\frac{8}{16} = \frac{1}{2}$	$\frac{2}{6} = \frac{1}{3}$	$\frac{8}{12} = \frac{2}{3}$	$\frac{6}{8} = \frac{3}{4}$	$\frac{5}{10} = \frac{1}{2}$	$\frac{75}{100} = \frac{3}{4}$

Problem Solving Answer the question below.

Problem: Each of the identically painted cubes has one face of each color: yellow, orange, red, green, blue, and purple. How must the net be colored to create another identical cube?

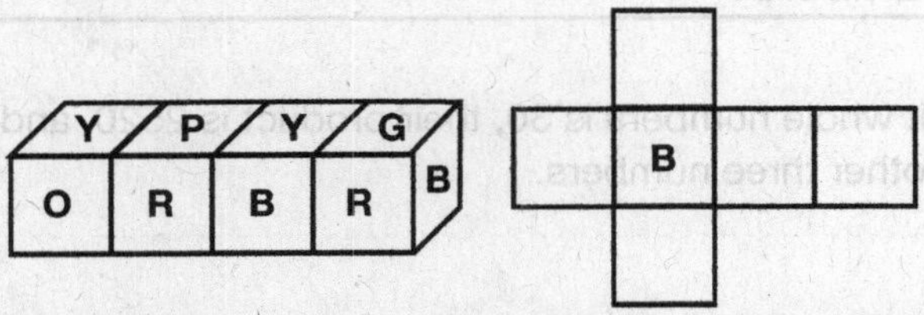

Understand

4 cubes are painted the same way. I need to draw a net that would create an identically painted cube.

Plan

Strategy: Draw a picture or diagram; Guess and check.

Use a net of the cube and fill in the corresponding colors.

Solve

B shares edges with G, R, Y and a fourth color.

Therefore, B is opposite O or P.

Two of eight possible solutions are shown.

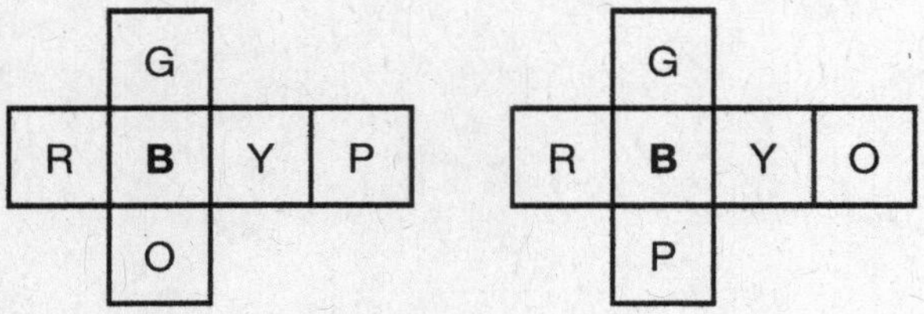

Check

Name ____________________ Time ____________

Power-Up Test 10

Math Course 1

Facts Multiply or divide as indicated.

$\begin{array}{r}4\\ \times 9\\ \hline 36\end{array}$	$\begin{array}{r}4\\ 4\overline{)16}\end{array}$	$\begin{array}{r}6\\ \times 8\\ \hline 48\end{array}$	$\begin{array}{r}4\\ 3\overline{)12}\end{array}$	$\begin{array}{r}5\\ \times 7\\ \hline 35\end{array}$	$\begin{array}{r}8\\ 4\overline{)32}\end{array}$	$\begin{array}{r}3\\ \times 9\\ \hline 27\end{array}$	$\begin{array}{r}9\\ 9\overline{)81}\end{array}$	$\begin{array}{r}6\\ \times 2\\ \hline 12\end{array}$	$\begin{array}{r}8\\ 8\overline{)64}\end{array}$
$\begin{array}{r}9\\ \times 7\\ \hline 63\end{array}$	$\begin{array}{r}5\\ 8\overline{)40}\end{array}$	$\begin{array}{r}2\\ \times 4\\ \hline 8\end{array}$	$\begin{array}{r}7\\ 6\overline{)42}\end{array}$	$\begin{array}{r}5\\ \times 5\\ \hline 25\end{array}$	$\begin{array}{r}2\\ 7\overline{)14}\end{array}$	$\begin{array}{r}7\\ \times 7\\ \hline 49\end{array}$	$\begin{array}{r}1\\ 8\overline{)8}\end{array}$	$\begin{array}{r}3\\ \times 3\\ \hline 9\end{array}$	$\begin{array}{r}0\\ 6\overline{)0}\end{array}$
$\begin{array}{r}7\\ \times 3\\ \hline 21\end{array}$	$\begin{array}{r}5\\ 2\overline{)10}\end{array}$	$\begin{array}{r}10\\ \times 10\\ \hline 100\end{array}$	$\begin{array}{r}8\\ 3\overline{)24}\end{array}$	$\begin{array}{r}4\\ \times 5\\ \hline 20\end{array}$	$\begin{array}{r}6\\ 9\overline{)54}\end{array}$	$\begin{array}{r}9\\ \times 1\\ \hline 9\end{array}$	$\begin{array}{r}2\\ 3\overline{)6}\end{array}$	$\begin{array}{r}7\\ \times 4\\ \hline 28\end{array}$	$\begin{array}{r}8\\ 7\overline{)56}\end{array}$
$\begin{array}{r}6\\ \times 6\\ \hline 36\end{array}$	$\begin{array}{r}9\\ 2\overline{)18}\end{array}$	$\begin{array}{r}3\\ \times 5\\ \hline 15\end{array}$	$\begin{array}{r}6\\ 5\overline{)30}\end{array}$	$\begin{array}{r}2\\ \times 2\\ \hline 4\end{array}$	$\begin{array}{r}3\\ 6\overline{)18}\end{array}$	$\begin{array}{r}9\\ \times 5\\ \hline 45\end{array}$	$\begin{array}{r}4\\ 6\overline{)24}\end{array}$	$\begin{array}{r}2\\ \times 8\\ \hline 16\end{array}$	$\begin{array}{r}8\\ 9\overline{)72}\end{array}$

Problem Solving Answer the question below.

Problem: Find the missing digits in this problem:

$$\begin{array}{r}\_37\_\\ -\ 2\_65\\ \hline 59\_7\end{array}$$

Understand

A four-digit number is being subtracted from another 4-digit number, but some of the digits are missing. I need to find the missing digits to complete the operation.

Plan

Strategy: Work backwards; Use logical reasoning.
Reverse the step-by-step process of subtraction using logic and math knowledge to find the missing digits.

Solve

If the ones place in the difference is 7 and the ones place in the subtrahend is 5, the ones place in the minuend must be 12 because 7 + 5 = 12. The ones place holds 2 and 1 tens-unit carries to the tens place of the subtrahend. The tens place is then 7, which is subtracted from a 7 in the minuend's tens place to create a 0 in the tens place of the difference. Using the same logic, if the hundreds place in the difference is 9, and the hundreds place in the minuend is 3, the subtrahend must be 4 because 9 + 4 = 13 and 1 hundreds-unit is carried to the thousands place in the subtrahend, making it 3. Finally, if subtracting that 3 from the minuend creates a difference of 5 in the thousands place, the thousands place in the minuend must be 8.

Check

$$\begin{array}{r}\underline{8}37\underline{2}\\ -\ 2\underline{4}65\\ \hline 59\underline{0}7\end{array}$$

Name ______________________ Time ______________

Power-Up Test 11

Math Course 1

Facts Write each improper fraction as a mixed number. Reduce fractions.

$\frac{5}{4} = 1\frac{1}{4}$	$\frac{6}{4} = 1\frac{1}{2}$	$\frac{15}{10} = 1\frac{1}{2}$	$\frac{8}{3} = 2\frac{2}{3}$	$\frac{15}{12} = 1\frac{1}{4}$
$\frac{12}{8} = 1\frac{1}{2}$	$\frac{10}{8} = 1\frac{1}{4}$	$\frac{3}{2} = 1\frac{1}{2}$	$\frac{15}{6} = 2\frac{1}{2}$	$\frac{10}{4} = 2\frac{1}{2}$
$\frac{8}{6} = 1\frac{1}{3}$	$\frac{25}{10} = 2\frac{1}{2}$	$\frac{9}{6} = 1\frac{1}{2}$	$\frac{10}{6} = 1\frac{2}{3}$	$\frac{15}{8} = 1\frac{7}{8}$
$\frac{12}{10} = 1\frac{1}{5}$	$\frac{10}{3} = 3\frac{1}{3}$	$\frac{18}{12} = 1\frac{1}{2}$	$\frac{5}{2} = 2\frac{1}{2}$	$\frac{4}{3} = 1\frac{1}{3}$

Problem Solving Answer the question below.

Problem: What is the largest 2-digit number that is divisible by 3 and whose digits differ by 2?

Understand

I need to find the largest 2-digit number that is divisible by 3 and whose digits differ by 2.

Plan

Strategy: Make an organized list; Work backwards.

Starting with the largest 2-digit number, 99, list the multiples of 3 in reverse order to find the answer.

Solve

The largest 2-digit multiple of 3 is 99. List backwards from 99 (99, 96, 93, 90, 87, 84, 81, 78, 75, …) until there's a multiple whose digits differ by 2: 75 ($75 \div 3 = 25$, $7 - 5 = 2$).

Check

Name ______________ Time __________

Facts Multiply or divide as indicated.

$4 \times 9 = 36$	$\begin{array}{r} 4 \\ 4\overline{)16} \end{array}$	$6 \times 8 = 48$	$\begin{array}{r} 4 \\ 3\overline{)12} \end{array}$	$5 \times 7 = 35$	$\begin{array}{r} 8 \\ 4\overline{)32} \end{array}$	$3 \times 9 = 27$	$\begin{array}{r} 9 \\ 9\overline{)81} \end{array}$	$6 \times 2 = 12$	$\begin{array}{r} 8 \\ 8\overline{)64} \end{array}$
$9 \times 7 = 63$	$\begin{array}{r} 5 \\ 8\overline{)40} \end{array}$	$2 \times 4 = 8$	$\begin{array}{r} 7 \\ 6\overline{)42} \end{array}$	$5 \times 5 = 25$	$\begin{array}{r} 2 \\ 7\overline{)14} \end{array}$	$7 \times 7 = 49$	$\begin{array}{r} 1 \\ 8\overline{)8} \end{array}$	$3 \times 3 = 9$	$\begin{array}{r} 0 \\ 6\overline{)0} \end{array}$
$7 \times 3 = 21$	$\begin{array}{r} 5 \\ 2\overline{)10} \end{array}$	$10 \times 10 = 100$	$\begin{array}{r} 8 \\ 3\overline{)24} \end{array}$	$4 \times 5 = 20$	$\begin{array}{r} 6 \\ 9\overline{)54} \end{array}$	$9 \times 1 = 9$	$\begin{array}{r} 2 \\ 3\overline{)6} \end{array}$	$7 \times 4 = 28$	$\begin{array}{r} 8 \\ 7\overline{)56} \end{array}$
$6 \times 6 = 36$	$\begin{array}{r} 9 \\ 2\overline{)18} \end{array}$	$3 \times 5 = 15$	$\begin{array}{r} 6 \\ 5\overline{)30} \end{array}$	$2 \times 2 = 4$	$\begin{array}{r} 3 \\ 6\overline{)18} \end{array}$	$9 \times 5 = 45$	$\begin{array}{r} 4 \\ 6\overline{)24} \end{array}$	$2 \times 8 = 16$	$\begin{array}{r} 8 \\ 9\overline{)72} \end{array}$

Problem Solving Answer the question below.

Problem: Six friends are organizing themselves by age. Zelda is older than Frank, but younger than Juan. Juan is younger than Celia, but older than Frank. Frank is older than Gina and Marcos. Marcos is younger than Celia and Gina. Who is the oldest and who is the youngest?

Understand

Given individual relationships between people of different ages, I need to find which person is the oldest and which is the youngest.

Plan

Strategy: Draw a picture or diagram; Use logical reasoning.

Use lists to compare the known information from statements side by side. Use logic to fill gaps and draw conclusions.

Solve

Statement 1:	Statement 2:	Statement 3:	Statement 4:
	Celia		Celia
Juan	Juan		
Zelda			
Frank	Frank	Frank	
		Gina	Gina
		Marcos	Marcos

Celia is the oldest, and Marcos is the youngest.

Check

Name ______________________ Time __________

Facts Write each mixed number as an improper fraction.

$2\frac{1}{2} = \frac{5}{2}$	$2\frac{2}{5} = \frac{12}{5}$	$1\frac{3}{4} = \frac{7}{4}$	$2\frac{3}{4} = \frac{11}{4}$	$2\frac{1}{8} = \frac{17}{8}$
$1\frac{2}{3} = \frac{5}{3}$	$3\frac{1}{2} = \frac{7}{2}$	$1\frac{5}{6} = \frac{11}{6}$	$2\frac{1}{4} = \frac{9}{4}$	$1\frac{1}{8} = \frac{9}{8}$
$5\frac{1}{2} = \frac{11}{2}$	$1\frac{3}{8} = \frac{11}{8}$	$5\frac{1}{3} = \frac{16}{3}$	$3\frac{1}{4} = \frac{13}{4}$	$4\frac{1}{2} = \frac{9}{2}$
$1\frac{7}{8} = \frac{15}{8}$	$2\frac{2}{3} = \frac{8}{3}$	$1\frac{5}{8} = \frac{13}{8}$	$3\frac{3}{4} = \frac{15}{4}$	$7\frac{1}{2} = \frac{15}{2}$

Problem Solving Answer the question below.

Problem: The teacher asked for three volunteers. Adam, Blanca, Chad and Danielle raised their hands. How many different combinations of three students could the teacher select?

Understand

The teacher will select 3 students from 4 volunteers, I need to find how many combinations are possible.

Plan

Strategy: Use logical reasoning; Make an organized list.

Solve

Because there are only four students who volunteered, if just one student "sits out" there will be three volunteers for the teacher. There are four possible combinations of three students.

~~Adam~~	Adam	Adam	Adam
Blanca	~~Blanca~~	Blanca	Blanca
Chad	Chad	~~Chad~~	Chad
Danielle	Danielle	Danielle	~~Danielle~~

Check

Name ______________________ Time ____________

Power-Up Test 14

Math Course 1

Facts Write each improper fraction as a mixed number. Reduce fractions.

$\frac{5}{4} = 1\frac{1}{4}$	$\frac{6}{4} = 1\frac{1}{2}$	$\frac{15}{10} = 1\frac{1}{2}$	$\frac{8}{3} = 2\frac{2}{3}$	$\frac{15}{12} = 1\frac{1}{4}$
$\frac{12}{8} = 1\frac{1}{2}$	$\frac{10}{8} = 1\frac{1}{4}$	$\frac{3}{2} = 1\frac{1}{2}$	$\frac{15}{6} = 2\frac{1}{2}$	$\frac{10}{4} = 2\frac{1}{2}$
$\frac{8}{6} = 1\frac{1}{3}$	$\frac{25}{10} = 2\frac{1}{2}$	$\frac{9}{6} = 1\frac{1}{2}$	$\frac{10}{6} = 1\frac{2}{3}$	$\frac{15}{8} = 1\frac{7}{8}$
$\frac{12}{10} = 1\frac{1}{5}$	$\frac{10}{3} = 3\frac{1}{3}$	$\frac{18}{12} = 1\frac{1}{2}$	$\frac{5}{2} = 2\frac{1}{2}$	$\frac{4}{3} = 1\frac{1}{3}$

Problem Solving Answer the question below.

Problem: Two families have moved into a neighborhood. Each has a rectangular backyard garden, with a perimeter of 24 yards. However, one garden has an area that is 8 sq. yd more than the other. What are the areas of the two gardens?

Understand

I know there are two rectangular gardens with the same perimeter, 24 yd. But the area of one garden is 8 sq. yd. larger than the other. I need to calculate the areas of the two gardens.

Plan

Strategy: Make or Use a Table, Chart or Graph.

Make a table of addends that total 12 (half the perimeter) as lengths and widths of rectangles to compare the areas of possible rectangles. Find two pairs whose products differ by 8.

Solve

Length (yd)	Width (yd)	Area (sq. yd)
11	1	11
10	2	20
9	3	27
8	4	32
7	5	35
6	6	36

35 sq. yd − 27 sq. yd = 8 sq. yd

One garden is 9 yd × 3 yd, and the other garden is 7 yd × 5 yd.

Check

Name ______________________ Time ______________

Power-Up Test 15

Math Course 1

Facts Write each mixed number as an improper fraction.

$2\frac{1}{2} = \frac{5}{2}$	$2\frac{2}{5} = \frac{12}{5}$	$1\frac{3}{4} = \frac{7}{4}$	$2\frac{3}{4} = \frac{11}{4}$	$2\frac{1}{8} = \frac{17}{8}$
$1\frac{2}{3} = \frac{5}{3}$	$3\frac{1}{2} = \frac{7}{2}$	$1\frac{5}{6} = \frac{11}{6}$	$2\frac{1}{4} = \frac{9}{4}$	$1\frac{1}{8} = \frac{9}{8}$
$5\frac{1}{2} = \frac{11}{2}$	$1\frac{3}{8} = \frac{11}{8}$	$5\frac{1}{3} = \frac{16}{3}$	$3\frac{1}{4} = \frac{13}{4}$	$4\frac{1}{2} = \frac{9}{2}$
$1\frac{7}{8} = \frac{15}{8}$	$2\frac{2}{3} = \frac{8}{3}$	$1\frac{5}{8} = \frac{13}{8}$	$3\frac{3}{4} = \frac{15}{4}$	$7\frac{1}{2} = \frac{15}{2}$

Problem Solving Answer the question below.

Problem: In a typical newspaper, 4 pages are printed on one sheet of newsprint. If the last page of a section of a newspaper is page 24, how many sheets of newsprint are in that section of the newspaper?

Understand

4 pages are printed on 1 sheet of paper, creating a ratio 4:1. I need to know how many sheets of newsprint are in a 24-page section of a newspaper.

Plan

Strategy: Write a number sentence or equation,
Use the ratio of pages to newsprint to set up an equation.

Solve

Based on the ratio 4:1, a 24-page section of a newspaper is made up of $24 \div 4 = 6$ sheets of newsprint.

Check

Name ______________________ Time ____________

Power-Up Test 16

Math Course 1

Facts

Complete each equivalent measure.		Write a unit for each reference.
		Metric Units:
1. 1 cm = 10 mm	13. 10 cm = 100 mm	25. The thickness of a dime: millimeter
2. 1 m = 1000 mm	14. 2 m = 200 cm	
3. 1 m = 100 cm	15. 5 km = 5000 m	26. The width of a little finger: centimeter
4. 1 km = 1000 m	16. 2.5 cm = 25 mm	
5. 1 in. = 2.54 cm	17. 1.5 m = 150 cm	27. The length of one big step: meter
6. 1 mi ≈ 1610 m	18. 7.5 km = 7500 m	
		U.S. Customary Units:
7. 1 ft = 12 in.	19. $\frac{1}{2}$ ft = 6 in.	28. The width of two fingers: inch
8. 1 yd = 36 in.	20. 2 ft = 24 in.	
9. 1 yd = 3 ft	21. 3 ft = 36 in.	29. The length of a man's shoe: foot
10. 1 mi = 5280 ft	22. 2 yd = 6 ft	
11. 1 m ≈ 39 in.	23. 10 yd = 30 ft	30. The length of one big step: yard
12. 1 km ≈ 0.62 mi	24. 100 yd = 300 ft	

Problem Solving

Answer the question below.

Problem: In 1883, a cowboy in Tombstone, Arizona bought a horse for $80, sold it for $90, bought it back for $100, and sold it again for $110. How much money did the cowboy make overall?

Understand

A cowboy bought and sold a horse and made a profit, I need to find out how much money he made overall.

Plan

Strategy: Write a number sentence or equation.
Use the dollar amounts in the problem to set up a number sentence, then calculate the result.

Solve

–$80 + $90 – $100 + $110 = $20

or

The cowboy made $10 on the first buy-sell transaction and another $10 on the second buy-sell transaction.

Check

Name ____________ Time ____________

Power-Up Test 17

Math Course 1

Facts

Complete each equivalent measure.		Write a unit for each reference.
		Metric Units:
1. 1 cm = 10 mm	13. 10 cm = 100 mm	25. The thickness of a dime: millimeter
2. 1 m = 1000 mm	14. 2 m = 200 cm	
3. 1 m = 100 cm	15. 5 km = 5000 m	26. The width of a little finger: centimeter
4. 1 km = 1000 m	16. 2.5 cm = 25 mm	
5. 1 in. = 2.54 cm	17. 1.5 m = 150 cm	27. The length of one big step: meter
6. 1 mi ≈ 1610 m	18. 7.5 km = 7500 m	
		U.S. Customary Units:
7. 1 ft = 12 in.	19. $\frac{1}{2}$ ft = 6 in.	28. The width of two fingers: inch
8. 1 yd = 36 in.	20. 2 ft = 24 in.	
9. 1 yd = 3 ft	21. 3 ft = 36 in.	29. The length of a man's shoe: foot
10. 1 mi = 5280 ft	22. 2 yd = 6 ft	
11. 1 m ≈ 39 in.	23. 10 yd = 30 ft	30. The length of one big step: yard
12. 1 km ≈ 0.62 mi	24. 100 yd = 300 ft	

Problem Solving

Answer the question below.

Problem: When two people shake hands, there is just one handshake. If three people shake hands, there are three handshakes. If four people each shake hands with one another once, how many handshakes will take place?

Understand

Given relationships between the number handshakes between two and three people, determine how many handshakes will take place between four people.

Plan

Strategy: Use logical reasoning or make a diagram.
Count and sum the number of handshakes person by person to find the total.

Solve

Person A will shake the hands of people B, C, and D. Person B will still need to shake the hands of people C and D. Person C will still need to shake the hand of Person D, who will have now already shaken the hands of people A, B, and C. 3 + 2 + 1 = 6 handshakes.

or

2 people—1 shake 3 people—3 shakes 4 people—6 shakes

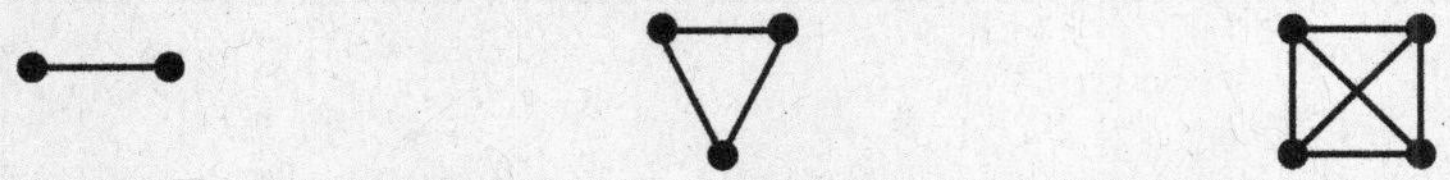

Check

Name ____________________ Time __________

Power-Up Test 18

Math Course 1

Facts

Write the abbreviation.	Complete each equivalence.	Complete each conversion.
Metric Units:	Metric Units:	14. 2 liters = 2000 milliliters
1. liter L	7. 1 liter = 1000 milliliters	15. 2 liters ≈ 2 quarts
2. milliliter mL	U.S. Customary Units:	16. 3.78 liters = 3780 milliliters
U.S. Customary Units:	8. 1 cup = 8 ounces	17. 0.5 liter = 500 milliliters
3. ounces oz	9. 1 pint = 16 ounces	18. $\frac{1}{2}$ gallon = 2 quarts
4. pint pt	10. 1 pint = 2 cups	19. 2 gallons = 8 quarts
5. quart qt	11. 1 quart = 2 pints	20. 2 half gallons = 1 gallon
6. gallon gal	12. 1 gallon = 4 quarts	21. 8 cups = 2 quarts
	Between Systems:	
	13. 1 liter ≈ 1 quart	22–23. A two-liter bottle is a little more than 2 quarts or $\frac{1}{2}$ gallon.

Problem Solving

Answer the question below.

Problem: Matthew and Mark bought several kinds of flowers for their mother on Mother's Day. 20% were carnations, 5% were roses, half were daisies, one-tenth were lilies and 15 were sunflowers. How many daisies did they buy?

Understand

The kinds of flowers in a bouquet are represented by their percents or fractions of the total number in the bouquet. I need to find how many daisies were in the bouquet.

Plan

Strategy: Write a number sentence or equation.

Convert known fractions to percents. Add the known percents to find the percent remaining. Use that percent and the known number of sunflowers to calculate the total number of flowers in the bouquet. Half of this number represents the number of daisies.

Solve

$\frac{1}{2}$ = 50%, $\frac{1}{10}$ = 10%. 20% + 5% + 50% + 10% = 85% of the bouquet;
100% − 85% = 15%. So the 15 sunflowers represent 15% of the bouquet. This means there were 100 flowers in the bouquet. Matthew and Mark bought 50 daisies.

Check

Name ______________________ Time ____________

Power-Up Test 19

Math Course 1

Facts

Write the abbreviation.	Complete each equivalence.	Complete each conversion.
Metric Units:	Metric Units:	14. 2 liters = 2000 milliliters
1. liter L	7. 1 liter = 1000 milliliters	15. 2 liters ≈ 2 quarts
2. milliliter mL	U.S. Customary Units:	16. 3.78 liters = 3780 milliliters
U.S. Customary Units:	8. 1 cup = 8 ounces	17. 0.5 liter = 500 milliliters
3. ounces oz	9. 1 pint = 16 ounces	18. $\frac{1}{2}$ gallon = 2 quarts
4. pint pt	10. 1 pint = 2 cups	19. 2 gallons = 8 quarts
5. quart qt	11. 1 quart = 2 pints	20. 2 half gallons = 1 gallon
6. gallon gal	12. 1 gallon = 4 quarts	21. 8 cups = 2 quarts
	Between Systems:	
	13. 1 liter ≈ 1 quart	22–23. A two-liter bottle is a little more than 2 quarts or $\frac{1}{2}$ gallon.

Problem Solving

Answer the question below.

Problem: A pentagon is formed from a 6-cm square of paper folded along the dashed lines. What is the area of the pentagon?

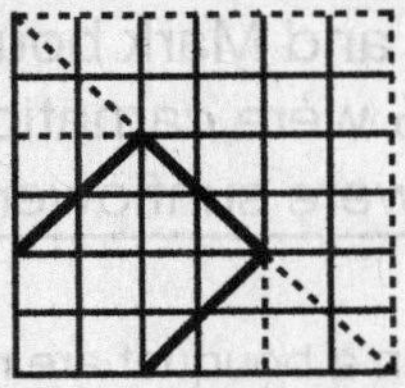

Understand

A new shape is created by removing two triangular areas from a larger triangle. I need to calculate the area of the new shape based on the dimensions of the original triangle.

Plan

Strategy: Write a number sentence or equation.
Use the given measurements to calculate the area of the triangle and subtract from it the areas of the smaller triangles.

Solve

The area of the original triangle was $\frac{1}{2}(6 \times 6) = 18$ sq. cm. By folding the corners over we have eliminated 4 sq. cm from each corner. $18 - 2(4) = 10$ sq. cm, which is the area of the patterned section that remains visible.

Check

Name ____________________ Time ______________

Power-Up Test 20

Math Course 1

Facts Write each percent as a reduced fraction and decimal number.

Percent	Fraction	Decimal	Percent	Fraction	Decimal
5%	$\frac{1}{20}$	0.05	10%	$\frac{1}{10}$	0.1
20%	$\frac{1}{5}$	0.2	30%	$\frac{3}{10}$	0.3
25%	$\frac{1}{4}$	0.25	50%	$\frac{1}{2}$	0.5
1%	$\frac{1}{100}$	0.01	$12\frac{1}{2}\%$	$\frac{1}{8}$	0.125
90%	$\frac{9}{10}$	0.9	$33\frac{1}{3}\%$	$\frac{1}{3}$	Rounds to 0.333
75%	$\frac{3}{4}$	0.75	$66\frac{2}{3}\%$	$\frac{2}{3}$	Rounds to 0.667

Problem Solving Answer the question below.

Problem: A ball is dropped from a height of 32 meters and bounces back $\frac{1}{2}$ of the height. The ball continues to bounce back $\frac{1}{2}$ the height until it stops bouncing after making a bounce that is less than 3 cm high. How many times does the ball bounce?

Understand

Starting at 32 meters, the height that a ball bounces continually decreases until the ball stops bouncing. I need to determine how many times the ball bounces before it stops.

Plan

Strategy: Make or use a table, chart or graph.

Create a chart or list that shows the height of each bounce. Find the bounce (term in a sequence) that equals $<$ 3 cm.

Solve

Height:	32 m	16 m	8 m	4 m	2 m	1 m	50 cm	25 cm	12.5 cm	6.25 cm	3.125 cm	1.5 cm
Bounces:	0	1	2	3	4	5	6	7	8	9	10	11

The ball will bounce *less than* 3 cm on the eleventh bounce.

Check

Name ____________________ Time __________

Power-Up Test 21

Math Course 1

Facts Write each percent as a reduced fraction and decimal number.

Percent	Fraction	Decimal	Percent	Fraction	Decimal
5%	$\frac{1}{20}$	0.05	10%	$\frac{1}{10}$	0.1
20%	$\frac{1}{5}$	0.2	30%	$\frac{3}{10}$	0.3
25%	$\frac{1}{4}$	0.25	50%	$\frac{1}{2}$	0.5
1%	$\frac{1}{100}$	0.01	$12\frac{1}{2}\%$	$\frac{1}{8}$	0.125
90%	$\frac{9}{10}$	0.9	$33\frac{1}{3}\%$	$\frac{1}{3}$	Rounds to 0.333
75%	$\frac{3}{4}$	0.75	$66\frac{2}{3}\%$	$\frac{2}{3}$	Rounds to 0.667

Problem Solving Answer the question below.

Problem: Carpeting is sold by the square yard. If carpet is priced at $25 per square yard (including tax and installation), how much would it cost to carpet this office that is currently tiled with 1 square foot tiles?

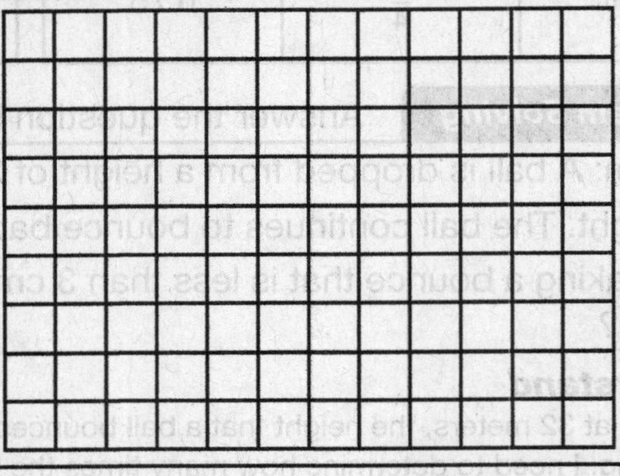

Understand

Given a rectangular shape, I need to find the area to calculate the cost of carpet based on $25 per square yard.

Plan

Strategy: Write a number sentence or equation.

Count the number of tiles in the length and width of the office to calculate the area. Convert the area to square yards. Use the result to find the cost to carpet the office.

Solve

The office is 12 feet long and 9 feet wide. These measurements can be converted to a length of 4 yards (12 ft = 4 yd) and a width of 3 yards (9 ft = 3 yd). 4 yd × 3 yd = 12 square yards.

12 sq. yd × $25 = $300.

Check

Facts Write each percent as a reduced fraction and decimal number.

Percent	Fraction	Decimal	Percent	Fraction	Decimal
5%	$\frac{1}{20}$	0.05	10%	$\frac{1}{10}$	0.1
20%	$\frac{1}{5}$	0.2	30%	$\frac{3}{10}$	0.3
25%	$\frac{1}{4}$	0.25	50%	$\frac{1}{2}$	0.5
1%	$\frac{1}{100}$	0.01	$12\frac{1}{2}$%	$\frac{1}{8}$	0.125
90%	$\frac{9}{10}$	0.9	$33\frac{1}{3}$%	$\frac{1}{3}$	Rounds to 0.333
75%	$\frac{3}{4}$	0.75	$66\frac{2}{3}$%	$\frac{2}{3}$	Rounds to 0.667

Problem Solving Answer the question below.

Problem: Dana and Liz are in a chess tournament. There are two ways to win the match: (1) win two games in a row, or (2) win a total of three games. What are the possible outcomes of play that would determine a winner?

Understand

To win a chess match, a player has to win 2 games in a row or any 3 games. I need to find the combinations of possible outcomes than allow a player to win.

Plan

Strategy: Make an organized list.
List possible combinations of wins in a row and totals of 3 wins.

Solve

The list of possible outcomes can be organized by the total number of games it would be possible to play to determine a winner:

Two games:	DD or LL
Three games:	DLL or LDD
Four games:	DLDD or LDLL
Five games:	DLDLD, DLDLL, LDLDL, or LDLDD

Check

Name ______________ Time ____________

Power-Up Test 23

Math Course 1

Facts Complete each equivalence.

1. Draw a segment about 1 cm long.
2. Draw a segment about 1 inch long.
3. One inch is how many centimeters? 2.54
4. Which is longer, 1 km or 1 mi? 1 mi
5. Which is longer, 1 km or $\frac{1}{2}$ mi? 1 km
6. How many ounces are in a pound? 16
7. How many pounds are in a ton? 2000
8. A dollar bill has a mass of about one gram.
9. A pair of shoes has a mass of about one kilogram.
10. On Earth a kilogram mass weighs about 2.2 pounds.
11. A metric ton is 1000 kilograms.
12. On Earth a metric ton weighs about 2200 pounds.
13. The Earth rotates on its axis once a day.
14. The Earth revolves around the Sun once in a year.

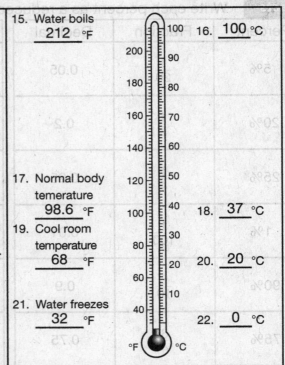

15. Water boils 212 °F
16. 100 °C

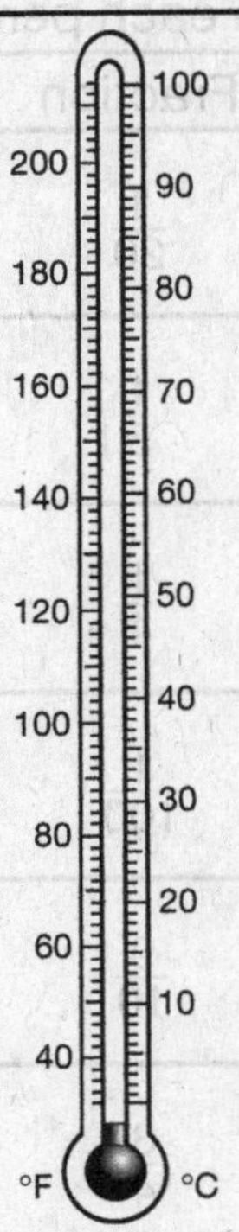

17. Normal body temerature 98.6 °F
18. 37 °C
19. Cool room temperature 68 °F
20. 20 °C
21. Water freezes 32 °F
22. 0 °C

Problem Solving Answer the question below.

Problem: Analyze the following two graphs, and describe the progress of the two academic teams. Do the graphs misrepresent the data?

Math Club Team A

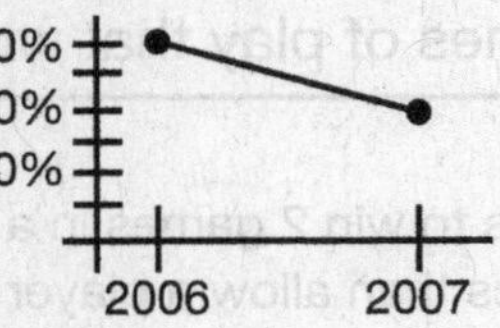

Slight Decrease in Scores

Math Club Team B

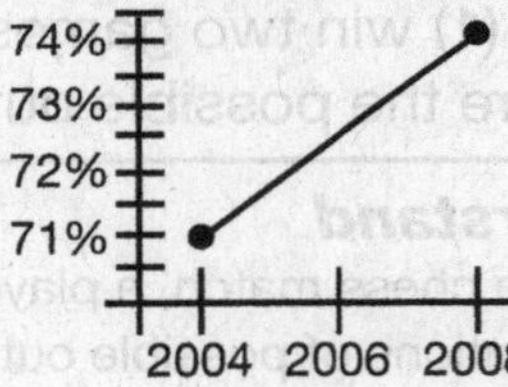

Large Increase in Scores

Understand

Data in two graphs describes the progress of two teams. I need to analyze the graphs to describe each teams' progress and to determine if the graphs misrepresent the data.

Plan

Strategy: Use logical reasoning.

Read the graphs to determine whether the graph represent the data accurately.

Solve

Team A's decrease of about 30 percentile points over one year is not a slight decrease. The graph misrepresents the data by extending the values on the *x*-axis (years) and condensing the values on the *y*-axis (percents). Team B's increase of about 3 percentile points over 4 years is not large. The graph misrepresents the data by condensing the values on the *x*-axis (years), and extending the values on the *y*-axis (percents).

Check

Performance Task 1

1. **Average Measured Height of Sample Grass 1**

Week (W)	**5**	**6**	**7**
Height (h)	11 cm	13 cm	15 cm

a. *New Height = Old Height* + 2 cm

c. *Answers will vary. Sample:* The grass grows quickly the first week, but then grows the same amount each week during weeks 2–4.

d. *Answers will vary. Sample:* the grass may be using food stored in the seeds during the first week of growth.

2. a. **Average Measured Height of Sample Grass 2**

Week (W)	**5**	**6**	**7**
Height (h)	75 mm	90 mm	105 mm

b. *New Height = Old Height* + 15 mm

c. addition sequence

d. Sample: 15 × (*Week Number*) = *Height*

3. *Answers will vary. Sample:* The grass in Exercise 1 grows 2 cm each week. The grass in Exercise 2 grows 15 mm each week. I know that 2 cm is the same as 20 mm. So the grass in Exercise 1 grows about 5 mm more each week than the grass in Exercise 2.

4. a. **Pounds of Grass Seed Needed to Grow New Grass**

	Area in Square Feet
Grass	**5000**
Zoysia	$7\frac{1}{2}$
Rye grass	45
Kentucky bluegrass	15
Bermuda grass	10

b. 24 lbs

Performance Activity 2

1. Sample: 3 + (2 × 6) = 15; (3 + 2) × 6 = 30; Therefore, $x + (y \times z)$ will not always have the same answer as $(x + y) \times z$.

2. Sample: 9 × 2 = 18; if you multiply any odd number between 0 and 10 by 2 the result is an even number. It follows that any odd number greater than 10 multiplied by 2 is also an even number.

3. Sample: If $n = 8$, then $2n = 16$ and 16 is a number in the sequence. Therefore, if n is a number in the sequence 2, 4, 6, 8, 10, 12, . . ., the expression $2n$ will always give a number in the sequence when n is a positive whole number.

4. Sample: 2 + 5 > 3 but 2 is not greater than 3. Therefore, if $a + b > c$, then a is not always greater than c.

5. Sample: "If $a > b$ and $b > c$, then $a > c$"; 9 > 7, 7 > 3, and 9 > 3; −4 > −6, −6 > −8, and −4 > −8

Performance Task 3

1. **Land Areas of *The Four Corner States***

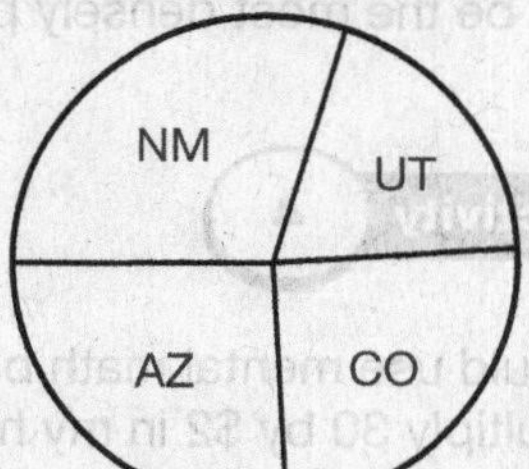

Land Areas of *The Four Corner States*

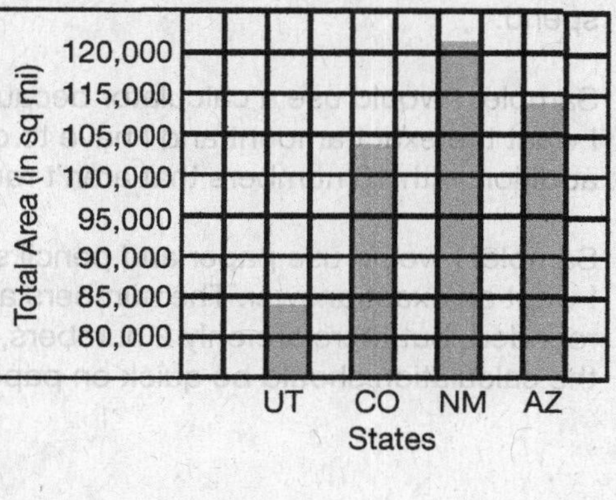

Solutions

2. Sample: The bar graph makes it easy to compare the areas of the states and to quickly read area measurements. The circle graph shows each state's area compared to the total area better; the circle graph could display the percent (value) of each state's area relative to the total.

3. Sample: Because the number of visitors to the Grand Canyon in Arizona is so much greater than the number of visitors to the other states' parks, it would be difficult to find a scale on a bar graph that wouldn't distort the data. The number of visitors to parks in Colorado and New Mexico might appear to be identical.

4. Sample: Mt. Elbert in Colorado has the highest point at approximately 14,000 ft. In fact, the highest elevation points of *The Four Corners States* are closer in measurement—all between 12,000 and 14,000 ft.—than the states' lowest points. The lowest point among the states is in Arizona, at 70 ft, while the lowest points in Utah, Colorado, and New Mexico are all between 2000 and 3000 ft.

5. Sample: Some students may realize they can divide the population by the area to find population density. Other students may indicate that the areas of all the states are close in size. The population of Arizona is much larger than the other states. Therefore, Arizona must be the most densely populated state.

Performance Activity 4

1. Sample: I would use mental math because I can easily multiply 30 by $2 in my head.

2. Sample: I would use estimation since I only need to find out about how much I would spend.

3. Sample: I would use a calculator because I want the exact amount and I have to do addition with 10 numbers that aren't rounded.

4. Sample: I would use paper and pencil since I want an exact answer. The numbers aren't rounded, but there are only 2 numbers, so the calculation should be quick on paper.

Performance Task 5

1. Sample: I chose a desk. I thought about how long a foot was and then I marked off feet along the edge of the desk. I did this four times, so I thought it was about 4 feet long.

2. Sample: $3\frac{1}{2}$ feet

3. Sample: Yes. $3\frac{1}{2}$ feet is close to 4 feet.

4. Sample: Yes. I would find an object like a book that I think is about 1 foot long and then see how many times I can fit it across the length.

5. Sample answers in table below.

Object	Estimate	Actual
Height of a window	40 inches	36 inches
Width of door	40 inches	36 inches
Length of your desk	20 inches	24 inches

6. Sample: I chose a waste-paper basket. I think it is about 60 centimeters around the rim.

7. Sample: 89 centimeters

8. Sample: No. 60 centimeters and 89 centimeters are not very close.

9. Sample: I remember from last year that the distance around a circle is about 3 times the distance across. I would estimate the distance across and then multiply by 3.

10. Sample answers in table below.

Object	Estimate	Actual
Length of your arm	50 centimeters	47 centimeters
Heigth of a table	70 centimeters	65 centimeters
Length of your desk	35 centimeters	40 centimeters

Performance Activity 6

1. Sample: 1001 − 1; Check students' work.

2. Sample: One way I represented 1000 is with the expression 1001 − 1. I could keep changing that one expression indefinitely to get 1000. For example, 1002 − 2 and 1003 − 3. There are an infinite number of ways I could represent 1000 just using the operation of subtraction.

Performance Task 7

1. $5\frac{3}{4}$ pounds

2. $1\frac{1}{3}$ pounds

3. 6.3 pounds

4. 22.7 pounds

5. $7.20; Sample: The phrase "per pound" told me I needed to multiply the cost by the weight. I multiplied 2.4 by 3, keeping the decimal in place so my answer was 7.2. Expressed as money, that's $7.20.

6.

Item	Amount sold
Apples	$6\frac{3}{4}$ pounds
Oranges	$5\frac{1}{12}$ pounds
Grapes	12.6 pounds
Bananas	3.7 pounds

7. $\frac{25}{100}$ or $\frac{1}{4}$

8. $\frac{60}{100}$ or $\frac{3}{5}$

9. a. $\frac{12}{48}$ or $\frac{1}{4}$

   b. $\frac{12}{60}$ or $\frac{1}{5}$; Sample: I added 12 and 48 to find the total number of jars of olives was 60. The number of small jars of olives is 12 so the ratio of small jars of olives to total jars of olives is $\frac{12}{60}$ or $\frac{1}{5}$.

Performance Activity 8

Sample representations are drawn on the diagrams below:

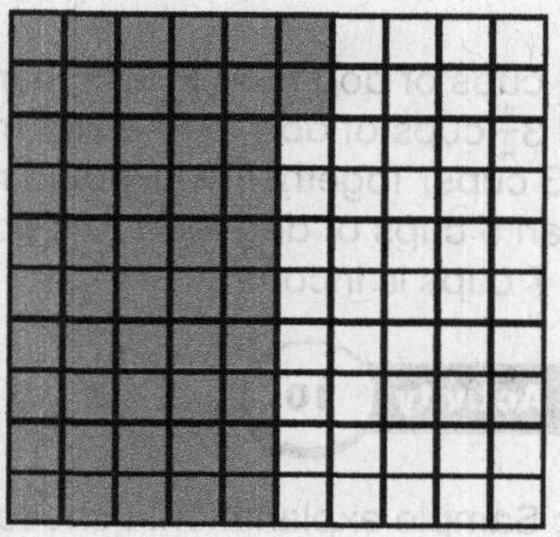

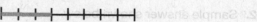

1. Sample: I would use Diagram 3 for Statement 1 because a line divided into eighths is a good way to represent a linear measure, like a mile, divided into eighths. I would use Diagram 1 for Statement 2 because the model is divided into 100 equal parts, and the statement involves percent. I would use Diagram 2 for Statement 3 because the 8 circles can represent 8 individual people and I can shade three of the circles to show 3 out of 8.

2. Sample: 48% of the bike riders were not women.

3. Sample: Diagram 2; 5 out of 8 people in the bike race have been in more than one race.

Performance Task 9

1. **Zelda's Weight Chart**

Age	Weight Gain from Previous Month
2 months	$3\frac{3}{4}$ pounds
3 months	$3\frac{3}{4}$ pounds
4 months	$3\frac{1}{2}$ pounds
5 months	$3\frac{1}{2}$ pounds
6 months	$3\frac{1}{2}$ pounds

2. Sunshine and Pine Tree; Pine Tree and Rocky; Pine Tree and Sea View.

3. $5\frac{3}{8}$ cups

4. $5\frac{1}{6}$ cups

5. Sample: $1\frac{2}{3}$ cups of dog food is less than 2 cups and $3\frac{1}{4}$ cups of dog food is not much more than 3 cups. Together, you would need no more than 5 cups of dog food to feed both dogs. 7 cups is incorrect.

Performance Activity 10

1. Line graph; Sample explanation: I chose a line graph because line graphs work well for showing change over time.

2. Sample answer shown below.

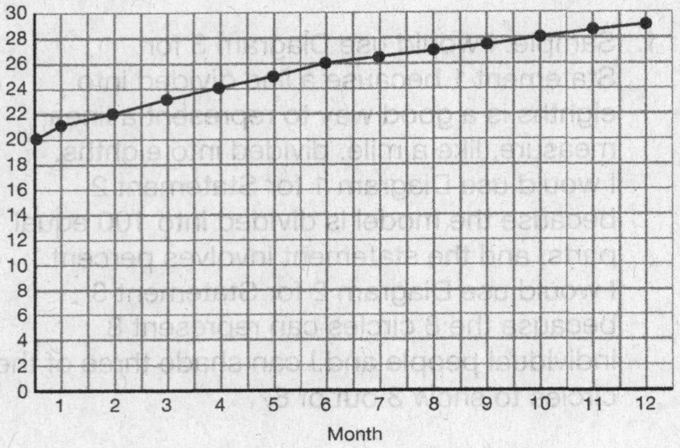

3. Sample: The growth in the length of a baby slows down in the second half of the first year of life.

Performance Task 11

1. a. Mean

   b. Mean = 4 points

2. a. Median

   b. Sample: Arrange the players from shortest to tallest. The median is the height halfway between the sixth- and seventh-tallest players' heights. The six players whose heights are less than the median are on Squad B. The six players whose heights are greater than the median are on Squad A.

   c. Median = 5 ft $8\frac{1}{2}$ in.

   d. Range = 6 inches

3. a. Mode

   b. Mode = 8.5

4. a. Mean = 5

   b. Range = 7

Performance Activity 12

1. Check students' work. The folded paper should have 10 approximately equal sections and each section should be labeled with $\frac{1}{10}$, 0.10 and 10%.

2. Sample: I divided 11 in. by 10 to get 1.1 inches (a little less than $1\frac{1}{8}$ in.) per section or about 28 cm ÷ 10 = 2.8 cm per section. I made folds at each of those marks.

3. Sample: I can fold the paper up so I just see one section. When I do that I can see that all of the sections are the same.

4. 100%

5. 50%

6. $\frac{1}{10}$

7. $\frac{3}{10}$

Performance Task 13

1. 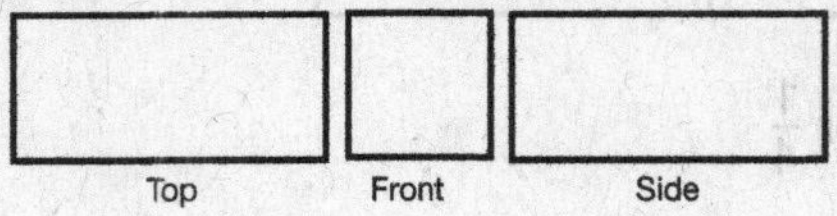

2. 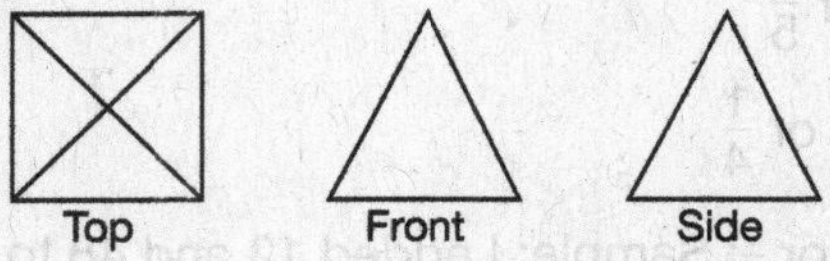

3. Sample: Each has a rectangle as a base.

4. Sample: The right prism has parallel sides and the sides don't come to a point (vertex). The square pyramid does not have parallel sides and the sides come to a point (vertex).

5.

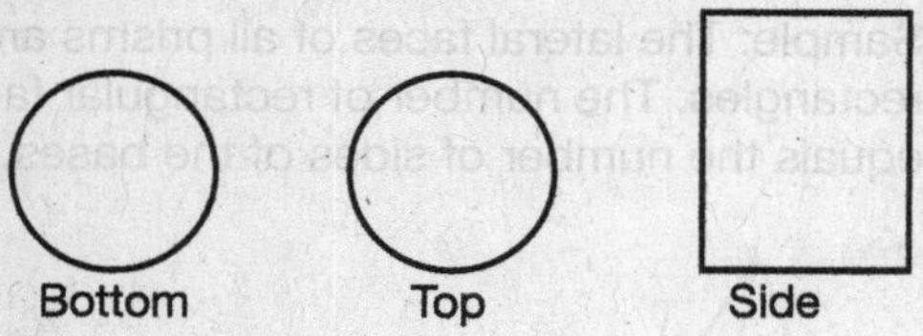

6.

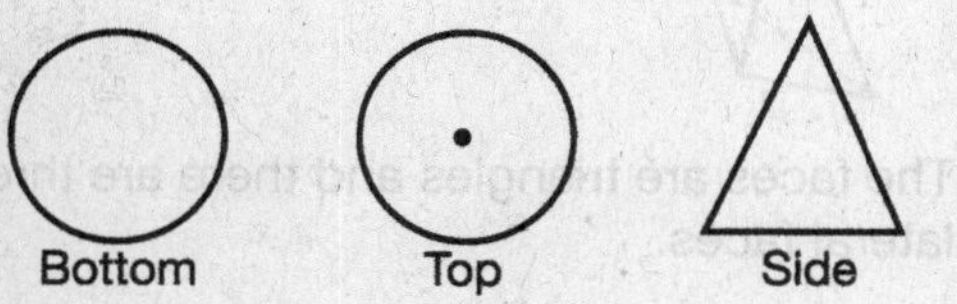

7. Sample: Each has a circle as a base.

8. Sample: The cone comes to a point (vertex) and the cylinder does not.

Performance Activity 14

1. Sample: The formula for the circumference of a circle is πd. If you double the diameter of that circle the circumference is $\pi 2d$. For example, a circle with a diameter of 3 in. has a circumference of 9.42 in. and a circle with a diameter of 6 in. has a circumference of 18.84 in., which is double 9.42 in.

2. Sample: If you have a 1 in. by 2 in. rectangle, its area is 2 square inches. If you triple the sides of that rectangle, you have a 3 in. by 6 in. rectangle. The area of the new rectangle is 18 square inches. The new rectangle is 9 times the area of the original rectangle. So if you triple both the length and width of a rectangle, you multiply its area by 9. ($lw = A$, $3l \cdot 3w = 9A$)

3. Sample: The faces of all cubes are squares. All squares are rectangles. Therefore, the faces of all cubes are rectangles and a cube is a rectangular prism. For example, a cube with 4 in. square faces is a rectangular prism.

4. Sample: All of the faces are congruent. For cubes, all of the faces are squares with the same dimensions so all the faces are congruent. For example, if one face of a cube is a 3 in. square all of the faces are 3 in. squares. For rectangular prisms that are not cubes, at least two faces will not be congruent to the other four faces. For example, in a rectangular prism with four 3 in. by 2 in. faces and two 3 in. by 3 in. faces, the 3 in. by 2 in. faces are not congruent to the 3 in. by 3 in. faces.

Performance Task 15

1.

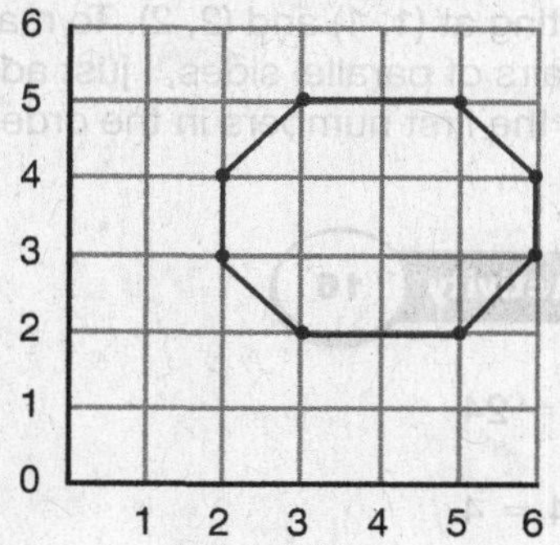

octagon

2.

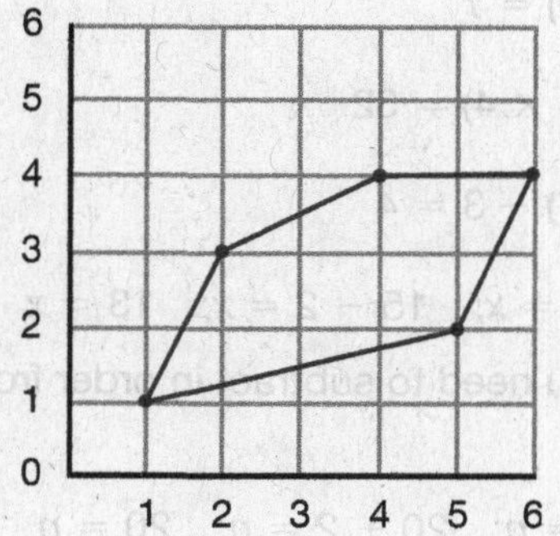

pentagon

3.

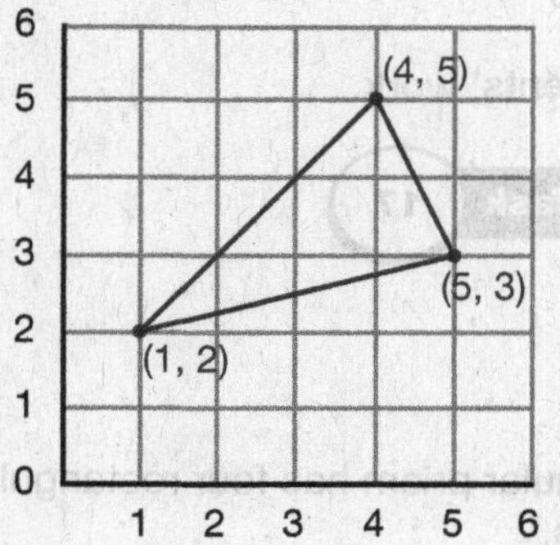

4.

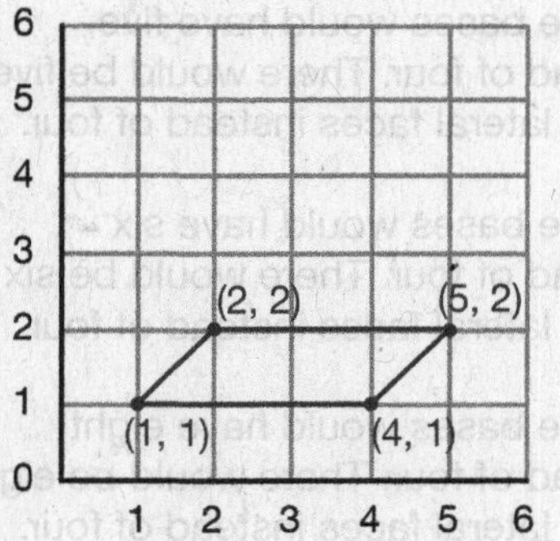

Solutions

Sample: I know the figure I drew is a parallelogram because I drew two sides parallel to the horizontal axis on the lines of the grid starting at (1, 1) and (2, 2). To make sure I had pairs of parallel sides, I just added 3 to each of the first numbers in the ordered pair.

Performance Activity 16

1. $6 \times (3 + 1) = 24$
2. $(13 + 3) \div 4 = 4$
3. $(4 + 6) \times 2 = 20$
4. $5 + (18 \div 9) = 7$
5. $(4 \times 3) + (5 \times 4) = 32$
6. $5 + (14 \div 7) - 3 = 4$

1. $20 - 5 - 2 = x;\quad 15 - 2 = x;\quad 13 = x$

   Sample: You need to subtract in order from left to right.

2. $5 \times 4 + 2 = n;\quad 20 + 2 = n;\quad 20 = n$

   You need to use the order of operations and multiply 5 by 4 first and then add 2.

3. Check students' work.

Performance Task 17

1. 

   The rectangular prism has four rectangular lateral faces.

2. Sample: The bases would have five sides instead of four. There would be five rectangular lateral faces instead of four.
3. Sample: The bases would have six sides instead of four. There would be six rectangular lateral faces instead of four.
4. Sample: The bases would have eight sides instead of four. There would be eight rectangular lateral faces instead of four.
5. Sample: The lateral faces of all prisms are rectangles. The number of rectangular faces equals the number of sides of the bases.
6. 

   The faces are triangles and there are three lateral faces.

7. Sample: The base would have four sides instead of three. There would be four triangular faces instead of three.

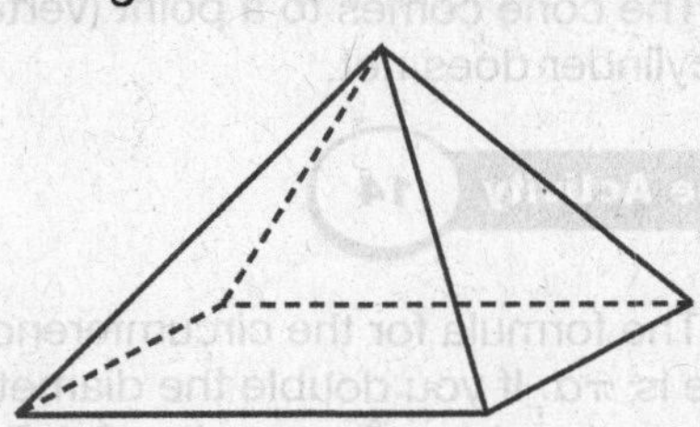

8. Sample: The base would have six sides instead of three. There would be six triangular faces instead of three.
9. Sample: Pyramids have one base that is a polygon. The lateral faces are always triangles. The number of lateral faces equals the number of sides of the base.

Performance Activity 18

1. $6s = P$
2. regular hexagon
3. $s^2 = A$
4. square
5. $e^3 = V$
6. cube

Performance Task 19

1. Check students work.

2. Sample: You multiply the length by the width to find the area of a rectangle. There are 6 rectangles that make up the surface area of a rectangular prism. Two of them have area *lw*, two of them have areas *lh*, and two of them have area *wh*.

3.

Figure	Surface Area	Volume
Rectangular Prism	about $77\frac{1}{2}$ cm^2	about $43\frac{3}{4}$ cm^3
Pyramid	about 48 cm^2	about $21\frac{1}{3}$ cm^3
Cylinder	about 40 cm^2	about $18\frac{3}{4}$ cm^3
Cone	about 33.75 cm^2 or $33\frac{3}{4}$ cm^2	about $13\frac{1}{2}$ cm^3

Performance Activity 20

1. $\frac{2}{50} = \frac{x}{300}$ 12 packets

2. $\frac{30}{100} = \frac{x}{50}$ 15 square yards

3. $y = 1.50x$; $10.50

4. Sample: $\frac{3}{12} = \frac{6}{x}$; 6 packets should cost $24, so the clerk's calculation is incorrect; $\frac{3}{12} = \frac{1}{4}$ or $\frac{2}{8} = \frac{1}{4}$, so the rates are equal ($4 per packet).

Performance Task 21

1. 4 lines of symmetry, *HD*, *BF*, *CG* and *AE*: 90° rotational symmetry

2. 2 lines of symmetry, *CG* and *AE*: 180° rotational symmetry

3. Sample:

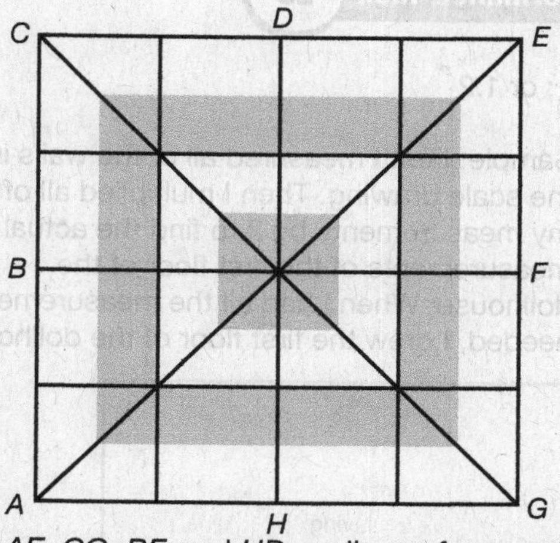

AE, *CG*, *BF*, and *HD* are lines of symmetry.

Sample:

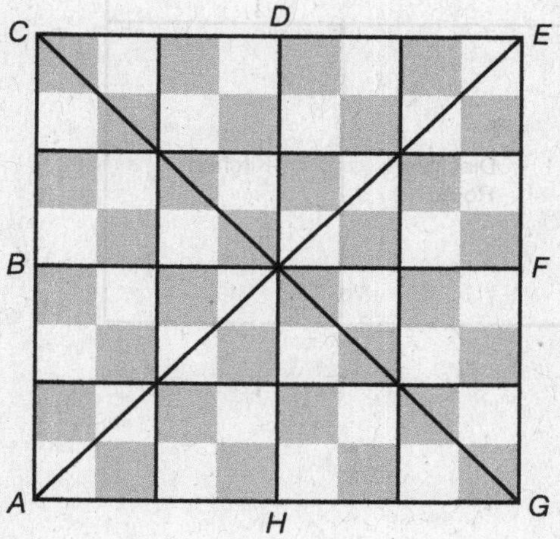

AE and *CG* are lines of symmetry.

5. Sample: If I fold across the lines of symmetry, everything in the design matches. There are only two lines with which I can do this. If I rotate the design one half turn it looks exactly the same as before I turned it.

Performance Activity 22

1. $\frac{5}{15} = \frac{4}{y}$; $y = 12$ inches
   $\frac{5}{15} = \frac{3}{x}$; $x = 9$ inches

2. $\frac{3}{6} = \frac{2}{x}$; $x = 4$ inches

3. Sample: Yes. The ratio of the length to the width of any square can be reduced to 1:1.

Solutions

Performance Task 23

2. $\frac{1}{2}$; or 1:2

3. Sample: First I measured all of the walls in the scale drawing. Then I multiplied all of my measurements by 2 to find the actual measurements of the first floor of the dollhouse. When I had all the measurements I needed, I drew the first floor of the dollhouse.

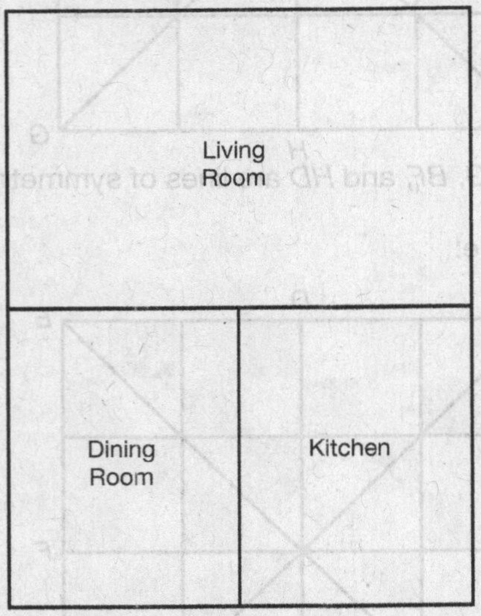

Benchmark Test 1

1. $4\overline{)28}$ = 7; 28; 0

D. 7 inches

2. $28 - 12 = 16$ girls

$\frac{\text{boys}}{\text{girls}} = \frac{12}{16} = \frac{3}{4}$

C. $\frac{3}{4}$

3. $\frac{117}{29} \approx \frac{120}{30}$

A. $\frac{120}{30}$

4. $360 \div 4 = 90$

$360 \div 5 = 72$

$360 \div 6 = 60$

$360 \div 7 = 51\frac{3}{7}$

D. 7

5. $\frac{38 + 42 + 41}{3} = \frac{121}{3} = 40\frac{1}{3}$

C. between 38 yd and 42 yd

6. Factors of 24: 1, 2, 3, 4, 6, 8, 12, 24

C. 10

7. Factors of 24: 1, 2, 3, 4, **6,** 8, 12, 24

Factors of 18: 1, 2, 3, **6,** 9, 18

B. 6

8. **D. diameter**

9. $\frac{5}{\cancel{6}_1} \times \frac{\cancel{12}^2}{1} = 10$

D. 10

10. $\left(\frac{2}{7} + \frac{3}{7}\right) - \frac{1}{7} = \frac{5}{7} - \frac{1}{7} = \frac{4}{7}$

B. $\frac{4}{7}$

11. $1 - \frac{1}{8} = \frac{8}{8} - \frac{1}{8} = \frac{7}{8}$

C. $\frac{7}{8}$

12. $\frac{1}{2} \times \frac{3}{4} = \frac{3}{8}$

D. $\frac{3}{8}$

13. $\frac{2}{3} + \frac{2}{3} = \frac{4}{3} = 1\frac{1}{3}$

C. $1\frac{1}{3}$

14. $3\frac{1}{4} + 2\frac{3}{4} = 5\frac{4}{4} = 6$

D. 6

15. $\frac{7}{8} - \frac{1}{8} = \frac{6}{8} = \frac{3}{4}$

C. $\frac{3}{4}$

16. Multiples of 6: 6, 12, **18,** 24, 30, 36...

Multiples of 9: 9, **18,** 27, 36, 45, 54...

C. 18

17. 64 cm ÷ 4 = 16 cm

C. 16 cm

18. $\frac{3}{4} \times \frac{4}{3} = 1$

C. $\frac{4}{3}$

19. 8, 16, 24, 32, 40, 48, 56, <u>64</u>,...

These are the multiples of 8.

D. 64

20. **C. obtuse**

21. $4w = 320$

$w = \frac{320}{4} = 80$

C. 80

22. $\frac{1}{4} = 25\%$

B. 25%

23. $\frac{3}{6} \div \frac{3}{3} = \frac{1}{2}$

$\frac{4}{8} \div \frac{4}{4} = \frac{1}{2}$

$\frac{50}{100} \div \frac{50}{50} = \frac{1}{2}$

$\frac{7}{12} \neq \frac{1}{2}$

D. $\frac{7}{12}$

24. $\frac{6}{15} \div \frac{3}{3} = \frac{2}{5}$

B. $\frac{2}{5}$

25. Maricruz $= \frac{2}{5} = 0.4$

Ting $= \frac{3}{8} = 0.375$

Molly $= \frac{1}{2} = 0.5$

Jasmine $= \frac{2}{3} = 0.66...$

D. Jasmine

Benchmark Test 2

1. Numbers > 2 = 3, 4, 5, 6 (4 possibilities)

$P(>2) = \frac{4}{6} = \frac{2}{3}$

D. $\frac{2}{3}$

2. 6 × 6 in. = 36 in.

C. 36 inches

3. $12 \text{ cm} \times 8 \text{ cm} = 96 \text{ cm}^2$

D. 96 cm^2

4. C. 5

5.
$$\begin{array}{r} 2.00 \\ 3.40 \\ +\ 0.56 \\ \hline 5.96 \end{array}$$
A. 5.96

6.
$$\begin{array}{r} \overset{0}{\cancel{1}}.\overset{9}{\cancel{0}}\overset{10}{\cancel{0}} \\ -\ 0.24 \\ \hline 0.76 \end{array}$$
C. 0.76

7.
$$\begin{array}{r} 0.16 \\ \times\ 0.4 \\ \hline 0.064 \end{array}$$
D. 0.064

8. $C = \pi d$

$C = (3.14)\ (20 \text{ in.})$

$C = 62.8 \text{ in.} \approx 5 \text{ feet}$

C. 5 ft

9. B. 9

10. 18 − 12 = 6 lost

$\frac{\text{won}}{\text{lost}} = \frac{12}{6} = \frac{2}{1}$

A. $\frac{2}{1}$

11.
$$\begin{array}{r} 6 = 5\frac{4}{4} \\ -\ 3\frac{3}{4} = 3\frac{3}{4} \\ \hline 2\frac{1}{4} \end{array}$$
B. $2\frac{1}{4}$

12.
$$\begin{array}{r} 0.24 \\ 5\overline{)1.20} \\ 1\,0 \\ \hline 20 \\ 20 \\ \hline 0 \end{array}$$
C. 0.24 pounds

13.
$$\begin{array}{r} 20 \\ 6\overline{)120} \\ 12 \\ \hline 00 \\ 00 \\ \hline 0 \end{array}$$
B. 20

14. 1 gal ≈ 3.78 liters

10 gal ≈ 37.8 liters

C. 37.8 liters

15.
$$\begin{array}{r} \frac{1}{2} = \frac{5}{10} \\ +\ \frac{4}{5} = \frac{8}{10} \\ \hline \frac{13}{10} = 1\frac{3}{10} \end{array}$$
C. $1\frac{3}{10}$

16.
$$\begin{array}{r} \frac{2}{5} = \frac{6}{15} \\ -\ \frac{1}{3} = \frac{5}{15} \\ \hline \frac{1}{15} \end{array}$$
D. $\frac{1}{15}$

17. D. $\frac{1}{6}, \frac{1}{2}, \frac{2}{3}$

18.
$$\begin{array}{r} 3\frac{3}{4} = 3\frac{3}{4} \\ +\ 2\frac{1}{2} = 2\frac{2}{4} \\ \hline 5\frac{5}{4} = 6\frac{1}{4} \end{array}$$
B. $6\frac{1}{4}$

19.
$$\begin{array}{r} 6\frac{1}{3} = 5\frac{4}{3} \\ -\ 1\frac{2}{3} = 1\frac{2}{3} \\ \hline 4\frac{2}{3} \end{array}$$
C. $4\frac{2}{3}$

20.
$$\begin{array}{r} \$9.29 \\ \times\ 0.08 \\ \hline 0.7432 \end{array} \rightarrow 74¢$$
C. 74¢

21. B. 100 by 4

22. $(3\text{ ft})^2 = (1\text{ yd})^2$
$9\text{ ft}^2 = 1\text{ yd}^2$
C. 9

23. $\dfrac{\overset{1}{\cancel{2}} \cdot 3 \cdot \overset{1}{\cancel{3}} \cdot \overset{1}{\cancel{5}}}{\underset{1}{\cancel{2}} \cdot 2 \cdot 2 \cdot \underset{1}{\cancel{3}} \cdot \underset{1}{\cancel{5}}} = \dfrac{3}{4}$
B. $\frac{3}{4}$

24. B. $\frac{1}{4}$ **(60 – 48)**

25. $\frac{1}{2}\left(\frac{1}{2}\text{ gal}\right) = \frac{1}{4}\text{ gal} = 1\text{ qt}$
$\frac{1}{2}\left(\frac{1}{4}\text{ gal}\right) = \frac{1}{8}\text{ gal} = 1\text{ pt}$
$\frac{1}{2}\left(\frac{1}{8}\text{ gal}\right) = \frac{1}{16}\text{ gal} = 1\text{ cup}$
$$\begin{array}{r} \frac{1}{16} = \frac{1}{16} \\ \frac{1}{8} = \frac{2}{16} \\ +\ \frac{1}{4} = \frac{4}{16} \\ \hline \frac{7}{16} \end{array}$$
A. $\frac{7}{16}$

Benchmark Test 3

1. $\dfrac{2}{\underset{1}{\cancel{3}}} \times \dfrac{\overset{200}{\cancel{600}}}{1} = 400$ sprouted
600 − 400 = 200 did not sprout
B. 200

2. $\dfrac{\text{boys}}{\text{girls}} = \dfrac{3}{4}$
$\dfrac{3}{4} = \dfrac{12}{g}$
$3g = 48$
$g = 16$ girls
D. 16

3. Perimeter = 9 cm + 15 cm + 12 cm = 36 cm
B. 36 cm

4. Area $= \dfrac{9\text{ cm} \times 12\text{ cm}}{2} = 54\text{ cm}^2$
B. 54 cm^2

5.
$$\begin{array}{r} \overset{3}{\cancel{4}}.\overset{9}{\cancel{0}}\overset{10}{\cancel{0}}\text{ m} \\ -\ 3.08\text{ m} \\ \hline 0.92\text{ m} \end{array}$$
A. 0.92 m

6.
$$\begin{array}{r} 2.5 \\ \times\ 0.03 \\ \hline 0.075 \end{array}$$
C. 0.075

7. $0.3 \div \sqrt{36} = 0.3 \div 6$
$$\begin{array}{r} 0.05 \\ 6\overline{)0.30} \\ \underline{30} \\ 0 \end{array}$$
B. 0.05

8.
$$\begin{array}{r} 40 \\ 7\overline{)280} \\ \underline{28} \\ 00 \\ \underline{00} \\ 0 \end{array}$$
C. 40

9. $\sqrt{36} < \sqrt{40} < \sqrt{49}$
$\sqrt{36} = 6$
$\sqrt{49} = 7$
D. 6 and 7

10.
$$\begin{array}{r} \frac{1}{2} = \frac{5}{10} \\ +\ \frac{7}{10} = \frac{7}{10} \\ \hline \frac{12}{10} = 1\frac{2}{10} = 1\frac{1}{5} \end{array}$$
C. $1\frac{1}{5}$

11.
$$\begin{array}{r} 4\frac{1}{4} = 3\frac{5}{4} \\ -\ 2\frac{1}{2} = 2\frac{2}{4} \\ \hline 1\frac{3}{4} \end{array}$$
B. $1\frac{3}{4}$

12. $4\frac{1}{2}\text{ ft} \times 3\frac{1}{3}\text{ ft} = \frac{\overset{3}{\cancel{9}}}{\underset{1}{\cancel{2}}}\text{ ft} \times \frac{\overset{5}{\cancel{10}}}{\underset{1}{\cancel{3}}}\text{ ft} = 15\text{ ft}^2$

D. 15 ft^2

13. $10 \div 3\frac{1}{3} = 10 \div \frac{10}{3} = \frac{\overset{1}{\cancel{10}}}{1} \times \frac{3}{\underset{1}{\cancel{10}}} = 3$

A. 3

14. $5y = 12$

$y = \frac{12}{5} = 2\frac{2}{5} = 2.4$

B. 2.4

15. $d = 2r = 2(5\text{ cm}) = 10\text{ cm}$

$C = \pi d$

$C = (3.14)(10\text{ cm})$

$C = 31.4\text{ cm}$

C. 31.4 cm

16. $A = \pi r^2$

$A = (3.14)(5\text{ cm})^2$

$A = 78.5\text{ cm}^2$

B. 78.5 cm^2

17. $75\% = \frac{75}{100} \div \frac{25}{25} = \frac{3}{4}$

B. $\frac{3}{4}$

18. $V = lwh$

$V = (12\text{ in.})(6\text{ in.})(5\text{ in.})$

$V = 360\text{ in.}^3$

D. 360 in.^{3}

19. B. 12 edges

20.

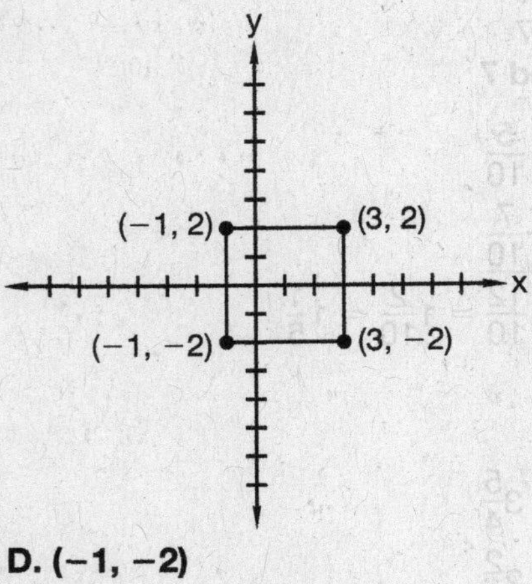

D. (−1, −2)

21. 118 minutes = 1:53

$$\begin{array}{r} 4{:}25\text{ p.m.} \\ +\ 1{:}53 \\ \hline 5{:}83 \rightarrow 6{:}23\text{ p.m.} \end{array}$$

A. 6:23 p.m.

22. C. $-2, 0.3, \frac{1}{2}, 1$

23.

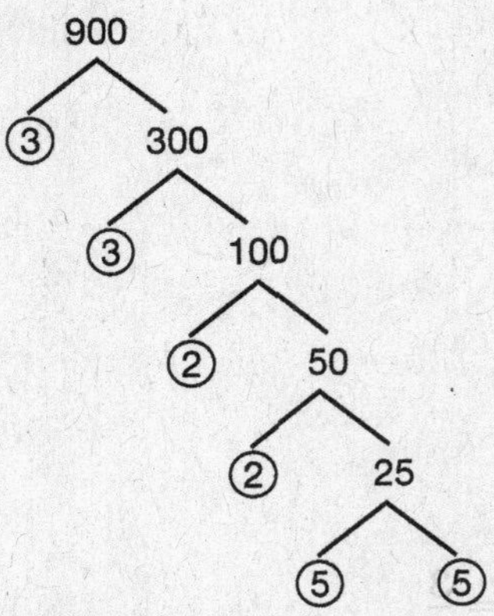

B. $2^2 \cdot 3^2 \cdot 5^2$

24. $P(\text{blue}) = \frac{2}{10} = 20\%$

B. 20%

25. $3 + 3 \times 3 - 3 \div 3 = 3 + 9 - 1 = 11$

D. 11

End-of-Course Exam

1. $\begin{array}{r} 304\frac{10}{25} \\ 25\overline{)7610} \\ \underline{75} \\ 11 \\ \underline{0} \\ 110 \\ \underline{100} \\ 10 \end{array}$ $\quad 304\frac{10}{25} = 304\frac{2}{5}$

C. $\mathbf{304\frac{2}{5}}$

2. $\begin{array}{r} \overset{1}{8}.75 \\ 6.00 \\ \underline{+\ 4.50} \\ 19.25 \end{array}$

D. 19.25

3. $\begin{array}{r} 1.\overset{7}{\not{8}}0 \\ \underline{-\ 0.25} \\ 1.55 \end{array}$

A. 1.55

4. $\begin{array}{r} 0.15 \\ \underline{\times\ \ 4.2} \\ 030 \\ \underline{060\ } \\ 0.630 \end{array}$

A. 0.63

5. $\begin{array}{r} 5.2 \\ 0\underset{\frown}{7})3\underset{\frown}{6}4 \\ \underline{35} \\ 14 \\ \underline{14} \\ 0 \end{array}$

B. 5.2

6. $1\frac{2}{3} + 2\frac{5}{6} = 1\frac{4}{6} + 2\frac{5}{6} = 3\frac{9}{6} = 4\frac{3}{6} = 4\frac{1}{2}$

B. $\mathbf{4\frac{1}{2}}$

7. $3\frac{2}{5} - 1\frac{1}{2} = 3\frac{4}{10} - 1\frac{5}{10} = 2\frac{14}{10} - 1\frac{5}{10} = 1\frac{9}{10}$

C. $\mathbf{1\frac{9}{10}}$

8. $\frac{4}{5} \times 3\frac{1}{3} = \frac{4}{\underset{1}{\not{5}}} \times \frac{\overset{2}{\not{10}}}{3} = \frac{8}{3} = 2\frac{2}{3}$

C. $\mathbf{2\frac{2}{3}}$

9. $2\frac{2}{5} \div 1\frac{1}{2} = \frac{12}{5} \div \frac{3}{2} = \frac{\overset{4}{\not{12}}}{5} \times \frac{2}{\underset{1}{\not{3}}} = \frac{8}{5} = 1\frac{3}{5}$

A. $\mathbf{1\frac{3}{5}}$

10. $\frac{60}{84} = \frac{\not{2^2} \cdot \not{3} \cdot 5}{\not{2^2} \cdot \not{3} \cdot 7} = \frac{5}{7}$

C. $\mathbf{\frac{5}{7}}$

11. B. 4

12. A. 2,500,000

13. $1.2 \text{ m} \cdot \left(\frac{1 \text{ km}}{1000 \text{ m}}\right) = 0.0012 \text{ km}$

$1.2 \text{ m} \cdot \left(\frac{100 \text{ cm}}{1 \text{ m}}\right) = 120 \text{ cm}$

$1.2 \text{ m} \cdot \left(\frac{1000 \text{ mm}}{1 \text{ m}}\right) = 1200 \text{ mm}$

C. 1200 mm

14. B. 2 m

15. $0.4 \times 100\% = 40\%$

$2 \div 5 \times 100\% = 40\%$

$40 \div 100 \times 100\% = 40\%$

$0.04 \times 100\% = 4\%$

D. 0.04

16. $10^3 \cdot 10^4 = 10^{3+4} = 10^7$

B. $\mathbf{10^7}$

17. $\sqrt{100} = 10$, so $\sqrt{199} > 10$.

$14 \times 14 = 196$

$15 \times 15 = 225$

C. 14 and 15

18. Twenty-five thousandths = 0.025

E. None correct

19. $17.36 + 8.7 \approx 17 + 9 = 26$

D. 26

20. $33\% = 0.33$

$33\frac{1}{3}\% = \frac{1}{3}$

$\frac{1}{3} > 0.33$

$\begin{array}{r} 0.333 \\ 3\overline{)1.000} \\ \underline{9\ \ } \\ 10\ \\ \underline{9\ } \\ 10 \\ \underline{9} \\ 1 \end{array}$

C. $\mathbf{0.3, 33\%, \frac{1}{3}}$

21. $\frac{8}{12} = \frac{12}{n}$
$8n = (12)(12)$
$8n = 144$
$n = \frac{144}{8}$
$n = 18$
C. 18

22.

	Ratio	Actual Count
Boys	2	*B*
Girls	3	18
Total	5	*T*

$\frac{3}{5} = \frac{18}{T}$
$3T = 90$
$T = 30$
D. 30

23. $3(25) = 75$
$75 - 22 - 22 = 75 - 44 = 31$
D. 31

24. The measures, in order, are 6, 8, 8, 8, 9, 9, 10, 11, 12, 16. Because the number of measures is even, the median is the average of the two middle values:
$\frac{9 \text{ in.} + 9 \text{ in.}}{2} = \frac{18 \text{ in.}}{2} = 9 \text{ in.}$
B. 9 in.

25. 3 favorable outcomes
6 total outcomes
So, the probability is $\frac{3}{6}$, or $\frac{1}{2}$.
C. $\frac{1}{2}$

26. $\begin{array}{r} \$2.89 \\ \times\ 0.08 \\ \hline 0.2312 \end{array}$ → \$0.23 tax $\begin{array}{r} \$2.89 \\ +\ \$0.23 \\ \hline \$3.12 \end{array}$
B. \$3.12

27. $32\overline{)4.16}$ = 0.13
$\begin{array}{r} 3\,2 \\ \hline 96 \\ 96 \\ \hline 0 \end{array}$
C. 13¢/oz

28.

	%	Actual Count
Original	100	\$36
Change	25	*C*
New	75	*S*

$\frac{100}{75} = \frac{\$36}{S}$
$100S = \$2700$
$S = 27.00$
C. \$27.00

29. $25\overline{)21.00}$ = $0.84 = 84\%$
$\begin{array}{r} 20\,0 \\ \hline 1\,00 \\ 1\,00 \\ \hline 0 \end{array}$
B. 84%

30. $400 \times \left(2\frac{1}{2}\right) = 1000$
D. 1000 miles

31. **B.**

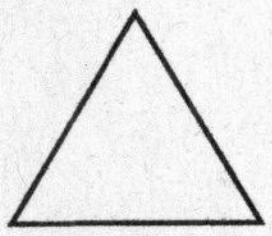

32. $m\angle x + m\angle y + 90° = 180°$
$m\angle y = 180° - 90° - m\angle x$
$m\angle y = 90° - 38°$
$m\angle y = 52°$
A. 52°

33. Perimeter = 7 cm + 11 cm + 8 cm + 9 cm + 15 cm + 20 cm = 70 cm
D. 70 cm

34. Circumference $= 2\pi(r) \approx 2(3.14)(10 \text{ inches})$
$= 62.8$ in.
B. 62.8 in.

35. Area $= \frac{1}{2}bh = \frac{1}{2}(9 \text{ m})(12 \text{ m}) = 54 \text{ m}^2$
B. 54 m^2

36. Area $= \pi r^2 = \pi(4)^2 = 16\pi \approx 16(3.14) = 50 \text{ ft}^2$
A. 50 ft^2

37. Volume = *lwh*
= 8 cm × 5 cm × 2 cm
= 80 cm^3
A. 80 cm^3

38. **C.**

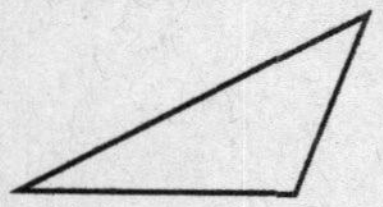

39. **D.** $\overline{TS}$

40. $3^2 + 4^2 = c^2$

$25 = c^2$

$5 = c$

A. 5

41. $(-6) + (-3) + (+2) = (-9) + (2) = -7$

B. −7

42. $4(3)(12) = 12(12) = 144$

D. 144

43. $3[16 - 2(5 - 3)] = 3[16 - 2(2)] = 3(16 - 4)$
$= 3(12) = 36$

C. 36

44.

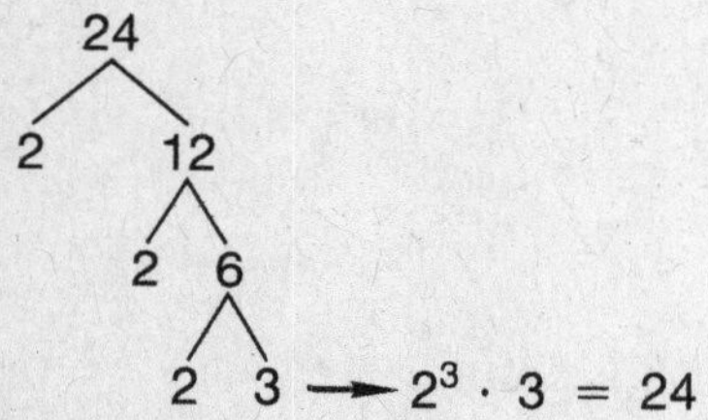

A. $\mathbf{2^3 \cdot 3}$

45. **B. X**

46. $3m - 1 = 35$

$3m = 36$

$m = \frac{36}{3}$

$m = 12$

B. 12

47. **A.** $\sqrt{9} < 2^2$

48. $(-10)(-10) = 100$

B. 100

49. Since $-3 < -2$, x cannot be -3.

D. −3

50.

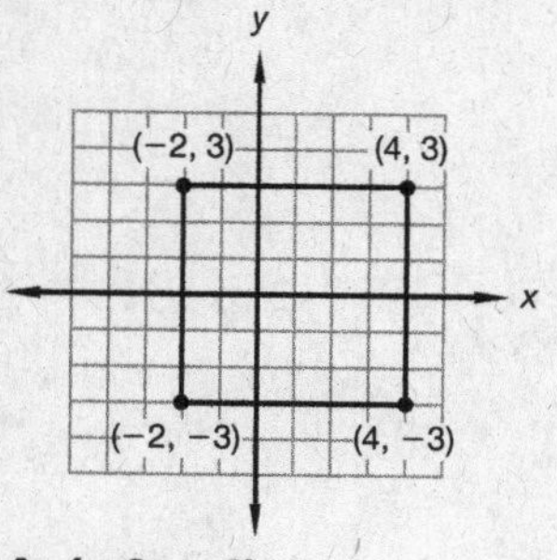

A. (−2, −3)

